Preserving Islamic Tradition

Preserving Islamic Tradition

Abū Naṣr Qūrṣāwī and the Beginnings of Modern Reformism

NATHAN SPANNAUS

OXFORD
UNIVERSITY PRESS

OXFORD
UNIVERSITY PRESS

Oxford University Press is a department of the University of Oxford. It furthers the University's objective of excellence in research, scholarship, and education by publishing worldwide. Oxford is a registered trade mark of Oxford University Press in the UK and certain other countries.

Published in the United States of America by Oxford University Press
198 Madison Avenue, New York, NY 10016, United States of America.

CIP data is on file at the Library of Congress

ISBN 978–0–19–025178–9

1 3 5 7 9 8 6 4 2

Printed by Sheridan Books, Inc., United States of America

To Alex,

[add heartfelt and witty comment here]

Contents

Preface ix

Acknowledgments xi

Transliteration, Dates, Ethnonyms xiii

Timeline of Volga-Ural History xv

Map: Central Eurasia, ca. 1800 xvii

1. Introduction—Historiography of Reform and Tradition 1
   - Jadidism and Historiography 3
   - Eighteenth-Century Reformism 7
   - Tradition and Institutions 16
   - The Current Study 21
2. An *ʿĀlim* in the Russian Empire 29
   - *Sharīʿa* and the *ʿUlamāʾ* 34
   - Tsarist Rule, Persecution, and Tolerance 38
   - Sanction and Scholarship 46
   - Bukhara 52
   - The Spiritual Assembly 68
   - Conflicts in Bulghar Islam 82
3. An Epistemological Critique 91
   - Postclassical Scholarship 93
   - Reforming the Scholarly Tradition 108
4. *Ijtihād* and the Function of Legal Theory 112
   - Qūrṣāwī's Conception of *Ijtihād* 113
   - The Prevalence of *Taqlīd* 128
   - The Social Function of *Ijtihād* 135

5. The Question of the Divine Attributes 144
Qūrṣāwī's Critique 145
Divine Transcendence 162
Orthodoxy and Condemnation 169

6. Postclassical *Kalām* 175
Wujūdī Influence 176
Approaching Sirhindī 187
Qūrṣāwī as *Mutakallim* 193

7. Reform Within the Scholarly Tradition 201
Eighteenth-Century Reformism 204
A Response to Tsarist Rule 214

8. Modernity 219
Disembedding and Individualism 221
Secularity 227
Modern Reformism 232

9. The Transformation of the Religious Environment 237
Reforming Muslim Education 238
Printing 247
The Fragmentation of Authority 261
Jadidism and the Post-1905 Religious Environment 273

10. Conclusion—Separating Qūrṣāwī and Jadidism 288

Bibliography 299

Index 321

Preface

THIS PROJECT BEGAN as idle browsing in the DK section of the library in my first semester of graduate school, where I first became aware of Qūrṣāwī, and it eventually settled on two questions: What is Qūrṣāwī's reformism about? And why is it remembered so differently in most historical sources?

Answering these questions required wading into Volga-Ural history and postclassical Islamic studies, two fields that have long been overlooked and underinvestigated, but also rarely brought together. While both have seen significant advancements since the 1990s, the study of Volga-Ural Muslims remains hindered by the ideological influence of the Soviet academy and flawed, outdated ideas about Islam and Islamic history.

The field itself is divided among experts in social sciences, Soviet nationalities, security studies, and varied historiographical trends, as well as between researchers with facility in different languages—too many, I would argue, in only Russian, and too few in Arabic and Persian. It also has suffered from reliance on a narrow range of primary sources, interpreted with a sparse methodological toolbox.[1]

In all, the field has been left ill-equipped to analyze and contextualize the religious, social, and cultural developments that mark Volga-Ural history, particularly in the imperial period. (The Soviet period, too, though that is beyond the scope of this study.) Much of the work has overwhelmingly focused on Jadidism, the early 20th-century modernist movement in the region, leaving other topics alternately ignored and disregarded, such that any picture of the broader context remains incomplete, and persistent methodological shortcomings mean that even Jadidism remains poorly understood.

---

1. See Devin DeWeese's insightful diagnosis of the problems facing the study of Islam in the former Soviet Union: Devin DeWeese. "Islam and the Legacy of Sovietology: A Review Essay on Yaacov Ro'i's *Islam in the Soviet Union*." *Journal of Islamic Studies*, vol. 13, no. 3, 2002. 298–330.

Research into this history in all periods is at a relatively early stage, especially in terms of religious issues. Nevertheless, the immense strides made in recent years are encouraging, and our understanding will doubtless improve into the foreseeable future, necessitating revisions and emendations to the present literature. (Also true for postclassical Islamic studies, if for different reasons, to be addressed in the Introduction.)

This is my intended contribution—to expand and deepen our understanding of the forms and currents of Islamic thought in the Volga-Ural region in the 19th century and its religious and intellectual environment through the analysis of one important figure's thought. But rather than an attempt to engage equally with the fields of Volga-Ural history and Islamic studies, addressing the conventions and conversations of both, this monograph is squarely aimed at the latter. It is a work of Islamic intellectual history, which I believe is the field that offers the best approach for investigating and analyzing the subject matter. It is this literature and its contours that I engage with, and this audience that I am speaking to. (Accordingly, I err toward explaining for the reader aspects of Russian history or governance more than Islam or Islamic history.)

This field, to be sure, is far from perfect. There are critical gaps in its periodization, primarily the separation between premodern and modern Islamic studies, as well as in the related issue of dealing with European influence on Islamic thought (discussed in the Introduction). In addition, the Volga-Ural region is a periphery of the Islamic world, and such areas are not always given their due in scholarship, to the detriment of the field. Indeed, the region not only sits on the edge of both the Islamic world and Europe but is a part of the former long under the rule of the latter, and the chronological focus of the book—the turn of the 19th century—falls at the very transition from the premodern to the modern. As such, this topic is peripheral multiple times over, with all attendant complexities.

This monograph is an effort to move beyond these gaps, but also to advance the extant literature in new directions. This will certainly involve choices, interpretations, and conclusions that some readers may not agree with. That's okay. This book should be seen as an *essai*, a sincere attempt to make sense of the historical, religious, social, and intellectual phenomena under study, in a still-developing area of inquiry. It is a worthwhile task, but not a straightforward one.

Acknowledgments

THIS BOOK REPRESENTS several years of study, research, and contemplation that would not have been possible without the generous help and support of many people. Every teacher (especially language instructors), classmate, librarian, secretary, bookstore, and friend along the way, from Ann Arbor to St. Petersburg, St. Louis, Cambridge, Montreal, Tempe, Kazan, Damascus, Princeton, Knoxville, Oxford, and all places in between, has made this book what it is. I don't really do effusive (and will soon run out of synonyms for "supportive"), but know that although I cannot list all of you here, nor possibly repay your kindness, I am forever grateful.

The project that eventually became this book first took shape at Harvard under the invaluable guidance of the late Shahab Ahmed, Khaled El-Rouayheb, Roy Mottahedeh, and John Schoeberlein. At McGill, I benefited immensely from working and studying with Malek Abisaab, Wael Hallaq, Laila Parsons, and Uner Turgay. Special mention is due to Robert Wisnovsky, who has been an unfailing source of guidance, support, and productive disagreement. I couldn't ask for a better supervisor and mentor. And thanks to everyone at the Institute of Islamic Studies, which provided both an unparalleled intellectual environment and funding for language study, writing time, and manuscript research.

My work at Tennessee and Oxford allowed me to think seriously about the relevant theoretical and comparative issues arising from my research, particularly my time with the European Research Council–funded project "Changing Structures of Islamic Authority," under the supervision of Masooda Bano, who offered motivation and probing questions in equal measure. And special thanks to Christopher Pooya Razavian for his support, friendship, and constant mentions of philosophers whom I may or may not have eventually looked into.

(And I must of course acknowledge the collegiality and feedback from Jari Kaukua and Davlat Dadikhoda, Yusuf Daşdemir, Hadel Jarada, Kutlu Okan, and everyone in Jyväskylä.)

I also would like to thank the librarians, archivists, interlibrary loan staff, and assistants who made the research for this book possible, including those at Harvard, McGill, the New York Public Library, and Oxford, and particularly the respective staffs at the Institute of Oriental Manuscripts in St. Petersburg, the Department of Manuscripts and Rare Books at Kazan Federal University, the Tiumen State Museum, and the Sinor Research Institute for Inner Asian Studies at Indiana University.

Over the years, I have received immeasurable help from friends, colleagues, peers, conference attendees, co-presenters, and correspondents, who have generously and studiously read drafts, asked questions, made suggestions, and offered feedback and insights. Thanks (in alphabetical order) to Rainer Brunner, Alfrid Bustanov, Alireza Doostdar, Allen Frank, Rozaliya Garipova, Robert Gleave, Frank Griffel, Bilal Ibrahim, Kamran Karimullah, Edward Lazzerini, Reza Pourjavady, Junaid Quadri, Danielle Ross, Paolo Sartori, and Uli Schamiloglu. The two anonymous reviewers of the manuscript made critical comments and suggestions that only improved the final product, and Cynthia Read and everyone at Oxford University Press have shown great enthusiasm, patience, and skill in shepherding the book to publication. Of course, all errors are my own.

Finally, to my brother, parents, grandparents, aunts, uncles, cousins, nieces, nephews, and friends, without whom none of this would have been possible: thank you for supporting and inspiring me, distracting me when necessary, letting me talk at you, and smiling along politely. I apologize for any untoward reactions when asked what exactly my book is about or when it'll be done. Here it is. And Alex, who's shown more patience, interest, and support during this process than could reasonably be expected of anyone: thank you for everything.

Transliteration, Dates, Ethnonyms

FOR ALL QUOTATIONS and references in Arabic script, the transliteration scheme from the *International Journal of Middle East Studies* for Arabic-language materials will be used. While a significant proportion of the primary sources used here are not in Arabic, the prevalence of Arabic terminology and vocabulary and the intermixing of Arabic, Persian, and Turkic elements in the sources complicate the process of transliteration. In the interest of avoiding a situation where a term such as *ijtihād* would also, depending on the language, be rendered as *ejtehād, ictihâd,* or *izhtikhad,* despite the fact it would be written in exactly the same way across the original sources, I've chosen to use one scheme for all writing in Arabic script, regardless of language.

For Cyrillic script, Russian-language materials will be transliterated according to the Library of Congress system. Other transliteration from Cyrillic will follow the conventions for each language.

All references and citations will be made to the original language and script of the source, while mentions of figures within the text will use the most common spelling of their name. The same applies in the bibliography, where works by the same author are grouped together, regardless of spelling. (For instance, the 20th-century Tatar historian Gaziz Gubaidullin, whose name is most widely known in this Cyrillic form, will be indicated as such, while citations for his Arabic-script writings will be attributed to ʿAzīz ʿUbaydullīn but listed under "Gubaidullin.")

Technical terms and uncommon proper nouns will always be transliterated with diacritics, and the former italicized (e.g., *kalām,* Qūrṣā), but common proper nouns will not carry diacritics (e.g., Sufi, Hanafi, Prophet Muhammad). For well-known geographical terms, English versions will be used (Cairo, Moscow, steppe).

Both *hijrī* and Christian dates were employed during the period under study here. However, for the sake of simplicity, *hijrī* dates will be given only infrequently, when called for by primary source documents.

Until 1900, "Bulghar" (*bulghārī*) was the main identifier used by Volga-Ural Muslim peoples for themselves, in reference to the ancient city of Bulghār, to which they trace their origins as Muslims. Current ethnonyms such as "Tatar" or "Bashkir" did not become common for self-identification until the 20th century, though they had long been used by the tsarist government as administrative categories. In the interest of avoiding anachronism, and to identify these people as they identified themselves, "Bulghar" will be the term predominantly used here. (This usage, it should be noted, is unconnected with the debate in post-Soviet Tatarstan—on which I take no position—between "Tatarism" and "Bulgharism" as the focal point of Tatars' national identity.)

Timeline of Volga-Ural History

EARLY 10TH CENTURY

First conversion to Islam of the kingdom of Bulghār, solicitation of religious and military assistance from the Abbasid caliphate in Baghdad

921–922 Embassy of Aḥmad ibn Faḍlān from Baghdad to Bulghār

988 Conversion of the Rus to Orthodox Christianity by St. Vladimir, Grand Prince of Kiev (r. 980–1015)

1223–1240 Mongol invasions across Eurasian steppe into Eastern Europe; sack of Kiev; establishment of Chinggisid rule in the Golden Horde, centered on the lower Volga

1313 Establishment of Islam in the Golden Horde by Ūzbak Khān (r. 1313–1341)

1328 Appointment by Ūzbak Khān of Ivan I of Moscow (1288–1340) as Grand Prince; beginning of Muscovite predominance among the Rus

1394–1396 Invasion of the Golden Horde by Timur; sack of Bulghār

1431 Destruction of Bulghār by Muscovite armies

Mid-15th century Disintegration of Golden Horde into Chinggisid khanates—Kazan, Astrakhan, Crimea, Siberia, Kazakh

1460s–1540s Constant warfare and intrigue between Moscow and Kazan; end of Chinggisid suzerainty over Moscow

1475 Ottoman suzerainty established over khanate of Crimea

1547 Grand Prince of Moscow Ivan the Terrible (r. 1533–1584) declares himself Tsar of All Russia

1552 Conquest of khanate of Kazan by Moscow; Russian entrance into the Urals

1556 Conquest of khanate of Astrakhan by Moscow

1586 Conquest of khanate of Siberia by Moscow

1598–1613 The interregnum, famine, and invasion of Russia by Poland, known as the Time of Troubles, ending with establishment of Romanov dynasty

1703 Founding of St. Petersburg by Tsar Peter the Great (r. 1682–1725) as new capital

1721 Peter declares himself Emperor of All Russia, establishing Russian Empire

Mid-18th century–1840s Russian absorption of nomadic hordes and settlement of the steppe

1743 Founding of Orenburg fortress as center for trans-steppe trade and stage for Russian invasion of Central Asia

1773 Act of religious tolerance by Empress Catherine the Great (r. 1762–1796)

1783 Russian annexation of khanate of Crimea

1788 Foundation of Spiritual Assembly of Mohammedan Law in Ufa

1860s–1870s "Great Reform" era of Russian government; end of serfdom

1864–1873 Russian conquest and colonization of Central Asian khanates

1905–1907 First Russian Revolution; promulgation of civil rights and constitutional reforms by Tsar Nicholas II (r. 1894–1917)

1917 February Revolution ends Romanov dynasty and inaugurates nonmonarchical Provisional Government; October Revolution dissolves Provisional Government and institutes Marxist Bolshevik government, beginning Russian Civil War

Central Eurasia, ca. 1800

Imperial borders ——— Undefined frontiers – – – –
Central Asian Khanates ———
Limit of Orenburg Assembly jurisdiction ············

Preserving Islamic Tradition

1

Introduction

HISTORIOGRAPHY OF REFORM AND TRADITION

ABŪ NAṢR QŪRṢĀWĪ (1776–1812) is a seminal figure in the history of the Muslim communities of the Russian Empire. One of the greatest scholars of the Volga-Ural region, he was an active and influential participant in the scholarly debates of the beginning of the 19th century. He wrote extensively, engaging with significant questions of religious authority and the role of scripture, and his works on law (*fiqh*) and theology (*kalām*) stand as notable contributions to Islamic intellectual history in the postclassical period (13th–19th centuries).

In these writings, he articulated ideas that ran counter to conventional views among the *ʿulamāʾ* that he considered not only flawed and incorrect but also religiously detrimental; he criticized overreliance on *taqlīd* and widespread limitation on the exercise of legal reasoning (*ijtihād*), and he called for renewed scrutiny toward theological issues. In doing so, he articulated a broad reformist stance that sought to maintain the moral foundations of the community and emend or exclude practices and beliefs that he saw as scripturally unjustified.

This reformist project was undoubtedly controversial, drawing the ire of many of Qūrṣāwī's fellow scholars. The controversy reached its apex in 1808, when the *ʿulamāʾ* of Bukhara condemned him for heresy and he was nearly executed by the ruling amir, who exiled him from the amirate. But Qūrṣāwī's reformism had importance that extended beyond *ʿulamāʾ*. His lifetime fell within a transitional historical era, one that saw the relationship between the Russian state and its Muslim subjects irrevocably altered. The role of the

ʿ*ulamāʾ*, who had previously been the foremost authorities within their communities, was transformed in the process. Muslims, scholars and laypeople alike, were grappling with these changes, which were unprecedented within their society. It was within this context that Qūrṣāwī developed his reformist project, which was aimed at the Muslim community as a whole.

Qūrṣāwī's significance continued long after his death, and his ideas and the controversy surrounding them shaped the discourse among the Muslims of the Russian Empire into the 20th century. He attracted a number of ʿ*ulamāʾ* to his views, none more important than Shihāb al-Dīn Marjānī (1818–1889), the single most prominent scholar of the region, who put forward his own project of religious reform, based in large part on Qūrṣāwī's.

There are broad implications to research into Qūrṣāwī's reformism. Questions of the interaction between European imperialism and Islamic thought and how the latter is shaped by Western political domination are significant historiographical issues within Islamic studies. The Russian Empire was one of the very earliest European states to implement direct rule over large Muslim populations, and an analysis of how Volga-Ural Muslims, particularly the ʿ*ulamāʾ*, responded to tsarist rule has much to contribute to these discussions of the transformation of Islamic tradition and its adaptation in the modern period. These issues are of marked relevance for the relationship between Islamic discourses and institutions and the modern state. The study of Qūrṣāwī can help expand our understanding of the intersection of postclassical thought, religious reformism, and early modernist movements.

The Islamic scholarly tradition—described in detail in this chapter—represents an essential lens for understanding Qūrṣāwī's reformist project, and it is accordingly a main focus of the present study. The postclassical scholarly tradition formed the intellectual repertoire for his views and also the framework in which he developed and articulated his ideas and arguments. As an ʿ*ālim*, he argued his positions from within; he was deeply enmeshed in the tradition, and his reformism cannot be properly understood removed from this framework. My primary goal is to locate Qūrṣāwī's thought within its proper intellectual and historical context in an effort to formulate an in-depth analysis of the content and contributions of his reformist project. This analysis relies on Qūrṣāwī's own writings, along with those of his contemporaries, and it is connected to, and compared with, relevant trends within the broader Islamic world. Posthumous developments and treatments of his thought, while certainly relevant, are addressed separately.

Jadidism and Historiography

Such an approach to Qūrṣāwī is at odds with the extant literature on him and his contributions. The prevailing historical image not only ignores the role of Islamic tradition in his thought, but in fact positions him against it. He is presented as calling for Muslims to reject the Islamic scholarly establishment and instead adopt *ijtihād* as an individualistic, open-minded approach to the Qurʾan and Sunna, an idea that flew in the face of the *ʿulamāʾ*'s insistence upon *taqlīd*, understood here as the blind acceptance of centuries-old dogmas, the inflexibility of which allowed for no engagement with the foundational texts of the religion.

This portrayal is part of a larger narrative of the history of Russia's Muslims, which has viewed them as irrationally clinging to Islamic doctrine. Qūrṣāwī's criticism of the *ʿulamāʾ* and *taqlīd* is considered a turning point in this history, as it showed Muslims that they did not have to accept scholars' teachings, which were based on medieval ways of thinking no longer suited to contemporary circumstances. Qūrṣāwī's rejection of the *ʿulamāʾ*'s authority thus allowed these communities to move away from scholars' influence and develop a new modus vivendi that was modern, rational, and secular.[1]

Such is the picture of Qūrṣāwī presented in the historiography of Jadidism, the Muslim modernist movement that flourished in the Russian Empire at the beginning of the 20th century, and it has since become established in the broader historiography of Russian/Soviet Islam.[2] (Indeed, it has taken on remarkable political significance in the post-Soviet period, particularly among Tatars, who consider Qūrṣāwī one of their national heroes.)[3] This narrative views Qūrṣāwī's call for reform as initiating the process of Muslims'

1. Serge A. Zenkovsky. *Pan-Turkism and Islam in Russia*. Cambridge, MA: Harvard UP, 1960; Hélène Carrère d'Encausse. *Islam and the Russian Empire: Reform and Revolution in Central Asia*. 1966. London: I. B. Tauris, 1988; Ia. G. Abdullin. *Tatarskaia prosvetitel'skaia mysl'*. Kazan: Tatarskoe knizhnoe izd-vo, 1976; A. N. Khairullin. "Mesto G. Kursavi v istorii obschestvennoi mysli." *Iz istorii tatarskoi obschestvennoi mysli*. Ed. Iakh"ia Abdullin. Kazan: IIaLI AN SSSR, 1979. 72–78; Azade-Ayşe Rorlich. *The Volga Tatars: A Profile in National Resilience*. Stanford, CA: Hoover Institution P, 1986.

2. Dzhamaliutdin Validov. *Ocherk istorii obrazovannosti i literatury Tatar*. 1923. Oxford: Society for Central Asian Studies, 1986; ʿAbdraḥmān [*sic*] Saʿdī. *Tātār adabiyātī tārīkhī*. Kazan: Tātārstān dawlat nashriyātī bāsmāsī, 1926; G. Gubaidullin. "K Voprosu ob ideologii Gasprinskogo." 1929. *Gasırlar awazı/Ekho vekov*, vol. 4, nos. 3–4; 1998. 98–118; A. M. Arsharuni and Kh. Gabidullin. *Ocherki panislamizma i pantiurkizma*. Moscow: izd-vo Bezobozhnik, 1931.

3. E.g., A. Iu. Khabutdinov. *Lidery natsii*. Kazan: Tatarskoe knizhnoe izd-vo, 2003, pp. 11–15; Gul'nara Idiiatullina. "Gabdennasir Kursavi, 1776–1812." *Tatarskii mir/Tatar dön'yası*, no. 9; 2009. 4. This historical image of Jadidism plays a central role in the formulation of "Euro-Islam," a secularized form of Muslim identity put forward by Rafael Khakimov, a prominent

"enlightenment" (*prosvetitel'stvo*), wherein great reformist intellectuals who were labeled, accordingly, as "enlighteners"—namely, Qūrṣāwī, Marjānī, and Ismail Gasprinskii (see Chapter 9)—led Muslims out of their benighted past dominated by the reactionary *ʿulamāʾ* into a modern, progressive, westernized future. Jadidism stands as the culmination of this process, presented as a popular movement devoted to Muslims' social, economic, and cultural development.[4]

Soviet Marxist historiography has deeply shaped this narrative (as evinced by much of the terminology employed). Many Jadids were themselves Marxists or influenced by Marxism, and the ideological impact only became stronger as the narrative was reified in Soviet academia. Within this historiographical framework, Muslims' enlightenment was a necessary part of their society's passing from a feudal to a capitalist stage of development, which culminated in the formation of a national bourgeoisie.[5] Jadidism as a cultural and political movement was understood as an expression of this new social class.[6] It was no longer, however, a part of *Muslims'* enlightenment, but rather part of Tatars' distinctive national enlightenment (alongside Bashkirs', Kazakhs', Uzbeks', Tajiks', etc.). The development from a feudal to a capitalist society was understood explicitly as a process of secularization, wherein religious identity and affiliation were to be abandoned in favor of national identity. Religious adherence was a sign of feudalism, while modern capitalist society was inevitably secular. Therefore, Qūrṣāwī's putative break with the *ʿulamāʾ* takes on greater significance than a mere intra-religious debate. Instead, it serves as the beginning of the secularization of this society and the historical emergence of the modern Tatar nation.

Despite its prominence, this narrative is deeply flawed, and it suffers from a number of historiographical and analytical shortcomings. As Adeeb Khalid points out, it is unavoidably teleological, viewing every development through the lens of Jadidism, such that Qūrṣāwī's significance is reduced to his

academic and political figure in contemporary Tatarstan; see, e.g., Rafael Khakimov. "Islam's Modernization: How Plausible Is It?" *Russia in Global Affairs*, vol. 2, no. 3; Dec. 2003. 126–139.

4. The broad outlines of this narrative (i.e., a break with tradition leads to secular enlightenment) is not unique to Qūrṣāwī or the Tatars, but is found in the historiography of all former Soviet Muslim peoples; see Franz Wennberg. *On the Edge: The Concept of Progress in Bukhara During the Rule of the Later Manghits*. Uppsala: Acta Universitatis Upsaliensis, 2013, pp. 15–17.

5. Wennberg notes that a uniform historical trajectory was sought for all Soviet national groups; ibid., pp. 13–15.

6. L. I. Klimovich. *Islam v tsarskoi Rossii*. Moscow: Gosudarstvennoe antireligioznoe izd-vo, 1936; S. G. Batyev. "Tatarskii dzhadidizm i ego èvoliutsiia." *Istoriia SSSR*, no. 4; 1964. 53–63.

supposed contribution to the movement.[7] This misappropriation of Qūrṣāwī's ideas, as Alfrid Bustanov and Michael Kemper argue, is made possible only by stripping them of their original religious meaning and context and employing them for entirely separate ideological purposes.[8] Whole aspects of his thought have thus been elided and/or ignored in order to fit this portrayal, which, critically, is not based on his own writings: virtually none of the secondary literature has made use of his works, instead relying on 20th-century Jadidist texts written by authors engaged in their own social and ideological struggles.[9]

In the post-Soviet period, new research into Volga-Ural Islam has shed some of the shortcomings of this earlier literature, particularly reemphasizing the religious component of these reform movements and utilizing a wider range of primary sources. Most important is Michael Kemper's 1998 monograph on the religious history of Volga-Ural Muslims in the 18th and 19th centuries.[10] An analysis of changes in the "Islamic discourse" of the region (a concept adopted from the work of Reinhard Schulze[11]), Kemper's study of fifteen prominent Muslim authors—Qūrṣāwī among them—has contributed greatly to our understanding of the issues, debates, and controversies that were most socially and culturally salient during this period. Accordingly, it is overwhelmingly a local history, its analysis focusing only on issues that had broad significance among Volga-Ural Muslims. In this way, Kemper is one of the very first scholars to meaningfully engage with specifically religious matters within Volga-Ural Muslim society, and he makes extensive use of previously

---

7. Adeeb Khalid. "What Jadidism Was, and What It Wasn't: The Historiographical Adventures of a Term." *Central Eurasian Studies Review*, vol. 5, no. 2; 2006. 3–7.

8. Alfrid Bustanov and Michael Kemper. "From Mirasism to Euro-Islam: The Translation of Islamic Legal Debates into Tatar Secular Cultural Heritage." *Islamic Authority and the Russian Language: Studies on Texts from European Russia, the North Caucasus and West Siberia*. Eds. Alfrid Bustanov and Michael Kemper. Amsterdam: Pegasus, 2012. 29–54; also Michael Kemper. "Šihabaddin al-Marǧani als Religionsgelehrter." *Muslim Culture in Russia and Central Asia from the 18th to the Early 19th Centuries*. Eds. Michael Kemper et al. Berlin: Klaus Schwarz Verlag, 1996. 129–166.

9. On these ideological struggles and their influence on the reception of Jadidism, see Allen J. Frank. *Muslim Religious Institutions in Imperial Russia: The Islamic World of Novouzensk District and the Kazakh Inner Horde, 1780–1910*. Leiden: Brill, 2001, pp. 5–16, also 218. Notably, two of the major Soviet-era works on Jadidism (those by Arsharuni and Gabidullin and Klimovich, respectively) were published by official anti-religious presses.

10. Michael Kemper. *Sufis und Gelehrte in Tatarien und Baschkirien, 1789–1889: Der islamische Diskurs unter russischer Herrschaft*. Berlin: Klaus Schwarz Verlag, 1998.

11. Reinhard Schulze. *A Modern History of the Islamic World*. 1994. Trans. Azizeh Azodi. New York: I. B. Tauris, 2000.

unstudied manuscript sources (including those in Arabic, largely ignored by researchers of Islam in Russia). His study is thus of unquestionable value.

Alongside Kemper's history is the work of Gul'nara Idiiatullina, who has authored the only monograph study of Qūrṣāwī.[12] She has also produced an introduction and Russian translation of his sole published work, the *Irshād li-l-ʿibād*.[13] However, as with the conventional historiography, she presents Qūrṣāwī's reformism as rejecting major elements of the Islamic scholarly tradition and explicitly connects him with the emergence of Jadidism. Moreover, Idiiatullina's monograph focuses only on the *Irshād*, the text that serves as the basis for the misappropriation of Qūrṣāwī's views in Jadidist historiography, to the exclusion of the rest of his oeuvre.[14]

Also of note is Ahmet Kanlidere's 1997 monograph on Jadidism, which uses a number of primary sources published in the Ottoman Empire and republican Turkey.[15] While this work is valuable as a study of Jadidism—its discussion of the movement's similarities with contemporary Salafism in particular—its treatment of Qūrṣāwī is cursory and relies exclusively on Jadidist sources for a presentation of his views. As a result, its analysis suffers from many of the same flaws as earlier works, linking Qūrṣāwī to Jadidism and anachronistically attributing to him the positions of the latter.

By approaching Qūrṣāwī's reformism as quintessentially religious in nature and, especially in the case of Kemper, utilizing his own writings as primary sources, these studies have moved away from some of the most glaring problems in the secondary literature.[16] Despite their contributions, however,

12. Gul'nara Idiiatullina. *Abu-n-Nasr Kursavi*. Kazan: Fen, 2005. Here I utilize the similar analysis in her introduction to Qūrṣāwī's *Irshād*; Gul'nara Idiiatullina. "Vvedenie." In Abu-n-Nasr Abd an-Nasir al-Kursavi. *Nastavlenie liudei na put' istiny*. Intro. and trans. Gul'nara Idiiatullina. Kazan: Tatarskoe knizhnoe izd-vo, 2005. 10–88.

13. Abū al-Naṣr ʿAbd al-Naṣīr Qūrṣāwī. *al-Irshād li-l-ʿibād*. Kazan: lito-tipografiia I. N. Kharitonova, 1903. Reprinted with introduction and Russian translation as Abu-n-Nasr Abd an-Nasir al-Kursavi. *Nastavlenie liudei na put' istiny*. Intro. and trans. Gul'nara Idiiatullina. Kazan: Tatarskoe knizhnoe izd-vo, 2005.

14. Cf. Nathan Spannaus. "The Ur-Text of Jadidism: Abu Nasr Qursawi's *Irshad* and the Historiography of Muslim Modernism in Russia." *Journal of the Economic and Social History of the Orient*, vol. 59; 2016. 93–125; also Bustanov and Kemper, "From Mirasism to Euro-Islam," p. 39. It is often cited without any discussion of its specific contents; e.g., Rorlich, *Volga Tatars*, p. 49.

15. Ahmet Kanlidere. *Reform Within Islam: The Tajdid and Jadid Movement Among the Kazan Tatars (1809–1917): Conciliation or Conflict?* Istanbul: Eren, 1997.

16. Aidar Iuzeev has also taken this approach, but his work nevertheless repeats the same flawed Jadidist-centered narrative and contains a number of misconceptions about Islamic intellectual history; Aidar Iuzeev. *Mirovozzrenie Sh. Mardzhani i arabo-musul'manskaia*

the scholarly understanding of Qūrṣāwī's reformist project and its place within the history of Islamic thought remains limited, focused on Jadidism and heavily influenced by Soviet academia.

It is not my intention to critique this historiography (as I have done elsewhere), nor is it my aim to amend or revise it.[17] Rather, I believe it should be thrown out entirely, and a new historical understanding of Qūrṣāwī's thought and his role in the broader history of Russia's Muslim communities must be crafted in its place. Instead of approaching Qūrṣāwī from the perspective of this 20th-century movement, it is far more appropriate to view him and his reformist project as part of premodern Islamic intellectual history. The hundred years between 1750 and 1850 constitute perhaps the single most transformative period in the history of Volga-Ural Muslims—indeed, in the history of the Islamic world more generally—and it witnessed remarkable changes to virtually all aspects of society. Qūrṣāwī's thought represents an early example of the intellectual dimensions of these changes. His reformism is grounded within postclassical scholarly discourse, even as he departs from it. The constituent elements of that discourse were operative within his thought, but they were no longer authoritative for many scholars who lived in later eras. Herein lies the issue. Given the transitional nature of the period, we cannot expect that the discourse current in 1800 would remain current in 1850 or 1875, much less in 1900 or 1925. If the discourse has changed, then we may assume that the way elements of the discourse are understood has changed. Therefore, any treatment of Qūrṣāwī's thought by later scholars could reasonably be considered an appropriation, reflecting not Qūrṣāwī's viewpoint, but a later one. And in fact this is quite clearly the case with the Jadids, for whom aspects of his reformist project had very different meanings than they had in their original setting.

Eighteenth-Century Reformism

In order to craft a more accurate understanding of Qūrṣāwī's thought and contributions, a new framing is needed, not merely of his ideas but of his context as well, with both connected to the broader Islamic environment of the period. Indeed, any study of the Muslim communities of Russia must begin with the premise—uncontestable, in my view—that the Volga-Ural region, at least

---

filosofiia. Kazan: RAN IIaLI, 1992; Aidar Iuzeev. *Filosofskaia mysl' tatarskogo naroda*. Kazan: Tatarstan knizhnoe izd-vo, 2007.

17. Spannaus, "Ur-Text."

prior to the Soviet period, was part of the Muslim world and Bulghar Muslims were full participants within the global Islamic community. Though shaped by their particular circumstances within the Russian Empire, they were hardly cut off from other Muslim regions or the collective Islamic discourse current at the time.[18] As Robert Crews writes:

> Though important localized factors gave form to religious controversies, these did not occur in isolation. Networks of scholars and Sufis linked village and small-town mosque communities through trade, study, preaching, pilgrimage, and the circulation of manuscript literature in Tatar, Arabic, and Persian to regional centers of learning, the *madrasas*, whose number increased in the late eighteenth and early nineteenth centuries. Their ties extended to cosmopolitan hubs of scholarship and piety in Bukhara, Samarkand, Kabul, Istanbul, Baghdad, Cairo, Mecca, and other locales. Through these channels, Russia's Muslims shared in the conflicts and concerns of their co-religionists throughout the community of Islam. How Muslims in the Russian empire experienced and made sense of these broader dialogues and disputes turned on their adaptation of resources from both a cosmopolitan repertoire of Islamic norms and imperatives and the political context of the tsarist empire.[19]

In this way, Qūrṣāwī, though living much of his life closer to Moscow than, say, Baghdad, should be viewed primarily within the context of the 18th- and early 19th-century Islamic world, as manifested in this particular geographic setting.

This approach is borne out by the content of Qūrṣāwī's reformist project, which is not directed toward the tsarist state or Russian society but rather focused on reforming the Muslim community from within. (In fact, his writings are virtually devoid of any mention of Russia or Russians.) It is centered around religious correctness and Muslims' adherence to scriptural norms, and as such, it represents a type of *tajdīd* (renewal), a notion of uniquely religious reform long established in Islamic tradition.[20]

---

18. They were/are certainly peripheral, but no more so than Muslims in Southeast Asia or sub-Saharan Africa.

19. Robert Crews. *For Prophet and Tsar: Islam and Empire in Russia and Central Asia.* Cambridge, MA: Harvard UP, 2005, pp. 96–97.

20. Qūrṣāwī, *Irshād*, p. 29. Stemming from a prophetic hadith, *tajdīd* as conventionally understood is the idea that the moral trajectory of the community will periodically drift off course, and a *mujaddid* (a "renewer," a figure of great piety, wisdom, and learning) will

By advocating for *tajdīd*, Qūrṣāwī falls alongside several contemporary scholars in other parts of the Islamic world who were engaged in similarly oriented reformist projects—namely, Shāh Wālī Allāh al-Dihlawī (1703–1762) in Mughal India, Aḥmad b. Idrīs (1760–1837) and Muḥammad b. ʿAlī al-Sanūsī (1787–1859) in North Africa, and Muḥammad b. ʿAlī al-Shawkānī (1760–1834) in Yemen.

The scholarly attention directed toward these figures, and 18th-century developments generally, has increased in recent decades, beginning largely with the work of John Voll, who has argued for the existence of a particular reformist trend cultivated by a global network of scholars centered in the Hijaz.[21] This literature has focused primarily on a small handful of select figures (and to a lesser extent on those associated with them), including those listed above, as well as Muḥammad b. ʿAbd al-Wahhāb (1703–1787), the founder of Wahhabism in central Arabia. This approach, particularly for Voll, seeks to articulate a single rubric of reformism encompassing all of these scholars, premised upon the student-teacher connections linking them and the commonalities within their respective outlooks, as well as affiliation with reform-minded Sufi orders such as the Naqshbandiyya and Khalwatiyya.[22] In fact, there is a strong connection between this view and "neo-Sufism," a historiographical concept that describes a reformist trend emerging among some Sufi orders in the 17th and 18th centuries that promoted legalism and conventional piety against the mystical excesses found in certain forms of Sufism.[23] Voll explicitly links it with the 18th-century Hijaz network, calling

be needed to get it back on track, religiously speaking—to expunge incorrect beliefs and practices and return the community toward righteousness; see John Voll. "Renewal and Reform in Islamic History: Tajdid and Islah." *Voices of Resurgent Islam*. Ed. John L. Esposito. New York: Oxford UP, 1983. 32–47; Ella Landau-Tasseron. "The 'Cyclical Reform': A Study of the Mujaddid Tradition." *Studia Islamica*, no. 70; 1989. 79–117.

21. John O. Voll. "Muhammad Hayya al-Sindi and Muhammad ibn ʿAbd al-Wahhab: An Analysis of an Intellectual Group in Eighteenth-Century Madina." *Bulletin of the School of Oriental and African Studies, University of London*, vol. 38, no. 1; 1975. 32–39. On the Hijaz network, see also Basheer M. Nafi. "Tasawwuf and Reform in Pre-Modern Islamic Culture: In Search of Ibrahim al-Kurani." *Die Welt des Islams*, vol. 42, no. 3; 2002. 307–355.

22. John O. Voll. *Islam: Continuity and Change in the Modern World*. Boulder, CO: Westview Press, 1982; John O. Voll. "Hadith Scholars and Tariqahs: An Ulama Group in the 18th Century Haramayn and Their Impact in the Islamic World." *Journal of Asian and African Studies*, vol. 15, no. 3/4; July/Oct. 1980. 264–273.

23. Fazlur Rahman. *Islam*. 2nd ed. Chicago: U of Chicago P, 2002, pp. 193–211.

its reformist outlook "an apparent coming together of hadith scholarship and Neo-Sufism."[24]

Voll's work has led to a model that is at least tacitly accepted as illustrative of 18th-century reformism generally. According to this model, it is activist in nature, concerned with matters of broad religious significance and social-communal transformation. This is expressed in general terms of scripturalism, a "return to" Qurʾan and Sunna, and a renewed focus on their role in Islamic piety and religiosity. Additionally, there is the prominence of hadith scholarship, which has a central place in this model. Looking beyond the standard hadith canon, reformers stressed the importance of earlier collections—especially Mālik's *Muwaṭṭāʾ*—and emphasized oral transmission and memorization for prophetic reports.[25] *Ijtihād* is a main feature of this model as well, and part of 18th-century reformers' scripturalism involves renewed engagement with the texts of revelation and scholars' ability to interpret them without relying on *taqlīd*. There is also considerable skepticism—if not downright hostility—directed toward the *madhhab* as an institution and its role in shaping legal doctrine.

However, Ahmad Dallal has pointed out a number of serious shortcomings with this model. He notes that it is based on the views of a limited set of scholars and thus cannot be considered representative, and in fact there is little in the writings of these scholars to warrant grouping them together under a single rubric of reform. He argues instead that greater research is needed into the specific content of these disparate intellectual projects.[26] Bernard Haykel echoes this critique in his study of Shawkānī, writing that "the substantive content of the ideologies of Islamic revival needs to be thoroughly researched before any broad generalizations can be made about the nature of Islamic thought in a given period or across a vast expanse of geographic space." Moreover, due regard must be placed upon the particularities of setting for

24. Voll, *Islam*, p. 38; see also Voll, "Hadith Scholars," pp. 264–266; Nehemia Levtzion and John O. Voll. "Introduction." *Eighteenth-Century Renewal and Reform in Islam*. Eds. Nehemia Levtzion and John O. Voll. Syracuse, NY: Syracuse UP, 1987. 3–20; Bernd Radtke. "Sufism in the 18th Century: An Attempt at a Provisional Appraisal." *Die Welt des Islams*, vol. 36, no. 3; 1996. 326–364.

25. This was partly involved in the collection of so-called elevated *isnāds*; see John Voll. "ʿAbdallah ibn Salim al-Basri and 18th Century Hadith Scholarship." *Die Welt des Islams*, vol. 42, no. 3; 2002. 356–372; Basheer M. Nafi. "A Teacher of ibn ʿAbd al-Wahhab: Muhammad Hayat al-Sindi and the Revival of *Ashab al-Hadith*'s Methodology." *Islamic Law and Society*, vol. 13, no. 2; 2006. 208–241.

26. Ahmad Dallal. "The Origins and Objectives of Islamic Revivalist Thought, 1750–1850." *Journal of the American Oriental Society*, vol. 113, no. 3; July/Sept. 1993. 341–359.

each reformer, which is largely passed over in Voll's approach: "Given that ideas are not formed in a vacuum, one must attempt to link a given scholar's ideology with the political and social contexts in which he is developing his views."[27] Indeed, Dallal notes that shared student-teacher relationships hardly entail shared views and, contrary to the literature that seeks to locate 18th-century reformism in broad *ʿulamāʾ* networks, intellectual movements that were primarily regional in character were the more important drivers of reform. He writes:

> The main intellectual contributions were made by scholars who, in addition to their direct and deep involvement in the political and social affairs of their own regions, were locally educated; their ideas were definitely hybrid and heavily indebted to diverse elements of the vast Islamic legacy, but were not the product of a universal pan-Islamic movement.[28]

Thus, though broad reformist trends may be important, they should be subordinated to the study of local trends and movements, in which the true intellectual vigor of this period manifested itself. Focusing on particular contexts and the specific content of scholars' views—rather than simply grouping all contemporary instances of "reformism" together—will contribute to more accurate representations of the varieties and diversity of reformist thought in this period. (Though not focused on the 18th century, Khaled El-Rouayheb's recent study of postclassical scholarship is remarkably valuable in this regard.)[29]

This is especially true of reform movements whose origins lay outside the Arab Middle East, which are largely ignored in scholarship.[30] Indeed, of the major reformist figures studied, only Shāh Wālī Allāh comes from a non-Arab

---

27. Bernard Haykel. *Revival and Reform in Islam: The Legacy of Muhammad al-Shawkani*. Cambridge: Cambridge UP, 2003, p. 13.

28. Ahmad Dallal. "The Origins and Early Development of Islamic Reform." *The New Cambridge History of Islam*. Vol. 6: *Muslims and Modernity: Culture and Society since 1800*. Ed. Robert Hefner. Cambridge: Cambridge UP, 2010. 107–147, pp. 135–136.

29. Khaled El-Rouayheb. *Islamic Intellectual History in the Seventeenth Century: Scholarly Currents in the Ottoman Empire and the Maghreb*. Cambridge: Cambridge UP, 2015.

30. As Nikki Keddie has noted, "One reason why there have been few comparative studies of Islamic revivalist movements is that scholars of Islam tend to be divided by geographic specialty, with Middle East specialists happy to ignore the great majority of the world's Muslims who live outside the Middle East"; Nikki R. Keddie. "The Revolt of Islam, 1700 to 1903: Comparative Considerations and Relations to Imperialism." *Comparative Studies in Society and History*, vol. 36, no. 3; July 1994. 463–487, p. 468. One important exception is Azmyumardi Azra. *The Origins of Islamic Reformism in Southeast Asia: Networks of*

background, yet is often grouped under this rubric on the basis of his very brief period of study in Arabia.[31]

I agree with Dallal and Haykel that any conclusions about reformism in the 18th century must focus on more substantive criteria than scholarly background or Sufi affiliation and be based on a wider scope of research than it has been up to this point.[32] Questions of the existence of a coherent reformist trend centered around scholarly networks in the Hijaz, which scholars were involved therein and what was the content of their views are all historiographically important, but it is much too premature to declare this reformist trend broadly representative. The period spanning the 15th through 18th centuries is by far the least-studied era of Islamic history (particularly in terms of intellectual history), and stereotypes of "decline" and "stagnation" in its cultural and intellectual production remain common; our current understanding of any reformist trends in this period is too limited and atomized for a portrayal that is both broad and accurate to be developed.

I do not attempt to answer these questions, which are beyond the scope of a study devoted to a single scholar. Rather, my analysis of Qūrṣāwī is intended to contribute to these discussions by providing a point of comparison for 18th-century reformism that falls outside the contours of the current understanding in a number of important respects but also shares significant overlap.

Reformism and European Influence

One way that the study of Qūrṣāwī's project is uniquely suited to add to the scholarship on Islamic reformism is regarding the European impact on reformist movements. Much of the analysis of 18th-century reform is premised on a dichotomy between types of reformism that were wholly indigenous in character and those that were subject to Western influence. The former are classified as part of 18th-century reform, understood—often implicitly—as

Malay-Indonesian and Middle Eastern Ulama *in the Seventeenth and Eighteenth Centuries.* Honolulu, HI: U of Hawaii P, 2004.

31. E.g., Voll, "Muhammad Hayya al-Sindi," p. 39; Voll, *Islam*, p. 59.

32. I would also agree with Dallal that the scholarship on Islamic reformism in general too frequently uses Wahhabism as a benchmark for evaluating other movements, rather than treating it as anomalous within Islamic history; Dallal, "Origins and Early Development," esp. pp. 108–109.

part of the long 18th century.[33] The latter, on the other hand, are treated as an entirely separate genus: "Shaped, as it were, by the encounter with Europe, nineteenth-century reform was first triggered by the increasing material threat of expanding European powers, but gradually reflected an increasing awareness of the cultural and intellectual challenges brought about by this encounter."[34] Similarly, R. S. O'Fahey argues that 18th-century reformers should be considered "ignorers" of the West, free from European influence,[35] and John Esposito and Voll treat reformism that is part of the *tajdīd* tradition as "internal" reform, separate from considerations of any Western impact.[36]

This dichotomy seems to have developed out of scholarly debates over the question of Islamic civilization's decline in later centuries. In an effort to show the cultural vibrancy of post–"golden age" Islam, authors pointed to intellectual developments in the 17th and 18th centuries while emphasizing their independence from simultaneous phenomena in Europe.[37] Out of these efforts came Schulze's idea of an indigenous Islamic "enlightenment," characterized by the emergence of new cultural, religious, and economic forms.[38]

Although Schulze's highly controversial view has largely disappeared from scholarship, some aspects of it have been adopted by other scholars of reform. Most notably, O'Fahey has utilized it in service of his treatment of Sufi-inspired reformism in 18th-century North Africa. He combines characteristics of Schulze's enlightenment with the concept of neo-Sufism to address the

33. In this sense, the long 18th century could be very long indeed. Dallal extends it to include ʿAbd al-Qādir al-Jazāʾirī, whose life (1808–1883) falls entirely in the 19th century; ibid., p. 129.

34. Ibid., p. 140, also 133.

35. R. S. O'Fahey. *Enigmatic Saint: Ahmad ibn Idris and the Idrisi Tradition.* Evanston, IL: Northwestern UP, 1990, p. 5.

36. John Esposito and John Voll. *Makers of Contemporary Islam.* Oxford: Oxford UP, 2001, p. 18.

37. Cf. on this literature Stefan Reichmuth. "Arabic Literature and Islamic Scholarship in the 17th/18th Century: Topics and Biographies: Introduction." *Die Welt des Islams*, vol. 42, no. 3; 2002. 281–288.

38. Reinhard Schulze. "Das Islamische 18. Jahrhundert. Versuch einer historiographischen Kritik." *Die Welt des Islams*, vol. 30, no. 1; 1990. 140–159; Reinhard Schulze. "Was ist die islamische Aufklärung?" *Die Welt des Islams*, vol. 36, no. 3; 1996. 276–325. For one critique (of many), see Rudolph Peters. "Reinhard Schulze's Quest for an Islamic Enlightenment." *Die Welt des Islams*, vol. 30, no. 1; 1990. 160–162. The idea of an Islamic Enlightenment is linked with Peter Gran's theory of capitalist-mercantilist development in 18th-century Egypt; Peter Gran. *The Islamic Roots of Capitalism: Egypt, 1760–1840*. Austin: U of Texas P, 1979.

emergence of what he sees as an individualistic emphasis on piety among some Sufi orders.[39] O'Fahey conceptualizes this type of piety—"pietism," he calls it—in Weberian terms, and he views it as an effort to reshape Islamic religiosity along rationalistic and humanistic lines.[40]

There are important similarities between O'Fahey's approach and the one employed by Kemper, whose analysis of the Islamic discourse of the Volga-Ural region is based on Weber's idea of the "Protestant ethic." Accordingly, he focuses on the appearance among Bulghar Muslims of moralistic, ascetic forms of religious practice—in particular the spread of sober, legalistic Sufism—as an indication of cultural development, which he links with the emergence of a "spirit of Islamic capitalism" among these communities. He connects these changes in religious practice and discourse to the simultaneous growth and development of industry and commerce in the Volga-Ural region.[41] However, these developments are not separate from the West, but rather are caused by exposure to European society. Kemper here blurs the distinction between 18th- and 19th-century reformism. Following Voll's analysis, he links Qūrṣāwī's advocacy of *ijtihād* with a broad revitalizing trend across the Islamic world at the time, citing figures such as Shawkānī and Sanūsī as examples.[42] But he also

39. Like the Islamic enlightenment, the concept of neo-Sufism has been widely criticized by scholars, including O'Fahey himself. It has been argued that neo-Sufism does not constitute a distinct or coherent trend, rather its specific ideas either are widely attested across a range of Sufis or the putative neo-Sufis understand those ideas among themselves in inconsistent or contradictory ways; Bernd Radtke. "Ijtihad and Neo-Sufism." *Asiatische Studien: Zeitschrift der Schweizerischen Gesellschaft für Asienkunde*, vol. 48, nos. 3–4; 1994. 909–921; Dallal, "Origins and Early Development," pp. 127–128. Moreover, O'Fahey and Radtke contend that neo-Sufism has an insufficient foundation in the neo-Sufis' own writings, but is based on suppositions taken from the reports of colonial administrators about the activities of Sufi orders under surveillance; R. S. O'Fahey and Bernd Radtke. "Neo-Sufism Reconsidered." *Der Islam*, vol. 70; 1993. 52–87; see also Alexander Knysh. "Sufism as an Explanatory Paradigm: The Issue of the Motivations of Sufi Resistance Movements in Western and Russian Scholarship." *Die Welt des Islams*, vol. 42, no. 2; 2002. 139–173. Voll for his part defends neo-Sufism on the basis of organizational developments among reformist-minded Sufi orders in the 18th century; John Voll. "Neo-Sufism: Reconsidered Again." *Canadian Journal of African Studies*, vol. 42, no. 2/3; 2008. 314–330.

40. Rex Sean O'Fahey. "Pietism, Fundamentalism and Mysticism: An Alternative View of the 18th and 19th Century Islamic World." *Festskrift til Historisk Institutts 40-ars jubileum 1997*. Ed. Geir Atle Ersland. Bergen: Historik institutt, Universitetet i Bergen, 1997. 151–166.

41. Kemper, *Sufis*, esp. pp. 168–172.

42. Ibid., pp. 302–304, also 170. Kemper, following Rudolph Peters, characterizes this revitalization as "fundamentalist," a view (also taken by Voll) that has rightly drawn criticism for being anachronistic; Dallal, "Origins and Early Development," pp. 132–133; Rudolph Peters. "Ijtihad and Taqlid in 18th and 19th Century Islam." *Die Welt des Islams*, vol. 20, no. 3; 1980. 131–145; Voll, *Islam*, pp. 29–30. See also Chapter 7.

places Qūrṣāwī's reformism within the same Weberian framework, including it as part of Bulghars' 19th-century modernization and secularization.

Although Kemper excludes from his analysis the subject of Jadidism (the historiography of which he has critiqued), this approach mirrors that of earlier Soviet Marxist scholars, who sought to place the development of Jadidism within the domain of economic development.[43] Idiiatullina, who also adopts a Weberian perspective, goes further than Kemper in her analysis, linking Qūrṣāwī with Jadidism explicitly and placing him within a clear narrative of secularization.[44] In addition, Mustafa Tuna's recent study of Volga-Ural history relies on similar notions of Muslims' modernization through exposure to European economic, technological, and cultural advancement.[45] The approach these authors employ thus continues to rely on the Eurocentric and specifically secularist notions of "progress" and modernization found in the narrative of Jadidism.[46]

While I disagree with this theoretical framework and its emphasis on modernization, Kemper is right to ignore the dichotomy between indigenous expressions of Muslim reformism and reformist projects shaped by the interaction with Europe. Bulghar Muslims' circumstances were such that Western influence was utterly inevitable. Unlike other parts of the Islamic world where the European presence was diffuse, indirect, or marginal at the turn of the 19th century, Volga-Ural Muslims, under Russian political rule since 1552, were by this time firmly incorporated into the fabric of the tsarist state. (See Chapter 2.) According to the dichotomous view, indigenous reform would have been impossible in this context. Yet, as we will see, there were many ways in which the Bulghar religious and cultural modus vivendi was not substantively different from that of other Muslim societies. (This modus vivendi would change drastically by the 20th century, of course, but this, too, was the case in virtually all Muslim societies.)

---

43. Alexander Knysh, in an insightful review of the work, notes that, given the emphasis Kemper's study places on the interaction of economic and industrial development and ideological changes (in this case, in terms of religious thought), his analysis is not far from classical Marxism; Aleksandr Knysh. "Razmyshleniia po povodu russkogo perevoda knigi Mikhaèlia Kempera." *Ab Imperio*, no. 2; 2011. 333–344.

44. Idiiatullina, "Vvedenie."

45. Mustafa Tuna. *Imperial Russia's Muslims: Islam, Empire, and European Modernity, 1788–1914*. Cambridge: Cambridge UP, 2015.

46. Cf. Wennberg, *On the Edge*, p. 14. To be sure, this theoretical shortcoming is hardly limited to the study of Jadidism, but is a much larger problem within scholarship on Muslim societies and history.

Qūrṣāwī's reformist project thus straddles the two sides of the dichotomy. Though shaped by European presence, it is indigenous in form and content. The impact of Russian rule does not negate the ways that Qūrṣāwī fits in with other 18th-century reformers. This does not mean that his thought is incoherent or self-contradictory; rather, it means that differentiating between the two types of reformism is less straightforward—and there is more overlap between them—than the dichotomous view allows. While distinguishing the two can be analytically useful, they should not be treated as wholly or self-evidently separate.[47]

Tradition and Institutions

Implicit in the distinction between indigenous and European-influenced reformism is an opposition between tradition and modernity: indigenous reformism, by virtue of its basis in the Islamic past, is tied to tradition in ways that European-influenced reformism, which is linked with Western modernity, cannot be. This opposition, however, is misleading. Islamic reformism of either type is necessarily articulated in reference to beliefs, practices, and terms established in the past but which continue to have meaning and relevance for Muslims, regardless of the advent of modernity. This is particularly important in regard to Qūrṣāwī's reformist project, which, as I argue, is both indigenous and shaped by Western impact, grounded entirely within the Islamic scholarly tradition.

The scholarly tradition is part of the broader Islamic tradition, as defined by Talal Asad: a combination of elements that at their most basic possess meaning in reference to a conception of the "Islamic" that is considered authoritative. This discursive space encompasses the forms, symbols, practices, genres, texts, terms, and tropes through which the religion is understood and transmitted. This notion of tradition is seen as

> consist[ing] essentially of discourses that seek to instruct practitioners regarding the correct form and purpose of a given practice that, precisely

47. Part of the logic behind this separation is to contradict the widespread (and I believe incorrect) notion that modern religious phenomena in Muslim societies—namely Islamism, Salafism, even Jadidism—are continuations of much earlier trends, rather than novel developments tied to modernity; e.g., Voll, *Islam*; Ira Lapidus. "Islamic Revival and Modernity: The Contemporary Movements and the Historical Paradigms." *Journal of the Economic and Social History of the Orient*, vol. 40, no. 4; 1997. 444–460; Ingeborg Baldauf. "Jadidism in Central Asia Within Reformism and Modernism in the Muslim World." *Die Welt des Islams*, vol. 41, no. 1; 2000. 72–88.

> because it is established, has a history. These discourses relate conceptually to *a past* (when the practice was instituted, and from which the knowledge of its point and proper performance has been transmitted) and *a future* (how the point of that practice can best be secured in the short or long term, or why it should be modified or abandoned), through *a present* (how it is linked to other practices, institutions, and social conditions).

According to Asad, then, tradition represents a set of discourses existing diachronically, connected to social and historical circumstances. He goes on, "An Islamic discursive tradition is simply a tradition of Muslim discourse that addresses itself to conceptions of the Islamic past and future, with reference to a particular Islamic practice in the present."[48]

It is incorrect to speak of tradition as the antecedent or antipode of modernity, whether in historical or conceptual terms. Tradition, as a set of diachronic, socially established discourses and practices, represents a separate philosophical category from modernity, a particular historical period. The "traditional" is not equivalent to the "premodern," nor does modernity supplant tradition; tradition, as a means of cultural transmission through time, continues across eras. (Indeed, Kwame Gyekye argues that every society is necessarily traditional in this sense, and the idea that tradition could be comprehensively replaced would require the drastic, utter abandonment of a society's total culture and way of life.)[49] Modernity, which affects virtually every aspect of society, inevitably transforms tradition, but it does not negate nor even alter the notion of a discursive tradition. To return to Asad's definition, discourses are both socially grounded in a present and simultaneously related "to a past (when the practice was instituted, and from which the knowledge of its point and proper performance has been transmitted) and a future (how the point of that practice can best be secured in the short or long term, *or why it should be modified or abandoned*)."[50] As he notes, particular discourses do not continue perpetually unchanged, but their alteration or abandonment is itself part of the diachronic continuum of tradition stretching through the present back to

48. Talal Asad. "The Idea of an Anthropology of Islam." *Qui Parle*, vol. 17, no. 2; 2009. 1–30. [Re-edition of *The Idea of an Anthropology of Islam*. Washington, DC: Center for Contemporary Arab Studies, Georgetown University, 1986], p. 20; emphasis in original.

49. Kwame Gyekye. *Tradition and Modernity: Philosophical Reflections on the African Experience*. New York: Oxford UP, 1997, esp. pp. 217–232.

50. Asad, "Idea," p. 20; emphasis added.

the discourses' establishment. That they change over time is itself evidence of their continuous existence as part of a tradition, a fact that is not negated by their (eventual) abandonment.

Subsumed within this tradition is the Islamic scholarly tradition, which constitutes what Alasdair MacIntyre calls a "practice," defined as any cooperative, complex, formal activity.[51] MacIntyre, whose work forms the basis for Asad's idea of tradition, describes how practices proceed and develop over time as practitioners work toward the advancement of their practice, necessarily in reference to its past forms. These efforts are sustained and structured by institutions, which provide a framework for engaging in a practice and to connect practices to broader society.[52] Islamic scholarship, both in general and in specific fields—say, *kalām* or *tafsīr*—is a collective endeavor to understand and articulate the moral substance of Islam, with its own parameters, methodologies, and internal dynamics. It is guided and supported by particular institutions, with its own practitioners in *ʿulamāʾ*. And it has a history; its contours and dynamics have been created and developed over the centuries, with different (though not discrete) phases of evolution.[53] Sherman Jackson, speaking of *fiqh*, refers to this diachronic development as the "scaffolding" of legal discourse, wherein *fuqahāʾ* could rely on the work of earlier scholars to advance their own interpretations.[54] (See Chapter 3.) Scholarship is characterized by scholars' constant conversation and disputation with their contemporaries and predecessors, part of, as MacIntyre describes, their continuous striving to further the field.[55] Islamic scholarship is therefore also a discursive tradition—or multiple, constituent discursive traditions—within the broader Islamic tradition, as defined by Asad.

---

51. Like an academic subject, artistic genre, sport, or trade.

52. Alasdair MacIntyre. *After Virtue: A Study in Moral Theory*. 1981. 3rd ed. Notre Dame, IN: U of Notre Dame P, 2007, esp. p. 187.

53. On the applicability of MacIntyre's approach to *ʿulamāʾ*, see Muhammad Qasim Zaman. *The Ulama in Contemporary Islam: Custodians of Change*. Princeton, NJ: Princeton UP, 2002, pp. 4–6.

54. Jackson, who equates scaffolding with *taqlīd*, uses the analogy that scholars working within such a framework are freed from continuously having to reinvent the wheel and can "devote themselves to the more practical enterprise of building a car"; Sherman Jackson. "Taqlid, Legal Scaffolding and the Scope of Legal Injunctions in Post-Formative Theory: Mutlaq and ʿAmm in the Jurisprudence of Shihab al-Din al-Qarafi." *Islamic Law and Society*, vol. 3, no. 2; 1996. 165–192, p. 172.

55. MacIntyre, *After Virtue*, esp. p. 194, 221–222.

It's difficult to draw a firm distinction between the Islamic scholarly tradition and Islamic tradition as a whole. Asad describes the latter in normative terms of a hegemonic orthodoxy, encompassing above all that which Muslims qua Muslims believe should be taught and learned.[56] *ʿUlamāʾ* and their scholarship obviously play an important role in not only teaching but also articulating these hegemonic discourses and their epistemic underpinnings, but they are not alone in crafting or upholding orthodoxy, which is somewhat different from the elite discourses that circulate among *ʿulamāʾ* and within scholarly institutions. MacIntyre argues that practices are embedded in broader traditions within society and necessarily connected to the morality of society, its norms, values, and priorities, and they must maintain this connection in order to remain viable.[57] They are thus subsumed within the overarching moral tradition of their society; simply put, the Islamic scholarly tradition could not exist apart from Islamic tradition, but not vice versa.

(This moral component is crucial to understanding the scholarly tradition. Scholarship was seen as ultimately and primarily benefiting the community, for whom *ʿulamāʾ* served as learned guides, and such guidance was considered a necessity [*farḍ*] for the community's moral and religious standing. See Chapter 4.)

As the scholarly tradition is tied to, and operates within, society, it is altered by societal shifts. Discursive change is itself necessarily part of a practice, MacIntyre argues, as practitioners engage in the continuous articulation of its discourses.[58] But such change inexorably falls within the tradition, regardless of whether it is driven by external factors or emerges out of the tradition's internal dynamics. As Asad states, between discourses' origins in the past and the continuum of the tradition into the future stands a present, the historical moment in which discourses are connected to broader circumstances. This forms the crux where the discourses of the tradition interact with social reality, in regard to which they are continued, altered, or abandoned, but nevertheless in conversation with the tradition's past.

This is the case even in instances of significant historical transformation. As Mansoor Moaddel argues, authoritative discourses in a social and cultural setting play a role in the formulation of new discourses spurred by historical shifts within that setting. Although employing a different theoretical approach than Asad and MacIntyre, Moaddel's analysis offers important

---

56. Rather than *anything* Muslims do, say, or believe; Asad, "Idea," pp. 20–22.

57. MacIntyre, *After Virtue*, pp. 222–223.

58. Ibid., esp. p. 194.

nuance in understanding how circumstances shape discursive and ideological production. He puts forward what he calls an "episodic discourse model," wherein moments of historical change—episodes—warrant the production of new discourses. He divides the factors affecting discursive production into two types, deductive and inductive, with the former affecting the *content* of discourses and the latter the *context* of their formulation.[59]

In this model, changes to sociohistorical circumstances—an inductive factor—help explain how new ideas come to be developed and accepted, while preexisting ideas current in the environment—a deductive factor—help determine their precise content. The role of prior discourse is equivalent to tradition (a term Moaddel does not use himself) in Asad's conception, in the sense of a framework for discourses that are authoritative and thus determinative of future forms. Indeed, Moaddel writes that "ideological production is a function of the kinds of discourses that are dominant in the social environment," indicating the effect the discursive norms that underlie tradition have on the formulation of new ideas.[60]

Institutions, especially with a practice such as Islamic scholarship, play an important role in upholding tradition, maintaining the parameters for authoritative discourses. This essential normative function of institutions is carried out within society and is susceptible to societal changes. As noted, MacIntyre holds that institutions link a practice to its society, and they facilitate and shape the continuous articulation of its discourses by its practitioners; they therefore serve as the point of inflection at which the circumstances of society can impact the future of the tradition. The parameters of tradition remain only as long as institutions uphold them; if an institution is altered or abandoned, then the parameters relying upon its authority would be altered or abandoned as well. Thus changes within a society—Moaddel's episodes—affect tradition, both allowing for and warranting the articulation of new ideas within the discourse.

As we will see, the Muslim communities of the Russian Empire experienced a number of historical episodes in the 18th century that brought with them significant social, economic, and religious changes. These episodes were largely the result of measures undertaken by the Russian imperial state, and the changes wrought by them directly affected the authority and function

59. Mansoor Moaddel. *Islamic Modernism, Nationalism, and Fundamentalism: Episode and Discourse*. Chicago: U of Chicago P, 2005, pp. 14–23.

60. Ibid., p. 15. It is more useful, I think, given the essentially religious nature of Qūrṣāwī's thought, to think of it as a "discursive tradition," rather than "socially dominant discourses," as Moaddel would have it.

of Islamic institutions under its rule. The changes to the community's institutions thus paved the way for the significant transformation of Islamic thought that took place over the course of the 18th and 19th centuries and in which Qūrṣāwī played an important role. It is a main argument of this study that Qūrṣāwī's reformist positions were simultaneously facilitated by and a response to the alteration of these institutions. This is not to say, however, that his thought was inspired by the interaction with the Russian state. Rather, Qūrṣāwī's works are entirely of the Hanafi-Maturidi tradition in the postclassical period and have no relevance to Russians or Russian society. (In this respect, Qūrṣāwī is truly an "ignorer" of the West.) The key to understanding the connection between his reform project and Russian rule lies within Moaddel's distinction between inductive and deductive factors. The societal changes to Islamic institutions at the hands of the government fall strictly into the former category. As such, they affect the circumstances for Qūrṣāwī's reformism while bearing no direct influence on the content of that reformism, which is instead determined by the discursive and institutional parameters of the Islamic scholarly tradition.

The differences between the two broadly constitutive elements of his thought—law and theology—reflect this fact. His stance on Islamic law represents a more radical departure than his stance on theology, which, I will argue, is due to the fact that Islamic institutions suffered greater interference by the tsarist government in terms of law than in terms of theology. Nevertheless, his stance on the former is no less grounded in Islamic tradition than his stance on the latter; the greater degree of transformation in the legal sphere merely allowed for the formulation of a wider range of ideas.

The Current Study

For Qūrṣāwī, the transformation of Islamic institutions under Russian rule was a moral concern. He saw the scholarly tradition as the foremost domain of orthodoxy and Islamic normativity, and it was an absolute religious necessity that it remain operative, with functional institutions capable of upholding it. The weakening of Islamic institutions jeopardized the maintenance of the tradition, thus warranting its alteration in the interest of preserving it.

Indeed, the scholarly tradition is the focal point of Qūrṣāwī's reformism, the main thrust of which is oriented toward emending erroneous practices and beliefs among *ʿulamāʾ*—who both articulate and maintain the tradition—to ensure its viability to serve the moral and religious needs of the community. In this regard, his thought is wholly internal to the tradition, relying upon its discourses, which continued to serve as the predominant, orthodox frame of reference for Bulghar Muslims. In responding to the circumstances under the Russian Empire, Qūrṣāwī's reformism also reflects European domination, which formed the broader environment. The present study focuses on each of these aspects to his thought—the response to Russian rule and the internal reform of Islamic scholarship—in particular how the latter forms a coherent whole for his reformist project, shaping the former.

The specific focus on Qūrṣāwī is intentional. Although he is certainly an important historical figure whose historiographical portrayal is in need of revision, I have chosen to look specifically at one scholar's thought in order to avoid the reductionism and teleology frequently encountered in works of Islamic intellectual history. Such an approach is particularly important in the history of the Muslims of the Russian Empire, where the scholarly picture of the broader context is still developing, and which, as noted, has been so far dominated by studies looking at these communities through the lens of modernization and the "development" or "emergence" of aspects therein—nationalism, capitalism, secularism, "enlightenment"—leading to research that is markedly teleological and overemphasizes "modernist" reform. Even Kemper's monograph, despite its praiseworthy contributions, nevertheless utilizes such a perspective; its Weberian approach places Qūrṣāwī into a narrative of the emergence of "rationalistic" and "pietistic" forms of religiosity, linked with capitalist development.[61] The association of particular categories of religious expression with modernization is characteristic of this literature, often in analytically problematic ways.[62] In addition, the focus on modernization frequently obscures and/or excludes religious and intellectual phenomena that are not continued or relevant in modernity, despite any earlier significance they may have. For instance, Qūrṣāwī's theological views, which constitute the most important element of his thought for contemporaries and take up the bulk of his writings, are almost entirely ignored in later historiography.

The present study thus focuses on Qūrṣāwī's thought as a whole, the discussions and debates in which he participated, and his particular milieu, in order to better understand the broader context. Here, one person's thought is used to shed light on the intellectual environment, as representative of the types of Islamic discourses circulating, the authoritative sources

---

61. Kemper, *Sufis*, esp. pp. 168–172, 301–304.

62. "Rationalistic" Islam, for instance, is commonly used to characterize positions that break with tradition, which is implicitly presented as irrational or unthinking; cf. Asad, "Idea," p. 22.

and antecedents, the topics of contemporary currency, the arguments his peers found persuasive (or not), and, in terms of the posthumous treatment of his thought, the subsequent changes to that environment. His reformist project serves as a specific example of views that were articulated within, and in reference to, Islamic tradition, but also—like the Bulghar environment—shaped by a context of significant historical change external to that tradition.

Despite this focus, I don't hold Qūrṣāwī to be paradigmatic nor the discourses current in the Bulghar environment to be univocal. Islamic tradition has always comprised varied symbols and discourses supporting myriad conflicting interpretations, and, as I will argue, changes to Islamic institutions led to a greater diversity of views; as such, the Bulghar environment was marked by vibrant and contentious debate, even between scholars of almost identical background and school affiliation (as Hanafi-Maturidis and the Naqshbandi-Mujaddidiyya were predominant). Qūrṣāwī's reformism was influential, but not overwhelmingly so, and a great many of his contemporaries differed with its premises and prescriptions. Though important, it represented one possibility among many others, including the eschewing of reform altogether. In this environment, the postclassical scholarly tradition was impacted by the shifting sociohistorical circumstances, eliciting the alteration of the former. Qūrṣāwī's thought and its reception show in specific terms the internal continuity of the tradition and how Bulghar *ʿulamāʾ* responded to their environment and adapted to the realities of Russian rule.

The analysis of Qūrṣāwī and the Bulghar intellectual environment, based on the study of his own writings and those of his contemporaries—in both manuscript and published form—leads to these main arguments: Qūrṣāwī's reformism is oriented toward emending what he sees as widespread shortcomings in the *ʿulamāʾ*'s scholarly understanding and approach, specifically a lack of a sound epistemological basis for their scholarship. He criticizes methodologies they use as fostering misguidance and beliefs that are erroneous or unfounded.

His critique, however, does not represent a rejection of the edifice of Islamic scholarship, but rather focuses on what he sees as a lack of vigilance and inquiry on scholars' part, leading them to accept and extend, rather than contest and exclude, flawed interpretations. And it is contemporary and recent scholars' insufficient knowledge that had allowed these errors to become established. Such positions must therefore be corrected and sound religious knowledge promoted.

Qūrṣāwī's thought is thus deeply grounded within the postclassical scholarly tradition (particularly Central Asian Hanafism and Maturidism), which he considers the sole normative framework for Islamic religious authority. As such, it is essential for the moral and religious well-being of the community, as is the continued existence of scholars learned in its discourses. The changes to Islamic institutions under Russian rule, however, altered and undermined the *ʿulamāʾ*'s function, especially in terms of law, and Qūrṣāwī puts forward a radical rethinking of the relationship between the *ʿulamāʾ* and the community in order to preserve the tradition in light of these institutional shifts.

There is no connection between Qūrṣāwī's reformism and Jadidism. They are separate phenomena, lacking any genealogical link, with goals that are in many ways diametrically opposed: Jadidism is overwhelmingly a rejection of the Islamic scholarly tradition in favor of intellectual and epistemic frameworks derived from European thought. It emerges as a movement only after significant changes to the intellectual environment—largely postdating Qūrṣāwī—have taken place.

Finally, the incorporation of Islamic institutions into the structures of the tsarist state represents a seismic shift in Bulghar Muslim society, which thus marks the beginning of modernity (defined specifically in Chapter 8) for these communities. Qūrṣāwī's reformism, as a response to these changes, is therefore a very early example of Islamic modernism. Any similarities or overlap between his thought and Jadidism can be attributed to fact that both, as forms of Islamic modernism, fall within, and speak to, the same broad historical context.

The question of modernity is one area where this analysis of Qūrṣāwī has much to contribute to the broader study of Islam and Islamic intellectual history. It touches upon the transformation of religious authority under state control and the types of responses articulated by *ʿulamāʾ*, as well as the impact of modernity and secularity upon Islamic tradition. His reformist project complicates the still-predominant perspective that identifies Islamic modernism and reform with the self-conscious embrace of westernization or Salafi fundamentalism. His approach to *ijtihād* has no connection to either, nor do his theological views, which are wholly characteristic of postclassical *kalām* (the validity of which was widely rejected by both European-inspired modernists and fundamentalists).

Yet Qūrṣāwī describes himself as following the doctrine of the *salaf* (*madhhab al-salaf*).[63] This comprises the views of both the major figures of

---

63. Abū Naṣr ʿAbd al-Naṣīr b. Ibrāhīm al-Qūrṣāwī. *Sharḥ jadīd li-l-ʿAqāʾid al-nasafiyya*. Ms. SPb IVR, no. A1241. Fols. 92b–147a, fol. 94b.

early Sunnism and the masters of the Hanafi-Maturidi and Naqshbandi Sufi traditions, which, along with the differences between his thought and characteristically "Salafi" beliefs, suggests the term was utilized in a manner broader than generally defined and quite distinct from its 20th-century meanings.[64] These discrepancies have relevance regarding Voll's model of 18th-century reformism, which he (and others) have put forward as the origins of modern Salafism.

It is Qūrṣāwī's reliance upon the existing structures of the scholarly tradition, both with law and—especially—theology that most sets him apart from Voll's model, as well as from Salafism. In fact, Qūrṣāwī views the scholarly tradition not only as an essential part of the religion but also as a viable discursive and moral paradigm. Unlike many modernist reformers, for whom it serves as a mere foil or frame of reference, for him it serves as an active, functional intellectual framework.

That such a stance toward the tradition coexists in a coherent way with a radical response to European imperialism speaks to both the mutability of scholarly discourse and the potential overlap between Western-influenced and indigenous reform. Indeed, Qūrṣāwī's reformism is simultaneously shaped by European rule and articulated without any reference to Europe. As such, it stands as an example of Islamic reformism responding to the European impact in a way that neither resists nor accommodates westernization. It can thus help us explore imperial rule and how Islamic institutions and discourses are thereby altered. Imperialism creates a distinct context that is shaped by state power, reorienting the Islamic religious environment (and therefore linking it with secularity). I argue that it wasn't the mere fact of non-Muslim political rule that brought about this impact but rather the specific ways that the Russian state approached Islamic institutions and the structures into which it fit them. (In this regard, diachronic changes to the tsarist government are certainly relevant, moving beyond static Muslim-state or Muslim-Christian relations.)

The study of Qūrṣāwī's reformism is thus one of the interaction between postclassical scholarship and a new historical context, and it is important for understanding the intellectual and religious changes that result from that interaction and the types of discourses and adaptations of tradition that emerge.

---

64. On the often-confused uses of "*salafi*," see Henri Lauzière. *The Making of Salafism: Islamic Reform in the Twentieth Century*. New York: Columbia UP, 2015.

Chapter Outline

The present study starts with a broad historical scope, narrowing to Qūrṣāwī's milieu and the specific analysis of his thought and its discursive context. From there it broadens again to address the issue of modernity and Bulghar intellectual history in the long 19th century, and finally Jadidism.

Chapter 2 presents both the history of Bulghar Muslims' relationship to the Russian state and a description of the *ʿulamāʾ* and their changing roles in society in the 18th and early 19th centuries. It addresses the structural changes to Islamic institutions resulting from their incorporation into the tsarist bureaucracy and its impact on religious discourse, which frames the discussion of Qūrṣāwī's biography and interactions with other scholars, including his condemnation in Bukhara.

The next four chapters are devoted to the analysis of Qūrṣāwī's thought. Chapter 3 establishes the contours of postclassical scholarship and locates the basic premises of his reformist project within them. Chapter 4 is an investigation of the legal aspects of his reformism and his approach to *ijtihād*, which is shaped by state control of Islamic institutions. Chapter 5 describes in detail Qūrṣāwī's stance on the divine attributes and his critique of the established position, analyzing the philosophical and metaphysical dimensions of his stance. Chapter 6 is devoted to the historical development of postclassical *kalām* and situates his stance within the later stages of that tradition, arguing that it reflects changes in theological discourse unique to this period. Chapter 7 concludes this section, discussing his thought as a whole in historical context and its implications for Islamic intellectual history, particularly in reference to the literature on 18th-century reformism.

Chapters 8 and 9, in contrast to the preceding, adopt a broader, more interpretive perspective, looking at the changing historical environment from the second half of the 18th century up to World War I. Chapter 8 addresses the issue of modernity in Bulghar history from a theoretical perspective, tying the institutional changes of the late 18th century to profound religious and social shifts that mark a new historical period, with a discussion of religious and intellectual developments that follow from this transition. Chapter 9 then looks at the modern intellectual history of Volga-Ural Muslims, including the emergence of Jadidism within this history. It shows how Volga-Ural Islamic discourse was transformed over the course of the 19th century, focusing on changes to the scholarly tradition and its place within this environment, and the growing diversity and contestation in the exercise of religious and social authority. Finally, Chapter 10 addresses Qūrṣāwī's thought in light of the discussion of Jadidism and its historical development, showing that the historiographical narrative locating the movement's origins in Qūrṣāwī and Marjānī's embrace of *ijtihād* cannot be sustained.

FIGURE 1 First Admiralteiskaia (Bīshbālta) Mosque, constructed on the outskirts of Kazan between 1805 and 1825 (Anonymous, undated photo)

2

An ʿĀlim *in the Russian Empire*

ʿABD AL-NAṢĪR ABŪ al-Naṣr b. Ibrāhīm b. Yārmuḥammad al-Qāzānī al-Bulghārī al-Ḥanafī al-Qūrṣāwī was born in 1776 (1190 AH) in the village of Qūrṣā (Russ. Verkhniaia Korsa), northeast of Kazan. Educated locally, he traveled to Bukhara in about 1798 to pursue further studies.[1] While there he was initiated into the Naqshbandi-Mujaddidiyya Sufi order. After four years in Bukhara he returned to Qūrṣā, becoming imam and *mudarris* in the village mosque. He again traveled to Bukhara in 1808, and his criticisms of the city's *ʿulamāʾ* regarding theological questions led him afoul of the ruling amir, who sentenced him to death for heresy. Narrowly avoiding execution, he left the city, once again settling in Qūrṣā. He continued to espouse his reformist views and attack opposing voices in writing, in public disputations, and in his teaching, becoming a widely known and controversial figure among Bulghar Muslims and drawing to his *madrasa* a small following of students and companions. In 1812 he set out on hajj, heading first to Istanbul, where he died of cholera shortly after arriving.

The accounts of Qūrṣāwī's life come from the three main biographical dictionaries of the Volga-Ural *ʿulamāʾ*: Shihāb al-Dīn Marjānī's *Mustafād al-akhbār*, Riḍāʾ al-Dīn Fakhr al-Dīn's (1859–1936) *Āthār*, and Muḥammad Murād Ramzī's (1853–1934) *Talfīq al-akhbār*. Of these sources, only Fakhr al-Dīn's *Āthār* is a conventional biographical dictionary, and it is by far the largest, providing information on hundreds of scholars, virtually all of whom lived in the key period under study.[2] But the work's historical value goes beyond mere *tarājim*. Included within its biographical entries are numerous documents,

1. On dating Qūrṣāwī's first journey to Bukhara, see note 153.

2. Riḍāʾ al-Dīn Fakhr al-Dīn. *Āthār*. 15 parts. Part 1: Kazan: Tipo-litografiia imperatorskogo universiteta, 1900. Parts 2–15: Orenburg: Tipografiia G. I. Karimova, 1901–1908. In addition,

which provide a substantial level of detail and documentary information found nowhere else. Most of these sources came from the archives of the state religious hierarchy (discussed in this chapter), which Fakhr al-Dīn used while composing *Āthār*, but he also included a significant number of documents and letters sent to him by private individuals.[3] These represent important primary sources in their own right, and they augment the richness of the historical material present.

Ramzī's *Talfīq al-akhbār wa-talqīḥ al-āthār fī waqāʾiʿ Qazān wa-Bulghār wa-mulūk al-Tatār*, by contrast, features a relatively small amount of biographical material.[4] Written in Mecca, where Ramzī settled between the 1880s and 1910s, it contains important information on the activities of Bulghar scholars while on hajj or otherwise traveling in the Middle East. In addition, the bulk of the work is a narrative history of Bulghar Muslims, providing their perspectives on a number of events before and after the Russian conquest. In doing so, it adds considerable nuance to the history of the relationship between the tsarist government and its Muslim subjects. (Ramzī's generally critical stance toward this relationship did not go unnoticed by the imperial censors, who rejected the book.)[5]

Lastly, Marjānī's *Mustafād al-akhbār fī aḥwāl Qazān wa-Bulghār* is, like the *Talfīq al-akhbār*, divided between narrative history and biographical entries.[6] The biographical material, however, is arranged in a unique way. Unlike the standard *ṭabaqāt* model, in which entries are ordered by the date of the

---

the third and fourth volumes, which were never published originally, have recently been edited in Cyrillic-script Tatar; Rizaéddin Fäxreddin. *Asar*. Vols. 3–4. Kazan: Ruxiyät, 2010.

3. On its composition, see Liliia Baibulatova. *<Asar> Rizy Fakhreddina: Istochnikovaia osnova i znachenie svoda*. Kazan: Tatarskoe knizhnoe izd-vo, 2006.

4. Muḥammad Murād Ramzī. *Talfīq al-akhbār wa-talqīḥ al-āthār fī waqāʾiʿ Qazān wa-Bulghār wa-mulūk al-Tatār*. 2 vols. 1908. Ed. Ibrāhīm Shams al-Dīn. Beirut: Dār al-kutub al-ʿilmiyya, 2002.

5. Hamid Algar. "Shaykh Zaynullah Rasulev: The Last Great Naqshbandi Shaykh of the Volga-Urals Region." *Muslims in Central Asia: Expressions of Identity and Change*. Ed. Jo-Ann Gross. Durham, NC: Duke UP, 1992. 112–133, p. 126; Il'ia Zaitsev. "Murad Ramzi i Arminii Vamberi." *Gasırlar awazı/Ekho vekov*, no. 3/4; 2001. n.p. Ramzī is the main source for the entries on Qūrṣāwī and his brother ʿAbd al-Khāliq (see *infra*) included in the Syrian Khayr al-Dīn al-Ziriklī's (1893–1976) massive biographical dictionary; Khayr al-Dīn al-Ziriklī. *al-Aʿlām: qāmūs tarājim li-ashhar al-rijāl wa-l-nisāʾ min al-ʿarab wa-l-mustaʿribīn bayn al-mustashriqīn*. 8 vols. Beirut: Dār al-ʿilm li-l-milāyīn, 1980, iv, p. 171; iii, p. 291.

6. Shihāb al-Dīn Marjānī. *Mustafād al-akhbār fī aḥwāl Qazān wa-Bulghār*. 2 vols. Vol. 1: Kazan: tipografiia B. L. Dombrovskago, 1897. Vol. 2: Kazan: tipografiia Universitetskago, 1900. Reprinted as Şehabeddin Mercani. *Müstefad'ül-ahbar fi ahval-i Kazan ve Bulgar*. 2 vols. Ankara: Ankara Üniversitesi basımevı, 1997.

scholar's death, Marjānī here groups scholars by the villages where they served as imams (or, in the case of Kazan, by the particular mosque). This remarkable arrangement reflects the importance of the *maḥalla* (mosque community), which became the foundational Islamic institution under the Russian state.

Marjānī began collecting historical reports while still a student in Central Asia, and the *Mustafād al-akhbār* provides a wealth of information on the Bulghar *ʿulamāʾ*. It is compiled from a wide variety of sources, including Russian chronicles.[7] As with *Āthār*, there are whole documents recorded verbatim in the work, though to a much lesser extent.

The *Mustafād al-akhbār* is often pointed to as a seminal work of Bulghar/Tatar historiography, and indeed, both Fakhr al-Dīn and Ramzī cite it frequently as a source.[8] But Marjānī wrote other historical works relevant to this topic. The final volume of his magnum opus, a six-volume biographical dictionary covering the entire span of Islamic history, the *Wafiyat al-aslāf wa-taḥiyat al-akhlāf*, focuses on the *ʿulamāʾ* of the 18th and 19th centuries.[9] Unlike the *Mustafād al-akhbār*, it is organized by scholars' death dates.

Also of note is Marjānī's first work, the *Tanbīh abnāʾ al-ʿaṣr ʿalā tanzīh anbāʾ Abī Naṣr*, written in 1849.[10] This short work is an account, drawing on reports from Central Asian scholars with whom Marjānī was associated, of the events surrounding Qūrṣāwī's condemnation in Bukhara, offering an explicit defense

---

7. ʿAzīz ʿUbaydullīn. "Marjānīniñ tārīkhī khidmatlarī." *Marjānī*. Ed. Ṣāliḥ b. Thābit ʿUbaydullīn. Kazan: Maʿārif, 1333 [1915]. 333–359, pp. 343–346; see also Mirkasym Usmanov. "Istochniki knigi Sh. Mardzhani 'Mustafad al-akhbar fi akhval Kazan va Bulgar.'" *Ocherki istorii povolzh'ia i priural'ia*, no. 2/3; 1969. 144–154.

8. Marjānī himself prefers "Tatar" as an ethnonym; Marjānī, *Mustafād*, i, p. 4. On the importance of the work, see Allen Frank. *Islamic Historiography and "Bulghar" Identity Among the Tatars and Bashkirs of Russia*. Leiden: Brill, 1998, pp. 149–150; Azade-Ayşe Rorlich, *The Volga Tatars: A Profile in National Resilience*. Stanford, CA: Hoover Institution Press, 1986, p. 51; M. Kh. Iusupov. *Shigabutdin Mardzhani kak istorik*. Kazan: Tatarskoe knizhnoe izd-vo, 1981; Uli Schamiloglu. "The Formation of a Tatar Historical Consciousness: Şihabaddin Marcani and the Image of the Golden Horde." *Central Asian Survey*, vol. 9, no. 2; 1990. 39–49.

9. Shihāb al-Dīn Marjānī. *Wafiyat al-aslāf wa-taḥiyat al-akhlāf.* 6 vols. Ms. KFU, nos. A-609 through A-615.

10. Shihāb al-Dīn Marjānī. *Risālat Tanbīh abnāʾ al-ʿaṣr ʿalā tanzīh anbāʾ Abī Naṣr*. Published in Michael Kemper. "Şihabaddin al-Marğani über Abu n-Nasr al-Qursawis Konflikt mit den Gelehrten bucharas." *Muslim Culture in Russia and Central Asia. Vol. 3: Arabic, Persian and Turkic Manuscripts (15th – 19th Centuries)*. Eds. Anke von Kügelgen et al. Berlin: Klaus Schwarz Verlag, 2000. 353–383, pp. 372–383. [Cited as Marjānī, *Tanbīh*.]

of the former. As such, it is a useful, if obviously biased, source on this critical episode in Qūrṣāwī's biography.[11]

In addition, there is Ḥusayn b. Amīrkhān's (1816–1893) *Tawārīkh-i bulghāriyya*.[12] Much like the *Mustafād al-akhbār* and *Talfīq al-akhbār*, this work is predominantly a narrative history, with two relatively brief sections of biographical material, composed by a prominent member of the Bulghar *ʿulamāʾ*. Indeed, the *Tawārīkh-i bulghāriyya* is quite similar to the *Talfīq al-akhbār* in scope, combining information on the history of Muslims under Russian rule with scholars' biographies.[13] There is also an anonymous biography of Qūrṣāwī contained in the main manuscript codex of his writings, which was produced in his *madrasa* in Qūrṣā within a few years of his death.[14] This work, although very brief, gives some valuable information about Qūrṣāwī's time in Bukhara, and it appears to have been used by Fakhr al-Dīn as a source in *Āthār*.

Though by no means comprehensive, these works collectively provide us with a mostly clear picture of the Bulghar *ʿulamāʾ* from the mid-18th through the late 19th centuries, and through them we can trace scholarly interactions—teacher-student connections, major disputes and subjects of study, bibliographical links—that formed Qūrṣāwī's context, both intellectually and socially.

The *ʿulamāʾ* are the only group within Bulghar society about whom we possess detailed historical accounts from this period.[15] The historical record for Bulghar *ʿulamāʾ*, however, is limited by their particular circumstances post-1552. As Allen Frank has noted, notwithstanding the handful of chronicles and local histories produced by Muslims from the 16th and 17th

---

11. Much of the work is devoted to praising Qūrṣāwī's virtues and implicitly linking his struggle against the Bukharan *ʿulamāʾ* with Prophet Muhammad's struggle against the Meccans. See Kemper's discussion of Marjānī's presentation of Qūrṣāwī in the work; Kemper, "Şihabaddin al-Marğani über Abu n-Nasr al-Qursawis Konflikt," pp. 353–357.

12. Ḥusayn b. Amīrkhān. *Tawārīkh-i bulghāriyya*. Kazan: Maṭbaʿat Wiyācheslāf, 1883. Reprinted with Russian translation as Khusain Amirkhanov. *Tavarikh-e Bulgariia (Bulgarskie khroniki)*. Intro. and trans. A. M. Akhunov. Moscow: izd-vo Mardzhani, 2010.

13. For a detailed discussion of the work, see Frank, *Islamic Historiography*, pp. 125–139.

14. *Manāqib Abī Naṣr ʿAbd al-Naṣīr b. Ibrāhīm al-Bulghārī al-Qāzānī*. Ms. SPb IVR, no. A1241. Fols. 68a–70a. This text is undated, but the other works contained in the codex range from 1233 to 1237 AH (1818–1822).

15. This fact is not unique to the Volga-Ural region but is an almost standard feature of Islamic historiography, which was, not incidentally, largely written by scholars themselves; cf. R. Stephen Humphreys. *Islamic History: A framework for inquiry*. Rev. ed. Princeton, NJ: Princeton UP, 1991, pp. 187–192.

centuries, this record prior to the late 18th century is slight.[16] It was only with the changes in the relationship between the *ʿulamāʾ* and the tsarist state at that time that Bulghar scholars and the institutions under their purview began to operate on firmer footing, allowing for the creation of a renewed historical record.

These histories, which really begin their post-conquest accounts in the middle of the 18th century, are inextricably tied to state sanction. Aside from Ramzī, who wrote the *Talfīq* while living in Mecca, all of these authors were prominent figures in the Volga-Ural *ʿulamāʾ*: Marjānī and Amīrkhān were imams in two of Kazan's major mosques, and Fakhr al-Dīn was a well-known author and publisher who would become head of the state religious hierarchy in 1921. They are all reliable sources, but because of the character of these works and their authors, they focus primarily on official *ʿulamāʾ*—that is, scholars who had been licensed (Russ. *ukaznyi*, Tat. *ūqāzlī* or *manshūrlī*) by the government—while unofficial *ʿulamāʾ* remain largely outside their scope, particularly for the 18th and early 19th centuries. As state approval was required for anyone holding a religious position, *ʿulamāʾ* lacking a license found themselves on legally dubious footing. Nevertheless, there were not-insignificant numbers of unlicensed *ʿulamāʾ*, due either to administrative gaps or to a willful rejection of government oversight, about whom extant historical information is generally limited.[17]

This lacuna is part of broader shortcomings in our historical understanding of Bulghar society in the imperial period. These mainly result from a lack of study so far into available sources, the overwhelming majority of which exist only in manuscript form. In addition to the sheer dearth of materials predating the 18th century, thousands, if not tens of thousands of codices remain unstudied and uncatalogued in archives and collections across Russia and former Soviet republics, comprising not merely biographical and historical texts but the bulk of Bulghar Muslims' pre-Soviet intellectual production. Continued research into these sources will almost certainly lead to new insights and approaches into Bulghar history, as well as a much more detailed and comprehensive understanding of the intellectual context in the 18th and 19th centuries. Our current picture of this context is only partial, and further analysis into manuscript sources will only help deepen and refine it, making future revisions of the present understanding likely.

16. Frank, *Islamic Historiography*, esp. p. 22.

17. Robert Crews. *For Prophet and Tsar: Islam and Empire in Russia and Central Asia*. Cambridge, MA: Harvard UP, 2005, pp. 100–101; Frank, *Islamic Historiography*, pp. 37–38.

Sharīʿa *and the* ʿUlamāʾ

Nevertheless, with these caveats, we can approach the Volga-Ural social and intellectual environment with a degree of certainty. The *ʿulamāʾ* played a central role in this society. After the conquest of the khanate of Kazan in 1552 and the subsequent removal of most forms of Muslim political rule, the *ʿulamāʾ* became the focal point for the Muslim community.[18] They served to maintain Islamic religious and social structures in the region, despite significant migration away from the areas of Russian conquest in the 16th and 17th centuries.[19] As Matthew Romaniello has shown, Russian state control wasn't fully established in the Middle Volga until the end of the 17th century (and in the Urals not until the mid-18th century).[20] Thus, under the aegis of the *ʿulamāʾ*, the preexisting social order was continued.

This social order was synonymous with the *sharīʿa*. Although it is frequently equated strictly with *fiqh* and the work of Islamic legal scholars, this is too narrow a conception of the term. The *sharīʿa* instead should be understood as representing the moral-legal framework for Islamic society, coterminous with the social order itself, as well as the discursive content of that framework. As Wael Hallaq writes, the *sharīʿa* "represented a complex set of social, economic, cultural, and moral relations" comprising a web of institutional interactions and discursive practices that "involved a cultural rendering of law in practice, where cultural categories meshed into *fiqh*, legal procedure, moral codes, and much else." Not limited to the function of law *sensu stricto*, it "structurally and organically tied itself to the world around it in ways that were vertical and horizontal, structural and linear, economic and social, moral and ethical, intellectual and spiritual, epistemic and cultural, and textual and poetic."[21]

---

18. Frank notes, "The continuation of the society's Islamic traditions and its self-definition ultimately came to be the responsibility of the *ʿulamāʾ*"; Frank, *Islamic Historiography*, p. 21.

19. Ibid., p. 25 n. 17.

20. Matthew Romaniello. *The Elusive Empire: Kazan and the Creation of Russia, 1552–1671*. Madison: U of Wisconsin P, 2012; also Alton S. Donnelly. *The Russian Conquest of Bashkiria 1552–1740: A Case Study in Imperialism*. New Haven, CT: Yale UP, 1968.

21. Wael Hallaq. *Shari'a: Theory, Practice, Transformations*. New York: Cambridge UP, 2009, pp. 543–544; also Wael Hallaq. "What Is Shari'a?" *Yearbook of Islamic and Middle Eastern Law, 2005–2006*, XII. Leiden: Brill, 2007. 151–180, pp. 155–156. Both Asad and Hallaq rely on Foucauldian notions of discourse and power in their discussions, if in distinct ways. Asad's view of tradition focuses on how discourses are supported and extended throughout time, while Hallaq's understanding of *sharīʿa* is concerned with the relationship between discourses and social actors within society. For the latter, the *sharīʿa* was comprised of normative Islamic discourses put into broad action, thereby ordering society. On viewing the *sharīʿa* as a discursive tradition, see Muhammad Qasim Zaman. *The Ulama in Contemporary Islam: Custodians of Change*. Princeton, NJ: Princeton UP, 2002, p. 6.

As such, the *sharīʿa* permeated and ordered society. And the *ʿulamāʾ*, accordingly, were not limited to legal or theological scholars, but included hadith transmitters, leaders of Sufi orders (*shaykhs* or *pīrs*), Qurʾan reciters and memorizers (*ḥuffāẓ*), and prayer leaders—those whose knowledge and piety gave them a degree of authority regarding this framework. (In the Volga-Ural region, the catchall title of *mullā*, a term denoting authority, encompassed the breadth of the category.) The task of continuously articulating, maintaining, and embodying the norms of the *sharīʿa*, determining how it should be manifested within society and accordingly guiding and educating the community, fell to them.

The scholarly tradition was part of this larger framework, comprised of the formalized discourses of Islamic sciences (*ʿulūm*)—such as *fiqh*, *kalām*, grammar, logic, hadith, rhetoric, *tafsīr*, and Sufism—mastery of which stood as the basis for some scholars' stature as the foremost religious authorities. For the Volga-Ural *ʿulamāʾ*, this chief role was held by the *ākhūnds*, the title for the most expert legal scholars and leading religious authorities in the region. The learned, elite discourse of these leading *ʿulamāʾ*—constituting, as noted, a practice in MacIntyre's sense—represented the vehicle for not only the formulation of norms for moral action and orthodox belief in reference to the texts of scripture but also for the very construction of that discourse and its methodologies. These scholars thus served as interpreters and arbiters of the *sharīʿa*, legitimated by their knowledge and expertise to speak for it regarding issues and concerns both mundane and transcendent.

The difference between these elite scholars and other *ʿulamāʾ* existed in the *degree* of knowledge that the former possessed, rather than the *kind*, and likewise with the distinction between *ʿulamāʾ* and the community as a whole. The authority of all *ʿulamāʾ* was grounded in their understanding of Islamic tradition, knowledge of which was prevalent throughout society. Indeed, Frank notes, speaking specifically of the Volga-Ural region in the early 19th century, that *ʿulamāʾ* and members of the broader community shared the same basic knowledge, while scholars "simply had a deeper knowledge of the same texts and ideas that the villagers had themselves studied in their *maktab*s and *madrasas*."[22] The knowledge of the *sharīʿa* and its discourses linked the community and the *ʿulamāʾ*, whose religious roles were deeply intertwined with the quotidian function of society. Manifesting the *sharīʿa* within society was not the responsibility of the *ʿulamāʾ* alone, but was borne out by their complex interactions with other segments of society.[23]

---

22. Allen Frank. *Muslim Religious Institutions in Imperial Russia: The Islamic World of Novouzensk District and the Kazakh Inner Horde, 1780–1910*. Leiden: Brill, 2001, p. 227.

23. Cf. Hallaq, *Shari'a*, p. 544.

(The pervasiveness of the framework of the *sharīʿa* within society and the importance of interactions between *ʿulamāʾ* and other social actors—particularly elites—as part of the social order contradicts the notion, widespread in the scholarship on Muslims of the Russian Empire, that *ʿādat* [custom] was in mutual conflict with the *sharīʿa* as distinct legal regimes for Muslim peoples, particularly nomads. As Virginia Martin's insightful study of 19th-century Kazakh customary law shows, *ʿādat* and *sharīʿa* were not firmly differentiated in Kazakhs' eyes, instead forming a "syncretic relationship," with *sharīʿa* constituting Kazakhs' moral order and *ʿādat* oriented toward the preservation of justice, cultural norms, and the function of the nomadic economy, but encompassed within that same moral order.[24] That *qāḍīs*' judgments were derived from *fiqh* and the adjudication carried out by tribal leaders [*biys* or *āqsaqals*] was not was less an indication of competition than merely a distinction between different institutional actors. Indeed, even in a narrow understanding of *sharīʿa* as *fiqh* were customary norms accounted for; postclassical Hanafis explicitly acknowledged a role for custom [synonymously labeled *ʿurf*] in *fiqh* reasoning, often as a means of accommodating political and military elites' administering of commercial and criminal matters—precisely those areas in which *ʿādat* was most applicable.)[25]

The lack of sources notwithstanding, it seems by all indications that the socioreligious framework of the *sharīʿa* continued into the 18th century in the Volga-Ural region under the leadership of the *ʿulamāʾ*, who maintained to the extent possible the Islamic social order after the Russian conquest. For instance, the *ākhūnd* Yūnus b. Īwānāy (1636–1688?), perhaps the most important Bulghar scholar of the 17th century, composed a *fatwā* asserting that payment of the *ʿushr* tax (a traditional Islamic tax on agriculture) was an obligation (*wājib*) for Bulghar Muslims.[26] Yūnus considered the region part of the

24. In fact, any sharp distinction between the two was largely a creation of tsarist administrators seeking to undermine preexisting Kazakh legal structures with Russian law; Virginia Martin. *Law and Custom in the Steppe: The Kazakhs of the Middle Horde and Russian Colonialism in the Nineteenth Century*. Richmond, UK: Curzon, 2001. On Russian Orientalist uses of *ʿādat*, see also Michael Kemper. "*ʿAdat* Against *Shariʿa*: Russian Approaches Toward Daghestani 'Customary Law' in the 19th Century." *Ab Imperio*, vol. 3, no. 3; 2005. 147–174.

25. Cf. Gideon Libson. "On the Development of Custom as a Source of Law in Islamic Law." *Islamic Law and Society*, vol. 4, no. 2; 1997. 131–155. Particularly in Ottoman domains, customary law (*ʿurf* and *ʿādat*, but also *qānūn*, *siyāsa*, and the Mongol *yasa*) complemented, and often overlapped with, *ʿulamāʾ* institutions; see the discussion on terminology in Uriel Heyd. *Studies in Old Ottoman Criminal Law*. Oxford: Clarendon, 1973, pp. 167–171. Qūrṣāwī himself includes *ʿurf* as well as *ʿādat* as basic parts of Hanafi legal theory; Abū al-Naṣr ʿAbd al-Naṣīr b. Ibrāhīm [al-Qūrṣāwī] al-Ghazānī [*sic*] al-Ḥanafī. *Sharḥ mukhtaṣar al-Manār*. Ms. TGM VF 6765, no. 19064, p. 263. [Pagination has been added to this manuscript codex, which is used here in citations.]

26. The *fatwā* is recorded in Marjānī, *Mustafād*, ii, p. 188.

dār al-Islām, and this *fatwā* further points to the semblance of a functioning Islamic society, led by scholars.[27]

The *ākhūnd*s themselves, who fulfilled the roles of both *qāḍī* and *muftī*, differed little from *fuqahā*ʾ elsewhere. They were of course deeply educated in the Islamic sciences, and they composed books and traveled in pursuit of scholarship: Yūnus, whose father was also an *ākhūnd*, studied for a time in Bukhara, penned a commentary on the major Hanafi *furū*ʿ work *Farāʾiḍ sirājiyya*, and twice went on pilgrimage to Mecca.[28] Such a career was noteworthy, but not anomalously so. Rather, it speaks to the *ākhūnds*' part in continuing an active—if perhaps not thriving—environment of Islamic scholarship.[29] Their knowledge was of course inextricable from their exercise of religious authority, and scholarship underpinned their role within society of interpreting and articulating the *sharīʿa*.

This function made the *ākhūnd*s, and the *ʿulamāʾ* more broadly, as well as their institutions, an integral part of the Bulghar community, of which they had become the primary leaders in the aftermath of the Russian conquest. As Frank notes, "*Maktab*s and *madrasas*, together with mosques and the *ʿulamāʾ*, were fundamentally important parts of the community because they were part of what made the community Muslim."[30] Scholars' social importance gradually drew the attention of tsarist administrators, who first began to recognize the *ʿulamāʾ* as a significant group within the Muslim population around the turn of the 18th century and whose approach toward governing that population came to focus on them—a shift that coincided with a change in the makeup of the Russian state.[31]

---

27. Alfrid Bustanov. "The Bulghar Region as a 'Land of Ignorance': Anti-Colonial Discourse in Khvarazmian Connectivity." *Journal of Persianate Studies*, vol. 9; 2016. 183–204, pp. 184–185. On the debate over *ʿushr* in the Russian empire, see Michael Kemper, *Sufis und Gelehrte in Tatarien und Baschkirien, 1789–1889: Der islamische Diskurs unter russischer Herrschaft*. Berlin: Klaus Schwarz Verlag, 1998, esp. pp. 290–294; see also Khaled Abou El Fadl. "Islamic Law and Muslim Minorities: The Juristic Discourse on Muslim Minorities from the Second/Eighth to the Eleventh/Seventeenth Centuries." *Islamic Law and Society*, vol. 1, no. 2; 1994. 141–187, esp. pp. 158–159, 161–162.

28. Marjānī, *Mustafād*, ii, pp. 187–189; Fakhr al-Dīn, *Āthār*, i, p. 30; ii, pp. 38–39; Ramzī, *Talfīq*, ii, p. 338; Kemper, *Sufis*, pp. 217, 290–291.

29. Nathan Spannaus. "The Decline of the *Akhund* and the Transformation of Islamic Law Under the Russian Empire." *Islamic Law and Society*, vol. 20, no. 3; 2013. 202–241, pp. 208–211.

30. Frank, *Institutions*, p. 227.

31. Frank, *Islamic Historiography*, pp. 22, 24–25.

Tsarist Rule, Persecution, and Tolerance

Following the conquest of Kazan, Russian control was gradually extended over the newly acquired territory through the twin institutions of the tsarist government and the Russian Orthodox Church. Large numbers of monasteries and fortresses, with accompanying towns, were founded as a means of establishing a Russian presence on the ground. Civil and religious institutions, however, represented distinct administrative regimes, with both providing a measure of governance in the area. Local officials naturally exerted legal authority within their jurisdictions, but monasteries also controlled territory and enjoyed separate commercial and legal privileges, and monastic villages served as focal points for Russian settlement.[32]

The burgeoning Russian state in the 16th and early 17th centuries functioned through what Romaniello calls layered or composite sovereignty, wherein the autocracy and the Orthodox hierarchy operated in parallel fashion—often in concert, but not necessarily so—with differing goals and methods. There were four separate "poles" of administrative authority at work in the Volga region in this period: the tsar and government in Moscow, the local administration, the Orthodox leadership in Moscow, and the archbishopric of Kazan, established in 1555.[33]

The distinct interests and approaches of these bodies led to occasionally dissonant relationships between them, resulting in a certain degree of inconsistency in the governance of the region. Muslims in turn were able to navigate the gaps in nascent Russian power, particularly the discrepancies between Muscovite ideals and the realities of local conditions: "Constructing a new political and economic system, imperfectly monitored by the four poles of authority, created a liminal space on the frontier, which allowed the tsar's new non-Russian and non-Orthodox populations to prosper."[34]

Despite claims from Moscow of Orthodoxy's definitive defeat of Islam, Muslim military elites (Russ. *murza*, Tat. *mīrzā*) were welcomed into tsarist service, quickly becoming indispensable for securing the former territory of the khanates. Moreover, Russian rule of the region continued Chinggisid forms of organization, which remained in place until the late 17th century.[35]

---

32. Romaniello, *Elusive Empire*, pp. 38–42, 72–82. One such town was Arsk, located very near to Qūrṣā, which was founded in 1576 and served as a regional administrative center to help project Russian control beyond Kazan's city walls.

33. Ibid., pp. 8–14.

34. Ibid., p. 15.

35. Ibid., esp. pp. 118–124.

Moscow's use of landholding elites who received tax privileges in exchange for military service was little different from the model of Turkic military dynasties that dominated much of the postclassical Muslim world. In fact, Muscovite rulers had earlier adopted some of these practices from the khanate of Kazan, of which the tsars considered themselves successors.[36] In this type of rule, dynasties were divorced from much of the subject population, exercising indirect political authority.[37] As such, the replacement of one dynasty at the hands of another was not hugely disruptive in terms of the broader society, and the similarities between Chinggisid and Muscovite structures allowed for the "largely seamless maintenance of social order in the region," as Romaniello describes it. "The conquest itself had been violent, but within a generation many [Muslims] simply substituted service to the tsar for service to the khan."[38]

In this way, Russian rule operated at arm's length, peripheral to the quotidian existence of the overwhelming majority of Muslims.[39] Rather than interfering in the affairs of their communities, the civil and ecclesiastical administrations were concerned primarily with promoting physical security and economic activity within the region. Muslims' cooperation was essential for doing so, giving them the ability to negotiate space between the distinct poles of Russian power. It was within this space that the *sharīʿa* as societal framework continued under tsarist rule and the *ʿulamāʾ*, despite the loss of political patronage, continued to exercise religious authority and social leadership.

Circumstances for Muslims began to change in the mid-17th century, as the Volga region became more closely aligned with the government in Moscow and began to lose its frontier character. This shift was accompanied by an increased promotion of Russian Orthodoxy. Despite the important role of church authorities in the extension of tsarist control, the conversion of non-Christians does not seem to have been a significant concern following the conquest of Kazan. While converts were certainly encouraged and welcomed by the Church, the government's somewhat tenuous hold on the territory

36. Donald Ostrowski argues for seeing the Muscovite *pomest'e* landholding system as influenced by the quite similar institution of *iqṭāʿ*; Donald Ostrowski. "The Military Land Grant Along the Muslim-Christian Frontier." *Russian History*, vol. 19, no. 1–4; 1992. 327–359; cf. Michael Khodarkovsky. *Russia's Steppe Frontier: The Making of a Colonial Empire, 1500–1800*. Bloomington: Indiana UP, 2002.

37. Cf. Hallaq, *Shari'a*, pp. 147–149.

38. Romaniello, *Elusive Empire*, p. 121.

39. Non-Russians' legal status following the conquest "limited almost entirely their contact with Muscovite officials to their yearly [tax] payments"; ibid., p. 151.

and dependence on Muslim soldiers made local officials wary of provoking Muslims through dedicated missionary activities, and the government accordingly limited proselytization measures.[40] To be sure, discriminatory policies based on religion were enacted, but these were small in scale, for instance restricting the sale of land between Christians and non-Christians or barring non-Christians from certain categories of state service. Overall, however, remaining Muslim did not represent a significant disadvantage.[41]

This ceased to be the case during the reign of Tsar Aleksei (r. 1645–1676), who implemented more discriminatory, explicitly anti-Muslim measures. Alongside smaller gestures such as burning Islamic books in Kazan in 1653,[42] Aleksei introduced policies that formally distinguished Orthodox and non-Orthodox elites, with attendant restrictions on the latter's place in tsarist society and a decrease in their status, excluding Muslims from higher positions. Additional measures, such as the potential seizure of non-Christians' lands, further strengthened the economic and social incentives for conversion.[43]

The push for the conversion of the Muslim elite—the primary target for this approach—was part of a larger project of consolidating the government under the tsarist autocracy. It is no coincidence that many of these measures enacted under Aleksei were contained in his 1649 legal code (*ulozhenie*), which had the effect of expanding the reach of state power and the institutional basis for state service while standardizing legal practice throughout the tsar's domains.[44]

---

40. Chantal Lemercier-Quelquejay. "Les missions orthodoxes en pays musulmans de moyenne- et basse-Volga." *Cahiers du Monde Russe et Soviétique*, vol. 8; 1967. 369–403, pp. 371–382.

41. Romaniello, *Elusive Empire*, pp. 125–126, 129–130, 155.

42. Amīrkhān, *Tawārīkh-i bulghāriyya*, p. 3.

43. Romaniello, *Elusive Empire*, pp. 126–128, 136–137, 144–145; see also Michael Khodarkovsky. "'Not by Word Alone': Missionary Policies and Religious Conversion in Early Modern Russia." *Comparative Studies in Society and History*, vol. 38, no. 2; Apr. 1996. 267–293; also Khodarkovsky, *Steppe*, esp. pp. 191–193. A 1675 law, for instance, declared that landholdings belonging to Muslims and other minorities were to be seized and distributed to Russians and new Orthodox converts; *Polnoe sobranie zakonov Rossiiskoi Imperii* (hereafter *PSZ*). Series 1. 40 vols. St. Petersburg: Gosudarstvennaia tipografiia, 1830, i, no. 616; also James Cracraft. *The Church Reform of Peter the Great*. Stanford, CA: Stanford UP, 1971, p. 64.

44. Cf. Valerie Kivelson. "Kinship Politics/Autocratic Politics: A Reconsideration of Early-Eighteenth-Century Political Culture." *Imperial Russia: New Histories for the Empire*. Eds. Jane Burbank and David Ransel. Bloomington: Indiana UP, 1998. 5–31; George Weickhardt. "Modernization of Law in Seventeenth-Century Muscovy." *Modernizing Muscovy: Reform and Social Change in Seventeenth-Century Russia*. Eds. Jarmo Kotillaine and Marshall Poe. London: Routledge, 2004. 76–92. Among other measures, the code instituted the penalty of immolation for proselytization by Muslims; *PSZ*, i, art. 22.24.

The 1649 code brought Muslims more directly under tsarist control, removing many of the privileges and spaces for negotiation that had existed previously. The extension of state power was continued by Peter the Great (r. 1689–1724) as part of his sweeping reforms, which included the reorganization of civil and military structures, establishment of new taxation and commercial regimes, forced introduction of Western European cultural models, and founding of St. Petersburg as capital of the newly christened Russian Empire. For Peter, as for Aleksei, the conversion of non-Christians was an important component in the consolidation of tsarist rule, and missionary activities, no longer limited to the non-Orthodox gentry, were made a priority for the government during his reign.[45]

Not only did the reforming emperor personally believe in the importance of proselytization,[46] but, more critically, the promotion of Orthodoxy served his political aims for the empire. As part of his reforms, Peter headed a reorganization of the Orthodox Church that brought it formally under imperial control (a process begun under Aleksei) through the establishment of the Orthodox Synod, a lay body replacing the Patriarchate of Moscow. Rather than standing as an independent institution within Russian society as it had for centuries, it was made part of the tsarist bureaucracy, subordinate to the Imperial Senate and effectively subject to the emperor himself.[47]

The subordination of the Church marks the beginning of confessional governance, which would come to characterize imperial rule under the Romanov dynasty (1613–1917).[48] Under Peter, the Church was made a vehicle for administering the Russian peasantry. It had long stood as the one institution that had direct contact with the empire's rural population, and its incorporation into the tsarist state allowed the government to use this position for its own administrative purposes.[49] This fact is most evident in the introduction of the parish register (*metricheskaia kniga*) in 1722. A comprehensive record of births,

45. A decree by the tsar, dated November 3, 1713, states that "in Kazan and Azov governorates Bessurmen [*sic*; < Tat. *busurmān* 'Muslim'] of the Mohammedan faith are to be baptized in a half year at most"; qtd. in E. V. Anisimov. *The Reforms of Peter the Great: Progress Through Coercion in Russia*. Intro. and trans. John T. Alexander. Armonk, NY: M. E. Sharpe, 1993, p. 208.

46. Cracraft, *Church Reform*, pp. 65–66.

47. Ibid., pp. 165–218.

48. Robert Crews. "Empire and the Confessional State: Islam and Religious Politics in Nineteenth-Century Russia." *American Historical Review*, vol. 108, no. 1; 2003. 50–83.

49. Anisimov, *Reforms*, pp. 208–210.

deaths, marriages, and divorces for all members of a congregation, the register not only provided the government with sorely needed demographic information (necessary for conscription, among other things) but also served to establish peasants' civil status within the empire. In so doing it "represented an indispensable instrument for the inclusion of various population groups in the empire's emerging civil order."[50]

As the Church was transformed into a vehicle for asserting state power, imperial subjects outside the Church became a larger political concern. As Michael Khodarkovsky writes of the Petrine period, "During this time the Russian government pursued policies that encouraged the non-Christians' conversion to Orthodox Christianity as a way of homogenizing the society into a single political and religious identity under one tsar and one God."[51] Accordingly, stronger financial and material benefits for converts, designed to bring more Muslims (as well as other minorities, to be sure) into the Orthodox fold were introduced.[52] Punitive taxes played a large role: a 1704 decree issued in the Ural region, for instance, instituted new levies on (respectively) mosques, imams, and every individual attending communal prayers. Attached to this decree, which precipitated the Muslim uprising of 1705–1711, was an official request that Muslims register marriages and deaths with an Orthodox priest.[53]

Efforts to entice Muslim converts met with relatively meager results, and they gradually intensified up to the 1740s, a decade that witnessed the height of official anti-Muslim persecution.[54] The rise in persecution was due primarily to the activities of the newly formed Kontora novokreshchenskikh del

---

50. Paul Werth. "In the State's Embrace: Civil Acts in an Imperial Order." *Kritika*, vol. 7, no. 3; 2006. 433–458, p. 437.

51. Khodarkovsky, "Word," p. 269; cf. Paul Werth. *The Tsar's Foreign Faiths: Toleration and the Fate of Religious Freedom in Imperial Russia*. Oxford: Oxford UP, 2014, esp. pp. 39–40; Lemercier-Quelquejay, "Missions," pp. 382–383.

52. Anisimov, *Reforms*, p. 284; Lemercier-Quelquejay, "Missions," pp. 383–385.

53. Danil' Azamatov. *Orenburgskoe magometanskoe dukhovnoe sobranie v kontse XVIII-XIX vv.* Ufa: Gilem, 1999, pp. 14–15.

54. Khodarkovsky describes this period as "one of the most violent assaults on non-Christians' religious beliefs"; Khodarkovsky, *Steppe*, p. 194. For a discussion of anti-Muslim governmental policies and measures, see ibid., esp. pp. 189–201; Khodarkovsky, "Word"; Lemercier-Quelquejay, "Missions"; Paul Werth. "Coercion and Conversion: Violence and the Mass Baptism of the Volga Peoples, 1740–1755." *Kritika*, vol. 4, no. 3; 2003. 543–569; Rorlich, *Volga Tatars*, pp. 37–47; see also Ramzī, *Talfīq*, ii, pp. 168–174.

(Agency of Convert Affairs).[55] This government office, "having a character simultaneously religious and civil," was intended to convert the non-Orthodox to Christianity as well as prevent the newly converted from reverting to their prior faith.[56] Headquartered in the Uspenskii-Bogoroditskii monastery in the city of Sviiazhsk (founded in 1551 as a staging point for the siege of Kazan), the Kontora was placed under the leadership of the archbishop of Kazan, Luka Konashevich (r. 1738–1755). Described as an intractable enemy of Islam, Konashevich approached missionary work with particular zeal, employing methods such as razing mosques, kidnapping Muslim children, and baptizing adults by force.[57] The harshness of his missionary exploits was such that, according to Ramzī, his infamy among local Muslims persisted into the 20th century.[58]

Severe measures came from St. Petersburg as well. In 1742 the Imperial Senate issued a decree calling for the destruction of mosques in Kazan district (*uezd*); 418 of the area's 536 mosques were destroyed on the pretext they were located too near to Christian homes. (The remaining 118 mosques were spared because they predated the 1552 conquest.) The decree was eventually carried out across the areas of the empire where Muslims were numerous: in Siberia, 98 out of 133 mosques were destroyed (though 35 were soon rebuilt), and 29 out of 40 in Astrakhan and the neighboring steppe.[59] (Only in the Urals did officials, wary of popular revolt, resist, sparing that region's mosques.)[60] In 1750 the Imperial Senate evicted Muslims from Kazan's old Tatar quarter (Russ. *staraia tatarskaia sloboda*, Tat. *īskī bīsta*), a neighborhood outside the city walls founded after the Muslim population was expelled in response to an uprising in 1556.[61] The government also continued its coercive economic policies that weighed heavily upon Muslims but from which converts were exempt.[62]

55. On its establishment under Empress Anna, see *PSZ*, xi, no. 8236.

56. Lemercier-Quelquejay, "Missions," pp. 387–388.

57. Ibid., pp. 375–376, 389; Rorlich, *Volga Tatars*, p. 41.

58. Ramzī, *Talfīq*, ii, p. 171.

59. *PSZ*, xiv, no. 10597; Khodarkovsky, *Steppe*, p. 194; Azamatov, *Orenburgskoe*, p. 18.

60. Frank, *Islamic Historiography*, pp. 29–30.

61. Rorlich, *Volga Tatars*, pp. 39, 41.

62. Khodarkovsky, "Word," pp. 279–281, 288. Economic incentives for conversion of varying levels of coerciveness were employed by the Russian government throughout the imperial period; see, for instance, Rorlich, *Volga Tatars*, pp. 41–42, 44; Alan W. Fisher. "Enlightened Despotism and Islam Under Catherine II." *Slavic Review*, vol. 27, no. 4; Dec. 1968. 542–553, pp. 543–545.

These measures, harsh though they were, were applied for a short time, and by the mid-1750s anti-Muslim persecution began to lessen. In 1755 Konashevich—since 1748 no longer head of the Kontora—was removed from his post as archbishop of Kazan and sent to Belgorod, near Ukraine. He was replaced by Gavriil Kremenitskii (r. 1755–1762), a theologian with little interest in missionary work.[63] Muslims were again allowed to reside in the old Tatar quarter, and in 1756 the Imperial Senate granted permission for the construction of new mosques. (There were strict conditions on where these new mosques could be built, however, with only those located in exclusively Muslim villages with at least two hundred adult male residents expressly approved.)[64]

Under Catherine the Great (r. 1762–1796), new, more tolerant policies regarding Muslims and Islamic institutions were put in place. The Kontora was abolished in 1764.[65] In 1767 Catherine personally approved the construction of Kazan's First Mosque (now known as Marjānī Mosque, located in the old Tatar quarter) while on a visit to the city.[66] Moreover, the Orthodox Synod issued an edict in Catherine's name in 1773, entitled "On the tolerance of all faiths (*veroispovedanii*) and on the forbidding of bishops to enter into actions involving non-Orthodox (*inovernykh*) faiths and the construction of houses of worship according to their law[s], leaving all of this to secular authorities."[67] This act, which was primarily concerned with loosening the restrictions on the construction of mosques (specifically regarding the two mosques in Kazan that had already been built under Catherine), had two far-reaching implications: it tacitly provided government sanction for Islamic institutions (reinforced by a 1783 decree allowing Muslim communities to choose their own imams and *ākhūnds*),[68] and it explicitly asserted the imperial administration's exclusive right to oversee and regulate those institutions.

These measures served to extend state power to the empire's Muslim subjects (while also precluding interference by the Church), and they did so as part of a

---

63. Lemercier-Quelquejay, "Missions," pp. 385, 392.

64. *PSZ*, xiv, no. 10597. On the Russian government's approach toward mosques, see Frank, *Institutions*, pp. 165–176.

65. *PSZ*, xvi, no. 12126; Fisher, "Enlightened Despotism," p. 543; Rorlich, *Volga Tatars*, p. 42.

66. Ramzī, *Talfīq*, ii, p. 172; Marjānī, *Mustafād*, ii, p. 12; Amīrkhān, *Tawārīkh-i bulghāriyya*, p. 73; Fakhr al-Dīn, *Āthār*, ii, p. 50; Kemper, *Sufis*, p. 35. Frank notes that there had been a number of mosques in Kazan prior to this at various times, though none had any permanent existence; Frank, *Institutions*, pp. 166, 172.

67. *PSZ*, xix, no. 13996.

68. Ibid., xxi, no. 15653.

FIGURE 2 First Mosque, Kazan (V. Turin, 1834)

broader project to incorporate them into the bureaucratic structures of the empire. Religious tolerance was a prerequisite, but the policies enacted had a much wider scope, removing barriers to Muslims' participation in tsarist government and society. Muslims were officially allowed into the merchant estate in 1776 and accepted as officers in the imperial army in 1783, and in 1784 a small number of Muslim hereditary elites were admitted into the Russian nobility.[69] Most importantly, in 1788 an official hierarchy for the Bulghar *ʿulamāʾ*, modeled on the Orthodox Synod, was established on Catherine's order, forming the Spiritual Assembly of Mohammedan Law (Dukhovnoe sobranie magometanskogo zakona).[70]

---

69. Cf. Ramil Khayrutdinov. "The Tatar *Ratusha* of Kazan: National Self-Administration in Autocratic Russia, 1781–1855." *Islam in Politics in Russia and Central Asia (Early Eighteenth to Late Twentieth Centuries)*. Eds. Stéphane Dudoignon and Hisao Komatsu. London: Kegan Paul, 2001. 27–42, p. 29. Merchants were one of the official estates (*sosloviia*), along with (respectively) nobles, Orthodox clergy, townspeople, and peasants, which determined a person's—and their descendants'—legal status, taxation, and privileges within the empire. Prior to the 1770s, Muslims were peasants or townspeople. The *ʿulamāʾ* were never admitted into the clerical estate. For a detailed discussion of the official status and rights of the *ʿulamāʾ*, see Paul Werth. "*Soslovie* and the 'Foreign' Clergies of Imperial Russia: Estate Rights or Service Rights?" *Cahiers du Monde Russe*, vol. 51, no. 2–3; 2010. 419–440.

70. On the Spiritual Assembly's founding, see *PSZ*, xxii, nos. 16710, 16711; xxiii, no. 16759; *Materialy po istorii Bashkirskoi ASSR*. 5 vols. Moscow/Leningrad: izd-vo Akademii Nauk SSSR, 1936–1960, v, pp. 563–566. This body was often called the Orenburg Assembly, due

Sanction and Scholarship

The granting of tolerance and official sanction marked a significant shift in the relationship between the tsarist government and its Muslim subjects, fostering among many of the latter a sense of goodwill: Amīrkhān writes in his history that the tsars "were enemies of the people of Islam" before Catherine, whom he calls the "Mother-Tsar" (*abī-pādishāh*).[71] More than anything, however, it brought recognition and stability to Muslim communities, which largely welcomed these policies.[72]

Catherine's measures actually expanded an approach first implemented in the Urals, where government acceptance for *ʿulamāʾ* had begun much earlier. In 1736, Empress Anna (r. 1730–1740), in response to requests from local officials, allowed the recognition of four *ākhūnds* as the sanctioned *ʿulamāʾ* for the region's Muslims.[73] The Urals at the time were still a frontier area in which imperial power was spread thin and anti-Russian revolts were common, and the local government was looking for ways to strengthen its administration of the region. Noting that, despite efforts to stop them, *ʿulamāʾ* from Siberia and the Middle Volga were operating freely in the area and building new mosques, officials proposed enlisting them in pro-government activities in exchange for recognition of their status.[74] Ultimately, sanction for courts under the authority

---

to its location within Orenburg governorate; Azamatov, *Orenburgskoe*, pp. 24–25. Crews renders the name in English as "Ecclesiastical Assembly," noting—quite correctly—that "this institution was devoted not to the cultivation of 'spirituality,' but to regulation and discipline"; Crews, *Prophet*, p. 385 n. 32. I choose to use the more common (and more literal) translation of *dukhovnoe* as "spiritual" simply in an effort to conform to the conventional usage in English-language scholarship. It was the first of four tsarist spiritual assemblies, with others founded in Simferopol in the Crimea (1794, reorganized 1831) and two in Tbilisi for Sunnis and Shiʿa in the Caucasus (1872); cf. Elena I. Campbell. "The Autocracy and the Muslim Clergy in the Russian Empire (1850s–1917)." *Russian Studies in History*, vol. 44, no. 2; 2005. 8–29. Each of the assemblies functioned differently, and their respective relationships to the government—on both the local and imperial levels—varied considerably. Only the Orenburg Assembly, whose jurisdiction covered the geographic area under study here, will be addressed.

71. Amīrkhān, *Tawārīkh-i bulghāriyya*, p. 73.

72. Indeed, there were calls from Muslims for patronage of Islamic institutions dating back to the 1730s; Frank, *Islamic Historiography*, pp. 26–27; Azamatov, *Orenburgskoe*, p. 19.

73. *PSZ*, ix, no. 6890, art. 14.

74. *Materialy po istorii Bashkirskoi ASSR*, iii, pp. 493–494; Azamatov, *Orenburgskoe*, pp. 16–17; see also Danil' Azamatov, "Russian Administration and Islam in Bashkiria (18th–19th Centuries)." *Muslim Culture in Russia and Central Asia from the 18th to the Early 20th Centuries*. Vol. 1. Eds. Michael Kemper et al. Berlin: Klaus Schwarz Verlag, 1996. 91–112; Frank, *Islamic Historiography*, pp. 21–39; Spannaus, "Decline," pp. 211–212. On imperial activities in the Urals in the first half of the 18th century, see Donnelly, *Russian Conquest*.

of the four *ākhūnds* was granted alongside tribunals headed by tribal elders and notables. The division of power between these two types of judicial bodies for Muslims was made explicit, with criminal proceedings falling under the purview of the tribunals, and *ākhūnds*' courts having exclusive competence over matters of family law and inheritance.[75]

Sanction brought with it a flourishing of Islamic scholarship. There are records of a number of *ʿulamāʾ* in the region serving as *qāḍīs* and issuing *fatwās*, opening *madrasas*, and copying and composing texts.[76] The town of Qarghālī (Russ. Seitovskii Posad) was an example of how state support (or at the very least noninterference) allowed Islamic institutions to thrive. It was established by imperial decree in 1744 next to the newly founded Russian city of Orenburg, and it was intended to be a hub for trade with the Kazakh steppe and Central Asia, conducted primarily by Muslims.[77] The town was originally settled by two hundred families of Kazan origin, and residents were granted certain privileges by the government, among them the operation of Islamic legal and religious institutions. Its first mosque was built by Major-General Aleksei Ivanovich Tevkelev (né Quṭlūgh Muḥammad b. Tawakkul), an important tsarist official who converted to Orthodoxy during his career in the imperial service.[78] The *ākhūnd* Ibrāhīm b. Muḥammad Tūluk b. Bīkmuḥammad (fl. 18th century) was appointed as imam.[79]

Qarghālī quickly became a center for Islamic scholarship—by 1788 there were four mosques in operation, each with its own *madrasa*—and it drew prominent *ʿulamāʾ* to settle there.[80] The *ākhūnd* ʿAbd al-Salām b. Ūrāzmuḥammad b. Qulmuḥammad (fl. mid-18th century), an expert in Hanafi *fiqh*, moved to Qarghālī in 1750.[81] Īshniyāz b. Shīrniyāz al-Khwārizmī (?–1791), a native of

---

75. Azamatov, *Orenburgskoe*, p. 17. As noted, the use of extrajudicial mediation by tribal elders was not an uncommon feature in Islamic societies and should not be seen (as Azamatov does) as something outside the *sharīʿa* legal order; cf. Hallaq, *Shariʿa*, pp. 160–164.

76. Cf. Spannaus, "Decline," pp. 213–215.

77. On the history of Qarghālī and the relationship between it and the imperial government, see Mami Hamamoto. "Tatarskaia Kargala in Russia's Eastern Policies." *Asiatic Russia: Imperial Power in Regional and International Contexts*. Ed. Tomohiko Uyama. London: Routledge, 2012. 32–51. The order establishing the town is *PSZ*, xii, no. 8893.

78. On Tevkelev, see Donnelly, *Russian Conquest*; Khodarkovsky, *Steppe*.

79. Marjānī describes Ibrāhīm as an exemplary *qāḍī* and *muftī*; Marjānī, *Mustafād*, ii, p. 209; Fakhr al-Dīn, *Āthār*, ii, pp. 40–41; Kemper, *Sufis*, pp. 25–26.

80. Azamatov, *Orenburgskoe*, p. 20; Frank, *Islamic Historiography*, p. 30. For the mosques and *ʿulamāʾ* in Qarghālī, see Marjānī, *Mustafād*, ii, pp. 209–213.

81. Marjānī, *Mustafād*, ii, p. 127; Fakhr al-Dīn, *Āthār*, ii, p. 42.

Urgench and one of the most important scholars of the 18th century, also settled in Qarghālī in this period, as did the Bukharan *shaykh* ʿAbd al-Karīm b. Bālṭāy (?–1757), one of the earliest representatives of the Naqshbandi-Mujaddidiyya in Russia.[82]

As state support for *ʿulamāʾ* was extended across much of the empire under Catherine, and without the existential threat posed by militant missionary policies, Islamic institutions proliferated and thrived. Scholarly networks were allowed to form and expand, as student-teacher and familial ties linked *ʿulamāʾ* from different parts of the empire, stretching across the Middle Volga, the southern Urals, Siberia, the Caucasus, the Crimea, and the Kazakh steppe. These networks also extended abroad, most importantly to Central Asia, which in the 18th century became a frequent destination for Bulghar students. The result was a vibrant Islamic scholarly culture emerging in new mosques and *madrasas* spread throughout these regions, but particularly the Volga-Urals. Indeed, Kemper notes a number of villages and towns other than Kazan and Qarghālī that had become important centers of scholarship and education by 1800: Qūrṣā, Machkara, Ūrā, Ṭāshkichū, Āshiṭ, Mangār, Tūntār, Ṣabā, Istarlīṭamaq, and Istarlībāsh.[83]

Qūrṣāwī was educated in Machkara, in a *madrasa* established in 1759.[84] There he studied under the renowned scholar and *ākhūnd* Muḥammad Raḥīm b. Yūsuf al-Āshiṭī (?–ca. 1817), one of the most accomplished *ʿulamāʾ* of the region. Āshiṭī had previously spent ten years in Dagestan studying with a number of preeminent *shaykhs*.[85] He traveled there with Ibrāhīm b. Khūjāsh (1750s–1826), perhaps the most prominent scholar of the era, who would go on to become senior *ākhūnd* and imam of Kazan's First Mosque.[86] Āshiṭī, upon his return to the Middle Volga in 1781, was appointed imam and *mudarris* in Machkara by some village notables.[87]

Students received a relatively broad education in Āshiṭī's *madrasa*, where he taught the subjects of logic, *fiqh*—*uṣūl* and *furūʿ*—hadith, and *kalām*, as well as

82. See Fakhr al-Dīn, *Āthār*, ii, p. 44; Ramzī, *Talfīq*, ii, p. 338.

83. Kemper, *Sufis*, p. 57.

84. Marjānī, *Mustafād*, ii, p. 161; also Fäxreddin, *Asar*, iii, p. 144/fol. 114a.

85. Ramzī, *Talfīq*, ii, p. 347.

86. See Fakhr al-Dīn, *Āthār*, v, pp. 226–238; Marjānī, *Mustafād*, ii, pp. 24–39; Ramzī, *Talfīq*, ii, pp. 352–353.

87. It seems that the notables gave him this position at the expense of the previous imam, ʿAbd al-Ḥamīd b. Ūtkān al-Tūntārī (?–1806), who was forced to move to another village; Marjānī, *Mustafād*, ii, p. 161.

disputation (*ādāb-i munāẓara*).[88] Such breadth was unusual, as most *mudarris*es taught only one or two subjects, a fact that speaks to Āshiṭī's standing as a scholar.[89] Indeed, there were a number of his students who became accomplished *ʿulamāʾ* in their own right.[90]

Āshiṭī's *madrasa*, like virtually all Islamic institutions in the empire, was supported financially by the local community, upon which it relied for not only its founding but its continued operation as well.[91] State sanction did not entail funding, and the *waqf*, so prevalent elsewhere in the Muslim world, was virtually nonexistent prior to the establishment of the Spiritual Assembly and remained quite limited after that. As such, direct support for mosques and *madrasa*s generally had to come from wealthier members of the community, and, as Frank points out, such funding was viewed as an almost expected beneficence, without which institutions struggled to even remain open.[92]

The proliferation of Islamic institutions was thus intimately connected with another byproduct of tolerance—the rise of a Muslim merchant class.[93] Volga-Ural Muslims were actively engaged in commerce across Eurasia and came to dominate the trans-steppe trade with Central Asia, enterprises that made them valuable to the tsarist government, which took an active role in promoting Muslim mercantilism. In 1763, traders were allowed to live in a section of Kazan previously restricted to Muslims in government service (the so-called *sluzhilo-tatarskaia sloboda*), and, as noted, Muslims were allowed to hold the legal status of merchant beginning in 1776.[94] Qarghālī was of course founded for the purpose of encouraging Muslim commerce with Central Asia.

One of the most significant steps was the establishment of a dedicated administrative body for Muslim merchants. The *ratusha* (from the German *rathaus*) was a municipal institution for the self-regulation of the empire's urban merchant

---

88. Marjānī, *Mustafād*, ii, p. 162; Fakhr al-Dīn, *Āthār*, iii, p. 142; Amīrkhān, *Tawārīkh-i bulghāriyya*, p. 43.

89. Cf. Mustafa Tuna, *Imperial Russia's Muslims: Islam, Empire, and European Modernity, 1788–1914*. Cambridge: Cambridge UP, 2015, p. 23.

90. Including Marjānī's grandfather Ṣubḥān b. ʿAbd al-Karīm (1749–1833). For a list of some of Āshiṭī's students, see Marjānī, *Mustafād*, ii, p. 162; also Fakhr al-Dīn, *Āthār*, iii, p. 142.

91. *Madrasas* at this time, it should be noted, were not schoolhouses—instruction usually took place in attached mosques—but consisted largely of lodging for students; cf. Frank, *Institutions*, pp. 251–252.

92. Ibid., pp. 179–180, 195–203, 232–235; Tuna, *Imperial*, p. 22.

93. For a detailed description of Muslim mercantilism in this period, see Tuna, *Imperial*, pp. 127–134.

94. Khayrutdinov, "Tatar *Ratusha* of Kazan," pp. 29, 31.

class, introduced in 1728, but in 1781 the imperial government, acting on specific orders from Catherine, created a separate *ratusha* for the Muslim traders of Kazan, who had previously been excluded from the city's *ratusha*. A second Muslim *ratusha* was founded in Qarghālī three years later.[95] The *ratusha*s were part of the broader structure of municipal governance, and they provided a venue for the growth of Muslim commerce under the auspices of the state, which, according to Ramil Khayrutdinov, "was clearly interested in establishing a means both for encouraging [Muslim] commerce and making sure that this commerce remained under the control of the central administration."[96] The merchants involved used the institution to serve their own commercial and entrepreneurial goals, and the *ratusha*s played an important part in fostering Muslims' prosperity.[97]

Muslim merchants were integral in Kazan's growth as a major manufacturing center; by the mid-19th century, it had become easily the third-largest commercial and industrial center in Russia, behind only Moscow and St. Petersburg.[98] In this time, the merchant class had replaced the landed nobility as the primary social elites alongside the *ʿulamāʾ*.[99] This burgeoning bourgeoisie for its part was keen on using their wealth for religious purposes, and many of them founded new mosques and *madrasa*s and supported scholars and *mudarris*es.[100] This was a necessary function for sustaining the religious infrastructure of the region, and a great many mosques mentioned in the sources had at least one patron associated with them. For instance, Qūrṣā's mosque had its *qibla* rebuilt in 1839 with the

95. Ibid., pp. 28–29, 33.

96. Ibid., p. 32.

97. Cf. Robert Geraci. *Window on the East: National and Imperial Identities in Late Tsarist Russia*. Ithaca, NY: Cornell UP, 2001, pp. 23–24.

98. Khayrutdinov, "Tatar *Ratusha* of Kazan," pp. 28, 32.

99. Tuna, *Imperial*, p. 125; Christian Noack. "State Policy and Its Impact on the Formation of a Muslim Identity in the Volga-Urals." *Islam in Politics in Russia and Central Asia (Early Eighteenth to Late Twentieth Centuries)*. Eds. Stéphane Dudoignon and Hisao Komatsu. London: Kegan Paul, 2001. 3–26, p. 6; see also Christian Noack. "Les musulmans de la région Volga-Oural au XIXe siècle. L'arrière-plan économique, social et culturel du mouvement d'émancipation." *L'Islam de Russie: Conscience communautaire et autonomie politique chez les Tatars de la Volga et de l'Oural depuis le XVIIIe siècle*. Eds. Stéphane Dudoignon et al. Paris: Maisonneuve et Larose, 1997. 89–114; D. M. Iskhakov. "O nekotorykh aspektakh formirovaniia gorodskoi kul'tury volgo-ural'skikh tatar na natsional'nom ètape (XVIII–nachalo XX vv.)." *Kazan, Moscow, St. Petersburg: Multiple Faces of the Russian Empire*. Eds. Catherine Evtuhov et al. Moscow: OGI, 1997. 249–264; also G. S. Gubaidullin. *Istoriia Tatar*. 1925. 3rd ed. Moscow: Moskovskii litsei, 1994, pp. 164–184.

100. Noack, "State Policy," pp. 6–7, 15; see also Marjānī, *Mustafād*, esp. ii, pp. 333–348.

support of a pair of brothers, ʿUbayd Allāh and ʿAbd al-Karīm of the powerful Āpānāy (Apanaev) family of Kazan.[101] The stone mosque in Ūrā was constructed by the wealthy Tūqṭāmish family (see section "The Religious Hierarchy").[102] All of Kazan's mosques had merchant families as patrons.[103] And nowhere was the link between Muslim merchants and Islamic institutions more evident than in Qarghālī, which developed simultaneously as a trading and scholarly center.

It was common for merchants and scholars to be bound by familial ties, often in marriage, as well as patronage. Qūrṣāwī was no exception. His father was a trader, as was his older brother ʿAbd al-Khāliq (?–1843), who, Marjānī writes, traveled repeatedly to Bukhara on merchant business.[104] Their sister Marḥab (?–1828) married the Machkara merchant ʿAbd Allāh b. ʿAbd al-Salām (1735–1832), who was descended from the important Ūtāmish (Utiamishev) family and who financially supported Machkara's stone mosque.[105] Their daughter, Ḥusnā (?–1843), married into the Āpānāy family, and at least one of their sons, Mūsā b. ʿAbd Allāh (?–1835), became a member of the *ʿulamāʾ* (in addition to working as a trader), as did Mūsā's son, Ismāʿīl (1805–1888).[106]

Such connections between families of scholars and patrons could be extensive, and they shaped the Bulghar institutional landscape. Qūrṣāwī's brother-in-law ʿAbd Allāh funded the reconstruction in stone of Kazan's Sixth Mosque in 1802, with Qūrṣāwī calculating the direction of its *qibla*. As patron, ʿAbd Allāh took the liberty of appointing its imam, naming Faḍl b. Sayf Allāh Kīzlawī (1747–1812), who was at the time imam in Qūrṣā.[107] Qūrṣāwī, who had shared teachers with Kīzlawī, took over this position.[108] ʿAbd Allāh and

---

101. Marjānī, *Mustafād*, ii, p. 167.

102. Ibid., p. 191.

103. Noack, "Les musulmans," p. 104.

104. Marjānī, *Wafiyat*, vi, fol. 145b; Marjānī, *Mustafād*, ii, p. 176. Qūrṣāwī had two other brothers, ʿAbd al-Karīm and ʿAbd al-Rashīd, and while they may also have been scholars (particularly ʿAbd al-Karīm), all that is explicitly recorded about them is that the former died in Cairo and the latter in Bukhara; Marjānī, *Mustafād*, p. 177; Ramzī, *Talfīq*, ii, p. 367.

105. Marjānī, *Mustafād*, ii, pp. 98, 157–159; Fakhr al-Dīn, *Āthār*, iii, p. 95.

106. Marjānī, *Mustafād*, ii, pp. 184, 336–337; Kemper, *Sufis*, p. 239 n. 92. On both Mūsā and Ismāʿīl, see Marjānī, *Mustafād*, ii, pp. 99–100, 184–185; Fäxreddin, *Asar*, iii, pp. 144–149/fol. 114a–118b; see also Ramzī, *Talfīq*, ii, p. 402.

107. Amīrkhān, *Tawārīkh-i bulghāriyya*, p. 74; Marjānī, *Mustafād*, ii, pp. 98, 101, 168; Fakhr al-Dīn, *Āthār*, ii, p. 87; also Kemper, *Sufis*, p. 56.

108. Marjānī, *Mustafād*, ii, p. 168.

his sons then helped Qūrṣāwī build a large *madrasa* attached to the mosque. When Qūrṣāwī returned to Bukhara in 1808, it was another of Āshiṭī's students (and son-in-law), Amīrkhān b. ʿAbd al-Mannān Ṭālqishī (1766–1828), who temporarily replaced him.[109] After Kīzlawī's death, Ṭālqishī took over the post of imam for the Sixth Mosque, and Kīzlawī's son, Muḥammad Wafā (?–1847), was appointed imam there after Ṭālqishī's death. In 1838 Baymurād b. Muḥarram Mangārī (?–1849) was appointed co-imam.[110] Then, in 1847 Ṭālqishī's son Ḥusayn Amīrkhān—author of the *Tawārīkh-i bulghāriyya*—in turn became imam, serving in that position until 1889. (He also would later marry Mangārī's daughter.)[111]

Qūrṣāwī himself married not into a merchant family but rather into a family of *ʿulamāʾ* when he married Fāṭima bt. Saʿīd of the prominent Shirdānī family.[112] He had become close with three of her brothers, ʿAbd al-Sattār (?–1830), ʿAbd al-Ghaffār (?–1830), and Aḥmad (1790–1867), during their time studying together under Āshiṭī. Their father, Saʿīd b. Aḥmad Shirdānī (1744–1830), had studied in Qarghālī under Īshniyāz Khwārizmī (among others) and became imam of Kazan's Fifth Mosque in 1810.[113] After this, the position became the exclusive domain of the family until the 1880s, with all four of his sons and two of his grandsons serving as imam or co-imam.[114]

Bukhara

Tolerance, state sanction, and elite patronage all contributed to the vibrant Islamic scholarly environment. But, in addition to the circumstances under

---

109. Ibid., pp. 101–102, 176; Fakhr al-Dīn, *Āthār*, v, p. 250; Amīrkhān, *Tawārīkh-i bulghāriyya*, pp. 74–76.

110. Marjānī, *Mustafād*, ii, p. 102. On Mangārī, see ibid., pp. 102–103; Fakhr al-Dīn, *Āthār*, xi, pp. 191–201; Ramzī, *Talfīq*, ii, pp. 375–376.

111. Kemper, *Sufis*, pp. 56–57; Marjānī, *Mustafād*, ii, p. 102; Amīrkhān, *Tawārīkh-i bulghāriyya*, p. 75.

112. Virtually nothing is known about their marriage. There is simply an oblique reference in Fakhr al-Dīn stating that Saʿīd b. Aḥmad Shirdānī's daughter Fāṭima was Qūrṣāwī's ex-wife; Fakhr al-Dīn, *Āthār*, v, p. 261; cf. Gul'nara Idiiatullina. "Vvedenie." In Abu-n-Nasr Abd an-Nasir al-Kursavi. *Nastavlenie liudei na put' istiny*. Kazan: Tatarskoe knizhnoe izd-vo, 2005. 10–88, p. 52.

113. Fakhr al-Dīn, *Āthār*, v, p. 261.

114. Ibid., p. 260; Ramzī, *Talfīq*, ii, p. 355; Marjānī, *Mustafād*, ii, pp. 96–97. ʿAbd al-Sattār, ʿAbd al-Ghaffār and their father Saʿīd all died within weeks of each other in the cholera epidemic of 1830–1831, and Aḥmad, who was in Bukhara at the time, returned to Kazan to take over as imam.

the Russian Empire, this environment was shaped by extensive ties to Bukhara as a cultural and religious center. As Frank has shown, Bulghar Muslims had long viewed Bukhara (frequently understood as the whole of Transoxiana rather than just the city itself) as a sacral heartland, to which they traced their ancestral and spiritual heritage. Eurasian trade strengthened the connection with Bukhara in the 18th century, as Bukharan merchants established trading communities in Bulghar cities (with tsarist support), and vice versa.[115]

Most significant for our purposes, however, is the considerable prestige attached to Bukhara in terms of Islamic scholarship. Bukharan education was held in very high regard among Bulghars, and by 1800 it had become common for aspiring *ʿulamāʾ* to travel there in pursuit of learning, and ubiquitous among the most prominent scholars. Bulghar students studying under the same *shaykhs* and *mudarrises* formed ties that remained after they returned to Russia, shaping to a degree their subsequent work as *ʿulamāʾ*.

Sufism was closely linked with the prestige attributed to Bukharan education. Sufi affiliation was overwhelmingly prevalent in Bukhara, and chains of Sufi authority, overlapping with scholarly networks, connected *ʿulamāʾ* (in the broadest sense) throughout the Russian Empire to Central Asia and to each other.[116] The Naqshbandi-Mujaddidiyya was central in this regard as the predominant affiliation among Bulghar scholars.[117] The suborder had spread steadily since its emergence in 17th-century India, becoming one of the most important *ṭarīqas* in Central Asia in the 18th century, particularly in the amirate of Bukhara under the Manghit dynasty (r. 1785–1920).[118] From there it was brought to Russia.

---

115. Allen Frank. *Bukhara and the Muslims of Russia: Sufism, Education, and the Paradox of Islamic Prestige*. Leiden: Brill, 2012. For a broad perspective on scholarship and society in post-Timurid Bukhara, see Robert McChesney. "Islamic Culture and the Chinggisid Restoration: Central Asia in the Sixteenth and Seventeenth Centuries." *New Cambridge History of Islam. Vol. 3: The Eastern Islamic World Eleventh to Eighteenth Centuries*. Eds. David Morgan and Anthony Reid. Cambridge: Cambridge UP, 2010. 239–265.

116. On the importance of personal interactions between the *shaykh/pīr* and disciple (*murīd*) among Naqshbandis, see J. G. J. ter Haar. "The Importance of the Spiritual Guide in the Naqshbandi Order." *The Heritage of Sufism*, Vol. II: *The Legacy of Medieval Persian Sufism (1150–1500)*. Ed. Leonard Lewisohn. Oxford: Oneworld, 1999. 311–322.

117. See Kemper, *Sufis*, pp. 82–98; Algar, "Shaykh Zaynullah Rasulev."

118. See Hamid Algar. "A Brief History of the Naqshbandi Order." *Cheminements et situation actuelle d'un ordre mystique musulman: actes de la Table ronde de Sèvres, 2–4 mai 1985*. Eds. Marc Gaborieau et al. Istanbul: Editions ISIS, 1990. 3–44, pp. 24–28; also Kemper, *Sufis*, pp. 86–88; Baxtiyor M. Babadžanov. "On the History of the Naqšbandiya Muǧaddidiya in Central Mawara'annahr in the Late 18th and Early 19th Centuries." *Muslim Culture in Russia and Central Asia from the 18th to the Early 19th Centuries*. Eds. Michael Kemper et al. Berlin: Klaus Schwarz Verlag, 1996. 385–414, pp. 385–386; Anke von Kügelgen. "Die Entfaltung der

Qarghālī was an early center for the order, under the leadership of the above-mentioned *shaykh* ʿAbd al-Karīm b. Bālṭāy. ʿAbd al-Karīm was initiated into the order by Ḥabīb Allāh al-Balkhī (or Bukhārī) (?–1699), who was one of the most important Mujaddidi *shaykhs* in Central Asia and the *khalīfa* of Muḥammad al-Maʿṣūm (1597–1668), the son and chosen successor of Aḥmad Sirhindī (1564–1624), founder of the Mujaddidiyya.[119] ʿAbd al-Karīm taught a number of students in Qarghālī, helping disseminate the order, as did his son, Isḥāq (?–1801).[120] Among Isḥāq's students and close companions was the Mujaddidi ʿAbd al-Raḥmān b. Muḥammadsharīf Khān-Kirmānī (1746?–1827), an imam and *mudarris* in Qarghālī whom Kemper calls one of the most influential *ʿulamāʾ* of the region.[121]

Large numbers of Bulghar scholars were also initiated into the order while studying in Central Asia, including prominent figures such as Muḥammadjān b. Ḥusayn (1758–1824), the first Mufti of the Spiritual Assembly, as well as the brothers Fatḥ Allāh b. Ḥusayn al-Ūriwī (1767–1843) and Ḥabīb Allāh b. Ḥusayn al-Ūriwī (1762–1818).[122] These three were adepts of Fayḍ Khān Kābulī (?–1802), as was ʿAbd al-Raḥīm b. ʿUthmān al-Ūtiz-Īmānī (1754–1834), a scholar who would become a main opponent of both Qūrṣāwī and Fatḥ Allāh Ūriwī.[123]

Qūrṣāwī studied in Bukhara with Niyāzqulī al-Turkmānī (?–1821), a prominent member of the Bukharan *ʿulamāʾ* and, along with Fayḍ Khān Kābulī, one of the two most important Mujaddidi *shaykhs* for Bulghar *murīds*.[124] According to

---

Naqšbandiya Muǧaddidiya im mittleren Transoxanien vom 18. bis zum Beginn des 19. Jahrhunderts: Ein Stück Detektivarbeit." *Muslim Culture in Russia and Central Asia from the 18th to the Early 20th Centuries. Vol. 2: Inter-Regional and Inter-Ethnic Relations.* Eds. Anke von Kügelgen et al. Berlin: Klaus Schwarz Verlag, 1998. 101–151.

119. Kemper, *Sufis*, pp. 87–88; von Kügelgen, "Entfaltung," pp. 114–116.

120. See Fakhr al-Dīn, *Āthār*, ii, pp. 74–75; Ramzī, *Talfīq*, ii, p. 338.

121. Kemper, *Sufis*, p. 241; see Marjānī, *Mustafād*, ii, p. 231; Ramzī, *Talfīq*, ii, p. 354; Fakhr al-Dīn, *Āthār*, v, pp. 241–246.

122. On Fatḥ Allāh, see Marjānī, *Mustafād*, ii, pp. 193–195; Fakhr al-Dīn, *Āthār*, ix, pp. 7–72; Ramzī, *Talfīq*, ii, p. 367; Amīrkhān, *Tawārīkh-i bulghāriyya*, p. 42. On Ḥabīb Allāh, see Marjānī, *Mustafād*, ii, pp. 190–193; Fakhr al-Dīn, *Āthār*, iii, pp. 144–149; Ramzī, *Talfīq*, ii, pp. 347–348; Amīrkhān, *Tawārīkh-i bulghāriyya*, pp. 42–43.

123. On this important scholar, see Marjānī, *Mustafād*, ii, pp. 239–241; Fakhr al-Dīn, *Āthār*, vi, pp. 300–316; Ramzī, *Talfīq*, ii, pp. 360–361; Kemper, *Sufis*, esp. pp. 172–212; G. Idiiatullina. "Dukhovno-religioznaia atmosfera v Povolzh'e v XVII–XVIII vv." *Islam v srednem povolzh'e: istoriia i sovremennost'*. Kazan: IIIaL AN Tatarstana, 2001. 176–201; Aidar Iuzeev. *Filosofskaia mysl' tatarskogo naroda*. Kazan: Tatarskoe knizhnoe izd-vo, 2007, pp. 60–66.

124. Kemper, *Sufis*, pp. 90–98; Algar, "Shaykh Zaynullah Rasulev," esp. pp. 113–117; Frank, *Bukhara*; Ramzī, *Talfīq*, ii, p. 343; Marjānī, *Mustafād*, ii, p. 168; Fakhr al-Dīn, *Āthār*, iii, p. 96.

Ramzī, Qūrṣāwī was fully initiated into the order under Turkmānī, becoming a Mujaddidi *shaykh* in his own right.[125]

The Naqshbandi order is marked by its emphasis on strict adherence to the norms of orthodoxy, which is encompassed in one of the central tenets of the order, *naẓar bar qadam*—"watching one's step," being mindful of following the example of the Prophet.[126] The Mujaddidiyya, originated by Sirhindī—known among his followers as "the Renewer of the Second Millennium" (*mujaddid-i alf-i thānī*), from which the suborder takes its name—formed as an offshoot of the Naqshbandiyya in India around 1600.[127] Concerned with upholding strict Sunnism and adherence to the prophetic example, Sirhindī put forward a vision of Sufism that combined the *ʿulamāʾ*'s emphasis on scholarly knowledge and correctness with religious and political activism.[128] Herein lies Sirhindī's ultimate contribution to the Naqshbandi order, according to Hamid Algar, who writes that his importance stems from his insistence on "obedience to the *sunna* and the [legalistic] *sharīʿa* as being itself the prime method of spiritual realization and advancement. This theme was not, of course, new in the history of the order, but it was elaborated more fully and systematically by Sirhindī than had been the case hitherto."[129] For Sirhindī, however, correctness and propriety regarding belief were more important than they were regarding praxis. This distinction, which J. G. J. ter Haar describes as orthodoxy over orthopraxy, is based on the idea that deviation in belief is far worse than deviation in, for instance, ritual, which is more easily corrected.[130] Despite this distinction between belief and praxis, Sirhindī considered correctness in both

---

Turkmānī was also called Abū Ṣāliḥ al-Khalajī Khalīfa al-Turkmānī, *Pīr-i Dastgīr*; ibid., iv, p. 284; Kemper, *Sufis*, p. 234 n. 73; cf. Babadžanov, "History," pp. 398–399.

125. Ramzī, *Talfīq*, ii, p. 343. Ramzī writes that he reached the stage of perfection (*martabat al-kamāl*) in the Sufi path, which, along with initiating *murīds*, makes one a *shaykh* of the order; see ter Haar, "The Importance of the Spiritual Guide," p. 318.

126. Arthur F. Buehler. *Sufi Heirs of the Prophet: The Indian Naqshbandiyya and the Rise of the Mediating Sufi Shaykh*. Columbia: U of South Carolina P, 1998, p. 234. For the eleven main articles of the Naqshbandi *ṭarīqa*, see ibid.; ter Haar, "Importance of the Spiritual Guide," p. 313; also Algar, "Brief History."

127. On the formation of the Mujaddidiyya and relation to the Naqshbandi order as a whole, see Arthur Buehler. "The Naqshbandiyya in Timurid India: The Central Asian Legacy." *Journal of Islamic Studies*, vol. 7, no. 2; 1996. 208–228.

128. Ibid., p. 221; Buehler, *Sufi Heirs*.

129. Algar, "Brief History," p. 22.

130. J. G. J. ter Haar. *Follower and Heir of the Prophet: Shaykh Ahmad Sirhindi (1564–1624) as Mystic*. Leiden: Het Oosters Instituut, 1992, pp. 47–48, 59, 61–62.

to trump strictly mystical concerns. As a result, Sirhindī held that (legal, theological) *ʿulamāʾ*, as those who determined proper doctrine and action, were much more important than Sufis for the community as a whole.[131]

This exceedingly positive stance toward *ʿulamāʾ* made the order popular with scholars. A number of Mujaddidiyya were important figures in the Bukharan *ʿulamāʾ*, and many Mujaddidi *shaykhs* became deeply involved in the politics of the amirate.[132] Among them, for instance, were ʿAṭāʾ Allāh Khwāja b. Hādī Bukhārī and ʿInāyat Allāh Bukhārī, *shaykh al-Islām* and chief *qāḍī* (*qāḍī-yi kalān*), respectively, under Amir Ḥaydar (r. 1800–1826).[133] Indeed, the *ʿulamāʾ*'s close involvement in politics was cultivated by Ḥaydar and his predecessor, Shāh Murād (r. 1785–1800), who based their rule upon piety and a support for religious morality and learning, with both amirs being active in the order.[134]

Niyāzqulī Turkmānī was another such Mujaddidi with political connections.[135] In addition to serving as *khaṭīb* in the city's great central mosque, he served as spiritual advisor to the two Bukharan amirs while operating his own *madrasa* and *khānqāh*.[136] Turkmānī is described as exceptionally zealous in his adherence to orthodoxy and rejection of deviation in belief, standing out even among other Mujaddidiyya. According to Baxtiyor Babadžanov, he appears in his writings to be primarily concerned with legal and ritual questions, rather than mysticism, and he used his position within the amirate to inveigh against immoral conduct by the political elite.[137]

Articulating Reform

Qūrṣāwī shared this outlook with Turkmānī. He writes, for instance, that to be a Sufi means "limiting oneself to worshipping (*iqāmat al-ʿubūdiyya*) according

131. Ibid., pp. 50–52.

132. Babadžanov, "History," p. 405; see also von Kügelgen, "Entfaltung"; Anke von Kügelgen. *Die Legitimierung der mittelasiatischen Mangitendynastie in den Werken ihrer Historiker (18.–19. Jahrhundert)*. Istanbul: Ergon Verlag Würzburg, 2002; Anke von Kügelgen. "Manghits." *EIr.*

133. Kemper, *Sufis*, p. 51; Sayyid Muḥammad Naṣīr al-Dīn [al-Bukhārī] b. Sayyid Amīr Muẓaffar. *Tuḥfat al-zāʾirīn*. Ed. Mullā Muḥammadī Makhdūm. Bukhara: n.p., 1328 [1910], p. 98.

134. Von Kügelgen, "Entfaltung," pp. 114, 130; von Kügelgen, *Legitimierung*, pp. 281–292.

135. Marjānī writes that Amir Ḥaydar read the *janāza* prayer at Turkmānī's funeral; Marjānī, *Mustafād*, i, p. 183.

136. Ibid., i, p. 180; ii, p. 170; Ramzī, *Talfīq*, ii, p. 344 n. 1. See Bukhārī, *Tuḥfat al-zāʾirīn*, p. 99; von Kügelgen, "Entfaltung," pp. 111, 131–136; Babadžanov, "History," pp. 398–399, 406–407.

137. Babadžanov, "History," pp. 390, 398, 407.

to the example of the Prophet within the [bounds of the] *sharīʿa* and . . . requires action by the *sharīʿa* in accordance with the *Sunna*."[138] Turkmānī was known to keep political elites at arm's length, never accepting presents or rewards from them, and Qūrṣāwī appears to have been the same way.[139] Yet, despite this attitude toward political power, Qūrṣāwī's primary moral criticisms were reserved for the *ʿulamāʾ*. While in Bukhara he was outspoken in denouncing what he considered to be their excesses and deviations, particularly their overreliance on rationalist beliefs in *kalām*, and these criticisms were a pervasive feature in his written works.

It seems, however, that Qūrṣāwī did not always have this stance toward *kalām* and the leading *ʿulamāʾ*. It is reported that as a young man he delved deeply and unreservedly into the study of *kalām*, in line with the most prominent scholars in Bukhara.[140] But, Fakhr al-Dīn writes, Qūrṣāwī realized one day while at the *madrasa* that *kalām* was "nothing more than delusions and suppositions (*awhām wa-ẓunūn*)" based on "the wisdom of the Greeks" (*ḥikmat-i yūnāniyya*).[141] Instead, he saw that belief must be based primarily on Qurʾan and Sunna, and that knowledge of, and adherence to, scripture was the basis of religious correctness. Qūrṣāwī then devoted himself to the study of the works of "the noble Qurʾan-commentators, the great scholars of hadith, the Qurʾan-memorizers and the Sufis (*ahl-i taṣawwuf*)."[142]

Qūrṣāwī's views provoked a significant degree of controversy in Bukhara, and many people were calling for his condemnation.[143] Among his main opponents was Fakhr al-Dīn b. Ibrāhīm b. Khūjāsh (1757–1844), the son of Ibrāhīm b. Khūjāsh and Āshiṭī's sister, Munawwar, who had settled in Bukhara.[144]

138. Qūrṣāwī, *Irshād*, p. 51.

139. Babadžanov, "History," pp. 406–407; cf. Marjānī, *Tanbīh*, p. 376.

140. *Manāqib*, fol. 68a.

141. Fakhr al-Dīn, *Āthār*, iii, p. 119. Fakhr al-Dīn seems to take his account at least partially from the *Manāqib*, which frequently uses the phrase "*ḥikma yūnāniyya*" to describe *kalām*; e.g., *Manāqib*, fol. 68b.

142. Fakhr al-Dīn, *Āthār*, iii, p. 119. Although less explicit, the other sources imply a similar transition in Qūrṣāwī's thought, though with different timing. Ramzī states that Qūrṣāwī adopted his way of thinking after his first time in Bukhara and makes an oblique reference to him ignoring criticisms of his past; Ramzī, *Talfīq*, ii, p. 343. Marjānī, for his part, also writes that Qūrṣāwī developed his views after returning to Qūrṣā, though he says little at all about him prior to his second time in Bukhara; Marjānī, *Mustafād*, ii, p. 168.

143. Marjānī, *Mustafād*, i, p. 180; Marjānī, *Tanbīh*, p. 374.

144. Marjānī, *Tanbīh*, p. 376; also Fakhr al-Dīn, *Āthār*, x, pp. 109–114; Ramzī, *Talfīq*, ii, pp. 370–371.

A learned scholar in his own right, Fakhr al-Dīn was connected with the elite of the Bukharan *ʿulamāʾ*, serving as Amir Ḥaydar's teacher of Qurʾanic recitation.[145] He also studied under ʿAṭāʾ Allāh Bukhārī, who, as noted, was *shaykh al-Islām* in Bukhara, and who was descended from a line of prominent theologians dating back to the 16th century.[146]

It was precisely such scholars that Qūrṣāwī continued to criticize for what he considered deviant views. In this he would have had many opportunities. Amir Ḥaydar fancied himself a scholar, and he frequently held public debates between members of the *ʿulamāʾ*.[147] Marjānī writes that Qūrṣāwī excelled in these debates, where he expressed his criticisms of scholars' errors in *kalām*.[148] He would have presumably been supported in doing so by Turkmānī, who, according to Babadžanov, was likewise an outspoken proponent of doctrinal purity.[149]

Qūrṣāwī seems to have had a close relationship with Turkmānī, who continually protected him from persecution.[150] Much of Qūrṣāwī's time in Bukhara revolved around his activities with the *shaykh*, and it is telling that no other teachers from Bukhara are named in connection with him, even though he was known to have studied under other scholars.[151] In addition to his brother ʿAbd al-Khāliq, Qūrṣāwī's companions Muḥammad Āmīn al-Nalāsāwī (?–1833), Niʿmat Allāh b. Bīktimur (1774–1843), and Dawlatshāh b. ʿĀdilshāh (1768–1832) were all students of Turkmānī, as were two of his brothers-in-law, ʿAbd al-Ghaffār and Aḥmad Shirdānī.[152]

---

145. Fakhr al-Dīn, *Āthār*, x, p. 109; Ramzī, *Talfiq*, ii, p. 370; Marjānī, *Mustafād*, i, p. 183.

146. Kemper, *Sufis*, p. 221. ʿAṭāʾ Allāh is the author of three known works on theology. The first is a supercommentary on the *Tatimma* by Yūsuf Qarabāghī (fl. 17th cent.) and the second a short work on the problem of eternality and contingency; ibid., p. 221 n. 33. The third is a supercommentary on an excerpt from the *ʿAqāʾid ʿaḍudiyya* (discussed *infra*) dealing with the creation of the world; ʿAṭāʾ Allāh Bukhārī. *Ḥāshiya ʿalā al-ʿAḍudiyya*. Ms. SPb IVR, no. B4038. Fols. 128b–137b.

147. Ṣadr al-Dīn ʿAynī. *Tārīkh-i amīrān-i Manghitiyya-i Bukhārā*. Tashkent: Turkestanskoe gosudarstvennoe izd-vo, 1923, p. 19; Marjānī, *Mustafād*, i, p. 184.

148. Marjānī, *Tanbīh*, pp. 379–380; see also Kemper, *Sufis*, pp. 233–234.

149. Babadžanov, "History," p. 398.

150. Ramzī, *Talfiq*, ii, p. 344.

151. Marjānī, *Mustafād*, ii, p. 169; Fakhr al-Dīn, *Āthār*, iii, p. 96.

152. On these figures, see Marjānī, *Mustafād*, ii, pp. 100, 177, 238, 254–255; Ramzī, *Talfiq*, ii, pp. 358, 366–369; Fakhr al-Dīn, *Āthār*, vi, pp. 292–295; viii, p. 477; ix, 77–93; xii, p. 450; Amīrkhān, *Tawārīkh-i bulghāriyya*, pp. 45–46, 52–53.

In about 1802, after four years with Turkmānī in Bukhara, Qūrṣāwī returned to Qūrṣā, where he became imam and *mudarris*.[153] We can assume, based on his own works, that he taught *uṣūl al-fiqh*, Qurʾan, hadith, and theology (labeled *ʿilm al-tawḥīd wa-l-ṣifāt*, lit. "the science of [God's] oneness and the [divine] attributes").[154] A number of students studied in his *madrasa*, among them ʿAbd al-Khāliq Qūrṣāwī, Niʿmat Allāh b. Bīktimur, and Nuʿmān b. Amīr b. ʿUthmān al-Thamanī (?–1846?).[155] These three, along with Dawlatshāh b. ʿĀdilshāh and Muḥammad Nalāsāwī, would become Qūrṣāwī's closest companions and most ardent supporters. He also initiated adepts into the Mujaddidi order.[156]

While in Qūrṣā Qūrṣāwī continued his scholarly work. According to both Marjānī and Ramzī, he read a number of texts by early scholars (*mutaqaddimūn*) and studied "the doctrine of the ancestors" (*madhhab al-salaf*) in order to refute the errors of later generations. These texts/authors are not specified, but both sources note that he engaged in extensive study of Abū Ḥāmid al-Ghazālī's

153. There is some question as to when he was in Bukhara the first time, as a date is not recorded in the primary sources, only that he spent four years there; cf. Fakhr al-Dīn, *Āthār*, iii, p. 120; *Manāqib*, fol. 68b. Kemper places it at 1800–1804, based on a manuscript source from 1802 describing the recent arrival in Bukhara of an unnamed Bulghar scholar who broadly resembles the general portrayal of Qūrṣāwī, but who is also praised by known opponents of Qūrṣāwī, including Ūtiz-Īmānī, who authored the text; Kemper, *Sufis*, pp. 226–227; see also the discussion in Idiiatullina, "Vvedenie," p. 42. Alfrid Bustanov has placed Qūrṣāwī's arrival in Bukhara before 1800, relying on somewhat stronger evidence: a manuscript that mentions a Bulghar scholar named Abū Naṣr attending a debate held by Amir Shāh Murād, who dies in 1800. This reference is contained in a biography of Muḥammad Sharīf Bayrakawī (?–1841), a reformist scholar and Sufi from the Volga-Ural region who was also a student of Turkmānī (in fact, Bustanov states that it's likely Bayrakawī is Kemper's unnamed scholar); Bustanov, "Bulghar Region," esp. pp. 190–191; see also Fakhr al-Dīn, *Āthār*, viii, pp. 458–469; Ramzī, *Talfīq*, ii, pp. 364–366. I lean toward placing Qūrṣāwī's time in Bukhara at 1798–1802 for circumstantial reasons connected with his return to the Middle Volga, namely the reconstruction of Kazan's Sixth Mosque in 1802 (mentioned earlier): his calculation of the mosque's *qibla*, and Faḍl b. Sayf Allāh Kīzlawī's appointment as imam, vacating his position in Qūrṣā, which Qūrṣāwī filled. (It's worth noting that Qūrṣāwī's brother-in-law ʿAbd Allāh was integral in both of these events.) Although this fits with Bustanov's timeline, it is of course possible that some time elapsed between these events and Qūrṣāwī's return (particularly the mosque's construction, which could be a drawn-out process); cf. Marjānī, *Mustafād*, ii, pp. 98, 101.

154. According to Fakhr al-Dīn, it was a subject also taught by Āshiṭī and some of Qūrṣāwī's students; cf. Fakhr al-Dīn, *Āthār*, iii, p. 142; ix, p. 79. On the significance of *ʿilm al-tawḥīd wa-l-ṣifāt*, see Chapter 5.

155. Ramzī, *Talfīq*, ii, pp. 367, 374; Fakhr al-Dīn, *Āthār*, iii, p. 96; x, pp. 146–151. Both Ramzī and Fakhr al-Dīn estimate Thamanī's death in around 1262 AH (1846) but state explicitly that the date is unknown.

156. Ramzī, *Talfīq*, ii, p. 343.

(1058–1111) *Iḥyāʾ ʿulūm al-dīn* while in Qūrṣā.[157] This work, widely considered Ghazālī's magnum opus, links proper knowledge with moral comportment: "From the start," John Renard writes, "Ghazālī makes it very clear that becoming a person of knowledge is a foundational religious calling, one that outranks even devotion and martyrdom. . . . The quality of one's knowledge directly affects one's spiritual life," due to the "essential links of knowledge to faith and action."[158] In this way, the "*ʿulūm al-dīn*" of the title does not, according to Mohamed Ahmed Sherif, necessarily refer to the conventional religious sciences of law or theology but rather to "a discipline whose central concern is how to establish and maintain a special spiritual relation with God."[159] This discipline connects knowledge with behavior, benefiting the believer's soul and constituting, as Ghazālī writes, the "science of the way to the hereafter" (*ʿilm ṭarīq al-ākhira*).[160]

For Qūrṣāwī, sound religious knowledge—especially knowledge of scripture—is essential for every Muslim so that they are responsible for their own behavior and, by extension, salvation. The *ʿulamāʾ*, Qūrṣāwī repeatedly emphasizes, cannot necessarily be relied upon, as their never-ending squabbling and philosophizing have led them away from certain knowledge into error. This is a reflection of what we find in the *Iḥyāʾ*, where Ghazālī makes note of the "disputations (*khilāfiyyāt*) which have been created (*uḥdithat*) in the current age," writing that most arguments and disputes are irrelevant and can lead to deviation.[161] As evidence, he cites a hadith: "A people who have been guided go astray only when they have been afflicted by argumentation," and indeed Qūrṣāwī quotes this very same hadith in his own attacks against misguided scholars.[162]

---

157. Ibid.; Marjānī, *Mustafād*, ii, p. 168. This is the only book he studied that is mentioned by name. It was extraordinarily popular among Bulghar Muslims, a fact evinced by the sheer number of extant manuscript copies of the original, as well as commentaries; cf. Kemper, *Sufis*, pp. 49, 126, 216.

158. John Renard. "Introduction." *Knowledge of God in Classical Sufism: Foundations of Islamic Mystical Theology*. New York: Paulist Press, 2004. 11–64, p. 46.

159. Mohamed Ahmed Sherif. *Ghazali's Theory of Virtue*. Albany: State U of New York P, 1975, pp. 8–10.

160. Abū Ḥāmid Muḥammad al-Ghazālī. *Iḥyāʾ ʿulūm al-dīn*. 5 vols. Beirut: Dar Sader, 2000, i, p. 16.

161. Ibid., p. 65.

162. *Mā ḍalla qawm^{un} baʿd huda^{n} kānū ʿalayh illā utū al-jadāla*; Abū Naṣr ʿAbd al-Naṣīr b. Ibrāhīm al-Qūrṣāwī. *Mabāḥith al-ism wa-l-ṣifa*. Ms. SPb IVR, no. A1241. Fols. 153b–170b, fol. 154b.

Qūrṣāwī's emphasis on religious knowledge led him, quite naturally, to interrogate the bases for correct belief, which he also explored in his own works at this time. According to Ramzī, while in Qūrṣā he composed the *Kitāb al-Lawāʾiḥ* and his first commentary on the *ʿAqāʾid nasafiyya* (the *Sharḥ qadīm*), both of which deal with significant theological and philosophical matters. The *Lawāʾiḥ* was written precisely against those criticized in the *Iḥyāʾ* who go too far in argumentation and those who "persist in thinking themselves above knowledge and action."[163] The "prescriptions" (*lawāʾiḥ*, sing. *lāʾiḥa/lawḥ*) of the title refer to the structure of the work, which consists of the elucidation and explanation of several principles regarding belief, the recording of which Qūrṣāwī considers an important matter in order to help the mass of people who cannot distinguish between truth and ignorance.[164]

Importantly, these principles are not dogmatic, but rather philosophical in nature. For example, the first principle given addresses the difference between two types of eternality (*qidam*)—persistence in time and transcendence of time—with a discussion of how the latter type applies only to God.[165] Though concerned with matters of belief, this work puts forward a rational basis for them, and it is clear that it is intended to explain these principles to people in order to correct what Qūrṣāwī sees as deviant beliefs. He writes that misguidance (*ḍalāla*) is widespread, and people should study these matters, rather than relying on parents or teachers whose knowledge might be defective.[166]

In the *Sharḥ qadīm*, Qūrṣāwī addresses such teachers'—that is, other scholars'—defective knowledge. As a commentary on the *ʿAqāʾid nasafiyya* of Najm al-Dīn ʿUmar al-Nasafī (ca. 1068–1142), a central work in the Hanafi-Maturidi canon, the *Sharḥ qadīm* constitutes direct engagement on Qūrṣāwī's part with the *kalām* tradition. The *ʿAqāʾid nasafiyya* is best known through Saʿd al-Dīn Maṣʿūd b. ʿUmar al-Taftāzānī's (1322–1390) commentary, which was widely used in Central Asian scholarly circles (as well as in India and the Ottoman Empire) and formed the basis for theological education in the Volga-Ural region at the time.[167] Qūrṣāwī, however, bypasses Taftāzānī and

163. Abū Naṣr ʿAbd al-Naṣīr b. Ibrāhīm al-Qūrṣāwī. *al-Lawāʾiḥ li-l-ʿaqāʾid*. Ms. SPb IVR, no. A1241. Fols. 76b–86a, fol. 76b.

164. Ibid., fols. 76b–77a.

165. Ibid., fol. 77a–81b.

166. Ibid., fol. 85b.

167. Kemper, *Sufis*, p. 216; also Frank, *Institutions*, p. 244; Saʿd al-Dīn Taftāzānī. *Sharḥ al-ʿaqāʾid al-nasafiyya*. Ed. Aḥmad Ḥijāzī al-Saqqā. Cairo: Maktabat al-Kulliyyāt al-azhariyya, 1407/1988.

instead comments directly upon Nasafī, whom he holds in very high regard.[168] Although Qūrṣāwī only comments on a tiny fragment from Nasafī's original text,[169] he presents in his commentary all of the major criticisms he has of the predominant position on the divine attributes.[170]

The discussion contained in the *Sharḥ qadīm*, however, is for the most part cursory and not as detailed and thorough as the arguments found in his later works. This is not an indication that his ideas were not well developed at this time—indeed, the arguments in the *Lawā'iḥ* do delve into very complex theological issues in a more or less systematic fashion—but rather that Qūrṣāwī had most likely not yet fully articulated those ideas in writing. This would not come until after his second journey to Bukhara, when the bulk of his textual production likely took place.

Condemnation in Bukhara

Qūrṣāwī again left Qūrṣā for Bukhara, arriving in early 1808.[171] Why he returned is unknown, although Ramzī speculates that he traveled there to "guide (*irshād*) and admonish (*naṣīḥa*)" the people of the city.[172] This is not an implausible explanation: if, as both Ramzī and Marjānī suggest, Qūrṣāwī developed his critical stance toward the *ʿulamā'* while in Qūrṣā, then it stands to reason that he might well have wanted to extol the moral virtues of his beliefs to the scholars in Bukhara, the center of prestige and learning for Bulghar Muslims. Indeed, Qūrṣāwī himself writes that it is a duty to debate those who have gone astray in belief.[173] Another possible, even related reason for his return is the establishment of Turkmānī's *madrasa*—the Chār-minār, so named

168. Qūrṣāwī, *Sharḥ jadīd*, fol. 92b; Marjānī, *Tanbīh*, p. 377.

169. "And the creator of the world is God Exalted, the One, the Eternal" (*wa-l-muḥdith li-l-ʿālam huwa Allāhu taʿālā al-wāḥid al-qadīm*).

170. He rejects the attributes' multiplicity (*taʿaddud*), contingency (*imkān*), differentiation (*taghāyur*) and superaddition (*ziyāda ʿalā*), in addition to asserting God's oneness (*tawḥīd*) and transcendence (*tanzīh*); Abū Naṣr ʿAbd al-Naṣīr b. Ibrāhīm al-Qūrṣāwī. *Sharḥ al-ʿAqā'id al-nasafiyya al-qadīm*. Ms. KFU, no. A-1347. Fols. 17a–18b, fol. 18a. See Chapter 5.

171. Qūrṣāwī left on the journey in very late 1222 AH (1807); Fakhr al-Dīn, *Āthār*, iii, pp. 96, 120; also Marjānī, *Mustafād*, ii, p. 168; Ramzī, *Talfīq*, ii, p. 343. Audrey Burton describes the journey from Kazan to Bukhara as taking approximately nine weeks in the 17th century (though presumably longer in the winter); Audrey Burton. *The Bukharans: A Dynastic, Diplomatic, and Commercial History, 1550–1702*. Richmond, UK: Curzon, 1997, pp. 396–397.

172. Ramzī, *Talfīq*, ii, p. 343.

173. Qūrṣāwī, *Irshād*, p. 27.

for its four minarets—which, according to Anke von Kügelgen, opened in Shawwāl 1222 (December 1807).[174] It is certainly plausible that Qūrṣāwī could have traveled again to Bukhara to study with, or teach alongside, his old mentor.[175]

Whatever the reason, Qūrṣāwī began criticizing the city's *ʿulamāʾ* almost immediately upon arrival.[176] Ramzī writes, "He made clear to them that they had deviated (*inḥarafū*) from the way of the *salaf* in belief and action (*al-iʿtiqād wa-l-ʿamal*) and abandoned adherence to the Book and Sunna."[177]

This led to a situation where the *ʿulamāʾ* of the city were widely set against Qūrṣāwī. According to Marjānī, they slandered and unfairly criticized him and attributed to him radically heretical—and, Marjānī makes a point of noting, contradictory—theological positions, accusing him of leaving the bounds of Sunnism.[178] And many people, including Fakhr al-Dīn b. Ibrāhīm b. Khūjāsh, took their concerns to the amir, seeking punishment for Qūrṣāwī for his ideas.[179] According to a certain Yaḥyā b. Īshmuḥammad, a scholar from Qizilyār in Dagestan whose account supports the *ʿulamāʾ*, the most prominent scholars advised the amir to condemn him for unbelief.[180] As the mood among the *ʿulamāʾ* seems to have been darkening, Turkmānī futilely suggested to Qūrṣāwī that he leave the city for his own safety.[181]

In response to the situation, a meeting (*majlis*) was called between the amir and the *ʿulamāʾ* on one side and Qūrṣāwī on the other.[182] According to Ramzī, the meeting was held with the goal of executing him, a fact that

174. Von Kügelgen, "Entfaltung," pp. 135–136; also Kemper, *Sufis*, p. 226 n. 50.

175. This has also been speculated by Idiiatullina; Idiiatullina, "Vvedenie," pp. 45–46.

176. Marjānī, *Mustafād*, ii, p. 168; Marjānī, *Tanbīh*, pp. 373–374; Fakhr al-Dīn, *Āthār*, iii, p. 120.

177. Ramzī, *Talfīq*, ii, p. 344.

178. Namely, that Qūrṣāwī both denied the existence of the divine attributes and asserted the distinct existence of several eternal attributes; Marjānī, *Tanbīh*, p. 374; Marjānī, *Mustafād*, ii, p. 169; also Ramzī, *Talfīq*, ii, p. 344.

179. Marjānī, *Tanbīh*, p. 374; Ramzī, *Talfīq*, ii, p. 344.

180. His account is recorded in Fakhr al-Dīn, *Āthār*, iii, pp. 116–117. I have been unable to locate biographical information for this person.

181. Marjānī, *Tanbīh*, pp. 374–375.

182. Ibid., p. 376; Fakhr al-Dīn, *Āthār*, iii, p. 117; Marjānī, *Mustafād*, ii, p. 168; Ramzī, *Talfīq*, ii, p. 344. These four sources represent the main accounts of the events. Amīrkhān only gives a rough outline, in addition to quoting the main *fatwā* condemning Qūrṣāwī; Amīrkhān, *Tawārīkh-i bulghāriyya*, pp. 53–55.

Marjānī corroborates.[183] Fakhr al-Dīn, on the other hand, relates Yaḥyā's account, which states that Qūrṣāwī himself asked the amir for a debate with the *ʿulamāʾ*.[184]

Sixteen people, plus Qūrṣāwī, participated in the meeting, and each attached his name to the primary *fatwā* condemning him.[185] In addition to Amir Ḥaydar, these were the most prominent members of the amirate's *ʿulamāʾ*, and among them were the major scholars ʿAṭāʾ Allāh Bukhārī, ʿInāyat Allāh Bukhārī, and Qāḍī Tursūn Bāqī.[186] It is stated that civil and military leaders were also present, though it seems they did not participate.[187]

The meeting was intended to feature a debate between Qūrṣāwī and the *ʿulamāʾ* over his position on the divine attributes, but, as shown in Marjānī's detailed account in the *Tanbīh*, it more resembled an inquisition, with Qūrṣāwī constantly questioned about his statements. The amir began the meeting while brandishing a sword, and the *ʿulamāʾ*, primarily a certain Shams al-Dīn Balkhī, proceeded to interrogate Qūrṣāwī on the attributes in an ultimately unsuccessful attempt to provoke a heretical statement from him.[188]

The accounts generally agree regarding the outcome of the matter. The amir and the *ʿulamāʾ* declared Qūrṣāwī guilty of unbelief (*kufr*) and condemned

---

183. Ramzī, *Talfīq*, ii, p. 344; Marjānī, *Tanbīh*, pp. 375, 376.

184. Fakhr al-Dīn, *Āthār*, iii, p. 117. Though corroborating many of the details in Yaḥyā's account, Tursūn Bāqī's subsequent letter to the Bulghar *ʿulamāʾ* about the condemnation states that Qūrṣāwī was summoned to the amir's palace; ibid., p. 101; Marjānī, *Mustafād*, ii, p. 174.

185. Fakhr al-Dīn, *Āthār*, iii, p. 100; Marjānī, *Mustafād*, ii, p. 173; Amīrkhān, *Tawārīkh-i bulghāriyya*, p. 54. For a transcription of the *fatwā* and English translation, see Nathan Spannaus. "Islamic Thought and Revivalism in the Russian Empire: An Intellectual Biography of Abu Nasr Qursawi (1776–1812)." Diss. McGill University, 2012, pp. 228–230.

186. 1. Amir Ḥaydar; 2. Qāḍī Mīr Zayn al-Dīn b. Qadī-īshān Qurbān Badal; 3. Khwāja ʿAṭāʾ Allāh [al-Bukhārī]; 4. Qāḍī ʿInāyat [Allāh]; 5. Muftī Abū Naṣr Khwāja; 6. Qāḍī Mīrzā Faḍīl; 7. Qāḍī Mīr ʿAbd Allāh, *muftī-yi jūybār*; 8. Qāḍī Tursūn Bāqī; 9. Qāḍī Mīrzā Niʿmat Allāh Muftī b. Mīrzā Niyāz Muḥammad ʿAlī; 10. Qāḍī Mīrzā Shams al-Dīn b. Mīrshāh al-Ḥusaynī [al-Balkhī]; 11. Qāḍī Niyāz Birdī; 12. Muftī Mīrzā ʿAbd al-Raḥmān *aʿlam*; 13. Mīr ʿAbd al-Raḥīm Khwāja, *muftī-yi ʿaskar*; 14. Muḥammad Ḍiyāʾ *muftī*; 15. Shaykh al-Islām ʿAlawī Mīrza Raḥmat Allāh Khwāja b. ʿAṭāʾ Allāh Khwāja Nāṣirī; 16. Mīr ʿAbd Allāh Khwāja al-Ḥusaynī. There are minor discrepancies between the lists of participants in the sources, mostly due to different forms of names. Kemper notes the paucity of biographical sources of Bukharan *ʿulamāʾ* in this period, and as such, very few of these scholars can be otherwise identified; Kemper, "Şihabaddin al-Marğani über Abu-Nasr Qursawis Konflikt," p. 356; also Kemper, *Sufis*, p. 230 n. 64. Some are mentioned in Marjānī's account of the history of the Manghit dynasty, but without identifying details; Marjānī, *Mustafād*, i, pp. 172–193.

187. Marjānī, *Mustafād*, ii, p. 174; Fakhr al-Dīn, *Āthār*, iii, p. 101.

188. Marjānī, *Tanbīh*, pp. 376–378.

him to death if he did not renounce his views (*rujūʿ ʿan madhhabih*). Qūrṣāwī, seeing no other option, repented (*tāba*) and recited from memory the *ʿAqāʾid nasafiyya*, stating that it was his belief (*muʿtaqad*). The amir let him go, ordering his books burned and issuing a proclamation that anyone in Bukhara found holding his beliefs or possessing his writings could be executed. Urged by Turkmānī, Qūrṣāwī left the city for good.[189]

The Aftermath

His theological views roundly rejected and his life nearly lost, Qūrṣāwī headed to Khiva, where, according to Marjānī, he was warmly welcomed. From there he went to Astrakhan before traveling up the Volga to Qūrṣā.[190] The controversy, however, did not end with his departure. In Bukhara, several of the scholars who condemned Qūrṣāwī issued a letter to the Bulghar *ʿulamāʾ* describing his doctrinal errors and the reasons for his condemnation.[191] Yaḥyā b. Īshmuḥammad states that this letter was sent directly to the *ʿulamāʾ* in Kazan,[192] while Kemper suggests that it was addressed to ʿAbd al-Raḥmān

189. Ramzī, *Talfīq*, ii, p. 344; Fakhr al-Dīn, *Āthār*, iii, pp. 117–118, 121; Marjānī, *Mustafād*, ii, pp. 168–169. The divergences between the accounts are for the most part minimal. Ramzī writes that the *ʿulamāʾ* condemned Qūrṣāwī before the meeting, which was summoned to allow him the opportunity to repent, which he did only partially. Ramzī implies that it was Turkmānī's influence that saved his life; Ramzī, *Talfīq*, ii, p. 344. Yaḥyā b. Īshmuḥammad, who omits any mention of the *ʿAqāʾid nasafiyya*, writes that Ḥaydar only sought the *fatwā* from the *ʿulamāʾ* after the debate had ended. Qūrṣāwī then "repented and returned to the way of the people of the Sunna out of fear of the sword"; Fakhr al-Dīn, *Āthār*, iii, p. 117. In the *Mustafād*, Marjānī states that the *ʿulamāʾ* were summoned by Ḥaydar to discuss Qūrṣāwī. Only after this did the meeting take place, during which they condemned him and threatened him with death. Qūrṣāwī in this account does not repent but rather only recites the *ʿAqāʾid nasafiyya*, which sufficiently placates the amir; Marjānī, *Mustafād*, ii, p. 168. Only Marjānī's portrayal of the events in the *Tanbīh* differs significantly. Here Marjānī presents Qūrṣāwī as besting the *ʿulamāʾ* in the debate, which ends with the scholars turning on each other and the amir leaving in a huff. No mention is made of his condemnation or threatened execution, and only later does Qūrṣāwī heed Turkmānī's advice and leave the city; Marjānī, *Tanbīh*, pp. 376–378. Marjānī here does not mention the *fatwā*s condemning Qūrṣāwī by the Bukharan *ʿulamāʾ*, even though he later records them verbatim in the *Mustafād*; Marjānī, *Mustafād*, ii, pp. 172–175. On the differing portrayals of the events in the *Tanbīh* and *Mustafād* and an analysis of Marjānī's account, see Kemper, "Şihabaddin al-Marğani über Abu-Nasr Qursawis Konflikt," pp. 353–357.

190. Marjānī, *Tanbīh*, pp. 378–379; Marjānī, *Mustafād*, ii, p. 179; Fakhr al-Dīn, *Āthār*, iii, p. 96; Ramzī, *Talfīq*, ii, p. 344. Turkmānī was a native of Khiva, and Bustanov notes that there was a Bulghar community of Mujaddidiyya there; Bustanov, "Bulghar Region," esp. pp. 195–200.

191. The letter is quoted in full in Marjānī, *Mustafād*, ii, p. 174; Fakhr al-Dīn, *Āthār*, iii, p. 101.

192. Fakhr al-Dīn, *Āthār*, iii, p. 118.

Khān-Kirmānī (mentioned earlier) in Qarghālī, who, Fakhr al-Dīn notes, was known to correspond with Amir Ḥaydar.[193] Sometime after leaving the city, Yaḥyā writes, Qūrṣāwī recanted his repentance, which prompted another letter from the Bukharan *ʿulamāʾ* declaring Qūrṣāwī guilty of apostasy (*irtidād*).[194] This is almost certainly the letter by Qāḍī Tursūn Bāqī (dated 22 Jumādā Ūlā 1225 [June 14, 1810]), which condemns Qūrṣāwī in markedly harsher terms than other writings from Bukhara.[195]

It is reported in several places that Ḥaydar always regretted not executing Qūrṣāwī,[196] and the *ʿulamāʾ* continued to attack his positions. A certain "Afandī Dāghistānī," for instance, composed a refutation of his views on the divine attributes that includes effusive praise for Ḥaydar.[197] Qūrṣāwī remained *persona non grata* in Bukhara at least through the 1840s. Marjānī, who studied there between 1838 and 1849, writes that it was forbidden to discuss Qūrṣāwī's positions at that time.[198] Though curious, Marjānī did not become acquainted with his thought until traveling to Samarqand in 1844.[199] (This despite studying under Turkmānī's son ʿUbayd Allāh [?–1852] in Bukhara.[200] Marjānī also studied under Dāmullā ʿAbd al-Muʾmin Khwāja al-Afshanjī [?–1866], who reportedly was receptive to Qūrṣāwī's views but apparently unwilling to discuss them.)[201] In Samarqand, Marjānī studied with Qāḍī Abū Saʿīd b. ʿAbd al-Ḥayy al-Samarqandī (?–1849), who gave him an accurate idea of Qūrṣāwī's thought, rather than the scorn with which it was often treated.[202] Upon

193. Ibid., v, p. 241; Kemper, *Sufis*, p. 241.

194. Fakhr al-Dīn, *Āthār*, iii, p. 118.

195. Ibid., p. 101; Marjānī, *Mustafād*, ii, pp. 174–175; transcription and translation in Spannaus, "Islamic Thought," pp. 231–232.

196. Ramzī, *Talfīq*, ii, p. 344; Marjānī, *Wafiyat*, vi, fol. 145b; Marjānī, *Mustafād*, i, p. 185; ii, p. 170; ʿAynī, *Tārīkh-i amīrān*, p. 19.

197. Afandī al-Dāghistānī. *Radd ʿalā Abī al-Naṣr al-Qūrṣāwī*. Ms. SPb IVR, no. B2750. Fols. 1b–7a, fol. 2a. The identity of this author is unknown. It is possible he is Yaḥyā b. Īshmuḥammad, as similarities exist between the two documents, but this is purely speculative.

198. Ramzī, *Talfīq*, ii, p. 403; Marjānī, *Wafiyat*, vi, fol. 145b. However, Frank notes that some copies of his *Sharḥ jadīd* (see *infra*) were produced in Bukhara in the 1840s; Frank, *Bukhara*, p. 128.

199. Marjānī, *Wafiyat*, vi, fol. 146a; Marjānī, *Mustafād*, ii, p. 43; Shahr Sharaf. "Marjānīniñ tarjima-i ḥālī." *Marjānī*. Ed. Ṣāliḥ b. Thābit ʿUbaydullīn. Kazan: Maʿārif, 1333 [1915]. 2–193, pp. 46–51; see also Kemper, *Sufis*, pp. 436–437.

200. Sharaf, "Marjānīniñ tarjima-i ḥālī," pp. 33, 71.

201. Ibid., p. 34.

202. Marjānī, *Tanbīh*, p. 375; Kemper, *Sufis*, p. 436.

returning to Bukhara, he was able to locate copies of some of Qūrṣāwī's theological writings belonging to Ismāʿīl b. Mūsā, the son of Qūrṣāwī's nephew Mūsā b. ʿAbd Allāh.[203] Ismāʿīl himself had no use for Qūrṣāwī's works and believed them to contain the same heretical ideas that the Bukharan *ʿulamāʾ* had accused him of holding, a fact that Marjānī notes with some frustration.[204]

Having returned to Qūrṣā, Qūrṣāwī resumed writing and expounding his views. He wrote extensively in this period, producing a number of texts in a relatively short time. He wrote focused theological works, such as the *Mabāḥith fī al-ism wa-l-ṣifa* and the *Kitāb al-Naṣāʾiḥ*, which explore the relationship between Qūrṣāwī's view of the attributes and Sirhindī's. (See Chapter 6.)[205] It was in Qūrṣā that he also completed a full commentary on the *ʿAqāʾid nasafiyya* (the *Sharḥ jadīd*), as well as a commentary on the *Mukhtaṣar al-Manār* (the *Sharḥ Manār*).[206] The latter deals with the *mukhtaṣar* (summary, abridgement) of Abū al-Barakāt ʿAbd Allāh al-Nasafī's (ca. 1224–1310) *Kitāb al-Manār fī uṣūl al-fiqh* by Ṭāhir ibn Ḥabīb al-Ḥalabī (1340–1406), an important work of Hanafi legal theory,[207] and Qūrṣāwī's commentary goes into great detail about the hermeneutical process for deriving legal norms and determining religious obligations. Many of these works expand upon arguments previously formulated, as the *Sharḥ jadīd* does with the *Sharḥ qadīm* and the *Mabāḥith* does with the *Lawāʾiḥ*.

Qūrṣāwī also elucidated the practical elements and implications of his reformism in the *Irshād li-l-ʿibād*, which addresses many of the same themes found in the *Iḥyāʾ*.[208] The primary concern of the work is the relationship between religious knowledge and action, and the importance of true knowledge for every believer. Knowledge for Qūrṣāwī is particularly important in avoiding religious or moral deviation, to distinguish between the correct and

---

203. Marjānī, *Wafiyat*, vi, fol. 146b–147a; Sharaf, "Marjānīniñ tarjima-i ḥālī," p. 57.

204. Marjānī, *Wafiyat*, vi, fol. 147a.

205. Abū Naṣr ʿAbd al-Naṣīr b. Ibrāhīm al-Qūrṣāwī. *Kitāb al-Naṣāʾiḥ*. Ms. KFU, no. A-1347. Fols. 18a–22b.

206. Rezeda Safiullina writes that the *Sharḥ Manār* was published in 1905 by the Kharitonov press in Kazan, although this is not attested elsewhere; R. R. Safiullina. *Arabskaia kniga v dukhovnoi zhizni tatarskogo naroda*. Kazan: izd-vo Alma-Lit, 2003, pp. 98, 168.

207. Aron Zysow notes that the *Kitāb al-Manār* was among the most frequently commented-upon *fiqh* works; Aron Zysow. "Muʿtazilism and Maturidism in Hanafi Legal Theory." *Studies in Islamic Legal Theory*. Ed. Bernard G. Weiss. Leiden: Brill, 2002. 235–266, p. 238 n. 11.

208. Ramzī, *Talfīq*, ii, p. 343; Fakhr al-Dīn, *Āthār*, iii, p. 97. According to the *Manāqib*, the *Irshād* was one of the last works that Qūrṣāwī wrote; *Manāqib*, fol. 70a. Kemper, for his part, presumes it was written between 1808 and 1812; Kemper, *Sufis*, p. 237.

the incorrect, and the *Irshād* was explicitly composed to help regular people (*al-ʿāmma*) understand the bases for correct action and belief. At the very opening of the work, he states, speaking of the deviation he sees everywhere around him, that "widespread *bidʿa* and complete error (*ḍalāla mustawʿiba*)" have warranted his writing, to explain in perhaps difficult detail why they are wrong, as "the situation with the withering of religion and understanding among most people makes it necessary."[209]

Qūrṣāwī also composed his first work for a broader audience, rather than other *ʿulamāʾ*, with his partial Qurʾan translation-*cum*-commentary, the *Haftiyak tafsīrī*. Though the *Irshād* was ostensibly written for everyone, it was written in Arabic (like the rest of his works), thus excluding less-educated readers. Qūrṣāwī's *tafsīr*, on the other hand, was intended to increase popular understanding of the Qurʾan, and accordingly it was written in Tatar-Turkic, making it accessible to all literate people.[210]

The controversy surrounding his views continued, however, and he worked actively to promote them and persuade other *ʿulamāʾ*. For instance, he wrote a letter (unfortunately undated) to Khān-Kirmānī, the influential Qarghālī scholar, in which he explains and champions his own position on the attributes.[211] He cites in the letter a number of authorities, including Nasafī and Sirhindī, seemingly in an attempt not merely to defend himself but to win Khān-Kirmānī over.[212] He also frequently participated in scholarly debates, as he had in Bukhara.[213]

The Spiritual Assembly

But this was a distinct phase of the controversy surrounding him, involving different issues and—critically—a very different setting. The divine attributes obviously remained a point of contention, but there was no condemnation or official response as there had been in Bukhara. *ʿUlamāʾ* in the Russian

209. Qūrṣāwī, *Irshād*, p. 3.

210. Abū Naṣr ʿAbd al-Naṣīr b. Ibrāhīm al-Qūrṣāwī. *Haftiyak tafsīrī*. Ms. KFU, no. T-36, fol. 1b, 2b. Marjānī praises the work as "making the Qurʾan comprehensible and depicting it in clear language"; Marjānī, *Mustafād*, ii, p. 172.

211. Fakhr al-Dīn, *Āthār*, iii, p. 98; transcription and translation in Spannaus, "Islamic Thought," pp. 235–237.

212. The *Naṣāʾiḥ*, which is clearly addressed to another scholar, may have been written for Khān-Kirmānī as well; see the marginal note in Qūrṣāwī, *Naṣāʾiḥ*, fol. 19a; cf. Marjānī, *Wafiyat*, vi, fols. 167a–167b.

213. Marjānī, *Mustafād*, ii, p. 169.

Empire had a far different relationship to political power than in the amirate of Bukhara, as well as different institutional structures. State sanction for *ʿulamāʾ* and the establishment of the Spiritual Assembly, while providing stability to Islamic institutions and allowing scholarship to flourish, also brought restrictions upon those institutions and their function. The result was a transformed context for the exercise of religious authority. Even as Islamic discourses continued, the shifting circumstances under Russian rule precipitated a range of new questions faced by the Muslim community within a profoundly altered religious and social landscape.

The very structure of the Spiritual Assembly was aimed toward state control of Islamic institutions. The government retained the power to limit the number of *ʿulamāʾ* and determine who received official support. Unlike the earlier situation in the Urals, where only *ākhūnd*s were subject to tsarist oversight, the Spiritual Assembly extended government control to all ranks of the *ʿulamāʾ*—*ākhūnd*s, imams, and *mudarris*es, as well as all other mosque employees—headed by the Mufti, who was appointed by the state.[214] Candidates for religious positions required approval by both the government and the Spiritual Assembly leadership, located in Ufa. A scholar nominated by a *mahalla* first had to be approved by the local administration in order to ensure his loyalty to the empire and acceptability for the position.[215] If accepted, he then was examined by the Spiritual Assembly to test his knowledge in religious matters.[216] Scholars were barred from performing any role without official approval, and once in place they were required to serve only in their *maḥalla* (a regulation, Fisher argues, intended to limit itinerant *ʿulamāʾ*, who were seen as a threat to imperial order and stability).[217]

---

214. *Materialy po istorii Bashkirskoi ASSR*, v, p. 563. The title *muftī* was not current in the Volga-Ural region at this time, and, according to Azamatov, it was most likely the first Mufti, Muḥammadjān b. Ḥusayn, who suggested it as the title for this position; Azamatov, *Orenburgskoe*, pp. 22–23. In discussions of Islamic legal practice in this study, a distinction will be drawn between a *muftī* (one who issues a *fatwā*) and the Mufti, (the head of the Spiritual Assembly, the Russian title for which was *mufti* or *muftii*). Similarly, I will use *fatwā* to indicate a legal opinion (i.e., the end result of a *muftī*'s juridical interpretation) in order to distinguish between this traditional legal activity and the pronouncements and decrees of the Russian state Mufti, which were also called *fatwā*s, but which bore little to no relation to the juridical activity of *fiqh*. The latter will be labeled *fetvas*, using the Russian term.

215. *Materialy po istorii Bashkirskoi ASSR*, v, pp. 563–564; Crews, *Prophet*, p. 53; Azamatov, *Orenburgskoe*, p. 89; Tuna, *Imperial*, pp. 43–44.

216. Examinations were used as a condition for government sanction for *ākhūnd*s as early as 1771; Azamatov, *Orenburgskoe*, p. 20.

217. Fisher, "Enlightened Despotism," p. 550; see also Azamatov, *Orenburgskoe*, pp. 21, 22–23; Crews, *Prophet*, p. 54; *Materialy po istorii Bashkirskoi ASSR*, v, p. 564.

The whole of the Spiritual Assembly hierarchy was thus explicitly placed under the government. As stated in its founding plan, "the Spiritual Assembly of Mohammedan Law is subordinate to the Ufa provincial administration (*Ufimskago namestnicheskago pravleniia*) and is therefore equivalent to an intermediate judicial rank." It was given the power to "resolve and decide matters regarding the religious part (*dukhovnaia chast'*) of Mohammedan law, including: circumcision, marriages, divorces and mosque services," as well as control over questions of religious doctrine.[218] As was the case in the Urals, the *ʿulamāʾ*'s legal competence was restricted to matters of family law and inheritance, with only these areas administered by the Spiritual Assembly. All other legal matters, even cases only involving Muslims, were made the purview of Russian courts.[219]

The hierarchy itself was set up to have an appellate function. Muslims would take their disputes falling under the Spiritual Assembly's jurisdiction to their imam, and if they disagreed with the imam's resolution of the matter, they could then appeal to an *ākhūnd*, to whom all imams in a given location were subordinate.[220] If they disagreed with the *ākhūnd*, the claimants could then appeal to the Mufti, whose decision was final.[221] Though it was not stated at the time of the Spiritual Assembly's founding, the first Mufti, Muḥammadjān b. Ḥusayn (r. 1789–1824), insisted on the legally binding nature of the judgments and *fetva*s he issued. In the 1820s this de facto power was explicitly granted by the government.[222]

---

218. *Materialy po istorii Bashkirskoi ASSR*, v, pp. 563–564.

219. Azamatov, *Orenburgskoe*, pp. 17–18.

220. Ibid., pp. 27–28. The imam (conventionally referred to as *mullā* in the Volga-Ural region, though the term was used broadly) was an official rank subordinate to the *ākhūnds*, as well as to the *muḥtasibs* (a primarily administrative rank originally below *ākhūnd*). Given that the *maḥalla*, the imam's jurisdiction, was the primary locus of the Spiritual Assembly's activity, imams were by far the most important position within the *ʿulamāʾ* hierarchy for the Muslim community, and all *ʿulamāʾ* except the Mufti and his assistants in Ufa served as an imam in addition to any other offices.

221. *Materialy po istorii Bashkirskoi ASSR*, v, pp. 564–565; *PSZ*, xxii, no. 16711, xxiii, no. 16759; Crews, *Prophet*, p. 55; Azamatov, *Orenburgskoe*, pp. 21, 28. Besides Muḥammadjān, the Muftis were to be chosen by the Muslim community, though in practice all of the pre-Revolutionary Muftis were appointed by the imperial government; see ibid., pp. 40–69, esp. pp. 48–49, 52–53; also Danil' Azamatov. "The Muftis of the Orenburg Spiritual Assembly in the 18th and 19th Centuries: The Struggle for Power in Russia's Muslim Institution." *Muslim Culture in Russia and Central Asia from the 18th to the Early 20th Centuries. Vol. 2: Inter-Regional and Inter-Ethnic Relations*. Eds. Anke von Kügelgen et al. Berlin: Klaus Schwarz Verlag, 1998. 355–384.

222. Crews, *Prophet*, pp. 59, 66, 158. On Muḥammadjān, see ibid., pp. 55–60; Marjānī, *Mustafād*, ii, pp. 287–298; Fakhr al-Dīn, *Āthār*, iv, pp. 181–200; Ramzī, *Talfīq*, ii, p. 181; Kemper, *Sufis*, pp. 50–55; Azamatov, *Orenburgskoe*, pp. 40–48; also Azamatov, "Muftis," pp. 356–364.

The *ākhūnds* were the *ʿulamāʾ* most affected by the introduction of the bureaucratic hierarchy. Traditionally the elite of the *ʿulamāʾ*, the *ākhūnds* had, for at least the previous fifty years, been the focal point for tsarist efforts at managing the Muslim population. More importantly, the *ākhūnds*, as specialists in Islamic law, served as *qāḍīs* and *muftīs*—in the traditional sense—for their communities, settling disputes and offering guidance on legal questions.[223] The *ākhūnds*' shifting relationship with the government, however, left their ability to carry out these tasks increasingly limited. The restriction of the *ʿulamāʾ*'s jurisdiction narrowed the scope for their legal activity, and through the Spiritual Assembly the *ākhūnds* were forced into an appellate role, under government control via the Mufti. This arrangement saw the *ākhūnds*' authority and autonomy significantly limited and their very role as legal experts marginalized, with the responsibility for settling disputes among Muslims taken over by imams, who did not necessarily have the same degree of legal education and expertise.[224]

The Muftiate

When the *ākhūnds* did issue judgments on cases brought before them, their decisions were subject to oversight by the Mufti. Officially the highest-ranking Islamic authority, the Mufti was selected by the government more for his loyalty to the state than for any scholarly qualifications. Mufti Muḥammadjān in fact spent much of his life in imperial service. Before his appointment in 1789, he had served as a foreign affairs official in Ufa and, after returning from study in Central Asia, as a tsarist officer in Orenburg. It was as an officer in 1785 that he was named *ākhūnd* for the Frontier Commission, an imperial body established in Orenburg to administer the Kazakh Little Horde.[225]

As *ākhūnd* in the commission, his primary duty was to project both Russian authority as well as religious tolerance to the Kazakhs in an attempt to win their loyalty toward St. Petersburg. He also negotiated on the government's behalf, seeking an end to the Kazakh uprising of 1785.[226] For this task Muḥammadjān

223. For examples of pre–Spiritual Assembly *ākhūnds* performing these duties, see Marjānī, *Mustafād*, ii, pp. 100, 127, 187–189, 209; Fakhr al-Dīn, *Āthār*, ii, pp. 42, 45–46, 52–54; Ramzī, *Talfiq*, ii, p. 340.

224. Some imams barely knew how to write; Tuna, *Imperial*, p. 49.

225. Fakhr al-Dīn, *Āthār*, iv, p. 183.

226. *Istoriia Kazakhskoi SSR s drevneishikh vremen do nashikh dnei*. 5 vols. Alma-Ata: izd-vo Nauka Kazakhskoi SSR, 1979. iii, p. 117. For these services Muḥammadjān was paid by the state 150 rubles in 1785 and 300 in 1786; *Materialy po istorii Bashkirskoi ASSR*, v, p. 683. On other imperial duties performed by Muḥammadjān, see Fakhr al-Dīn, *Āthār*, iv, p. 183; Kemper, *Sufis*, pp. 51–53.

was appointed "First *Ākhūnd*," a rank especially created for him to raise his personal prestige for such diplomatic missions. These missions did not cease with his appointment as Mufti. In fact, the scope of his foreign activity only grew, with him pressing the empire's claims among the Kazakh hordes and Caspian Turkmen, as well as in the Caucasus.[227]

However, Muḥammadjān did have a *madrasa* education, having studied with the well-regarded *ākhūnd* Muḥammad b. ʿAlī al-Dāghistānī (?–1796) in Qarghālī, then traveling to Central Asia, where he studied under ʿAṭāʾ Allāh Bukhārī (among other prominent *ʿulamāʾ*) as well as (as noted) the Naqshbandi-Mujaddidi *shaykh* Fayḍ Khān Kābulī.[228] Despite this education, Muḥammadjān did not stand out as a scholar, and his extensive state service raised eyebrows among Muslims. An unnamed contemporary quoted by Fakhr al-Dīn suggests that Muḥammadjān did not go to Central Asia to study but rather was sent by the government for political purposes.[229] (Danil' Azamatov confirms this innuendo, noting that, in addition to studying, Muḥammadjān collected intelligence for the empire while in Central Asia.)[230]

Muḥammadjān's career resembled that of an ambitious tsarist official more than that of a Muslim scholar. The military governor of Orenburg, Grigor Volkonskii, one of the Mufti's superiors in government, described him as "a greedy, sly person, disliked by even his co-religionists, a person at first displaying before the authorities a great concern for the common good, but always yearning for the satisfaction of his personal interests."[231] Frequent charges of corruption dogged the Mufti. Muḥammadjān was accused of soliciting bribes from candidates for religious positions in 1803 and again in 1804. In the latter case, an *ākhūnd*, a certain Yanibāy b. Īshmuḥammad, named four *ʿulamāʾ* from whom Muḥammadjān extorted bribes under the threat of removal from their posts. Yanibāy was willing to testify openly against the Mufti

---

227. Azamatov, *Orenburgskoe*, pp. 23–24. Muḥammadjān's appointment was part of a series of reforms that called for using trustworthy Bulghar *ʿulamāʾ* to encourage the Kazakhs' loyalty to the empire and press Russian interests; *PSZ*, xxii, nos. 15,991, 16,292. See *Istoriia Kazakhskoi SSR*, iii, pp. 117–120; Khodarkovsky, *Steppe*, pp. 175–176, 217; Crews, *Prophet*, pp. 52, 200; Allen Frank. "Tatarskie mully sredi kazakhov i kirgizov v XVIII i XIX vv." *Kul'tura, isskustvo tatarskogo naroda: istoki, traditsii, vzaimosviazi*. Eds. M. Z. Zakiev et al. Kazan: AN Tatarstana, IIaLI, 1993. 124–128.

228. Fakhr al-Dīn, *Āthār*, iv, p. 181. On Dāghistānī, see ibid., ii, pp. 66–69; Marjānī, *Mustafād*, ii, pp. 219–220; Ramzī, *Talfīq*, ii, p. 340.

229. Fakhr al-Dīn, *Āthār*, iv, p. 183.

230. Azamatov, *Orenburgskoe*, p. 23. It was not unheard of at this time for the government to employ members of the *ʿulamāʾ* as spies; ibid., pp. 22–23.

231. Qtd. in Azamatov, "Muftis," p. 360; Azamatov, *Orenburgskoe*, p. 45.

in court, but the case never went forward, and he was eventually dismissed from his position. Muḥammadjān constantly resisted attempts to investigate and prosecute charges against him, and in 1811 he received privileges from the government making him effectively immune from judicial proceedings.[232]

Furthermore, the Mufti strove to augment his personal authority within the Spiritual Assembly; according to Azamatov, Muḥammadjān "sought to achieve one-man rule" over the religious hierarchy.[233] He would issue his rulings unilaterally, without consultation with other members of the *ʿulamāʾ*, despite government directives to the contrary. Although the Spiritual Assembly was originally intended as a consultative body, under its ambitious first Mufti it operated in a much more imperious fashion, with those immediately subordinate to Muḥammadjān—three scholars given the title of *kadi*—contributing little.[234] And it was he who insisted upon the binding nature of his *fetvas*, going so far as to assert that anyone who rejected a ruling by the Mufti should not be considered a Muslim.[235]

Personally, Muḥammadjān was very successful in his ambitions. He was accepted into elite circles of imperial Russia: for his service to the empire he was awarded the Order of St. George and even admitted into the Russian Bible Society.[236] After repeated petitions to the empress, he received special rights to hold property and own serfs that by law were otherwise not granted to Muslims.[237]

Being a good servant of the empire, however, did not necessarily make one a good Islamic scholar, and Muḥammadjān was widely seen by Muslims as undeserving of the authority and standing granted him by the state.[238] Marjānī names three of Muḥammadjān's contemporaries who, he notes explicitly, were superior scholars.[239] Fakhr al-Dīn also disparages Muḥammadjān's abilities as an *ʿālim*, as well as his service to the empire's Muslims.[240] Ramzī, for

232. Azamatov, *Orenburgskoe*, pp. 42–44.

233. Ibid., p. 42; Azamatov, "Muftis," p. 357.

234. Azamatov, *Orenburgskoe*, p. 42. As with "mufti," this title bore little relation to its traditional usage; Tuna, *Imperial*, p. 43 n. 29.

235. Crews, *Prophet*, p. 59.

236. Ibid., p. 61.

237. Azamatov, *Orenburgskoe*, p. 24.

238. Cf. Crews, *Prophet*, p. 57.

239. Marjānī, *Mustafād*, ii, p. 289.

240. Fakhr al-Dīn, *Āthār*, iv, pp. 182, 187.

his part, shows very little regard for Muḥammadjān at all, giving him only the most perfunctory of biographical entries.[241]

The Religious Hierarchy

The power claimed by Muḥammadjān and his approach to the Muftiate show how the new roles and positions for *ʿulamāʾ* altered the application of Islamic law. The beginning of patronage for Islamic scholars initiated a gradual process of bureaucratization of the *ʿulamāʾ* in the empire, furthered by the establishment of the Spiritual Assembly. The *ākhūnds*—whose specialized legal knowledge underpinned their traditional social role—found themselves and their function marginalized under the religious hierarchy, less like *qāḍīs* and *muftīs* and more like government functionaries, tasked with transmitting and implementing directives from above and passing along edicts to the imams subordinate to them, whether from the Mufti or the government. (Which were often functionally indistinguishable: in 1826 ʿAbd al-Sattār Shirdānī, then *ākhūnd* in Kazan, sent an official letter to an imam under his supervision informing him of a decree—a *fetva*—from the Mufti stating that imams and mosque employees were obligated to read a prayer in Russian for the health of the emperor at all communal prayers.)[242]

Indeed, the bureaucratization of the *ʿulamāʾ* was spurred by government backing for their authority. Once appointed, a scholar was protected in his position by state sanction, and removing him became an official matter.[243] *ʿUlamāʾ* who were considered incompetent or unfit or fell into conflict with members of their *maḥalla* could not simply be ignored or replaced. For instance, in 1815 a group from the village of Kūkcha-Bīriza had (for unspecified reasons) insulted and shunned their imam, a certain ʿAbd al-Fayḍ Amīnūghlū, and prayers were instead being led by a different, unlicensed person. Ibrāhīm b. Khūjāsh, the senior *ākhūnd* for the area, sent an official letter to the villagers restoring ʿAbd al-Fayḍ and reminding them that, per decree no. 283 from the Minister of Religious Affairs, they were required to respect and listen to the official imam and forbidden from praying behind anyone lacking a license.[244]

---

241. Ramzī, *Talfīq*, ii, p. 181.

242. Fakhr al-Dīn, *Āthār*, v, pp. 258–259.

243. Frank, *Institutions*, p. 140.

244. Fakhr al-Dīn, *Āthār*, v, pp. 231–232.

Under the Spiritual Assembly, individual *ʿulamāʾ* exercised their authority by virtue of their office—that is, derived from the hierarchy itself—and not by virtue of their scholarly aptitude or moral comportment. An *ākhūnd* could overrule a subordinate imam for any reason, without needing to appeal to an argument based in *fiqh*. Likewise, the Mufti could overrule an *ākhūnd* or imam because he was the Mufti, and his legally binding rulings superseded any *ākhūnd*'s by virtue of coming from the highest-ranking figure in the hierarchy, whose judgment on all Islamic matters was officially supreme.[245]

Such reliance on the office, rather than scholarly competence, is more characteristic of a bureaucracy than the premodern *ʿulamāʾ*, and in fact the Spiritual Assembly was part of the tsarist bureaucracy from its very founding. It was established under the oversight of the Ufa provincial administration, but quickly transferred to imperial control, first under the Ministry of Foreign Religions and eventually under the massive Ministry of Internal Affairs.[246]

Importantly, however, the Spiritual Assembly also operated alongside other parts of the tsarist administration, creating parallel legal structures. Muslims were free—if not encouraged—take their cases to Russian legal bodies, often with each of the disputing parties addressing their claims to different venues in search of the most favorable outcome.[247]

The option to pursue their cases elsewhere lessened Muslims' reliance on the *ʿulamāʾ*, undermining the Spiritual Assembly's authority, and in practice judgments by *ʿulamāʾ* were not necessarily final. Muslims pursued unfavorable decisions in tsarist courts or sought help from Russian administrators for cases within the religious hierarchy. Indeed, in 1815 Muḥammadjān petitioned St. Petersburg requesting that municipal-level administrators and lower courts—that is, bodies officially inferior to the Spiritual Assembly's judicial standing within the government—be barred from interfering in Spiritual Assembly business. The request was denied.[248] Eventually, a series of reforms were implemented in the 1820s in order to strengthen the *ʿulamāʾ*'s legal standing, requiring Muslims to address all disputes within the Spiritual Assembly's competence to an imam. Those cases could then be appealed to an *ākhūnd*, whose ruling on the matter was final. If the *ākhūnd* encountered any

245. E.g., ibid., iv, pp. 191–192; v, pp. 233–235; cf. Spannaus, "Decline," pp. 222–224.

246. *Materialy po istorii Bashkirskoi ASSR*, v, p. 563; Crews, *Prophet*, p. 23.

247. Cf. Werth, *Foreign Faiths*, p. 69. In *Āthār*, there are reports from a number of cases brought before members of the *ʿulamāʾ* in which claimants had gone to various government departments in addition to the Spiritual Assembly, or the case was referred to the *ʿulamāʾ* by a government official who was unwilling to hear it.

248. Azamatov, *Orenburgskoe*, p. 22.

difficulty with the case, he could refer it to the Mufti, who would issue a *fetva* on the matter, thus settling the case.[249] In reality, however, it seems that many cases did not follow this neat path up the hierarchy, as Muslim disputants continued to seek out the most advantageous venue in which to press their claims. The question of the Spiritual Assembly's standing vis-à-vis the rest of the government remained an issue throughout the imperial period.

Moreover, the religious hierarchy was largely dependent on tsarist institutions to enforce its rulings. Officials could overrule or simply ignore a judgment by a member of the *ʿulamāʾ*, and the enforcement of Spiritual Assembly decrees and decisions was always contingent on the local authorities' willingness to do so.[250] The conflict between Mufti Muḥammadjān and Ḥabīb Allāh Ūriwī illustrates this point. In 1787, Ḥabīb Allāh returned from studying in Central Asia to his home village of Ūrā, where he became imam of the village's stone mosque, newly built by the wealthy Tūqṭāmish family, into which he had married. At some point afterward, the relationship between Ḥabīb Allāh and the family soured, and they sought from the Mufti his dismissal as imam.[251] It is not clear if the Mufti did in fact order his dismissal or if Ḥabīb Allāh quit of his own accord, but Muḥammadjān appointed his brother Fatḥ Allāh Ūriwī to the position in 1799.[252] Whatever the reason behind Ḥabīb Allāh's replacement, he and his followers responded by successfully petitioning the local government for permission to build a second, wooden mosque in the village for himself. In 1800, Muḥammadjān ordered the mosque sealed (and, possibly, burned).[253] Although the Mufti's order was approved by the imperial government, by 1801 the mosque had been unsealed by local administrators, and Ḥabīb Allāh was again acting as imam there.[254]

Ḥabīb Allāh, it seems, had found support within the local government, and, as a prominent Naqshbandi *shaykh*, his considerable following bolstered his position in the conflict. The number of petitions on his behalf submitted to the provincial governor swayed the administration, going so far as to convince an official to grant Ḥabīb Allāh permission to return to his original position as imam of the stone mosque, thereby displacing the Mufti's chosen replacement.[255] The dispute eventually broke out into street fights in Ūrā between

---

249. Crews, *Prophet*, pp. 154–158.

250. Ibid., p. 98; Tuna, *Imperial*, p. 46.

251. Marjānī, *Mustafād*, ii, pp. 190–191; Crews, *Prophet*, p. 62; Kemper, *Sufis*, p. 58.

252. Marjānī, *Mustafād*, ii, p. 193; Fakhr al-Dīn, *Āthār*, ix, p. 7; Crews, *Prophet*, pp. 62–63.

253. Kemper, *Sufis*, pp. 58–59; Crews, *Prophet*, p. 63.

254. Marjānī, *Mustafād*, ii, p. 191; Crews, *Prophet*, pp. 61, 63.

255. Crews, *Prophet*, p. 63.

factions supporting each brother, ending only when Ḥabīb Allāh quit the village in 1802.[256]

What's interesting for our purposes is less the conflict between Muḥammadjān and Ḥabīb Allāh than the apparent struggle between Muḥammadjān and the government to get his way. Even though he ostensibly had the authority to dictate who could open a mosque and who could be imam, this seems to have mattered little to the administration in Ūrā. Concerned with the dispute within the village, and presumably influenced by Ḥabīb Allāh's large following, which continually petitioned officials on his behalf, the local government took measures it thought necessary, whether they conformed to the jurisdictional status of the Spiritual Assembly or not. As Crews states, the Mufti was reliant on officials located in the villages and towns to enforce his orders. If they chose not to, as in this case, there was little he could do.[257]

Promoting State Power

At its most basic, the Spiritual Assembly was created to serve the ends of the state, co-opting the *ʿulamāʾ*'s religious authority to extend tsarist control to the Muslim subjects of the empire. It was modeled on the recognition for *ākhūnd*s introduced in the Urals in the 1730s, which was grounded in the pragmatic aims of governance: the *ʿulamāʾ* operating in the region were governing a population where the tsarist administration had found little success. By bringing the *ākhūnd*s into the imperial fold, their social and religious functions (which they were carrying out regardless), once recognized and endorsed by the state, could be used to further tsarist aims, while sanction had the effect of controlling their number and enlisting them in pro-government activities.[258] The initial 1736 decree granted recognition to four *ākhūnd*s (rather than the ten originally identified by local officials) and obliged them to swear an

---

256. Marjānī, *Mustafād*, ii, p. 191. The dispute progressed to such a point that even the emperor became involved, in addition to other prominent imperial officials; see the letters from the officials to Muḥammadjān in Fakhr al-Dīn, *Āthār*, iv, pp. 186–189. See also Crews, *Prophet*, pp. 63–66; Kemper, *Sufis*, pp. 59–61; Azamatov, *Orenburgskoe*, p. 22.

257. Cf. Crews, *Prophet*, p. 98. The dispute in Ūrā was not the only instance of a local government body siding with Ḥabīb Allāh over Muḥammadjān's order. In 1810, despite a decree from St. Petersburg confirming the appointment of a certain Abū Shaḥma b. Raḥmānqulī as imam for the trading fair in Makar'ev (near Nizhnii Novgorod), the civil governor of Kazan instead installed Ḥabīb Allāh in the position; Fakhr al-Dīn, *Āthār*, iv, p. 196. Controversy regarding this influential appointment seems to have been fairly common; see Frank, *Institutions*, pp. 123–124.

258. Azamatov, *Orenburgskoe*, pp. 16–18, 20–21; Frank, *Islamic Historiography*, pp. 34–35; Crews, *Prophet*, p. 51. Fisher, on the other hand, considers the empire's efforts at occupying the Crimea in the 1770s to be the model for the Spiritual Assembly; Fisher, "Enlightened Despotism," pp. 547–548.

oath pledging that they would not attempt to convert anyone to Islam nor build mosques or *madrasas* without special permission. Upon the death of an *ākhūnd*, any candidate to succeed him was required to produce a petition attesting to his loyalty to the empire.[259] In addition, the *ākhūnds* were required to report any anti-government activity, and officials recommended that *ʿulamāʾ* suspected of the slightest offense were to be swiftly punished and/or exiled.[260] Thus, while granting recognition to the *ʿulamāʾ*, the government explicitly asserted its power to set conditions for receiving patronage and determine which scholars would be recognized.

The government's aim in offering sanction to *ʿulamāʾ* was to better administer the population. In fact, the decree contained a list of policies for governing the region, including measures for dealing with fugitive serfs, flood defenses, and taxation.[261] The recognition for the four *ākhūnds* was itself based on the administrative divisions of the region, with one *ākhūnd* appointed for each of its four districts.[262]

These earlier efforts formed the basis for the Spiritual Assembly and came to be applied throughout the Muslim areas of the empire. The government's aims for the Spiritual Assembly, however, were much larger than merely governing a territory. Instead, it was designed to bring Islamic institutions into the established imperial bureaucracy and, in so doing, employ those institutions to better incorporate the Muslim population into the administrative fabric of the empire.[263] The reasoning behind it was straightforward: if the *ʿulamāʾ*, whose religious and social authority Muslims recognized and accepted, were made part of the government, then Muslims would accept the government's authority. Indeed, not only had this approach been implemented in the Urals, but *ʿulamāʾ* were used in the 1770s–1780s in the administration of newly acquired Muslim territories of the Crimea and in the Kazakh steppe as well.[264]

As a vehicle for state power, the Spiritual Assembly was necessarily subordinate to the government. Crews notes that the cameralist attitudes

259. *PSZ*, ix, no. 6890, art. 14.

260. *Materialy po istorii Bashkirskoi ASSR*, iii, p. 494.

261. *PSZ*, ix, no. 6890, arts. 9, 11, 15.

262. Ibid., art. 14.

263. Fisher, "Enlightened Despotism," p. 549.

264. In the 1780s the government began materially supporting some mosques and *madrasas* in critical regions within its domains; ibid., pp. 547–549; Crews, *Prophet*, pp. 51–52; Frank, "Tatarskie mully."

underpinning Romanov rule (particularly Catherine's) considered religion beneficial to the state's fortunes by motivating subjects to work hard and serve the dynasty—the basis of confessional governance. When controlled and moderated by the government, piety could be deployed in the formation of (in the words of Immanuel Kant) "useful citizens, good soldiers, and loyal subjects," and therefore was of great utility for the state.[265] "To realize Islam's potential contribution to the empire, Catherine's administrators set out to find a mode of organization to discipline the faith and its officiants and draw them into state service."[266] The mode found by the government was an official religious hierarchy, based on the Orthodox Synod, through which the government sought to regulate the *ʿulamāʾ* and, through them, the whole of the empire's Muslim community.[267]

The Spiritual Assembly's purpose was therefore tied to its benefit to the autocracy, primarily its ability to promote order and loyalty among Muslims. It served as the main focal point for the interaction between the state and its Muslim subjects, creating a distinct institutional structure that Russian officials could manage and control. It was for this reason that the government supported the Spiritual Assembly as the sole Islamic authority, as any Islamic institutions outside tsarist oversight would be in competition with the hierarchy and feared by administrators as a potential vehicle for disloyalty.

It also allowed the government to limit the scope of Islamic authority, delineating the *ʿulamāʾ*'s competence. By assigning a particular jurisdiction to the Spiritual Assembly, the government effectively defined what was, and more importantly what was not, an Islamic matter. Although the *ʿulamāʾ* retained authority over matters of family and personal status law, all other types of cases—thefts, debts, assaults, property disputes, sales, contracts—were the purview of the tsarist administration; officially speaking, they were no longer subject to Islamic law. Moreover, the separation of Islamic and Russian legal spheres was used to reinforce the predominance of the latter, as all cases not clearly within the Spiritual Assembly's competence were considered government matters.[268]

The impact on Islamic religious institutions was marked. The establishment of the Spiritual Assembly contributed directly to the dismantling of

265. Crews, *Prophet*, pp. 40–43.

266. Ibid., p. 50.

267. Ibid., pp. 49–55.

268. Ibid., p. 164.

FIGURE 3 Nineteenth-century headquarters of the Orenburg Spiritual Assembly, Ufa (Anonymous, undated photo)

the structure and edifice of established forms of Islamic law within the empire. While state sanction allowed scholarship to flourish, the introduction of the hierarchy imposed formal roles upon scholars that significantly altered the makeup of the *ʿulamāʾ* and their function. The Muftiate was of course a wholly new rank, crafted by the government and out of Muḥammadjān's maneuvering, but the position of imam was itself reconstituted under the Spiritual Assembly. Imams obviously long predated the hierarchy as prayer leaders, preachers, and educators, yet under tsarist control they were allotted a much wider range of responsibilities that also included conducting marriages and divorces, dividing inheritances, offering legal judgments (*qaḍāʾ*) in family law disputes, and (after 1828) keeping official records of members of their *maḥalla*. Except for the latter two, these were not necessarily rare functions for an imam to perform, historically speaking. But the Spiritual Assembly made all of them an imam's required duties, encompassing the breadth of the religious hierarchy's purview. These changes to the imam's role thus represent the formation of a new, institutionalized *office*, distinct from the various roles conventionally fulfilled by imams. Lastly, the *ākhūnd*s, the traditional elite of the *ʿulamāʾ*, found themselves with little place within the hierarchy. Their function as *qāḍī*s—already limited to family law—was primarily taken over by imams, and their appellate role under the Spiritual Assembly was undermined by the Muftis' legally binding judgments. Indeed, there was no dedicated place for *fiqh* expertise in the religious hierarchy, reinforcing its officially bureaucratic character.[269]

The transfer of authority from legal experts, whose mastery of the texts and methodologies of *fiqh* was recognized as authoritative for the Muslim community, to a state-backed bureaucracy directly contributed to significant transformations in how the *sharīʿa* was applied in the Russian Empire and how Muslims conceived of it.[270] From "a complex set of social, economic, cultural, and moral relations" (as per Hallaq), it was rendered a strictly legal ethic exercised by an official hierarchy with a bounded jurisdiction within the tsarist government. Asad describes such a shift, "when the *sharīʿa* is structured essentially as a set of legal rules defining personal status," as a transmutation (rather than curtailment), wherein the *sharīʿa* "is rendered into a subdivision of legal norms (*fiqh*) that are authorized and maintained by the centralizing state."[271] No longer the primary domain of scholars, Islamic institutions became another arm of the imperial legal structure, utilized in support of the tsarist autocracy.

In this respect the Spiritual Assembly was little different from the post-Petrine Orthodox Church. Many of the conditions the government placed on Islamic institutions were also applied to the Orthodox Synod, including state approval for church construction and appointments for members of the clergy, civil interference in ecclesiastical affairs, and the obligation for churchmen to pledge their loyalty to the tsar and report any anti-government activity among their parishioners.[272] Just as the Church was turned into a vehicle for extending tsarist rule to rural Christians, the Islamic hierarchy now brought the government to rural Muslims. The formation of analogous institutions for the empire's Catholic, Protestant, Jewish, and Buddhist subjects as well solidified confessional governance, through which each official community was administered.

---

269. The position of *ākhūnd* was gradually abandoned beginning in the 1850s; Spannaus, "Decline," pp. 233–234.

270. The usurpation of legal authority by the government is a central feature of the alteration of Islamic law in the modern period; see Hallaq, *Shariʻa*; Wael Hallaq. "Can the Shariʻa Be Restored?" *Islamic Law and the Challenges of Modernity*. Eds. Yvonne Yazbeck Haddad and Barbara Freyer Stowasser. Walnut Creek: Alta Mira Press, 2004. 21–53; Zaman, *Ulama*; Nathan Brown. "Sharia and State in the Modern Muslim Middle East." *International Journal of Middle East Studies*, vol. 29, no. 3; 1997. 359–376; Aharon Layish. "The Transformation of the Shariʻa from Jurists' Law to Statutory Law in the Contemporary Muslim World." *Die Welt des Islams*, vol. 44, no. 1; 2004. 85–113.

271. Talal Asad. *Formations of the Secular: Christianity, Islam, Modernity*. Stanford, CA: Stanford UP, 2003, p. 227.

272. Cracraft, *Church Reform*, esp. pp. 198–210, 214–215, 236–240.

State control of Islamic institutions, it should be noted, did not entail Russification, nor did it immediately transform Muslim communities, which were predominantly rural and socially cut off from Russian communities. The incorporation of these institutions into tsarist structures created a space for Islam within the imperial bureaucracy, which allowed for significant continuity—cultural, social, religious—for Muslims, now with a more stable position within the empire. Muslims' agency within this space should not be overlooked. Both lay Muslims and *ʿulamāʾ* shaped the function of the Spiritual Assembly and used it for their own ends, and it served as an important means of negotiation with the government. Crews writes that tsarist involvement in the *maḥalla*, while occasionally seen as intrusive, was also seen by Muslims as an avenue for pursuing their claims toward each other and toward the administration, with officials frequently drawn into Muslims' affairs.[273] Moreover, the Mufti, as the official head of the Muslim community, became its primary spokesman and representative within the government, to whom Muslims continually turned to press and defend their interests.

Muslims on the whole quickly adapted to the situation and accepted state support for Islamic institutions. Frank notes that resistance to the Spiritual Assembly was minimal, and very few writings against it have so far come to light.[274] (ʿAbd al-Raḥīm Ūtiz-Īmānī, Qūrṣāwī's opponent, was a prominent exception, rejecting both the hierarchy and acquiescence to Russian rule.)[275] Indeed, the acceptance of the idea of government backing for Islamic institutions was such that there were calls from Muslims for the founding of new, additional assemblies on the local level as early as 1802.[276]

Conflicts in Bulghar Islam

The establishment of the Spiritual Assembly and Muslims' incorporation into tsarist governing structures altered the Bulghar religious landscape. Official sanction bolstered some *ʿulamāʾ*'s standing as Islamic authorities, but it also marginalized religious experts and granted exclusive control over a bounded and narrowed jurisdiction for Islamic law. All other areas of law were controlled by the tsarist government, which ordered society as a whole and to which Islamic institutions were subordinate.

---

273. Crews, *Prophet*, esp. pp. 93–94.

274. Frank, *Islamic Historiography*, pp. 37–38; cf. also Bustanov, "Bulghar Region."

275. Kemper, *Sufis*, pp. 175–176.

276. Azamatov, *Orenburgskoe*, pp. 33–34; Azamatov, "Russian Administration," pp. 108–109. These calls elicited considerable support from provincial administrators; however, the Spiritual Assembly in Ufa was ultimately able to retain its original authority. Ḥabīb Allāh Ūriwī was a major supporter of these efforts, which suggests that his struggle with the Mufti did not stem from questions of the Spiritual Assembly's legitimacy.

Crews locates the major religious change in the use of state power to enforce the Spiritual Assembly's decrees, which he argues led to a standardization of Islamic orthodoxy. While this was possible in theory, given the makeup of the Spiritual Assembly and its official purview, there are only isolated instances of attempts by the Muftiate to regulate matters of "orthodoxy"—itself a broad and complicated category in terms of Islam.[277] Nor was there much inclination for tsarist officials to wade into intra-Muslim religious disputes when imperial order and stability were not in jeopardy. The *ʿulamāʾ*'s juridical function did come to be regulated under the Spiritual Assembly, primarily through its appellate structure and state oversight, but religious discourse beyond this strictly "legal" sphere became more diverse in this period, not less, with the scope of contestation over what is "orthodox" and how that should be determined only increasing across the 19th century. (See Chapters 8 and 9.)

Bulghar religious discourse was necessarily shaped by these circumstances, leading *ʿulamāʾ* and, increasingly, lay Muslims into conflict over a range of issues related to religious authority and Islamic tradition and the nature of a Muslim society, in ways specific to the Bulghar setting. Qūrṣāwī played a central part in these debates, alongside his main antagonists, Ūtiz-Īmānī and Fatḥ Allāh Ūriwī, and the controversies between these three would color the religious discourse in the region into the 20th century.[278]

One prominent issue was the question of the *ʿishāʾ* prayer (Tat. *yastū namāzī*). In extreme latitudes, the allotted time for this prayer—when the night sky reaches complete darkness—does not occur in summer, and for centuries it was a point of dispute among Hanafi *ʿulamāʾ* whether the obligation to perform it falls *only* at its set time, meaning the prayer should be omitted during summer when that time never comes.[279] Entering this debate, Qūrṣāwī stated that the scriptural duty to carry out all the daily prayers superseded the

277. As an example, Crews highlights the dispute between two licensed imams in 1860 over one's leading some villagers in a vocal *dhikr* following prayers in the mosque. The police were eventually called in to investigate the charges of heretical behavior (the vocal *dhikr* is broadly rejected among Naqshbandis), and the Spiritual Assembly in Ufa officially ruled that this practice violated the *sharīʿa*, declaring anyone who continued to take part in it an apostate who should be barred from the mosque by police; Crews, *Prophet*, pp. 129–131. It should be noted, however, that this case was highly unusual, with such official interventions in religious disputes quite rare, but also that Sufi orders were treated with particular suspicion in Russian governing circles, out of fear that they fostered "fanaticism" and anti-Russian sentiment; see Alexander Knysh. "Sufism as an Explanatory Paradigm: The Issue of the Motivations of Sufi Resistance Movements in Western and Russian Scholarship." *Die Welt des Islams*, vol. 42, no. 2; 2002. 139–173, pp. 146–157.

278. Kemper, *Sufis*, p. 59; Tuna, *Imperial*, p. 34.

279. Kemper, *Sufis*, pp. 278–283; also Michael Kemper, "Imperial Russia as Dar al-Islam? Nineteenth-Century Debates on Ijtihad and Taqlid Among the Volga Tatars." *Encounters: An International Journal for the Study of Culture and Society*, vol. 6; 2015. 95–124.

fiqh reasoning that held the prayer to be contingent on the correct time. He writes that it is absolutely obligatory to perform the prayer, while its timing in summer is a question to be answered through *ijtihād*.[280] This position was opposed by both Ūriwī and Ūtiz-Īmānī, who stuck by the more established doctrine against the prayer's performance.[281]

The issue of *ʿishāʾ* attracted widespread attention as a contentious subject, and the view that the prayer must always be performed became associated with Qūrṣāwī, growing in acceptance in the first half of the 19th century.[282] Muḥammadjān issued a *fetva* in 1819 agreeing that the prayer should not be omitted, but—critically, in light of Crews' argument—there does not seem to have been any effort to enforce this directive, and the controversy continued long after.[283]

Although ostensibly an issue of straightforward ritual importance, the question had significant implications for religious authority in the Volga-Ural region. The disagreement between Qūrṣāwī and his opponents focused on the determination of the correct time for the prayer. For the latter, it had already been settled within the broader Hanafi *corpus juris*, and it was simply a matter of Muslims praying only at the proper times. For the former, however, the short summer nights invalidated the conventional position, necessitating the articulation of a new one suited to the setting. The controversy thus hinged upon different visions of who can make this determination: a contemporary scholar individually or the earlier generations of Hanafis collectively. By declaring it a matter for *ijtihād*, Qūrṣāwī implies that he, or any qualified scholar, has the authority to determine the time. Moreover, he criticizes the conventional position as absolutely unfounded.[284] (See Chapter 4.)

Qūrṣāwī's critical stance on *ʿishāʾ* reflects his basic position that all religious views must be investigated and verified to ensure their scriptural correctness and that scholars cannot be relied upon necessarily or absolutely. (See Chapter 3.) This skepticism is a fundamental aspect of his reformist project, extending equally to *ʿulamāʾ* and lay Muslims, whom he expects to become

---

280. Cf. Qūrṣāwī, *Irshād*, pp. 58–59; Qūrṣāwī. [On Prayer.] Ms. KFU, no. A-841. Fols. 3b–4a.

281. Cf. Kemper, *Sufis*, pp. 280–283.

282. See, for instance, the biographies for minor Siberian scholars who adopted this position in Alfrid Bustanov. "ʿAbd al-Rashid Ibrahim's Biographical Dictionary on Siberian Islamic Scholars." *Kazan Islamic Review*, no. 1; 2014. 10–78, pp. 22, 52 (original); 28–29, 67 (trans.); also Fakhr al-Dīn, *Āthār*, iii, pp. 139–140.

283. Marjānī, *Mustafād*, ii, p. 290. Marjānī records two decrees from the Mufti on the prayer's performance; ibid., 291–293.

284. Qūrṣāwī, *Irshād*, esp. pp. 58–59.

educated enough to make some determinations themselves and whom he exhorts against following *ʿulamāʾ* or elders blindly.[285]

Ūtiz-Īmānī took this skepticism to a more extreme degree, condemning the Bulghar *ʿulamāʾ* as untrustworthy and arguing that Muslims must follow the extant norms of Hanafi *furūʿ* instead of relying upon contemporary scholars. Although diametrically opposed, both his and Qūrṣāwī's positions represent responses to the alteration of Islamic institutions under Russian rule and reconceptualize the relationship between the *ʿulamāʾ* and the community. Ūriwī, on the other hand, staunchly supported the *ʿulamāʾ*'s traditional function and social role.[286]

Theological issues were central to these debates. As noted, Qūrṣāwī continued to criticize what he saw as the religious and philosophical deficiencies of the predominant forms of *kalām*, particularly regarding the divine attributes, both in writing and in public disputations. This set him apart from both Ūtiz-Īmānī, who rejected theological reasoning per se and condemned the majority of Bulghar *ʿulamāʾ* who engaged in it, and Ūriwī, who was deeply involved in mainstream *kalām* and staunchly opposed Qūrṣāwī's stance on the attributes as a violation of Sunni theological orthodoxy.

Ūriwī's opposition to Qūrṣāwī led him to write a letter to Mufti Muḥammadjān, dated November 11, 1810,[287] seeking Qūrṣāwī's removal from his position as imam and *mudarris* in Qūrṣā. He describes in this letter what he considers to be Qūrṣāwī's serious doctrinal and religious errors, and he attacks Qūrṣāwī for considering himself a *mujtahid* and spurning established books of *kalām*.[288]

Ūriwī was well connected to the Bukharan *ʿulamāʾ*, having studied with several of its prominent scholars, and this letter came only a few months after Tursūn Bāqī's missive to the Bulghar *ʿulamāʾ* harshly condemning Qūrṣāwī's apostasy. Although Ūriwī's letter does not refer to the events in Bukhara, it does contain some of the same language used by Tursūn Bāqī, and Ūriwī perhaps hoped that he could sway Muḥammadjān against Qūrṣāwī. (The two shared

---

285. Qūrṣāwī, *Lawāʾiḥ*, fol. 85b.

286. Cf. Nathan Spannaus. "Formalism, Puritanicalism, Traditionalism: Approaches to Islamic Legal Reasoning in the 19th-Century Russian Empire." *Muslim World*, vol. 104, no. 3; 2014. 354–378.

287. This date is in the Old Style (Julian) calendar.

288. Fakhr al-Dīn, *Āthār*, iii, pp. 108–109; transcription and translation in Spannaus, "Islamic Thought," pp. 232–234. See also Ūriwī's critique in Fatḥ Allāh b. Mullā Ḥusayn [Ūriwī]. *Risāla fī al-mabāḥith al-mutaʿalliqa bi-ṣifāt al-bārī*. Ms. SPb IVR, no. C234. Fols. 35b–43a; cf. Kemper, *Sufis*, pp. 235–236, 270 n. 214.

teachers in Bukhara, including some of the same scholars who had condemned Qūrṣāwī.)[289] There were other calls to rebuke or remove Qūrṣāwī as well. Yet despite these efforts, the Mufti seems not to have taken any action against him.[290]

Qūrṣāwī was not without defenders. Saʿīd Shirdānī, his father-in-law and imam of Kazan's Fifth Mosque, rejected the views regarding the attributes of his teacher, Īshniyāz Khwārizmī, in favor of Qūrṣāwī's.[291] Saʿīd's sons likewise supported Qūrṣāwī, and his main companions joined him at his *madrasa* in Qūrṣā: ʿAbd al-Khāliq Qūrṣāwī, Dawlatshāh b. ʿĀdilshāh, Muḥammad Nalāsāwī, Niʿmat Allāh b. Bīktimur, and Nuʿmān b. Amīr Thamanī. But he also had supporters who had no personal connection with him.[292]

Only a few years after returning from Bukhara, Qūrṣāwī, perhaps weary of the constant struggle of defending himself and his views, decided to go on hajj. In Shaʿbān 1227 (beginning August 9, 1812), he left Qūrṣā with his brothers ʿAbd al-Khāliq and ʿAbd al-Karīm, arriving in Istanbul in the second half of that month. Thamanī temporarily took over as imam and *mudarris* in Qūrṣā. Reaching Istanbul, Qūrṣāwī, stricken with cholera during the journey, died in the last ten days of Ramaḍān (September 28–October 7, 1812) and was buried in the cemetery in Üsküdar.[293]

Dawlatshāh b. ʿĀdilshāh became imam in Qūrṣā, a position he held until moving to a nearby village in 1821.[294] Qūrṣāwī's other companions likewise moved on to become *ʿulamāʾ* in other cities and villages in the region. His brothers completed the pilgrimage, then traveled in the Middle East, staying for several years in Cairo, where ʿAbd al-Khāliq studied hadith and Qurʾanic recitation. (ʿAbd al-Karīm died in Cairo, but nothing else of his time there is known.) ʿAbd al-Khāliq then returned to Qūrṣā and became imam and *mudarris* in his brother's mosque. He achieved renown as a Naqshbandi-Mujaddidi *shaykh* and initiated a number of adepts into the order.[295]

289. Kemper, *Sufis*, pp. 58–59; Fakhr al-Dīn, *Āthār*, iv, p. 181.

290. Kemper, *Sufis*, p. 238.

291. Marjānī, *Mustafād*, ii, p. 93.

292. See the list in ibid., p. 169. Among them is Niẓām al-Dīn b. Sirāj al-Dīn Qurūjī, a scholar who studied texts of *kalām* and philosophy and wrote a work in support of Qūrṣāwī commenting on some of his writings. Niẓām al-Dīn traveled extensively, studying in Mecca, India, Herat, and Bukhara, and he died in Baghdad in 1273 AH (1856); ibid., pp. 263–265; Fakhr al-Dīn, *Āthār*, vi, pp. 267–279; Ramzī, *Talfīq*, ii, pp. 381–383.

293. Fakhr al-Dīn, *Āthār*, iii, pp. 96, x, p. 146; Ramzī, *Talfīq*, ii, pp. 344, 367; Marjānī, *Mustafād*, ii, pp. 168–169, 177; Marjānī, *Wafiyat*, vi, fol. 145b; *Manāqib*, fol. 69b.

294. Fakhr al-Dīn, *Āthār*, vi, p. 284; Marjānī, *Mustafād*, ii, p. 176.

295. One such adept was Ḥasan b. Ḥāmid al-Muslimī (?–1872), who succeeded ʿAbd al-Khāliq as imam in Qūrṣā; Marjānī, *Mustafād*, ii, p. 177.

Qūrṣāwī's companions continued the ongoing debates, defending and promulgating his views. Dawlatshāh wrote a work asserting the correctness of Qūrṣāwī's position on the attributes and its agreement with the standard *kalām* orthodoxy. (Kemper calls it a "whitewashing" of Qūrṣāwī's theology.)[296] Thamanī completed Qūrṣāwī's *tafsīr* for the remainder of the Qurʾan, which was first published in Kazan in 1861.[297] Ūriwī, Qūrṣāwī's intractable opponent, wrote a refutation of this work that doubles as a refutation of Qūrṣāwī's thought.[298] Ūriwī's critique is written in vernacular Turkic, and he attached it to his commentary on the *Tawārīkh-i bulghāriyya*, one of the most important and widely read texts at the time, which, Kemper notes, is surely evidence of the growing influence of Qūrṣāwī's views.[299]

Baymurād Mangārī (mentioned earlier), imam of Kazan's Sixth Mosque, also wrote works against Qūrṣāwī's view of the attributes.[300] He was closely connected with the Bukharan *ʿulamāʾ*, studying under ʿAṭāʾ Allāh Bukhārī (among others), and he wrote a eulogy in praise of Amir Ḥaydar upon his death in 1826.[301] He engaged in debates on these questions, both in writing and in person, with Muḥammad Nalāsāwī, who himself had criticized Ūriwī on theological grounds.[302]

These debates drew in new generations of scholars, none more historically prominent than Marjānī, who became Qūrṣāwī's most important supporter. His first written work, the *Tanbīh*—composed upon his return from Bukhara in 1849—is an explicit defense of Qūrṣāwī, asserting the correctness of his views and extolling his virtues with extravagant praise. (For instance, he refers to Qūrṣāwī as such a scholar who appears once every five hundred years.)[303] Although his later theological writings would

296. Kemper, *Sufis*, pp. 239–240.

297. *Tafsīr-i nuʿmānī*. Mss. KFU, nos. T-33, T-34; Kemper, *Sufis*, p. 242; Iuzeev, *Filosofskaia*, p. 68.

298. Fatḥ Allāh b. Mullā Ḥusayn [Ūriwī]. [Untitled work.] Ms. KFU, no. T-3571. Fols. 1a–3a; cf. Kemper, *Sufis*, pp. 354–358.

299. Kemper, *Sufis*, p. 358. This text, which is different from Amīrkhān's history of the same name, itself had significance for these debates; cf. ibid., pp. 324–358; Spannaus, "Formalism," p. 375; and, broadly, Frank, *Islamic Historiography*.

300. Baymurād b. Muḥarram al-Mangārī. *Risāla fī al-ṣifāt*. Ms. KFU, no. A-1004. Fols. 122b–128a; see Kemper, *Sufis*, pp. 221, 257.

301. Cf. Kemper, *Sufis*, pp. 221, 237–238.

302. Marjānī, *Mustafād*, ii, pp. 102–103, 238; Fakhr al-Dīn, *Āthār*, vi, pp. 292–293; xi, pp. 191–194. Fakhr al-Dīn notes that one of Mangārī's local teachers, Fayḍ b. ʿAbd al-ʿAzīz b. ʿĪsā al-Kinārī (?–after 1834), engaged in debates with Qūrṣāwī and Nalāsāwī; ibid., pp. 293, 297.

303. Marjānī, *Tanbīh*, p. 373. See also Kemper, "Şihabaddin al-Marğani über Abu-Nasr Qursawis Konflikt," pp. 353–358; Kemper, *Sufis*, p. 453.

be less explicitly attached to Qūrṣāwī, Marjānī's own stance was based on Qūrṣāwī's, which he refined and advanced in his works. Most importantly, he wrote two commentaries that further elaborated the connection between Qūrṣāwī's theological principles and the established *kalām* tradition: his own commentary on the *ʿAqāʾid nasafiyya*, which more fully explains their position on the attributes, and a supercommentary on Jalāl al-Dīn Dawānī's (1427–1502) *Sharḥ al-ʿaqāʾid al-ʿaḍudiyya*, which places it into a more detailed philosophical-theological discourse.[304] (These two works were the most important texts for Central Asian *kalām*, ubiquitous in Bukharan and Bulghar *madrasas*.)

Beyond theology, which, as with Qūrṣāwī, was a major focus of his thought, Marjānī was also concerned with the issue of *ʿishāʾ*. He took the position that it was absolutely obligatory—confirmed extensively by scripture—and that it should be performed in summer with the preceding *maghrib* prayer. He describes his stance in the *Nāẓūrat al-ḥaqq fī farḍiyyat al-ʿishāʾ wa-in lam yaghib al-shafaq* ("A View of the Truth on the Absolute Obligation of *ʿIshāʾ*, Even If Dusk Does Not Disappear"), which, as the title shows, is devoted to the issue, including a lengthy history of the debates regarding it. However, like Qūrṣāwī, Marjānī considers the timing of the prayer to be a question for *ijtihād*, and the *Nāẓūrat al-ḥaqq* begins with an extensive treatment of the permissibility of *ijtihād*, its religious importance, who can exercise it, and how.[305]

In this way, Marjānī was participating in broader discussions over *ijtihād* that had been ongoing among Bulghar *ʿulamāʾ* since Qūrṣāwī.[306] The persistence of these debates—over *ijtihād*, *ʿishāʾ*, and the attributes especially—shows the continuation and vibrancy of postclassical discourse throughout the 19th century. (Indeed, the controversy over the attributes had a long life. Manuscript copies of the *Tanbīh* were produced at least as late as 1887,[307] and

---

304. Shihāb al-Dīn al-Marjānī. *al-Ḥikma al-bāligha al-jāniyya fī sharḥ al-ʿaqāʾid al-ḥanafiyya*. Kazan: Maṭbaʿat Wiyācheslāf, 1888; Shihāb al-Dīn al-Marjānī. *Ḥāshiya ʿalā sharḥ al-ʿaqāʾid al-ʿaḍudiyya*. Printed alongside Ismāʿīl b. Muṣṭafā Kalanbawī. *Ḥāshiya ʿalā sharḥ Jalāl al-Dīn Dawānī ʿalā al-ʿaqāʾid al-ʿaḍudiyya*. Dersaadat [Istanbul]: Maṭbaʿa ʿUthmāniyya, 1316 [1898]; cf. Nathan Spannaus. "Šihab al-Din al-Marǧani on the Divine Attributes: A Study in *Kalam* in the 19th Century." *Arabica*, vol. 62, no. 1; 2015. 74–98.

305. Shihāb al-Dīn al-Marjānī. *Nāẓūrat al-ḥaqq fī farḍiyyat al-ʿishāʾ wa-in lam yaghib al-shafaq*. Kazan: n.p., 1870. On Marjānī's understanding of *ijtihād*, see Natan Spannaus. "Iuridicheskii i religioznyi avtoritet v kontseptsii *idzhtikhada* u Mardzhani." *Minbar*, forthcoming.

306. Kemper, *Sufis*, p. 304.

307. Kemper, "Šihabaddin al-Marǧani über Abu-Nasr Qursawis Konflikt," p. 357.

accusations of heresy against Marjānī and Qūrṣāwī were made into the 20th century.)[308]

But the contours of these debates reflect the unsettled religious environment under the Spiritual Assembly, highlighting the degree to which issues of ritual correctness, theological orthodoxy, and the continuity of the scholarly tradition were increasingly called into question. From the end of the 18th century on, growing contestation and controversy over religious authority and interpretation led to profound transformations among Bulghar *ʿulamāʾ* and lay Muslims. Qūrṣāwī's reformist project represents an important element of this controversy, and it speaks to the concerns Muslims had about their changing religious landscape under the Russian Empire.

The transformation of the relationship between the tsarist government and its Muslim subjects that occurred under Catherine provided Muslims with greater stability and prosperity, offering *ʿulamāʾ* a defined role and position in society and allowing Islamic scholarship to flourish and develop. Scholarly discourse, a central part of the broader Islamic tradition and integral to the *sharīʿa*, had long pervaded Bulghar Muslim communities, tying them together and to each other. It also connected them with Bukhara, representing their shared intellectual and educational heritage, as well as with their co-religionists around the world. And Qūrṣāwī's life was in many ways conventional for a premodern Muslim scholar. His condemnation notwithstanding, it was common for scholars from all over the Islamic world to travel for their education, to teach in a *madrasa*, to debate other scholars, to be initiated into a Sufi order, to go on hajj. Indeed, virtually all of the scholars mentioned in this chapter followed a similar path.

What sets the Bulghar case apart, of course, is that this vibrant Islamic intellectual environment existed under an autocratic, non-Muslim political order. Confessional governance both created a space for the *sharīʿa* within tsarist society and subordinated it to tsarist power, which formed the backdrop for the continuation of Islamic religious discourse. From the very beginning of this period scholars sought to make sense of this context, altering this discourse to fit the new state structures. Government control bore a significant influence on the Bulghar *ʿulamāʾ*. Restrictions to the function of Islamic institutions narrowed the scope of the *sharīʿa* and its manifestation within society, while the religious hierarchy marginalized learned experts, empowering the Mufti and imams while undermining *ākhūnd*s and the role of *fuqahāʾ* and turning the *ʿulamāʾ* into bureaucrats. These are the circumstances in which Qūrṣāwī developed his reformist project.

308. Dzhamaliutdin Validov. *Ocherk istorii obrazovannosti i literatury Tatar*. 1923. Oxford: Society for Central Asian Studies, 1986, p. 62; Iusupov, *Shigabutdin Mardzhani*, p. 69; e.g., ʿAbd Allāh b. ʿAbd Allāh al-Bulghārī. *ʿUjāla marḍiya fī bayān al-ashʿariyya*. Kazan: Tipo-litografiia imperatorskago universiteta, 1905. Refutations along these lines seem to have been common across this period; Frank, *Bukhara*, pp. 18–19.

FIGURE 4 Incipit to Qūrṣāwī's *Sharḥ jadīd* (Saint Petersburg Institute of Oriental Manuscripts)

3

An Epistemological Critique

Knowledge is religion, so pay heed to those from whom you take your religion.[1]

Qūrṣāwī's reformism is premised upon a basic claim, which forms a coherent whole out of the many different discussions in which he was engaged. The foundation for his thought is the insistence upon a sound epistemological basis for religious belief and knowledge, which manifests itself in an emphasis on the supremacy of scripture, as the most epistemologically reliable source, and on the believer's reliance upon and adherence to the Qurʾan and prophetic Sunna. This outlook, which Qūrṣāwī calls "the way of the righteous ancestors" (*madhhab al-salaf al-ṣāliḥ*), is at the heart of his position on every other issue—legal and theological, social and moral.[2] It is essential for the articulation of *ʿaqīda* (beliefs, creed) and establishing correct action, as determined through *fiqh*.[3] Anything else is error and innovation.[4]

The aim of this stance is the elimination of doubt. Scholars may err and put forward incorrect views, while the only unerring sources of knowledge are scripture and the consensus of the *salaf* and the great scholars of the past.[5] They serve as the foundation for all legitimate religious knowledge. Any scholar's position is correct only if it is properly derived from them and conforms to them in content.[6] Truth and error can be mixed together in scholars' pronouncements, Qūrṣāwī writes, and so everything must

1. *al-ʿIlm dīn*[un] *f-anẓurū ʿamman taʾkhudhūn dīnakum*—hadith reported by Muslim (*muqaddimat Ṣaḥīḥ Muslim*), quoted by Qūrṣāwī; Qūrṣāwī, *Irshād*, p. 6.

2. Cf. Qūrṣāwī, *Sharḥ jadīd*, fol. 94b; also Ramzī, *Talfīq*, ii, p. 343; Marjānī, *Mustafād*, ii, p. 168.

3. Qūrṣāwī, *Irshād*, p. 35.

4. Ibid., pp. 35–36; Qūrṣāwī, *Lawāʾiḥ*, fol. 85b.

5. Qūrṣāwī, *Sharḥ jadīd*, fol. 94b; cf. Marjānī, *Tanbīh*, p. 373.

6. Qūrṣāwī, *Irshād*, p. 32.

be verified (*taḥqīq*) such that it does not contradict these sources.[7] A good Muslim cannot simply accept another's wisdom, but should only follow that which is known to stem ultimately from the prophets, their books, and their companions.[8] To follow a position without ensuring its scriptural basis is therefore to fall into error and misguidance. Anything lacking such support must be rejected.[9]

This stance was necessarily oppositional, reflecting a significant degree of skepticism and mistrust directed toward his fellow scholars, and it is likely that much of the conflict between him and his contemporaries stems from this attitude. Indeed, his harsh criticisms of other *ʿulamāʾ*, which are frequent in his writings, were remembered long after his death.[10]

But beyond scholarly disputes, there is an important social element to Qūrṣāwī's thought. As he sees it, the *ʿulamāʾ* have failed to properly uphold these norms, and therefore they have failed in their essential function as moral guides for the community. By reforming scholarship and emending the erroneous positions and ideas *ʿulamāʾ* have allowed to spread, he intends to strengthen the scholarly tradition and with it the community's adherence to Islamic norms.

His view of the contemporary *ʿulamāʾ* was shaped to a degree by state control of Islamic institutions, specifically regarding their role in supporting scholarship and exercising religious authority. The bureaucratization of the *ʿulamāʾ* and attendant marginalization of learned scholars altered their function, and elements of Qūrṣāwī's reformism can be seen as responding to these changes, as can his critiques of his contemporaries: he writes, for instance, that the knowledge even of learned people—*ʿulamāʾ*, teachers, *mullās*—cannot necessarily be relied upon.[11]

Muslims' relationship with the tsarist government is not a direct concern for him, however, and his works focus only on issues internal to the Muslim community. His engagement with the Islamic scholarly tradition revolves around its importance for the community's moral well-being. This is the focus of his epistemological critique, on the necessity of reestablishing the correctness of the prevalent discourses therein, against what he perceives as the failures and shortcomings of fellow *ʿulamāʾ*. Fundamentally, it represents

7. Ibid., p. 30; Qūrṣāwī, *Lawāʾiḥ*, fols. 85a–85b.

8. Qūrṣāwī, *Sharḥ jadīd*, fol. 94b.

9. Qūrṣāwī, *Irshād*, p. 36; Qūrṣāwī, *Mabāḥith*, fol. 153b, 156b, 169a.

10. E.g. Ramzī, *Talfīq*, ii, p. 344; Marjānī, *Tanbīh*, p. 373.

11. Qūrṣāwī, *Lawāʾiḥ*, fol. 85b.

a critique of postclassical scholarship and the construction of the tradition over the preceding centuries.

Postclassical Scholarship

To begin with, Qūrṣāwī takes aim at *taqlīd*, which he considers the main source of religious error. He defines *taqlīd* as the acceptance of another's position or assertion (*qawl*) "without evidence" (*dalīl*)—that is, without ascertaining its epistemological basis.[12] As such, it (perhaps indirectly) separates Muslims from scripture; if the Qurʾan and Sunna represent the absolute sources for sound religious knowledge, then studying them to determine correct action and belief is a moral obligation. *Taqlīd*, however, prevents this. It replaces the true, errorless object of Muslims' adherence with scholars' fallible pronouncements, cutting the community off from its moral foundations.[13] Truth is thereby obscured, harming the community's religious standing.[14]

Such a stance was anomalous for the time. Scholarship in the postclassical period was oriented around what Jackson has termed the "regime of *taqlīd*" as the predominant framework of authority. Underpinning the regime of *taqlīd* was the overwhelmingly prevalent view that it was essential for maintaining both the correctness and coherence of scholarship (discussed further on in this chapter).[15] Indeed, much of Qūrṣāwī's notoriety can be attributed to his criticisms of *taqlīd* in the face of contemporaries' unwavering insistence upon it. Ūriwī, for instance, attacks him repeatedly for disregarding the great scholars of preceding generations, presenting it, as in his 1810 letter to Mufti Muḥammadjān, as a sign of his religious deviance.[16]

---

12. Qūrṣāwī, *Sharḥ jadīd*, fol. 102b; Qūrṣāwī, *Mabāḥith*, fol. 154b; cf. Marjānī, *Ḥāshiya*, p. 5.

13. Qūrṣāwī, *Irshād*, pp. 3, 5, 30.

14. Ibid., p. 7.

15. Sherman Jackson. "Taqlid, Legal Scaffolding and the Scope of Legal Injunctions in Post-Formative Theory: Mutlaq and ʿAmm in the Jurisprudence of Shihab al-Din al-Qarafi." *Islamic Law and Society*, vol. 3, no. 2; 1996. 165–192; Sherman Jackson. *Islamic Law and the State: The Constitutional Jurisprudence of Shihab al-Din al-Qarafi*. Leiden: Brill, 1996; Wael Hallaq. *Authority, Continuity, and Change in Islamic Law*. Cambridge: Cambridge UP, 2001; Lutz Wiederhold. "Legal Doctrines in Conflict: The Relevance of Madhhab Boundaries to Legal Reasoning in the Light of an Unpublished Treatise on Taqlid and Ijtihad." *Islamic Law and Society*, vol. 3, no. 2; 1996. 234–304.

16. Fakhr al-Dīn, *Āthār*, iii, pp. 108–109; Ūriwī, [Untitled], fol. 1a; also Michael Kemper, *Sufis und Gelehrte in Tatarien und Baschkirien, 1789–1889: Der islamische Diskurs unter russischer Herrschaft*. Berlin: Klaus Schwarz Verlag, 1998, p. 270. It's worth noting that Ūriwī in the letter does not draw a firm distinction between *fiqh* and *kalām* in terms of Qūrṣāwī's deviance, but criticizes him generally for his disregard of earlier authorities.

Qūrṣāwī, however, saw *taqlīd* as allowing error, rather than precluding it. His objection is to following scholars' pronouncements to the exclusion of other, more certain sources of religious knowledge. This, he argues, obscures the foundation of a given position, making it difficult to determine its correctness. But it is not accepting another's position per se that is problematic; he writes that *taqlīd* is forbidden *only* when the opinion being followed runs counter to scripture. But following (*ittibāʿ*) a scholar's judgment (*ḥukm*), if it is based on a firm understanding of the *sharīʿa* (*mudrak sharʿī*), is like following revelation (*mā anzala Allāhu*).[17] The issue is knowing if a judgment has such a basis, which must be verified through *taḥqīq* to determine its correctness. Otherwise, it must be rejected.[18]

Qūrṣāwī's position on *ʿishāʾ* serves as an example of *taḥqīq* at work. Because the duty to perform all five prayers daily is known with certainty, the view that *ʿishāʾ* should be omitted, no matter how well established it is among *ʿulamāʾ*, cannot be correct. Although there is room for interpretation as to the precise timing of the prayer, the obligation to perform it is beyond doubt and cannot be abandoned.[19] Yet, in addition to this basic objection, Qūrṣāwī also interrogates the legal justification for the prayer's omission, arguing against it as a matter of legal theory. Thus, *taḥqīq* into the issue belies the position's unfoundedness, both as a matter of a known obligation and in its *fiqh* rationale, rendering it invalid.

Taḥqīq

Qūrṣāwī in this way holds up *taḥqīq* as the primary opposite of *taqlīd*. (He praises God for preserving him from the fire [*ḥuṭama*] of *taqlīd* and guiding him "to the Eden of *taḥqīq*.")[20] *Taqlīd*'s conventional opposite, *ijtihād*, is treated as an interpretive activity, a type of derivation (likened to *istidlāl* or *istinbāṭ*),[21] and though Qūrṣāwī opposes it to *taqlīd*, there are ways in which the two can overlap or coexist (see here and Chapter 4). *Taḥqīq*, however, as the investigation into the underlying premises and basis of a position, decisively contradicts the "acceptance of a statement without evidence" that

17. Qūrṣāwī, *Irshād*, p. 32.

18. Qūrṣāwī, *Mabāḥith*, fol. 153b, 156b, 169a; Qūrṣāwī, *Lawāʾiḥ*, fols. 85a–85b.

19. Cf. Qūrṣāwī, [Prayer], fol. 3b.

20. Qūrṣāwī, *Mabāḥith*, fol. 153b.

21. E.g., ibid., fols. 154b–155a; Qūrṣāwī, *Irshād*, p. 62.

is *taqlīd*. It serves as a means of engaging deeply with a position, exploring its implications and analyzing and critiquing its logical and philosophical grounding.[22] For Qūrṣāwī especially, it also requires determining its scriptural foundations.

In his understanding of *taḥqīq*, Qūrṣāwī subordinates matters of *ʿaql* (reason, intellect) to *naql* (tradition; lit. "passing along").[23] The latter, which is comprised of scripture and scholarly consensus, serves as the source of certain religious knowledge. He writes that Sunnism (*madhhab ahl al-sunna wa-l-jamāʿa*) is based on "placing *naql* above reason in the sense that what is confirmed by the text of the Book, widespread (*mutawātir*) hadith, or the consensus of the *umma* among the ancestors (*salaf*) and the legal scholars requires belief in it and the cessation of dispute [on it]."[24] Other sources of knowledge—weaker hadith, forms of logical interpretation such as *qiyās*—though still valid, do not impart certain (*qaṭʿī*) knowledge, but only probable (*ẓannī*) knowledge, and therefore must be subordinate to these stronger sources of *naql*.[25]

Naql therefore represents the proper epistemological—and, indeed, moral—basis for any religious belief or action. Reason, by contrast, has inherent limitations in its capacity to comprehend certain religious matters and cannot be relied upon alone. *Naql* acts as a safeguard against error, and knowledge of it prevents deviation in belief, as reason itself is prone to leading people into mistaken ideas.[26] Since reason can be used to support many different things, people use it to justify their own whims (*ahwāʾ*). Consequently, it leads to dissension and division (*tafarruq*) among people: "The root of disagreement in belief (*ʿaqīda*) is difference of opinion and the whims which are molded by human desires (*nufūs al-insān*). Therefore, prohibiting [people]

22. Cf. Khaled El-Rouayheb. *Islamic Intellectual History in the Seventeenth Century: Scholarly Currents in the Ottoman Empire and the Maghreb*. Cambridge: Cambridge UP, 2015, esp. pp. 28, 32–33, 124; Dimitri Gutas. *Avicenna and the Aristotelian Tradition*. Leiden: Brill, 1988, pp. 187–193; Robert Wisnovsky. "Towards a Genealogy of Avicennism." *Oriens*, vol. 42, no. 4; 2014. 323–363, p. 347.

23. *Naql*, the transmission of scriptural materials, religious praxis, and beliefs, which I translate here as "tradition," should not be confused with the "scholarly tradition" as described in the Introduction—that is, the practice of Islamic scholarship mediated diachronically through religious institutions. For the sake of clarity, *naql* will remain untranslated.

24. *Ad "al-ʿilm al-thābit bi-l-ḍarūra fī al-tayaqqun wa-l-ithbāt"*; Qūrṣāwī, *Sharḥ jadīd*, fol. 99b, also 94b.

25. Cf. Qūrṣāwī, *Naṣāʾiḥ*, fols. 19a, 21a; Qūrṣāwī, *Mabāḥith*, fol. 170a; Qūrṣāwī, *Sharḥ Manār*, pp. 13–14.

26. Qūrṣāwī, *Mabāḥith*, fol. 153b; Qūrṣāwī, *Lawāʾiḥ*, fol. 84a; Qūrṣāwī, *Sharḥ jadīd*, fol. 99b.

from following their whims is stated repeatedly in the Qur'an, and [God] says, 'Do not follow whim, it will lead you astray from God's path.'"[27] Qūrṣāwī explicitly links whim with *bidʿa*, defining the latter as the work of "one who inclines toward what he wishes for in religion (*man māla ilā mā yahwāh fī al-dīn*)," which can be prevented through reliance on *naql*.[28] Accordingly, he also connects *bidʿa* with uncertainty in religious matters.[29]

Taḥqīq, then, for Qūrṣāwī serves as a means of validating scholars' pronouncements in terms of *naql*, providing certainty as to what is and is not correct. However, his belief that reason must be subordinate to *naql* does not entail an outright rejection of reason or its role in articulating religious views. Rather, *taḥqīq* must also take into account a position's philosophical and/or interpretive basis as part of ensuring its correctness. We can see this approach in his stance on the *ʿishāʾ*, but also in his rejection of the widely held view that there are seven or eight essential attributes of God (discussed in Chapters 5 and 6): Qūrṣāwī argues both that this position is logically untenable in its premises and implications *and* that there is neither scholarly consensus on it nor a scriptural basis for it.[30] Thus he rejects it on the grounds of *ʿaql* as well as *naql*, and the bulk of his argumentation focuses on the former.

Taḥqīq as such represents a form of engagement with all facets of scholarship. It stands as a means of critique, of evaluating a position's validity and correctness. But it isn't necessarily negative. *Taḥqīq* also requires deep familiarity with the underlying foundation of a position, and it serves as a way to revise and improve arguments, to expand upon them and extrapolate from them.

In this regard, *taḥqīq* was intimately connected with the commentary (*sharḥ*), one of the primary textual vehicles for postclassical scholarship.[31] Extensive engagement with a scholar's views was the raison d'être of this genre, whose form and structure allowed for both the critique and expansion

---

27. Q 38:26; Qūrṣāwī, *Sharḥ jadīd*, fol. 94a, also 96b.

28. Qūrṣāwī, *Irshād*, p. 12.

29. Ibid., p. 27.

30. See, e.g., Fakhr al-Dīn, *Āthār*, iii, p. 98.

31. On the relationship between *taḥqīq* and postclassical scholarship, see esp. Robert Wisnovsky. "Avicennism and Exegetical Practice in the Early Commentaries on the *Isharat*." *Oriens*, vol. 41, no. 3/4; 2013. 349–378; also El-Rouayheb, *Islamic Intellectual History*.

of an author's positions.[32] It also served as a platform for the continuous articulation of new ideas based on established texts. As a text (*matn*) engendered commentaries, which in turn engendered supercommentaries (sing. *ḥāshiya*), with further addenda and attached remarks (termed *taʿlīqāt*), new views were formulated, and this type of textual engagement became a major venue for the development and evolution of scholarly discourse.[33]

It is thus within the commentary that much of the intellectual dynamism and vibrancy of the postclassical period is to be found.[34] The scholarly acumen on display in the commentary tradition belies the widespread image of these texts as comprising little more than sterile repetition.[35] The ideas and positions contained in commentaries, however, are to some degree rooted in the original text, and the innovations therein are often quite subtle. (The commentary was rarely the place for putting forward a wholly new stance.) Such an approach was characteristic of postclassical scholarship in general, which did not lend itself to radical or sweeping revisions of discourse; Hossein Ziai notes, for instance, that it is marked by scholars' efforts to "*refine*, rather than *refute*, a range of philosophical propositions and problems," resulting in the small-scale emendation of positions instead of their wholesale replacement.[36]

The frequently factional nature of scholarship was certainly a contributing factor. Scholars self-consciously and often explicitly attached themselves and their ideas to earlier scholars, often as part of a certain (if, outside of the legal *madhhab*, largely informal) school, *ṭarīqa*, group (*aṣḥāb*), or scholarly chain as a means of legitimation, and it was common, Stephen

---

32. Wisnovsky, "Towards a Genealogy"; Wisnovsky, "Avicennism," esp. pp. 354–357; Asad Ahmed. "Post-Classical Philosophical Commentaries/Glosses: Innovation in the Margins." *Oriens*, vol. 41, no. 3/4; 2013. 317–348.

33. Cf. Baber Johansen. "Legal Literature and the Problem of Change: The Case of Land Rent." *Islam and Public Law: Classical and Contemporary Studies*. Ed. Chibli Mallat. London: Graham and Trotman, 1993. 29–47.

34. El-Rouayheb notes that commentaries underwent a significant shift in the 14th century—with scholars like Taftāzānī at the forefront—expanding the breadth and extensiveness of commentarial treatments of a text, such that the genre became "a standard vehicle for scholarly writing in Islamic civilization"; El-Rouayheb, *Islamic Intellectual History*, p. 122.

35. Ahmed, "Post-Classical"; see further the articles dedicated to the commentary in *Oriens*, vol. 41, no. 3/4; 2013.

36. Hossein Ziai. "Recent Trends in Arabic and Persian Philosophy." *The Cambridge Companion to Arabic Philosophy*. Eds. Peter Adamson and Richard C. Taylor. Cambridge: Cambridge UP, 2005. 405–425, p. 406; emphasis in original.

Humphreys notes, for them to present their activities as a collective, rather than individual, enterprise.[37] Attaching themselves to a faction bolstered scholars' authority by linking them with the collective authority of the faction. Yet scholars could share in this authority only to the degree that their views aligned with the established discourse of the group. As Jackson writes, scholars had to maintain "a discernably genetic relationship" between their views and those of their predecessors, limiting their autonomy to articulate variant and novel positions and thereby precluding radical changes.[38] The commentary, which facilitated extensive engagement with an argument while maintaining discursive coherence, was particularly well suited to such an approach.

Taqlīd

This scholarly modus operandi is part and parcel of Jackson's "regime of *taqlīd*." Yet *taqlīd*, even more than the commentary, is at the center of the skewed characterization of postclassical scholarship as stagnant and repetitive. This view is based on the widespread misunderstanding of *taqlīd* as blind acceptance or unthinking imitation. Rather, as just described, *taqlīd* functioned as a means for scholars to gain authority for their scholarly/interpretive activity by connecting that activity to an established discourse, granting them legitimacy. It was not in any sense passive, Jackson points out, nor did it entail lesser forms of scholarship.[39] As Muhammad Qasim Zaman writes, "That jurists often professed strict adherence to the established doctrines of their school of law" in no way diminished their abilities as scholars, "for the very effort to sort out the complexities of a rich, multi-layered tradition as it existed at a particular time and place was itself not a small measure of legal acumen and of the recognition that went with it." Scholarship in this period was "an on-going conversation with forebears and contemporaries" in which earlier

37. R. Stephen Humphreys, *Islamic History: A Framework for Inquiry*. Rev. ed. Princeton, NJ: Princeton UP, 1991, p. 195. One example is the so-called school of ibn ʿArabī, which pursued certain metaphysical aspects of his thought in new directions distinct from his own views; cf. James Morris. "Ibn ʿArabi and His Interpreters Part II: Influences and Interpretations." *Journal of the American Oriental Society*, vol. 106, no. 4; 1986. 733–756; James Morris. "Ibn ʿArabi and His Interpreters Part II (Conclusion): Influences and Interpretations." *Journal of the American Oriental Society*, vol. 107, no. 1; 1987. 101–119. See Chapter 6.

38. Jackson, *Islamic Law*, p. 98.

39. Ibid., pp. 80–81.

precedents were utilized in novel ways and engaged in continuing Islamic scholarly discourse.[40]

Jackson (as noted in the Introduction) characterizes *taqlīd* as "scaffolding," a conception of authority in which the work of earlier scholars was accepted by later scholars to facilitate their own scholarship. There was little need or incentive for the latter to revisit larger, more structural issues, he argues, and *taqlīd* allowed them to instead devote their energies to addressing more minute but also more advanced questions, leading to more sophisticated scholarship.[41] *Taqlīd* thus served as a paradigm for scholarship, in which the positions of earlier scholars were utilized as premises for the formulation of new positions within the same discourse.[42]

A significant benefit of the *taqlīd* framework was that it limited the potential for the formulation of deviant or anomalous views. Coherence was a major goal of *taqlīd*, and as scholars were generally obliged to conform to the established positions of their school or faction, they were restrained in their interpretive activity and the possible scope for any new position was narrowed. Scaffolding was understood to safeguard (though not necessarily ensure) the correctness of scholars' formulations, which could depart only so much from the views of their predecessors. A direct connection with scripture was thus seen as unnecessary, as any new stance would have to align with positions that had been previously legitimated as correct. Indeed, the interpretation of scripture without the limits imparted by the *taqlīd* framework was considered more likely to breed erroneous, unpredictable, and/or incoherent views.[43]

Although much of the attention devoted to *taqlīd* in secondary literature is focused on its role in the area of law, its place in *kalām* was not

---

40. Muhammad Qasim Zaman. "Transmitters of Authority and Ideas Across Cultural Boundaries, Eleventh to Eighteenth Centuries." *New Cambridge History of Islam. Vol. 3: The Eastern Islamic World, Eleventh to Eighteenth Centuries.* Eds. David Morgan and Anthony Reid. Cambridge: Cambridge UP, 2010. 582–610, pp. 592–593. Zaman's perspective is indebted to MacIntyre; Zaman, *Ulama*, p. 4.

41. Jackson, "Taqlid," esp. pp. 167–172.

42. Jackson, *Islamic Law*, p. 97.

43. Cf. Norman Calder. "al-Nawawi's Typology of Muftis and Its Significance for a General Theory of Islamic Law." *Islamic Law and Society*, vol. 3, no. 2; 1996. 137–164; Mohammad Fadel. "The Social Logic of Taqlid and the Rise of the Mukhtasar." *Islamic Law and Society*, vol. 3, no. 2; 1996. 193–233.

altogether distinct.[44] Postclassical *kalām* reflects a similar use of scaffolding, as *mutakallimīn* incorporated into their positions different approaches from earlier scholars, building off them to articulate novel views on existing theological issues, while legitimating their interpretations in part through association with established authorities. To be sure, *taqlīd* in *kalām* was less formalized than in *fiqh*, which was institutionalized in the *madhhab* as "guild," strictly enforcing its boundaries and operating within society.[45] Yet, as Jackson argues, scaffolding is a part of any advanced and mature field, which would certainly apply to *kalām* in this period.[46]

Theology

In terms of *kalām*, argumentation that was rationally sound and conformed to established religious premises could be considered correct and incorporated into the framework for theological discourse. *Kalām*'s essentially logical character allowed for the formulation of views based on deductive principles alone.[47] Earlier theological disputes paved the way for this type of intellectual endeavor, and, as Oliver Leaman and Sajjad Rizvi point out, "later *kalām* texts were well equipped to present a systematic theology which progressed on strictly ratiocinative lines to prove the truths of religion, as well as deploying reason to interpret the content of revealed doctrine."[48] As a result, postclassical *kalām* discourse consisted

44. In contrast to the extensive literature on legal dimensions of *taqlīd*, much of the work on *taqlīd* in *kalām* focuses on the relationship between knowledge and faith with regard to laypeople; see, for instance, Richard Frank. "Knowledge and Taqlid: The Foundations of Religious Belief in Classical Ash'arism." *Journal of the American Oriental Society*, vol. 109, no. 1; 1989. 37–62; also El-Rouayheb, *Islamic Intellectual History*, pp. 173–188, 204–215. An exception, however, is Frank's discussion of Ghazālī's critique of theological scholars who accept the teachings of their lineage or school as fact, without rational examination or verification; Richard Frank. "al-Ghazali on *Taqlid*: Scholars, Theologians, and Philosophers." *Zeitschrift für Geschichte der Arabisch-Islamischen Wissenschaften*, no. 7; 1991/1992. 207–252; see also Frank Griffel. "*Taqlid* of the Philosophers: al-Ghazali's Initial Accusation in His *Tahafut*." *Ideas, Images, and Methods of Portrayal: Insights into Classical Arabic Literature and Islam*. Ed. Sebastian Gunther. Leiden: Brill, 2005. 273–296.

45. Cf. Jackson, *Islamic Law*, esp. pp. 103–112; also George Makdisi. "The Guilds of Law in Medieval Legal History: An Inquiry into the Origins of the Inns of Court." *Cleveland State Law Review*, vol. 34, no. 3; 1985. 3–18.

46. Jackson, "Taqlid," pp. 167–168.

47. Cf. Richard Frank. "The Science of *Kalam*." *Arabic Sciences and Philosophy*, vol. 2; 1992. 7–37, esp. pp. 26–30.

48. Oliver Leaman and Sajjad Rizvi. "The Developed *Kalam* Tradition." *The Cambridge Companion to Classical Islamic Theology*. Ed. Timothy Winter. Cambridge: Cambridge UP, 2008. 77–96, p. 78.

of positions rationally derived from beliefs established by earlier theologians. Indeed, it's written in one of the Bukharan *fatwās* condemning Qūrṣāwī that reason is superior to *naql*, "although surety (*iʿtidād*) only comes through *naql*," evincing the dogmatic foundations for *kalām* reasoning.[49]

Postclassical *kalām*, then, operated within a rational framework constructed upon an established religious basis. A clear textual example of this is the widespread genre of the creed (*ʿaqīda*/*ʿaqāʾid*), in which positive statements of proper belief were enumerated.[50] The texts were often very brief and elliptical, but this allowed for extensive commentary, as theologians explained, elaborated, and extended the points of dogma contained in the original text. The two most important works of postclassical *kalām* in Central Asia were in fact commentaries on creeds: Saʿd al-Dīn Taftāzānī's *Sharḥ al-ʿaqāʾid al-nasafiyya* and Jalāl al-Dīn Dawānī's commentary on the *ʿAḍudiyya*, the creed of ʿAḍud al-Dīn al-Ījī (1281–1356). Both feature extensive theological reasoning that builds significantly upon their base texts, which serve as platforms for the further articulation of ideas. And both spawned lengthy commentarial traditions, facilitating even greater theological interpretation within a coherent discourse tied to the original *matn*.[51]

This use of the commentary stands as an example of *taqlīd* in the form of scaffolding, as scholars could carry out their interpretive activities legitimated by their connection to an established source of authority (in this case, the authors and texts commented upon). Qūrṣāwī of course also commented on Nasafī's creed, and he presents himself quite explicitly in the text as following Nasafī's guidance and acknowledging his authority.[52] But his commentary also stands as a rebuke of Taftāzānī, representing a new commentarial tradition that excises the other's work and by implication denies his connection with Nasafī. Qūrṣāwī takes issue with how Taftāzānī builds off Nasafī, seeing his positions as unfounded and therefore negating the ostensible genealogical link between the two scholars' ideas.[53]

---

49. Marjānī, *Mustafād*, ii, p. 172; Fakhr al-Dīn, *Āthār*, iii, p. 99.

50. See Frank, "Science," pp. 25–26.

51. Dawānī's work in particular was the subject of further commentary, especially among Central Asian scholars whose teacher-student lineage stretched back to Dawānī (including ʿInāyat Allāh Bukhārī and ʿAṭāʾ Allāh Bukhārī, both of whom composed supercommentaries on it); see Nathan Spannaus. "Theology in Central Asia." *Oxford Handbook of Islamic Theology*. Ed. Sabine Schmidtke. Oxford: Oxford UP, 2016. 587–605, p. 592.

52. Qūrṣāwī, *Sharḥ jadīd*, fol. 92b.

53. Ahmed notes the use of commentaries to engage—tacitly or explicitly—with other commentaries on the same level (what he calls a "horizontal" reference, e.g., a supercommentary with another supercommentary) on the same text; Ahmed, "Post-Classical," pp. 330, 345. While Ahmed is here discussing commentaries in horizontal conversation with each other, Qūrṣāwī's treatment of Taftāzānī is a clear example of horizontal refutation.

Qūrṣāwī's critique of *kalām* focuses on the acceptance of scholars' positions without verifying their correctness—his definition of *taqlīd*—and the further use of those positions in the articulation of new beliefs that are justified only through reason, without a direct connection to *naql*. Such use of *taqlīd* relied upon the discursive framework of *kalām* itself (particularly its logical underpinnings) to guarantee correctness, rather than ensuring every position's conformity with certain religious knowledge. The subordination of *naql* to reason made rational or philosophical viability the primary criterion for acceptance. This left the possibility that a religiously incorrect but logical view could become accepted and widespread, and consequently used for the formulation of further incorrect positions, assumed to be legitimate due to their reliance on a recognized earlier stance. It was in this way that *taqlīd* propagated error and increased misguidance. Without recourse to *naql* and verification of positions, invalid beliefs could proliferate unchecked.[54]

According to Qūrṣāwī, theological views produced in this manner were nothing more than logical extrapolation without any sound religious basis. He attacks *kalām* as a discipline along these lines, alleging that it perpetuates this type of ostensibly rational yet scripturally meaningless speculation about God. (As with *taqlīd* in general, his attacks on *kalām* are at times more rhetorical than actual, as we will see.) Rather, every point of belief must be based on an epistemologically sound foundation, yet *ʿulamāʾ* have allowed erroneous and unfounded views to spread and then obliged others to follow them through *taqlīd*.[55]

Law

The implications of Qūrṣāwī's critique were more pronounced in terms of theology (which had more stringent standards for validity than *fiqh*), but there were overlapping concerns with the sphere of law, where he sought to rein in the use of *taqlīd* for similar reasons. Just as he saw Muslims basing their beliefs on flawed theological positions that had been allowed to spread through *taqlīd*, he saw Muslims' actions determined by *fiqh* reasoning that relied wholly on scholars' work, to the exclusion of scripture.[56]

54. Cf. Qūrṣāwī, *Lawāʾiḥ*, fols. 85a–85b; Qūrṣāwī, *Naṣāʾiḥ*, fols. 18b–19a.

55. Cf. Qūrṣāwī, *Sharḥ jadīd*, fols. 99b–100a; Qūrṣāwī, *Mabāḥith*, fol. 155a, 167a.

56. Qūrṣāwī, *Irshād*, p. 2.

The predominance of *taqlīd* in postclassical *fiqh* was most evident in the object of scholars' interpretations. In formulating their positions, *fuqahāʾ* in this period utilized the judgments of earlier scholars of their *madhhab*. These judgments constituted the school's *corpus juris*, its collective body of *furūʿ* (points of positive law), which within the framework of *taqlīd* served as the textual materials from which their judgments could be derived. As Norman Calder writes, noting the sources utilized by scholars, "Jurists within a *madhhab* draw the law out of the texts and structures of the *madhhab* and not out of the texts of revelation."[57]

Hallaq has termed this "secondary" legal reasoning, a category of interpretation "that is based on an already formulated set of established rules" within a legal school.[58] (With its opposite, primary reasoning, scriptural texts themselves are the object of interpretation.) Limiting scholars to secondary reasoning served a critical purpose in the Islamic legal order and its application in society. As noted, restricting scholars' direct interpretation of scripture narrowed the scope of possible positions that could be articulated, thus providing coherence, which was particularly important in the domain of law. It was a widely held view that a *mujtahid* was forbidden from following another scholar's *ijtihād*, but instead must address every question anew within the sources of revelation.[59] Therefore, a proliferation of *mujtahids* would lead to a proliferation of potentially widely (and wildly) varying positions on a single issue. With the limitation of scholars to secondary reasoning within the *madhhab*, the variance

---

57. Calder, "Typology," p. 156.

58. Hallaq, *Authority*, p. 140. As both Hallaq and Jackson have noted, this type of interpretation allowed later jurists to delve critically into the law as elaborated, thus creating new theoretical and hermeneutical conceptions within *fiqh*; ibid., pp. 86–120; Jackson, "Taqlid," esp. pp. 172–173. Calder, citing the prominent 13th-century Shafiʿi Nawawī, also makes note of this; Calder, "Typology," p. 156.

59. Cf. Hallaq, *History*, pp. 118–119; Bernard Weiss. "Interpretation in Islamic Law: The Theory of Ijtihad." *American Journal of Comparative Law*, vol. 26, no. 2; Spring 1978. 199–212, p. 207; Mirza Kazem Beg. "Notice sur la marche et les progrès de la jurisprudence parmi les sectes orthodoxes musulmanes." *Journal Asiatique*, ser. 4, no. 15; Jan. 1850. 154–214, p. 190. This author, Mirza Aleksandr Kazem Bek (1802–1870), was a prominent Russian Orientalist who worked at Kazan and St. Petersburg universities. Of Persian origin from the south Caucasus, Kazem Bek converted to Protestant Christianity as a young man before immigrating to Russia. His expertise in Muslim languages and Islamic law, particularly Hanafism, was utilized by the imperial government, for which he provided oversight of the Spiritual Assembly; see Robert Crews. *For Prophet and Tsar: Islam and Empire in Russia and Central Asia*. Cambridge, MA: Harvard UP, 2005, esp. pp. 177–189; also David Schimmelpenninck van der Oye. "Mirza Kazem-Bek and the Kazan School of Russian Orientology." *Comparative Studies of South Asia, Africa and the Middle East*, vol. 28, no. 3; 2008. 443–458.

of possible outcomes was decreased. In this way, the scope of juristic opinions was narrowed, thereby reducing changes in legal norms based on the result of every new act of *ijtihād*. This in turn led to greater predictability and stability in the law, which is essential for the function of any society.[60]

One of the main interpretive vehicles for secondary reasoning was the process of *tarjīḥ* (evaluation), a broad hermeneutical category for weighing multiple pieces of evidence in legal opinions. Scholars would engage with the *corpus juris* of their *madhhab* by analyzing and comparing its multivarious, differing judgments through a number of criteria focusing on a judgment's scriptural basis, underlying principles, and conformity to school doctrine.[61] *Tarjīḥ* served as the primary method by which postclassical scholars approached *furūʿ*, utilizing legal theory to distinguish (*tamyīz*) stronger and weaker opinions and determining the most legally compelling (*rājiḥ*) position among conflicting interpretations (a process also labeled *taṣḥīḥ*).[62] As an analysis of the scriptural and interpretive basis for a position, there is a clear conceptual linkage between *tarjīḥ* and *taḥqīq*, and indeed the two have been connected in scholarship.[63]

Grouped under *tarjīḥ* was the process of *takhrīj*, the derivation or extrapolation of new legal norms within the *madhhab*, either from the existing body of *furūʿ* or—less commonly—from scripture regarding previously unanswered issues. *Takhrīj*, and *tarjīḥ* more generally, represented an avenue for active legal reasoning within the regime of *taqlīd*, a form (as it were) of *ijtihād*.[64]

Secondary legal reasoning, utilizing the *corpus juris* of the *madhhab* to formulate new opinions, Jackson argues, was tied in with the *madhhab* itself. As noted, scholars attached themselves to the school through *taqlīd* as a means of gaining authority for their interpretations, and we can see this arrangement at work with *tarjīḥ*. The authority that scholars derived from their association with a *madhhab* (and by extension with its founder) brought with it limitations

60. Fadel, "Social Logic," esp. pp. 197–201.

61. See Hallaq's detailed description (where he translates *tarjīḥ* as "preponderance"); Hallaq, *Authority*, pp. 126–133; also Jackson, *Islamic Law*, pp. 84–86.

62. Hallaq, *Authority*, esp. pp. 134–146.

63. See the quote in ibid., p. 136.

64. Jackson, *Islamic Law*, pp. 91–96; cf. Qūrṣāwī, *Irshād*, p. 62.

to their autonomy and how they could innovate—much less deviate from—their school's doctrine.[65]

These limitations were manifested in ranks for scholars, based on the structure of the *madhhab* as an institution, which regulated the type and scope of reasoning a jurist was allowed to carry out, the topics upon which he could give responsa, and his ability to give responsa conflicting with those of other scholars of the *madhhab*.[66] While jurists were classified according to their expertise and ability among their contemporaries, the primary factor, most notably among Hanafis, was chronological: a scholar's place in the ranks was determined by his historical proximity to the founding members of the school. As the ranks descended across the generations, later scholars were strictly confined in their ability to carry out legal reasoning, restricted almost exclusively to secondary interpretation.[67]

The prominence of these ranks in postclassical Hanafism was due to the importance of *taqlīd* within the makeup of the school, specifically in its legal theory. More so than the other *madhhab*s, Hanafism is based on what Aron Zysow has labeled legal formalism, an approach to *uṣūl al-fiqh* that relies on the precise methodology of legal reasoning for the validity of its judgments. With formalism, the correct exercise of the legal hermeneutic minimizes the possibility for errors in interpretation, thereby legitimating judgments derived through that hermeneutic (in contrast to legal materialism, in which the soundness of the [scriptural] textual materials utilized by the jurist determines a judgment's validity).[68]

---

65. Jackson, *Islamic Law*, p. 98.

66. See Fadel, "Social Logic," p. 200; Calder, "Typology," pp. 143–149; Kazem Beg, "Notice," pp. 205–213. Hallaq connects the creation of *madhhab* ranks with the development of the schools as guilds; Hallaq, *Authority*, pp. 19–20.

67. Kazem Beg, "Notice," pp. 202–206; Hallaq, *Authority*, pp. 14–17; see also Wael Hallaq. "Was the Gate of Ijtihad Closed?" *International Journal of Middle East Studies*, no. 16; 1984. 3–41. [Reprinted in Wael B. Hallaq. *Law and Legal Theory in Classical and Medieval Islam*. Brookfield, VT: Variorum, 1995], pp. 29–30.

68. As Zysow notes, there is a degree of uncertainty inherent to *fiqh*, such that any judgment or ruling is in and of itself only probable in its correctness. Accordingly, *uṣūl al-fiqh* developed in order to minimize uncertainty and limit the possibility for error. The more probable a judgment, the more likely it is to be considered valid and followed; Aron Zysow. "An Economy of Certainty: An Introduction to the Typology of Islamic Legal Theory." Diss. Harvard University, 1984.

Formalist *fiqh* is thus centered around the process of *uṣūl al-fiqh*, which is given institutional form in the *madhhab*, the very name for which (literally "way") reflects its essentially methodological orientation: the foundation of the *madhhab* of Abū Ḥanīfa is (at the risk of tautology) Abū Ḥanīfa's *madhhab*—that is, his "way" of legal interpretation, his *fiqh* methodology.[69] To be a Hanafi *faqīh*, then, is to do Hanafi *fiqh*.[70] The *madhhab* as an institution maintains the integrity and coherence of the founder's hermeneutical approach. Although this applies to all the schools, the importance of this function is heightened in Hanafism by virtue of its formalist character; as the process imparts validity to a judgment, preserving methodological correctness becomes, as Zysow notes, a "paramount concern."[71] It is for this reason that the Hanafi insistence upon *taqlīd* was so pronounced. The school's very authority was derived through its continued conformity to Abū Ḥanīfa's method, any deviation from which risked undermining its legitimacy. Hanafi *fuqahā*ʾ were thus obliged to align their judgments with the main doctrine of the school, not only methodologically but also in terms of content. If all Hanafis duly applied Abū Ḥanīfa's hermeneutic, then there was little reason for their judgments to conflict with his. (By the same token, rulings on issues not addressed by Abū Ḥanīfa were nevertheless attributed to him, on the grounds that had he addressed them he would have reached the same opinion.)[72]

The Hanafis' strict, chronological ranks for scholars reflect this logic. Later *fuqahā*ʾ were restricted from returning to already settled questions because allowing them to do so served little purpose; any methodologically correct interpretation would merely confirm the established view, while any conflicting opinion would be understood as improperly derived, and therefore invalid. Limiting the scope of later scholars' autonomy helped maintain the coherence

---

69. "A madhhab is always fundamentally the doctrine or method of an individual scholar. Scholars belonging to the collectivity of adherents of a particular madhhab may, of course, propound doctrines not found within the body of doctrine of the eponymic founder. No matter how divergent these doctrines may be, they are viewed as falling within the doctrinal space framed by the madhhab of, say, Abū Ḥanīfa, even if only by reason of adhering to the guiding principles laid down by him. The madhhab remains throughout all development of doctrine the madhhab of the founder"; Bernard Weiss. "The Madhhab in Islamic Legal Theory." *The Islamic School of Law: Evolution, Devolution, and Progress*. Eds. Peri Bearman et al. Cambridge, MA: Harvard UP, 2005. 1–9, p. 2.

70. Cf. Calder, "Typology," p. 145; Jackson, "Taqlid," p. 169.

71. Zysow, "Economy," p. 4.

72. Hallaq, *Authority*, pp. 54–55. These ranks, it should be noted, were not unique to Hanafis; see, broadly, ibid., pp. 1–23.

of the *madhhab*, which, as the institutional manifestation of Abū Ḥanīfa's method, was the very locus of Hanafi authority.

(Materialist scholars, on the other hand, derive validity for their judgments from the textual materials themselves, and therefore have less need to strictly maintain their methodological coherence, and by extension less need for extensive restrictions on scholars' interpretive autonomy. Accordingly, materialists take a more lenient stance toward *ijtihād* than formalists, while viewing *madhhab* adherence and the attendant framework of *taqlīd* as less important.)[73]

These structures built into the Hanafi school were predominant in the Bulghar scholarly environment, where they were widely viewed as essential aspects of *fiqh* practice. Qūrṣāwī, however, rejects many of the assumptions underlying this framework and the attendant insistence upon *taqlīd*. His primary objection is to the idea that limiting scholars to secondary reasoning minimizes the possibility for error. As he sees it, such a view relies on the absolute correctness of the established *furūʿ*; otherwise, any judgment derived from a flawed *farʿ* would likewise be flawed. (Something entirely possible, as any interpretation or judgment was itself considered only of probable veracity [*ẓannī*].)[74] In this way, rather than minimizing error, *taqlīd* can allow it to proliferate, as erroneous positions are perpetuated within the school. The same holds true for faulty beliefs, spread by the overreliance on logic in *kalām*.

It is for this reason that Qūrṣāwī espouses the need for *taḥqīq*. All positions, he argues, must be verified to ensure their correctness. If conforming to *naql* and of sound interpretation, they should be accepted and followed without issue, but if not, they must be rejected absolutely.[75] Accordingly, Qūrṣāwī does away in his reformist project with scholarly ranks and their attendant restrictions, writing that any earlier scholar's positions, including Abū Ḥanīfa's, can be countered and rejected if found to lack a sound basis.[76]

---

73. On the relationship between *taqlīd*, *ijtihād*, and the *madhhab* in the materialist Hanbali school, see Abdul-Rahman Mustafa. *On Taqlid: Ibn al Qayyim's Critique of Authority in Islamic Law*. Oxford: Oxford UP, 2013.

74. Cf. Qūrṣāwī, *Mabāḥith*, fols. 153b, 155a; also Qūrṣāwī, *Sharḥ jadīd*, esp. fol. 96b.

75. Qūrṣāwī, *Irshād*, pp. 30, 36.

76. Ibid., pp. 29, 32.

Reforming the Scholarly Tradition

The issue for Qūrṣāwī is that the rigid structures of *taqlīd* maintained coherence at the expense of religious correctness. By obliging conformity to school doctrine and restricting scholars' ability to approach scripture, the regime of *taqlīd* made the *madhhab* itself, and by extension the judgments of the founder, upon which the entire edifice of the school was based, the foremost source of religious authority.[77] As a result, the true, unerring knowledge contained in scripture and consensus was replaced as the point of religious adherence by scholars' fallible opinions. Indeed, Qūrṣāwī criticizes the *ʿulamāʾ* for holding that adherence to the Book and the Sunna is the exclusive province of the founders of the four schools of law, consigning everyone else to reliance upon their judgment.[78]

Consequently, scholars' knowledge was not of sound scripture and established consensus but of other scholars' pronouncements, thereby divorcing their interpretive activities from the texts of revelation.[79] To say that scholars in the *madhhab* can no longer interpret scripture as part of their legal reasoning, Qūrṣāwī writes, is to say that "we have no need for the meanings (*maʿānī*) of the Qurʾan in our time."[80] Qūrṣāwī viewed their reliance upon *taqlīd* as a grave mistake and moral failing on their part as *ʿulamāʾ*. For him, the insistence upon *taqlīd* was a sign of arrogance by scholars, as it served as a way to place themselves ahead of the Qurʾan and Sunna, to a degree that bordered on the nonsensical. As he asks rhetorically in the *Irshād*: "What forbids a *muqallid* from acting by the text of the Book and Sunna [as though] there is proof (*dalīl*) that limits him to [following] the position of a *mujtahid*? How is [this possible when] the Qurʾanic verses and hadith requiring adherence (*iʿtiṣām*) to the Book and Sunna from everyone are more than can be counted?"[81] More

77. See the Iraqi Hanafi Abū al-Ḥasan al-Karkhī's (863–952) view that school doctrine should be preferred to any Qurʾanic verse or prophetic hadith that may conflict with it; Mustafa, *On Taqlid*, p. 14.

78. Qūrṣāwī, *Irshād*, pp. 2–3, also 35.

79. See Bernard Weiss's discussion of the tension in Islamic legal theory between the need for scriptural basis and the intellectual construction of legal reasoning; Bernard Weiss. "The Primacy of Revelation in Classical Islamic Legal Theory as Expounded by Sayf al-Din al-Amidi." *Studia Islamica*, no. 59; 1984. 79–109.

80. Qūrṣāwī, *Irshād*, p. 29.

81. Ibid., p. 30.

significantly, it rendered *ʿulamāʾ* incapable of fulfilling their essential duty to understand and interpret scripture on the community's behalf, leaving the community's moral and religious well-being in compromise.[82]

Yet, despite his railing against *taqlīd* in this way, the *madhhab* as the preserve of proper *fiqh* methodology nevertheless retains marked importance for Qūrṣāwī. He argues for the necessity of legal theory and the methods of interpretation in understanding scripture and determining morally correct action from it, and his discussion of legal reasoning conforms entirely to the tradition of Hanafi *uṣūl*.[83] In fact, it is not the *madhhab* as an institution that Qūrṣāwī objects to, but rather the overreliance upon *taqlīd* that places school doctrine above *naql* and limits scholars' ability to approach revelation. Qūrṣāwī sees no problem with accepting and following the judgments of Abū Ḥanīfa and the early masters of the Hanafi school, provided there is no conflicting scriptural evidence.[84] It was later scholars, he argues, who went too far in their insistence upon *taqlīd*, contradicting the known consensus of earlier authorities, Abū Ḥanīfa included.[85]

Qūrṣāwī's view toward the *madhhab* is reflective of his understanding of the Islamic scholarly tradition as a whole. The importance of the *madhhab* for Qūrṣāwī is connected to its function in maintaining *uṣūl* methodology and scholars' proper exercise of it. As the hermeneutic through which scripture is interpreted and moral action is determined, *uṣūl al-fiqh* is indispensable for any Muslim society, as are people trained in its methods and processes. Therefore the *madhhab*, as the institutional basis for legal reasoning, fulfills a critical need within the edifice of the *sharīʿa*. For Qūrṣāwī, Islamic legal discourse represents the only valid paradigm for determining correct action based on the texts of revelation, and *uṣūl al-fiqh* and, by extension, the *madhhab*—as constituent elements of that paradigm—play a critical role within the moral foundations of society.

In a similar fashion, theological scholars articulate correct beliefs and defend them through rational argumentation, based on dogmatic and philosophical

---

82. Ibid., pp. 28–29, 31, 40–41.

83. Cf. ibid., p. 6.

84. Ibid., p. 29; Qūrṣāwī, *Lawāʾiḥ*, fol. 86a.

85. Qūrṣāwī, *Irshād*, pp. 2–3, 5.

principles devised within established schools of *kalām*. Therefore theological discourse is likewise essential for society's religious standing.

By accepting the importance of the *madhhab*, Qūrṣāwī implicitly accepts the utility of *taqlīd*, lending important nuance to his stance. His epistemological critique manifests itself in the need for verification of scholars' positions as the means for ensuring correctness, but within the established frameworks of postclassical scholarship. Although he may have directed his skepticism and mistrust toward fellow *ʿulamāʾ*, he did not question the essential importance of their shared venture, nor their standing as the foremost religious authorities.

It is clear, then, that the Islamic scholarly tradition is central within Qūrṣāwī's reform project. As the broad framework in which the content of revelation can be articulated and made manifest, it is a vital part of a Muslim society. Indeed, the *ʿulamāʾ* utilize their expertise to interpret and understand the true sources of religious knowledge on behalf of the community; Qūrṣāwī emphasizes the need for Muslims to abide by sound scholarship, and he praises one who follows (*yuqallid*) the true scholars and imams.[86]

The issue was not with *ʿulamāʾ* per se, but with the flawed and erroneous views and practices they had allowed to spread, diminishing their basic function as moral and religious guides for the community. Moreover, the realities of Russian rule and state control of Islamic institutions in the 18th century had marginalized scholars and their ability to promote correct guidance and knowledge.

For Qūrṣāwī, then, it was imperative to preserve Islamic scholarship's scriptural validity and religious legitimacy, which had been compromised by excessive reliance upon *taqlīd*—itself rendered a larger problem by the structural changes to the *ʿulamāʾ* under tsarist auspices. As a result, *ʿulamāʾ* could not necessarily be relied upon, and so scholars' opinions and positions warranted verification to show their correctness with regard to scripture and *naql*, to halt the spread of error and misguidance.

Qūrṣāwī's epistemological critique revolved around the elimination of flawed or unfounded religious knowledge and—more significantly—the types of scholarship that allowed it to proliferate. For him, the uncritical reliance on the regime of *taqlīd*, though intended to ensure correctness, served only to separate scholarship from the scriptural foundations of the religion and its sources of certain knowledge. This failing on the *ʿulamāʾ*'s part required

---

86. Qūrṣāwī, *Lawāʾiḥ*, fol. 86a.

greater vigilance and insistence upon the verification of scholars' positions and judgments to determine their correctness, so that the tradition itself remained viable and capable of providing the necessary guidance to the Muslim community. In response, Qūrṣāwī focused on two main areas of reform: the reassertion of primary legal reasoning through *ijtihād* and the continued articulation of *fiqh* norms, and the elimination of specious and false beliefs about the nature of God and His attributes.

4

Ijtihād *and the Function of Legal Theory*

QŪRṢĀWĪ'S EPISTEMOLOGICAL REFORM calls for increased certainty in the sphere of law (and therefore in the quotidian function of society), which requires moving away from *taqlīd* through *taḥqīq* and the renewed exercise of primary legal reasoning—that is, *ijtihād*, necessary for the articulation of legal norms. This is the role of the *faqīh*, Hallaq writes: to expend "his utmost effort in extracting a rule from the subject matter of revelation while following the principles and procedures established in legal theory."[1] The scholar thus formulates, through his *ijtihād*, rules derived from scripture.[2] As the textual-interpretive process through which points of law are derived, *ijtihād* is the essence of *fiqh*, the method by which legal norms are formulated and elucidated by scholars.[3]

Ijtihād serves as the link between the texts of revelation and mundane action, allowing for the articulation of specific norms for behavior and interaction out of the moral content of scripture: "To the extent that the Law of God may be found at all in the mundane realm, it is only found in the formulations of jurists. It is primarily by virtue of the *ijtihād* of jurists that Islamic law exists

1. Wael Hallaq. *A History of Islamic Legal Theories: An Introduction to Sunni Usul al-Fiqh*. New York: Cambridge UP, 1997, p. 117; also Wael Hallaq. *Authority, Continuity and Change in Islamic Law*. New York: Cambridge UP, 2001, p. 192.

2. Bernard Weiss. "Interpretation in Islamic Law: The Theory of Ijtihad." *The American Journal of Comparative Law*, vol. 26, no. 2; 1978. 199–212, pp. 199–200.

3. Mohammad Hashim Kamali. *Principles of Islamic Jurisprudence*. 3rd ed. Cambridge: Islamic Texts Society, 2003, pp. 1–2.

at all as a body of positive rules."[4] In addition, *ijtihād* represented the way *fiqh* could be adapted to new cases and circumstances. In this way it served as "the main instrument of interpreting the divine message and relating it to the changing conditions of the Muslim community."[5] In fulfilling this function, *ijtihād* formed "the only true means by which Islamic law historically developed."[6] This adaptability was necessary so that the law could remain relevant and operative in different contexts. Without *ijtihād*, some scholars argued, the *sharīʿa* would cease to exist and Muslim society would plunge into anarchy.[7] Thus, *ijtihād* was widely considered to be a *farḍ kifāya*, an obligation upon the (or an) entire Muslim community.[8] The existence of qualified scholars engaging in *ijtihād* was seen as critical to the moral life of the community, ensuring proper guidance.[9]

Qūrṣāwī's Conception of Ijtihād

This is how Qūrṣāwī understands *ijtihād*. For him, it is the method through which legal reasoning is carried out, *uṣūl al-fiqh* in practice. He writes, "*Ijtihād* . . . in the technical language (*iṣṭilāḥ*) of the *sharīʿa* is the [act] of the jurist (*faqīh*) giving forth his ability in order to form an opinion on a legal norm (*li-taḥṣīl ẓann bi-ḥukm sharʿī*)."[10] As the process by which the law was articulated and determined by scholars and adapted to changing conditions, it is a necessity that must be present in all Muslim societies at all times. Indeed, it is an essential part of what makes a society Muslim. Learned interpretation

4. Weiss, "Interpretation," p. 201.

5. Kamali, *Principles*, p. 468.

6. Weiss, "Interpretation," p. 202.

7. Cf. Wael Hallaq. "Was the Gate of Ijtihad Closed?." *International Journal of Middle East Studies*, no. 16; 1984. 3–41. [Reprinted in Wael B. Hallaq. *Law and Legal Theory in Classical and Medieval Islam*. Brookfield, VT: Variorum, 1995], pp. 4–5, 20–23.

8. For a discussion of the importance of *ijtihād* within a society, see ibid., esp. p. 27; Hallaq, *Authority*, pp. 166–235; Hallaq, *History*, p. 117; Norman Calder, "al-Nawawi's Typology of Muftis and Its Significance for a General Theory of Islamic Law." *Islamic Law and Society*, vol. 3, no. 2; 1996. 137–164, p. 144; Kamali, *Principles*, pp. 471–472.

9. Wael B. Hallaq. "Ifta' and Ijtihad in Sunni Legal Theory: A Developmental Account." *Islamic Legal Interpretation: Muftis and Their Fatwas*. Eds. Muhammad Khalid Masud et al. Cambridge, MA: Harvard UP, 1996. 33–44, p. 38.

10. Qūrṣāwī, *Irshād*, p. 24; also Qūrṣāwī, *Sharḥ Manār*, pp. 187–188; Qūrṣāwī, *Sharḥ jadīd*, fol. 102b.

of scripture, utilizing an established hermeneutic, is indispensable for the community's moral foundations.[11]

The communal religious implications of *fiqh* play an important role in Qūrṣāwī's reformist project. It is telling that he offers a detailed discussion of *ijtihād* in the *Irshād*, which, as noted, was intended for a broad audience. Although it contains three chapters devoted to legal reasoning and interpretation, it is not a systematic legal work, and its discussion of *fiqh* is incorporated into a broader treatment of fairly basic religious issues, including fasting and pilgrimage. That this discussion is contained here indicates something of Qūrṣāwī's aim regarding *ijtihād*. For him, *ijtihād* should not be the exclusive domain of the *ʿulamāʾ*, consigning everyone else to reliance upon their judgment.[12] Instead, he broadens the scope of who should engage in *ijtihād* and how they should go about it. Quite simply, he holds that *ijtihād* is an obligation upon individuals, not just the community as a whole, with the degree to which one exercises *ijtihād* based on one's ability to do so. He writes: "Know that it is obligatory for everyone (*wājib li-kull aḥad*) to engage in *ijtihād* in the search for what is correct to the extent of one's ability. So absolute *ijtihād* (*al-ijtihād al-muṭlaq*) is obligatory for whoever is capable of absolute *ijtihād*, and *ijtihād* within the *madhhab* is obligatory for whoever is capable of that."[13]

Not only are individuals obliged to exercise *ijtihād*, but Qūrṣāwī also puts forward an expanded conception of what constitutes *ijtihād*. He draws a distinction between "legal *ijtihād*" (*ijtihād sharʿī*)—that is, *ijtihād* in the conventional sense just described—and more limited forms of *ijtihād*, which serve as a type of analysis and verification, through *tarjīḥ* and *taḥqīq*.[14] For him, *ijtihād* in some form or other is obligatory for all those who are capable. Those with the necessary scriptural and hermeneutical knowledge to do absolute *ijtihād* must always do so (as an absolute *mujtahid* is forbidden from following any other person's *ijtihād*), while others are obliged to carry out *ijtihād* to the extent of their knowledge of the scriptural sources and legal theory.[15] Absolute *taqlīd*

---

11. Qūrṣāwī, *Irshād*, pp. 29, 31.

12. Ibid., p. 2. Indeed, the *Sharḥ Manār*, which was intended for a scholarly audience, does not contain the same detailed treatment of *ijtihād* or its exercise.

13. Ibid., p. 29; transcription and translation in Nathan Spannaus. "Islamic Thought and Revivalism in the Russian Empire: An Intellectual Biography of Abu Nasr Qursawi (1776–1812)." Diss. McGill University, 2012, pp. 238–239.

14. Qūrṣāwī, *Irshād*, p. 29.

15. Ibid., p. 24.

is acceptable only for those incapable of any sort of legal reasoning, as their (lack of) ability makes it necessary (*ʿind al-ḍarūra*).[16]

Legal *Ijtihād*

The purpose behind this stance is the renewed exercise of scriptural interpretation, in order to lessen reliance on scholars' pronouncements. Qūrṣāwī presents the capacity for *ijtihād* as something readily attainable, even unremarkable.[17] Describing the requisite knowledge for legal *ijtihād*, he writes:

> The condition[s] (*sharṭ*) for *ijtihād* are [having] a natural strength of understanding and a knowledge (*ʿilm*) of the Book and Sunna—the text (*matn*), *isnād*[s], their linguistic and legal (*sharīʿatan*) meanings—such that [a *mujtahid*] is acquainted with (*yaʿrif*) the meaning of the words (*mufradāt*) and sentences (*murakkabāt*) and their particulars (*khawāṣṣ*) and content (*ifāda*). And he [should be] acquainted with the meanings that are operative for legal norms (*al-maʿānī al-muʾaththira fī al-aḥkām*) along with their classifications into the specific and general (*al-khāṣṣ wa-l-ʿāmm*), and clear and vague (*al-mufassar wa-l-mujmal*), and so on. An acquaintance with all of the Book and Sunna is not required, only what is relevant to an understanding of legal norms. Memorization is not required, but it is sufficient to have a verified source (*aṣl muṣaḥḥaḥ*) available that includes the legal hadith (*aḥādīth al-aḥkām*), such as the *Ṣaḥīḥayn* or others. And he [should be] acquainted with points of consensus (*mawāqiʿ al-ijmāʿ*), so that a *fatwā* is not given that contradicts established opinion (*al-naṣṣ*) or consensus. And an understanding of all the points of established opinion and consensus is not necessary, only of what is relevant to every question he will address, so that he knows (*yaʿlim*) that his *fatwā* does not contradict [them]. And [lastly]

16. Ibid., p. 32. Qūrṣāwī predominantly uses "*taqlīd*" to indicate absolute *taqlīd* (i.e., no *ijtihād* whatsoever), while legal reasoning short of absolute *ijtihād*—which necessarily involves some degree of *taqlīd*—is described simply as *ijtihād*, or with more specific terms (*tarjīḥ*, mainly, or *takhrīj*).

17. This is in contrast to most scholars, who, according to Kazem Bek, considered the conditions for absolute *ijtihād* to be so difficult as to be impossible (a view that Hallaq rejects); Mirza Kazem Beg. "Notice sur la marche et les progrès de la jurisprudence musulmane parmi les sectes orthodoxes." *Journal asiatique*, ser. 4, no. 15; Jan. 1850. 154–210, p. 184; Hallaq, "Gate," p. 4.

> he should be acquainted with the methods (*ṭuruq*) of *qiyās* and its conditions.[18]

In addition to these requirements, an extensive knowledge of the methods of hadith interpretation and criticism is also necessary for every Muslim (not just *mujtahids*), which Qūrṣāwī describes earlier in the *Irshād*.[19]

These requirements are for the most part conventional, in line with conditions normally stipulated for *ijtihād*.[20] But the description Qūrṣāwī gives here is rather vague, and he doesn't specify what different abilities for *ijtihād* might be—for instance, what distinguishes an absolute *mujtahid* from a limited *mujtahid* (*mujtahid muqayyad* or *mujtahid fī al-madhhab*—that is, one whose *ijtihād* is exercised within a *madhhab*).[21] Yet this ambiguity makes sense in the context of his reformist project. To delineate what qualifies a *faqīh* for what degree of interpretive autonomy would entail setting limits on the extent to which he can carry out his *ijtihād*. This of course would be functionally equivalent to the restrictive ranks for scholars in the *madhhab*, which Qūrṣāwī rejects. Rather, it is much more important for Qūrṣāwī that *ijtihād* is carried out at all. Accordingly, he does away with ranks for *mujtahids* so that they are not confined in the scope of their legal reasoning by rigid frameworks.

The limits to scholars' exercise of *ijtihād* thus stem from their own abilities and knowledge; if faced with a complex legal question beyond his understanding or about an area of law with which he is not familiar, a *faqīh* would then follow the judgment of another scholar. Qūrṣāwī leaves it to the individual *mujtahid* to determine the limits of his abilities, to discern, through moral and conscientious introspection, the degree to which he can carry out *ijtihād*.[22]

In this way, scholars are not obliged toward *taqlīd*, as is conventional within the postclassical *madhhab*, but rather toward *ijtihād*, which becomes the default. Indeed, for Qūrṣāwī the very exercise of legal reasoning becomes synonymous with *ijtihād*; he writes, "Whoever answers questions from the

---

18. Qūrṣāwī, *Irshād*, p. 24; transcription and translation in Spannaus, "Islamic Thought," pp. 237–238.

19. See Qūrṣāwī, *Irshād*, pp. 6–24.

20. See Kazem Beg, "Notice," pp. 184–186, 202–206; Hallaq, "Gate," pp. 5–7; Calder, "Typology," pp. 143–147.

21. Though the "limited *mujtahid*" is a recognized rank of *ijtihād*, I use "limited" here in contradistinction to "absolute"; cf. Calder, "Typology," p. 146; Hallaq, "Gate," p. 17.

22. Cf. Weiss, "Interpretation," p. 207.

Book, Sunna, consensus, and *qiyās*" is a *muftī*, and by extension a *mujtahid*.[23] A *faqīh* is required to follow another *faqīh*'s judgment only in cases where he has not reached his own decision through the full exercise of *ijtihād*, and he is forbidden from following another *mujtahid* in any matter on which he has formulated his own judgment.[24]

Equating *ijtihād* with legal reasoning in general promotes jurists' interpretive autonomy, and even limited *mujtahids* have the ability to perform *ijtihād* to its fullest extent, without undue restriction. Qūrṣāwī states that a scholar who follows through *taqlīd* the eponymous founder of a *madhhab* can nullify (*qayyala*) the founder's position if there is definitive evidence (*dalīl qaṭʿī*) to do so. In that case, he must disregard the founder's opinion, since it is obligatory to follow more certain sources of knowledge. He writes that Hanafis "follow (*yuqallidūn*) Abū Ḥanīfa whenever there is no sound evidence (*dalīl*) contradicting a position of his (*ʿalā khilāf qawlih*) that is stronger than his evidence. And if evidence more compelling (*rājiḥ*) than his is apparent, then do not follow his position." If, however, Abū Ḥanīfa's position can be verified as scripturally correct and sound in its reasoning, then there is no issue with following it.[25]

Here conforming to scripture is shown to be of paramount importance, even at the expense of coherence in *madhhab* doctrine. Qūrṣāwī thus puts forward a vision of the exercise of *ijtihād* that is broader and more open than conventionally understood. Unencumbered by rigid structures within the *madhhab*, *mujtahids* instead can pursue legal questions to the fullest extent of their ability, fulfilling their purpose of articulating scriptural norms for the community.

However, this ability to carry out *ijtihād* unfettered by hierarchical ranks does not make all *mujtahids* absolute *mujtahids*. Rather, the *madhhab* framework remains operative for most scholars. Limited *mujtahids*, despite the lack of restrictions on their interpretation, must nevertheless take their

---

23. "*al-Muftī huwa al-mujtahid, ay man yaʾkhudh jawāb al-masʾila ʿan al-kitāb wa-l-sunna wa-l-ijmāʿ wa-l-qiyās*"; Qūrṣāwī, *Irshād*, p. 30.

24. Ibid., p. 24. This is because the outcome of an act of *ijtihād* is necessarily what the *mujtahid* believes to be the correct view on the matter, as a full and complete act of *ijtihād* leads to a preponderance of belief (*rujḥān al-iʿtiqād*) within the *mujtahid* that his opinion is correct. Since a *mujtahid* must believe his opinion is correct, he can follow another *mujtahid*'s opinion only if he is incapable of formulating his own on the matter; ibid.; cf. Weiss, "Interpretation," pp. 203–208; Hallaq, *History*, pp. 118–119; Aron Zysow. "The Economy of Certainty: An Introduction to the Typology of Islamic Legal Theory." Diss. Harvard University, 1984, pp. 460–461, 471.

25. Qūrṣāwī, *Irshād*, p. 32; also Qūrṣāwī, *Lawāʾiḥ*, fol. 86a.

school's doctrine into account. As Qūrṣāwī writes in his description of the requirements for *ijtihād*, scholars must be acquainted with the established positions of the *madhhab* (*naṣṣ/manṣūṣ ʿalayh*).[26] Although they are not required to follow it or conform to it, it is clear that Qūrṣāwī does not intend the autonomy to interpret scripture directly to mean that scholars can simply disregard preexisting *furūʿ*.

In this respect, the *madhhab* still holds considerable importance for Qūrṣāwī, a fact that is even more pronounced in terms of *uṣūl*. The major distinction between a limited *mujtahid* and an absolute *mujtahid* is that the latter employs his own legal hermeneutic, while the former uses that of his *madhhab* (which is a form of *taqlīd*). Therefore, even if a limited *mujtahid* reaches a decision that goes against a position of his school's founder, by employing the founder's method, his reasoning falls within the framework of the *madhhab*, which is underpinned by *taqlīd*.[27] At its most basic, this framework is built upon a particular methodology of legal interpretation, one that is shared among its members: to be a Hanafi *faqīh* is to do Hanafi *fiqh*, which is to utilize Abū Ḥanīfa's *uṣūl*. The *madhhab* thus represents an established hermeneutic of *uṣūl al-fiqh*, necessary for the proper exercise of legal reasoning. Without it, Qūrṣāwī argues, there is no way to understand scriptural norms and translate them into moral action, leading to *bidʿa*.[28] All scholars must therefore follow a *madhhab* in *uṣūl*. (Indeed, this point is implicit throughout Qūrṣāwī's discussions of *fiqh*.) Only an absolute (also called independent) *mujtahid* relies on no one else's method in *ijtihād*.[29] But he must nevertheless utilize an interpretive methodology, if one of his own devising. An absolute *mujtahid* thus follows his own *madhhab*.

The Master Rule of Legal Reasoning

Such a view of the importance of *uṣūl* methodology is characteristic of Hanafi formalism. As noted, formalism relies on the process of *ijtihād* itself to confer legitimacy upon an act of legal interpretation. *Ijtihād* in this way represents the "master-rule" from which legal validity is derived: "By applying this rule, the jurist can be certain that his result is valid. . . . Certainty is no longer

---

26. Qūrṣāwī, *Irshād*, pp. 24, also 32.

27. Jackson argues that since the scholar operating within the *madhhab* derives his authority for interpretation from the founder, the founder "in effect stands between him and scripture," even if it's only in terms of methodology; Jackson, "Taqlid," p. 169.

28. Cf. Qūrṣāwī, *Irshād*, esp. pp. 35–36.

29. Kazem Beg, "Notice," pp. 195–196; also see, for instance, Hallaq, "Gate," pp. 15–17.

sought in the specific case, but the [result] of the case derives its validity from the certainty of the master-rule."[30]

This notion of *ijtihād* as the master rule that extends legal interpretation its legitimacy is at the heart of Qūrṣāwī's sociolegal stance. He states explicitly that any position that is not derived from Qur'an, Sunna, consensus, or *qiyās* is *bid'a*, and these four sources of law—the *uṣūl al-fiqh*—are confirmed by unanimous consensus (*bi-ijmā' al-fuqahā' kāfat*[an]) as the sound basis of the *sharī'a*.[31] Anything that is derived from these sources—that is, through *ijtihād*—constitutes a sound judgment, and any judgment formulated through the proper exercise of *ijtihād* is correct.[32] For Qūrṣāwī, *ijtihād* as a process represents that which confers legitimacy and validity upon a responsum—that is, Zysow's master rule.

Because of this, the performance of *ijtihād* is raised in status, making its very exercise significant, while the result derived through it is in many ways incidental. This position is most fully expressed in the notion of juristic infallibility, which plays an important role in Qūrṣāwī's stance. Juristic infallibility is the view that no matter what the outcome of an individual act of *ijtihād*, its result (*mujtahad*) is, by virtue of having been derived from the *uṣūl*, correct.[33] This is based on the principle that "every *mujtahid* is correct" (*kull mujtahid muṣīb*), stemming from a prophetic hadith that states: "If a judge (*ḥākim*) exercises *ijtihād* and is correct [in his interpretation] then he receives two rewards [in the hereafter], and if he is wrong, he receives one."[34] This doctrine, Zysow writes, "recognizes an inherent value in *ijtihād*" and holds it to be morally praiseworthy per se.[35]

Qūrṣāwī does not hold that all legal responsa are absolutely correct (a widespread Mu'tazili view that Zysow calls "extreme infallibilism"). Instead Qūrṣāwī evinces agreement with aspects of two related doctrines on the issue, labeled by Zysow as "fallibilism" (*takhṭī'a*) and "verisimilitude" (*ashbāh*). In

---

30. Zysow, "Economy," p. 469; cf. also Weiss, "Interpretation," p. 203.

31. Qūrṣāwī, *Irshād*, p. 35. Qūrṣāwī also holds that *ijtihād* is subordinate to consensus, thus making the *uṣūl* inviolable; ibid., p. 24.

32. Ibid., pp. 24–25; Qūrṣāwī, *Sharḥ Manār*, pp. 13–14.

33. See Zysow, "Economy," esp. pp. 463–483; Aron Zysow. "Mu'tazilism and Maturidism in Hanafi Legal Theory." *Studies in Islamic Legal Theory*. Ed. Bernard Weiss. Leiden: Brill, 2002. 235–266, pp. 239–247.

34. Qūrṣāwī, *Irshād*, p. 24; Qūrṣāwī, *Sharḥ jadīd*, fol. 146b; see also Hallaq, *History*, p. 120.

35. Zysow, "Economy," p. 475.

contrast to extreme infallibilism, these doctrines posit that there is a single correct answer for a legal issue, known only to God. A *mujtahid* is rewarded for doing *ijtihād* because of his attempt to discern the truth, insofar as it is possible. This reward is merely for carrying out the act of interpretation. If the result of his *ijtihād* is correct (that is, it matches the one answer known to God), then he is rewarded again. If it is not correct, then he is either wrong (in fallibilism) or simply not right (in verisimilitude).[36]

For Qūrṣāwī, the *mujtahid* who has reached an incorrect result is, in fact, wrong (*mukhṭiʾ*). But *mujtahids*, he writes, are not tasked with reaching what is with God, only with reaching a result they themselves consider correct. Consequently, the incorrect *mujtahid* is forgiven for his error.[37] He is understood to have been right in the beginning and to have gone wrong only at the end.[38] Because it is not the *mujtahid*'s duty to reach the correct result, the correctness of the ensuing judgment is incidental to the act of *ijtihād*. The *mujtahid* is right in carrying out *ijtihād*, regardless of the result.

Zysow writes that Central Asian Hanafi-Maturidis were virtually unanimous in holding fallibilism, in contrast to Iraqi Hanafis, most of whom were proponents of verisimilitude. (The importance of this debate for the Central Asians bordered on the theological. Nasafī includes the point that *mujtahids* are fallible as an article of belief in his *ʿaqāʾid*.)[39] Qūrṣāwī, however, does not hold to pure fallibilism, and it seems that the inspiration for his partial adoption of verisimilitude may come from another source.

One Central Asian scholar who does profess infallibilism was the Bukharan Sufi Abū Bakr Muḥammad b. Abī Isḥāq al-Kalābādhī (?–ca. 995). As we will see, Kalābādhī strongly influenced Qūrṣāwī's theological thought, and there are some important similarities between his stance on juristic infallibility and Qūrṣāwī's. Kalābādhī's position itself evinces a synthetic character that, Zysow notes, is "not easily reconciled with true infallibilism."[40] Kalābādhī writes: "And [Sufis] see the differences [among] the legal scholars (*al-fuqahāʾ*)

---

36. Zysow considers verisimilitude to be a form of infallibilism; see ibid., pp. 459–484; Zysow, "Muʿtazilism," pp. 240–244.

37. Qūrṣāwī, *Irshād*, pp. 24–25; also Qūrṣāwī, *Sharḥ jadīd*, fol. 146b.

38. Qūrṣāwī, *Irshād*, p. 27; Qūrṣāwī, *Sharḥ Manār*, pp. 188–189. This position was associated with verisimilitude; see Zysow, "Muʿtazilism," p. 242 n. 28.

39. Qūrṣāwī, *Sharḥ jadīd*, fol. 146b; Saʿd al-Dīn al-Taftāzānī. *Sharḥ al-ʿaqāʾid al-nasafiyya*. Ed. Aḥmad Ḥijāzī al-Saqqā. Cairo: Maktabat al-Kulliyyāt al-azhariyya, 1407/1988, p. 111; cf. Zysow, "Muʿtazilism," pp. 241–243.

40. Zysow, "Muʿtazilism," p. 241 n. 23.

as correct, and one of them does not contradict (*yaʿtariḍ*) another. Every *mujtahid* among them is correct (*muṣīb*), [as is] everyone who follows a *madhhab* in the *sharīʿa*."[41] Kalābādhī's infallibilism is based on the acceptance of the *madhhabs* as the repositories of proper legal reasoning. This he makes explicit, stating that what is correct (the verb *ṣaḥḥa* here indicating a greater level of epistemological certainty than the verb *aṣāba*) according to one *madhhab* is similar to what is correct in another, in that it ultimately comes from the Book and Sunna.[42]

This underlying principle for Kalābādhī's infallibilism is at the heart of Qūrṣāwī's. For the latter, it is the application of proper legal reasoning that ensures certainty. This is the foundation of Hanafi formalism, and it underpins Qūrṣāwī's entire stance on *ijtihād*: a responsum derived through *ijtihād* can necessarily be considered correct, and the mere act of *ijtihād* is supported by God.

This outlook reinforces the significance Qūrṣāwī places on the *madhhab* (beyond being based in Hanafi formalism), the authority of which rests on its doctrine of *uṣūl al-fiqh*. Indeed, he writes that the locus of the *madhhab* is not in any substantive position but rather in its method of "*ijtihād* and *tarjīḥ*." He goes on:

> It is the way *to* something (*madhhab ilayhā*), not the way *in* something (*madhhab fīhā*). But [now] it is only allowed [to be] the way in something, not the way to something. But the way of the person headed to Kufa, for example, is the route to Kufa, not Kufa itself. And [correct] Hanafi *ʿulamāʾ* see the necessity of following the ways and methods of Abū Ḥanīfa in *ijtihād* and [legal] derivation (*istinbāṭ*).[43]

That the individual scholars within a school may disagree on a given ruling is insignificant (or, in the case of Hanafism, encouraged[44]); their authority is

41. Abū Bakr Muḥammad b. Ishāq al-Kalābādhī. *Kitāb al-Taʿarruf li-madhhab ahl al-taṣawwuf.* Ed. A. J. Arberry. Cairo: Maktabat al-khānjī, 1934, pp. 55–56.

42. Ibid., p. 56.

43. Qūrṣāwī, *Irshād*, p. 62; emphasis added; cf. Kemper, "Imperial Russia," pp. 116–118.

44. Cf. Qūrṣāwī, *Sharḥ jadīd*, fol. 146b. See also the article by Brannon Wheeler, where he argues that juristic disagreement and plurality of opinion was a central aspect of Hanafism; Brannon Wheeler. "Identity in the Margins: Unpublished Hanafi Commentaries on the *Mukhtasar* of Ahmad b. Muhammad al-Quduri." *Islamic Law and Society*, vol. 10, no. 2; 2003. 182–209.

derived from their adherence to the school's interpretive method.[45] This authority is based on the consensus that the method of each of the four *madhhabs* is sound, and insofar as a *faqīh* conforms to one of these methods, his interpretive manipulation of *uṣūl al-fiqh* is considered valid. It is the *madhhab* that ensures the proper application of *ijtihād*.

This last point, of course, does not apply to absolute *mujtahids*, who are above the *madhhab*. But absolute *mujtahids* are by definition the foremost masters of *uṣūl al-fiqh*, and it would be absurd if their *ijtihād* were not properly carried out. They are, however, inevitably a minority among *mujtahids*.[46] All other *mujtahids* must utilize the method of a *madhhab*.

But absolute *ijtihād* is not a particular concern for Qūrṣāwī. In fact, he hardly mentions it. What's more important for him is promoting *ijtihād* of any type in order to counteract the proliferation of errors through the secondary reasoning of *taqlīd* and maintain the link between the community and the texts of revelation. The continuous interpretation of scripture to serve people's practical needs is one of the major goals for his reformist project. Accordingly, legal theory, as the necessary methodology for determining morally correct action, is a significant point of emphasis within his thought. Both of his works dealing specifically with legal issues focus primarily on *uṣūl*, and the *Irshād* is intended to help increase knowledge of Hanafi legal theory within the community.

Lesser Ijtihād

Qūrṣāwī promotes knowledge of *uṣūl al-fiqh* as a way to counteract the overreliance on *taqlīd* and bring about the renewed exercise of primary legal reasoning, to preserve and strengthen the community's moral foundations. Critically, he does not limit this knowledge to scholars alone; rather, he argues in the *Irshād* that *all* Muslims must have an understanding of the methods of textual interpretation and hadith criticism so that they can base their actions upon sound scriptural knowledge.[47]

With this, Qūrṣāwī puts forward a way for lay Muslims to exercise *ijtihād*, which, though distinct from legal *ijtihād* carried out by *fuqahā*ʾ, is nevertheless

45. For Jackson, this is the essence of *taqlīd*, not, as many would have it, the blind adoption of the content of the *mujtahid*'s reasoning; Jackson, "Taqlid," pp. 170–172.

46. To become an absolute *mujtahid*, a scholar must first master all the requisite aspects of the law. Until he attains such mastery, he is not an absolute *mujtahid*, and thus must exercise his *ijtihād* within a *madhhab*; cf. Shihāb al-Dīn al-Marjānī. *Nāẓūrat al-ḥaqq fī farḍiyyat al-ʿishāʾ wa-in lam yaghib al-shafaq*. Kazan: n.p., 1870, esp. pp. 56–57.

47. Qūrṣāwī, *Irshād*, pp. 4–5.

obligatory. The type of reasoning and interpretation at the heart of this lay *ijtihād* is *tarjīḥ*, which is (as noted) the hermeneutical process for weighing multiple pieces of evidence or legal opinions. Through it, a person can consider various elements within scripture or legal judgments in order to determine which among them is most compelling (*rājiḥ*). Though *tarjīḥ* is predominantly an expert activity, Qūrṣāwī considered it, like legal *ijtihād*, to be an obligation upon everyone capable of it.[48]

There are two dimensions to *tarjīḥ*—the evaluation of scripture (primarily *aḥādīth*) and the evaluation of *mujtahids' fatwās*—and Qūrṣāwī understands both as important parts of lay Muslims' engagement with legal reasoning. The two aspects, of course, are linked, as one of the most salient ways of evaluating *fatwās* is to weigh the scriptural sources used in their formulation. Qūrṣāwī treats the evaluation of *fatwās* as a way for a *muqallid* to actively engage with *ijtihād* through its end product. As Hallaq notes, *tarjīḥ* was one of the methods by which the theoretical value of the *fatwā* was transferred into the domain of positive law; if a *fatwā* was evaluated and deemed compelling, it would then be put into practice by the *muqallid*.[49] For Qūrṣāwī, this constitutes an active form of reasoning:

> For whomever is not capable of legal *ijtihād* (*al-ijtihād al-sharʿī*) and is compelled towards *taqlīd*, inquiry (*taḥarrī*) into the *ʿulamāʾ* is obligatory, [to determine who is] most learned and pious in order to be confident in his *fatwā*[s] and rely upon his opinion. And what is absolutely obligatory is [following] God's statement: "And do not follow that of which you have no knowledge,"[50] which is understood [to mean knowledge] by a compelling belief (*bi-l-iʿtiqad al-rājiḥ*). So whoever is capable of evaluation by evidence (*al-tarjīḥ bi-l-dalīl*) should do so, and whoever is not capable of it should evaluate the opinion of whoever is most just, reliable, and knowledgeable (*al-aʿdal wa-l-awraʿ wa-l-afqah*), since the obligation is [based] only on the extent of [one's] ability.[51]

Qūrṣāwī enumerates, with respect to evaluating *fatwās*, an interpretive process for determining preponderance. He writes that in terms of *furūʿ*, the

---

48. Ibid., pp. 6, 29.

49. Hallaq, *Authority*, p. 133.

50. Q 17:36.

51. Qūrṣāwī, *Irshād*, p. 29; transcription and translation in Spannaus, "Islamic Thought," pp. 238–239.

most weight is given to those positions upon which there is consensus (*mujma*ʿ *ʿalayh*). Barring that, the most judicious (*al-aḥwaṭ*) is favored, then the strongest in terms of evidence (*al-awthaq dalīl*^an), and last the position of whoever is considered most learned and reliable.[52]

In this way, a *muqallid* can evaluate both *mujtahids*' judgments as well as the *mujtahids* themselves. Though incapable of his own *ijtihād*, the *muqallid* can still expend significant interpretive effort in applying the law, in ways that overlap with scholars' interpretation. Indeed, when discussing a limited *mujtahid*'s evaluation of the *fatwās* of other scholars, Qūrṣāwī enumerates the same steps for *tarjīḥ* as he does for a *muqallid*.[53] This form of reasoning, which is employed by *fuqahā*ʾ in the determination of judgments, constitutes part of *qiyās*.[54]

Here we have the first type of *tarjīḥ*—the evaluation of scriptural evidence in order to weigh the merits of various legal responsa, which can be done by analyzing the sources used in their formulation. It is connected to *takhrīj*, which involves the interpretation and analysis of scriptural sources (primarily, but not exclusively, hadith) in order to derive principles that can be used as the basis for correct action.[55] This is based on the premise that a sound hadith necessitates action (*al-ḥadīth al-ṣaḥīḥ wājib al-*ʿ*amal*).[56] But even sound *aḥādīth* are not necessarily straightforward, and rules of interpretation (*ta*ʾ*wīl*) and abrogation (*naskh*) as well as linguistic concerns play a large role in complicating the interpretive process. It is for this reason that *tarjīḥ* is necessary, as it allows for the evaluation of individual reports so that one can act upon what he deems to be most compelling.[57]

Abū Yūsuf (731–798), one of the early masters of the Hanafi school, was of the opinion, quoted by Qūrṣāwī, that to deduce principles from hadith is not for laypeople (*al-*ʿ*āmmī*), who do not know the various methods of interpreting and analyzing hadith that "are needed in the evaluation (*tarjīḥ*) of reports vis-à-vis one another."[58] This, however, entails relying upon the ʿ*ulamā*ʾ alone to

52. Qūrṣāwī, *Irshād*, p. 30.

53. Ibid., p. 32.

54. Hallaq, *Authority*, p. 131; Weiss, "Interpretation," p. 202.

55. Kazem Beg, "Notice," p. 208.

56. Qūrṣāwī, *Irshād*, p. 4.

57. "And if one is capable of evaluating (*tarjīḥ*) one of the probable meanings [of a hadith] by opinion (*bi-l-ra*ʾ*y*), then he [should] act upon what is most compelling to him (*bi-mā tarjaḥ* [sic] ʿ*indah*)"; ibid., p. 5.

58. Ibid.

determine proper action from hadith, which Qūrṣāwī, of course, does not accept. For him the issue, as with all forms of *taqlīd*, is one of knowledge. If laypeople are forced to rely on the *ʿulamāʾ* to determine which hadith are operative for action and how they are to be interpreted, then a person's knowledge is not of hadith but rather of a scholar's position. Instead, Qūrṣāwī writes, "it is obligatory upon everyone who is able to distinguish (*tamyīz*) sound from weak reports and [distinguish] reliable transmitters (*nāqilīn*) from others, to act only upon what they know to be correct."[59]

Qūrṣāwī then sets out to describe in detail the interpretive process for evaluating scriptural evidence. (Although this discussion is explicitly addressed toward hadith, as Hallaq notes, the methodological tools for interpreting the text of a hadith are just as applicable for interpreting the Qurʾan.)[60] Indeed, it seems that explaining and elaborating upon this form of *tarjīḥ* is one of Qūrṣāwī's primary concerns. The chapter dealing with it takes up nearly a third of the *Irshād*'s total length, and it is a major focus of the *Sharḥ Manār*.

Qūrṣāwī begins the *Irshād* arguing that the ability to distinguish between different types of hadith and their obligations for proper action has been taken away from common people, but that this knowledge is necessary for their proper guidance and avoiding error (*ḍalāla*).[61] The discussion of scriptural interpretation that follows is an attempt to rectify this situation, emphasizing the evaluation of scriptural evidence in order to determine correct action. If one can ascertain, through *tarjīḥ* and *takhrīj*, a principle from hadith that is determinative for action, then the corresponding action can reasonably be considered correct, in the sense that it was properly derived from hadith. The methods of *tarjīḥ* provide a framework for formulating this knowledge.

For example, Qūrṣāwī describes the process for weighing multiple *āḥād* reports (sing. *khabar wāḥid*), which are among the most problematic types of hadith in their determinative value for action.[62] *Āḥād* reports are hadith that have only a single transmitter at some point along their *isnād* and so carry less certainty than *mutawātir* reports, which have so many transmitters as to be beyond doubt, conveying certain knowledge (*ʿilm ḍarūrī* or *qaṭʿī*), and *mashhūr* reports, whose epistemological value, though less than that of the *mutawātir*,

---

59. Ibid., pp. 5–6.

60. Hallaq, *Authority*, pp. 130–131.

61. Qūrṣāwī, *Irshād*, p. 3.

62. Zysow, "Economy," p. 32. Zysow refers to this type of report as a "unit tradition."

imparts trusted knowledge (*ʿilm ṭamānīna*).[63] *Āḥād* reports, on the other hand, convey only an opinion (*ẓann*).[64]

Due to their relative weakness in terms of *isnād, āḥād* reports, though still considered sound, necessitate a certain degree of hermeneutical attention in order to constitute a sufficiently reliable basis for action. Qūrṣāwī enumerates eight criteria for evaluating a *khabar wāḥid*—four regarding the report's content, and four regarding its transmitters.

The first criterion of the content is that it does not contradict the text of the Qurʾan in its apparent or basic meaning (*al-ẓāhir wa-l-ʿumūm*), and the second is that it does not contradict a more authoritative hadith (i.e., a *mashhūr* or *mutawātir* report).[65] The third condition is that it cannot concern a broad or universal matter. The reason for this, as Qūrṣāwī writes, is that the prophet would not have spoken of an issue of general significance to only small numbers of people: "He [Muhammad] did not limit himself in addressing individuals (*āḥād*) about what is of general concern, [but] went to great lengths to disseminate it due to people's need for it."[66] The fourth condition is that the Companions did not cease to make use of the hadith due to disagreement among themselves over its meaning. For Qūrṣāwī, such disagreement shows that either the meaning of that hadith was not fixed (*ghayr thābit*) or the report had been abrogated. In either case it should be disregarded.[67]

In addition, Qūrṣāwī lays out four qualities the transmitter (*mukhbir*) of a hadith must have. A transmitter must be noted for his or her reason (*ʿaql*), reliability (*ʿadāla*), precision (*ḍabṭ*), and devotion to Islam for any hadith transmitted by that person to be accepted. The presence of anyone not evincing

---

63. Qūrṣāwī, *Irshād*, p. 9; also Qūrṣāwī, *Sharḥ Manār*, pp. 99–100. That *mutawātir* reports carry this degree of epistemological certainty is even found in the *ʿAqāʾid nasafiyya*; cf. Qūrṣāwī, *Sharḥ jadīd*, fols. 97b–98a. On the three categories of reports in Hanafi *fiqh*, see Zysow, "Economy," pp. 13–42; Kamali, *Principles*, pp. 92–108.

64. Qūrṣāwī, *Sharḥ Manār*, p. 101, also 62.

65. Qūrṣāwī, *Irshād*, p. 10. These first two conditions are commonsensical; more epistemologically sound sources obviously take precedence over sources that are less so, and the latter should conform to the former.

66. Ibid., pp. 10–11. The purpose of this condition is to prevent an anomalous hadith, whose content does not conform to a fundamental tenet of the religion (*aṣl*), from being used to preclude that tenet; ibid., p. 11. This is a standard Hanafi interpretive doctrine; Zysow, "Economy," pp. 64–67.

67. Qūrṣāwī, *Irshād*, p. 11. According to Qūrṣāwī, it was the position of some from among his Hanafi predecessors, as well as most of his contemporaries, that such reports are rejected. Hadith scholars, however, as with the third condition, accept those hadith whose *isnād*s are valid, regardless of any other concerns.

these characteristics within a chain of transmitters precludes action on the basis of that report. For instance, someone noted for forgetfulness would be considered as lacking both reliability and precision, thus eliminating all *aḥādīth* transmitted by them. Within these categories, transmitters are separated further into those who are known for their legal knowledge and those who are not, as a report transmitted by one of the former group is considered to be more accurate in terms of precision and wording, and thus more compelling (*rājiḥ*).[68]

A *khabar wāḥid* meeting all necessary conditions becomes suitable for action.[69] If there are two conflicting yet sound reports, then they are evaluated according to the relevant criteria until one is determined to be more compelling than the other. For instance, Qūrṣāwī writes that if two otherwise valid *āḥād* reports have ambiguity (*shubha*) within their texts, the lesser ambiguity should be preferred.[70] (In addition to *tarjīḥ* as a means for evaluating preponderance for a report, Qūrṣāwī also details the hermeneutical means for interpreting the meanings of scriptural language, particularly for parsing ambiguous or obscure words.)[71]

In this way, an educated Muslim—and not necessarily a scholar—can evaluate and engage directly with scripture, while determining a scriptural basis for correct action. Significantly, this discussion of *tarjīḥ* precedes the discussion of *ijtihād* in the *Irshād*. As not everyone meets the requirements for *ijtihād*, Qūrṣāwī's treatment of it is less relevant for some people than for others. *Tarjīḥ*, on the other hand, is relevant for everyone, since it deals with Muslims' interaction with scripture and the *ʿulamāʾ*. It provides a way for laypeople to evaluate the *ʿulamāʾ*'s positions and derive evidence (*dalīl*) from scripture, and both of these aspects of *tarjīḥ* work to dispel *taqlīd*, thereby constituting a form of *ijtihād*. Indeed, Qūrṣāwī explicitly understands it this way, as he writes, "*Ijtihād* in evaluating (*tarjīḥ*) reports (*riwāyāt*) from hadith and *fatwās*, through its methods [i.e., the methods of *ijtihād*], is obligatory."[72]

The emphasis here is on the application of the interpretive method, which is directly connected with Qūrṣāwī's insistence upon epistemological

---

68. Ibid., pp. 11–13.

69. Ibid., p. 10. *Āḥād* reports only convey opinion (*ẓann*) or probable knowledge (*mufīd al-ʿilm*), which do not by themselves oblige action; Qūrṣāwī, *Sharḥ Manār*, pp. 101–103; see Zysow, "Economy," p. 91.

70. Qūrṣāwī, *Irshād*, p. 13.

71. Ibid., pp. 17–18.

72. Ibid., p. 6.

certainty. Evaluating *fatwās* serves to minimize the possibility for error by directing greater scrutiny toward scholars' judgments from lay Muslims who rely upon them for guidance, lessening the chances that unfounded and incorrect interpretations will be followed. However, it is not mere scrutiny but the exercise of *uṣūl* methodology specifically that minimizes the possibility for error. In line with Hanafi formalism, as it is the process of legal theory that confers legitimacy upon a judgment, it is also the process that must be used to verify that judgment. Accordingly, Qūrṣāwī argues that lay Muslims must know the principles of *fiqh* interpretation, and his discussion of *tarjīḥ* and the methods through which a proof (*dalīl*) can be derived is taken entirely from traditional Hanafi hermeneutics.[73]

The primary concern is complying with the divine *sharīʿa*, but since the *sharīʿa* cannot be determined with certainty, a Muslim is obliged to exercise *ijtihād* in order to discern correct action with as much certainty as possible. This *ijtihād* can range from evaluating which *mujtahid* is the most learned and pious all the way to absolute *ijtihād*. The goal of all degrees of *ijtihād*, however, is the same: the determination of compelling evidence (*dalīl rājiḥ*) that obliges action. And regardless of whether a Muslim determines this through his own act of *ijtihād* or through another's that he has verified, such evidence must be followed.[74]

The Prevalence of Taqlīd

This stance, holding *ijtihād* to be obligatory and allowing for the possibility of absolute *ijtihād*, represents a significant break with convention. Law in the postclassical period was marked by Jackson's regime of *taqlīd*, which served as the hegemonic form of legal authority from the 11th century on. This hegemony was expressed in the "closure of the gate of *ijtihād*" (*insidād bāb al-ijtihād*), the view that there were no longer absolute *mujtahids*. Legal reasoning continued after this putative closure, but it could be carried out only within the *madhhab*, governed by the bonds of *taqlīd*. As a result, there was a gradual separation in

---

73. Qūrṣāwī's treatment of the methods of hadith interpretation is grounded within Hanafi *fiqh* to such a degree that it includes a description of a debate among early Iraqi Hanafis over the respective positions of Abū Bakr al-Jaṣṣāṣ (917–981) and ʿĪsā b. Abān (?–835) regarding the epistemological value of a *mashhūr* report. Qūrṣāwī does not in any way challenge the view that came to predominate among Hanafis—ibn Abān's—but describes the debate in detail while affirming ibn Abān's position; ibid., p. 9; see Zysow, "Economy," pp. 24–31. This regard for Hanafi *fiqh* is also present in the *Sharḥ Manār*, which includes a more detailed discussion of Hanafi scriptural and linguistic interpretation than is found in the *Irshād*.

74. Qūrṣāwī, *Irshād*, p. 32.

legal literature of the titles *muftī* and *mujtahid*, with the requirements of the former decreasing over time and the latter considered to have ceased to exist. While *muftī*s continued to carry out legal reasoning and interpretation, it was no longer called "*ijtihād*," whether by *muftī*s themselves or by others.[75] *Muftī*s and *fuqahā*ʾ instead saw themselves as bound by their position within the ranks of their *madhhab*, which, as noted, limited later scholars' interpretive autonomy and obliged deference to earlier figures, reinforcing the regime of *taqlīd*.

This was certainly the case in the Volga-Ural region, where the regime of *taqlīd* predominated. An anonymous text from Kazan copied in the early 19th century describes the strict hierarchy of scholars in the Hanafi school, based on the progression of generations (*ṭabaqāt*): after Abū Ḥanīfa, the second generation includes the *mujtahids fī al-madhhab*, who must engage in *taqlīd* on the fundamentals (*qawāʿid*) of *uṣūl al-fiqh*, and the third generation is allowed *ijtihād* only regarding otherwise unsettled questions. Beyond these first three generations, scholars are mere *muqallids*, limited to *tarjīḥ* in the fourth and fifth generations, and after that having the ability only to distinguish (*tamayyuz*) between strong and weak opinions.[76]

Although the current paucity of sources makes it difficult to state definitively how *fiqh* was carried out in this region, the extant legal writings we have suggest that from at least the 17th century it was overwhelmingly characterized by secondary interpretation.[77] Similarly, the recorded rulings and opinions of official imams and *ākhūnd*s show that this continued widely under the Spiritual Assembly. Fatḥ Allāh Ūriwī is a case in point: his rulings as *ākhūnd* evince an approach to interpretation strictly grounded within the *madhhab* framework and the Hanafi *corpus juris*.[78]

---

75. Cf. Jackson, "Taqlid," pp. 170–173; Hallaq, "Gate," pp. 24–25, 30–33; Hallaq, "Ifta'."

76. *Ṭabaqāt al-ḥanafiyya*. Ms. KFU, no. A-1010. Fols. 21b–45a, fols. 21b–22b. This fits with Kazem Bek's description, where he considers the *taqlīd* practiced by the *muqallid* generations an elevated form of the *taqlīd* of laypeople; Kazem Beg, "Notice," pp. 207–213.

77. See, for instance, the 17th-century *fatwā* by *ākhūnd* Yūnus b. Īwānāy requiring the *ʿushr* tax for Bulghar Muslims (mentioned in Chapter 2); Marjānī, *Mustafād*, ii, p. 188. See also the judgment (*ḥukm*) of the *ākhūnd* Amīr b. Nūrmuḥammad (?–after 1779), where he utilizes both Hanafi *furūʿ* and an opinion from Mālik b. Anas to settle a case regarding a woman's divorce from her missing husband (which was a particularly thorny topic in the Hanafi school); Fakhr al-Dīn, *Āthār*, ii, p. 53; also Nathan Spannaus. "The Decline of the *Akhund* and the Transformation of Islamic Law Under the Russian Empire." *Islamic Law and Society*, vol. 20, no. 3; 2013. 202–241, pp. 209 n. 27, 210.

78. A number of his rulings are recorded in Fakhr al-Dīn, *Āthār*, ix, pp. 12–72; see also Nathan Spannaus. "Formalism, Puritanicalism, Traditionalism: Approaches to Islamic Legal

Ūriwī, it should be noted, was one of the most important figures among the Bulghar *ʿulamāʾ*, and he was deeply knowledgeable in *fiqh*. He issued *fatwās*, and he is described by Marjānī as engaging with "*fiqh* reports (*riwāyāt-i fiqhiyya*) and *furūʿ* questions (*masāʾil-i furūʿiyya*)."[79] This reasoning, however, did not constitute *ijtihād*, and Ūriwī, despite his extensive learning in Islamic law, was still considered a *muqallid*. Describing Ūriwī's stature as an *ʿālim*, Amīrkhān writes, "If the gate of *ijtihād* had not been closed, he of course would have been a *mujtahid*."[80]

Indeed, Ūriwī was a staunch proponent of *taqlīd*, and he flatly rejected the permissibility of *ijtihād*. He held that it allowed for incoherence in the law by not limiting the potential responses to any legal question. Moreover, to carry out *ijtihād* is to disregard the established scholars of earlier eras, while following them through *taqlīd* is equivalent to following the prophets.[81] Accordingly, he criticizes Qūrṣāwī for his support of *ijtihād*, and his 1810 letter to Mufti Muḥammadjān seeking Qūrṣāwī's removal gives "claiming to be a *mujtahid*" (*mujtahidlik daʿwāsinī qīlūb*) first among his religious errors.[82]

ʿIshāʾ

The question of the *ʿishāʾ* prayer was part of this conflict over *taqlīd*. Qūrṣāwī, as noted, considered the timing of the prayer a matter for *ijtihād*, but Ūriwī—as well as the majority of Bulghar *ʿulamāʾ*—held that there was no question at all, since the proper approach to the prayer had been settled among most Hanafi *fuqahāʾ*: it should not be performed in the short summer nights at extreme latitudes because its proper time—the disappearance of twilight (*shafaq*)—never arrives. And because the proper time was considered the determining cause (*sabab*) or condition (*sharṭ*) for each of the five daily prayers, its lack of occurrence meant *ʿishāʾ* was not obligatory in summer (that is, because twilight

---

Reasoning in the 19th-Century Russian Empire." *Muslim World*, vol. 104, no. 3; 2014. 354–378, esp. pp. 372–374.

79. Marjānī, *Mustafād*, ii, p. 193; Ramzī, *Talfiq*, ii, p. 367.

80. "*Agar bāb-i ijtihād masdūd dīmasik albatta mujtahidlardān ūlmaqī*"; Ḥusayn Amīrkhān. *Tawārīkh-i bulghāriyya*. Kazan: Maṭbaʿat Wiyācheslāf, 1883. [Reprinted with Russian translation as Khusain Amirkhanov. *Tavarikh-e Bulgariia (Bulgarskie khroniki)*. Intro. and trans. A. M. Akhunov. Moscow: izd-vo Mardzhani, 2010], p. 42.

81. Ūriwī, [Untitled], fol. 1a; Ūriwī, *Risāla*, fols. 36a–36b; Fakhr al-Dīn, *Āthār*, iii, pp. 108–109.

82. Fakhr al-Dīn, *Āthār*, iii, p. 108.

does not disappear, the necessary conditions for the prayer's performance do not come about).[83]

Qūrṣāwī objects to this view on epistemological grounds. Separating the prayer's obligation (*wujūb*) from its timing, he argues that the latter is merely one of the conditions signaling its proper performance.[84] The obligation to perform *ʿishāʾ*, like all daily prayers, is known, backed by multiple *mutawātir* hadith. As *mutawātir* sources convey certain knowledge, they are stronger than legal interpretation (*qiyās*), and therefore the *fiqh* determination that the coming of the correct time is the prayer's cause—at times a point of controversy among Hanafis—cannot contravene the obligation to perform the prayer every day.[85]

Beyond asserting the scriptural basis for the prayer's obligation, Qūrṣāwī also criticizes the rationale behind the argument for its omission. Even if time is an element of an obligation, he writes, there are conditions for how and when to fulfill it that require specification (*taʿayyun/taʿyīn*) for particular circumstances. But those circumstances do not affect the underlying obligation, which comes from divine commandment (*amr*). (He gives the example of travelers, for whom the timing and performance of daily prayers are altered, but the prayers are nevertheless obligatory.)[86] Moreover, conditions for prayer times—like the disappearance of twilight—are merely signs (*ʿalāmāt*) for

83. The issue hinged on the understanding of a prophetic hadith that the prayer should be performed after the disappearance of twilight (*ghaybūbat al-shafaq*); e.g., *Ṣaḥīḥ Bukhārī*, i:x, no. 544; cf. Qūrṣāwī, *Irshād*, pp. 57–58. Hanafis from various regions and eras disagreed as to the meaning of *shafaq*, but also over the relationship between this astronomical point and the performance of the prayer. Since the 12th–13th centuries, however, most Volga-Ural scholars had adopted the view that the disappearance of twilight signified the complete darkening of the night sky, which does not occur in the region year-round (also confusing the timing of the *fajr* prayer, which falls before dawn). With no arrival of the allotted time for the prayer in summer, there was no obligation to perform it; Michael Kemper. *Sufis und Gelehrte in Tatarien und Baschkirien, 1789–1889: Der islamische Diskurs unter russischer Herrschaft*. Berlin: Klaus Schwarz Verlag, 1998, pp. 278–282; see Shams al-Dīn Quhistānī's (?–1546) *Jāmiʿ al-rumūz*, a Hanafi *furūʿ* work popular in the Volga-Ural region, which directly (and approvingly) mentions the omission of the prayer among Bulghars; Shams al-Dīn Muḥammad al-Quhistānī. *Jāmiʿ al-rumūz*. Intro. Qāḍīzāda Sharīf Makhdūm. Kazan: Maṭbaʿat Kūkūbīn 1299 [1882], pp. 69–70.

84. Qūrṣāwī, *Irshād*, pp. 57, 59.

85. Ibid., pp. 58–60; Qūrṣāwī, [Prayer], fols. 3b–4a; cf. Qūrṣāwī, *Sharḥ Manār*, p. 81.

86. Cf. Qūrṣāwī, *Sharḥ Manār*, pp. 33–35, also 42. This discussion here is not made in explicit reference to the *ʿishāʾ* debate, but rather is part of an extensive analysis of the relationship between time and the performance of religious obligations, such as hajj and Ramadan, and (more broadly) the fulfillment of obligations per se. He does raise this point specifically for the prayer in Qūrṣāwī, *Irshād*, p. 59.

performing it, to aid believers in fulfilling their obligations. The obligations, however, are themselves distinct: "The causes (*asbāb*) of religious prescriptions (*mashrūʿāt*) in reality refer to the Lawgiver's [act of] obligation (*ījāb al-shāriʿ*), not that they truly entail the obligation [itself]."[87] Time is not a cause of an obligation, even if timing affects and limits its correct fulfillment.[88]

The continual duty to perform *ʿishāʾ* is therefore inarguable, as it is known by certain scriptural proof. But the particular circumstances in summer in the Volga-Ural region render its precise timing a matter of interpretation—a question, he writes explicitly, to be settled through *ijtihād*, which is both warranted and necessary as the established view is clearly flawed and untenable.[89] (He makes a similar point about the necessity of holding congregational prayers wherever possible, which Abū Ḥanīfa himself believed should be performed only in or near cities [*amṣār*] with Muslim governors and judges. Establishing the prayers' obligation through Qurʾan, hadith, and consensus, he then argues that, without such cities in the region, it becomes a matter of *ijtihād* to determine how this obligation should be fulfilled.)[90]

Here the link for Qūrṣāwī between *ijtihād* and *taḥqīq* becomes apparent. Interrogating the extant position on *ʿishāʾ*, he finds it incorrect, both on scriptural-*cum*-epistemological grounds and in terms of legal theory. This is *taḥqīq* at work, in the verification of scholarship. But the rejection of a widely held view necessitates its replacement with a sound position, conforming to what is certain and falling within the limits for interpretation and acceptable disagreement—that is, a position articulated through *ijtihād*.

Rethinking *Taqlīd*

The objections to Qūrṣāwī's stance on *ʿishāʾ* followed a generally conservative tack, holding to the generally accepted position as the necessarily correct one. This is, respectively, Ūriwī and Baymurād Mangārī's argument, and it is also the one put forward by ʿAbd al-Raḥīm Ūtiz-Īmānī, who went into great detail

87. Qūrṣāwī, *Irshād*, p. 58.

88. Qūrṣāwī, *Sharḥ Manār*, p. 33.

89. Qūrṣāwī, [Prayer], fols. 3b–4a; Qūrṣāwī, *Irshād*, p. 59.

90. Qūrṣāwī, *Irshād*, pp. 61–62; cf. Michael Kemper. "Imperial Russia as Dar al-Islam? Nineteenth-Century Debates on Ijtihad and Taqlid Among the Volga Tatars." *Encounters: An International Journal for the Study of Culture and Society*, vol. 6; 2015. 95–124, pp. 114–118. On this issue, see Quhistānī, *Jāmiʿ al-rumūz*, esp. pp. 159–163, 167.

regarding the history of the position in the Hanafi school in a work directed against Qūrṣāwī.[91]

But Ūtiz-Īmānī's view, though overlapping with that of scholars such as Ūriwī, had quite different underlying premises. Rather than simply the straightforward adherence to a prevailing position, it was part of a sweeping, radical stance on *taqlīd* and its practical application: rejecting any possibility for *ijtihād*, he argued that Muslims in later periods must follow established *furūʿ* to ensure correct action. For him, the *corpus juris* of a *madhhab* represented the locus of legal authority. The content of *furūʿ* texts had been accepted over centuries by the community, and Muslims could depend on them for guidance. *Ijtihād*, by contrast, led to results that were uncertain and prone to error and deviation.[92] Moreover, Ūtiz-Īmānī maintained, in response to Qūrṣāwī, that *mujtahids* had long disappeared by this time, and so *taqlīd* of an eponymous founder was an absolute obligation (*farḍ*).[93] Particularly in later eras, he argues, those claiming to be *mujtahids* were responsible for serious errors and misleading the people.[94] The way to prevent such misguidance was to rely only upon legal norms whose veracity had been established within the *madhhab* and the community. New legal interpretation was thus impossible and must be rejected.[95]

In order to preserve adherence to the *sharīʿa* and avoid the possibility for wrong action, Ūtiz-Īmānī held, people must abstain from anything not explicitly sanctioned as permissible. This approach, which he called "prudence" (*iḥtiyāṭ*), precluded any action whose legal acceptability might be in question or dispute; the presence of doubt or contradictory evidence regarding an act's permissibility, he argued, should lead Muslims to consider it illicit.[96] To declare something licit requires proof that is beyond mere probability, he argues, as

91. Kemper, *Sufis*, pp. 278–282; also Kemper, "Imperial Russia." On the differing views of legal authority between Qūrṣāwī and Ūtiz-Īmānī, as well as Ūriwī, in context, see Spannaus, "Formalism."

92. ʿAbd al-Raḥīm b. ʿUthmān al-Bulghārī [Ūtiz-Īmānī]. *Risāla-i Dibāghāt*. Ms. Institut iazyka literatury i istorii Akademii nauka Respublika Tatarstan (IIaLI RT), fond 39, no. 46. Facsimile printed in G. Utyz-Imiani al-Bulgari. *Izbrannoe*. Ed. R. Adygamov. Kazan: Tatarstan knizhnoe izd-vo, 2007. n.p; also Fakhr al-Dīn, *Āthār*, vi, p. 303.

93. Fakhr al-Dīn, *Āthār*, vi, pp. 308–309. Hanafis consider a *farḍ* obligation absolutely certain and beyond any doubt or ambiguity; cf. Zysow, "Economy," p. 90; see also later in this chapter.

94. Ūtiz-Īmānī, *Dibāghāt*, [p. 4].

95. Ibid., [pp. 11–12]; Fakhr al-Dīn, *Āthār*, vi, p. 309.

96. Ūtiz-Īmānī, *Dibāghāt*, [p. 9]; Kemper, *Sufis*, pp. 187–194.

"the *sharīʿa* does not definitively decide a thing [based on] probability" (*al-sharʿ lā yajzim maʿ al-iḥtimāl bi-shayʾ*).[97] In this way, impermissibility becomes the default, and he writes that "the forbidden supersedes the permitted (*al-ḥarām yaghlib ʿalā al-ḥalāl*), and the unclean (*najis*) supersedes the pure (*ṭāhir*)."[98] Even actions categorized as *mubāḥ* (morally neutral) are proscribed, he states, as they could potentially lead to transgression.[99]

Some Sufi orders, including the Mujaddidiyya, called for a similar form of asceticism for their members, and Ūtiz-Īmānī explicitly links this strict understanding of morality with the order through the writings of Aḥmad Sirhindī.[100] But Ūtiz-Īmānī holds it to be obligatory (*wājib*) for all Muslims[101]—an unquestionably radical stance, which can be understood as shaped by the contemporary circumstances in the Volga-Ural region. As he saw it, Bulghar society was in a state of moral crisis, and he criticized Muslim elites for their failure to properly serve and support the community.[102] He rejected Russian rule generally and the Spiritual Assembly specifically, and he particularly singled out the *ʿulamāʾ* for censure, denouncing them as poor scholars incapable of properly interpreting the *sharīʿa* and preoccupied with religiously dubious forms of knowledge (*kalām*, namely).[103]

His response to this situation was for lay Muslims to cease relying upon the incompetent contemporary *ʿulamāʾ* and instead follow the moral and legal guidance of earlier scholars, maintained exclusively through *taqlīd*. By adopting the positions contained in the sound collections of Hanafi *furūʿ*,

---

97. Ūtiz-Īmānī, *Dibāghāt*, [pp. 6–9].

98. Ibid., [p. 9].

99. ʿAbd al-Raḥīm b. ʿUthmān al-Bulghārī [Ūtiz-Īmānī]. *Jawāhir al-bayān*. Ms. IIaLI RT, fond 39, no. 2982. Fols. 23–87. Facsimile printed in G. Utyz-Imiani al-Bulgari. *Izbrannoe*. Ed. R. Adygamov. Kazan: Tatarstan knizhnoe izd-vo, 2007. n.p., [p. 4].

100. This approach was also inspired by the 16th-century Ottoman scholar Pīr Muḥammad Birgivī (1522–1573), whose notion of the *Ṭarīqa muḥammadiyya* was based on strict conformity to a prophetic model of behavior; cf. Ūtiz-Īmānī, *Jawāhir*; Kemper, *Sufis*, esp. pp. 185–196, 208–212.

101. Ūtiz-Īmānī, *Dibāghāt*, [pp. 8, 13].

102. ʿAbd al-Raḥīm b. ʿUthmān al-Bulghārī [Ūtiz-Īmānī]. *Risāla-i Irshādiyya*. Kazan: èlektrotipografiia Ürnäk, 1910. Reprinted in G. Utyz-Imiani al-Bulgari. *Izbrannoe*. Ed. R. Adygamov. Kazan: Tatarstan knizhnoe izd-vo, 2007.

103. E.g., ibid.; Ūtiz-Īmānī, *Dibāghāt*, [pp. 14–15]; Ūtiz-Īmānī. *Inqādh al-hālikīn min al-mutakallimīn*. This last work is unfortunately available to me only in Russian translation: G. Utyz-Imiani al-Bulgari. "Spasenie pogibaiushchikh." *Izbrannoe*. Ed. and trans. R. Adygamov. Kazan: Tatarstan knizhnoe izd-vo, 2007. 132–165; cf. also Kemper, *Sufis*, pp. 175–176, 196–199.

in combination with strict prudence and avoidance of anything whose permissibility was not certain, laypeople could maintain their own adherence to the *sharīʿa* through *taqlīd*, separate from the *ʿulamāʾ*'s flawed and uncertain interpretations.

This stance renders Muslims' correct behavior a solely individual responsibility, to the exclusion of the *ʿulamāʾ*, who, in Ūtiz-Īmānī's estimation, could no longer serve as moral guides for the community. For him, this shift toward the individual was made necessary by the circumstances in Bulghar society and the *ʿulamāʾ*'s inability to fulfill their scholarly and religious role.

In this regard, Ūtiz-Īmānī's position shares an important similarity with Qūrṣāwī's view on *ijtihād*, which likewise focuses on the individual. By arguing that *ijtihād* is obligatory upon everyone, not merely scholars, and by putting forward types of legal reasoning expressly for laypeople, Qūrṣāwī lessens the need for reliance on the *ʿulamāʾ*, thereby shifting the necessary exercise of *fiqh* away from scholars to the broader community.

Although the two take diametrically opposed positions on legal interpretation, the similarity between their stances reflects the fact that both are responding to the shortcomings of the contemporary *ʿulamāʾ* (of whom they each offer harsh criticism) and the marginalization of Islamic institutions under Russian rule. Convinced that the *ʿulamāʾ* could not fulfill their moral and legal functions within society, each scholar sought a way to maintain the community's correct adherence to the *sharīʿa*: Ūtiz-Īmānī seized upon the established body of *furūʿ* as the repository of legitimate legal guidance, while Qūrṣāwī, by contrast, put forward *uṣūl*, arguing that the continuous exercise of legal interpretation serves as the valid link between the community and its scriptural foundations.

The Social Function of Ijtihād

The focus for Qūrṣāwī is the determination of correct principles that can be acted upon. This comes through equally in the *Irshād* and in the *Sharḥ Manār*, the latter of which is almost entirely devoted to hermeneutical techniques for deriving evidence (*dalīl*) for action from scripture. This is the essence of *ijtihād*, which Qūrṣāwī equates with all legal reasoning, and which must be continually carried out to ensure the community's moral and religious well-being.

This form of hermeneutic (which, Zysow points out, was particularly sophisticated and subtle in the Hanafi school, due to its emphasis on formalistic interpretation)[104] required a certain degree of learning, not only in terms of

104. Zysow, "Economy," pp. 89, 91.

fiqh but also in areas such as Arabic grammar and lexicography. Consequently, interpretive activity was traditionally the domain of legal scholars who had the time and training to elaborate and develop this method and also to employ and apply it in order to formulate interpretations and judgments for cases as they arose in their myriad permutations. This was the essential social function that *fuqahāʾ* served, to determine correct action through the exercise of *ijtihād* and "communicate the mundane results of their legal constructions" to the people, which, Hallaq writes, gave *fiqh* its existential purpose.[105] The duty to interpret and articulate the law was almost universally recognized as a *farḍ kifāya*, a collective obligation that must be carried out for the society as a whole. Ghazālī in the *Iḥyāʾ* likens *fiqh* in this way to medicine, in that both are necessary for the health of the community.[106]

Imperial Islamic Institutions

For Volga-Ural Muslims, this obligation on behalf of the community was discharged by the *ākhūnds*. But, as we have seen, the *ākhūnds* in the 18th century faced a number of restrictions upon their religious and legal authority, and by 1800 the function of Islamic law within Bulghar society had been transformed at the hands of the tsarist state. The most salient way in which the law had been altered was the marginalization of the *ākhūnds* and their traditional role as legal experts. In the 1750s their ability to rule on legal disputes (*qaḍāʾ*) was severely curtailed, limited only to areas of family law. With the founding of the Spiritual Assembly, even this restricted *qaḍāʾ* was further changed as they were forced into an appellate role, with their position as the foremost legal authorities usurped by the Mufti, who was chosen more for his loyalty and political acumen than for his qualifications as a jurist (which were at best minimal).

On the other hand, issuing *fatwās* (*iftāʾ*), which was a much more informal process, remained within the *ākhūnds*' capabilities. An imam, too, could issue *fatwās*, if a Muslim deemed him learned enough to request one from him. But this aspect of Islamic law was also subjected to disruption by social circumstances. Although not specifically directed at the practice of *iftāʾ*, state interference weakened Islamic legal institutions of all kinds, whose function relied upon their authoritativeness and comprehensiveness in the eyes of Muslims. *Iftāʾ*, of course, traditionally played a central role within the holistic

---

105. Hallaq, "Ifta'," p. 32.

106. Ghazālī, *Iḥyāʾ*, i, p. 34.

entity of Islamic law, and, Hallaq notes, was intimately connected with that of *qaḍāʾ*.[107] (This is particularly true with the pre-Assembly *ākhūnds*, as *qaḍāʾ* and *iftāʾ* were combined within their duties.)[108] Any drastic change to *qaḍāʾ*—and the foundation of the Spiritual Assembly brought with it many—would necessarily lead to changes within *iftāʾ*. (On the broader ramifications for legal discourse, see Chapters 8 and 9.)

It is difficult to overstate the impact of these developments for the application of Islamic law within society. Not only did the incorporation of Islamic institutions into imperial governing structures introduce the element of the coercive state into the Muslim communities under its rule—which itself has had immense consequences for the practice and function of Islamic law—but this particular coercive state had little interest in upholding the norms of the *sharīʿa*.[109] Thus was created for Muslims a significant, even predominant social space external to Islamic law, to say nothing of a societal order whose social and legal puissance far outstripped that of Islamic institutions. Combined with the marginalization of legal experts within the religious hierarchy and the bureaucratization of scholars, this left the *ʿulamāʾ* with a drastically altered (to say nothing of reduced) position within society.

The Preservation of the *Sharīʿa*

Qūrṣāwī's stance on *ijtihād* can be seen as a response to these shifts.[110] Through the government's actions, a constituent element of the Islamic legal

---

107. Wael Hallaq. *Shari'a: Theory, Practice, Transformations.* New York: Cambridge UP, 2009, esp. pp. 159–221; see also Baber Johansen. *Contingency in a Sacred Law: Legal and Ethical Norms in the Muslim* Fiqh. "The Muslim *Fiqh* as a Sacred Law." Leiden: Brill, 1999. 1–76.

108. Cf. Spannaus, "Decline," esp. pp. 204–205, 209–210.

109. It did have *some* interest, as the imperial government attempted to co-opt adherence to the *sharīʿa* as loyalty to the state; cf. Robert Crews. *For Prophet and Tsar: Islam and Empire in Russia and Central Asia.* Cambridge, MA: Harvard UP, 2005. For a discussion of the interaction between the modern state and Islamic legal structures, see Hallaq, *Shari'a*, pp. 357–370.

110. Kemper puts forward Ghazālī as a possible inspiration for Qūrṣāwī's call for obligatory *ijtihād*, writing that Ghazālī in the *Mustaṣfā* also holds that *ijtihād* is required for whomever is capable; Kemper, *Sufis*, p. 275. Ghazālī, while stating that *mujtahids* are forbidden from *taqlīd* and must perform *ijtihād*, writes that a layperson (*ʿāmmī*) may became learned enough to carry out *ijtihād*, but he would not be compelled (*yulzim*) to do so; Abū Ḥāmid Muḥammad al-Ghazālī. *al-Mustaṣfā fī ʿilm al-uṣūl.* 2 vols. Baghdad: Maktabat al-muthannā, 1970. [Reprint, 1324 Būlāq edition], ii, p. 384. This seems to me a very different—and much more conventional—proposition than Qūrṣāwī's, which states that *ijtihād* is obligatory for everyone, and the degree to which they are to carry out *ijtihād* is then determined by their ability.

system—the *ʿulamāʾ*—was marginalized, and their ability to carry out their sociolegal function was altered, restricted, and undermined. Within the state religious hierarchy, educated *faqīh*s were limited in number, power, and competency, reduced to applying the *sharīʿa* only insofar as it aligned with the purposes of the imperial government.

Simply put, if the *ʿulamāʾ* were no longer capable of sufficiently carrying out the *farḍ kifāya* of administering the *sharīʿa* for the Bulghar Muslim community, something would have to take up this essential duty. And this duty was essential.[111] Qūrṣāwī viewed the failure to maintain legal interpretation as placing all members of the community in moral compromise. He writes in the *Irshād* that if the most learned scholar of a country is incapable of *ijtihād* or *tarjīḥ*, he must instead recount in toto the positions of the founder of his *madhhab*. Such a scholar, Qūrṣāwī notes, cannot be considered a *muftī*, as he merely transmits others' opinions.[112] He is thus rendered an utter *muqallid*, incapable of offering the necessary legal guidance to the community. This, according to Qūrṣāwī, has significant negative ramifications, since the lack of a *mujtahid* separates the community from the meanings of scripture and results in the spread of ignorance.[113]

The discussion of the absence of *mujtahid*s speaks directly to the situation among Bulghar Muslims, and it is perhaps telling that it is preceded in the *Irshād* by a discussion of the ignorance of a Muslim living outside the *dār al-Islām*.[114] Although Qūrṣāwī clearly considers the Volga-Ural region part of the *dār al-Islām*, he sees the *ʿulamāʾ* as the community's rightful leaders, and measures undertaken by the Russian government toward its Muslim subjects made the disappearance of *fiqh* experts a distinct possibility.[115]

---

111. In the Hanafi school, there is a distinction between obligations that are *farḍ* and *wājib*, with failure to fulfill the former linked with nonbelief (*kufr*). (A *wājib* obligation is of a lesser status, and its nonperformance does not remove one beyond the pale of Islam); Kevin Reinhart. "'Like the Difference Between Heaven and Earth': Hanafi and Shafiʿi Discussions of *Wajib* and *Fard*." *Studies in Islamic Law and Society*. Ed. Bernard Weiss. Leiden: Brill, 2002. 205–234; Zysow, "Economy," p. 90.

112. Qūrṣāwī, *Irshād*, p. 31.

113. Ibid., p. 29.

114. Ibid., pp. 28–29.

115. Qūrṣāwī in fact argues in the *Sharḥ jadīd* that the *ʿulamāʾ* fulfill the role of the Imam (i.e., caliph); Qūrṣāwī, *Sharḥ jadīd*, fol. 141b. Ūtiz-Īmānī, for his part, considers the Russian Empire *Dār al-ḥarb*, linking this view in part with the *ʿulamāʾ*'s shortcomings; Ramzī, *Talfīq*, ii, pp. 360–361; cf. Kemper, *Sufis*, p. 296; also Kemper, "Imperial Russia."

However, if *ijtihād* is obligatory (*wājib*) upon everyone, the performance of the *farḍ kifāya* to interpret and apply the law devolves from the *ʿulamāʾ* to the community *collectively*, rather than resting with the *ʿulamāʾ* to carry it out *on the community's behalf*. The performance of legal interpretation remains incumbent, but its performance is ensured by the obligation on the individual level.

Such a stance reshapes the nature of the relationship between the *ʿulamāʾ* and the community. Traditionally, the former articulated, interpreted, and applied the law on behalf of the latter, who were by definition *muqallids*, bound to follow the *ijtihād* of a jurist or *madhhab*.[116] By rendering *ijtihād* an individual obligation, however, Qūrṣāwī makes its exercise not the domain of a select segment of the *ʿulamāʾ* (i.e., *mujtahids*) but something taken up by *all* educated Muslims, blurring the line separating the *ʿulamāʾ* from the community as a whole.

Importantly, however, the application and elaboration of the *sharīʿa* are not changed for Qūrṣāwī, whose reform does not concern the construction of *fiqh* itself. Rather, he understands the exercise of *ijtihād* as falling within the hermeneutical framework of the *madhhab*, with a conventional view of *uṣūl al-fiqh*. In his promotion of *ijtihād* as an individual obligation, Qūrṣāwī is putting forward Hanafi formalism as a means for preserving the practice of the *sharīʿa* in light of the weakening of the *ʿulamāʾ* and the changes in their function. The critical interpretation and elaboration of the *sharīʿa* by the *ʿulamāʾ* for the community, being unfeasible, is replaced by the collective exercise of *ijtihād* by individuals for themselves. In this way, the master rule of *uṣūl al-fiqh* is utilized in the preservation of the community's religious and moral standing, providing a way to ensure the continued interpretation and application of Islamic law.

In fact, Qūrṣāwī's stance could be seen as markedly beneficial for the community's adherence to the *sharīʿa*. As already noted, within Hanafi formalism it is the application of the hermeneutic of *fiqh*—the exercise of *ijtihād*—that conveys validity and legitimacy upon the results of legal interpretation. Therefore, the result of any and all individual acts of *ijtihād* is necessarily valid and constitutes a concrete part of the *sharīʿa*. Furthermore, *ijtihād* as a vehicle for legal reasoning exists for the derivation of norms that can be acted upon. (Qūrṣāwī frequently emphasizes this practical aspect.) As such, once an individual act of *ijtihād* has been completed—once the person exercising *ijtihād*

116. Bernard Weiss. "The Madhhab in Islamic Legal Theory." *The Islamic School of Law: Evolution, Devolution, and Progress*. Eds. Peri Bearman et al. Cambridge, MA: Harvard UP, 2005. 1–9, p. 4.

has done so to the fullest extent—the result reached is considered to be the correct course of action, insofar as *ijtihād* carried out to the fullest extent necessarily results in a prevailing opinion (*ghalabat al-ẓann*) that the right answer to the issue at hand has been ascertained. Since the person exercising *ijtihād* must believe that the answer is correct, they must then act on it.[117] Indeed, Qūrṣāwī writes that, if lacking sound evidence on a given legal issue, a person is obliged to act according to the "proof of the heart" (*dalīl al-qalb*)—the view they truly feel is correct.[118]

Thus, every single act of *ijtihād* results in a course of action that can be considered valid within the *sharīʿa and* which must be carried out. In holding *ijtihād* to be obligatory upon everyone, Qūrṣāwī is not only creating a way for lay Muslims to exercise legal reasoning on their own (in light of the *ʿulamāʾ*'s marginalization) but also ensuring that they act in accordance with the *sharīʿa*.

That was not an insignificant concern, given the community's standing under the rule of a powerful non-Muslim state. This sort of formalism provided a means for reasserting the *sharīʿa* within the social space from which it had been excluded by the government. As Jackson writes:

> [*Uṣūl al-fiqh*'s] essential function is to establish and maintain the parameters of a discourse via which views can be validated by rendering them identifiably *legal*, both in the sense of passing muster as acceptable (if not true) embodiments of scriptural intent *and* in the sense of being rendered distinct from views that are, say, scientific, ideological or simply pragmatic.[119]

In this way, a Bulghar Muslim who for instance conducts his business affairs in accordance with principles derived from scripture through *ijtihād* is necessarily acting within the framework of Islamic law, even though his business dealings are officially not subject to Islamic law or any Islamic institution. Therefore, by insisting upon the obligation of both applying *uṣūl al-fiqh* and acting upon the results, Qūrṣāwī is requiring reasoning and action that are necessarily connected with the *sharīʿa*.

---

117. Qūrṣāwī, *Irshād*, p. 2; cf. Kamali, *Principles*, p. 472.

118. Qūrṣāwī, *Sharḥ Manār*, p. 41. Interestingly, the copyist of the manuscript has highlighted this point in the margin.

119. Sherman A. Jackson. "Fiction and Formalism: Toward a Functional Analysis of *Usul al-fiqh*." *Studies in Islamic Legal Theory*. Ed. Bernard Weiss. Leiden: Brill, 2002. 177–204, pp. 178–179; emphasis in original.

Alongside his call for individual *ijtihād* was Qūrṣāwī's broader push for the epistemological reform of legal discourse, with both oriented toward the continuous articulation of the law and maintaining the necessary link between it and the texts of revelation. The possibility of absolute *ijtihād* plays an important role here as necessary for proper adherence to the *sharīʿa*. It comprises both primary legal reasoning and *taḥqīq*, and, although Qūrṣāwī does not state this explicitly, the continued existence of absolute *mujtahids* seems to serve for him as a needed corrective for the practice of *fiqh*, to prevent the proliferation of errors and deviation through *taqlīd*. This is linked with the notion of *tajdīd*, which (tellingly) Qūrṣāwī understands in terms of *uṣūl al-fiqh*. For him, *tajdīd* involves uniting "the sciences (*ʿulūm*) of the Book, Sunna, consensus, and the ways of *qiyās* (*ṭuruq al-muqāyas* [sic])," leading to the elimination of *bidʿa*.[120] Absolute *mujtahids* serve to preserve and reassert the master rule of *ijtihād* for the betterment of the community. Qūrṣāwī writes that it is a *farḍ kifāya* to prevent deviation from the Qurʾan and spread true knowledge of the religion, and in this respect absolute *mujtahids* (whether *mujaddids* or not) and the obligatory exercise of *ijtihād* play an essential role.[121] (Qūrṣāwī, it should be noted, at no point refers to himself as a *mujaddid*, even if others, including Marjānī, did.)[122]

Other 18th-century figures presented their reformist projects in terms of *tajdīd*, and there is significant overlap between their views toward *ijtihād* and Qūrṣāwī's, which are all based on the belief that juristic and scholarly constructions are not sufficient for ensuring scriptural correctness and that the renewed exercise of *ijtihād* is necessary for maintaining the link between the community and the texts of revelation. Although they shared this underlying motivation for reform, the specific approaches they put forward are quite distinct, reflecting their differing intellectual orientations and shaped by their diverse environments and circumstances. (See Chapter 7.)

We can to a degree separate Qūrṣāwī's call for *tajdīd* and the renewed exercise of *ijtihād*, which are based on concerns internal to scholarly discourse, from his stance that *ijtihād* is an obligation upon everyone, which is a response to the transformation of Islamic institutions by the Russian imperial state. The latter is nevertheless consistent with the former, as both pertain to

---

120. Qūrṣāwī, *Irshād*, p. 29.

121. Qūrṣāwī, *Sharḥ jadīd*, fol. 96a.

122. Marjānī, *Tanbīh*, p. 382; also Fakhr al-Dīn, *Āthār*, viii, pp. 477–478.

the importance of the *ʿulamāʾ* and scholarly tradition in providing religious guidance for the community. Although he relies upon established aspects of Hanafi scholarship in his reformism, the social circumstances in which Bulghar Muslims found themselves at the beginning of the 19th century were such that maintaining legal discourse unchanged had become unfeasible. Indeed, faced with the threat to the application of the *sharīʿa* that the marginalization of the *ʿulamāʾ* presented and the potential nonfulfillment of the attendant *farḍ kifāya*, Qūrṣāwī offered a radical reformulation of who can carry out *ijtihād*, forgoing the predictability in the elaboration of the *sharīʿa* entailed by *taqlīd* in favor of the continued elaboration of the *sharīʿa* itself. (Ūtiz-Īmānī makes a similarly radical reformulation of legal authority, if in a manner opposite Qūrṣāwī's.)

Here we can see the significant social element to Qūrṣāwī's stance on *ijtihād*. With the bureaucratization and undermining of the *ʿulamāʾ*, the *farḍ kifāya* of legal reasoning devolves to Muslims on a truly individual level to ensure the continuation of normative legal discourse within their community. This is done through the application of *ijtihād* as the master rule of Islamic law. If this obligation were not fulfilled, the community's moral and religious standing would be put in doubt; thus the exercise of *ijtihād* becomes essential.

In this light, the view that *ijtihād* is obligatory can be seen as a response to historical circumstances, necessitated by the impact of tsarist policies on the community's religious institutions. It is also grounded in the underlying foundation of Qūrṣāwī's thought—the moral imperative of basing belief and action upon certain sources of knowledge. *Ijtihād* therefore serves as the method for determining proper action and maintaining adherence to the *sharīʿa*. In order to promote the exercise of legal reasoning and scriptural interpretation, Qūrṣāwī argues for the removal of restrictions on scholars' autonomy, while putting forward ways for lay Muslims to engage in their own legal interpretation and determine their own actions based on sound religious knowledge.

This stance is deeply grounded in Hanafism and its *uṣūl* paradigm. Despite his misgivings about the *ʿulamāʾ*, it is clear that Qūrṣāwī considers the Islamic scholarly tradition to be the best—or, perhaps more accurately, the only—way for the *sharīʿa* to be put into practice. Indeed, the notion that the law could be elaborated by any means other than *uṣūl al-fiqh* would have been unthinkable to Qūrṣāwī. Rather, the interpretive method of *ijtihād* is the medium through which the *sharīʿa* is made manifest in society.

His reformism thus does not represent a rethinking or alteration of *fiqh* itself, but rather an adaptation of how it is articulated and applied in a changed context, in order to continue to serve the community's moral needs. As an essential part of any Muslim society, maintaining the framework for the elaboration of the *sharīʿa*—the scholarly tradition—becomes imperative, and the radical reformulation of the relationship between the *ʿulamāʾ* and the community becomes warranted.

5

The Question of the Divine Attributes

QŪRṢĀWĪ'S INSISTENCE ON sound religious knowledge is asserted most strongly in his discussions on theology. He considers belief (the domain of theology) to require more certainty than action (the domain of law), as errors in belief were seen as far more serious and far more morally harmful than errors in legal interpretation. Accordingly, a narrower range of sources was allowed in theology in order to ensure certainty, excluding some sources acceptable for *fiqh* because they convey only probable, rather than definite, knowledge.[1] There was also a far smaller scope for legitimate disagreement in terms of belief, as any position had to be known as certain, precluding other possibilities with less sound backing. There was no theological equivalent of the idea that "every *mujtahid* is correct."

The implications of the epistemological critique that underpins Qūrṣāwī's reformism are thus more evident regarding *kalām*. Aside from his view on *ʿishāʾ*, which is a relatively minor concern within his writings, he takes issue primarily with the predominant approach to legal reasoning, rather than any particular substantive positions. With *kalām*, however, he in equal measure criticizes the methodology utilized in theological interpretation and rejects certain widespread beliefs as incorrect. He argues that the speculative nature of *kalām* renders it unacceptable for determining matters of belief. He considers *kalām* to be based primarily on reason rather than on sound scriptural sources, and therefore not productive of the requisite certainty. As such, it predisposes the *mutakallimīn*, who formulate opinions about God and His

1. Such as *qiyās* and *āḥād* reports; Qūrṣāwī, *Naṣāʾiḥ*, fols. 19a, 21a; Qūrṣāwī, *Mabāḥith*, fol. 170a.

nature and essence based on rational speculation, to profess opinions unfounded in scripture and *naql*.[2]

For Qūrṣāwī, nowhere have the *mutakallimīn* gone so wrong as on the question of the divine attributes. He saw the prevailing orthodoxy on the issue—expressed in Saʿd al-Dīn Taftāzānī's commentary on the *ʿAqāʾid nasafiyya*, ubiquitous in Central Asian and Volga-Ural scholarly circles—as absolutely incorrect, rejecting points of it as both scripturally unfounded and logically and philosophically untenable. It was Qūrṣāwī's attacks on this position that led to his condemnation at the hands of the Bukharan *ʿulamāʾ*, who accused him of holding heretical beliefs on the subject.

A central issue in the theological tradition, the attributes held a place of prominence in Sunni scholarship and religious identity. But Qūrṣāwī did not reject the basic Sunni position. Despite this (highly) critical posture, his stance on the attributes, and his theological views in general, are firmly grounded within the Hanafi-Maturidi *kalām* tradition. As with *fiqh*, this tradition represented for him the only legitimate framework in which matters of belief could be articulated and justified, and his critiques fall not on the tradition itself but rather on those aspects of *kalām* reasoning that he believed to be erroneous, lacking scriptural basis, and in violation of the central tenets of the religion. His own stance on the attributes conforms entirely to the principles of Sunni *kalām*.

Qūrṣāwī's Critique

Dating back to the 9th century, the Sunni view of the attributes was that they are real, eternal, and distinct from the divine essence, of which they are predicated.[3] Qūrṣāwī adhered to this general position, but within it there was considerable room for interpretation, and its precise contours shifted significantly over the centuries. Qūrṣāwī's critique revolves around the question of the attributes' distinctiveness. For him, Taftāzānī presented the attributes as so distinct from the divine essence that they risked being seen as multiple eternal entities separate from God, thus violating *tawḥīd* (divine oneness).[4] Though the

2. Cf. Qūrṣāwī, *Naṣāʾiḥ*, fol. 19a.

3. Robert Wisnovsky. "Avicenna and the Avicennian Tradition." *The Cambridge Companion to Arabic Philosophy*. Eds. Peter Adamson and Richard C. Taylor. New York: Cambridge UP, 2005. 92–136, p. 121.

4. That it was Taftāzānī's understanding of the attributes that was at issue for both sides of this debate is evident. In Qūrṣāwī's commentary on the *Nasafiyya*, he makes his attacks on Taftāzānī explicit; Qūrṣāwī, *Sharḥ jadīd*, fol. 92b; transcription and translation in Nathan

standard view was unproblematic for many scholars—as the rebuttals against him clearly show—Qūrṣāwī rejected parts of it outright, putting forward instead his own understanding that lessened the attributes' distinctiveness. This understanding emphasized God's oneness in both of its aspects—uniqueness and simplicity—and His transcendence (*tanzīh*).[5]

Qūrṣāwī's critique, however, does not constitute a radical reformulation of the attributes' status. Rather, it is primarily couched in terms laid out in the *ʿAqāʾid nasafiyya*. (Qūrṣāwī held its author, Najm al-Dīn Nasafī, in particularly high regard.) In the work, Nasafī affirms the attributes' reality and eternality, writing that "He [God] has eternal attributes subsisting in His essence (*wa-lahu ṣifāt azaliyya qāʾima bi-dhātih*)." Nasafī goes on to describe their distinctiveness in relation to the divine essence, stating that "they are neither it nor other than it (*lā huwa wa-lā ghayruh*)."[6] This formula, developed in the 8th century, denies both that the attributes are one and the same with the essence (a concept labeled *ʿayniyya*) and that they are entirely other (its opposite, *ghayriyya*), and it became a central element in the Sunni conception of the attributes.[7]

Both Taftāzānī and Qūrṣāwī accept this description of the attributes' status in their respective commentaries on Nasafī.[8] And regarding the attributes' real and eternal existence, the two are in virtual agreement. Qūrṣāwī's description, that "He has not ceased and will not cease to exist with [or in] all of His names and attributes" (*wa- huwa lam yazal wa-lā yazāl mawjūd*^{an} *bi-jamīʿ asmāʾih wa-ṣifātih*), mirrors that of Taftāzānī, who states that "God is eternal with [or in] His attributes" (*Allāhu qadīm*^{un} *bi-ṣifātih*).[9] Each of these positions resembles

---

Spannaus. "Islamic Thought and Revivalism in the Russian Empire: An Intellectual Biography of Abu Nasr Qursawi (1776–1812)." Diss. McGill University, 2012, pp. 248–249. Likewise, Dāghistānī's refutation of Qūrṣāwī doubles as an implicit defense of Taftāzānī (see *infra*).

5. Uniqueness represents God's singularity, while simplicity entails that God has no compositeness or complexity; see Wisnovsky, "Avicenna," p. 121.

6. That is, the attributes are neither identical to the essence nor other than it; Qūrṣāwī, *Sharḥ jadīd*, fols. 111a–112a; Saʿd al-Dīn al-Taftāzānī. *Sharḥ al-ʿaqāʾid al-nasafiyya*. Ed. Aḥmad Ḥijāzī al-Saqqā. Cairo: Maktabat al-Kulliyyāt al-azhariyya, 1407/1988, pp. 36–37.

7. See Daniel Gimaret, "Muʿtazila," *EI*^{2} and Wilferd Madelung, "Sulaymān b. Jarīr al-Rakkī," *EI*^{2}.

8. Qūrṣāwī, *Sharḥ jadīd*, fol. 112a; Taftāzānī, *Sharḥ*, p. 37.

9. Qūrṣāwī, *Sharḥ jadīd*, fol. 110a, also 107a. Similarly, he writes that "God is one with [or in] His attributes" (*Allāhu taʿālā wāḥid bi-ṣifātih*); Qūrṣāwī, *Risāla fī Ithbāt al-ṣifāt*. Ms. SPb IVR, no. A1241. Fols. 148b–152a, fol. 150b; cf. Taftāzānī, *Sharḥ*, p. 38.

the formula for God's eternality originated by the early Sunni theologian ʿAbd Allāh ibn Kullāb (?–855), who wrote that "He is an eternal [entity] that never ceases to be with [or in] His names and His attributes" (*wa-innahu qadīm*^{un} *lam yazal bi-asmāʾih wa-ṣifātih*).[10]

Over the precise significance of the attributes' eternality, however, they begin to differ, specifically in terms of how the attributes' eternal existence relates to God's eternal existence. The discrepancy revolves around the attributes' causal dependence. For both scholars, the attributes are necessary of existence by, or in, the divine essence (*wājibat al-wujūd bi-l-dhāt*). This formula is expressly linked with eternality, because, as Robert Wisnovsky writes, when something is described as eternal, what is really meant "is that an eternal thing *cannot possibly not exist*, and that therefore an eternal thing *is necessary of existence*."[11] According to Avicenna, entities could be grouped into three modalities of existence: the necessary, which must exist; the contingent (*mumkin*), which may or may not exist; and the impossible (*mumtaniʿ*), which cannot exist.[12] The swift adoption of the modalities into Sunni *kalām* represents the Avicennian Turn, and such a view allowed Muslim theologians to consider the divine attributes eternal without infringing upon God's uniqueness, by holding that they are necessary of existence by, or through, the divine essence. Thus, Taftāzānī writes that although the attributes are eternal, this does not violate *tawḥīd* because the attributes are causally dependent upon God.[13] As God is the only being that is necessary of existence in Himself, His uniqueness is

10. Abū al-Ḥasan al-Ashʿarī. *Maqālāt al-islāmiyyīn wa-ikhtilāf al-muṣallīn*. 2nd ed. Ed. Hellmut Ritter. Wiesbaden: Franz Steiner Verlag, 1963, p. 169. The critical common element in all of these statements is that God is eternal "bi-*ṣifātih*"; see Robert Wisnovsky. "One Aspect of the Avicennian Turn in Sunni Theology." *Arabic Sciences and Philosophy*, vol. 14; 2004. 65–100, pp. 71–75, 98.

11. Wisnovsky, "One Aspect," p. 67; emphasis in original.

12. I have chosen to translate *mumkin* (and related terms), which is usually rendered as "possible," as "contingent," because it is the attributes' causal dependence that is at issue here. The distinction is based on the terms of the debate. As we will see, *mumkin* and *mumtaniʿ* are conceptually linked insofar as an entity that is possible relies on something else for its existence, rendering it impossible in itself. In other words, its existence is contingent upon something else. (See Chapter 6.) The controversy over the attributes, therefore, focuses on the relationship between necessity as causal self-sufficiency and possibility as causal dependence. Thus, when Taftāzānī writes that the attributes are necessary of existence through God and possible in themselves, he is stating that the attributes are not causally self-sufficient, and their existence is contingent upon God; see Robert Wisnovsky. *Avicenna's Metaphysics in Context*. Ithaca, NY: Cornell UP, 2003, esp. pp. 212–217; Wisnovsky, "Avicenna," pp. 115–118.

13. Whereas the existence of multiple independent, eternal beings would surely violate God's uniqueness.

upheld, while the attributes, though eternal, are in themselves only contingent of existence (*mumkinat al-wujūd*), while relying upon God for their necessity and eternality.[14]

Qūrṣāwī, however, has a slightly different understanding. For him, eternality and necessity are synonymous.[15] Every eternal entity is necessary, and vice versa, so to state that the attributes are eternal but not necessary is absurd.[16] So while Taftāzānī understands the attributes as ontologically subordinate to God, Qūrṣāwī understands them to be ontologically equivalent; both God and the attributes are together necessary of existence in, or through, the divine essence. To avoid the problem of presenting the attributes as necessary, eternal entities (and thus violating *tawḥīd*), Qūrṣāwī relies on the notion that the attributes are *lā huwa wa-lā ghayruh*: if the attributes are not other than God, then they do not constitute separate entities whose existence infringes upon God's uniqueness. Likewise, they cannot be causally dependent upon the divine essence because they are not something other than the essence.

The two scholars' respective understandings of eternality are at the crux of their disagreement over the attributes, and they are present in virtually all of Qūrṣāwī's criticisms of Taftāzānī's position. In particular, this discrepancy underlies their debate over how exactly the attributes are distinct from the divine essence. Although both accept that the relationship between the attributes and the essence is *lā huwa wa-lā ghayruh*, their disagreement over how to understand this relationship is significant and unequivocal. Qūrṣāwī's critique of Taftāzānī focuses on three particular points regarding distinctiveness that he considers unacceptable implications of Taftāzānī's position and which he rejects categorically: the attributes' multiplicity (*taʿaddud*), mutual differentiation (i.e., among each other) (*mughāyara*), and superaddition to (*ziyāda ʿalā*) the divine essence. Qūrṣāwī understands these three positions, in addition to the attributes' contingency (*imkān*), as resulting in a conception of the attributes that renders them too distinct from God (*ghayriyya*). The rejection of these four points constitutes his break with Taftāzānī and thus his criticism of the established view.

---

14. Taftāzānī, *Sharḥ*, p. 38.

15. Qūrṣāwī, *Sharḥ jadīd*, fols. 104b–105a, 112a; Qūrṣāwī, *Lawāʾiḥ*, fols. 79b–80a; Qūrṣāwī, *Ithbāt*, fol. 149a; Qūrṣāwī, *Sharḥ qadīm*, fols. 17b, 18a.

16. Qūrṣāwī, *Sharḥ jadīd*, fol. 106a; Qūrṣāwī, *Lawāʾiḥ*, fol. 79a.

Contingency

As with all aspects of his theological thought, Qūrṣāwī's primary concern is upholding God's oneness and transcendence, and His eternality and necessity are essential aspects of both. He puts forward two possible definitions of the eternal: infinite precedence in time and "transcendence from time, change, and cessation . . . So there is no distinction between pre-eternality and post-eternality [with the second type], but rather [it] is first without an end and last without a beginning."[17] He explicitly links this second type of eternality with necessity, writing that "the eternal is that which has no beginning to its existence, and the necessary is that for which nonexistence is impossible . . . [so therefore] everything that is eternal is necessary."[18] God's eternality is of this type, which is an expression of His transcendence.[19]

By holding God to be eternal and necessary in this way, Qūrṣāwī is asserting two things: that God is causally independent—that is, He has no creator or originator outside of Himself—and that He cannot but exist and does not change. Neither of these claims is particularly remarkable; they are at the heart of the position that God is necessary of existence in Himself (*wājib al-wujūd bi-l-dhāt*). The issue at hand, however, is how the attributes relate to His necessity. Though both Qūrṣāwī and Taftāzānī agree with the formula that God is eternal with, or in, His attributes (*bi-ṣifātih*) and that the attributes are necessary of existence by, or on account of, the essence (*wājib al-wujūd bi-/li-l-dhāt*), Taftāzānī holds that the attributes, while still eternal, are only contingent in themselves (as noted).[20] Drawing a distinction between eternality and necessity, Taftāzānī writes (*ad "lā huwa wa-lā ghayruh"*) that

> [the attributes] are necessary by the essence of the Necessary [i.e., God], and in themself [*sic*] they are contingent. And there is no impossibility (*istiḥāla*) in the eternality of the contingent. If it subsists in the essence of the Eternal (*qā'im bi- dhāt al-qadīm*), then it is necessary by it (*wājib*[an] *lahu*) [while] not separable from it. So not every eternal [entity] is a

17. Qūrṣāwī, *Sharḥ jadīd*, fol. 106a, *ad "al-qadīm"*; transcription and translation in Spannaus, "Islamic Thought," pp. 239–242; also Qūrṣāwī, *Lawā'iḥ*, fol. 82b; Qūrṣāwī, *Sharḥ qadīm*, fol. 17b.

18. Qūrṣāwī, *Sharḥ jadīd*, fol. 106a; see also Qūrṣāwī, *Sharḥ qadīm*, fol. 18a.

19. A similar stance can be found in Abū Shukūr al-Sālimī. *Tamhīd*. Delhi: al-Maṭba' al-Fārūqī, 1309 [1892], esp. pp. 35, 36, 39.

20. Taftāzānī, *Sharḥ*, p. 38.

god, nor is the existence of [multiple] eternals or [multiple] divinities entailed [by it].[21]

Taftāzānī, by holding that the attributes are necessary by the essence of the Necessary (*wājiba li-dhāt al-wājib*) and contingent in themselves, puts forward causal dependence upon God for the attributes, thus preserving God's uniqueness.

Qūrṣāwī, for his part, accepts Taftāzānī's premise: if the attributes are contingent, then they must depend upon God for their existence, which avoids the problem of a plethora of eternal pseudo-divinities.[22] However, Qūrṣāwī rejects their contingency, and he does so based on his understanding of eternality and necessity.[23] He considers them to be equivalents (*mutasāwiyān*), and, as a result, createdness (*ḥudūth*) and contingency (*imkān*)—their respective opposites—are equivalents as well.[24] He gives a logical explanation for this position: he writes that if a thing does not exist eternally, it must come into being (be created) at some time. Likewise, if a thing does not exist necessarily, it (if it can exist at all) can only exist contingent upon another. Dependence (*iḥtiyāj*) is linked to createdness in the sense that if a thing is created, it depends upon a creator to bring it into existence. Such an entity therefore must be contingent. To think otherwise, Qūrṣāwī writes, "is an absurdity."[25]

Taftāzānī asserts that the attributes, while not necessary in themselves, are nevertheless eternal. But by Qūrṣāwī's reckoning this is impossible: if the attributes are contingent, not only must they be dependent (which Taftāzānī accepts), but they cannot be eternal, and must instead be created (which Taftāzānī rejects). Moreover, the existence of a created entity (*muḥdath*) that is *lā huwa wa-lā ghayruh* with the divine essence is a logical impossibility and wholly unacceptable.

---

21. Ibid.

22. Qūrṣāwī, *Ithbāt*, fols. 149a–149b.

23. Qūrṣāwī, *Sharḥ jadīd*, fol. 105a; Qūrṣāwī, *Ithbāt*, fols. 149a–149b; Fakhr al-Dīn, *Āthār*, iii, p. 98.

24. Qūrṣāwī, *Sharḥ jadīd*, fols. 104b–105a, 112a; Qūrṣāwī, *Lawāʾiḥ*, fols. 79b–80a; Qūrṣāwī, *Ithbāt*, fol. 149a; Qūrṣāwī, *Sharḥ qadīm*, fols. 17b, 18a.

25. Qūrṣāwī, *Mabāḥith*, fol. 166a, explicitly contra Aḥmad Sirhindī; cf. Aḥmad Sirhindī. *Maktūbāt-i imām-i rabbānī ḥaḍrat mujaddid-i alf-i thānī*. 3 vols. Ed. Nūr Aḥmad Amritsarī. Istanbul: Ishīq, 1397/1977. [Reprint (with altered pagination) of 1392/1972 Karachi edition by H. M. Saʿīd Kampanī], 2:3, pp. 18–19.

Qūrṣāwī gives many reasons for this last point. He states, first of all, that "the necessary of existence in itself [i.e., the divine essence] is necessary in all aspects" (*wājib al-wujūd bi-l-dhāt wājib^{un} min jamīʿ al-jihāt*).[26] As such, it is impossible for any created entities (*ḥādithāt*) to subsist (*qiyāma*) in it.[27] This alone would violate God's simplicity.

However, according to Qūrṣāwī, it leads to other problems with *tawḥīd*. If the attributes were contingent of existence, and thus not eternal, as far as he is concerned, they would depend upon a cause (*taḥtāj ilā al-muʾaththir*), and they must therefore be created (*ḥāditha*)—again, not eternal.[28] This is both impossible and absurd, as the divine essence is necessary in every respect.

But it also infringes upon God's transcendence. Qūrṣāwī writes that "[God] is not associated (*tushārik*) or likened (*tushābih*) to creation, either in His essence, His attributes, or His actions."[29] The existence within the divine essence of dependence, which describes created things, entails *tashbīh* (the opposite of *tanzīh*), since everything other than the essence is dependent and created.[30] Similarly, it is due to His transcendence and eternality that God is unknowable; He exists beyond any form or state that could be understood.[31] (See the section "Knowing the Essence.") On the other hand, "contingent realities" (*ḥaqāʾiq imkāniyya*), which are not eternal, can be comprehended.[32] Consequently, if the attributes are contingent, then something that subsists within the divine essence can be comprehended, rendering it like created beings.

Qūrṣāwī writes, "Every contingent [thing] is created" (*kull mumkin muḥdath*), and, since createdness and eternality are contradictories, the presence of something created (*muḥdath* or *ḥādith*) within the eternal divine essence leads to absurdities.[33] Created entities have the potential to change (*tabaddul* or *taghayyur*) due to their contingency.[34] Were it the case that created

---

26. Qūrṣāwī, *Lawāʾiḥ*, fols. 79a–79b.

27. Ibid. Since Nasafī, Taftāzānī, and Qūrṣāwī all agree that the attributes subsist in the essence, this in itself would preclude the attributes' contingency; Taftāzānī, *Sharḥ*, p. 37; Qūrṣāwī, *Sharḥ jadīd*, fol. 111b.

28. Qūrṣāwī, *Ithbāt*, fol. 149b; Qūrṣāwī, *Sharḥ qadīm*, fol. 17b.

29. Qūrṣāwī, *Lawāʾiḥ*, fol. 82b.

30. Qūrṣāwī, *Sharḥ jadīd*, fol. 105a; Qūrṣāwī, *Lawāʾiḥ*, fol. 78b; Qūrṣāwī, *Mabāḥith*, fol. 166a.

31. Qūrṣāwī, *Lawāʾiḥ*, fols. 83b, 85a.

32. Ibid., fol. 81a; also Qūrṣāwī, *Sharḥ jadīd*, fols. 116a–116b.

33. Qūrṣāwī, *Lawāʾiḥ*, fol. 78a; also Qūrṣāwī, *Sharḥ jadīd*, fol. 104b.

34. Qūrṣāwī, *Sharḥ jadīd*, fol. 104b.

entities subsist in the essence (itself violating the eternality of the essence), the essence would therefore also have the potential for change, also violating eternality.[35] Change is directly connected with existence in time—temporality—which infringes upon God's eternality as well. Qūrṣāwī writes, "'Time does not occur with Him,' since a thing's being in time is inconceivable without change of state (*tabaddul al-aḥwāl*)."[36] Thus, "it is forbidden to describe the [divine] essence and attributes with entities renewing or elapsing [in time] (*al-mutajaddidāt wa-l-munṣarimāt*), since His essence does not change and His attributes do not renew."[37]

Change is inevitable for contingent entities, and Qūrṣāwī states that "the contingent (*al-mumkin*) is required in its existence to change (*yataghayyar*), so it shifts from one condition (*shaʾn*) to another." This, he goes on to say, includes the shift from nonexistence into existence. Indeed, that which is contingent of existence is possible of nonexistence, and contingent entities are created out of nonexistence, such that, as he writes, "whatever depends on creation (*mā yataʿallaq bi-l-takwīn*) is an existent (*kāʾin*) after [its] nonexistence."[38]

Consequently, the attributes, if contingent, must have been nonexistent prior to their coming into existence. Therefore, asserting the attributes' contingency contravenes their very existence: "Even if we remove ourselves from the view that contingency in itself is pure diminution [of existence] (*naqṣ ṣarīḥ*), there is no separating avowing [the attributes'] createdness (*ḥudūth*) and denying their existence (*taʿṭīl*)."[39]

This, of course, is not Taftāzānī's aim. Upholding the attributes' real, eternal existence—the opposite of denying their existence—is one of his primary goals, and indeed, when asserting the attributes' contingency in themselves, he explicitly affirms their eternal existence in the divine essence.[40] But this eternality seems to be closer to the first type described by Qūrṣāwī, that is, infinite precedence in time.[41] Taftāzānī, who was engaged in debate with Muʿtazilites, for whom maintaining *tawḥīd* and God's transcendence required denying the attributes' existence, believed that upholding the attributes' reality

35. Qūrṣāwī, *Lawāʾiḥ*, fols. 77b–78a.

36. Qūrṣāwī, *Sharḥ jadīd*, fol. 110a, *ad "wa-lā yajrī ʿalayh zamān."*

37. Qūrṣāwī, *Lawāʾiḥ*, fol. 84a.

38. Ibid., fols. 78a–81b.

39. Ibid., fol. 79a. On *taʿṭīl*, see Louis Gardet, "Allah," *EI*².

40. Taftāzānī, *Sharḥ*, p. 38.

41. Qūrṣāwī, *Sharḥ jadīd*, fol. 106a.

and distinctiveness was paramount.[42] This was accomplished by asserting their noncreatedness (i.e., their eternality), which Taftāzānī does.[43]

Qūrṣāwī, though still conforming to the general Sunni position on the attributes, focuses on asserting *tawḥīd* and transcendence, if at the expense of the attributes' distinctiveness. Upholding their necessity (in contrast to their causal dependence upon God), and by extension their eternality, was important because it more closely links the attributes' existence with that of the essence. Qūrṣāwī writes that "the types of eternality (*nuʿūt al-qidam*) required for the essence are required for the attributes,"[44] and it is clear that his aim is upholding the transcendence of God *and* His attributes together, while still upholding the reality and distinctiveness of the latter.

By asserting that the attributes' existence is equivalent to, rather than causally dependent upon, that of the essence, Qūrṣāwī relies on the attributes' being not other than the essence, in order to avoid infringing upon God's uniqueness. Indeed, this rejection of the attributes' otherness from the essence (*ghayriyya*) underlies his entire stance on the attributes.

Distinctiveness

The remaining points on which Qūrṣāwī criticizes Taftāzānī—the attributes' multiplicity, differentiation, and superaddition—all touch upon this issue of distinctiveness and represent important aspects of the controversy surrounding Qūrṣāwī. His arguments against them follow the same lines: these, along with the attributes' contingency, must be rejected because they entail too much of a distinction between the essence and the attributes.

Taftāzānī accepts all of these points as permissible. In his commentary on Nasafī, he asserts the attributes' multiplicity and differentiation: "Disagreement among the people of the Sunna on the plurality (*kathra*) of the attributes and their multiplicity (*taʿaddud*) is inconceivable, [as is] whether or not they are differentiated [from each other] (*mutaghāyira*)."[45] He

42. As the "upholders of the attributes" (*aṣḥāb al-ṣifāt*), a label by which some Sunnis referred to themselves to contrast with the Muʿtazila, who were seen as deniers of the attributes' existence; Wisnovsky, "One Aspect," 69; Gimaret, "Muʿtazila"; Wilferd Madelung, "Taftāzānī, Saʿd al-Dīn Masʿūd b. ʿUmar," *EI*².

43. See Daniel Gimaret, "Tawḥīd (a)," *EI*².

44. Qūrṣāwī, *Sharḥ jadīd*, fols. 113b–114a.

45. Taftāzānī, *Sharḥ*, p. 38.

also asserts the superaddition of the attributes to the divine essence.[46] For Qūrṣāwī, however, upholding these three aspects entails the attributes' otherness (*ghayriyya*), thus contradicting the second clause of the formula *lā huwa wa-lā ghayruh*. This in turn entails a multiplicity of eternal entities other than God, which is of course a violation of *tawḥīd*.

Multiplicity

Though Taftāzānī is aware in his commentary of the possible implications, he warns against such an interpretation. He attempts to avoid infringing upon God's uniqueness when he asserts that the attributes are necessary through God's existence. He writes that they are "necessary through the essence of the Necessary" (*wājiba li-dhāt al-wājib*), but in themselves only contingent.[47] Since he draws a distinction between eternality and necessity, a plurality of eternal attributes does not violate *tawḥīd* because they would nevertheless be causally dependent upon God.[48] It seems that for him only a plurality of uncaused, intrinsically necessary entities would violate *tawḥīd*, and since God is the only intrinsically necessary being, His uniqueness is preserved. Thus, the attributes can be multiple. Indeed, Taftāzānī writes, affirming their multiplicity, that God has eight attributes: knowledge (*ʿilm*), power (*qudra*), life (*ḥiyāt*), hearing (*samʿ*), sight (*baṣar*), will (*irāda*), creating (*takwīn*), and speech (*kalām*).[49] (That God has eight attributes became the standard Maturidi position. The Ashʿaris held there are only seven, omitting *takwīn* as an essential attribute.)[50]

For Qūrṣāwī, however, such a view was untenable. He dispenses with the notion of the attributes numbering seven or eight, stating that there is no report (*riwāya*) or Qurʾanic verse affirming that number, nor any consensus on it.[51] (This point on the lack of consensus is well taken; Nasafī, for example, does not give a number for the attributes, and in fact lists thirteen of them.[52] Ibn Kullāb, the forefather of the Sunni position on the attributes, himself lists

46. Ibid., p. 37.

47. Ibid., p. 38.

48. Ibid., p. 30.

49. Ibid., p. 40.

50. See Claude Gilliot, "Attributes of God," *EI*³.

51. Qūrṣāwī, *Ithbāt*, fol. 151b; Qūrṣāwī, *Sharḥ jadīd*, fol. 115b; Qūrṣāwī, *Mabāḥith*, fol. 169b; Fakhr al-Dīn, *Āthār*, iii, p. 98.

52. In addition to the eight given above, he adds might (*quwwa*), volition (*mashīʾa*), activity (*fiʿl*), creation (*takhlīq*), and sustaining (*tarzīq*); Qūrṣāwī, *Sharḥ jadīd*, fol. 112b; Taftāzānī, *Sharḥ*, pp. 40–41; see also Michael Kemper. *Sufis und Gelehrte in Tatarien und Baschkirien*,

thirty.)[53] But more important than the specific number for Qūrṣāwī is the negation of the attributes' multiplicity (*taʿaddud*), belief in which he calls "delusion" (*tawahhum*).[54]

The problem with multiplicity is that it violates God's uniqueness; since the divine essence is singular, the divine attributes cannot be many, as they are *lā huwa wa- lā ghayruh*. This formula, according to Qūrṣāwī, negates their multiplicity absolutely, because to uphold their multiplicity is to contravene *lā ghayruh*.[55] And, were they other than God, this would entail the existence of multiple eternal, pseudo-divine entities, a clear contradiction of monotheism.[56]

It was this reason that led the Muʿtazila to deny the attributes' real existence as distinct entities.[57] Qūrṣāwī accepts the Muʿtazilite premise that confirming the multiplicity of the attributes entails multiple eternal, pseudo-divine entities, while at the same time denying that the confirmation of the attributes' existence as *lā huwa wa-lā ghayruh* does so as well.[58] Taftāzānī, for his part, states that this violation of *tawḥīd* is not entailed by the attributes' multiplicity, which he upholds.[59] But Qūrṣāwī rejects this stance and explicitly blames the later Ashʿaris for inventing it.[60]

The presence of multiplicity within the divine essence would also violate God's transcendence.[61] Qūrṣāwī writes that Abū Ḥanīfa in the *Fiqh al-akbar* "said God is one, not in a numerical sense (*lā min ṭarīq al-ʿadad*), but rather in the sense that He has no partner [i.e., is unique].[62] And others among the

1789–1889: Der islamische Diskurs unter russischer Herrschaft. Berlin: Klaus Schwarz Verlag, 1998, p. 259.

53. Ashʿarī, *Maqālāt*, p. 169.

54. Qūrṣāwī, *Sharḥ jadīd*, fol. 106b.

55. Qūrṣāwī, *Ithbāt*, fols. 148b, 159a; Qūrṣāwī, *Mabāḥith*, fols. 164a, 165a; Qūrṣāwī, *Sharḥ jadīd*, fols. 106b, 112a.

56. Qūrṣāwī, *Ithbāt*, fols. 148b, 149a–149b; Qūrṣāwī, *Mabāḥith*, fol. 165a. On this issue, see Wisnovsky, "One Aspect," esp. pp. 71–77, 96–99.

57. Wisnovsky, "Avicenna," p. 121.

58. Qūrṣāwī, *Sharḥ jadīd*, fols. 100a–100b, 112a.

59. Taftāzānī, *Sharḥ*, p. 38.

60. Qūrṣāwī, *Ithbāt*, fol. 149a; Qūrṣāwī, *Mabāḥith*, fols. 165a, 170a–170b.

61. Qūrṣāwī, *Lawāʾiḥ*, fol. 79b; also Qūrṣāwī, *Sharḥ jadīd*, fol. 106b.

62. Cf. Mullā ʿAlī al-Qārī. *Sharḥ kitāb al-Fiqh al-akbar*. Beirut: Dār al-kutub al-ʿilmiyya, 1404/1984, p. 23; this is also quoted in Qūrṣāwī, *Sharḥ jadīd*, fol. 108b. The *Fiqh al-akbar* is traditionally attributed to Abū Ḥanīfa, and even though false, it will be referenced as such here.

ʿulamāʾ and *fuqahāʾ* have proved this in numerous works because number is quantity (*kamm*), and quantity is an accident (*ʿarḍ*), and an accident does not revolve around (*lā yuḥawwim fī ḥawl*) [i.e., cannot be present in] the essence or the attributes."[63] Were number or quantity present in the divine essence, this would lead to divisibility (*infiṣāl*) within it.[64] Elsewhere Qūrṣāwī makes this point about quantity more explicit, writing, "Quantity is an accident, and an accident cannot subsist in His essence, and quantity is a description (*waṣf*) that does not concern His essence."[65] Thus, to state that "God is one" in a numerical sense is to describe Him with the accident of quantity, and Qūrṣāwī warns against giving any consideration to *mutakallimīn* who do not consider quantity an accident.[66]

Qūrṣāwī is adamant in his refusal of any such infringement upon God's simplicity. He repeatedly states that there can be nothing resembling number (*ʿadad*), quantity (*kamm* or *kammiyya*), plurality (*kathra*), paucity (*qilla*), or even oneness (*waḥda*) with God. He writes, for instance, regarding Nasafī's statement that God is not numbered (*wa-lā maʿdūd*): "He is not described by number, nor only by oneness, since it is a quality (*kayfiyya*) entailing paucity and finiteness (*nihāya*). . . . And He is one not by way of number, but rather in that He has no partner."[67] Paucity, according to Qūrṣāwī, merely hides plurality, and oneness does not contradict plurality.[68] God's attributes, however, are above both paucity and plurality.[69]

The divine attributes also cannot be described by any type of number or quantity, by virtue of the fact that they are *lā huwa wa-lā ghayruh* with the divine essence. Qūrṣāwī writes *ad "wa-hiya lā huwa wa-lā ghayruh"*

> This means that the attributes in reality are not described as being few or many, since those are descriptions of numbers and quantity. So the

63. Qūrṣāwī, *Ithbāt*, fol. 149a (see also ms. SPb IVR, no. C1975, fol. 113b); Qūrṣāwī, *Naṣāʾiḥ*, fol. 20b.

64. Qūrṣāwī, *Lawāʾiḥ*, fol. 80a.

65. Qūrṣāwī, *Mabāḥith*, fol. 164a.

66. Ibid. About the view that there can be no accident in the divine essence, see Qūrṣāwī, *Sharḥ jadīd*, fol. 108b; Qūrṣāwī, *Lawāʾiḥ*, fols. 82b–83a, 85a.

67. Qūrṣāwī, *Sharḥ jadīd*, fol. 108b; also Qūrṣāwī, *Ithbāt*, fol. 149a; cf. Sālimī, *Tamhīd*, p. 43; also Ulrich Rudolph. *Al-Maturidi and the Development of Sunni Theology in Samarqand*. Leiden: Brill, 2012, pp. 274–277.

68. Qūrṣāwī, *Lawāʾiḥ*, fols. 79b–80a; Qūrṣāwī, *Sharḥ jadīd*, fol. 112a.

69. Qūrṣāwī, *Sharḥ jadīd*, fol. 116a.

> attributes and the essence are not one thing in reality, as that would entail finiteness and paucity; nor [are they] two things, as that would entail finiteness and plurality, and the negation of [the attributes'] existence is not entailed by the rejection of their being one and being many.[70]

Thus, being neither identical with the essence nor other than it means that the attributes are neither one with the essence nor something separate and multiple. They are therefore beyond number, as is the essence itself.

Differentiation

The tension between God's simplicity and the attributes' multiplicity is closely connected with the issue of the attributes' differentiation (*mughāyara*)—that is, whether or not the attributes are distinct from each other. This represents another of Qūrṣāwī's points of departure from the standard view. The reasoning linking differentiation and multiplicity is clear: if the attributes can be numbered, then each one must be distinct from the others. The converse is also true: if the attributes are not distinct, then they cannot be numbered or counted. For Qūrṣāwī, as we have seen, the attributes indeed cannot be numbered or counted, and so they cannot be differentiated. According to him, there can be no distinction or division between the attributes themselves.[71] Instead, their relationship to each other is also *lā huwa wa-lā ghayruh*.[72] He links this with denying multiplicity: "[The attribute of] power is neither [the attribute of] life and nor other than life, so [with] each attribute [in relation to] another attribute, we say it is not it and it is not other than it, because His attributes are not countable things (*maʿdūdāt*)."[73] Likewise, "they do not fall under [the category of] number (*lā tadkhul taḥta al-ʿadad*)."[74]

The attributes' differentiation, like their multiplicity, entails a plurality of pseudo-divinities. This Qūrṣāwī argues during his condemnation in Bukhara, as reported in Marjānī's *Tanbīh*: in response to the charge that his position leads to "a multiplicity of necessary entities and a plurality of eternals in the essence," Qūrṣāwī states, "That would follow for us only if we had asserted

70. Ibid., fol. 112a; transcription and translation in Spannaus, "Islamic Thought," p. 248.

71. Qūrṣāwī, *Sharḥ jadīd*, fols. 105a, 106b; Qūrṣāwī, *Sharḥ qadīm*, fol. 18a; Fakhr al-Dīn, *Āthār*, iii, p. 98.

72. Qūrṣāwī, *Ithbāt*, fol. 150b; Fakhr al-Dīn, *Āthār*, iii, p. 98.

73. Qūrṣāwī, *Ithbāt*, fol. 150b. Here Qūrṣāwī is citing Kalābādhī's *Kitāb al-Taʿarruf*; cf. Kalābādhī, *Kitāb al-Taʿarruf*, pp. 15–16.

74. Qūrṣāwī, *Ithbāt*, fol. 150b; Fakhr al-Dīn, *Āthār*, iii, p. 98.

the attributes' differentiation and superaddition."[75] Though he does not explicitly describe his reasoning on this point, his objection seems to be that multiplicity would necessarily follow from the attributes' being clearly distinguished from one another. As multiplicity violates God's uniqueness, then so too must their differentiation.

To hold that God's power is neither identical to God nor other than God, and that His knowledge is neither identical to Him nor other than Him, but that God's power *is* other than His knowledge, is to introduce division into the divine essence; here, an aspect of the attributes' existence or nature would differ from God's. This would make the attributes too distinct from God—too "other than" Him—and thus infringe upon *tawḥīd*. Indeed, Qūrṣāwī makes a connection between differentiation and otherness (*ghayriyya*), writing, "We say that the attributes are neither something differentiated from the essence (*mutaghāyirat*[an] *li-l-dhāt*), nor distinguished in themselves (*lā mutaghāyirat*[an] *fī anfusihā*)."[76] Elsewhere (somewhat inconsistently) he uses "distinction" (*taghāyur*) as a synonym for *ghayriyya*.[77]

Qūrṣāwī blames "some Ashʿaris" for inventing the attributes' differentiation, and there was indeed disagreement among early Sunnis over its acceptability, with scholars such as ibn Kullāb rejecting it.[78] However, Taftāzānī, who also links differentiation with multiplicity, holds that both are permissible. His reasoning on this point is telling. He writes that it is not possible for one of a set of ten to be separated from the ten, and the ten cannot exist without one, and one cannot exist without the ten. Hence, the attributes can be numbered and differentiated without being actually separable.[79]

Taftāzānī relies on a narrowed understanding of *ghayr* (other) when making this point. He states that *ghayriyya* means only the possibility of separation (*jawāz al-infikāk*) between two things, in the sense that one can exist entirely independent of the other. Likewise, identification (*ʿayniyya*) means complete unification (*ittiḥād*) of two things, such that there is no distinction between them. Thus, a thing can be other than another thing in the sense of different or distinct without it being wholly separate in its existence. He goes on to say, *ad "wa-lā huwa wa-lā ghayruh,"*

---

75. Marjānī, *Tanbīh*, pp. 377–378.

76. Qūrṣāwī, *Sharḥ jadīd*, fol. 106b.

77. Qūrṣāwī, *Lawāʾiḥ*, fol. 80.

78. Qūrṣāwī, *Sharḥ jadīd*, fols. 105a, 106b; Ashʿarī, *Maqālāt*, pp. 169–171.

79. Taftāzānī, *Sharḥ*, pp. 38–39.

> an intermediate [position] between [*ghayriyya* and *ʿayniyya*] can be imagined, that there is a thing, the concept (*mafhūm*) of which is not the [same] concept of the other, nor does it exist without [the other], like the part (*juzʾ*) with the whole, the attribute with the self (*dhāt*), or some attributes with others. So God's essence and His attributes are eternal (*azaliyya*), and the nonexistence of the eternal is impossible.[80]

Taftāzānī's argument here (related to his position on contingency) is that because the attributes depend upon the essence for their existence—they cannot exist without it—they cannot be fully other than it. Nevertheless, the attributes are distinct from the essence, just as they are different from each other (just as all the numbers in a set of ten are different but inseparable within the set).[81]

The implication of Taftāzānī's argument is that the relationship between the attributes themselves is the same as that between divine essence and the attributes. This would imply that the attributes among themselves are *lā huwa wa-lā ghayruh*. He explicitly rejects the possibility of the attributes' separation (*infikāk*) from the essence and from each other, as well as their identification with it, and so it would follow that the intermediate position he posits between those two extremes is *lā huwa wa-lā ghayruh*.

While this stance is very similar to Qūrṣāwī's, Taftāzānī also asserts the attributes' differentiation (*mutaghāyara*, semantically and conceptually related to *ghayr*). The narrowed meaning of *ghayr* allows Taftāzānī to do so, as they would not be seen as entirely separate and independent of each other. Such a position, however, would require two separate definitions of *ghayr*, since the sense that one divine attribute is other than the rest of the attributes (with regard to their mutual differentiation) is not the same as the sense that the attributes are not other than God. Indeed, Qūrṣāwī rejects Taftāzānī's understanding of *ghayriyya* and *ʿayniyya*, focusing his criticism on the narrowed meaning of *ghayr*. He writes that "two [things] are two different [things] (*al-ithnān humā al-ghayrān*), and vice versa," and that this is how most people (*al-jumhūr*) understand these terms.[82] He continues, citing Sirhindī, that some theologians have attempted to change the meaning of *ghayriyya*.[83]

---

80. Ibid., p. 39.

81. Ibid., pp. 37–38.

82. Qūrṣāwī, *Mabāḥith*, fol. 164a, citing Jurjānī's *Sharḥ al-Mawāqif*; also Qūrṣāwī, *Ithbāt*, fol. 148b.

83. Qūrṣāwī, *Mabāḥith*, fol. 164b; Sirhindī, *Maktūbāt*, 1:272, p. 504. Muḥammad Maʿṣūm states that the *mutakallimīn* have stumbled into *ghayriyya* because their definition of the

Qūrṣāwī adds that this change in meaning has particular implications for *lā huwa wa-lā ghayruh*. His objection is based on the ambiguity between the two senses of *ghayr* implied by Taftāzānī. In essence, the formula *lā huwa wa-lā ghayruh* relies upon the conventional meaning of *ghayr* as signifying duality. He writes that the prophetic Companions and early scholars have

> agreed that His attributes are *lā huwa wa-lā ghayruh*, and that upon which the *ʿulamāʾ* agree has the status of text (*naṣṣ*) [i.e., is certain], and texts rely upon their outward meanings (*ẓawāhir*), [that is,] what is understood in convention and expression. And it is confirmed that the understanding in convention and expression of *ghayriyya* is duality. So it [*lā huwa wa-lā ghayruh*] must refer to the negation of duality.[84]

According to Qūrṣāwī, the sole purpose of *lā ghayruh* is to negate duality between the attributes and the essence. To say that there is another sense of *ghayr* that is not negated by this formula, however, is to posit the attributes as meaningfully other than the essence. Were this the case, Qūrṣāwī writes, the attributes' multiplicity would not be negated, but would in fact logically follow, resulting in an obvious violation of God's oneness.[85]

Qūrṣāwī instead puts forward a broader understanding of *ghayr*. He writes that it has two meanings: "One is the negation of association (*salb al-shirka*) and the other is the possibility of separation (*jawāz al-infikāk*)."[86] He explicitly labels only the latter as duality, and it is that definition that matches Taftāzānī's understanding, but Qūrṣāwī considers both negated in regard to the attributes. With this conception of *ghayr* in place, it becomes clear that differentiation (*mughāyara*) of the attributes is unacceptable for him. Were the attributes in some way unassociated with, or separated from, each other, God's simplicity—to say nothing of His uniqueness—would unquestionably be violated. As Qūrṣāwī considers Taftāzānī's understanding of *ghayr* untenable, so too does he find his acceptance of differentiation.

---

term *ghayr* as "the possibility of separation" is too narrow and does not account for "general otherness" (*muṭlaq-i ghayriyya*) between two things; Khwāja Muḥammad Maʿṣūm. *Maktūbāt*. 3 vols. Karachi: Asrār Muḥammad Khān, 1977, 2:105, pp. 164–166.

84. Qūrṣāwī here blames Ashʿarī and the "innovators from the people of *kalām*" for promoting the altered sense of the term; Qūrṣāwī, *Mabāḥith*, fols. 164b–165a; transcription and translation in Spannaus, "Islamic Thought," pp. 242–244; cf. also Qūrṣāwī, *Ithbāt*, fol. 149a.

85. Qūrṣāwī, *Mabāḥith*, fol. 165a.

86. Ibid., fols. 168a–168b.

Superaddition

The respective problems of the attributes' differentiation and multiplicity, conceptually linked as they are, touch upon the issue of the attributes' distinctiveness from the divine essence. Related to these is the matter of the attributes' superaddition to the essence (*ziyāda ʿalā al-dhāt*), another point of departure between Qūrṣāwī and the standard orthodoxy. Upheld by Taftāzānī, Qūrṣāwī rejects it.[87] Qūrṣāwī does not make his reasoning explicit, however. He writes, for instance, "We affirm the basis of the attributes which the Book affirms and we negate the superaddition which imagination affirms."[88] Elsewhere he links superaddition with *tashbīh*, seemingly on the grounds that philosophical accidents are superadded to a being, and there can be no accident within the divine essence, due to God's simplicity.[89] And, as his responses to the questioning by the Bukharan *ʿulamāʾ* show, it seems that Qūrṣāwī considers superaddition to violate *lā ghayruh* much in the same way multiplicity and differentiation do.[90]

A possible inspiration for Qūrṣāwī's position comes from Muḥammad Maʿṣūm, Sirhindī's son (mentioned in Chapter 2), who argues that superaddition necessarily entails *ghayriyya*, and the Sunni *mutakallimīn* are wrong to uphold it.[91] Marjānī, for his part, goes into greater detail on the issue. He states that the later Ashʿaris, by accepting superaddition, "are forced (*udṭurrū*) to permit multiplicity," and he explicitly links all three issues—superaddition, multiplicity, and differentiation—as leading to a plurality of pseudo-divinities and violating *tawḥīd*.[92]

This connection between multiplicity and superaddition is evident in the unknown Afandī Dāghistānī's refutation of Qūrṣāwī, where he writes, "There is no impossibility in confirming that [the attributes'] number necessarily (*ḍarūratan*) entails that the concept (*mafhūm*) of the attributes is other than the concept of the essence, because [the attributes] are notions (*maʿānin*) superadded [to the essence], just as they subsist within the essence."[93] Since the attributes are superadded to, yet subsist within, the essence, the concept

87. Taftāzānī, *Sharḥ*, p. 37; Marjānī, *Tanbīh*, p. 378.

88. Qūrṣāwī, *Sharḥ jadīd*, fol. 106b.

89. Ibid., fol. 111b.

90. Marjānī, *Tanbīh*, pp. 377–378.

91. Muḥammad Maʿṣūm, *Maktūbāt*, 2:105, pp. 164–166.

92. Marjānī, *Ḥāshiya*, p. 47; Marjānī, *Ḥikma al-bāligha*, p. 31; see also Nathan Spannaus. "Šihab al-Din al-Marǧani on the Divine Attributes: A Study in *Kalam* in the 19th Century." *Arabica*, vol. 62, no. 1; 2015. 74–98, esp. pp. 83, 91.

93. Dāghistānī, *Radd*, fol. 6a.

of them is separate from the concept of the essence, and their multiplicity—as opposed to the essence's oneness—is possible.[94] Qūrṣāwī, for his part, would agree with the logic behind this line of reasoning: the attributes' superaddition entails their being other than the essence and, as such, allows for their multiplicity. However, he considers it an utterly unacceptable position, on the grounds that the attributes' superaddition and multiplicity are linked with their otherness, which violates *lā huwa wa-lā ghayruh* and which must therefore be rejected absolutely.

All of these points—the attributes' contingency, multiplicity, differentiation, and superaddition—are rejected because they entail too much of a distinction between the essence and the attributes. Whether they violate God's uniqueness, His simplicity, or His transcendence, they are, for Qūrṣāwī, entirely unacceptable and should be refuted. Indeed, he states repeatedly that belief in these is innovation or heresy (*bidʿa*) and error (*ḍalāla*), constituting unbelief (*kufr*).[95]

Divine Transcendence

Although God's oneness was universally regarded as the central tenet of Islam, scholars differed over its precise meaning and philosophical implications, as well as the degree to which it should be emphasized vis-à-vis other aspects of divinity. Qūrṣāwī considers God's oneness and transcendence to be primary principles of the religion, upholding God as utterly and categorically other than creation. He bases this view on the Qurʾanic statement "There is nothing like unto Him" (*laysa ka-mithlih shayʾ*[un]) (42:11), which appears in his works as scriptural justification.[96] This precept is also central to Sirhindī's thought, expressed in the formula that God is *bī-chūn wa chīgūnah* (which ter Haar renders as "beyond compare"), a Persian translation of *laysa ka-mithlih shayʾ*[un].[97] Although Qūrṣāwī breaks with Sirhindī over other theological

94. Dāghistānī here uses "number" (*ʿadad*) in a way synonymous with Qūrṣāwī's use of "multiplicity" (*taʿaddud*).

95. Cf. Qūrṣāwī, *Lawāʾiḥ*, fols. 85a–85b; Qūrṣāwī, *Mabāḥith*, fols. 166b, 167a; Qūrṣāwī, *Sharḥ jadīd*, fol. 101b.

96. E.g., Qūrṣāwī, *Haftiyak*, fol. 1b; Qūrṣāwī, *Naṣāʾiḥ*, fol. 20a.

97. Sirhindī, *Maktūbāt*, 1:38, p. 103; J. G. J. ter Haar. *Follower and Heir of the Prophet: Shaykh Ahmad Sirhindi (1564–1624) as Mystic*. Leiden: Het Oosters Instituut, 1992, p. 62. Sirhindī's formula is mentioned in a marginal note at the beginning of Qūrṣāwī's *Mabāḥith*, the work in which Sirhindī's importance to Qūrṣāwī is most evident; Qūrṣāwī, *Mabāḥith*, fol. 153b.

matters (see Chapter 6), he references Sirhindī's emphasis on *tanzīh* to defend his stance on the attributes.[98]

We find a similar focus on *tanzīh* regarding the attributes in the work of Abū Shukūr al-Sālimī (fl. 10th–11th cent.), an important Bukharan Hanafi who offers an argument for the attributes' eternality that revolves around divine simplicity, resembling Qūrṣāwī's. Like Qūrṣāwī, Sālimī relies heavily upon the attributes having a *lā huwa wa-lā ghayruh* relationship to the essence to justify his position.[99]

Sālimī cites *laysa ka-mithlih shayʾun* in his argument for *tanzīh*,[100] as does the Bukharan Sufi Abū Bakr Kalābādhī in his *Kitāb al-Taʿarruf*, where he presents a view of the attributes that emphasizes God's transcendence.[101] Kalābādhī served as a significant inspiration for both Qūrṣāwī and Sirhindī,[102] and his *Taʿarruf*, according to A. J. Arberry, who compares the work to Ghazālī's *Ihyāʾ*, represents a combination of Sufism and Central Asian Hanafi *kalām* with a focus on scripturally based piety.[103]

The thread linking Sālimī, Kalābādhī, and Sirhindī with Qūrṣāwī is an emphasis on God's utter transcendence, which provides the basis for Qūrṣāwī's critique. He saw the prevailing orthodoxy as infringing upon both *tawḥīd* and *tanzīh* by making the attributes too distinct from the divine essence. This is the focus of his criticisms and the point of departure for his own stance on the attributes. For him, the standard *kalām* position cannot be correct and is necessarily unfounded because it does not uphold God's oneness and transcendence. In violating these fundamental principles of the religion, Qūrṣāwī argues, it runs counter to God's descriptions of Himself.[104] Therefore, it is an invalid and illegitimate expression of Islamic belief that must be countered and rejected to prevent its spread.

---

98. E.g., Qūrṣāwī, *Mabāḥith*, fols. 166a, 169b; Qūrṣāwī, *Naṣāʾiḥ*, fol. 20a.

99. Sālimī, *Tamhīd*, pp. 35–41, 48–51. On Sālimī, see Rudolph, *Al-Maturidi*.

100. Sālimī, *Tamhīd*, p. 39.

101. Kalābādhī, *Kitāb al-Taʿarruf*, p. 14.

102. E.g., Sirhindī, *Maktūbāt*, 3:90, p. 479.

103. A. J. Arberry. *The Doctrine of the Sufis*. "Introduction." Cambridge: Cambridge UP, 1977. ix–xviii, pp. xiii–xv; also Kemper, *Sufis*, p. 268.

104. Qūrṣāwī, *Sharḥ jadīd*, fol. 96b.

Knowing the Essence

Qūrṣāwī's emphasis on upholding God's transcendence extended to the impossibility of knowing Him. He states that God, in His transcendence, is beyond comprehension.[105] As God lacks both form and any likeness to which He could be compared, His nature and essence cannot be understood, and, he writes, "Knowledge (*ʿilm*) and apprehension (*idrāk*) are the occurrence of the form (*ḥuṣūl al-ṣūra*) or the occurring form (*al-ṣūra al-ḥāṣila*), and so that which has no form or quality (*kayfiyya*)," as God does not, "is definitively not apprehended or comprehended."[106] Likewise, a thing is beyond definite understanding if its reality (*ḥaqīqa*) or a confirmed correspondence (*munāsaba muṣaḥḥaḥa*) to its reality cannot occur in the mind or be perceived. Thus, Qūrṣāwī states, "according to this principle, gnosis (*maʿrifa*) of the nature (*kunh*) and reality of the essence of [God] and His attributes is impossible."[107] There cannot be knowledge of the divine essence, only ignorance (*jahl*).[108]

The only possible sources of knowledge about the divine essence are God's descriptions of Himself or the prophets' descriptions of Him.[109] Scripture thus serves as the primary means for understanding God, but only in an oblique way. Qūrṣāwī explains through the analogy of calling fire "hot": "hot" cannot answer the question "What is fire?" because it does not refer directly to fire, but rather to heat. "So when we say 'knowing' or 'powerful,'" he writes, "it has the meaning of an obscure thing (*shayʾ mubham*) which has a description (*waṣf*) of knowledge or power." These descriptions seem to equate God with creation, but since actual *tashbīh* is impossible—since there is nothing like God—true descriptions can only be negative, such that, for instance, He is living not like living things (*huwa ḥayy lā ka-l-aḥyāʾ*).[110] Similarly, those

105. On the question of the knowability of the divine essence, see Binyamin Abrahamov. "Faḫr al-Din al-Razi on the Knowability of God's Essence and Attributes." *Arabica*, vol. 49, no. 2; 2002. 204–230.

106. Qūrṣāwī, *Lawāʾiḥ*, fols. 83b, 85a; also Qūrṣāwī, *Sharḥ jadīd*, fol. 104a. This idea that knowledge of a thing's form is linked with knowledge of that thing is also found in Avicenna, here by way of Sirhindī; e.g., Sirhindī, *Maktūbāt*, 3:48, pp. 382–383.

107. Qūrṣāwī, *Lawāʾiḥ*, fol. 81a.

108. Qūrṣāwī, *Mabāḥith*, fol. 170a. This, however, does not preclude seeing God in the afterlife, though this sight is not physical, but rather occurs in the heart; Qūrṣāwī, *Lawāʾiḥ*, fol. 83b.

109. Cf. Qūrṣāwī, *Lawāʾiḥ*, fol. 83a.

110. Qūrṣāwī, *Sharḥ jadīd*, fol. 109b. This reinforces Qūrṣāwī's position about the unknowability of the essence. If scripture is the only source of knowledge about the essence (and Qūrṣāwī is adamant about this), yet the descriptions contained in scripture do not actually

verses that mention anthropomorphic elements of God—His face or hand or mouth or proximity—cannot be understood literally, since He transcends such things.[111] However, there can be no interpretation (*taʾwīl*) into how God describes Himself, because He conceals the truth.[112]

In this respect, Qūrṣāwī's thought evinces a reliance upon the so-called *bi-lā kayfa* doctrine, in that he dismisses speculation about the essence and attributes, beyond affirming their existence.[113] For example, God's face is affirmed as an attribute because it is found in scripture, but its relationship to God is beyond human understanding.[114] A. J. Wensinck points out that *bi-lā kayfa* developed historically into a principle of transcendence, and we can see this principle at work in Qūrṣāwī's position on the attributes.[115] His reliance upon *bi-lā kayfa* does not stem from a rejection of reason (*ʿaql*) in theological inquiry but rather from what he sees as its limitations: it can lead one to affirm the existence of the essence and attributes, but comprehending anything beyond that exceeds its capability.[116] He writes, for instance, that *ʿaql* cannot lead to the inner realities (*ḥaqīqāt*) of the divine essence, as God in His transcendence is incomprehensible.[117] Therefore, *naql* should be relied upon exclusively for those questions reason cannot answer.[118]

Qūrṣāwī's view of reason deeply colors his view of *kalām* and its place within the Islamic scholarly tradition. For him, *kalām*, because it is based on reason, is subject to the same problems and limitations and is inextricably linked with it, to the point that he calls it *ʿilm al-kalām wa-l-naẓar* (the science

---

describe the essence, then there is absolutely no way, short of direct, divine inspiration, for one to know anything about the essence, other than it exists, it possesses attributes, and there is nothing like unto it.

111. Ibid., fols. 107a–107b.

112. Ibid., fols. 101a, 103b–104a.

113. Literally "without how," in the sense that humans can know and affirm perplexing or impenetrable aspects of God's being, without knowing their precise nature; see Binyamin Abrahamov. "The 'Bi-la Kayfa' Doctrine and Its Foundations in Islamic Theology." *Arabica*, vol. 42, no. 3; 1995. 365–379.

114. Qūrṣāwī, *Sharḥ jadīd*, fols. 99b, 110b; cf. ʿAlī Qārī, *Sharḥ*, pp. 58–61.

115. A. J. Wensinck. *The Muslim Creed: Its Genesis and Historical Development*. London: Frank Cass & Co., 1965, p. 207, also p. 86. In a similar fashion, Kalābādhī and ʿAlī Qārī consider God's face an attribute as well; Kalābādhī, *Kitāb al-Taʿarruf*, p. 15; ʿAlī Qārī, *Sharḥ*, p. 58.

116. Qūrṣāwī, *Lawāʾiḥ*, fol. 81b; Qūrṣāwī, *Mabāḥith*, fol. 170b; Qūrṣāwī, *Sharḥ Manār*, p. 173.

117. Qūrṣāwī, *Sharḥ jadīd*, fol. 109a.

118. Ibid., fol. 96a.

of disputation and speculation).[119] But he speaks much more harshly of *kalām*, and particularly its practitioners, than he does of reason itself. He condemns it as a field of knowledge and, citing the formative Hanafi scholar Abū Yūsuf, goes so far as to reject the possibility of one who does *kalām* leading prayer: "Prayer behind a *mutakallim* is not permissible, and this statement is true because he [the *mutakallim*] is an innovator (*mubtadiʿ*), and prayer behind an innovator is not permissible."[120]

But Qūrṣāwī's relationship to *kalām* is more nuanced than at first glance. This complexity is largely attributable to his use of the term *kalām* itself, which he employs exclusively in a pejorative sense, rather than his view toward theology as an intellectual endeavor. For him, *kalām* is not simply theology—in the sense of thinking systematically about God—or even rational theology; it is the excessive use of reason in theology, particularly at the expense of *naql*. Qūrṣāwī criticizes, for example, the Muʿtazila and some Ashʿaris for holding *naql* to be subordinate to reason, and he connects such a position with philosophy (specifically Avicenna).[121] He also defines *kalām* as "the science of those who plunge into philosophy and their whims" (having already identified whim as a central danger of relying upon reason).[122]

What Qūrṣāwī does is draw a distinction between *kalām*—as he sees it—and acceptable reasoning about God, which he calls *ʿilm al-tawḥīd wa-l-ṣifāt* (the science of *tawḥīd* and the attributes), despite the fact these two labels were traditionally synonymous.[123] He writes that the Companions and Followers of

119. Qūrṣāwī, *Mabāḥith*, fol. 155a.

120. Ibid., fols. 155a–156b; also Qūrṣāwī, *Sharḥ jadīd*, fols. 93a–93b.

121. Qūrṣāwī, *Sharḥ jadīd*, fol. 99a.

122. Ibid., fol. 93b.

123. Qūrṣāwī, *Sharḥ qadīm*, fol. 17a; cf. Gimaret, "Tawḥīd (a)," *EI*[2]. On Qūrṣāwī's use of this distinction, see also Kemper, *Sufis*, pp. 247–248. The origins of this distinction are obscure. The Bukharan scholar Abū al-Ḥasan ʿAlī b. Muḥammad al-Bazdawī (1010–1089) writes that *ʿilm al-tawḥīd wa-l-ṣifāt* is "adherence to the Book and Sunna and avoidance of whim and *bidʿa*," and it is what the *salaf* practiced. But he contrasts it with "*ʿilm al-sharāʾiʿ wa-l-aḥkām*"—i.e., law—suggesting that it merely signifies theology; ʿAlī b. Muḥammad al-Bazdawī. *Uṣūl al-Bazdawī: Kanz al- wuṣūl ilā maʿrifat al-uṣūl*. [Karachi]: Mīr Muḥammad kutubkhāna-yi markaz-i ʿilm wa-adab, n.d., pp. 3–4. However, ʿAlī Qārī, writing in the 16th century, makes a distinction in the *Sharḥ al-Fiqh al-akbar* (much in the same way as Qūrṣāwī) between his work (*ʿilm al- tawḥīd*) and the *kalām* of the *ahl al-bidʿa*, who rely too heavily on reason and logic; ʿAlī Qārī, *Sharḥ*, pp. 5–7. It is also mentioned by Fakhr al-Dīn in reference to scholars connected to Qūrṣāwī, though its connotations are unclear. He writes that Qūrṣāwī's teacher Āshiṭī taught *ʿilm al-tawḥīd wa-l-ṣifāt*, among other subjects, in his *madrasa*; Fakhr al-Dīn, *Āthār*, iii, p. 142. Qūrṣāwī's student Nuʿmān Thamanī describes the *Sharḥ jadīd* as a commentary "on the writing of ʿUmar al-Nasafī on *ʿilm al-tawḥīd wa-l-ṣifāt*;

the Prophet engaged in *ʿilm al-tawḥīd wa-l-ṣifāt* (explicitly not *kalām*), and that it is the basis of religious duties (*aṣl al-wājibāt wa-asās al-mashrūʿāt*) and the most beneficial type of knowledge (*anfāʿ al- ʿulūm*).[124]

This distinction seems to be grounded in the use of *naql*. For Qūrṣāwī, the extreme reliance on reason among *mutakallimīn* sets their intellectual endeavor apart from his, which is based on *naql*. Indeed, there does seem to have been a real disagreement between Qūrṣāwī and his opponents on the role of reason in determining belief. ʿInāyat Allāh Bukhārī writes that scripture is the basis (*asās*) for belief (*iʿtiqād*), but that *kalām* constitutes part of belief, and logical reasoning (*qiyās*) is the basis for *kalām*.[125] Qūrṣāwī's descriptions of *kalām* would suggest that he agrees, but the view that *qiyās* or other forms of rational deduction constitute part of belief runs directly counter to his epistemological position.

Qūrṣāwī objects to the idea that the use of sound logical principles provided certainty to theological reasoning, which underpinned postclassical *kalām*. Instead, he argues that matters of belief require certain knowledge, which comes only through *naql* sources.[126] *Qiyās* and *ijtihād* are therefore rejected in formulating matters of belief, on the grounds that they only impart

---

ibid., x, p. 150. In addition, Qūrṣāwī's companion Niʿmat Allāh b. Bīktimur, who, according to Fakhr al-Dīn, forbade the "sciences of the philosophers" (*ʿulūm al-falāsifa*)—logic, *kalām*, astronomy (*hayʾa*), and science/philosophy (*ḥikma*)—is said to have studied *ʿilm al-tawḥīd wa-l-ṣifāt* from the work; ibid., ix, pp. 79, 81; also Ramzī, *Talfīq*, ii, 368–369. On *ḥikma* in this context, see Mirza Kazem Beg. "Notice sur la marche et les progrès de la jurisprudence musulmane parmi les sectes orthodoxes." *Journal asiatique*, ser. 4, no. 15; Jan. 1850. 154–210, p. 160.

124. Qūrṣāwī, *Sharḥ jadīd*, fols. 93a, 105b; also Qūrṣāwī, *Sharḥ qadīm*, fol. 17a. *ʿIlm al-tawḥīd wa-l- ṣifāt* can best be encapsulated in Richard Frank's understanding of the Sunnis' "primary theological endeavor": "to describe the being of God in formally conceptual terms and to do so without sacrificing to the normal logic of common human language and discourse either the sense of the plenitude of the divine being that reveals itself symbolically in the language of the revelation or the doctrine of its transcendent unity"; Richard Frank. "The Science of *Kalam*." *Arabic Sciences and Philosophy*, vol. 2; 1992. 7–37, p. 32. Marjānī, for his part, considers this part and parcel of *kalām*, writing that "the foundations of *kalām* are the sources of its questions which produce the affirmation of His existence and of the rest of His attributes" (*uṣūl al-kalām ummahāt masāʾilih allatī tufīd al-taṣdīq bi-wujūdih wa-sāʾir ṣifātih*); Marjānī, *Ḥāshiya*, p. 6. He condemns *kalām* elsewhere, however; see Marjānī, *Nāẓūrat al-ḥaqq*, pp. 7–11.

125. ʿInāyat Allāh Bukhārī. [Untitled work.] Ms. SPb IVR, no. A914. Fols. 113a–117a, fol. 114a; also ʿInāyat Allāh Bukhārī. *Risāla ʿan qism ḥāshiyat al-Khayālī ʿalā sharḥ al-ʿAqāyid al-nasafiyya li-l-Taftāzānī*. Ms. SPb IVR, no. A914. Fols. 117a–122a, fol. 118a.

126. "Three of [the four *uṣūl*] necessitate knowledge (*ʿilm*) and action, and one of them—it is *qiyās*—necessitates action, but not knowledge"; Qūrṣāwī, *Naṣāʾiḥ*, fols. 19a, 21a; Qūrṣāwī, *Mabāḥith*, fol. 170a. The view that consensus necessitates knowledge runs counter to the Aristotelian perspective (important in the more philosophically oriented *kalām* of the post-classical period) that the intuitively necessary truths that provide the basis for syllogistic

probability (*ẓann*) and are subject to error.[127] Thus, the inclusion of *qiyās* as part of belief is simply unacceptable, a religious wrong.

But Qūrṣāwī's position was not strictly against rational sources. Because errors in belief were considered far more serious and morally harmful than errors in legal interpretation, theological reasoning demands absolute certainty, and it must be based on sources that fall beyond any doubt. Therefore, the *khabar wāḥid*, which is of course scriptural, is also excluded, due to its inherent uncertainty.[128] Indeed, Qūrṣāwī equates *qiyās* and the *khabar wāḥid* in terms of epistemological value.[129] Only that which can be directly found in the soundest, most certain scriptural sources, as well as in established consensus, can be admitted for belief. Everything else must be rejected.[130]

The conviction that belief requires absolutely certain knowledge is at the heart of Qūrṣāwī's view of *kalām*, the speculative nature of which renders it unacceptable for determining matters of faith. Reason by itself can lead people into mistaken beliefs, and the *mutakallimīn*, following their own fallible logic, cannot help but fall into error.[131] *Naql* acts as a safeguard: knowledge of it prevents deviation in belief, since anything not found in scripture or consensus can be rejected as error and innovation.[132] Reason therefore must be entirely subordinate to *naql*. It can be used to defend proper belief,[133] but those beliefs must not be themselves formulated through reason alone, and Qūrṣāwī writes that every theological position must be subject to verification (*taḥqīq*) that it conforms to sound knowledge.[134]

---

reasoning are more valid than consensus or generally accepted premises (endoxa, in philosophical terminology), which are instead the raw materials for rational argumentation. Yet, for Qūrṣāwī, logic is prone to individual error, while consensus has the weight of the community behind it. According to Zysow, this was the position of the ancient Samarqandi school of Hanafis; Aron Zysow. "The Economy of Certainty: An Introduction to the Typology of Islamic Legal Theory." Diss. Harvard University, 1984, p. 41.

127. Cf. Qūrṣāwī, *Ithbāt*, fol. 150a; Qūrṣāwī, *Irshād*, p. 27; Qūrṣāwī, *Sharḥ Manār*, esp. p. 173; also Zysow, "Economy," pp. 112, 116; Bernard Weiss. "Interpretation in Islamic Law: The Theory of Ijtihad." *American Journal of Comparative Law*, vol. 26, no. 2; 1978. 199–212, pp. 203–204.

128. Qūrṣāwī, *Naṣāʾiḥ*, fol. 19a.

129. Qūrṣāwī, *Sharḥ Manār*, p. 62.

130. Qūrṣāwī, *Mabāḥith*, fol. 169a.

131. Qūrṣāwī, *Lawāʾiḥ*, fol. 84a.

132. Qūrṣāwī, *Mabāḥith*, fol. 153b; Qūrṣāwī, *Irshād*, pp. 35–36; Qūrṣāwī, *Lawāʾiḥ*, fol. 85b.

133. Qūrṣāwī, *Mabāḥith*, fol. 154b.

134. Qūrṣāwī, *Lawāʾiḥ*, fols. 85a–85b.

Orthodoxy and Condemnation

For Qūrṣāwī, Taftāzānī's stance on the attributes is based on rational speculation, lacking sufficient grounding in *naql* and requisite certainty. (He writes, for instance, that a *mutawātir* source would be needed to declare that God possesses seven or eight attributes.)[135] Taftāzānī therefore posits things of God and the divine essence that cannot be known. And, given the criticisms Qūrṣāwī makes of Taftāzānī's reasoning, he also posits things that cannot be true. His stance, then, is invalid.

This is the gist of Qūrṣāwī's position, which is accordingly expressed largely in the negative, presented in terms of others' errors and misinterpretations. Although he makes it clear which views are beyond the pale, theologically speaking, he is less explicit about his own position. Nevertheless, a coherent picture of his view of the attributes can be constructed from his writings: the attributes are both eternal and necessary of existence, by virtue of their being *lā huwa wa-lā ghayruh* with the essence and subsisting within it.[136] The attributes have no dependence on the essence.[137] Their real existence is confirmed by scripture and *naql*, as are God's hand and face, which are attributes as well.[138] The attributes, innumerable and undifferentiated, are *lā huwa wa-lā ghayruh* among themselves. They therefore exist in a state where each attribute is not God and not other than God and concurrently not every other attribute and not other than every other attribute. Any difference between them, such as God's knowledge vis-à-vis His power or His life vis-à-vis His will, is a purely linguistic or conceptual distinction appearing in language or in human understanding.[139] The divine essence and attributes transcend everything.[140] They cannot be understood, and only revelation can lead to even partial knowledge of them.[141] They can therefore be described only in the negative.[142] Reason

135. Qūrṣāwī, *Mabāḥith*, fol. 169b.

136. E.g., "the established descriptions (*awṣāf*) and actions (*afʿāl*) of the Everlasting Real are necessary of affirmation [their existence] (*thubūt*) [and] impossible of cessation"; Qūrṣāwī, *Lawāʾiḥ*, fol. 82b.

137. Qūrṣāwī, *Mabāḥith*, fols. 165b–166a.

138. Qūrṣāwī, *Sharḥ jadīd*, fols. 111b, 107a, 110b.

139. Qūrṣāwī, *Ithbāt*, fol. 150b; Fakhr al-Dīn, *Āthār*, iii, p. 98; Qūrṣāwī, *Lawāʾiḥ*, fol. 83a; Qūrṣāwī, *Sharḥ jadīd*, fol. 107a.

140. Qūrṣāwī, *Lawāʾiḥ*, fols. 77a–78a.

141. Qūrṣāwī, *Sharḥ jadīd*, fol. 104a.

142. Ibid., fol. 109b.

(*ʿaql*) can do no more than affirm God and the attributes' existence, and people should not delve into the secrets of the divine, even though it is fruitless.[143]

As with his criticisms of others' beliefs, asserting God's oneness and transcendence are the overarching priorities of Qūrṣāwī's position. Thus, he posits that the attributes are undifferentiated within themselves in order to maintain both aspects of *tawḥīd*: God's simplicity is maintained by the fact that each attribute is not other than the other attributes, ruling out division within the essence, and His uniqueness is maintained by the fact that the attributes are not other than the essence. Qūrṣāwī's aim is as little separation or distinction between the essence and attributes, and among the attributes themselves, as possible, without undermining the attributes' real existence by identifying them with the essence (*ʿayniyya*) or each other. Thus, he puts forward a view verging on existential equivalence between the essence and the attributes: not only are they both eternal and necessary of existence, but the attributes' existence is not dependent upon the essence. Were they dependent upon the essence, then their existence would be subordinate or secondary to God's, leading to division within His being. By rejecting dependence, Qūrṣāwī maintains His oneness, but also asserts that God and the attributes have a single existence between them, which is made possible only by the fact that the attributes are not other than the essence.

Despite the fundamentally Sunni character of his stance, Qūrṣāwī's strong insistence on transcendence regarding the attributes opened him up to accusations of Muʿtazilism. According to mainstream Sunnism, the Muʿtazila had emphasized transcendence too strongly, leading them to deny the reality of the attributes.[144] Their conception of *tanzīh* had crossed the line into *taʿṭīl* (the negation of the attributes' very existence), a term used among Sunnis to signify the Muʿtazila's extreme position on the issue.[145] The Sunnis, in open theological conflict with the Muʿtazila, put forward a competing view focused around the attributes' reality, eternality, and distinctiveness.[146] This meant eight (or seven) differentiated attributes that were superadded to, and causally dependent upon, the divine essence. For Qūrṣāwī, however, this view went too far in the other direction. Sunni *mutakallimīn* such as Taftāzānī, in their

143. Ibid., fol. 109a; Qūrṣāwī, *Mabāḥith*, fol. 170a.

144. In their formulation, God does not possess an attribute of, say, knowledge, but rather God is knowing in Himself; cf. Ashʿarī, *Maqālāt*, p. 164.

145. Michel Allard. *Le problème des attributs divins dans la doctrine d'al-Asʿari et de ses premiers grands disciples*. Beirut: Imprimerie Catholique, 1965, esp. pp. 180–181.

146. See Wisnovsky, "One Aspect," pp. 68–69.

efforts to contradict *taʿṭīl*, had crossed the line into *ghayriyya*, which is tantamount to *shirk*, the violation of God's oneness. Qūrṣāwī's position in turn reemphasizes transcendence, based on the premise that the attributes are *lā huwa wa-lā ghayruh* (a formula intended, by its dual negation, to avoid both the Muʿtazilite identification of the attributes with the essence and holding the attributes to be entirely other than the essence).

To Qūrṣāwī's opponents, this attempt to reemphasize transcendence took him beyond the bounds of Sunnism. The question of the attributes was perhaps the most important theological issue in the history of *kalām*, and it was in many ways central to Sunni identity.[147] Thus, any perceived deviation from the prevailing view on the attributes could be seen as a break with Sunnism, particularly by a figure such as Ḥaydar, whose rule as amir of Bukhara relied upon maintaining religious legitimacy. His involvement in theological disputes was premised upon the protection of Sunni orthodoxy, to which the high-ranking *ʿulamāʾ* of the amirate contributed. Qūrṣāwī's critique that the orthodox position made the attributes too distinct from the essence, combined with his very pointed attacks against Taftāzānī and other revered *mutakallimīn*—to say nothing of his contemporaries—was destined to draw negative attention.

Qūrṣāwī's stance was widely seen as a rejection of mainstream Sunni *kalām*, and, as recorded by Marjānī in the *Tanbīh*, his interrogation at the hands of the *ʿulamāʾ* shows their attempts to place him outside the bounds of Sunnism. The amir accuses him of "invent[ing] a creed contradicting the creeds of the [Sunnis]," and the main inquisitor, Shams al-Dīn Balkhī, constantly seeks to elicit or provoke from Qūrṣāwī a statement that would imply either a denial of the attributes' existence (*taʿṭīl*) or making the attributes a plurality of causally independent pseudo-divinities (*shirk*), as both would push Qūrṣāwī beyond the pale of orthodoxy. (Balkhī in fact begins by asking Qūrṣāwī about the attributes' necessity or contingency, knowing, it seems, the imprecise nature of the question.)[148]

Marjānī writes that some people in Bukhara thought Qūrṣāwī had negated the attributes' existence (*munkir-i ṣifāt*), while others thought he had espoused a multiplicity of necessary entities (*taʿaddud-i wājib*).[149] Yet it was the former charge—that he undermined the attributes' existence—that was

147. Cf. Muhammad Al-Shahrastani. *Book of Religious and Philosophical Sects.* Ed. William Cureton. London: Society for the Publication of Oriental Texts, 1846, pp. 64–65.

148. Marjānī, *Tanbīh*, pp. 376–378.

149. Marjānī, *Mustafād*, ii, p. 169. In the *Tanbīh*, Marjānī attributes the Bukharans' confusion to their ignorance; Marjānī, *Tanbīh*, pp. 374, 378.

most common. Dāghistānī, in his work denouncing Qūrṣāwī, states that his stance entails *ʿayniyya*, implicitly linking it with Muʿtazilism.[150] Tursūn Bāqī, in his 1810 letter to the Bulghar *ʿulamāʾ*, explicitly denounces him for following the Muʿtazila (*taqlīd-i ahl-i iʿtizāl*).[151] And Marjānī's primary work defending Qūrṣāwī, the *Risālat Tanbīh abnāʾ al-ʿaṣr ʿalā tanzīh anbāʾ Abī al-Naṣr* (The epistle informing contemporaries about transcendence in the reports of Abū al-Naṣr), as its title shows, addresses the controversy surrounding Qūrṣāwī's conception of *tanzīh*.

Qūrṣāwī, for his part, explicitly affirms the attributes' real existence and rejects the Muʿtazilite arguments against it.[152] Nevertheless, he does make statements and take positions on God's transcendence that resemble those of the Muʿtazila, who, for instance, also believed that God is beyond understanding.[153] Similarly, he writes, "The Divine Being (*al-huwiyya al-ālihiyya*) in Its majesty and sublimity cannot be described except that He is He (*lā yumkin an yuʿabbar ʿanhā illā bi-annahu huwa huwa*)."[154] This statement mirrors the position of the Zaydi Muʿtazilite al-Qāsim b. Ibrāhīm (785–860), who put forward as an answer to the question "What is God?" "He is He."[155] In fact, while making this point (*ad* "and He is not described by quiddity," [*wa-lā yūṣuf bi-l-māhiyya*]), Qūrṣāwī cites with some approval Wāṣil b. ʿAṭāʾ (?–748), one of the founders of the Muʿtazila.[156]

Speaking specifically of the attributes, Qūrṣāwī rejects the level of distinctiveness put forward by the standard Sunni position in favor of a stance closer to Muʿtazilism. Harry Wolfson writes that the Muʿtazilite understanding of divine unity relied upon absolute unity, such that anything that infringed upon it in any way was rejected. This was in contrast to the early Sunnis, who considered God's unity to be relative, thus allowing—as Taftāzānī does—for the existence of eternal entities that are distinct from God (namely, the

---

150. Dāghistānī, *Radd*, fol. 5a.

151. Marjānī, *Mustafād*, ii, p. 174; Fakhr al-Dīn, *Āthār*, iii, p. 101.

152. E.g., Qūrṣāwī, *Sharḥ jadīd*, fols. 100b, 101a; cf. Marjānī, *Tanbīh*, pp. 377–378.

153. Abrahamov, "Razi," , pp. 204–206, 211. Fakhr al-Dīn al-Rāzī (1149–1210), while putting forward one argument for the unknowability of God, grounds it in the limitations of human perception, rather than divine transcendence; ibid., pp. 212–213.

154. Qūrṣāwī, *Sharḥ jadīd*, fol. 109a.

155. Abrahamov, "Razi," p. 206; see also Wilferd Madelung, "al-Rassī, al-Ḳāsim b. Ibrāhīm b. al-Ḥasan b. al-Ḥasan b. ʿAlī b. Abī Ṭālib," *EI*².

156. Qūrṣāwī, *Sharḥ jadīd*, fol. 109a; Josef van Ess, "Wāṣil b. ʿAṭāʾ," *EI*²; Gimaret, "Muʿtazila," *EI*².

attributes).[157] Qūrṣāwī's stance of course falls squarely on the side of absolute unity, and accordingly his position on the attributes' relation to the divine essence verges on *ʿayniyya*. For Taftāzānī, holding the attributes to be contingent in themselves effectively affirms their existential dependence upon the essence. The attributes are necessary of existence, but only through the essence (*bi-l-dhāt*), whereas the essence is also necessary, but through itself. As such, the attributes' existence is clearly subordinate to, and distinct from, the existence of the essence. On Taftāzānī's account, there can be no conflating the attributes with the essence.

But by asserting that both God and attributes are necessary existents in the divine essence, without the attributes' unequivocal dependence upon God, Qūrṣāwī was positing that God and the attributes have the same existence by the essence. Such a position is logically impossible: the attributes are *lā huwa wa-lā ghayruh* with the divine essence, whereas God *is* the divine essence. Indeed, Baymurād Mangārī argues that because the attributes are not identical to the essence, they must depend on it for their existence, and therefore they must be contingent in themselves (even if they aren't created out of non-existence, which defines the contingency/createdness of all other existents).[158] Making the connection with Muʿtazilism clear, Dāghistānī points out that the attributes' existence cannot be the same as God's, as this could be true only if they themselves were identical with God—violating *lā huwa*, and tantamount to denying their existence.[159]

However, the similarities between Qūrṣāwī's stance and that of the Muʿtazila do not necessarily signal his adoption of Muʿtazilism. As seen with Sālimī, Kalābādhī, and Sirhindī, an emphasis on divine transcendence was hardly unusual among Sunnis, and Qūrṣāwī displays little agreement with the Muʿtazila over any other issue. He is, after all, very clear in his subordination of reason to *naql*, explicitly criticizing the Muʿtazila for holding otherwise.[160] On the attributes, his insistence upon their real existence as eternal, distinct entities places him firmly within the Sunni camp, following the premises laid out by ibn Kullāb, pioneer of Sunni orthodoxy on the issue. And he states

157. Harry A. Wolfson. *The Philosophy of the Kalam*. Cambridge, MA: Harvard UP, 1976, p. 139.

158. Mangārī, *Risāla*, esp. fol. 124b.

159. Dāghistānī, *Radd*, fol. 5a.

160. Qūrṣāwī, *Sharḥ jadīd*, fols. 94a, 99a; Qūrṣāwī, *Lawāʾiḥ*, fol. 85b; cf. Binyamin Abrahamov. *Islamic Theology: Traditionalism and Rationalism*. Edinburgh: Edinburgh UP, 1998, p. 33.

explicitly that the attributes' real existence is confirmed by scripture and the established consensus of the community.[161]

Qūrṣāwī's criticism focuses on the attributes' distinctiveness, which was a main element of the Sunni position and the source of its greatest ambiguity. As such, it represents a corrective from within the same theological framework as Taftāzānī's stance, articulated in response to what Qūrṣāwī sees as its shortcomings. It is therefore not a rejection of Sunnism, as any Muʿtazilite position would be. Rather it reflects Qūrṣāwī's critique of extant scholarship, *taḥqīq* at work. Taftāzānī's position on the attributes cannot be correct because it both fails logically and, like *kalām* generally, lacks the scriptural certainty necessary to make such claims about the divine. As we'll see in Chapter 6, however, this is not an attack on the entire edifice of *kalām* but on a part of it, a particular form of theological scrutiny directed at the prevailing orthodoxy, shaped by the evolution of Sunni *kalām* over the four centuries separating Taftāzānī and Qūrṣāwī.

---

161. E.g., Qūrṣāwī, *Sharḥ jadīd*, fol. 111a.

6

Postclassical Kalām

THE THEOLOGICAL TRADITION had undergone significant change from the 14th to 19th centuries. Contrary to much of the relevant scholarship, which views *kalām* in later eras as repetitive and derivative,[1] the tradition was constantly evolving as new ideas were formulated and incorporated into its preexisting discourses. Postclassical *kalām* was hardly isolated or stagnant, particularly in Central Asia and the Volga-Ural region, where influences from the Ottoman Empire, the Caucasus, India, and Iran were important in shaping the further development of Sunni theology well into the 19th century.

As noted, theological reasoning in this period was constructed around *taqlīd* in the form of "scaffolding": scholars accepted a number of basic premises that were necessary for shared theological discourse and which underpinned their arguments. These foundational premises served to maintain the coherence of the *kalām* tradition, as theologians adopted the positions of earlier scholars and in turn employed them as a basis for the articulation of their own views. New developments were thus built upon established ideas, and the theological tradition was constantly evolving, if in subtle ways, through the continuous refinement and emendation of *kalām* discourse.

One of the most significant developments was the metaphysical schema of Muḥy al-Dīn ibn ʿArabī (1165–1240), who introduced a new understanding of existence. Briefly, he posited that all being is a manifestation (*tajallī*) of

1. E.g., Majid Fakhry. *A History of Islamic Philosophy*. 2nd ed. New York: Columbia UP, 1983; Josef Van Ess. *The Flowering of Muslim Theology*. Cambridge, MA: Harvard UP, 2006. On Central Asia specifically: Claude Gilliot. "La théologie musulmane en Asie centrale et au Khorasan." *Arabica*, vol. 49; 2002. 135–203; M. Dinorshoev. "Philosophy, Logic and Cosmology." *History of Civilizations of Central Asia*. Vol. V: *Development in Contrast: From the Sixteenth to the Mid-Nineteenth Century*. Paris: UNESCO, 2003. 747–758.

God, who *is* existence itself.[2] This idea would come to be known as *waḥdat al-wujūd* (the unity of existence)—a term ibn ʿArabī did not himself use—and it represents a major part of his considerable contribution to postclassical thought.

A native of Andalusia who settled in Damascus, ibn ʿArabī's metaphysics quickly spread to Central Asia and India through his many followers and commentators. His putative "school," according to James Morris, seized primarily upon its ontological aspects, systematizing them and incorporating his conception of existence into established philosophical and theological discourse.[3] A prominent example is the *Durra al-fākhira* of ʿAbd al-Raḥmān Jāmī (1414–1492), which is an extensive comparison of the respective beliefs of the philosophers, the *mutakallimīn*, and "the Sufis" (here followers of ibn ʿArabī) on issues following from his thought.[4] A great many adherents of the school used ibn ʿArabī's writings as the starting point for their own metaphysical reasoning, developing views and arguments apart from his own, and the reformulation of his ideas into the language of Islamic scholarship (as opposed to his idiosyncratic use of terminology) furthered their tremendous spread among *ʿulamāʾ*, particularly in the Persianate world.[5]

Wujūdī *Influence*

Ibn ʿArabī's thought itself combines significant elements of Ashʿari *kalām* and Avicennian philosophy, and the diffusion of his *wujūdī* metaphysics among scholars furthered preexisting debates about the nature of existence. Ibn ʿArabī's ideas were hardly uncontroversial—many scholars viewed them as

2. The best treatment of ibn ʿArabī's thought is found in the many relevant works of William Chittick, namely William Chittick. *The Sufi Path of Knowledge: ibn al-ʿArabi's Metaphysics of Imagination*. Albany: State U of New York P, 1989; William Chittick. *The Self-Disclosure of God: Principles of Ibn al-ʿArabi's Cosmology*. Albany: State U of New York P, 1998.

3. James Morris. "Ibn ʿArabi and His Interpreters Part II: Influences and Interpretations." *Journal of the American Oriental Society*, vol. 106, no. 4; 1986. 733–756, esp. pp. 745–756; James Morris. "Ibn ʿArabi and His Interpreters Part II (Conclusion): Influences and Interpretations." *Journal of the American Oriental Society*, vol. 107, no. 1; 1987. 101–119, pp. 110–114; also Nathan Spannaus. "Theology in Central Asia." *Oxford Handbook of Islamic Theology*. Ed. Sabine Schmidtke. Oxford: Oxford UP, 2016. 587–605, pp. 593–595; Toby Mayer. "Theology and Sufism." *The Cambridge Companion to Classical Islamic Theology*. Ed. Timothy Winter. Cambridge: Cambridge UP, 2008. 258–287, pp. 277–279.

4. ʿAbd al-Raḥmān Jāmī. *al-Durra al-fākhira fī taḥqīq madhhab al-ṣūfiya wa-l-mutakallimīn wa-l-ḥukamāʾ al-mutaqaddimīn*. Eds. Nicholas Heer and ʿAlī Mūsāwī Bihbihānī. Tehran: Dānishgāh-i MakGīll, 1358/1980.

5. Morris, "Ibn ʿArabi," pp. 752–756.

deeply problematic for a number of reasons—but they were nevertheless influential, and they forced *ʿulamāʾ* of all stripes to contend with substantial ontological questions.[6]

One of the primary effects of the spread of ibn ʿArabī's thought, even among those who disagreed, was an increased emphasis on the relationship between (respectively) the divine essence, its existence, and the existence of everything else (labeled *mā siwā Allāh*, lit. "what is other than God"). For ibn ʿArabī, who relies on Avicenna's modalities of existence, God Himself is absolute existence (*al-wujūd al-muṭlaq*), as He is necessary of existence in Himself and therefore the only being that is inherently ontologically self-sufficient.[7] All other entities are in themselves nonexistent, brought into being only through God.[8] They are therefore distinguished from God as existents (*mawjūdāt*) whose being is qualified or circumscribed in some way.[9] They are made existent through the individuation (*taʿayyun/fī al-ʿayn*) of the primordial matter (*hayūlā/al-madda al-ūlā*), which comes from God and is God. (Hence the unity of existence, as all things share in the same existence, which is God.)[10]

That God is Himself existence that all other entities share in went too far for many scholars, and it is unfounded from the perspective of mainstream Sunni *kalām*, which in general viewed each entity's existence as identical with its essence or quiddity (*māhiyya*). Ibn ʿArabī was criticized on these grounds—namely, that the idea that God's existence and the existence of everything else are identical is logically absurd, as every existent is distinct in its existence and

---

6. See Alexander Knysh's study of the reactions to ibn ʿArabī, which for all its scope only addresses those responses written in Arabic; Alexander Knysh. *Ibn ʿArabi in the Later Islamic Tradition: The Making of a Polemical Image in Medieval Islam*. Albany: State U of New York P, 1999. For a more contextual approach to similar material, see Khaled El-Rouayheb. *Islamic Intellectual History in the Seventeenth Century: Scholarly Currents in the Ottoman Empire and the Maghreb*. Cambridge: Cambridge UP, 2015, esp. pp. 235–346.

7. Muḥy al-Dīn Ibn ʿArabī. *Inshāʾ al-dawāʾir*. In *Kleinere Schriften des Ibn al-ʿArabi*. Ed. H. S. Nyberg. Leiden: Brill, 1919. 1–39, esp. pp. 15, 20. The *Inshāʾ*, although one of ibn ʿArabī's minor works, is a representative summary of the ontological aspects of his thought.

8. Cf. ibid., p. 10. Ibn ʿArabī here writes, "there is no contingent in existence fundamentally, and it [existence] is restricted to necessity and impossibility" (*innahu mā fī al-wujūd mumkin aṣl^{an}, wa-innahu munḥaṣir fī al-wujūb wa-l-istiḥāla*), an idea that later members of his school would understand as distinguishing God's necessary existence from the nonexistence of everything else, insofar as the latter cannot exist without an external cause (see e.g. note 13).

9. Ibn ʿArabī, *Inshāʾ*, pp. 20–22; cf. Chittick, *Sufi Path*, p. 79.

10. Ibn ʿArabī, *Inshāʾ*, esp. pp. 7, 16–19.

the existence of contingent/possible entities (*mumkināt*) cannot be the same as the existence of the Necessary.[11]

The distinction between God's necessary existence and the basic nonexistence of everything else, however, proved far more influential. There is, first of all, nothing objectionable about it in terms of Sunni orthodoxy, and it follows as an implication of the Avicennian modalities.[12] It was an important focus in the writings of ibn ʿArabī's school,[13] and it appeared in works by Sunni theologians, who came to redefine contingent entities as inherently or primarily nonexistent, prior to their creation (*ḥudūth*).[14] Jalāl al-Dīn Dawānī, for instance, argued that God, as the only necessary existent, is in fact the only true existent.[15] These discussions contributed to necessity becoming God's main meta-attribute, replacing eternality in scholars' treatments of His

11. [Pseudo-]Taftāzānī. *Risāla fī waḥdat al-wujūd*. In *Majmūʿa rasāʾil fī waḥdat al-wujūd*. [Istanbul]: n.p., 1294 [1877]. 2–50, esp. pp. 8, 15–16; see Knysh, *Ibn ʿArabi*, pp. 141–158. This work is attributed to Taftāzānī, but its author is now considered to be his student ʿAlāʾ al-Dīn al-Bukhārī (1377–1437).

12. Cf. El-Rouayheb, *Islamic Intellectual History*, p. 239. In fact, it was discussed by Avicenna himself; see Herbert Davidson. *Proofs for Eternity, Creation and the Existence of God in Medieval Islamic and Jewish Philosophy*. New York: Oxford UP, 1987, pp. 291–292.

13. Jāmī, for instance, begins the *Durra al-fākhira* by praising the Necessary Existent in Itself (rather than any other epithets for God) and then writing, "Know that there is a necessary [entity] in existence, otherwise existent[s] would be limited to the contingent, and this would imply that nothing would exist at all, [because] the contingent, even if it is multiple (*mutaʿaddid*), is not itself sufficient in its existence. And it is clear that its creation [could not come] by another, because the stage of creation (*martabat al-ījād*) [only] follows the stage of existence. Since there [would be] neither existence nor creation, there [would be] no existent, neither in itself nor through another. Thus the existence of the Necessary is affirmed"; Jāmī, *Durra al-fākhira*, p. 1.

14. Previously, the contingent had been described as neutral in terms of existence and nonexistence, but in the later postclassical period nonexistence came to be seen as the contingent's default state, as we see in Sirhindī and Qūrṣāwī. This also appears in Yūsuf Qarabāghī's influential supercommentary on Dawānī; *Ḥāshiyat Yūsuf Qarabāghī ʿalā sharḥ ʿaqāʾid Mullā Jalāl*. Ms. University of Michigan, Isl. ms. no. 1027.

15. Reza Pourjavady. *Philosophy in Early Safavid Iran: Najm al-Din Mahmud al-Nayrizi and His Writings*. Leiden: Brill, 2011, pp. 88–99; also Spannaus, "Theology," pp. 594–595. This issue was first broached by Dawānī in his *Risālat al-Zawrāʾ*; Jalāl al-Dīn Muḥammad al-Dawānī. *Risālat al-Zawrāʾ*. In *Sabʿ rasāʾil*. Ed. Aḥmad Tūysirkānī. Tehran: Mīrāth-i maktūb, 1381/2002. 171–184. Dawānī explored it further in later works, such as the *Risālat Ithbāt al-wājib al-jadīda*, although it was primarily his earlier works, such as the *Risālat Ithbāt al-wājib al-qadīma* and—particularly—the *Sharḥ al-ʿAḍudiyya*, that were most widely circulated in the Volga-Ural region. (Editions of these two *risālas* are contained in ibid.) Interestingly, however, the *Risālat al-Zawrāʾ* is the only work by an author other than Qūrṣāwī contained in the main codex of his writings, which was produced at his *madrasa* in Qūrṣā shortly after his death; ms. SPb IVR, no. A-1241, fols. 86b–90a.

nature.[16] Most importantly for our purposes, it informs Qūrṣāwī's criticism of Taftāzānī, as when he states that holding the attributes' contingency posits their nonexistence and absolute dependence on a cause to bring them out of nonexistence.[17]

Sirhindī for his part used this idea as the basis for a new ontological schema that more comprehensively emphasizes God's transcendence and otherness from creation.[18] He argues that only God exists (as, like ibn ʿArabī, absolute existence, *al-wujūd al-muṭlaq*) and that the existence of every other entity is merely a shadow representation of that existence (*wujūd-i taṣawwurī ẓillī*).[19] This shadow existence is not real, but its connection to real existence is analogous to the relationship between a thing and its shadow. Sirhindī therefore posits two levels of existence: the level of reality, at which only God exists and any other being is absolutely inconceivable, and the level of shadow, at which all existents (*mawjūdāt*) receive their (pseudo-)existence from God.[20]

Although it differs from ibn ʿArabī's on certain issues, Sirhindī's stance relies on the same framework of *wujūdī* metaphysics. (He is often presented in scholarship as rejecting ibn ʿArabī's thought, but the differences between the two have been far overstated.)[21] Existence at the level of shadow operates in a manner very similar to ibn ʿArabī's ontology, as each scholar's view entails a hierarchy of existents brought into being through individuation by God. For

16. A meta-attribute is an attribute of God that describes both God and the other attributes (e.g., God is eternal, as is His knowledge); Robert Wisnovsky. "One Aspect of the Avicennian Turn in Sunni Theology." *Arabic Sciences and Philosophy*, vol. 14; 2004. 65–100, pp. 72–75; Robert Wisnovsky. "Essence and Existence in the Eleventh- and Twelfth-Century Islamic East (*Mašriq*): A Sketch." *The Arabic, Hebrew and Latin Reception of Avicenna's Metaphysics*. Eds. A. Bertolacci and D. Hasse. Berlin: de Gruyter, 2011. 27–50, pp. 33–35.

17. Qūrṣāwī, *Lawāʾiḥ*, fols. 78a–81a.

18. J. G. J. ter Haar. *Follower and Heir of the Prophet: Shaykh Ahmad Sirhindi (1564–1624) as Mystic*. Leiden: Het Oosters Instituut, 1992, pp. 125–126; cf. Chittick, *Self-Disclosure*, p. 8; see also Sirhindī, *Maktūbāt*, 2:1, pp. 5–13.

19. Sirhindī, *Maktūbāt*, 2:3, pp. 18–19.

20. See ter Haar, *Follower and Heir*, pp. 127–135; Burhan Ahmad Faruqi. *The Mujaddid's Conception of Tawhid: Study of Shaikh Ahmad Sirhindis* [sic] *Doctrine of Unity*. Lahore: Institute of Islamic Culture, 1989, pp. 55–57; Muhammad Abdul Haq Ansari. *Sufism and Shariah: A Study of Shaykh Ahmad Sirhindi's Effort to Reform Sufism*. Leicester, UK: Islamic Foundation, 1986, pp. 110–114.

21. Cf. Arthur Buehler. "Ahmad Sirhindi: A 21st-Century Update." *Der Islam*, vol. 86; 2011. 122–141. The literature on the relationship between Sirhindī and ibn ʿArabī is substantial, but frequently biased toward one or the other. For a historical discussion, see Yohanan Friedmann. *Shaykh Ahmad Sirhindi: An Outline of His Thought and a Study of His Image in the Eyes of Posterity*. Montreal: McGill-Queen's UP, 1971.

both, individuation takes place through the outward emanation of the divine names and attributes at the first stage of existence outside the divine essence.[22] (One primary discrepancy here is that creation for ibn ʿArabī is the individuation of the primordial matter, which is God, while for Sirhindī it is the individuation of pure nonbeing, unconnected to God.)[23] Significantly, Sirhindī, who writes in Persian, describes his ontology using the terminology of *wujūdī* metaphysics as developed by members of ibn ʿArabī's school, for whom he expresses admiration and praise (as he does for ibn ʿArabī) and to whose discourse he is indebted.

The Metaphysics of the Attributes

These discussions about ontology focused on the distinction between God and *mā siwā Allāh* in terms of existence. The attributes, however, hold an intermediate position (roughly speaking) between the two, and there was a tendency among proponents of *wujūdī* metaphysics to view the attributes as separate from God. Ibn ʿArabī himself argues that God as absolute existence is utterly transcendent and can have no essential attribute (*ṣifa nafsiyya*) predicated of Him.[24] The divine attributes are indeed present within his ontology, but they function outside the divine essence, connected with creation.[25]

Members of his school took this as their basic position on the issue, holding the attributes to be mental existents that are themselves individuated beings. Ṣadr al-Dīn Qūnawī (ca. 1207–1274), ibn ʿArabī's student and foremost disciple, writes that in one respect God as absolute existence is beyond any predication or attribution. However, since existence is one, there is another respect in which (His) existence can be defined within creation. This is through individuation, the act of bringing into being, and in this respect

22. Ibn ʿArabī, *Inshāʾ*, pp. 25–35; cf. Sirhindī, *Maktūbāt*, 1:234, pp. 381–392; 2:1, esp. pp. 9–13; 2:5, pp. 23–24; 3:26, pp. 334–338.

23. E.g., Sirhindī, *Maktūbāt*, 1:234, pp. 383–392; 2:99, p. 268.

24. Ibn ʿArabī, *Inshāʾ*, pp. 20–21, 32–33.

25. Ibid., pp. 33–38. Ibn ʿArabī posits that there are seven attributes (which he also calls names and prototypes [*aʾimma*]), declaring them settled by both reason and orthodoxy. He lists living, knowing, willing, speaking (*qāʾil*), powerful, generous (*jawād*), and apportioning (*muqassiṭ*) in the main text, and the more conventional life, speech (*kalām*), power, will, knowledge, hearing, and sight in a diagram; ibid., 33, 30; see also Jāmī's commentary on ibn ʿArabī's self-summary of his *Fuṣūṣ al-ḥikam*, the *Naqsh al-fuṣūṣ*, in which he explains the role of the seven essential attributes (called "names" here) in existence; ʿAbd al-Raḥmān b. Aḥmad Jāmī. *Naqd al-nuṣūṣ fī sharḥ Naqsh al-fuṣūṣ*. Ed. William Chittick. Tehran: Anjuman-i Shāhanshāhī-i Falsafa-i Īrān, 1398/1977, pp. 40–41.

His absolute existence becomes qualified (*muqayyad*). Within this existence, God has attributes, which are mentally individuated from the divine essence.[26] As with ibn ʿArabī, their individuation signaled their connection with creation.[27] Jāmī likewise affirms the attributes' perfect, eternal existence as mental constructs (*iʿtibarāt*), but he writes that they also are part of God's manifestation as qualified existence in the world, tying Him to creation. Nevertheless, the Necessary Existent is beyond any qualification, division, multiplicity, or attribution, without the individuation of His existence.[28]

For his part, Sirhindī, like ibn ʿArabī and the others, renders the attributes distinct, individuated existents.[29] He holds that, due to God's absolute transcendence, the attributes are one with the divine essence at the level of real existence, while they have their own external existence (*fī al-khārij*, rather than mental existence) separate from the essence at the level of shadow.[30] In this way, Sirhindī inverts *lā huwa wa-lā ghayruh*, such that the attributes are both identical to the essence and other than it. Indeed, regarding the level of reality, he describes God in characteristically Muʿtazili terms, writing that God is knowing by His essence, not by an attribute of knowledge, and likewise for all of His attributes. Sirhindī's statement (*wa bi-dhāt-i khūd dānā ast nah bi-ṣifat-i ʿilm*) is virtually identical to the classical Muʿtazili formula that God is a knower in Himself, not by an attribute of knowledge.[31] (This is ironic, as Sirhindī of perhaps all adherents of *wujūdī* metaphysics is most concerned with upholding strict Sunni orthodoxy, and he saw himself as taking an intermediate stance between the mainstream Sunni *ʿulamāʾ* and ibn ʿArabī.)[32]

The differences in their views notwithstanding, each of these scholars places the attributes in a position of existence secondary to the divine essence.

---

26. William Chittick. "Sadr al-Din Qunawi on the Oneness of Being." *International Philosophical Quarterly*, no. 21; 1981. 171–184, esp. pp. 173–174, 178.

27. William Chittick and Patrick Lamborn Wilson. "Introduction." In Fakhr al-Din Ibrahim ʿIraqi. *Divine Flashes*. New York: Paulist Press, 1982. 3–32, esp. pp. 8–10.

28. Jāmī, *Durra al-fākhira*, pp. 11–20, 30–31; Jāmī, *Naqd al-nuṣūṣ*, pp. 40–41, 72, 73–75.

29. See, for instance, Sirhindī, *Maktūbāt*, 1:209, pp. 330, where he calls the names of God derived from the attributes (*ʿālim, qādir*, etc.) *taʿayyunāt*; see also ter Haar, *Follower and Heir*, p. 126; Faruqi, p. 38.

30. Sirhindī, *Maktūbāt*, 2:5, pp. 23–24. The essence is necessary at the level of shadow, while the attributes, because of their dependence on the essence, are contingent, indicating the degree of difference between them; ibid., 2:3, pp. 18–19.

31. *Allāhu ʿālim*[un] *bi-nafsih lā bi-ʿilm* (employing the synonym *nafs* for *dhāt*); Ashʿarī, *Maqālāt*, p. 164.

32. Friedmann, *Sirhindi*, p. 64.

In and of itself, this is not so distinct from Sunni theological orthodoxy. The idea that the attributes are contingent in themselves and only necessary through the essence is to posit them as dependent on, and subordinate to, the essence (as we see in Taftāzānī's stance and Qūrṣāwī's critique). But in the Sunni position the attributes are *lā huwa wa-lā ghayruh* with the essence and different from any other existent.[33] In addition, the attributes' existence for Sunnis is real, rather than mental or conceptual. The *wujūdī* framework, by contrast, relied upon an existential distinction between God and *mā siwā Allāh*. To posit the attributes as apart from the essence, below it in the hierarchy of existents, was to render them on the latter side of that division, as separate entities individuated out of God's existence like everything else in creation (as ibn ʿArabī, Qūnawī, Jāmī, and Sirhindī all state). Despite claims that the attributes must be affirmed, the implication of this position was that their existence was both markedly other than God's and lesser than God's, that some degree of nonexistence or imperfection tainted their being, that they were intrinsically impossible of existence, or—for Sirhindī—that they had no real existence at all.

Therefore, the God/*mā siwā Allāh* distinction, as constructed in *wujūdī* metaphysics, contradicted *lā huwa wa-lā ghayruh*, by either negating the attributes or collapsing them into the essence (in terms of absolute existence) and presenting them as separate, individuated existents outside the essence, simultaneously positing both *ʿayniyya* and *ghayriyya*.

Some scholars seized upon this in their critiques of *wujūdī* metaphysics. Most notably, ʿAlī Qārī al-Harawī (?–1606), the Hanafi traditionist from Herat, wrote a refutation of *waḥdat al-wujūd* that focuses in large part on this problem with the attributes.[34] Engaging with members of ibn ʿArabī's school such as Qūnawī and Jāmī, he argues that the *wujūdī* stance errs in both its *ʿayniyya* and *ghayriyya*, comparing it with other sects holding heretical views on the attributes.[35] The correct Sunni position, he argues, falls in between these two extremes, and he states repeatedly that God is transcendent together with His attributes.[36]

---

33. Which we see, for instance, in Taftāzānī's statement that the attributes are eternal (*azaliyya*) with God, quoted in Chapter 5; Saʿd al-Dīn al-Taftāzānī. *Sharḥ al-ʿaqāʾid al-nasafiyya*. Ed. Aḥmad Ḥijāzī al-Saqqā. Cairo: Maktabat al-Kulliyyāt al-azhariyya, 1407/1988, p. 39.

34. ʿAlī Qārī. *Risāla fī waḥdat al-wujūd*. In *Majmūʿa rasāʾil fī waḥdat al-wujūd*. [Istanbul]: n.p., 1294 [1877]. 52–114. His view of ibn ʿArabī was not exclusively negative, and he does offer reserved praise for him elsewhere; cf. El-Rouayheb, *Islamic Intellectual History*, p. 246.

35. ʿAlī Qārī, *Risāla*, pp. 59–60.

36. Ibid., pp. 53, 56–57, 63, 64.

In response to such critiques, Muḥammad Maʿṣūm defends Sirhindī's understanding of the attributes by arguing that ibn ʿArabī and his followers have negated the attributes by holding them to have only mental existence, while asserting that the Sunni *ʿulamāʾ* have themselves failed to avoid *ghayriyya*, due to their belief in the attributes' superaddition.[37]

In light of these debates, the motivation behind Qūrṣāwī's position becomes apparent. The spread of *wujūdī* ideas had significantly shaped theology in this period, even among those who continued to rely on more conventional metaphysics.[38] That includes Qūrṣāwī, who argued against it in favor of Sunni *kalām* ontology. Nevertheless, the questions of the relationship between the divine essence, its existence, and the existence of everything else that followed from ibn ʿArabī's thought had shifted the discourse over the attributes.

The primary issue was no longer whether or not the attributes have existence but what their existence is vis-à-vis God and creation, respectively. For Qūrṣāwī, upholding their existence as *divine* attributes means that they are transcendent with God (as they are not other than Him). Therefore, they can have no connection with created beings; in the ontological distinction between God and everything else, the attributes fall strictly with the former.

---

37. Cf. Muḥammad Maʿṣūm, *Maktūbāt*, 2:105, pp. 164–166. Muḥammad Maʿṣūm states that the *mutakallimīn* have stumbled into *ghayriyya* because their definition of the term *ghayr* as "the possibility of separation" is too narrow and does not account for "general otherness" (*muṭlaq-i ghayriyya*) between two things. See the section "Differentiation" in Chapter 5.

38. Dawānī was hugely important for later theologians in Central Asia, with many of the most prominent scholars of the 19th century, including Ūriwī, Mangārī, and Fakhr al-Dīn b. Ibrāhīm b. Khūjāsh, possessing a scholarly lineage (*isnād* or *silsila*) that connects to him, through ʿAṭāʾ Allāh Bukhārī; Michael Kemper. *Sufis und Gelehrte in Tatarien und Baschkirien, 1789–1889: Der islamische Diskurs unter russischer Herrschaft*. Berlin: Klaus Schwarz Verlag, 1998, p. 221 n. 33; Spannaus, "Theology," p. 592; the *isnād* is recorded in Fakhr al-Dīn, *Āthār*, vi, p. 291. This lineage also connects these scholars with Yūsuf Qarabāghī, perhaps the most important scholar of 17th- and 18th-century Bukhara, who wrote—among many other works—a supercommentary on the *Sharḥ al-ʿAḍudiyya* that deals with questions of existence and non-existence stemming from *wujūdī* ideas; Spannaus, "Theology," pp. 592–593, 596–597. (In this article I wrote that the "Mawlānā Sharīf" listed in the *isnād* is unknown. In fact, this is likely Muḥammad Sharīf Bukhārī [?–after 1699], who was possibly a student of Qarabāghī; cf. Robert McChesney. "Islamic Culture and the Chinggisid Restoration: Central Asia in the Sixteenth and Seventeenth Centuries." *New Cambridge History of Islam. Vol. 3: The Eastern Islamic World Eleventh to Eighteenth Centuries*. Eds. David Morgan and Anthony Reid. Cambridge: Cambridge UP, 2010. 239–265, pp. 263–264.) As El-Rouayheb has shown, beginning in the 17th century leading Ottoman *ʿulamāʾ* similarly traced their scholarly lineage back to Dawānī in ways that overlap with these Central Asian scholars; El-Rouayheb, *Islamic Intellectual History*, pp. 43, 48, 50, 52–55. It's worth noting, however, that the influence of ibn ʿArabī's metaphysics in Central Asia and the Volga-Ural region seems to be quite different from the contemporaneous intellectual developments in Ottoman Arab lands that El-Rouayheb highlights.

Accordingly, Qūrṣāwī's stance is concerned mainly with lessening the attributes' distinctiveness. Indeed, the aspects of Taftāzānī's position that he focuses on are those that posit a degree of ontological separation between the attributes and the essence, rendering the attributes merely contingent of existence and therefore like created beings. While presenting it as an absurd violation of God's transcendence, Qūrṣāwī is also reinforcing the idea that the attributes share in that transcendence. He argues that the attributes are necessary, because they exist *by* or *in* the essence. As such, they have almost ontological equality, in that the attributes and the essence have the same existence. The existence of everything else, however, is separate, thereby removing any question of the attributes' link with creation. Qūrṣāwī in fact states this explicitly in the *Sharḥ jadīd*, writing about the world (*al-ʿālam*), "It is existents that are other than God (*siwā Allāh*), and [that] description (*taʿrīf*) does not comprise the attributes because they are not other than the essence (*laysat siwā al-dhāt*) in existence."[39]

Although Taftāzānī and Qūrṣāwī locate their respective positions within the framework of Sunni *kalām*, the differences between them reflect their different historical contexts and the evolution of *kalām* discourse over time. The Sunni stance on the attributes developed in large part in response to the Muʿtazili claim that the attributes have no real existence and are identical with the essence. Taftāzānī, following the lead of earlier Sunni *mutakallimīn*, emphasized the attributes' distinctiveness in order to counter this argument, which was still current in his time; according to Wilferd Madelung, the Muʿtazila remained prominent in Central Asia, particularly Khwārizm, well into the 14th century, and Taftāzānī himself debated Muʿtazili scholars at the Timurid court.[40]

Yet the Muʿtazila disappeared soon after. Their ideas were incorporated into other movements as new approaches were put forward and argued over. The theological discourse changed accordingly. Although the memory of the sect remained important, that the attributes exist ceased to be a point

39. Qūrṣāwī, *Sharḥ jadīd*, fol. 103a. Notably, Dawānī in the *Sharḥ al-ʿAḍudiyya* explicitly defines the world as "what is other than His essence and His attributes" (*mā siwā dhātih wa-ṣifātih*). Marjānī uses his phrasing to criticize the Ashʿari position on the attributes, stating that it posits them as so different from the divine essence that Dawānī was forced to mention them alongside the essence to make it clear they are not part of the world; Marjānī, *Ḥāshiya*, p. 47.

40. Wilferd Madelung. "The Spread of Maturidism and the Turks." *Actas IV congresso de estudos arabes e islamicos, Coimbra-Lisboa, 1968*. Leiden: Brill, 1971. 109–168, p. 116; Wilferd Madelung, "Taftāzānī, Saʿd al-Dīn Masʿūd b. ʿUmar," *EI*².

of contention.[41] Instead, the focus of debates over the attributes shifted to questions of how their existence relates to God's, spurred by the influence of *wujūdī* metaphysics. This was the polemical environment in which Qūrṣāwī formulated his stance. While both he and Taftāzānī aimed to uphold the attributes, the degree of separation between them and the essence that allowed Taftāzānī to argue for their distinct existence had by Qūrṣāwī's time led to the belief that the attributes were separate existents, connected to God's existence like everything else. Lessening their distinctiveness became important for upholding their status as divine attributes, not other than the divine essence. As noted, Qūrṣāwī's stance approximates the absolute unity posited of God by the Muʿtazila, in contrast to the early Sunnis' relative unity.[42] Though unusual, such an approach makes sense in this context. The idea that all beings share in God's existence had made a more definitive statement of divine unity and transcendence necessary as a response. We can see this with Sirhindī, who attempted to assert absolute unity at the level of real existence in order to maintain God's transcendence. But Sirhindī used Muʿtazili terms in doing so, undermining the attributes' real existence. Qūrṣāwī, by contrast, presents an understanding of God's unity and transcendence that simultaneously distinguishes Him from creation and upholds the attributes as existent with Him, thereby avoiding *ʿayniyya* (and Muʿtazilism) while arguing for God's absolute unity in reference to—but not in agreement with—the doctrines of ibn ʿArabī's school.

It seems that Qūrṣāwī was not alone in engaging with these questions. Fatḥ Allāh Ūriwī himself put forward the concept of *waḥda ʿadadiyya* (lit. "numerical oneness") as an understanding of the relationship between the essence and the attributes. Although the work describing it, the *Risāla fī ittiṣāf al-wājib bi-l-waḥda al-ʿadadiyya*, has not been located,[43] *waḥda ʿadadiyya* appears to have been a similar attempt to deal with the attributes in response to *wujūdī* metaphysics. While there's little indication that Ūriwī adopted this ontology outright, there is a possible correspondence between *waḥda ʿadadiyya* and the *wujūdī* idea that God has two types of oneness—absolute,

41. For instance, though he explicitly positions himself against the Sunni *mutakallimīn*, Jāmī argues that the existence of God's attributes is beyond doubt; Jāmī, *Durra al-fākhira*, pp. 12–14.

42. Cf. Harry Austryn Wolfson. *The Philosophy of the Kalam*. Cambridge, MA: Harvard UP, 1976, p. 139.

43. Kemper, *Sufis*, p. 221 n. 31, 258; see Fakhr al-Dīn, *Āthār*, ix, pp. 8–9; Ramzī, *Talfīq*, ii, p. 368. It of course may be found in the future, thereby impacting my admittedly speculative discussion here.

existential transcendence that no other being shares (*aḥadiyya*), and a lesser oneness through which God's existence is shared by all beings (*waḥidiyya*).[44] As described by Jāmī, the latter accepts plurality (*kathra*) and number, which follows logically, he writes, because *waḥid* is itself a number.[45] Ūriwī for his part states that the essence is not subject to number, but it is possible to describe the singular essence with many attributes.[46]

The similarities with Sirhindī's two levels of existence are clear, and Ūriwī, who frequently cites Sirhindī, perhaps relies on this line of reasoning to argue that the eight (numbered) attributes exist with the essence without violating God's oneness. Qūrṣāwī of course rejects *waḥda ʿadadiyya* as infringing upon divine simplicity and transcendence,[47] but Ūriwī does not appear concerned with this critique. The disagreement between the two scholars seems to be grounded in differing views of *tawḥīd*. For Qūrṣāwī, as we have seen, *tawḥīd* entails God's absolute uniqueness and simplicity, as well as His transcendence from all creation. Ūriwī, however, seems to conceive of *tawḥīd* strictly in terms of God's uniqueness, objecting to Qūrṣāwī's claim that God is beyond quantity on the grounds that His oneness is only in terms of His having no partner (*shārik*) or equivalent (*naẓīr*).[48]

Such a view is obviously unusual, but it's possible that, with this position, Ūriwī is attempting to combine elements of Sirhindī's stance with Sunni *kalām*. Regarding the attributes specifically, Ūriwī understands them in terms of the established orthodoxy, describing them in ways similar to Taftāzānī and upholding their contingency, multiplicity, and superaddition.[49] He cites the famous Ashʿari Imām al-Juwaynī (1028–1085) for the view that "the attributes are existents (*mawjūdāt*), and [the attribute of] knowledge along with the essence are two existents (*mawjūdān*)," thus maintaining their distinctiveness.[50]

---

44. Jāmī, *Naqd al-nuṣūṣ*, pp. 25–26, 29–32; cf. Yasushi Tonaga. "The School of Ibn Arabi in Mashriq and Turkey with Special Reference to Abd al-Karim al-Jili." *III. Uluslar Arasi Mevlana Kongresi, 5–6 Mayis 2003: Bildirler*. Ed. Nuri Şimşekler. Konya: Selcuk Universitesi Matbaasi, 2004. 315–330.

45. Jāmī, *Naqd al-nuṣūṣ*, pp. 35, 69.

46. Ūriwī, *Risāla*, fols. 41a, 40b.

47. He writes that as God transcends (*yatanazzah ʿan*) number, He and His attributes must be beyond *waḥda ʿadadiyya*; Qūrṣāwī, *Ithbāt*, fol. 148b; also Qūrṣāwī, *Mabāḥith*, fol. 167b; Qūrṣāwī, *Sharḥ qadīm*, fol. 118a; Qūrṣāwī, *Sharḥ jadīd*, fol. 108b.

48. Ūriwī, [Untitled], fol. 1b.

49. Ūriwī, *Risāla*, fols. 39b–41b.

50. Ūriwī, [Untitled], fol. 1b.

Ūriwī, however, does not accept the attributes' differentiation, stating, like Qūrṣāwī, that they have a *lā huwa wa-lā ghayruh* relationship with each other.[51]

This rejection of differentiation may point to a limit to the attributes' distinctiveness. By arguing that the attributes are discrete existents without being other than each other, Ūriwī seems to be positing the attributes as distinct while still closely linked to each other and the essence. Given the importance of the God/*mā siwā Allāh* dichotomy, we may understand this stance, like Qūrṣāwī's, as an attempt to more clearly assert the attributes' connection to the essence. (Indeed, Ūriwī argues that upholding their differentiation is tantamount to *shirk*.)[52] Unlike Qūrṣāwī, however, Ūriwī is also concerned with maintaining the position articulated by Taftāzānī, and it is possible that he incorporates aspects of *wujūdī* metaphysics into his efforts to do so.[53]

This possibility is bolstered by Qūrṣāwī's reaction. As noted, he rejects *waḥda ʿadadiyya* as contravening God's simplicity, but—importantly—he also explicitly links it with individuation (*taʿayyun*), the coming into being of existents other than God within the *wujūdī* framework. For him, individuation is inconceivable within the divine essence, as it would entail its connection with creation and posit the existence of separate entities within it.[54] Yet this response is quite different than his criticisms of the established position, indicating the degree to which *waḥda ʿadadiyya* is a departure.

Approaching Sirhindī

Whatever its basis, it seems that *waḥda ʿadadiyya* was articulated as a way to understand the attributes' relationship with the essence, and Ūriwī, like Qūrṣāwī, engages with questions raised by *wujūdī* metaphysics, primarily through Sirhindī's writings. As members of the Mujaddidiyya, both scholars justify their positions with references and allusions to the order's founder. Sirhindī's prominence and the importance of the Mujaddidiyya made him a

51. Ūriwī, *Risāla*, fol. 40b.

52. Ibid.

53. It is not clear when Ūriwī developed the notion of *waḥda ʿadadiyya*. According to Fakhr al-Dīn, it was intended to refute Qūrṣāwī's position, yet Qūrṣāwī himself mentions it in the *Sharḥ qadīm*, one of his earliest works, suggesting that Ūriwī formulated *waḥda ʿadadiyya* apart from Qūrṣāwī; Fakhr al-Dīn, *Āthār*, ix, pp. 8–9; Qūrṣāwī, *Sharḥ qadīm*, fol. 18a. It should be noted that Ūriwī returned from studying in Bukhara in 1795, so his time there did not overlap with Qūrṣāwī's; Fakhr al-Dīn, *Āthār*, ix, p. 7. It is only after Qūrṣāwī returned around 1802 that Ūriwī could likely have become directly acquainted with his ideas.

54. Qūrṣāwī, *Mabāḥith*, fols. 167b–168a.

major source of scholarly authority among the Bulghar *ʿulamāʾ*—particularly those who studied in Central Asia—and appealing to his positions could be very persuasive. Indeed, Ūriwī cites Sirhindī to buttress his own stance, contra Qūrṣāwī, in upholding the attributes' contingency, multiplicity, and superaddition.[55] (In this way, according to Kemper, Ūriwī attempts to turn Sirhindī into a Sunni *mutakallim*, which was possible only by focusing on Sirhindī's view of the attributes at the level of shadow existence, not on his metaphysics as a whole.)[56]

Qūrṣāwī felt compelled to cite Sirhindī as well. As with Ūriwī, however, his view of the attributes does not line up with Sirhindī's, so he was often forced to refer to particular positions taken by Sirhindī while ignoring—if not rejecting—whole aspects of his thought. This led Qūrṣāwī into somewhat disingenuous statements, such as in his undated letter to ʿAbd al-Raḥmān Khān-Kirmānī (mentioned in Chapter 2), where he writes:

> And what [Sirhindī] said, "And they say that the real attributes are eight attributes," is predicated upon their eight concepts (*mafhūmāt*). So when the attributes are described by the lack of multiplicity, what is meant is their real, existential reality (*ḥaqīqatuhā al-mawjūda fī al-khārij*). And when [they] are described by something entailed by created and originated beings in terms of [the attributes'] being eight or seven, what is meant is their concepts as they occur in the [human] mind.[57]

In this letter, Qūrṣāwī is clearly trying to prove the correctness of his positions to another Mujaddidi scholar regarding the negation of the attributes' multiplicity. But he has to do so in light of Sirhindī's position on the attributes, which is in many ways contradictory to his own. He therefore explains Sirhindī's statement that there are eight attributes by (correctly) limiting that only to the level of shadow existence, as well as to human understanding of the attributes, while stating that the lack of multiplicity occurs at the level of real existence. Though his claim is technically true—there is no multiplicity of the attributes in reality—that is because for Sirhindī the attributes do not exist in reality. Instead, they are identical with the divine essence, a position Qūrṣāwī rejects.

---

55. Ūriwī, *Risāla*, fols. 39b–41b.

56. Kemper, *Sufis*, p. 270.

57. Fakhr al-Dīn, *Āthār*, iii, p. 98; transcription and translation in Nathan Spannaus. "Islamic Thought and Revivalism in the Russian Empire: An Intellectual Biography of Abu Nasr Qursawi (1776–1812)." Diss. McGill University, 2012, pp. 235–237.

Consequently, Qūrṣāwī found himself in the awkward position of appealing to Sirhindī's authority while simultaneously refuting his views. In an attempt to sidestep this discrepancy, Qūrṣāwī presents some of Sirhindī's pronouncements as *shaṭaḥāt*, ecstatic utterances that are incomprehensible and not to be taken literally. He writes in the *Naṣā'iḥ* that Sirhindī's stance on the multiplicity of the attributes and their being mere aspects of the divine essence at the level of real existence is not found in the *sharīʿa*, but "only among his *shaṭḥiyyāt*, and by *shaṭḥ* we mean words that are incomprehensible to the speaker, or which are comprehensible to him but he is incapable of understanding them or their meaning (*īrād*) in an expression indicating [the state of] his inner being (*bi-ʿibāra tadall ʿalā ḍamīrih*), and there is no benefit (*fā'ida*) in this type of speech."[58]

Nevertheless, Qūrṣāwī does rely on Sirhindī in his theological reasoning. For instance, his argument that the definition of "other" (*ghayr*) put forward by Taftāzānī is flawed (noted earlier) comes from Sirhindī, who, like Qūrṣāwī, used it to critique the prevailing position on the attributes.[59] More often, however, Qūrṣāwī's reliance on Sirhindī happens in oblique ways. For instance, in a particularly illuminating and complex passage from the *Mabāḥith*, Qūrṣāwī engages with Sirhindī (as well as Muḥammad Maʿṣūm, whom he also cites here) regarding the argument that God cannot be described as necessary, because He, as existence itself, transcends the modalities of existence, which can apply only to existents. Qūrṣāwī addresses this point while making the case for the attributes' necessity, and he rejects Sirhindī's view while at the same time using Sirhindī's logic to further support his own stance.[60]

Qūrṣāwī begins by citing Sirhindī's position that God and the attributes are both existents in the essence not by a further attribute of existence (*mawjūdāt bi-dhātih lā bi-l-wujūd*), which underlies the idea that they are beyond the modalities of existence.[61] Qūrṣāwī readily accepts that God and the attributes exist in the essence, but he takes issue with the second half of Sirhindī's claim.

---

58. Qūrṣāwī, *Naṣā'iḥ*, fol. 21a; Kemper, *Sufis*, p. 271.

59. Sirhindī, *Maktūbāt*, 1:272, p. 504; see also Muḥammad Maʿṣūm, *Maktūbāt*, 2:105, pp. 164–166.

60. Qūrṣāwī, *Mabāḥith*, fols. 165b–166a; transcription and translation in Spannaus, "Islamic Thought," pp. 246–248; cf. Sirhindī, *Maktūbāt*, 2:3, pp. 14–21; see also Kemper, *Sufis*, pp. 269–270.

61. Cf. Sirhindī, *Maktūbāt*, 2:3, pp. 18–19; 3:26, p. 334. This statement, while strongly resembling a Muʿtazili claim, is equivalent to a position taken by ibn Kullāb, who asserted that God is eternal in Himself, rather than through an attribute of eternality (*Allāhu qadīm bi-nafsih lā bi-l-qidam*); Ashʿarī, *Maqālāt*, pp. 164, 170. The distinction between God's eternality and His knowledge or power is that eternality is a meta-attribute (like necessity); Wisnovsky,

Having summarized Sirhindī's position, Qūrṣāwī counters that "an existent is either dependent in its existence or not. [In] the latter [case] it is necessary, and [in] the former contingent." The two, he writes, are absolutely and a priori mutually exclusive, and they entail an existent's negation or affirmation (in that the existence of a necessary being must be affirmed, and a contingent being must ultimately be negated).[62]

Here Qūrṣāwī has subtly refuted Sirhindī's position by arguing that any being that exists is logically either necessary or contingent, and cannot be otherwise. Since the latter implies nonexistence (as all contingent beings must be brought into existence), the divine essence therefore has to be necessary. He goes on, stating that an existent without existence is a contradiction, like "a black thing without blackness," and this could be correct only in the sense that such a thing exists by a particular existence that "cannot be understood by reason or comprehended by knowledge" (i.e., that a thing exists but its precise existence is unknown). Otherwise, he writes, the denial of that entity's existence in general would entail its negation. While it is possible to assert the former regarding God, it is not possible to assert the latter, since to say that God is without existence is to deny His being.[63]

But Sirhindī also argues that the attributes exist without existence, even, Qūrṣāwī notes, if they are something other than essence—that is, at the level of shadow, where they are separate entities. At this level of being, the divine essence is itself existence, which it emanates outward; therefore, Qūrṣāwī writes, this would mean that the essence would represent the attributes' existence. However, their existence would be separate from them, and thus superadded to them. Were this the case, he states, then the attributes would depend upon the essence for their existence, rendering them contingent and (by extension) the essence necessary. Therefore, the very basis of Sirhindī's argument that the essence and attributes are beyond necessity and contingency is undermined.[64]

Qūrṣāwī's primary goal in this passage is supporting the idea that the attributes are necessary with the essence, and he uses Sirhindī to make this point. He begins with Sirhindī's claim that God and the attributes both exist in the essence without an attribute of existence. However, he accepts the first

---

"One Aspect," pp. 72–75. Existence is likewise a meta-attribute, and so stating that God is existent in Himself without an attribute of existence fits into this position.

62. Qūrṣāwī, *Mabāḥith*, fol. 165b.

63. Ibid., fols. 165b–166a.

64. Ibid.

half while rejecting the second, and he uses his argument against Sirhindī to bolster his own claim about the attributes. While showing how the essence must have an existence that is necessary, he simultaneously shows how the attributes cannot have an existence that is separate from them, so they must also have necessary existence with the essence.

In making this argument, Qūrṣāwī relies upon Sirhindī's position (at least partially) while implicitly refuting important aspects of his metaphysics. The disconnect between Sirhindī's metaphysical framework and Qūrṣāwī's stance is evident in this passage. The basic premises of Sirhindī's *wujūdī* ontology are at odds with the tradition of Sunni *kalām* from which Qūrṣāwī is arguing; in the former's understanding, God's utter transcendence places Him beyond even existence, while the latter relies on the modalities of existence to assert His transcendence, as it is His necessity that distinguishes Him from all other existents. Indeed, this discrepancy arises immediately following this passage, where Qūrṣāwī specifically rejects Sirhindī's claim that the attributes are contingent and dependent upon the essence while still eternal and uncaused, on the grounds that a being that is dependent in its existence must have a cause (*muʾaththir*), and anything that requires a cause must be caused, so Sirhindī's claim that the attributes are dependent yet eternal is impossible.[65] Sirhindī's view on this point makes some sense within his ontology, insofar as the attributes have two types of existence (in shadow and real existence, respectively). Qūrṣāwī, though, recognizes only one type of existence, rendering this dual nature for the attributes untenable.

As a result of these fairly significant differences between the two, Sirhindī's influence on Qūrṣāwī's thought seems to be more in the way of perspective and priorities than as a main source for his ideas. The most direct link between the two is in terms of the importance of God's transcendence, expressed in the formula "There is nothing like unto Him" (*laysa ka-mithlih shayʾ*[un]/*bī-chūn wa chīgūnah*), which is foundational for both scholars (but, it should be noted, not unique). Yet, as we've seen, even this they understand differently: for Qūrṣāwī, it is God and His attributes as utterly other than creation, encapsulated in their inherent necessity; for Sirhindī, it is God as the only real being.

Qūrṣāwī's stance instead relies primarily upon the ideas of more conventional Sunni scholars. Nasafī's *ʿAqāʾid* of course provides the main textual basis for elaborating his position on the attributes and God's existence. Qūrṣāwī recites it during his inquisition in Bukhara and refers to Nasafī by a number of honorifics (including, among other things, *al-Imām al-Rabbānī*, a title

65. Ibid., fol. 166a.

conventionally reserved among the Mujaddidiyya for Sirhindī).[66] Kalābādhī as well is particularly important, and he describes the attributes in a way that corresponds very closely with Qūrṣāwī's view. He writes that the attributes are not God and not other than God, but are affirmed in themselves while subsisting within God; He never ceases to exist eternally in or with His names and attributes (*lam yazal qadīm^an bi-asmāʾih wa-ṣifātih*), and they are not differentiated but are *lā huwa wa-lā ghayruh* among each other.[67]

Though this position is not identical with Qūrṣāwī's, the connection between the two is evident, and Qūrṣāwī relies upon Kalābādhī when making his case to other scholars. His letter to Khān-Kirmānī explaining his view on the attributes includes a phrase that is taken virtually verbatim from Kalābādhī: "And [the great scholars] have agreed that [the attributes] are not multiple and not differentiated, so His knowledge is neither His power nor other than His power, and likewise with all of His attributes among hearing, seeing, His face, and His hand."[68]

These figures and their ideas were influential for Qūrṣāwī, but they also were generally important for the Central Asian theological tradition. Appealing to them allowed Qūrṣāwī to situate his views within the preexisting discourse and (ideally) persuade fellow *ʿulamāʾ* of the correctness of his stance. Indeed, Qūrṣāwī's letter to Khān-Kirmānī includes not only this quote from Kalābādhī but also explicit references to Sālimī, Nasafī, Sirhindī, and (negatively) Taftāzānī. Connecting his views to these prominent scholars served to bolster his critique by grounding it within the established theological tradition.

Qūrṣāwī's opponents responded accordingly, undermining his arguments and/or disregarding his references. Ūriwī, as noted, attempted to use Sirhindī against Qūrṣāwī. Dāghistānī refuted the sources of Qūrṣāwī's position (namely, Kalābādhī and ʿAlī Qārī) either by rejecting their statements or by showing how Qūrṣāwī's understanding of them is wrong. Dāghistānī writes, for instance, that Abū Ḥanīfa's statement that "God is one not in terms of number" (emphasized by ʿAlī Qārī in the *Sharḥ al-Fiqh al-akbar*) refers only to the essence, not the attributes, thus negating Qūrṣāwī's use of it.[69] Likewise,

---

66. Qūrṣāwī, *Sharḥ jadīd*, fol. 92b; see also Kemper, *Sufis*, p. 252 n. 135. Qūrṣāwī in fact elsewhere refers to Sirhindī in this way; e.g., Qūrṣāwī, *Mabāḥith*, fol. 168a; also Qūrṣāwī, *Naṣāʾiḥ*, fol. 20a.

67. Kalābādhī, *Kitāb al-Taʿarruf*, pp. 13–16.

68. Fakhr al-Dīn, *Āthār*, iii, p. 98; Kalābādhī, *Kitāb al-Taʿarruf*, p. 16; transcription and translation in Spannaus, "Islamic Thought," pp. 235–237.

69. Dāghistānī, *Radd*, fols. 3b, 4b.

the *fatwā* condemning Qūrṣāwī by the Bukharan *ʿulamāʾ* argues (implicitly) that Qūrṣāwī has misunderstood Sālimī's argument that there is no multiplicity with the attributes, which, they write, actually means that each attribute is singular—that is to say, for instance, that God is living through one attribute of life.[70]

Qūrṣāwī as Mutakallim

Although Qūrṣāwī relies on these earlier scholars, his stance on the attributes represents a development of the *kalām* tradition (as perhaps does Ūriwī's *waḥda ʿadadiyya*). The ideas he takes from his sources serve as antecedents, and he uses them in unique ways to formulate an understanding of the attributes' precise relationship to the divine essence, one that is characteristic of postclassical *kalām*. His use of Kalābādhī and Nasafī is illustrative of this point. Despite the overlap in their respective positions, there are a number of important elements of Qūrṣāwī's stance that are absent in their work. Most prominent is the issue of the attributes' necessity, which is a major focus for Qūrṣāwī. Kalābādhī and Nasafī are instead concerned with the attributes' eternality, which would become subsumed under the issue of necessity following the Avicennian Turn (which they predate). Qūrṣāwī's insistence upon the attributes' necessity, however, is markedly post-Avicennian. Similarly, he deals with ontological issues that arose only with the spread of *wujūdī* metaphysics. These important changes in the *kalām* tradition rendered Qūrṣāwī's intellectual environment quite different from that of these earlier figures, thus distinguishing his stance from his sources and influences.

Moreover, Qūrṣāwī was engaged in debate over these issues, and the constant theological contestation certainly shaped his stance and how it was articulated and argued. Qūrṣāwī's contemporaries, scholars such as Ūriwī, Mangārī, Dāghistānī, and Fakhr al-Dīn b. Ibrāhīm b. Khūjāsh—advocates of more rationalist theology and more established positions in Sunni *kalām*—fought with him over these questions.[71] Mangārī and Dāghistānī of course

70. Marjānī, *Mustafād*, ii, pp. 172–173; Fakhr al-Dīn, *Āthār*, iii, pp. 99–100; translation and transcription in Spannaus, "Islamic Thought," pp. 228–230. Ūriwī makes similar use of Sālimī; Ūriwī, *Risāla*, fol. 41a. Sālimī in fact does not reject multiplicity explicitly, but rather states that the attributes are not subject to number, yet he also argues that each attribute is itself singular; cf. Sālimī, *Tamhīd*, pp. 39, 48–51.

71. These scholars, as noted, were all (save the unknown Dāghistānī) students of ʿAṭāʾ Allāh Bukhārī, who was one of the Bukharan *ʿulamāʾ* who condemned Qūrṣāwī. ʿAṭāʾ Allāh was himself a prominent *mutakallim* who had written his own work on the issue of the attributes' eternality and contingency, and he criticized Qūrṣāwī in a letter to the Bulghar *ʿulamāʾ* for

wrote criticisms of Qūrṣāwī (both dedicated to Amir Ḥaydar, incidentally)[72] defending Taftāzānī. Similarly, Ūriwī composed a number of works in opposition to Qūrṣāwī's stance, upholding the attributes' superaddition as well as their contingency, which he justifies by stating that the attributes, though contingent, are not created (*ḥāditha*).[73] Here he draws the same distinction between eternality and necessity as Taftāzānī, and he in fact defends this view by citing Taftāzānī, writing that the attributes "are not necessary by themselves, but are necessary by the essence of the Necessary [Being]."[74] As for their multiplicity, Ūriwī upholds it as well, and he states definitively that there are seven or eight attributes.[75] Indeed, in his 1810 letter to Mufti Muḥammadjān, Ūriwī gives Qūrṣāwī's negation of multiplicity and his upholding of the attributes' necessity among the examples of his religious error. By espousing these views, he writes, Qūrṣāwī contradicts the established positions of Sunni *kalām* and is thus guilty of *bidʿa* and unbelief (*kufr*).[76]

Ūriwī states in his letter that, in rejecting the teachings of renowned scholars such as Taftāzānī, Dawānī, and al-Sayyid al-Sharīf Jurjānī (1339–1413), Qūrṣāwī's views go against more than four hundred years of traditional *kalām*. While it's true that Qūrṣāwī rejects many of their positions, his stance is deeply grounded in postclassical *kalām*. Not only does it reflect the development of post-Avicennian theology and the influence of *wujūdī* metaphysics, but it is also shaped by Qūrṣāwī's immediate context and the ongoing contestation among the Bulghar *ʿulamāʾ*.

Even Qūrṣāwī's epistemological critique does not serve as a rejection of *kalām*. Despite his attacks on the use of reason, his specific criticisms against his opponents—on the attributes' contingency, multiplicity, differentiation, and superaddition—are all supported by extensive rational argument, based upon the premises of Sunni *kalām*. Indeed, the fact that Qūrṣāwī actively participated in debates about what are very subtle and minute theological

---

asserting the attributes' necessity and the negation of their multiplicity, as well as placing (*taqaddum*) *naql* over *ʿaql*; Marjānī, *Mustafād*, ii, pp. 173–174; Fakhr al-Dīn, *Āthār*, iii, p. 101; Kemper, *Sufis*, p. 221 n. 33.

72. Mangārī, *Risāla*, esp. fol. 124a; also Fakhr al-Dīn, *Āthār*, xi, pp. 194, 195; Dāghistānī, *Radd*, fol. 2a.

73. Ūriwī, *Risāla*, fols. 40a–40b.

74. Ūriwī here also quotes ʿInāyat Allāh Bukhārī; Ūriwī, *Risāla*, fols. 39a–39b; cf. Taftāzānī, *Sharḥ*, p. 38.

75. Ūriwī, *Risāla*, fol. 40b.

76. Fakhr al-Dīn, *Āthār*, iii, pp. 108–109.

distinctions—in many ways *kalām*'s raison d'être—shows that he did not reject it as an intellectual endeavor.

In fact, Qūrṣāwī's attacks on *kalām* appear to be little more than a polemical ploy directed at his opponents. By drawing the distinction between his own theological work (so-called *ʿilm al-tawḥīd wa-l-ṣifāt*) and his opponents' theological work ("*kalām*"), he is able to deride their positions as the result of overuse of reason, philosophy, and whim, at odds with scripture and *naql*. This aim is apparent from the very opening of his *Sharḥ jadīd*:

> *Ammā baʿd*: [Qūrṣāwī] says: Now the summary called the *ʿAqāyid nasafiyya*, by the divine imam ʿUmar al-Nasafī, encompasses scholarly questions and indisputable principles. The commentary of the *muḥaqqiq* Taftāzānī, even if it contains revisions and precisions and is not devoid of verifications (*taḥqīqāt*), most of them are based only on philosophical principles and intellectual fancies and the kind of mistakes and errors of delusion that are not to be believed—in contrast to following the Book and Sunna—and bring no guidance except toward [Taftāzānī's] desires—in contrast to following consensus. . . . So God forgive him for clinging frequently to the *madhhab* of *shaykh* Abū Ḥasan al-Ashʿarī.[77]

Here Qūrṣāwī is differentiating between Taftāzānī's work and that of Nasafī, who is no less of a *mutakallim* than Taftāzānī but with whom Qūrṣāwī agrees. With this distinction, Qūrṣāwī can issue a blanket condemnation of his opponents, asserting that they are engaged in *kalām* (with negative connotations and intimations of philosophy), while he is purely studying *tawḥīd*.

But the fact that many of his opponents were Hanafi-Maturidis, to say nothing of Mujaddidiyya, makes this distinction doubly important. Qūrṣāwī cannot simply condemn all Ashʿaris while extolling the rightness of Maturidis, so he must in some way separate himself from antagonists such as Ūriwī, whose scholarly lineage was very similar to his own. As a result, the primary target for Qūrṣāwī's theological ire is what he calls the *ahl al-kalām*, whom he sometimes labels "the people of innovation" (*ahl al-mubtadiʿ*).[78] It is these people who have immersed themselves only in the study of *kalām* and

77. Qūrṣāwī, *Sharḥ jadīd*, fols. 92b–93a; transcription and translation in Spannaus, "Islamic Thought," pp. 248–249. See Figure 4.

78. Qūrṣāwī, *Mabāḥith*, fol. 165a.

confused themselves with excessive rationality, and in the process deviated from correct doctrine.[79] This group includes the Muʿtazila and *falāsifa*, as well as many Sunni theologians. (Besides Taftāzānī, Fakhr al-Dīn Rāzī and ʿAḍud al-Dīn Ījī are singled out for their theological errors.)[80]

For all his criticisms of *kalām*, most of Qūrṣāwī's contemporaries treat him as merely another *mutakallim*. Amīrkhān, for instance, writes that Qūrṣāwī was "distinguished in rational and traditional subjects (*ʿulūm-i ʿaqliyya wa-naqliyya*), and *he immersed himself in* kalām *in particular*."[81] His theological opponents saw him as little more than a misguided scholar, albeit one whose ideas posed a moral danger to the community.

It is undeniable that his thought relies on premises from the *kalām* tradition, to which the disputes over the attributes were internal. In this respect he and his opponents were all equally engaged in *kalām* and, as such, were "speaking each other's language." (By contrast, Ūtiz-Īmānī attacked Qūrṣāwī from an entirely different standpoint, denouncing him as a "philosopher" [*faylasūf*] and rejecting the entire enterprise of *kalām*.)[82]

There was without doubt a sense of shared discourse between Qūrṣāwī and the "*mutakallimīn*." Although opponents, Qūrṣāwī and a figure such as Dāghistānī understand the other's position and arguments well, and they do not misrepresent them. One could go so far as to state that each concedes the other's point—that Qūrṣāwī's position makes the attributes less distinct from the essence, and that Dāghistānī's (and Taftāzānī's) makes them more so. That said, they do not agree, and they essentially accuse each other of violating *lā huwa wa-lā ghayruh* (which they both accept), Qūrṣāwī the first clause and Dāghistānī the second. But their disagreement stems from their differing approaches to the attributes. Dāghistānī, who is self-consciously taking the established position, is concerned primarily with upholding the attributes' existence—that is, negating Muʿtazilism, which he sees in Qūrṣāwī's stance.[83] Qūrṣāwī, on the other hand, is primarily concerned with upholding God's

79. Ibid., fols. 155b–156b, 167b; Qūrṣāwī, *Sharḥ jadīd*, fols. 96b–97a.

80. Qūrṣāwī, *Mabāḥith*, fol. 166b; Qūrṣāwī, *Sharḥ jadīd*, fols. 94a, 108b; Qūrṣāwī, *Ithbāt*, fol. 148b.

81. Ḥusayn Amīrkhān. *Tawārīkh-i bulghāriyya*. Kazan: Maṭbaʿat Wiyācheslāf, 1883. [Reprinted with Russian translation as Khusain Amirkhanov. *Tavarikh-e Bulgariia (Bulgarskie khroniki)*. Intro. and trans. A. M. Akhunov. Moscow: izd-vo Mardzhani, 2010], p. 53; emphasis added.

82. Kemper, *Sufis*, p. 238; cf. G. Utyz-Imiani al-Bulgari. "Spasenie pogibaiushchikh." *Izbrannoe*. Ed. and trans. R. Adygamov. Kazan: Tatarstan knizhnoe izd-vo, 2007. 132–165.

83. Cf. Dāghistānī, *Radd*, fol. 6a.

oneness and transcendence, which he sees as being undermined by the established position, and he set about attempting to prove its falsity.

It was not mere contrarianism that motivated this approach. As noted, Qūrṣāwī considered it a religious duty to confront error in belief, and he applied so much effort toward refuting these views precisely because he saw them as religiously unacceptable. Beyond his polemical claims that those who held them were guilty of *bidʿa* and error (*ḍalāla*) is an understanding of theology—in Qūrṣāwī's sense, *ʿilm al-tawḥīd wa-l-ṣifāt*—that is not simply academic. Rather, he writes that the roots or foundations (*uṣūl*) of the religion are indisputable, and there can be no dissension (*tafarruq*) regarding them, especially concerning the attributes.[84] Accordingly, he makes it clear that any deviation in terms of the attributes should be rejected absolutely:

> And as for one who errs (*mukhṭiʾ*) in *uṣūl* or in creed (*ʿaqāyid*), he is reprehensible, but he is not considered to be deviant (*yuḍallal*) or unbelieving like the people of whim (*ahl al-hawāʾ*), some of whom deny God's attributes and say that He is knowing without knowledge and powerful without power.[85] Some of them affirm [the attributes] but they compare them by *tashbīh*, so they say that they are contingent [and] possible of existence (*mumkinat jāʾizat al-wujūd*), or God created them. And some of them affirm some of [the attributes], comparing them with *tashbīh*, and deny others, so they say that there are seven of them, and others [say] that there are eight, so these [people] deny what is beyond the seven or eight [attributes], and do not consider them to transcend quantity in the sense of paucity and plurality and in the sense of limitation. And this type of ignorance, even if it is short of unbelieving ignorance (*jahl al-kāfir*), does not warrant absolution in the hereafter, since it is against obvious evidence, such as [Qurʾanic] verses affirming the attributes and their transcendence.[86]

For Qūrṣāwī, such views are unacceptable because they contradict the most central tenets of the religion. Each of his objections to incorrect beliefs about the attributes is based on the notion that they all violate God's transcendence and both aspects of *tawḥīd*, be it God's uniqueness or simplicity. Qūrṣāwī explicitly affirms that *tawḥīd* and *tanzīh* are essential elements of the faith; as

---

84. Qūrṣāwī, *Irshād*, p. 27; Qūrṣāwī, *Sharḥ jadīd*, fol. 96b.

85. This is of course the Muʿtazili position.

86. Qūrṣāwī, *Irshād*, p. 27.

such, all of these views regarding the attributes are, for him, beyond the pale.[87] He makes it clear that despite his embrace of *ijtihād* in terms of law, the tenets of the religion are not open to the same kind of interpretation or dispute. Rather, belief requires certainty that can only come through scripture: "And we do not trust *ijtihād* by opinion (*bi-l-raʾy*) on the fundamentals of religion (*uṣūl al-dīn*), but rather [we only call for] adherence to the Book and the Sunna."[88]

Bearing this in mind, Qūrṣāwī's emphasis on attacking his opponents' positions rather than asserting his own makes sense. For him, their views represent deviation and ignorance, and are undoubtedly wrong. He writes that whoever deviates (*alḥada*) regarding the attributes fabricates (*taqawwul*) falsehood about them and the divine essence.[89] He constantly maintains his views' basis in *naql*, stating how they are grounded in the Qurʾan and Sunna, or that the Companions agreed upon them, while presenting his opponents as diverging from sound sources of knowledge and the beliefs of earlier authorities. In terms of the latter, for instance, he writes that Abū Ḥanīfa's statement that "God is one not by way of number, but rather in that He has no partner" precludes *waḥda ʿadadiyya*.[90] His aim is to draw attention to the novelty and innovation of his opponents' views and, by contrast, to show the conventionality and orthodoxy of his own. Qūrṣāwī's position, in fact, is not stated outright because it is presented as *the* correct position on the attributes, upon which all of those who are saved (i.e., the *firqa nājiya*) agree, rather than the views of a single scholar.[91]

Of course, taken as a whole, Qūrṣāwī's position on the attributes is in fact the view of a single scholar. The issue of the attributes' existence and their relation to the essence was, historically speaking, not nearly as settled as he (or the Bukharan *ʿulamāʾ*) presents it. The question of the attributes' multiplicity—closely linked with the question of their differentiation—was by no means resolved.[92] Neither was the issue of their necessary or contingent

87. Qūrṣāwī, *Sharḥ jadīd*, fols. 96b, 105b.

88. Qūrṣāwī, *Irshād*, p. 27.

89. Qūrṣāwī, *Lawāʾiḥ*, fol. 85a; also Qūrṣāwī, *Mabāḥith*, fol. 166b.

90. Qūrṣāwī, *Sharḥ jadīd*, fol. 108b; cf. ʿAlī Qārī, *Sharḥ*, p. 22.

91. Qūrṣāwī, *Sharḥ jadīd*, fol. 93a; Qūrṣāwī, *Mabāḥith*, fol. 156b, 157b. This is not unusual; Humphreys writes that the *ʿulamāʾ*'s scholarly activities were viewed as a collective, rather than individual, enterprise; R. Stephen Humphreys. *Islamic History: A Framework for Inquiry*. Rev. ed. Princeton, NJ: Princeton UP, 1991, p. 195.

92. See Dāghistānī's description of differing opinions on the attributes' multiplicity and differentiation; Dāghistānī, *Radd*, , fol. 2b.

existence, which had been altered by the spread of ideas from *wujūdī* metaphysics. Qūrṣāwī viewed the established orthodoxy as simultaneously theologically incorrect (positing absurdities of the essence, contradictory in its logic) and religiously unfounded (lacking sufficient certainty, violating the central tenets of the faith); in its place he offered a new view of the attributes, formulated and articulated within the existing theological discourse but (he argues) avoiding these problems.

It is here that we have the basis of Qūrṣāwī's reformism in the sphere of theology. Faced with what he saw as religious deviation, he set about rectifying it by attacking both the particular views he found objectionable and the methods used to reach them. He also attacked his opponents' reliance on *taqlīd*, which he blamed for allowing these false views to proliferate.[93] His criticisms, based on *taḥqīq* through both rational argument and sound use of *naql*, were put forward with the goal of refuting the significant creedal error he found in the contemporary application and understanding of *kalām*.

From this oppositional, reformist stance, Qūrṣāwī emphasizes his (negative) criticisms of the established orthodoxy over his own (positive) view, presenting his position as a corrective of the prevailing orthodoxy, showing specifically which aspects of that orthodoxy he holds to be incorrect and why, using methods of argumentation characteristic of *kalām* in order to prove his point. Contingency, multiplicity, differentiation, and superaddition were all elements of postclassical *kalām* discourse on the attributes. By framing his stance as a reaction to them, Qūrṣāwī renders it part of the same discourse; by engaging with these elements—even though he rejects them—he locates his stance within the parameters and topoi of that tradition. Whether we consider him to be actively and fully participating in Sunni *kalām* or merely using its discourse to show the *mutakallimīn* the error of their ways, his theological thought forms part of that tradition.[94] He appeals to many of the same authorities as his opponents, and cites many of the same arguments. He engages with many of the same issues, and he does so within the same genre of the commentary. His emphasis on *tawḥīd* and *tanzīh* and his reformulation of some of the premises of the Sunni position on the attributes

93. Dāghistānī, for instance, holds that one *must* accept that the attributes number either eight or seven because that is the position of the orthodox theological schools; ibid., fol. 6a. Ūriwī makes a similar claim; Ūriwī, *Risāla*, fol. 40b.

94. Kemper believes it to be the latter; Kemper, *Sufis*, pp. 260–261.

represent creative and active theological reasoning on this very central issue. His position does not constitute a radical departure from Sunni theology but rather a critique of it, an argument for less reliance on rational speculation and greater epistemological certainty through *naql*, and—accordingly—an exercise of *taḥqīq* in verifying the prevailing orthodoxy and interrogating its shortcomings.

7

Reform Within the Scholarly Tradition

QŪRṢĀWĪ'S REFORMISM IS based on his epistemological critique, which calls for reforming law and theology so that action and belief are brought into conformity with scripture, the source of all sound religious knowledge. He argues for the primacy of *naql*, comprising Qurʾan, Sunna, and authoritative consensus, as the only way to ensure correctness, and that any position without a basis in it must be rejected. This outlook underlies virtually every aspect of his thought and informs his attack on *taqlīd*, which, as he sees it, obliges scholars to take their positions from other scholars, to the exclusion of the certain sources of religious knowledge. As such, it separates scholarship from the community's scriptural foundations. Though ostensibly limiting the possibility for error, Qūrṣāwī holds that the structures of *taqlīd* in fact merely limit scholars' use of sound sources, thereby disguising erroneous positions and allowing incorrect views to proliferate. In this way, *taqlīd* cannot but breed error and spread misguidance.

The overreliance upon *taqlīd* thus represents a moral danger. It divorces the main source of religious guidance for the community—the *ʿulamāʾ*'s articulation of Islamic norms—from its epistemological foundations, leaving scholars to promulgate views whose correctness is based on their conformity to school doctrine rather than the texts of revelation. Therefore, to prevent the continued acceptance of flawed views among the community, every position must be verified through *taḥqīq* to ensure that it conforms to *naql*. If there is a contradiction, the position must be emended or rejected entirely, but it can be accepted and followed if there is no objection to it.

Qūrṣāwī's views on the divine attributes and *ʿishāʾ* reflect this attitude toward *taqlīd* and the need for *taḥqīq*. Each is a critique of a position that had become well established among *ʿulamāʾ* and which Qūrṣāwī rejected on both *naql* grounds and in terms of their underlying rationales: that God possesses eight essential attributes is unfounded scripturally and absurd logically, and the omission of a daily prayer contradicts a known obligation established by scripture and consensus, while the legal justification for doing so is itself flawed. These positions are, in his eyes, wrong by any standard, and their spread is evidence of the failure of *taqlīd* to maintain correctness in scholarship.

Such an exercise of *taḥqīq* is most critical in terms of ritual and belief, which must be based on only the soundest sources of knowledge. *Mutakallimīn* in particular have pursued reason to the exclusion of *naql*, resulting in the spread of unfounded views. Thus, *taqlīd*, with its propensity for perpetuating error and undermining sound knowledge, is a more serious issue in theology. *Fiqh*, by contrast, allows for a degree of uncertainty in its *furūʿ*.[1] Nevertheless, legal positions must also be verified to ensure their correctness. The rigid structures of *taqlīd* that underlie the *madhhab* have kept *fuqahāʾ* from engaging with scripture and must therefore be altered to restore the connection between *fiqh* discourse and the texts of revelation, through the exercise of primary legal reasoning.

Such a view runs counter to the regime of *taqlīd* predominant in the postclassical period. These structures were developed in order to maintain coherence and validity within scholarship, to exclude anomalous interpretations. For Qūrṣāwī, however, they cannot ensure certainty, and the coherence and validity that they impart is upheld by the work of scholars and therefore susceptible to errors in judgment and understanding.

But this does not mean that these structures serve no purpose and should be abandoned. Rather, despite his explicit condemnation of *taqlīd*, Qūrṣāwī views it as an important element in scholarship. We can see this in his regard for the *madhhab* as an institution, but more profoundly in the reliance on scaffolding within his thought and his use of the commentary as the main genre for presenting his ideas. These ideas are not radical reinterpretations of legal or theological premises nor drastic departures from prevailing *ʿulamāʾ* discourse, but simply alterations and revisions of established aspects of the scholarly tradition.[2] Qūrṣāwī's thought can thus be described as distinctly postclassical, shaped by approaches and reflecting concerns unique to this period. His stance on the divine attributes deals with a central question in

1. Qūrṣāwī, *Sharḥ jadīd*, fol. 96b; also Qūrṣāwī, *Mabāḥith*, fol. 155a.

2. He thus favors refining, rather than refuting (in Ziai's words), characteristic of the postclassical period; Hossein Ziai. "Recent Trends in Arabic and Persian Philosophy." *The Cambridge Companion to Arabic Philosophy*. Eds. Peter Adamson and Richard C. Taylor. Cambridge: Cambridge UP, 2005. 405–425, p. 406.

the history of Islamic theology, addressed from within the framework of post-Avicennian *kalām* and in light of the influence of *wujūdī* metaphysics and its spread since the 13th century. Similarly, his views on *ijtihād* and *fiqh* rely on the formalist approach to legal theory characteristic of the Hanafi school and its developed *uṣūl* methodology.

Thus, his calls for scriptural correctness, spurning *taqlīd* and the primacy of *naql*, do not constitute a rejection of the scholarly tradition in favor of a more "fundamentalist" approach to scholarship that looks back to 7th-century Arabia, as Kemper has argued.[3] Instead, utilizing existing legal and theological discourse to argue for his stance, Qūrṣāwī seeks to reform the postclassical tradition from within. In addition, his emphasis on scripture, with his reliance on rational and formalist interpretation, does not align at all with materialist or traditionist approaches characteristic of fundamentalism.[4]

A closer comparison can be made with Aziz Al-Azmeh's Islamic fideism, an approach that seeks to maintain a "genealogy" with scripture by rejecting any position that "would discursively carry [points of dogma] beyond the bounds of their given textuality, on the grounds that the sense of the divine statement is *sui generis* and comprehensible to us only within the terms of this very statement," wherein any attempt to extrapolate from the scriptural text is to move away from it and its ineffable meaning. In this regard, "the opposition is not one of reason and unreason, but one of nomothetic discourse, this being the divine, and that which is not."[5] For Hanbalis, who are Al-Azmeh's focus and whose theology was as materialist as their *fiqh*, beliefs can be legitimated as "genealogical" only by the scriptural texts themselves. Qūrṣāwī, by contrast, accepts the role of nonscriptural interpretive frameworks (to understand the texts' meaning in other terms) in justifying a position's genealogy, but only insofar as that genealogy is foregrounded and not subordinated to the

---

3. Michael Kemper. *Sufis und Gelehrte in Tatarien und Baschkirien, 1789–1889: Der islamische Diskurs unter russischer Herrschaft*. Berlin: Klaus Schwarz Verlag, 1998, pp. 305–306; Michael Kemper. "Imperial Russia as Dar al-Islam? Nineteenth-Century Debates on Ijtihad and Taqlid Among the Volga Tatars." *Encounters: An International Journal for the Study of Culture and Society*, vol. 6; 2015. 95–124, pp. 108–109 (with some caveats).

4. *Pace* Kanlidere and Idiiatullina, who both argue that Qūrṣāwī embraced Hanbali or Salafi scripturalism; Ahmet Kanlidere. *Reform Within Islam: The Tajdid and Jadid Movement Among the Kazan Tatars (1809–1917): Conciliation or Conflict?* Istanbul: Eren, 1997, p. 35; Gul'nara Idiiatullina. "Vvedenie." In Abu-n-Nasr Abd an-Nasir al-Kursavi. *Nastavlenie liudei na put' istiny*. Kazan: Tatarskoe knizhnoe izd-vo, 2005. 10–88, pp. 72–73.

5. Aziz Al-Azmeh. "Orthodoxy and Hanbalite Fideism." *Arabica*, vol. 35, no. 3; 1988. 253–266, pp. 256, 257.

interpretive framework itself. *Naql* thus provides a limit that a given interpretation cannot contravene nor take precedence over.

The difference between his respective positions on *ʿishāʾ* and the divine attributes is illustrative here. In the case of the former, he objects to a *fiqh* interpretation that runs counter to an essential religious obligation. In this conflict between a legal rationale and a known obligation, the obligation must remain supreme and the rationale adjusted accordingly (or, indeed, rethought entirely). His critique of Taftāzānī's position on the attributes, however, focuses on a theological view that did not necessarily contradict an explicit scriptural norm but which *ʿulamāʾ* had consecrated as a matter of creedal orthodoxy. As something based on *kalām* interpretation, it does not have the epistemological status to stand as a point of orthodox belief, which would require certainty that logical methods cannot impart. Therefore, the attributes' number, as Qūrṣāwī points out, is purely speculative. But it also is logically untenable, and so must be rejected. The attributes' necessity, on the other hand, likewise lacks direct textual grounding, but it can be accepted because it conforms both logically and conceptually to the scriptural portrayal of the divine essence, particularly its transcendence from creation, which is characterized within the framework of post-Avicennian *kalām* by contingency.

Certainly not fundamentalist, Qūrṣāwī's epistemological critique is perhaps best described as a fideistic conception of Hanafi-Maturidism. Although premised on the supremacy of scripture in religious interpretation, his reformism relies on the legal and theological traditions—which constitute the valid interpretive frameworks for scholarship—as integral parts of the broader scholarly tradition.

Ultimately, his is a reformist project that is markedly formalist and engaged in rational theology, while simultaneously emphasizing scriptural conformity and adherence to *naql*. He seeks to restore the connection between scripture and scholarship that had been weakened by the overreliance on *taqlīd* through *taḥqīq* and the renewed exercise of *ijtihād*, constituting reform through *tajdīd*.

Eighteenth-Century Reformism

We find similar views of *tajdīd* and its religious implications put forward by the prominent 18th-century reformist figures who shared Qūrṣāwī's critique of *taqlīd* and embrace of *ijtihād*. Muḥammad ʿAlī Sanūsī and Shāh Walī Allāh argued that *taqlīd* prevented scholars from understanding scripture and fully serving the community's religious needs.[6] Shāh Walī Allāh and Muḥammad b. ʿAlī Shawkānī held that the disappearance of *mujtahids* and scholars' ability to carry out *ijtihād* would be a bane for the community, and they blamed later *ʿulamāʾ* for creating this notion.[7] Shawkānī reasoned that if *mujtahids* ceased to exist, it would mean that "there no longer remains anyone among the people of this Islamic community (*al-milla al-islāmiyya*) who understands the Book and the Sunna."[8] This, he writes elsewhere, would entail an absurd limit on God's grace and abundance toward those living in times and places without scholars who could approach scripture.[9]

The emphasis on *ijtihād* among these reformers was accompanied by a belief that scholarship should not contradict scriptural evidence. Indeed, Qūrṣāwī, Shāh Walī Allāh, Shawkānī, and Aḥmad ibn Idrīs all held the view that if a scholar, regardless of the level of legal knowledge he has attained, discovers a sound hadith contradicting an established position of his school, he must follow that hadith in his judgments, to the exclusion of any existing opinions negated by it. Each reformer justifies this position in the same way, by relating statements from the four founding eponyms that if there is a hadith that goes against one of their opinions, the hadith should be followed and the opinion ignored. (Ibn Idrīs, like Qūrṣāwī, explicitly links the failure to do so with following one's whims [*ahwāʾ*].)[10]

These reformers also sought to reshape the relationship between the community and the *ʿulamāʾ*, lessening the former's reliance upon the latter. Sanūsī and Shawkānī both argue that a lay person who asks a scholar's guidance is not a *muqallid* if they learn the scriptural evidence behind the scholar's

---

6. Shāh Walī Allāh Aḥmad b. ʿAbd al-Raḥīm al-Fārūqī al-Dihlawī. *ʿIqd al-jīd fī aḥkām al-ijtihād wa-l-taqlīd*. Ed. Muḥammad ʿAlī al-Ḥalabī al-Atharī. Sharjah: Dār al-fatḥ, 1415/1995; Muḥammad b. ʿAlī al-Sanūsī. *ʿIqāẓ al-wasnān fī al-ʿamal bi-l-ḥadīth wa-l-Qurʾān*. In *al-Majmūʿa al-mukhtāra*. Ed. M. A. ibn Ghalbūn. Manchester: n.p., 1990; cf. Ahmed Dallal. "The Origins and Objectives of Islamic Revivalist Thought, 1750–1850." *Journal of the American Oriental Society*, vol. 113, no. 3; 1993. 341–359.

7. Shāh Walī Allāh, *ʿIqd al-jīd*, pp. 20–24; Muḥammad b. ʿAlī al-Shawkānī. *al-Qawl al-mufīd fī adallat al-ijtihād wa-l-taqlīd*. Cairo/Beirut: Dār al-kutub al-miṣrī/Dār al-kutub al-lubnānī, 1411/1991, pp. 40–42, 51; Muḥammad b. ʿAlī al-Shawkānī. *al-Badr al-ṭāliʿ bi-maḥāsin man baʿd al-qarn al-sābiʿ*. 2 vols. Cairo: Dār al-kitāb al-islāmī, n.d., i, p. 2.

8. Shawkānī, *Qawl mufīd*, p. 51.

9. Shawkānī, *Badr al-ṭāliʿ*, i, p. 2.

10. Qūrṣāwī, *Irshād*, p. 5, also 34; Aḥmad ibn Idrīs. *Risālat al-Radd ʿalā ahl al-raʾy*. In *The Exoteric Ahmed ibn Idris: A Sufi's Critique of the Madhahib and the Wahhabis*. Eds. Bernd Radtke et al. Leiden: Brill, 2000. 47–131, pp. 56–61; Shāh Walī Allāh, *ʿIqd al-jīd*, p. 56; Shawkānī, *Qawl mufīd*, pp. 44–46.

opinion.[11] Sanūsī goes further, stating that all Muslims should (*lāzim*) exercise *ijtihād* with the Qurʾan and learn the meanings of hadith reports to derive norms for action (*ikhrāj al-aḥkām*) from them.[12]

Such calls for *ijtihād* and rejection of *taqlīd* are primary aspects in the model of 18th-century reformism.[13] Yet the central reformist figures rely on a markedly materialist approach to law, arguing against strong school affiliation in favor of hadith-centric scholarship characteristic of materialist *fiqh*. Shawkānī most clearly illustrates this trend, rejecting the (largely formalist) Zaydi-Hadawi school of his upbringing in favor of Sunni traditionism.[14] Ibn Idrīs also moved away from the Maliki school toward hadith scholarship, as did Sanūsī, his main student and disciple.[15] For Shawkānī and Sanūsī, *ijtihād* is virtually synonymous with hadith scholarship; they hold that prophetic reports form the basis for sound action, to the exclusion of *qiyās*, which both largely reject.[16] They also argue against the need for school affiliation on scriptural grounds.[17]

---

11. Sanūsī, *ʿIqāẓ*, p. 96; Shawkānī, *Qawl mufīd*, p. 73.

12. Sanūsī, *ʿIqāẓ*, p. 116; see also Dallal, "Origins and Objectives," p. 358. A similar view is frequently attributed to Shawkānī, but he in fact did not hold that *ijtihād* should be carried out by lay people, even if he does advocate for knowledge of *fiqh* to become more widespread within the community; Shawkānī, *Qawl mufīd*, esp. pp. 23–24, 83; also Bernard Haykel. *Revival and Reform in Islam: The Legacy of Muhammad al-Shawkani*. Cambridge: Cambridge UP, 2003, p. 103; Jonathan A. C. Brown. "Is Islam Easy to Understand or Not? Salafis, the Democratization of Interpretation and the Need for the Ulema." *Journal of Islamic Studies*, vol. 26, no. 2; 2015. 117–144, p. 137.

13. Cf. John O. Voll. *Islam: Continuity and Change in the Modern World*. Boulder, CO: Westview Press, 1982, p. 52; Dallal, "Origins and Objectives," p. 341; Fazlur Rahman. *Islam*. 2nd ed. Chicago: U of Chicago P, 2002, pp. 242–250.

14. Haykel, *Revival*, esp. pp. 86–96; Bernard Haykel. "Reforming Islam by Dissolving the Madhahib: Shawkānī and His Zaydi Detractors in Yemen." *Studies in Islamic Legal Theory*. Ed. Bernard Weiss. Leiden: Brill, 2002. 337–364; see his major work on legal theory: Muḥammad b. ʿAlī al-Shawkānī. *al-Irshād al-fuḥūl ilā taḥqīq al-ḥaqq min ʿilm al-uṣūl*. 2 vols. Riyadh: Dār al-faḍīla, n.d.

15. R. S. O'Fahey. *Enigmatic Saint: Ahmad ibn Idris and the Idrisi Tradition*. Evanston, IL: Northwestern UP, 1990, esp. pp. 34–37, 199–200; Knut Vikor. *Sufi and Scholar on the Desert Edge: Muhammad b. ʿAli al-Sanusi and His Brotherhood*. London: Hurst, 1995, esp. pp. 110–111, 219–222; Ahmed Dallal. "The Origins and Early Development of Islamic Reform." *The New Cambridge History of Islam. Vol. 6: Muslims and Modernity: Culture and Society Since 1800*. Ed. Robert Hefner. Cambridge: Cambridge UP, 2010. 107–147, pp. 131–132; cf. Sanūsī, *ʿIqāẓ*, pp. 116–117, 55–57, 89–90; also Muḥammad b. ʿAlī al-Sanūsī. *al-Masāʾil al-ʿashr al-musammā bughyat al-maqāṣid fī khulāṣat al-marāṣid*. In *al-Majmūʿa al-mukhtāra*. Ed. M. A. ibn Ghalbūn. Manchester: n.p., 1990.

16. Sanūsī, *ʿIqāẓ*, esp. pp. 116–117; Dallal, "Origins and Objectives," p. 357; Shawkānī, *Qawl mufīd*, p. 67; Shawkānī, *Irshād*, ii, pp. 848–862; Haykel, *Revival*, pp. 93–94.

17. Shawkānī, *Qawl mufīd*, pp. 46, 66–67; Haykel, "Reforming," pp. 340–341; Sanūsī, *ʿIqāẓ*, p. 98; Dallal, "Origins and Objectives," p. 357.

Shawkānī dispenses with the idea—foundational within the *madhhab*—that a jurist can be a *mujtahid* in his judgments but a *muqallid* in terms of methodology. Rather, he writes that *ijtihād* is indivisible (*lā yataba*ʿʿ*aḍ*), and that if a scholar is capable of following no one in his *furū*ʿ, then the idea that he must follow someone else in his *uṣūl* is absurd, thus rendering all *mujtahids* absolute *mujtahids*.[18] Even Shāh Walī Allāh, the only other of these reformers from a Hanafi background, bases his reformist project on lessening the importance of *madhhab* adherence and attendant factionalism between ʿ*ulamā*ʾ through reliance on hadith (praising the Hanbalis for their use of scripture).[19]

This more materialist approach was accompanied by an emphasis on hadith transmission, which is a major aspect of Voll's Hijaz network. Voll describes these reformist circles (including, notably, Shāh Walī Allāh and Sanūsī) as focusing on the continuation of extant hadith networks through oral transmission and memorization of *aḥādīth*, stressing the collection of reports bearing a so-called elevated *isnād* (ʿ*uluw al-isnād*)—comprising the smallest number of transmitters possible—and hadith not contained in the canonical collections.[20]

None of these elements, however, are present within Qūrṣāwī's reformism. His formalist approach to legal theory has considerable regard for the *madhhab*, of course, and he rejects literalist interpretation, stating explicitly that *qiyās* is an essential part of legal reasoning and scriptural sources are not in and of

18. Shawkānī, *Qawl mufīd*, pp. 69–70.

19. J. M. S. Baljon. *Religion and Thought of Shah Wali Allah Dihlawi 1703–1762*. Leiden: Brill, 1986, esp. p. 152; Dallal, "Origins and Objectives," pp. 348–349; cf. the discussion in Shāh Walī Allāh, ʿ*Iqd al-jīd*, pp. 24–39, 47–75; Shāh Walī Allāh al-Dihlawī. *al-Inṣāf fī bayān asbāb al-ikhtilāf*. Beirut: Dār al-nafāʾis, 1397/1977, p. 62; Muhammad Qasim Zaman. "Transmitters of Authority and Ideas Across Cultural Boundaries, Eleventh to Eighteenth Centuries." *New Cambridge History of Islam. Vol. 4: Islamic Cultures and Societies to the End of the Eighteenth Century*. Ed. Robert Irwin. Cambridge: Cambridge UP, 2010. 582–610, pp. 589–590. For his part, Shāh Walī Allāh allows for limitations in the scope of a scholar's *ijtihād*. Zaman notes that he, like other reformers, held a particular reverence for Mālik's *Muwaṭṭā*ʾ.

20. On the uses and importance of hadith scholarship for 18th-century reformism, see John Voll. "ʿAbdallah ibn Salim al-Basri and 18th Century Hadith Scholarship." *Die Welt des Islams*, vol. 42, no. 3; 2002. 356–372; Basheer M. Nafi. "A Teacher of ibn ʿAbd al-Wahhab: Muhammad Hayat al-Sindi and the Revival of *Ashab al-Hadith*'s Methodology." *Islamic Law and Society*, vol. 13, no. 2; 2006. 208–241; Daniel Brown. *Rethinking Tradition in Modern Islamic Thought*. New York: Cambridge UP, 1996, pp. 22–27. According to Voll, this religio-moral outlook reflects a "fundamentalist" character, with its emphasis on literalist interpretation of scripture; Voll, *Islam*, p. 38.

themselves sufficient for scholarship.[21] His view regarding hadith scholarship bears even less resemblance to these other reformers and the trends Voll cites. He argues that analyzing *isnāds* is impossible due to the historical distance between his age and the Prophet's, and instead of advocating for the oral transmission of hadith and the search for unfamiliar reports, he writes that it is sufficient for a *mujtahid* to use a collection as a reference, without memorization, and any hadith not found in the canonical collections should as a rule be rejected as fabricated.[22]

In terms of neo-Sufism, another important element in the scholarship on 18th-century reform, Qūrṣāwī was a member of the Mujaddidiyya—a central neo-Sufi order—and his stance on Sufism resembles the sober, legalistic piety characteristic of neo-Sufism. Nevertheless, the Sufi influence in his works is limited, and, as we have seen, his theological views were quite at odds with Sirhindī's. The content of Qūrṣāwī's reformist project thus appears largely separate from his attachment to the order. (It should be noted that Fatḥ Allāh Ūriwī was also a devoted Mujaddidi, and, as his example shows, mere affiliation with the order did not necessarily make one a reformer.)

Whatever similarities Qūrṣāwī's reformism shares with other reformers' projects, they cannot be attributed to any scholarly connection between him and Voll's Hijaz network. There's no evidence to link Qūrṣāwī with any of the Arab reformers, nor with Shāh Walī Allāh, whose scholarly and mystical lineages were separate from his own.[23] Kemper, who relies to an extent on Voll's analysis, speculates that there might be a connection through Āshiṭī, Qūrṣāwī's teacher in Machkara, who spent several years as a student in

21. Qūrṣāwī, *Sharḥ Manār*, esp. p. 172. He criticizes the defunct Zahiri school, which served as an inspiration for Shawkānī, on this point; Qūrṣāwī, *Irshād*, p. 36. Qūrṣāwī also maintained that Hanafi ritual practices were beyond question by *ijtihād*, in contrast to Sanūsī, who (following ibn Idrīs) diverged from established Maliki ritual practices, particularly regarding prayer, on scriptural grounds; cf. Vikor, *Sufi and Scholar*, esp. pp. 223–224.

22. Qūrṣāwī, *Irshād*, pp. 6, 7, 24. Interestingly, Taftāzānī makes the same point about too much time having passed for the inspection of *isnāds*; Aron Zysow. "The Economy of Certainty: An Introduction to the Typology of Islamic Legal Theory." Diss. Harvard University, 1984, p. 76. Kemper speculates that the social and religious dislocation that followed the conquest of Kazan eliminated networks of hadith transmission among Bulghar Muslims; Kemper, *Sufis*, p. 246. ʿAbd al-Khāliq Qūrṣāwī did study hadith in Cairo and collected an *arbaʿīn* work, which exists in multiple manuscript copies (some incorrectly attributed to his brother); e.g., ʿAbd al-Khāliq b. Ibrāhīm al-Qūrṣāwī. *Aḥādīth-i nabawiyya*. Ms. KFU, no. A-1268.

23. *Pace* Idiiatullina, who argues for a direct link between Qūrṣāwī's stance on *ijtihād* and that of Shāh Walī Allāh, based on the latter's view of its importance and their shared affiliation with the Mujaddidiyya; Idiiatullina, "Vvedenie," esp. pp. 58, 67.

Dagestan. Kemper points to Muḥammad b. Mūsā al-Qudūqī (1652–1717), a native of Dagestan who traveled extensively in the Middle East and settled in Aleppo, as introducing to his homeland *ijtihād*-centric reformism, which he adopted from his teacher Ṣāliḥ b. Mahdī al-Maqbalī (1638–1697), a Yemeni who settled in Mecca. Maqbalī, who was outspoken against *taqlīd*, was praised by Shawkānī and had his written works spread among Dagestani scholars by Qudūqī, who posthumously became a well-known figure in Dagestan. Kemper also notes that a work by Qudūqī was circulating in the Volga region at the turn of the 19th century.[24]

Kemper doesn't go so far as to claim that Qudūqī or Maqbalī influenced Qūrṣāwī, only that it is possible, if indirectly so. There is, however, little supporting evidence. Although both were apparently widely known in Dagestan, their views were not necessarily accepted; Qudūqī left permanently out of frustration with the *ʿulamāʾ* there, and Shawkānī reports meeting a Dagestani scholar who traveled to Yemen in search of a sound copy of one of Maqbalī's major texts on *fiqh*, which was unavailable in Dagestan, suggesting a lack of scholarly currency.[25] Āshiṭī's presence as a student in Dagestan does not link him with either scholar, and none of his own students—including Qūrṣāwī—seem to evince any inclination toward a Dagestani-inspired (much less Yemeni) scholarly trajectory. Moreover, the text by Qudūqī circulating in the Volga region was on Arabic rhetoric, not any legal subject, and it is known in a commentary by Mangārī, an opponent of Qūrṣāwī who showed little in the way of openness to *ijtihād*.[26] Fakhr al-Dīn does include a short biographical entry for Qudūqī in *Āthār* where he states that many Bulghar *ʿulamāʾ* trace their lineage to him, but he does not specify who.[27]

A second possible avenue is through ʿAlī Qārī, who bore considerable influence on Qūrṣāwī's thought. He had left his native Herat to settle in Mecca, where he became involved in scholarly debates and study circles—particularly on hadith—connected with major figures in the Hijaz network.[28] Although

24. Kemper, *Sufis*, pp. 303–304; cf. Shawkānī, *Badr al-ṭāliʿ*, i, pp. 288–292. On Qudūqī, see Rebecca Gould. "*Ijtihad* Against *Madhhab*: Legal Hybridity and the Meanings of Modernity in Early Modern Daghestan." *Comparative Studies in Society and History*, vol. 57, no. 1; 2015. 35–66. Qudūqī's prominence in later Dagestani historiography, particularly in the early 20th century, is similar to Qūrṣāwī's.

25. Shawkānī, *Badr al-ṭāliʿ*, i, p. 290; Gould, "*Ijtihad*," pp. 48–49.

26. Kemper, *Sufis*, pp. 303–304.

27. Fakhr al-Dīn, *Āthār*, i, p. 31.

28. Basheer Nafi in fact compares ʿAlī Qārī's reformist efforts with Maqbalī's; Basheer M. Nafi. "Tasawwuf and Reform in Pre-Modern Islamic Culture: In Search of Ibrahim

there's no doubt as to Qūrṣāwī's reliance on ʿAlī Qārī, the latter does not seem to have shaped the former's stance on *ijtihād*, nor did Qūrṣāwī adopt his focus on hadith. Additionally, ʿAlī Qārī was a Hanafi from Herat, and so his influence on Qūrṣāwī hardly serves as an example of global or transnational exchange mediated through the Hijaz. And, as with Qudūqī, there is no evidence of teacher-student connections—so important to Voll's argument—ultimately linking the two. There is such a link to the Hijaz through Muḥammad Maʿṣūm, who spread the Mujaddidiyya there during a brief residence.[29] His spiritual chain (*silsila*) was brought to Central Asia by his main disciple, Ḥabīb Allāh Balkhī, and includes Turkmānī as a prominent representative.[30] But Muḥammad Maʿṣūm's time in the Hijaz came late in life and seems to have been important only for the spread of the Mujaddidiyya, making any substantive Hijazi influence on his thought unlikely.[31]

It's impossible to say for certain, without knowing the identities of all of Qūrṣāwī's teachers and their scholarly lineages, if he in fact has any connection with the Hijaz network. It is notable, however, that Qūrṣāwī's two known teachers, despite possible links with global currents of Islamic scholarship, are presented in the historical sources as figures of decidedly local or regional importance (even by Ramzī, who lived in Mecca and was connected with transnational Naqshbandi circles), as is Qūrṣāwī himself. His education was overwhelmingly localized within Bulghar scholarly circles, even while in Bukhara, and his writings, in their focus on Hanafi *fiqh* and Maturidi *kalām* and in their references and sources, are almost exclusively limited to those two schools in their Central and South Asian strands, reflecting the indigenous character of his thought. Indeed, his reformism is tied directly to both the scholarly

---

al-Kurani." *Die Welt des Islams*, vol. 42, no. 3; 2002. 307–355, esp. pp. 326–327, 343–345; also Shawkānī, *Badr al-ṭāliʿ*, i, pp. 445–446; Khayr al-Dīn al-Ziriklī. *al-Aʿlām: qāmūs tarājim li-ashhar al-rijāl wa-l-nisāʾ min al-ʿarab wa-l-mustaʿribīn bayn al-mustashriqīn*. 8 vols. Beirut: Dār al-ʿilm li-l-milāyīn, 1980, v, pp. 12–13.

29. Nafi, "Tasawwuf," p. 320; Atallah Copty. "The Naqshbandiyya and Its Offshoot, the Naqshbandiyya-Mujaddidiyya in the Haramayn in the 11th/17th Century." *Die Welt des Islams*, vol. 43, no. 3; 2003. 321–348.

30. Itzchak Weismann. *The Naqshbandiyya: Orthodoxy and Activism in a Worldwide Sufi Tradition*. New York: Routledge, 2007, pp. 78–80; Hamid Algar. "Shaykh Zaynullah Rasulev: The Last Great Naqshbandi Shaykh of the Volga-Urals Region." *Muslims in Central Asia: Expressions of Identity and Change*. Ed. Jo-Ann Gross. Durham, NC: Duke UP, 1992. 112–133, p. 114.

31. Copty, "Naqshbandiyya," pp. 334–337; Nafi, "Tasawwuf," pp. 346–347.

environment of the Volga-Ural region and Bulghar Muslims' social and historical circumstances.[32]

The fact that Qūrṣāwī's reformism bears a resemblance to others' without seemingly any link between them casts doubt on the relevance of Voll's network in spreading reformist approaches, but it could be argued that no connection is needed at all. One factor shared by all the reformers is having lived and worked in environments of social and political upheaval: Shāh Walī Allāh and the collapse of Mughal rule; Shawkānī and the transformation of Zaydi political and religious authority; Sanūsī's foundation of a new, utopian religious community (to say nothing of the beginning of the French colonization of North Africa); and Qūrṣāwī and shifts in Bulghar Muslims' relationship to the Russian imperial state. Given the connection between *taqlīd* structures and social stability, it is perhaps not surprising that *taqlīd* would (independently) be called into question in these settings.

Theology and Reformism

The importance of theology in Qūrṣāwī's thought further sets him apart from the other 18th-century reformers, who largely ignored or rejected *kalām*.[33] There is nothing like his engagement with the attributes in Shawkānī's writings, for instance, much less the sheer significance that theological reasoning has within his oeuvre, far surpassing any legal matter or even *ijtihād*.

In fact, there is a danger of overemphasizing *ijtihād* and scriptural literalism in the study of reformism, to the exclusion of theological concerns and other kinds of interpretation. To wit, there are similarities between Qūrṣāwī's reform project and the views of the important North African scholar Muḥammad b. Yūsuf al-Sanūsī (1435–1490) regarding theological reasoning. Not to be confused with the 18th-century Sufi reformer Muḥammad b. ʿAlī Sanūsī, this *mutakallim* rejected *taqlīd* in belief, arguing that all Muslims (not just scholars) are required to engage in *taḥqīq* to understand the rational bases of *kalām* arguments, rather than accepting received positions.[34] Although they

32. It is worth pondering, though, how Qūrṣāwī's thought might have changed had he reached the Hijaz and/or stayed in the Middle East.

33. Shāh Walī Allāh engaged in extensive philosophical and metaphysical reasoning, but from an overwhelmingly Sufi perspective, distinct from the *kalām* tradition. But this too deserves more attention in the study of 18th-century reform.

34. Khaled El-Rouayheb. *Islamic Intellectual History in the Seventeenth Century: Scholarly Currents in the Ottoman Empire and the Maghreb*. Cambridge: Cambridge UP, 2015, pp. 175–188. Sanūsī declares such an exercise of *taḥqīq* a *farḍ ʿayn*; cf. Muḥammad b. Yūsuf al-Sanūsī.

had differing conceptions of *taḥqīq*, with Sanūsī relying on rational inquiry (*naẓar*) to a far greater extent, Qūrṣāwī was likewise against the use of *taqlīd* in creedal issues, seeing it as an avenue for misguidance.[35] To be sure, their stances are distinct: Sanūsī had a more conventional relationship with *kalām*, particularly in his use of reason, and Qūrṣāwī did not consider theological inquiry an obligation in the same way he did *ijtihād*. But both have a similar wariness of received views, and both offer strong arguments, based in scripture and *naql*, against their pro-*taqlīd* peers.[36] More to the point, Qūrṣāwī's differences with Sanūsī are no greater than those between him and the main 18th-century reformers. Sanūsī represents an example of a somewhat similar intellectual project that had absolutely no connection to Qūrṣāwī but rather was local to North Africa (where it became predominant). Instead, these various figures show how the repertoire of the scholarly tradition was used to criticize and emend elements of postclassical scholarship under different circumstances and within different cultural and religious environments.

Qūrṣāwī's reformist project thus has clear implications for the literature on 18th-century reform, and both the similarities and differences between his thought and that of his contemporary peers (and other reformers) suggest ways to revise our understanding of the subject. Any potential model of 18th-century or postclassical reformism must be expanded beyond hadith-centric and anti-*madhhab* approaches, encompassing a wider range of interpretive styles as well as forms of theological and metaphysical inquiry. It must also focus less on teacher-student interactions and the intellectual developments they can—but don't necessarily—engender.

The important overlap between Qūrṣāwī's and other reformers' beliefs in the necessity of *ijtihād* and attacks on *taqlīd* points to a shared premise: a critical posture toward postclassical scholarship and its reliance upon the structures of *taqlīd* to ensure correctness. This attitude represents the most salient point of agreement among 18th-century reformers, who, in this estimation, were most prominently set against the shortcomings of prevailing scholarly discourse, thus warranting the reform of the tradition through *tajdīd*.[37]

ʿUmdat ahl al-tawfīq wa-l-tasdīd fī sharḥ ʿaqīdat ahl al-tawḥīd. Cairo: Maṭbaʿat jarīdat al-Islam, 1316 [1898], esp. pp. 31–32. [Cited as *Sharḥ al-kubrā*.]

35. Qūrṣāwī, *Sharḥ jadīd*, fols. 95b–96b; Qūrṣāwī, *Mabāḥith*, esp. fols. 154b–155a.

36. Sanūsī, *Sharḥ al-kubrā*, esp. pp. 14–17; cf. El-Rouayheb, *Islamic Intellectual History*, pp. 186–188.

37. See the critiques of earlier scholars' insistence upon *taqlīd* by both Shāh Walī Allāh and Shawkānī; e.g., Shāh Walī Allāh, *ʿIqd al-jīd*, p. 39; Shawkānī, *Qawl mufīd*, pp. 25, 42, 46–47, 51.

In this regard, the description of Qūrṣāwī as following the "*madhhab al-salaf*" (doctrine of the *salaf*) is particularly significant.[38] While such a critical stance toward scholarly discourse is not at odds with the conventional understanding of Salafism, it is clear that Qūrṣāwī's notion of the *madhhab al-salaf* is. It is distinct in content and approach from Salafi reformism's characteristic literalism and reliance on hadith, the origins of which Voll (and others) have located in the works of figures such as Shawkānī. Moreover, Qūrṣāwī's understanding of the *salaf* encompasses a different, broader range of figures than those usually associated with Salafism. He describes the basis of true belief as "following the Book, the Sunna, and the consensus of the *umma* . . . and this is the way of the first predecessors (*al-sābiqīn al-awwalīn*), which is the way of the Followers (*tābiʿīn*), and after them the [four] *mujtahid*-imams, the Qurʾan commentators, the hadith scholars, and the leaders of the Sufis."[39] Indeed, the authorities to whom he most frequently attaches himself are of the Hanafi-Maturidi and Central Asian Sufi traditions specifically: Abū Ḥanīfa, Shaybānī, Māturīdī, Kalābādhī, Sālimī, Nasafī, and Bahāʾ al-Dīn Naqshband (1318–1389). These, it seems, are the *salaf* whose doctrine he studied and whom he wishes to emulate.

This usage of the term *madhhab al-salaf* complicates the view of Salafism as having premodern origins, showing that the term had a much different understanding and reference, at least in this setting.[40] It is therefore perhaps more appropriate to separate Salafism prior to the 20th century from the hadith-centric scripturalism of its current form, identifying it instead with a critical posture toward mainstream scholarship. This of course fits with the nature of *tajdīd*, which aims to correct and eliminate errors and misguidance in scholarship. While such a stance often brings with it an emphasis on hadith and literalist interpretation, Qūrṣāwī shows that this is not necessarily so.

---

38. Cf. Qūrṣāwī, *Sharḥ jadīd*, fol. 94b; also Marjānī, *Mustafād*, ii, p. 168; Ramzī, *Talfīq*, ii, p. 343.

39. Qūrṣāwī, *Sharḥ jadīd*, 94b; cf. also Fakhr al-Dīn, *Āthār*, iii, p. 119.

40. It is, however, notable that this description of Qūrṣāwī is repeated by Ramzī, who was writing in the turn-of-the-century Hijaz—precisely the setting in which contemporary Salafism developed. Compare Qūrṣāwī's understanding of the *madhhab al-salaf* with the discussion of Jadidism and Salafism in Chapter 9.

A Response to Tsarist Rule

Qūrṣāwī's example supports Dallal's claim that it was local figures and currents that held the most importance, rather than transnational networks.[41] Qūrṣāwī of course had immense importance in the Volga-Ural region, and his particular historical context is critical to understanding his reformism. Unlike other contemporary reformers, whose interactions with the West were at most peripheral, he lived under the rule of a powerful European state. In this regard, Qūrṣāwī blurs the dichotomy posited by Dallal (and others) between indigenous Islamic reform movements of the 18th century and European-influenced trends of the 19th century. He lived in an almost exclusively Muslim social and cultural space, and he largely ignores Russian society and government in his writings. His primary goal is reforming and preserving the scholarly tradition (and by extension bolstering the Muslim community's religious standing), rather than engaging directly with European imperialism. Nevertheless, the experience of Russian subjecthood was a salient aspect of the Bulghar setting, and there are elements of Qūrṣāwī's thought that can be seen as responding to tsarist rule, shaping the form of his reformist project.[42]

The changes in Russian policy in the 18th century incorporated Russia's Muslim subjects into the imperial bureaucracy, transforming in the process not only Bulghar society but also (through the Spiritual Assembly) the very function of Islamic institutions within it. The impact of these changes is evident in the scale of reforms put forward by Qūrṣāwī, which differ markedly in the spheres of law and theology. For the latter, his stance is wholly conventional, fitting squarely within the broader Sunni understanding of the issue, formulated within the *kalām* tradition, as a corrective to the widespread view of the attributes. By contrast, Qūrṣāwī's reformism in terms of law is far more sweeping. Beyond calling for the verification of *any* legal position to ensure its correctness, it involves a drastic rethinking of the role of the *ʿulamāʾ* in the application of *fiqh*. By both declaring *ijtihād* to be broadly obligatory and devolving this duty from scholars to the community as a whole, Qūrṣāwī reconceptualizes the *ʿulamāʾ*'s traditional function in formulating, upholding,

41. Dallal, "Origins and Objectives," pp. 341–343; also Dallal, "Origins and Early Development," pp. 109–110.

42. As Moaddel argues (noted in the Introduction), a distinction must be drawn between the *content* of discursive changes and the *context* that gives rise to them, allowing us to separate Qūrṣāwī's wholly Islamic reformism from its European imperial environment; Mansoor Moaddel. *Islamic Modernism, Nationalism, and Fundamentalism: Episode and Discourse.* Chicago: U of Chicago P, 2005, pp. 17–20.

and maintaining the *sharīʿa*, blurring the distinction between *ʿulamāʾ* and lay Muslims.[43]

This discrepancy can be attributed to the impact of the Russian state. As we have seen, Islamic law under the Spiritual Assembly was subject to limitation of the authority and competence of legal experts, to say nothing of the significant degree of government interference in the function of the legal sphere. However, there was far less transformation regarding issues of doctrine and belief, oversight of which was explicitly granted to the Spiritual Assembly by the tsarist administration. Thus, unlike legal matters, the vast majority of which were removed from their jurisdiction, the theological sphere largely remained the purview of the *ʿulamāʾ*.

To be sure, the establishment of the Spiritual Assembly and restrictions placed on scholars under the religious hierarchy affected virtually every aspect of the *ʿulamāʾ*'s social and religious function. (See Chapters 8 and 9.) Yet, because state intervention was kept to a minimum regarding doctrinal matters, scholars could pursue *kalām* in a manner mostly unfettered by the government. In addition, the *madrasa*, the institution most closely aligned with continuity in scholarly discourse (at least until the later 19th century), was directly helped by Muslims' changed relationship with the tsarist state.[44] The Muslim community's increased economic stature was used to support *madrasas* in the region, and legal sanction allowed greater stability for Islamic education. As Kemper notes, Bulghar Muslims became more active in *kalām* toward the end of the 18th century, and scholars could pursue theological inquiry and debates within the tsar's domains.[45] The lack of structural changes to scholarly institutions regarding the *kalām* tradition made the continuation of that element of scholarly discourse possible.

This was not the case with law. Islamic law—previously a comprehensive societal system, governing the full range of Bulghar Muslims' social, commercial, political, and moral interactions—was now limited strictly to matters of family law, and the imperial administrative order was imposed in its place. Moreover, Islamic legal institutions were rendered subordinate to,

43. Weiss argues that historically the salient division within the community is between *mujtahids* (i.e., those who formulate the content of the law) and non-*mujtahids*; Bernard Weiss. "The Madhhab in Islamic Legal Theory." *The Islamic School of Law: Evolution, Devolution, and Progress*. Eds. Peri Bearman et al. Cambridge: Harvard UP, 2005. 1–9, pp. 3–4.

44. In both the Volga-Ural region and Central Asia, *kalām* constituted an essential part of *madrasa* education; cf. Kemper, *Sufis*, pp. 217–220.

45. Ibid., p. 220.

and dependent upon, the government. Faced with such an imbalance of authority, Muslims began addressing their legal claims to the tsarist administration, even in matters of family law, further undermining these institutions. In addition, the *ākhūnds*—the legal experts whose duty it was to articulate and apply the law—were marginalized within the religious hierarchy. No longer the foremost legal authorities, they were made subordinate to the Mufti, whose position was based on serving the state. The *ākhūnds*' role in settling disputes among Muslims was in turn given to imams, who were not, generally speaking, learned legal scholars. Thus, *fuqahā*ʾ, those whose knowledge and training gave them the ability and religious standing to interpret and elaborate the *sharīʿa*, had their religio-legal authority usurped, replaced by *ʿulamā*ʾ who were empowered by their position in an official hierarchy and obligated to follow in their application of Islamic law the dictates and directives of the tsarist state.

Under these circumstances, the continuation of the modus operandi of Islamic law was unfeasible. The government both interfered in the function of legal institutions and restricted and undermined their authority. The transformation of the legal tradition was inevitable, in order to adapt to the particular setting.

Qūrṣāwī's reform of *ijtihād* was formulated to do just that: to alter aspects of the legal tradition to ensure continued adherence to Islamic law, which changes to Islamic institutions and the marginalization of *fuqahā*ʾ had placed in doubt. (Likewise with Ūtiz-Īmānī and his absolute insistence upon *taqlīd*.) Indeed, the abandonment—for all intents and purposes—of the legal tradition due to the marginalization of scholars was not an unthinkable outcome. Zaman notes that in British India, which shared some salient features with the Russian Empire in terms of governing Muslim populations, the application of Islamic law essentially came to a halt regarding some matters due to the absence of *qāḍī*s.[46]

While Qūrṣāwī does not explicitly describe his stance on *ijtihād* in terms related to Russian rule, his overt skepticism toward the contemporary *ʿulamā*ʾ and his disdain for what he saw as obvious errors and misjudgment on their part can be seen as reflecting the changes to the *ʿulamā*ʾ under the Spiritual Assembly and the degree to which tsarist rule had undermined their standing as religious authorities and weakened their ability to offer learned religious guidance. Similarly, the devolution of the *farḍ kifāya* of *ijtihād*, the

46. Muhammad Qasim Zaman. *The Ulama in Contemporary Islam: Custodians of Change*. Princeton, NJ: Princeton UP, 2002, pp. 25–29.

performance of which was absolutely essential for the community's religious standing, from the *ʿulamāʾ* to the community as a whole allowed for the fulfillment of this religious duty despite the transformation of legal institutions. Although Qūrṣāwī was certainly critical of *ʿulamāʾ* in Bukhara (which was not under Russian rule at the time), it is remarkable that none of the several condemnations of his thought by Bukharan scholars mention *ijtihād* at all, in contrast to Bulghar scholars such as Ūriwī and Ūtiz-Īmānī, who denounced specifically his acceptance of *ijtihād*.[47] Therefore, it seems that Qūrṣāwī did not emphasize or advocate for legal reform in Central Asia. It came to the fore only in the Volga-Ural region, which was subject to a vastly different institutional and administrative environment.

Beyond this response to the structures of tsarist rule, Qūrṣāwī's reformism focuses on the scholarly tradition, and he relies upon its discourses to maintain the community's religious standing. As *kalām* (at least in the guise of *ʿilm al-tawḥīd wa-l-ṣifāt*) was the only legitimate framework for articulating and defending correct belief, and likewise the *madhhab* (as the preserve of legal methodology) the only legitimate framework for determining proper action, any flawed or defective positions within them had to be excluded (through *taḥqīq*), and active engagement with them had to emphasized. In terms of the latter, his call for the renewed exercise of *ijtihād* sought to use the paradigm of *uṣūl al-fiqh* to serve and strengthen the community; when he writes that anyone who answers legal questions using *uṣūl* is a *mujtahid*,[48] he is putting forward legal theory itself as the medium for the community's moral guidance (in contrast to proponents of *taqlīd* who separated *ijtihād* from the act of granting legal advice). Indeed, the truly radical element of Qūrṣāwī's reformist project is his call for *ijtihād* as an individual obligation, which significantly alters the relationship between the *ʿulamāʾ* and the community but does not change legal discourse itself, and which was necessitated by the shifting circumstances of Bulghar society.

The underlying epistemological motivation of Qūrṣāwī's reformist project is wholly shaped by the concerns of the postclassical tradition. For him, this tradition was essential for the moral and religious health of every Muslim society. As he saw it, the maintenance and refinement of its discourses was a necessary religious duty, and its preservation among Bulghar Muslims was intended to preserve the Bulghar community itself. Any society lacking the continuous exercise of scholarly interpretation would be in serious moral peril;

---

47. E.g. Fakhr al-Dīn, *Āthār*, iii, p. 107; vi, pp. 308–309.

48. Qūrṣāwī, *Irshād*, p. 30.

without it, people risked falling into grave error and slipping away from Islam. The propagation of incorrect and unverified positions by scholars and teachers likewise threatened the community, thus warranting the reform of scholarly discourse in favor of greater certainty and connection with the sound sources of religious knowledge.

8

Modernity

THE CHANGES IN Volga-Ural Muslims' relationship with the Russian imperial state in the second half of the 18th century ushered in a new era in their history. Although they had long been subject to Russian rule, the nature of that rule, varying in its treatment toward the Muslim population and involvement in their affairs, kept Muslims largely apart from the government and broader Russian society. The alteration of the state's approach during the reign of Catherine the Great, however, resulted in new policies, distinct in their support of the empire's Muslim subjects: official religious tolerance, greater sanction for Muslim merchants and soldiers, backing for Islamic institutions, and, most significantly, the establishment of the Muftiate and religious hierarchy. These policies simultaneously created a space for Muslims as participants within the empire and brought them closer to the state.

(Importantly, this did not mean the replacement of Islam with Christianity. While earlier efforts at bringing Muslims into the imperial government relied upon conversion to Russian Orthodoxy, religious tolerance meant that Muslims could remain Muslims while participating in tsarist institutions and governance, as well as in the broader fabric of imperial society.)

These changes resulted in the incorporation of Bulghar Muslims into the bureaucratic structures of the Russian state. Granted membership in the social groupings of tsarist society—the estates, military, and recognized religious communities—they were integrated into the system of rights from, and obligations to, the tsar that underpinned the imperial system. The creation of the Spiritual Assembly extended confessional governance to the empire's Muslim subjects, a logical conclusion of the centralizing drive for sovereignty led by Peter the Great and exemplified by the subordination of the Orthodox

Church.[1] (Indeed, in this regard the takeover of Islamic institutions was inevitable; as an otherwise autonomous source of legal authority, their continued operation outside the purview of the government would infringe upon the state's exclusive sovereignty.)[2]

Prior to this shift, tsarist power, though certainly present, had been peripheral to Bulghar society, which continued to operate along the lines of the premodern Islamic social order, organized around the *sharīʿa*. Within this societal framework, *ʿulamāʾ* institutions were both religiously and socially predominant; scholars articulated and maintained the moral and legal basis for society and managed the community on behalf of God, the ultimate sovereign, whose reward and punishment were foundational for the entire social order. With the new approach to imperial rule, however, these institutions were subordinated to the government and thus made to serve the ends of the state. Rather than providing a comprehensive Islamic framework for society, they were restricted in the scope of their authority by the government, which also gave directives as to how they should carry out their religious and legal functions. Although St. Petersburg brought Muslims into the tsarist bureaucracy, allowing their communities to flourish, this was done with regard for the empire's purposes, and Islamic institutions were used to harness religious morality in service of the tsar, turning the empire's Muslims into "useful citizens, good soldiers, and loyal subjects."[3]

Upholding the moral dictates of the *sharīʿa* became a decidedly secondary concern. Russian law was supreme, because the Russian state and its institutions were supreme. The Spiritual Assembly, as noted, was established as subordinate to tsarist legal organs, and the scope for its authority was limited by the state, creating a bounded sphere in which the *sharīʿa* as law continued to operate. Hallaq has noted the frequency with which colonial regimes restricted Islamic legal institutions to matters of ritual and family law, arguing that doing so was primarily a matter of political expedience.[4] The imperial government's reliance on Islamic institutions as mediators between it and its

1. James Cracraft. *The Church Reform of Peter the Great*. Stanford, CA: Stanford UP, 1971, esp. pp. 207, 209–210.

2. On the theoretical point regarding the coercive state and religious institutions, see Wael Hallaq. *The Impossible State: Islam, Politics, and Modernity's Moral Predicament*. New York: Columbia UP, 2013. The subordination of religious institutions in Muslim societies is a virtually universal aspect of rule under both European empires and the modern nation-state.

3. Cf. Robert Crews. *For Prophet and Tsar: Islam and Empire in Russia and Central Asia*. Cambridge, MA: Harvard UP, 2005, p. 41.

4. Wael Hallaq. *Sharīʿa: Theory, Practice, Transformations*. New York: Cambridge UP, 2009, pp. 443–447.

Muslim subjects constituted the confessional model of governance, with the empire allotting Muslims—and all recognized religious groups—a space for their own institutions, but as part of state structures. Although the tsarist government presented itself as defender of Islamic morality through its promotion of the Spiritual Assembly and enforcement of its decrees and judgments, this was the case only insofar as doing so accommodated imperial policy. In practice, the government asserted its control over Islamic institutions in myriad ways, even interfering in Islamic religious matters—over which the Spiritual Assembly had been granted exclusive jurisdiction—to press its own agenda.[5]

Disembedding and Individualism

The impact of state involvement on Muslim society was profound. The subordination of Islamic institutions to the tsarist government and the attendant transformations in their function undermined and restricted the previously comprehensive moral and legal framework of the *sharīʿa*, replacing it with the imperial social order. As a result, much of society and its function were structurally divorced from Islamic norms and morality, altering the religious environment.

The attendant changes to the scope and function of the *sharīʿa* represent a moral reorientation of society away from the *sharīʿa* and toward the imperial social order. It marks Bulghar Muslims' disembedding, defined by Charles Taylor as the removal of societally operative modes of identity and belonging, thereby precluding the continued existence of an "inescapable framework for social life."[6] At the root of disembedding is a breaking of the connection between the social order, the cosmos, and notions of human good.[7] In the premodern edifice of the *sharīʿa*, these were intimately linked. Society was ordered according to Islamic morality as determined from the texts of divine revelation, fostering an environment conducive to human flourishing (which

---

5. For instance, an imperial law from 1827 ordered a three-day waiting period between a person's death and burial, thus requiring Muslims to violate the norm that a Muslim be buried within a day of death. Despite the fact that the Spiritual Assembly had control over Islamic ritual, the government enforced the measure, enlisting Mufti ʿAbd al-Salām b. ʿAbd al-Raḥīm (r. 1825–1840) to persuade Muslims of its necessity and acceptability in the face of a broad backlash among *ʿulamāʾ*; Crews, *Prophet*, pp. 67–71.

6. Charles Taylor. *Modern Social Imaginaries*. Durham, NC: Duke UP, 2004, p. 61; also Charles Taylor. *A Secular Age*. Cambridge, MA: Harvard UP, 2007, p. 155.

7. Taylor, *Modern*, esp. pp. 51–60; Taylor, *Secular Age*, pp. 147–153.

is pleasing to God) and delivering people to salvation in the hereafter. To use Taylor's language, the social order was oriented toward and promoted notions of human good understood in reference to the cosmos.

However, the incorporation of Islamic institutions into the governing structures of the tsarist state infringed upon this social order, which was dismantled under, subordinated to, and supplanted by the imperial social order. Upholding Islamic morality was thus no longer a manifest priority within society. Instead, society was oriented around serving the ends of the tsarist state, which developed institutions and structures conducive to the formation of loyal and productive subjects, rather than good, pious Muslims earning divine reward.[8]

Disembedding in the Bulghar context was thus a consequence of the interaction between Islamic institutions and the imperial government, brought about by the sweeping changes to the *sharīʿa* that resulted from this interaction. Its restriction by the state into a bounded sphere left Muslims with a social order divorced from their own moral norms. The result was an environment in which Muslims' political, civil, and economic interactions operated along imperial lines, separate from any necessarily religious basis.

Taylor argues that disembedding brings with it a new self-understanding that "gave an unprecedented primacy to the individual" as distinct from a person's communal existence,[9] and we can see this understanding emerge among Bulghars over the course of the 19th century. But Muslims' individualization was not simply a matter of self-perception (which developed only gradually). Rather, it was an inevitable consequence of governing structures put in place by the Russian state and the overlap between the Islamic and imperial legal spheres. Unlike in the Western Christianity of Taylor's focus, where disembedding grew out of aspects internal to the religion and its traditions, disembedding for Bulghar Muslims was driven by external factors—namely, the undermining of the *ʿulamāʾ* and the possibility of separation from established religious authorities.

---

8. Taylor in fact argues that strong, centralized states can in themselves contribute to disembedding "because the very existence of state power entails some attempt to control and shape religious life and the social structures it requires," thus shifting conceptions of human good and society, primarily toward goals of order and productivity; Taylor, *Modern*, p. 59; Taylor, *Secular Age*, pp. 153–154.

9. Taylor, *Modern*, p. 50; Taylor, *Secular Age*, p. 146. This is part of what Taylor calls the modern Western "social imaginary," a collective understanding of social existence that is fundamental to society.

The very construction of the Spiritual Assembly transformed Muslims' relationship with religious authorities. The function of the imam under the Assembly hierarchy encompassed the entire scope of the religious sphere within their duties, making them the primary authority for most Muslims. Although an imam's judgments could be appealed, he also served as the prayer leader, teacher, wedding officiant, divorce mediator, and legal arbiter for his *maḥalla*. Therefore, a Muslim who found themselves at odds with their imam could become estranged from the proximate institution of the Spiritual Assembly, who could be removed only by the government. While Muslims certainly sought out and followed other religious authorities, it was often a practical impossibility to switch mosques, and anyone carrying out an imam's duties without a license was subject to arrest and punishment by the state. Tsarist control thus reshaped Muslims' ability to choose their religious leaders (even if it was not able to exclude all unsanctioned *ʿulamāʾ*) and the considerations therein.

Moreover, as noted, the Spiritual Assembly had jurisdiction only over family law, while all other areas were subject to the tsarist legal system. The state, however, also allowed Muslims to address family law cases to the Russian administration.[10] A Muslim could choose to pursue a family law case within the imperial administration alone, bypassing the *ʿulamāʾ*. In addition, the appellate construction of the religious hierarchy and the possibility of appealing cases to Russian legal bodies (often encouraged by tsarist officials) created an alternative space for Muslims to pursue their cases based on their individual motives. Family disputes among Muslims contested in Russian courts were not rare, suggesting that Muslims were generally concerned with finding the most personally advantageous venue for themselves, rather than choosing an Islamic legal body specifically.[11]

It was therefore possible for a Muslim to disregard any and all Islamic institutions if they so desired and it served their interests, or, if so inclined, to have virtually the entirety of their legal life be subject only to Russian law, to

10. This de facto possibility was made official in 1836; Nathan Spannaus. "The Decline of the *Akhund* and the Transformation of Islamic Law Under the Russian Empire." *Islamic Law and Society*, vol. 20, no. 3; 2013. 202–241, p. 228; cf. also Paul Werth. *The Tsar's Foreign Faiths: Toleration and the Fate of Religious Freedom in Imperial Russia*. Oxford: Oxford UP, 2014, p. 69.

11. See the cases in Spannaus, "Decline," pp. 222–229; also Robert Crews. "Empire and the Confessional State: Islam and Religious Politics in Nineteenth-Century Russia." *American Historical Review*, vol. 108, no. 1; 2003. 50–83, pp. 74–76.

the exclusion of any Islamic institution.[12] And doing so had little impact on a person's status as a Muslim or observance of the moral dictates of Islam. The former was guaranteed under the confessional model of governance, where anything short of formal conversion to Christianity kept one within the fold of Islam, while the latter was rendered not a societal concern but an individual one.

The overall effect was a profound decoupling of the individual and the community, which had previously been in balance within the edifice of the *sharīʿa*. The community, led by the *ʿulamāʾ* and its institutions, worked to create a moral environment conducive to the salvation of its members, while everyone was subject to divine reward or punishment based on their own conduct. Personal conscience played a major role in following institutions, of course, but prior to these changes a Muslim's moral comportment was supported and guided by the entire social order, through the comprehensive framework of the *sharīʿa* (and its harmonization of the social order, cosmos, and notions of human good). Muslims strove to elicit divine reward by following the normative guidance of religious authorities.

Implicit in this balance was the possibility for tension. Although mundane transgressions or the disregard of certain norms by individuals were not necessarily a problem for the community as a whole, a more significant issue would arise when a person, driven by their religious conscience, diverged from the community *believing they were right and justified in doing so.* Faced with this situation, the community could accordingly adapt to them, bring them back into the fold, or exclude them.[13] The first would represent an example of successful reform: an alteration of the community's religious modus operandi and/or discourse in a way that was seen as more correct. The latter two, by contrast, would represent an intervention by the community to protect itself (and its other individual members) from deviation by either correcting

12. Only marriage, officially considered a sacrament (!) for all faiths, was absolutely required to be carried out by the *ʿulamāʾ*; Paul Werth. "Empire, Religious Freedom, and the Legal Regulation of 'Mixed' Marriages in Russia." *Journal of Modern History*, vol. 80; 2008. 296–331, pp. 301–302; Crews, *Prophet*, p. 156. (This, however, is a change from traditional practice, where an imam or *ʿālim* was not necessary to perform the *nikāḥ*.)

13. Ulrich Beck explores in some detail the relationship between the individual and the community through the lens of heresy. Although he focuses exclusively on Christianity, his discussion of the salvific importance of the individual is equally applicable to Islam, and his analysis informs my understanding of the alteration of the link between the individual and the community, despite the different historical causes at work; Ulrich Beck. *A God of One's Own: Religion's Capacity for Peace and Potential for Violence*. Cambridge: Polity, 2010, esp. pp. 93–115.

misguided and erroneous ideas or silencing those espousing them, lest they and their ideas corrupt others.

The link here between reform and heresy is evident, and it is present in the case of Qūrṣāwī's condemnation in Bukhara. From his perspective, he was attempting to emend the errors in prevailing theological discourse, while the Bukharans saw him as vocally rejecting known orthodoxy. Though both sides were unsuccessful in convincing the other to change, the Bukharan *ʿulamāʾ*, representing the community, were responsible for excluding potentially harmful individuals, thus warranting Qūrṣāwī's execution in their eyes.[14]

As his condemnation illustrates, institutions played an integral role in the balance/tension between the individual and the community by delineating through their authority what is and is not divergent and what degree of diversity is acceptable. Indeed, Asad links the delineation of correct and incorrect discourses with the necessary exercise of power as constituting orthodoxy.[15]

Bulghar institutions possessed that power, as granted to the Spiritual Assembly by the state. However, as they were dependent upon the tsarist government for its enforcement, their exercise of it was largely limited to the informal. In this regard, it is significant that even though Qūrṣāwī elicited similar controversy in the Volga-Ural region as he had in Central Asia, no official steps were taken to censure or punish him. Ūriwī's letter to Mufti Muḥammadjān seeking his removal was ignored, as were the *fatwā*s and missives from Bukhara, and calls among some Kazan *ʿulamāʾ* to hold meetings (*majlis*) about his views led to nothing.[16] While it's certainly possible that more Bulghar leaders found Qūrṣāwī's stance acceptable, it is also true that any attempt to condemn him beyond the rhetorical would have almost necessarily involved Russian officials (needed to validate and enforce any action taken), whose primary concern in the matter was that social stability was ensured. As such, the Mufti would have had to convince them that Qūrṣāwī's ostensible heresy was a threat to the Spiritual Assembly's standing and/or

---

14. The main *fatwā* from Bukhara states that "the arrest, even execution of one who speaks against this [Sunni] creed and does not turn away from [his erroneous position] would be necessary," due to his spreading of "dissension, disturbance and instability" by promoting *bidʿa* as part of the true creed; Marjānī, *Mustafād*, ii, p. 173; translation and transcription in Nathan Spannaus. "Islamic Thought and Revivalism in the Russian Empire: An Intellectual Biography of Abu Nasr Qursawi (1776–1812)." Diss. McGill University, 2012, pp. 228–230.

15. Talal Asad. "The Idea of an Anthropology of Islam." *Qui Parle*, vol. 17, no. 2; 2009. 1–30. [Re-edition of *The Idea of an Anthropology of Islam*. Washington, DC: Center for Contemporary Arab Studies, Georgetown University, 1986], pp. 21–22.

16. Cf. Marjānī, *Mustafād*, ii, p. 169.

public order and therefore warranted intervention (which is a much different task than convincing *ʿulamāʾ* that Qūrṣāwī's view of the attributes fell outside the bounds of Sunnism).

Yet in more quotidian terms than heresy and reform, the transformation of the function of Islamic institutions under the imperial government undermined the moral link between them and individual Muslims. The community was defined by the state, rather than by its institutions or discourses.[17] "Muslim" was a legal category, which only formal and official conversion could change. Adherence to the *sharīʿa* was thus made a personal matter and—most critically—a *choice.* Not only could Muslims choose Russian over Islamic legal institutions (but not, in most cases, vice versa) or whether to accept the judgments and guidance of *ʿulamāʾ*, but it would fall to them as individuals to determine if and how they were to abide by the *sharīʿa* in their actions. As long as they followed the laws of the tsarist empire, there was nothing beyond peer pressure from other Muslims to compel any degree or kind of Islamic adherence. While this type of peer pressure is significant within notions of Islamic morality, it could be only so effective without a societal basis, and it paled in comparison to the coercive power of the state. The career of Muḥammadjān is illustrative of this fact, as his personal scandals and the widespread resentment of the Muslim community did little to weaken his power as head of the religious hierarchy or diminish his stature within imperial society.

Without effective and broadly supported institutions, there was no mechanism within Bulghar society for maintaining the balance between the community and the individual, who, religiously and morally speaking, was left to their own devices. In fact, the only Islamic institution that had the ability to shape Muslims' collective religious outlook was the *madrasa*, which, not coincidentally, had remained largely free of state interference. But the *madrasa*'s power in this regard was limited, and, as discussed in Chapter 9, over the course of the 19th century decreasing numbers of Muslims were connected with this institution, and the nature of Islamic education underwent marked divergence, becoming the subject of immense and fraught controversy.

17. John Meyendorff has noted that, following Peter's reform of the Church, Russian Orthodoxy was less a faith community than a mere "body of beliefs shared by the emperor's subjects and requiring state-sponsored social and educational services"; John Meyendorff. "Russian Bishops and Church Reform in 1905." *Catholicity and the Church.* Crestwood, NY: St. Vladimir's Seminary P, 1983. 143–156, p. 143. Such a description is also applicable to Islam under the Spiritual Assembly, but, given Orthodoxy's far greater closeness to the government than Islam, with little state involvement in the articulation of Islam's "body of beliefs."

Instead, a Muslim's individual conscience was left untethered from the community. Virtually all forms of Islamic observance and adherence became matters of strictly personal piety. A Muslim could choose to follow the extant institutions and communal praxis, but only as a choice, and one that could be changed at any time. The foundational understanding of each Muslim as individually eliciting divine reward or punishment remained. Islamic institutions continued to serve as guides for the community and support the morality of the individuals within it, but they no longer shaped the social order and were undermined on all sides by the Russian state. The community had little ability to maintain its moral cohesion. The vast majority of Muslims' interactions fell beyond the purview of these institutions, whose judgments could be questioned and appealed elsewhere for virtually any reason. Adherence to the *sharīʿa* had become almost exclusively the responsibility of individual Muslims and, for all intents and purposes, had been structurally rendered optional.

Secularity

The transformation of the Bulghar religious landscape represents a form of secularity. Distinct from secular*ism*, the ideological belief that religion should not play a public role within society, or the social marginalization or decline of religion, secularity is best understood as an altered context for religious belief, praxis, and authority, reshaping religion without necessarily supplanting it.[18] Taylor posits three dimensions to secularity: the separation of different spheres of society from religion, a widespread decrease in personal religiosity, and a shift in the religious environment in which any given form of religious belief is seen as merely one option among many.[19]

Of these, the latter two emerged among Bulghar Muslims only at the end of the 19th century, if at all in the imperial period. The last, linked with disembedding, bears a strong resemblance to the religious changes in the Bulghar setting, where the weakening of the link between the individual and the community necessarily created a setting in which no particular religious orientation could be presupposed; rather, any form of religiosity required some measure of assent on the individual's part, with the possibility of their choosing otherwise. Taylor, however, presents it as an issue of perception—of

18. Cf. Jose Casanova. "The Secular, Secularizations, Secularisms." *Rethinking Secularism*. Eds. Craig Calhoun et al. New York: Oxford UP, 2011. 54–74.

19. Taylor, *Secular Age*, esp. pp. 1–3. He labels them Secularity 1, 2, and 3, respectively.

widespread "construal"—within a society that any belief is but one option,[20] and there's little evidence that Bulghar Muslims saw adherence to the *sharīʿa* as a matter of choice. But, as I argue here and in the following section, this religious optionality is a structural matter, regardless of any particular perception or construal. This is a significant difference between Taylor and Ulrich Beck, with the latter presenting religious and social individualism as a societal fact, divorced from subjectivity. (Instead, Beck considers subjective individualism to stem from Enlightenment notions of the self and ego.)[21] For Bulghar Muslims, attachment to Islam was the default, but they nevertheless inhabited an environment in which Islamic institutions or virtually any form of religious adherence could be disregarded as a matter of personal choice.

Rather, we can understand secularity here primarily in Taylor's first sense, as a seismic shift in the structure of a society, separating it from an overarching order that had previously been "in some way connected to, based on, guaranteed by some faith in, or adherence to God, or some notion of ultimate reality."[22] Secularity in this sense signifies the existence and operation of whole spheres of society—politics, economy, law, and so on—unconnected to religion and/or lacking a religious basis. This phenomenon is linked with the structures of the sovereign state as a political entity, and it is apt for the Bulghar context. Although the Russian Empire was officially Christian, with laws that explicitly promoted and preferred Russian Orthodoxy, its rule over its Muslim subjects had no religious foundation, but was based solely on the state's coercive power. For Muslims, then, the empire was functionally secular, with its spheres of society ordered by imperial law, rather than the *sharīʿa*, and markedly lacking any substantive reference to Islam.[23]

---

20. Ibid., pp. 14–15. Taylor describes the very belief in God as one option, but this would entail that any particular type of belief in God is likewise optional.

21. Beck, *God*, esp. pp. 93–95. It's important to note that both Beck and Taylor see individualism as ultimately stemming from fundamental aspects of religion—the former in Christianity, the latter in post-axial, monotheistic religion in general.

22. Taylor, *Secular Age*, p. 1.

23. Although focusing on a later historical period, Birol Başkan makes a similar claim, arguing that the secular is manifested in certain governing structures regardless of the particular religion or ideology of those in power, because the coercive state is itself inherently secular; Birol Başkan. *From Religious Empires to Secular States: State Secularization in Turkey, Iran, and Russia*. New York: Routledge, 2014; cf. also the apposite argument in Hallaq, *Impossible State*, esp. pp. 25–30, 37–73. The question of secularity in terms of the empire's Orthodox subjects is beyond the scope of the present study, but suffice it to say that although it's complicated by the state's very different relationship with, and approach to, Orthodoxy vis-à-vis Islam, the Petrine takeover of the Orthodox Church could similarly be seen as constituting the bounding of an Orthodox religious sphere, and there are subsequent religious

With this change came the creation of a religious sphere for Muslims, a sphere that, as noted, was defined by the imperial state. In establishing a bounded and restricted jurisdiction for the *ʿulamāʾ*, the government delineated what was a religious matter and (perhaps more importantly) what was not. Thus, the very category of the religious was articulated by the tsarist state, as part of the confessional model of governance. Indeed, Crews has described how the government linked Muslim piety with loyalty to the tsar, utilizing a language of "sin" adopted from Russian Orthodoxy and employed "when officials sought to invoke the cautionary prospect of divine reckoning to reinforce the prescriptions of imperial law."[24] Following the pronouncements of the Muftiate was presented as an act of devotion; disregarding them was considered a sin, but it was also tantamount to breaking imperial law. The reverse was also true: disobeying an imperial order, while obviously illegal, was declared a sin.[25]

The bounding of a religious sphere by the state and its shaping of conceptions of religion and its discourses form an important element of the secular, according to Asad, who links it with the exclusion of certain religious actors, ideas, and praxis from broader society based on considerations necessarily articulated by existing power structures.[26] This is precisely what we see in the Russian Empire. The imperial state determined the authority for the ranks of the *ʿulamāʾ* hierarchy and the standards for appointment, approving each candidate. Within this bureaucratic arrangement, religious considerations were superseded by concerns of the state, which guaranteed the standing of each rank of the hierarchy, enforced its decisions, and denied any role for unsanctioned religious leaders. The tsarist government thereby remade the *ʿulamāʾ* into a formal clergy modeled on the Orthodox Church, while also utilizing and shaping language and conceptions of *sharīʿa*.[27]

The transformation of the Bulghar religious environment is reflected in Qūrṣāwī's stance on *ijtihād*, particularly the change in the relationship between individuals and the community. By considering *ijtihād* a duty for

---

phenomena among Orthodox Christians that would seem to represent reactions to an environment of secularity.

24. Crews, *Prophet*, p. 76.

25. Ibid., p. 66, also 76–77, 82.

26. Talal Asad. *Formations of the Secular: Christianity, Islam, Modernity*. Stanford, CA: Stanford UP, 2003, esp. pp. 183–185.

27. Cf. James Meyer. "Speaking Sharia to the State: Muslim Protesters, Tsarist Officials, and the Islamic Discourses of Late Imperial Russia." *Kritika*, vol. 14, no. 3; 2013. 485–505.

each Muslim, he shifts the responsibility for maintaining the *sharīʿa* within society—which is for him inextricably linked with the exercise of *fiqh*—from the *ʿulamāʾ* to individuals, to maintain for themselves. In doing so, he relies on the notion that everyone is personally subject to divine judgment. He implores Muslims in the *Irshād* to take an active role in their religious obedience, which his stance compels: not only must Muslims adhere to the Qurʾan and Sunna, but obliging individuals to engage in *ijtihād*, as the exercise of legal reasoning, also obliges them to discern the precise form that that adherence should take. They are thus accountable for determining what is morally correct action and subsequently following that determination (but also receiving divine reward for doing so). As Qūrṣāwī acknowledges, not everyone has the knowledge or ability to exercise *ijtihād*, and for those unable to carry it out, he obliges lesser forms of legal reasoning, such as *tarjīḥ*, as well as verification to ensure scriptural correctness, which everyone must do. Even those who lack any legal knowledge are nevertheless compelled to investigate scholars' morality and expertise before accepting their judgments. In any case, it falls to each individual to decide if they are capable of *ijtihād* and to what degree,[28] and to nevertheless follow what they believe to be correct (as Qūrṣāwī emphasizes in the *Sharḥ Manār*).[29]

Qūrṣāwī's stance thus focuses on the role of the individual, who is responsible for their own adherence to the *sharīʿa* without necessarily relying on the *ʿulamāʾ* or even the broader community. In this way his stance addresses the disembedding of Bulghar society and the removal of the *sharīʿa* as a comprehensive societal framework. Qūrṣāwī doesn't, however, espouse individualism, much less that the community is no longer important or that abiding by the *sharīʿa* is optional, all of which he would absolutely reject. Rather, he seeks to adapt existing *fiqh* discourse to fit a situation in which the role of Islamic institutions and the *ʿulamāʾ* had been transformed, necessarily altering the exercise of religious authority.

Ūtiz-Īmānī's insistence on the avoidance of anything not explicitly permitted in established *fiqh* texts similarly reflects these shifts in religious authority. Such an approach is unnecessarily restrictive in a society ordered by the *sharīʿa*, as the general function of society would align with its moral norms. Extreme prudence or vigilance becomes important in a setting in which *sharīʿa*

---

28. Weiss writes that the determination of oneself as capable of *ijtihād* necessarily involves "an exercise of conscience"; Bernard Weiss. "Interpretation in Islamic Law: The Theory of Ijtihad." *American Journal of Comparative Law*, vol. 26, no. 2; 1978. 199–212, p. 207.

29. Qūrṣāwī, *Sharḥ Manār*, p. 41.

norms are not operative and/or not broadly manifest. His understanding of *taqlīd* is based on an attitude that considers the contemporary *ʿulamāʾ* unreliable as religious interpreters or guides, and Muslims as estranged from their institutions and the broader society. Its inflexibility is thus intended to ensure proper adherence to the *sharīʿa*, both in the current setting and in an uncertain future: by relying only upon *furūʿ* texts for determining the validity of an action, his stance precludes the possibility that Muslims will reconsider the previously impermissible as acceptable, or otherwise altering moral norms. Locating authority in established texts, which were written in a different context still oriented by the *sharīʿa*, prevents the influence of the contemporary non-*sharīʿa* society from affecting notions of Islamic morality as determined by scholars.[30]

Despite their marked disagreement, both Qūrṣāwī and Ūtiz-Īmānī articulated positions that were responding to the changes accompanying Russian state control. Kemper remarks upon the apparent paradox that a radically pro-*ijtihād* stance should emerge at the same historical moment as an extreme insistence on *taqlīd* (linking the former with a certain, more progressive religious ethos).[31] In fact, their simultaneous appearance makes perfect sense due to their shared focus on the individual, which was warranted by the historical moment itself. The impact of Russian imperial rule on Bulghars' societal environment had rendered adherence to the *sharīʿa* a matter of choice and personal piety, thereby separating the individual from the community, and thus

30. Ūtiz-Īmānī's stance mirrors what Hallaq has described as the "entexting" of the *sharīʿa*, a shift in Islamic law where its authentic nature was seen as grounded in classical legal manuals, distinct from scholars' continuous interpretation; Wael Hallaq. "What Is Shariʿa?" *Yearbook of Islamic and Middle Eastern Law, 2005–2006*, XII. Leiden: Brill, 2007. 151–180, pp. 169–176; Hallaq, *Shariʿa*, esp. pp. 547–550. While Hallaq views entexting primarily as driven by the modern state, particularly imperial administrators and Orientalists who sought to mold Islamic law into a form intelligible and usable by them through reliance on texts (which certainly took place in the Russian Empire), entexting also entails a separation of the *sharīʿa*'s link between the articulation of legal discourse and social reality, and viewing texts as containing the "correct" or "authentic" content of the *sharīʿa* represents a means of preserving it in the face of its diminution or displacement within society, as we see with Ūtiz-Īmānī's insistence upon *taqlīd*. See also Nathan Brown's observation that the structural transformation of Islamic legal institutions and their relationship with the state has led to a shift in the conception of *sharīʿa* toward an overwhelming focus on its content, rather than its processes of interpretation; Nathan Brown. "Sharia and State in the Modern Muslim Middle East." *International Journal of Middle East Studies*, vol. 29, no. 3; 1997. 359–376, esp. pp. 359, 370–372.

31. Michael Kemper. *Sufis und Gelehrte in Tatarien und Baschkirien, 1789–1889: Der islamische Diskurs unter russischer Herrschaft*. Berlin: Klaus Schwarz Verlag, 1998, p. 304.

driving the need to strengthen individual Muslims' attachment to the *sharīʿa* and proper moral behavior.

Modern Reformism

These changes mark the beginning of modernity in Bulghar society. Importantly, this is not the beginning of a *process* of modern*ization*; rather, the sweeping shifts wrought by Muslims' incorporation into the structures of the tsarist bureaucracy ushered in an entirely new context, and by extension a new historical period, one that begins with the structural transformation of their society and appearance of secularity at the end of the 18th century.[32] As Fredric Jameson argues, modernity in a society begins with a historical break, signifying a new period that is markedly distinct from the preceding era.[33] By undermining Islamic institutions and infringing upon the comprehensiveness of the *sharīʿa* as a societal framework, the Russian state brought about a seismic shift in Bulghar society, ushering in an altered religious environment and a profound reorientation of the social order. These changes stand as the break from which modernity follows.

For Jameson, the modern break is unique (distinct from other historical breaks) in its transformative impact. In his understanding, the difference in context pre- and post-break is so stark that it calls into question the continuity of past forms and their suitability for the present environment, as "the foregrounding of continuities, the insistent and unwavering focus on the seamless passage from past to present, slowly turns into a consciousness" of a new historical period.[34] As a result, continuity is rendered conspicuous in ways it had not been previously, thereby reinforcing the unprecedented nature of the new historical environment and facilitating greater discontinuity. Modernity thus has a particular underlying "cultural logic," with an overwhelming focus on the present as distinct from the past and in which discursive continuity and discontinuity are in constant interaction.

Accordingly, Jameson conceptually separates *modernity*, the historical period, from *modernism*, the cultural and intellectual production characteristic

32. There are myriad analytical shortcomings to theories of modernization as a process, with its problematic associations with technological-economic development and/or Europeanization; see, e.g., the critique in Dipesh Chakrabarty. *Provincializing Europe: Postcolonial Thought and Historical Difference*. 2nd ed. Princeton, NJ: Princeton UP, 2008.

33. Fredric Jameson. *A Singular Modernity*. 2nd ed. London: Verso, 2012.

34. Ibid., p. 24.

of this period and reflecting its cultural logic.[35] This distinction is especially important for the study of Islam, as it allows for an understanding of the "modern" that is not specific to any cultural background. Modernity here serves as a historical context, while modernism itself is not tied to any characteristically Western orientation, nor based on any type of outlook, psychology, or subjectivity—thus excluding liberal autonomy and the sovereign, rational, secular subject of the Enlightenment, the emergence of which is often held up as the standard for modernity.[36] With this approach, we can consider historical phenomena that fit the modernist cultural logic but do not conform to conventionally Western or Eurocentric notions of modernity as nevertheless modern.

Jameson equates modernity with global capitalism, and he views the transition from feudalism to capitalism within a society as constituting the break from which modernity follows.[37] While this is perhaps apt for the Bulghar setting, as tsarist support for Muslim mercantilism contributed to an environment of capitalist enterprise and industry,[38] I would argue instead that modernity's unique cultural logic can be more directly attributed to secularity.[39] With the separation of the individual from the community, the maintenance of a given practice or discourse ceases to be the default; rather, it is

35. The "related concept in the aesthetic sphere," as he puts it; ibid., p. 13.

36. Ibid., pp. 42–57. In arguing against attaching any particular subjectivity to modernity, Jameson explicitly rejects the notion that "individuality" is directly linked with the modern. He argues that no particular type of subjectivity can be posited of anyone, much less of an entire historical period, but he specifies that equating individuality with modernity undermines the personal autonomy of premodern people. I agree wholeheartedly with these points. The separation of the individual from the community that I posit is qualitatively distinct from the subjectivity that Jameson critiques. As I argue above, this separation is not a matter of perception (or subjectivity) but rather is structural, applying to all members of the community regardless of how they conceive of themselves or their relationship to that community.

37. Ibid., pp. 39–40.

38. Something Kemper emphasizes; Kemper, *Sufis*, pp. 168–171. Another definition of a modern society is one subject to what Bernard Cohn, speaking of British India, calls the modalities of colonial governance, the production of certain forms of knowledge about a society that project imperial dominance: the writing of its history; observational travelogues; compilation of geographic, anthropological, and zoological statistics and descriptions; "museological" research, for the purposes of presentation to popular audiences; and categorization and surveillance of its peoples; Bernard Cohn. *Colonialism and Its Forms of Knowledge: The British in India*. Princeton, NJ: Princeton UP, 1996, esp. pp. 5–12. Muslims under Russian rule became subject to each of these modalities of knowledge in the 18th and early 19th centuries.

39. This is not a total rethinking of Jameson's position, as secularity is linked with capitalism in Marxist theory.

made an option, alongside the possibility of breaking with it, based on the concerns of the present moment. To return to Asad's discussion of the diachronic function of tradition, discourses from the past are maintained, altered, or abandoned based on the concerns and circumstances of the present. Modernity, a new historical context, impacts the present moment in which elements of the tradition are operative. As the present also serves as the crux in Asad's diachronic understanding of tradition, modernity therefore affects both the conceptualization of the past from which elements stem and the determination of how, or if, those elements should be made operative into the future.[40] With disembedding, the determination whether to maintain, alter, or abandon an aspect of the tradition is made by individuals, in light of their understanding of their current context. While they certainly may choose to defer to communal institutions or convention, they have the option not to. Continuity and discontinuity become choices, equally requiring some form of assent. In this way, the separation of the individual from the community fosters the cultural logic of modernity, as it allows for the intermixing of continuity and discontinuity. As this stems from secularity, its occurrence within Bulghar society serves as the modern break.

The debates among Qūrṣāwī, Ūtiz-Īmānī, and Ūriwī (and others) evince this new cultural logic within the Islamic discourse of the region. Ūriwī's claim in his letter to Mufti Muḥammadjān that Qūrṣāwī had abandoned four hundred years of authoritative scholarship is illustrative in this regard, as Ūriwī insists upon the need for continuity in response to discontinuity (represented here by Qūrṣāwī's embrace of *ijtihād* and rejection of the standard view of the attributes).[41] Qūrṣāwī and Ūtiz-Īmānī's respective stances on legal reasoning most clearly reflect the altered societal context. By shifting the responsibility for ensuring correct action from the *ʿulamāʾ* to all Muslims to determine for themselves, each radically reimagines the relationship between the *ʿulamāʾ* and lay Muslims, who are treated as individuals, in line with Muslims' disembedding. Ūriwī in turn promotes continuity in the *ʿulamāʾ*'s authority, but that authority had itself been altered under the new religious hierarchy.

Modernism, the cultural and intellectual production that reflects the cultural logic of modernity, follows from modernity, and the appearance of modernist discourses signals the beginning of the modern period. In the Bulghar

40. Asad, "Idea," p. 20; also Asad, *Formations*, pp. 222–223. Jameson focuses strongly on this element of the relationship to the past, going so far as to define modernity itself as a "narrative category," based on the reorientation of one's present in terms of continuity or discontinuity with the past; Jameson, *Singular Modernity*, pp. 23–41.

41. Fakhr al-Dīn, *Āthār*, iii, p. 109.

setting, the new notions of Islamic authority and types of Islamic discourse that emerge at the turn of the 19th century represent examples of modernism, reinforcing the transformative nature of this era and the new historical context. Qūrṣāwī's stance on *ijtihād* thus stands as a (very early) form of modernism, reflecting the modernity of Bulghar society at this time. Ūtiz-Īmānī's position on *taqlīd* also relates to Bulghars' disembedding and therefore is likewise an example of modernism. Other scholars began to embrace new, European forms of knowledge at this time, on the grounds that older methods of Islamic education were ill-suited to the present (see Chapter 9). That these views were formulated within two decades of the founding of the Spiritual Assembly underlines the transformative nature of the break and the need for new discourses suited to the current context.

Importantly, however, modernity or the appearance of modernism does not eliminate all premodern forms of discourse. Instead, modern and premodern discourses coexist as part of the interaction between continuity and discontinuity. The premodern does not evolve into the modern; rather, new discursive forms gradually arise within the modern context and others are altered or abandoned.[42] Indeed, Asad describes the multiple, overlapping temporalities of modern discourses as they "invoke or distance themselves from the past" in the articulation of novel discursive elements.[43] These discourses refer to, and have meaning within, the tradition (which necessarily continues despite the beginning of modernity), regardless of their continuous or discontinuous character; Jameson notes that any discursive break can be understood as such only if it has meaning within a preexisting cultural framework (i.e., a tradition), as it "must both affirm its absolute novelty as a break and at one and the same time its integration into a context from which it can be posited as breaking."[44]

The postclassical scholarly tradition thus remained relevant, as it continued to serve as the predominant framework for religious reasoning into the 19th century. It formed the basis for Ūtiz-Īmānī's radical insistence on *taqlīd*, and it was central to Qūrṣāwī's reformist project. For scholars such as Ūriwī, its reform was unwarranted and its discourses could continue without radical

---

42. Jameson, *Singular Modernity*, pp. 74–80, 128. Jameson takes this argument from Foucault's discussion of overlapping epistemes in Michel Foucault. *The Order of Things: An Archaeology of the Human Sciences*. New York: Vintage, 1970.

43. Asad, *Formations*, p. 222.

44. Jameson, *Singular Modernity*, p. 57.

revision.[45] These were all different responses to the present historical and religious circumstances.

The altered context had a widespread influence, and this period saw myriad intellectual and cultural developments within this religious landscape—indeed, Kemper's monograph is devoted to the new religious discourses that began emerging at the turn of the 19th century. Thus, the discontinuity engendered by the cultural logic of modernity had become apparent, particularly as breaks with the scholarly tradition and the abandonment of its discourses increased across the 19th century, spurred by secularity. These changes were not unidirectional. While it would be correct to say that they brought about a decline in Muslims' religiosity, they did not necessarily or uniformly do so. More accurately, they resulted in the alteration of Muslims' religiosity: Muslims suffered a loss of discursive coherence, which Islamic institutions could no longer maintain, and they increasingly relied on their own, individual religious approaches and interpretations, leading to a wider range of positions being articulated and greater contestation among Muslim voices—scholars and laypeople alike—over issues of religious, social, cultural, and (toward the 20th century) political significance. This contestation included Muslims who openly rejected Islamic tradition and religious norms and those who saw strict adherence to the scholarly tradition as the only means of preserving correct religious practice, as well as myriad views in between.[46] Yet each of these positions, and others, represents a form of modernism, shaped by the environment of secularity and reflecting the modern historical context.

45. Nevertheless, Ūriwī's writings themselves evince the impact that institutional shifts had had on *ʿulamāʾ* discourse and the function of legal interpretation; cf. Nathan Spannaus. "Formalism, Puritanicalism, Traditionalism: Approaches to Islamic Legal Reasoning in the 19th-Century Russian Empire." *Muslim World*, vol. 104, no. 3; 2014. 354–378, pp. 376–377.

46. It's worth noting that MacIntyre links individualism with the collapse of a prevailing moral tradition; Alasdair MacIntyre. *After Virtue: A Study in Moral Theory*. 1981. 3rd ed. Notre Dame, IN: U of Notre Dame P, 2007, p. 222.

9

The Transformation of the Religious Environment

THE INCORPORATION OF Muslims into the structures of the Russian state marks the beginning of a new historical context—modernity, as defined in Chapter 8—warranting new ideas and discourses and engendering further changes, with myriad social, cultural, and religious transformations to come as Muslims adapted to a new environment in which the structures of Bulghar society—indeed, the very nature of Bulghar society[1]—were destabilized under the imperial state. These changes reflected the growing diversity within Volga-Ural Islamic discourse, not just in the sense of a wider range of opinion but also in the sense of a decrease in coherence to the discourse, as ideas and frameworks external to Islamic tradition grew in importance for Muslims.

This diversity has conventionally been subsumed under the dichotomous conflict between the proponents of Jadidism, the movement embracing European social and cultural models, and Qadimism, the conservative defense of extant Islamic tradition. This conflict, as noted in the Introduction, has dominated the historiography of Islam in the Russian Empire, which equates Jadidism with Muslims' modernization, led by individual reformers—"enlighteners"—and locates modernity in westernization. Neither aspect of this narrative is wholly wrong—both factors were important in Jadidism's emergence and spread—but they offer a limited, teleological view skewed

1. It could be argued that a distinct Muslim society really ceases to exist, as Muslims' incorporation into the imperial bureaucracy brings a corresponding incorporation into tsarist society. In addition, "Bulghār" was gradually abandoned as a broad self-description for Volga-Ural Muslims toward the 20th century, with "Tatar" and "Bashkir," as well as other ethnonyms, used more by subgroups.

toward a particular type of historical phenomenon, obscuring developments falling outside this narrow lens.[2]

The approach employed here instead offers a broader scope that focuses on the growing diversity more in terms of changes to Muslims' religious and intellectual environment across the 19th century. The history of this period is one of varied responses to a constantly shifting context, as Muslims of all stripes adopted new ideas, premises, priorities, and ways of thinking in an effort to understand and adapt to contemporary circumstances. In the process, the discourse of their communities was remade.

This chapter addresses how that happened—how modern Muslim discourse was articulated and shaped in the Volga-Ural region, not only by reformers, but also by those ambivalent about European influence as well as those set against reform. The key element of this narrative is the gradual diminishing of the normative weight and influence of the Islamic scholarly tradition and the shift away from it by growing numbers of Muslims, leading to a drastically altered religious and intellectual landscape in the 20th century in which Jadidism and other religious orientations emerge. This landscape and the developments therein were shaped by three primary phenomena, each following from the pivotal period at the end of the 18th century: changes to Islamic education, the introduction of Arabic-script printing, and the fragmentation of Islamic religious authority. Interacting and contributing to each other, these three were directly involved with the transformations in Volga-Ural intellectual history in the modern era.

Reforming Muslim Education

Education was one of the primary functions of Islamic institutions, part of maintaining the scholarly tradition and its continued operation into the future. The overwhelming majority of Muslims were schooled in this tradition in *maktab*s and *madrasa*s, and the knowledge and values conveyed in these schools—primarily the purview of the *ʿulamāʾ*—were shared throughout the community, tying it together. As Frank writes, this education "formed the canon and the idiom through which the political, social and religious discourse

2. The recent monographs by Mustafa Tuna and James Meyer, for all their strengths, repeat many of these same tropes, reinforcing much of the standard historiography of modernization and nationalism, either through the efforts of leading Jadid reformers (Meyer) or Muslims' exposure to the West through Russian society (Tuna); Mustafa Tuna. *Imperial Russia's Muslims: Islam, Empire, and European Modernity, 1788–1914*. Cambridge: Cambridge UP, 2015; James Meyer. *Turks Across Empires: Marketing Muslim Identity in the Russian-Ottoman Borderlands, 1856–1914*. New York: Oxford UP, 2014.

of Volga-Ural Muslim communities was debated and discussed; without a background in this basic Islamic knowledge, Muslims, both men and women, would be unable to comprehend, let alone participate in, the internal debates going on within their own society."[3]

But the form and purpose of Islamic education became a point of contestation from the very beginning of the 19th century. By 1900, schooling represented an object of controversy and source of division, as fewer and fewer Muslims were educated by *ʿulamāʾ*, instead participating in Russian education as well as founding new schools whose curriculum was quite distinct from that of conventional *madrasas*.

One of the first instances of a Muslim working in a Russian educational institution was Sagit Khal'fin (Saʿīd Khalīfa) (1732–1785), who began teaching Tatar-Turkic language as an academic subject at the Kazan Gymnasium in 1769.[4] Formerly a translator in imperial service, Khal'fin was selected for the newly created post by Catherine the Great.[5] He was succeeded in this position by his son Iskhak (Isḥāq) (?–1800) and his grandson Ibragim (Ibrāhīm) (1778–1828), who would become the first instructor of Turkic languages at Kazan University soon after its establishment in 1804.[6]

From its very founding, Kazan University was an important avenue for Muslims in Russian academia, and its Department of Oriental Languages was made the center for Oriental studies (*vostokovedenie*) in the Russian Empire. The university attracted a number of Western European (particularly German) Orientalists, such as Christian Frähn (1782–1851), but Orientalist research at the university regularly involved members of the local Muslim population as well. Indeed, much of Frähn's work was facilitated by Ibragim Khal'fin, and the

---

3. Allen Frank. *Muslim Religious Institutions in Imperial Russia: The Islamic World of Novouzensk District and the Kazakh Inner Horde, 1780–1910*. Leiden: Brill, 2001, p. 227.

4. Many of the individuals mentioned in this chapter are more commonly known by the Russified form of their name, which in those cases will be the primary form used, with the Arabic-script spelling following in parentheses.

5. Prior to Catherine's reign, translators had overwhelmingly been Christian converts; Michael Khodarkovsky. *Russia's Steppe Frontier: The Making of a Colonial Empire, 1500–1800*. Bloomington: Indiana UP, 2002, pp. 70–72.

6. Ibragim Khal'fin taught simultaneously at Kazan Gymnasium and Kazan University (which were connected institutions), but he wasn't formally admitted to the faculty of the latter until 1811. On the Khal'fin family and its place in the history of Orientalism in Kazan, see M. Z. Zakiev. "Vliianie kazanskogo universiteta na razvitie tiurkologii v pervoi polovine XIX veka (do 1855 g.)." *Voprosy tatarskogo iazykoznaniia*. Ed. M. Z. Zakiev. Kazan: izd-vo kazanskogo universiteta, 1965. 357–393.

two collaborated frequently.[7] Following Khal'fin, Khusain Faizkhanov (Ḥusayn b. Fayḍkhān) (1823–1866), who had studied with both Mangārī and Marjānī, became an important lecturer in Kazan and later St. Petersburg, where the Oriental section of Kazan University was moved in 1855 (and re-formed as the Institute of Oriental Studies).[8]

Orientalist research nevertheless continued in Kazan, both at the university and under the auspices of the Kazan Theological Academy (Kazanskaia Dukhovnaia Akademiia), which became a significant center for Orientalism in its own right.[9] Although the Theological Academy was operated by the Orthodox Church for the purpose of training Christian missionaries, Muslims were connected with the school, most notably Kaium Nasyri (ʿAbd al-Qayyūm Naṣrī) (1825–1902), a *madrasa*-educated scholar from Shirdān who taught at the academy from 1855 to 1871.[10]

Nasyri in 1871 opened his own Muslim school, which taught a number of nonreligious subjects (natural sciences, geography, world history) as well as more conventional *madrasa* subjects, such as grammar, in ways adapted from Russian academia.[11] In fact, many of the figures linked with the Russian academy advocated for Islamic educational reform through the adoption of European methods and subjects. Faizkhanov, for instance, worked toward incorporating new types of pedagogy and subject matter into Islamic education.[12] One of his major written works, *Iṣlāḥ-i madāris*, which went unpublished, focuses on reshaping Muslim schooling to suit contemporary circumstances. In it Faizkhanov proposes a formalized curriculum that includes mathematics, natural sciences, and geography alongside conventional subjects such as *fiqh*,

7. Ibid., pp. 368–369.

8. Fakhr al-Dīn, *Āthār*, xiv, pp. 432–443; Shahr Sharaf. "Marjānīniñ tarjima-i ḥālī." *Marjānī*. Ed. Ṣāliḥ b. Thābit ʿUbaydullīn. Kazan: Maʿārif, 1333 [1915]. 2–193, pp. 113–114.

9. Mirkasym Usmanov. "The Struggle for the Reestablishment of Oriental Studies in Twentieth-Century Kazan." *The Heritage of Soviet Oriental Studies*. Eds. Michael Kemper and Stephan Conermann. New York: Routledge, 2011. 169–202, pp. 170–171; David Schimmelpenninck van der Oye. "Know Thine Enemy: The Travails of the Kazan School of Russian Missionary Orientology." *Religion and Identity in Russia and the Soviet Union: A Festschrift for Paul Bushkovitch*. Eds. Nikolaos Chrissidis et al. Bloomington, IN: Slavica, 2010. 145–164.

10. Chantal Lemercier-Quelquejay. "Un réformateur tatar au XIXe siècle 'Abdul Qajjum al-Nasyri." *Cahiers du monde russe et soviétique*; vol. 4, 1963. 117–142.

11. Ibid., esp. pp. 121–122.

12. Ibid., p. 120; M. A. Usmanov. "Avtografy Mardzhani na poliakh podlinnika proekta Khusaina Faizkhanova o shkol'noi reforme." *Mardzhani: uchenyi, myslitel', prosvetitel'*. Ed. Ia. G. Abdullin. Kazan: Tatarskoe knizhnoe izd-vo, 1990. 119–128.

theology, and logic (*manṭiq*).[13] Marjānī, himself associated with Orientalist circles in Kazan, was also an advocate of educational reform, championing the study of Russian language in *madrasas*.[14] He also adopted some Western scholarly methodologies: he relied on Russian Orientalist scholarship in his historical writings, and he criticized traditional Islamic—particularly sacred—historiography on empiricist grounds.[15] (This contributed to his induction into the Russian Archaeological Society, which published a Russian version of one of his historical works.)[16]

Most prominently, Ismail Gasprinskii (1851–1914), a Crimean Tatar activist who had studied at Russian schools in Voronezh and Moscow and lived in Paris, opened a Muslim primary school in the Crimean city of Bakhchisarai in the early 1880s that combined instruction in nonreligious subjects with a novel way of teaching Arabic-script literacy that relied on phonetic learning. The name for this approach, the *uṣūl-i jadīd* (new method), would come to signify reformed pedagogy in general, lending its name to the broader reform movement, Jadidism.[17]

Significantly, Islamic education was not impacted by state control. Until the 1870s St. Petersburg treated education as a strictly religious matter for the Spiritual Assembly to look after, precluding direct intervention by the government. This approach began to change with the so-called Great Reforms

13. Khusain Faizkhanov. "Reforma medrese (Islakh madaris)." Trans. I. F. Gimadeev. *Khusain Faizkhanov: Zhizn' i nasledie*. Ed. D. V. Mukhetdinov. Nizhnii Novgorod: izd-vo Medina, 2008. 12–28; cf. Fakhr al-Dīn, *Āthār*, xiv, p. 437.

14. Azade-Ayşe Rorlich. *The Volga Tatars: A Profile in National Resilience*. Stanford: Hoover Institution Press, 1986, p. 50; Usmanov, "Struggle," p. 171; Sharaf, "Marjānīniñ tarjima-i ḥālī," pp. 126–134.

15. E.g., Marjānī, *Mustafād*, i, pp. 206–225; cf. M. Kh. Iusupov. *Shigabutdin Mardzhani kak istorik*. Kazan: Tatarskoe knizhnoe izd-vo, 1981; ʿAzīz ʿUbaydullīn. "Marjānīnıñ tārīkhī khidmatlārī." *Marjānī*. Ed. Ṣāliḥ b. Thābit ʿUbaydullīn. Kazan: Maʿārif, 1333 [1915]. 333–359; Mirkasym Usmanov. "Istochniki knigi Sh. Mardzhani 'Mustafad al-akhbar fi akhval Kazan va Bulgar.'" *Ocherki istorii povolzh'ia i priural'ia*, no. 2–3; 1969. 144–154; Rorlich, *Volga Tatars*, pp. 49–50; Allen Frank. *Islamic Historiography and "Bulghar" Identity Among the Tatars and Bashkirs of Russia*. Leiden: Brill, 1998, pp. 149–157.

16. Sharaf, "Marjānīniñ tarjima-i ḥālī," p. 128; Ahmet Kanlidere. *Reform Within Islam: The Tajdid and Jadid Movement Among the Kazan Tatars (1809–1917): Conciliation or Conflict?* Istanbul: Eren, 1997, p. 48.

17. Adeeb Khalid. *The Politics of Muslim Cultural Reform: Jadidism in Central Asia*. Berkeley: U of California P, 1998, pp. 89–90. Gasprinskii (frequently Gaspıralı in Turkish sources), unlike most of the figures discussed in this chapter, utilized the Russified form of his name even in Arabic script (Ghaṣprinskī). The best study of Gasprinskii in English remains Edward Lazzerini. "Ismail Bey Gasprinskii and Muslim Modernism in Russia, 1878–1914." Diss. University of Washington, 1973.

under Tsar Alexander II (r. 1855–1881), which further integrated Muslims into the imperial order and brought greater state involvement in their affairs.[18] An 1874 law placed Muslim schools under the control of the imperial Ministry of Education, with the aim of introducing mandatory Russian-language instruction and state supervision, but this measure was met with staunch resistance from Muslim communities, which, seeking to maintain the Spiritual Assembly's purview, successfully prevented the ministry from exercising any meaningful oversight. Efforts by the government to assert ministry control in 1882 and 1893 were met with similar results, leaving most *maktab*s and *madrasas* free of state interference until the Soviet period.[19] As a result, Islamic education largely retained its earlier form and character up to 1900.

Yet ideas of educational reform had been circulating since the very early 19th century. Ibragim Khal'fin unsuccessfully sought to reshape *madrasa* curricula while at Kazan University.[20] As early as 1818 Mufti Muḥammadjān proposed that two European-style schools be established in Kazan and Orenburg for the purpose of preparing Muslims for university study or work as civil servants, translators, or schoolteachers. Modeled after the Russian gymnasium, these schools were needed, the Mufti argued, due to the general lack of education among Muslims and the impractical and inefficient character of Islamic education.[21] Though Muḥammadjān's proposal was ultimately unsuccessful, a small number of *madrasas* in the 1820s began teaching nontraditional subjects, utilizing Russian textbooks to do so.[22]

As the Mufti's proposal shows, there developed the sense among some that Muslim schooling as conventionally practiced was both ineffective and ill-suited to contemporary circumstances. State service and mercantilism had

---

18. E.g., Stefan Kirmse. "Law and Empire in Late Tsarist Russia: Muslim Tatars Go to Court." *Slavic Review*, vol. 72, no. 4; 2013. 778–801.

19. Much of the resistance took the form of frequent petitions on the religious importance of Islamic schooling, sent to both provincial officials and the tsar himself, as well as ignoring and rebuffing the (admittedly small-scale and unsystematic) efforts by government inspectors to monitor Muslim schools. The latter was helped by the fact that the overwhelming majority of Islamic education took place in mosques and private houses, rather than dedicated school buildings, which made inspection nearly impossible to carry out without the community's cooperation; cf. Tuna, *Imperial*, pp. 63–96; Meyer, *Turks*, pp. 67–79; Wayne Dowler. *Classroom and Empire: The Politics of Schooling Russia's Eastern Nationalities, 1860–1917*. Montreal: McGill-Queen's UP, 2001.

20. Cf. Lemercier-Quelquejay, "Réformateur," p. 118 n. 2.

21. Michael Kemper. *Sufis und Gelehrte in Tatarien und Baschkirien, 1789–1889: Der islamische Diskurs unter russischer Herrschaft*. Berlin: Klaus Schwarz Verlag, 1998, pp. 61–64.

22. Ibid., pp. 64–66.

become two of the most important avenues for Muslims' economic success, and the religiously grounded training found in the traditional *madrasa* was seen as irrelevant or even counterproductive for these professions. (These were common careers in cities particularly, and reformed schooling was overwhelmingly an urban phenomenon.) If, these reformers reasoned, Muslims were to flourish socially and economically (and later politically) in Russia, new approaches to education would be necessary; both *what* Muslim schools taught their students and *how* they taught them would need to be altered.[23]

Similar notions of educational reform were circulating in different milieux in the Middle East. Throughout the Ottoman Empire and Egypt, new types of schools organized according to Western models were established, along with nonreligious subjects and modern pedagogical practices introduced into *madrasas*. Particularly in the late 19th century, Ottoman sources of reform became influential in reformist circles in Russia through Russian Muslims living and studying in Istanbul, Cairo, and the Hijaz.[24] Indeed, the *uṣūl-i jadīd* was itself an Ottoman innovation, dating from the 1850s.[25] These reforms were motivated by the belief—shared with Jadidism—that conventional Islamic schooling required wholesale reform, and the adoption of Western educational approaches was intended to make it more practical, more efficient, more formalized and standardized, and more in line with contemporary needs.[26]

In the Russian Empire, the number of new-method *madrasas* remained tiny before 1890, after which they began to appear with some frequency. Though these schools varied, they shared some physical characteristics, operating in dedicated buildings consisting of classrooms with desks, chairs,

23. Cf. Christian Noack. "State Policy and Its Impact on the Formation of a Muslim Identity in the Volga-Urals." *Islam in Politics in Russia and Central Asia (Early Eighteenth to Late Twentieth Centuries)*. Eds. Stéphane Dudoignon and Hisao Komatsu. London: Kegan Paul, 2001. 3–26; Tuna, *Imperial*, p. 138.

24. Meyer, *Turks*; Tuna, *Imperial*, esp. pp. 27–29, 165; on the global circulation of Volga-Ural Muslim students in the imperial period, see Zavdat Minullin. "Fraternal and Benevolent Associations of Tatar Students in Muslim Countries at the Beginning of the 20th Century." *Muslim Culture in Russia and Central Asia from the 18th to the Early 20th Centuries. Vol. 2: Inter-Regional and Inter-Ethnic Relations*. Eds. Anke von Kügelgen et al. Berlin: Klaus Schwarz Verlag, 1998. 271–280.

25. Selçuk Türkyılmaz. "Usul-i Cedid Türkçe Öğretim Kitapları ve İsmail Gaspıralı." *Modern Türklük Araştırmaları Dergisi*, vol. 11, no. 4; 2014. 47–78.

26. Ismail Bei Gasprinskii. *Russkoe musul'manstvo: Mysli, zametki, i nabliudeniia musul'manina*. 1881. Oxford: Society for Central Asian Studies, 1985; Youssouff Aktchoura oglu [Iusuf Akchurin]. *L'état actuel et les aspirations des Turco-Tatares Musulmans en Russie*. Lausanne: Imprimeries Réunies, 1916, esp. pp. 10–12; cf. Timothy Mitchell. *Colonising Egypt*. 2nd ed. Berkeley: U of California P, 1991, esp. pp. 69–71.

and blackboards, and their educational content was marked by offerings in religious and secular subjects and programmatic curricula divided into classes and course levels. (See the report card from Kazan's Muḥammadiyya [Figure 5].) In addition, the *uṣūl-i jadīd* became widespread in the region as *maktabs* began adopting it to teach literacy, as well as occasionally offering instruction in basic nonreligious fields.[27]

Until this point, education had been a primary source of cohesion for Muslims. Taught by imams and *ākhūnds*, the shared knowledge, discourse, and norms spread through Islamic schooling linked Muslims from St. Petersburg to Siberia.[28] Education connected lay Muslims and the *ʿulamāʾ*, as within a mosque community "the imam and the congregation shared essentially the same education," Frank notes, "the imam simply ha[ving] a deeper knowledge of the same texts and ideas that the villagers had themselves studied in their *maktabs* and *madrasas*."[29] In this way schools were the main institution that tied the community together.

This education was deeply grounded in the moral and epistemic framework of the Islamic scholarly tradition. Methods of instruction, subject matter, textual production, and modes of discourse were all intertwined, part of the process of articulating and instilling Islamic ethics, values, and knowledge across generations. To alter any component of that process was necessarily to alter what is passed down to students, instilling in them different norms and values.[30]

In fact, the spread of reformed schools resulted in separate strands of education. As Stéphane Dudoignon notes, there had developed by 1900

---

27. Tuna, *Imperial*, pp. 163–166. In fact, it seems that *maktabs* employing the new method were far more common than reformed *madrasas*.

28. Even as more Muslims studied in Russian institutions, their early education (like, for instance, Gasprinskii's) would have been in a *maktab* and possibly a *madrasa* as well.

29. Frank, *Institutions*, p. 227; also Khalid. *Politics*, esp. pp. 20–31.

30. Cf. Brinkley Messick. *The Calligraphic State: Textual Domination and History in a Muslim Society*. Berkeley: U of California P, 1993; also Talal Asad. "The Idea of an Anthropology of Islam." *Qui Parle*, vol. 17, no. 2; 2009. 1–30. [Re-edition of *The Idea of an Anthropology of Islam*. Washington, DC: Center for Contemporary Arab Studies, Georgetown University, 1986], pp. 21–22. Describing the situation with Russian confessional schooling, which at the same time saw a similar push for reform (including the introduction of a phonetic method of teaching literacy), Ben Eklof notes the significant normative element in education, not only in enforcing values but also defining deviance, merit, failure, and success. More so than the ethical and moral components of traditional religious schooling, modern schools compel standardization, subordination, discipline, and hierarchy; Ben Eklof. *Russian Peasant Schools: Officialdom, Village Culture and Popular Pedagogy, 1861–1914*. Berkeley: U of California P, 1986.

مکاتب ابتدائیه شهادتنامه‌سی

اوشبو شهادتنامه ایه‌سی ....

.... ده .... نك نظارتنده بولغان مکتب ابتدائی‌نی

بتروب توبه‌نده‌گی فنلردن امتحان بیردی. وعموماً حالی .... نچی

درجه‌ده کوریلوب امتحانسز رشدیه برنچی صنفغه قبول ایتلو

درجه‌سینه نائل بولدی.

فنلر	درجه	فنلر	درجه
قرآن کریم مع تجوید		علوم دینیه	
املا وقرائت		حسن خط	
حساب		حفظ الصحه	
علم اخلاق		کتابت	
جغرافیا		تاریخ	
صرف ونحو		رسم	

اسمی فامیلیه‌سی ....

یاشی طوغان یری ....

معلم: .... امتحان اعضالری: ....

ناظر: .... ۱۹۱ سنه

ناشری: صباح کتبخانه‌سی

FIGURE 5 A blank report card (*shihādatnāma*) for the Muḥammadiyya *madrasa*'s elementary school, ca. 1910. (National Archives, Republic of Tatarstan)

a distinction between *muʿallims* (i.e., teachers in new-method schools) and imams, who had previously held a virtual monopoly on Islamic education, with the former becoming more socially prestigious than the latter.[31] As evinced by the split between the two terms, new-method education was marked by its secular—nonreligious—character; although reformed *madrasas* included religious subjects within their curricula, these were limited to a particular part of a broader course of study, diminishing their significance. No longer foundational, they were rendered individual subjects among many others.[32] And proponents of new-method schooling often saw a different ethos to education, viewing its goal as instilling practical knowledge rather than religious morality, a stance that was criticized by their opponents, who argued that it elevated harmful, irreligious knowledge at the expense of piety.[33]

At the same time, state schools for Muslims, which taught modern subjects in Russian, were undergoing tremendous growth. In operation since the 1870s, these schools were initially perceived by Muslims as promoting Orthodoxy and therefore had attracted few students. As views toward European and European-derived education changed, however, they came to be seen as a viable, even preferable, alternative to traditional *maktab*s and *madrasa*s, particularly among reform-minded Muslims.[34]

From the very beginning of the 20th century, more and more Muslims were being educated outside of Islamic tradition and instilled with different

31. Stéphane Dudoignon. "Status, Strategies and Discourses of a Muslim 'Clergy' Under a Christian Law: Polemics About the Collection of the *Zakat* in Late Imperial Russia." *Islam in Politics in Russia and Central Asia (Early Eighteenth to Late Twentieth Centuries)*. Eds. Stéphane A. Dudoignon and Hisao Komatsu. London: Kegan Paul, 2001. 43–73.

32. On reformed curricula, see R. Majerczak. "Notes sur l'enseignement dans la Russie musulmane avant la révolution." *Revue du monde musulman*, vol. 34; 1917–1918. 179–248, pp. 196–197. A detailed description of the course of study at the new-method Bubī *madrasa* is given in Mustafa Tuna. "Russia's Muslims: Inroads of Modernity." Diss. Princeton University, 2009, pp. 209–212.

33. Cf. Majerczak, "Notes," pp. 193, 199.

34. These included the so-called Russo-Tatar (-Bashkir, -Kazakh) schools and the Kazan Tatar Teachers' School (founded to train to Muslims to serve as instructors in the former), as well as primary schools supported by municipal councils (*zemstvos*), which were outside the control of the imperial Ministry of Education and, particularly in the areas around Ufa and Orenburg, an important educational option for Muslims. On these schools, see Tuna, *Imperial*, esp. pp. 70–71, 76, 83, 98–101, 166; Dowler, *Classroom*, esp. pp. 104–110, 131–156; Robert Geraci. *Window on the East: National and Imperial Identities in Late Tsarist Russia*. Ithaca, NY: Cornell UP, 2001, pp. 136–157; Norihiro Naganawa. "Maktab or School? Introduction of Universal Primary Education Among the Volga-Ural Muslims." *Empire, Islam, and Politics in Central Eurasia*. Ed. Tomohiko Uyama. Sapporo: Slavic Research Center, 2007. 65–98.

knowledge and values.[35] The products of these institutions were intellectuals and professionals, rarely *ʿulamāʾ*, and the social and cultural—to say nothing of religious—ramifications were significant. Shifting educational trends brought about a generation of Muslims that no longer possessed the same education as their parents nor all of their peers. Rather, new-method students received qualitatively different knowledge, taught through different paradigms, than their counterparts in more conventional schools, largely separate from the knowledge of the scholarly tradition that was now no longer shared throughout the community. This situation, Danielle Ross rightly argues, "resulted in the replacement of a single uniform body of knowledge with multiple, competing ones." Instead of a source of communal cohesion, schooling now served as a marker of divergence, leading to varying attitudes and ideologies as well as conflicting claims to communal leadership (a point to which we will return).[36]

Printing

Efforts to reform Muslim education were furthered by the development of Arabic-script printing, which became a significant part of Muslims' intellectual life at this time, and also provided a venue for competing conceptions of Islamic knowledge. The first private Arabic-script press was established with imperial permission in 1800 by ʿAbd al-ʿAzīz Būrāsh, a prominent member of the Tūqṭāmish merchant family.[37] Located at Kazan Gymnasium, it published a handful of religious titles over its first few years of operation. In about 1804, the merchant Yūsuf Āpānāy began to publish books there as well, and in 1809 ownership of the press was transferred to the gymnasium. At the same time Kazan University established its own press issuing Arabic-script and Russian publications. It took over the gymnasium's press in 1829, becoming a major publisher in the Russian Empire, putting out hundreds of editions of books in Muslim languages throughout the imperial period.[38]

35. Rorlich notes that significant numbers of Muslims were taking part in European professional and trade schooling by this time, both in Russia and abroad in Europe; Rorlich, *Volga Tatars*, pp. 101–102.

36. Danielle Ross. "Caught in the Middle: Reform and Youth Rebellion in Russia's Madrasas, 1900–10." *Kritika*, vol. 16, no. 1; 2015. 57–89, p. 60.

37. Arabic-script presses had existed in St. Petersburg since the reign of Peter the Great, but, like all publishing in the empire, they were under government control until the very end of the 18th century.

38. There's some discrepancy between the sources over dates and the precise sequence of events, but suffice it to say Arabic-script printing began in Kazan in the first decade of the

Alongside the Qur'an, the most frequently published title was *Īmān sharṭī*, a moral didactic work for children widely used in Volga-Ural *maktabs*.[39] The majority of books printed were editions of common religious texts (like *Īmān sharṭī*), but printing bore a significant impact even when the texts themselves were not new. Printed books were cheaper and could be more widely distributed than manuscripts, making texts much more obtainable and therefore accessible than they had been previously.[40] In terms of schooling, the availability of printed materials lessened over time the emphasis on oral learning, which was the primary method of transmission in Islamic education. Increased popular literacy was an obvious consequence, but, as Elizabeth Eisenstein has shown in her study of the beginnings of printing in Europe, some of the most subtle and profound ramifications came not in terms of the spread of education and literacy but rather in alterations to intellectual life among scholars.[41]

Indeed, it was *ʿulamāʾ* for whom the widespread availability of books had the most immediate impact. Cheaper and more plentiful books allowed scholars access to a wider range of texts, without the need to travel in search of manuscript copies. Out of this accessibility came discursive changes. With greater numbers of books available, scholars could read much more broadly; with far less need to memorize or produce a new copy of a text and more books at their disposal, they could devote their time and attention to a wider variety of sources.[42] (This was particularly true for *madrasa* students, who often had

---

19th century, and Kazan University followed and soon surpassed any previous presses; A. G. Karimullin. *U istokov tatarskoi knigi: ot nachala vozniknoveniia do 60-kh godov XIX veka.* Kazan: Tatarskoe knizhnoe izd-vo, 1992; Gaziz Gubaidullin. *Istoriia Tatar.* 1925. 3rd ed. Moscow: Moskovskii litsei, 1994, pp. 183–184; Rezeda Safiullina. *Istoriia knigopechataniia na arabskom iazyke v Rossii u musul'man Povolzh'ia.* Kazan: izd-vo Alma-Lit, 2003; B. Dorn. "Chronologisches Verzeichniss der seit dem Jahre 1801 bis 1866 in Kasan gedruckten arabischen, türkischen, tatarischen und persischen Werke, als Katalog der in dem asiatischen Museum befindlichen Schriften der Art." *Mélanges asiatiques tirés du Bulletin de l'Académie impériale des sciences de St.-Pétersbourg*, vol. 5; 1866. 533–649; *Katalog knig otpechatannykh v tipografii imperatorskago kazanskago universiteta c 1800 do 1896.* Eds. N. F. Katanov and A. Solovev. Kazan: Tipografiia kazanskago universiteta, 1896.

39. Dorn, "Chronologisches," pp. 538–548; cf. Frank, *Institutions*, p. 241.

40. Even with only two presses in operation, more than 170,000 copies of Arabic-script books had been published in Kazan by 1829; Karimullin, *U istokov*, p. 136. By the mid-19th century, hundreds of titles on a wide range of subjects were being issued every year.

41. Cf. Elizabeth Eisenstein. *The Printing Revolution in Early Modern Europe.* Cambridge: Cambridge UP, 1983.

42. Ibid., pp. 47–48. The wider variety of accessible texts, Eisenstein writes, also meant that scholars engaged less deeply with any given work.

to share a single copy of a manuscript with their peers.)[43] Particularly toward the middle of the 19th century, the selection of published books in the Volga-Ural region increased significantly. According to Rezeda Safiullina, there were a large number of different texts just on Hanafi *fiqh* edited and published by authors from Central Asia and the Ottoman Empire, as well as Iraq and the Hijaz, and from varying eras. These texts were not necessarily exotic, but none were so widespread in manuscript form, and some, Safiullina notes, were not commonly used prior to their publication.[44]

From the bibliographic data, it's clear that Volga-Ural *ʿulamāʾ* had an ever-widening range of texts available and accessible to them, and, as Eisenstein has argued, exposure to a greater diversity of texts brings with it exposure to a greater diversity of ideas and approaches, with significant consequences. She writes:

> Not only was confidence in old theories weakened, but an enriched reading matter also encouraged the development of new intellectual combinations and permutations. . . . Once old texts came together within the same study, diverse systems of ideas and special disciplines could be combined. Increased [publishing] output directed at relatively stable markets, in short, created conditions that favored new combinations of old ideas at first and then, later, the creation of entirely new systems of thought.[45]

With more texts at their disposal, scholars could make connections and combinations that were otherwise impossible. *ʿUlamāʾ* in the Russian Empire could avail themselves of an increasingly broad spectrum of older Islamic texts, and over time a growing number of newly composed books begin to appear on a range of subjects—including conventional ones such as *fiqh, kalām,* Sufism, history, and language.[46]

In the process, new genres and types of publications emerged. Many of these new titles were on religious subjects, but pedagogical works on other topics appeared as well, covering new subjects of study and/or approaching established

---

43. Messick, *Calligraphic State*, pp. 90–91.

44. Cf. R. R. Safiullina. *Arabskaia kniga v dukhovnoi zhizni tatarskogo naroda*. Kazan: izd-vo Alma-Lit, 2003, pp. 85–100. It's important to note here that Safiullina's study is restricted only to books written in Arabic, and so does not include the numerous and certainly more popular books in Persian or Turkic languages.

45. Eisenstein, *Printing Revolution*, p. 49.

46. See, e.g., Safiullina, *Arabskaia*, pp. 152–177.

topics in novel ways. These authors—Muslim and non-Muslim—were frequently connected with Russian educational institutions, and their works show not only the new types of discourses emerging from these connections but also the ways that printing influenced existing forms of scholarship. Books on language and history were among the very first nonreligious titles published and composed. For instance, Ibragim Khal'fin edited Abū al-Ghāzī Bahādur Khān's (1605–1663) famed history of the Turkic peoples, the *Shajara-i tūrk*, and he also wrote a grammar of Tatar-Turkic.[47] Although engaging with a popular historical work and composing a grammar were common activities for *ʿulamāʾ*, Khal'fin's books were of a very different type. The process of editing an existing work and preparing it for publication—which Khal'fin did in concert with the Orientalist Frähn—is a venture distinct from the type of work with a text characteristic of the Islamic scholarly tradition. More significantly, Khal'fin's grammar was not composed along the lines of grammatical works by *ʿulamāʾ*, but instead was modeled after Mikhail Lomonosov's groundbreaking Russian grammar from 1755.[48]

As more presses were founded from the 1840s on,[49] books for Muslims on varied academic and popular topics became common.[50] Nasyri, for one, composed books on geography, mathematics, agronomy, local history, and hygiene as part of his expansive oeuvre.[51] Likewise, Gasprinskii used his own press in Bakhchisarai to publish dozens of new titles on religious, scientific, medical, and historical subjects, as well as works of fiction.[52]

Many of these new types of texts were produced under Russian auspices. Orientalist scholars in Kazan and St. Petersburg edited and published large numbers of books in Muslim languages and related works of academic scholarship.[53] Moreover, Orthodox missionaries produced a considerable

---

47. Dorn, "Chronologisches," p. 540 n. 5, 543 n. 11; Zakiev, "Vliianie," pp. 369–373.

48. Zakiev, "Vliianie," p. 369.

49. Karimullin, *U istokov*, pp. 119–120; also, for the late 19th century, Rorlich, *Volga Tatars*, pp. 73–75.

50. See Gasprinskii's detailed bibliography from 1900 of modern textbooks in Turkic languages; Edward Lazzerini. "Ǧadidism at the Turn of the Twentieth Century: A View from Within." *Cahiers du Monde russe et soviétique*, vol. 16, no. 2; 1975. 245–277, pp. 259–277.

51. Lemercier-Quelquejay, "Réformateur," esp. pp. 136–142; Tuna, *Imperial*, p. 155.

52. Lazzerini, "Ǧadidism," pp. 275–277.

53. Beyond scholarship, Orientalists assisted the government in disseminating bureaucratic documents to the Muslim population as well. Ibragim Khal'fin produced Turkic versions of numerous government directives, including, for instance, a notice on the usefulness of vaccinations that was first printed in Kazan in 1803; Karimullin, *U istokov*, pp. 135–136; Dorn, "Chronologisches," p. 584.

proportion of all the publications in Muslim languages.[54] These works—even older Islamic texts edited by Orientalists—were organized around different purposes than those produced from within the scholarly tradition, and they were influential in the spread of different textual and pedagogical approaches.

In the second half of the 19th century, missionaries began promoting Christianity and Russification through the use of vernacular Turkic languages in Cyrillic script, distinct from the written languages of the prevailing Islamic discourse (Arabic, Persian, literary Tatar-Turkic). The goal was to separate Muslim and Christian(ized) non-Russians from this discourse, thereby facilitating their inculcation into an Orthodox and ultimately Russian cultural framework.[55] This strategy was pioneered by the Kazan missionary leader Nikolai Il'minskii (1821–1891), who worked to develop written forms of local Turkic vernaculars to serve as languages of instruction in missionary schools.[56] Though anathema to most Muslims, Il'minskii's efforts bore a significant impact on non-Russian education in the empire. Orientalist scholars were directing their attention to the vernacular as well, producing not only collections of texts in different local Turkic varieties but also dictionaries and grammars.[57]

This focus on the vernacular dovetailed with efforts of Muslim pedagogical reformers, who, like Il'minskii, sought to make popular education more accessible and effective by using a language of instruction that matched people's spoken language.[58] Faizkhanov, for instance, advocated for education in Tatar-Turkic, rather than Arabic or Persian, to promote students' understanding of the material (and to increase the feasibility and spread of popular publishing). Arabic, Persian, and especially Ottoman should still be taught, he argued, but as distinct academic subjects, while religious subjects such as *fiqh* would be

---

54. Cf. Karimullin, *U istokov*, pp. 130, 134–135.

55. Schimmelpenninck van der Oye, "Know Thine Enemy," esp. p. 160. The influence of Islamic discourse on Christianized Tatars—labeled Kriashen (baptized)—was significant. As Agnès Kefeli has shown, the cultural and linguistic bonds between Kriashen and Muslim communities frequently contributed to the return to Islam by the former; Agnès Kefeli. "Constructing an Islamic Identity: The Case of Elyshevo Village in the Nineteenth Century." *Russia's Orient: Imperial Borderlands and Peoples, 1700–1917*. Eds. Daniel Brower and Edward Lazzerini. Bloomington, IN: Indiana UP, 1997. 271–291.

56. On the so-called Il'minskii method, see Dowler, *Classroom*; Geraci, *Window*, esp. pp. 117–136.

57. Cf. M. Kh. Gainullin, *Tatarskaia literatura XIX veka*. Kazan: Tatarskoe knizhnoe izd-vo, 1975, pp. 196–197.

58. Mustafa Tuna. "Gaspirali v. Il'minskii: Two Identity Projects for the Muslims of the Russian Empire." *Nationalities Papers*, vol. 30, no. 2; 2002. 265–289; Isabelle Kreindler. "Ibrahim Altynsarin, Nikolai Il'minskii and the Kazakh National Awakening." *Central Asian Survey*, vol. 2, no. 3; 1983. 99–116; cf. Geraci, *Window*, p. 140.

in Tatar-Turkic.[59] Nasyri's efforts also stand out in this regard, as much of his scholarly career was devoted to turning the Kazan dialect into a formal, standardized written language.[60] To that end, he authored a number of texts specifically on the language—grammars, dictionaries, writing guides—but he also composed all of his works in it, which, given their immense scope, necessitated the creation of a range of new scientific and technical terms.[61] His endeavors were furthered and certainly shaped by his connections with Orientalists and missionaries (two categories that in Kazan often overlapped): Il'minskii, for instance, assisted with his first Tatar grammar, published in 1860, and he was also supported by Vassilii Radlov (1837–1918), a scholar at Kazan University who himself produced several texts on vernacular Tatar, including the first Russian dictionary of the language.[62]

Nasyri's emphasis on the vernacular as a written language was instrumental in the emergence of Tatar prose literature, which began in the 1880s.[63] The first such novel was *Ḥisām al-Dīn Mullā* by Mūsā Āqyigit (1865–1923), published in Kazan in 1886. In the novel, the titular character, a young Muslim from a small Volga village, travels to Kazan, where he becomes enamored with an educated young woman and is exposed to reformist ideas, leading him to give up the conventionally religious ways of his upbringing.[64] Zagir Bigiev (Ẓāhir Bīgī) (1870–1902), older brother of the famed reformer Musa Bigiev

59. Faizkhanov, "Reforma."

60. Lazzerini, "Gasprinskii" (1973), p. 214.

61. Gainullin, *Tatarskaia literatura*, p. 178; cf. Tuna, *Imperial*, p. 155.

62. Dowler, *Classroom*, p. 156; Gainullin, *Tatarskaia literatura*, pp. 196–197. Radlov would serve as supervisor of Muslim schools during the aborted takeover by the government in the 1870s; on this role, see Tuna, *Imperial*, esp. pp. 74–91; Geraci, *Window*, pp. 140–150.

63. Cf. Gainullin, *Tatarskaia literatura*, esp. p. 163; also Lemercier-Quelquejay, "Réformateur," pp. 126–127. Tatar drama also developed at this time and would become a major element among reformers' messaging to the (often skeptical) Muslim public; see Madina Goldberg. "Russian Empire-Tatar Theater: The Politics of Culture in Late Imperial Kazan." Diss. University of Michigan, 2009.

64. Cf. A. Battal-Taymas. "La littérature des Tatars de Kazan." *Philologiae Turcica Fundamenta*. Vol. 2. Eds. Jean Deny et al. Aquis Mattiacis: Steiner, 1979. 762–778, p. 763; Lazzerini, "Gasprinskii" (1973), pp. 211–212; ʿAbdraḥmān Saʿdī. *Tātār adabiyātī tārīkhī*. Kazan: Tātārstān dawlat nashriyātī bāsmāsī, 1926, pp. 76–78; Gainullin, *Tatarskaia literatura*, pp. 198–208. Āqyigit (also written Akyigitzade) was educated in Russian schools, and he took a very progressive view of religion, arguing for a connection between Islam and global modern culture. Shortly after the novel was published he moved to the Ottoman Empire, where he became influential in ongoing economic and social debates; see Deniz Kilinçoğlu. *Economics and Capitalism in the Ottoman Empire*. London: Routledge, 2015; also Niyazi Berkes. *The Development of Secularism in Turkey*. London: Hurst, 1998, pp. 263–264.

(discussed later in this chapter), published his first novel, *Ulūf, yāki Gūzil qiz Khadīja*, in Kazan in 1887, and subsequently composed a handful of others. Like *Ḥisām al-Dīn Mullā*, Bigiev's novels dealt with issues of social and religious change through the eyes of young Muslim characters often possessing European educations.[65]

The Muslim Public Sphere

An even more significant development was the appearance of Arabic-script newspapers, which, like the novel, represented a new textual genre characteristic of the contemporary historical environment. Also like the novel, they were embraced by reformist-minded Muslims, such as Faizkhanov and Nasyri, both of whom attempted (unsuccessfully) to found journals in the mid-19th century.[66] The push for Muslim periodical printing was led in earnest by Gasprinskii's *Tarjumān*, one of the very first enduring Muslim newspapers in the Russian Empire.[67] Published regularly in the Crimea between 1883 and 1918, *Tarjumān* would prove hugely influential in spreading Gasprinskii's view of educational reform and the *uṣūl-i jadīd*. Primarily authored by Gasprinskii himself, *Tarjumān* was a beacon for proponents of Islamic reform, and figures such as Āqyigit and Fakhr al-Dīn contributed to it.[68]

But *Tarjumān* was particularly important in terms of the way that Gasprinskii attempted to shape the Muslim public sphere in the Russian Empire (and abroad). Written in a simplified form of Ottoman Turkic, *Tarjumān* and its

---

65. See Gainullin, *Tatarskaia literatura*, pp. 208–218. Unlike Āqyigit, Bigiev himself was a *madrasa*-trained imam. Nevertheless, he was deeply familiar with European culture, and his novels were influenced by the works of Tolstoy and Dostoyevsky, as well as French authors such as Victor Hugo and Émile Zola; ibid., pp. 208–209.

66. Karimullin, *U istokov*, pp. 196–197; Dilara Usmanova. "Die tatarische Presse 1905–1918: Quellen, Entwicklungsetappen und quantitative Analyse." *Muslim Culture in Russia and Central Asia*. Eds. Michael Kemper et al. Berlin: Klaus Schwarz Verlag, 1996. 239–278, pp. 242, 257. Nasyri did publish an annual almanac semiregularly between 1871 and 1897.

67. Cf. Lazzerini, "Gasprinskii" (1973), pp. 11–17; Meyer, *Turks*, pp. 39–40. The first lasting Muslim-language newspaper in the Russian Empire was the *Turkistān Wilāyātiniñ Gazitī*, published in Central Asia by the government from 1870. Khalid makes the important point that the publication of this journal was part of the Russian colonization of the region; Khalid, *Politics*, p. 117. No Arabic-script periodicals were published in the Volga-Ural region until the 20th century; cf. also Alexandre Bennigsen and Chantal Lemercier-Quelquejay. *La Presse et le mouvement national chez les musulmans de Russie avant 1920*. Paris: Mouton, 1964, pp. 21–32; Usmanova, "Die tatarische Presse," pp. 257–259.

68. Lazzerini, "Gasprinskii" (1973), pp. 211–212; Mahmud Tahir. "Rizaeddin Fahreddin." *Central Asian Survey*, vol. 8, no. 1; 1989. 111–115, p. 112.

language were intended to connect all Turkic peoples—"from Istanbul to Kashgar"—through a common idiom, accessible to every literate person.[69] Gasprinskii, who had married into the prominent Iunusov merchant family of Kazan, traveled extensively across the empire, drumming up support for his project and working to form connections with like-minded individuals.[70] Though generally met with indifference by Muslim audiences, he was able to spread the *uṣūl-i jadīd* and notions of educational reform in certain circles.

The public sphere that Gasprinskii was attempting to tap into was by this time well established in the Volga-Ural region. It had arisen with religious tolerance and state support for Islamic institutions at the end of the 18th century, to say nothing of the introduction of printing, as the circulation of texts and widespread discussions on religious and cultural topics among educated Muslims formed, as Kemper puts it, the Islamic discourse of the region. This discourse was articulated in the public sphere—a common discursive space constituted through disparate texts and group exchanges and understood as one big debate, carried out within society through a variety of media.[71] In the Volga-Ural region, the public sphere was formed in exchanges in mosques and *madrasas*, coffeehouses and markets, public disputations between *ʿulamāʾ*,

69. Lazzerini, "Gasprinskii" (1973), pp. 207–236; see Gaziz Gubaidullin's critical appraisal of Gasprinskii's project; G. Gubaidullin. "Ismail Gasprinskii i iazyk." 1927. *Gasırlar awazı/Ekho vekov*, no. 3/4; 1997. 205–214; also G. Gubaidullin. "K Voprosu ob ideologii Gasprinskogo." 1929. *Gasırlar awazı/Ekho vekov*, vol. 4, no. 3–4; 1998. 98–118.

70. Lazzerini, "Gasprinskii" (1973), pp. 29–30; Meyer, *Turks*, pp. 41–42.

71. The idea of the modern public sphere was articulated by Jürgen Habermas, as an element of bourgeois civil society; Jürgen Habermas. *The Structural Transformation of the Public Sphere: an Inquiry into a Category of Bourgeois Society*. Trans. Thomas Burger. Cambridge, MA: MIT Press, 1989. Taylor, building on Habermas, has incorporated the idea of the public sphere into his understanding of modern society; cf. Charles Taylor. *Modern Social Imaginaries*. Durham, NC: Duke UP, 2004, esp. p. 84. See Khalid's discussion of the related situation in Central Asia; Khalid, *Politics*, pp. 114–118; also Adeeb Khalid. "Printing, Publishing, and Reform in Tsarist Central Asia." *International Journal of Middle East Studies*, vol. 26, no. 2; 1994. 187–200. Tuna also touches upon the issue of the public sphere from Habermas' and Taylor's works, though he argues that there was no public sphere properly speaking in the Russian Empire because it was not "a democratic nation-state" and placed significant limits on public discourse; Tuna, *Imperial*, pp. 11–12. While that's certainly true about Russia, it has been pointed out that limits and restrictions on discourse are found in all settings, whether democratic or not, and such restrictions do not negate the broad participation in Volga-Ural Islamic discourse characteristic of a distinct public sphere, as well as a burgeoning civil society. For a helpful point of comparison, see Jeffrey Veidlinger. *Jewish Public Culture in the Late Russian Empire*. Bloomington, IN: Indiana UP, 2009. Asad also argues in light of Habermas that—for religious minorities particularly—the public sphere is not an empty or neutral space, but one whose discursive structures are articulated by existing power structures that necessarily place barriers to entry and on certain discourses; Talal Asad. *Formations of the Secular: Christianity, Islam, Modernity*. Stanford, CA: Stanford UP, 2003, esp. pp. 183–187.

and—increasingly toward the turn of the 20th century—civil associations and institutions, as well as in written texts and letters, the book trade, newspapers, and decrees from the Mufti and the government. Spurred on by the rise in publishing, the Volga-Ural Muslim public sphere became more extensive and more inclusive, beyond the *ʿulamāʾ* and educated elites, as the 19th century went on. It was not strictly bounded, but overlapped with other localized Muslim public spheres, such as in the Crimea and the Caucasus, as well as culturally and linguistically adjacent public spheres in Central Asia, China and the Ottoman Empire, extending even to India and Egypt.[72]

It also overlapped increasingly with the Russian public sphere.[73] Particularly in urban areas, many Muslims knew Russian, and presses owned by Russians in Kazan and Orenburg often published works in both Russian and Muslim languages. (Such publications stand as a very early avenue for European cultural influence, and they show the diversity of the urban intellectual environment; indeed, among the very first publications issued by Kazan University's press were an edition of the Qurʾan, Ibragim Khal'fin's Turkic grammar, and a Russian text on economics based on the work of Adam Smith.)[74] Writings in Russian by Muslims intended for both audiences began to appear in the second half of the 19th century. For instance, Ataulla Baiazitov (ʿAṭāʾ Allāh b. Bāyazīd) (1847–1911) penned *Otnosheniia Islama k nauke i k inovertsam* (Islam's relationship with science and non-Muslims), a text espousing Islam's embrace of learning and tolerance for people of other faiths. Baiazitov's book was published in St. Petersburg (where he was a prominent imam with connections to the government), and it presents a vision of Islam acceptable to Russian society while simultaneously exhorting Muslims toward similar attitudes on religious grounds.[75]

---

72. Cf. Stéphane Dudoignon. "Echoes to *al-Manar* among Muslim of the Russian Empire: A Preliminary Research Note on Riza al-Din b. Fakhr al-Din and the *Shura* (1908–1918)." *Intellectuals in the Modern Islamic World: Transmission, Transformation, Communication.* Eds. Stéphane Dudoignon et al. New York: Routledge, 2006. 85–116. For instance, Iusuf Akchurin wrote his *Ūch ṭarz-i siyāsat*, a work specifically on Ottoman politics, in Kazan, and it was first published in Cairo; Yūsuf Āqchūra. *Ūch ṭarz-i siyāsat.* New ed. Istanbul: Maṭbaʿa-yi Qadar, 1327 [1911].

73. To give one example, an early article in the journal *Bayān al-ḥaqq* from 1906 comments on Orthodox missionaries' reactions to the appearance of Muslim newspapers published in the Russian press; "Islām gazītalarī ḥaqqinda mīsiyānīrlarnañ fikrī." *Bayān al-ḥaqq*, no. 2; 24 Ṣafar 1324/5 April 1906. 5–6.

74. *Katalog*, pp. 1–2; cf. Rorlich, *Volga Tatars*, p. 71.

75. Ataulla Baiazitov. *Otnosheniia Islama k nauke i k inovertsam.* St. Petersburg: Tipografiia A. S. Suvorina, 1887. This work follows his response to the French Orientalist Ernest Renan's (1823–1892) famous lecture "L'Islamisme et la science," which Baiazitov published in Russian in 1883; cf. Dudoignon, "Echoes to *al-Manar*," p. 111 n. 35.

Gasprinskii likewise attempted to engage both audiences in this way.[76] One of his earliest works, *Russkoe musul'manstvo* (Russian Muslims), argued for the benefits Muslims could derive from their links with Russian society and culture, and the need for Muslims to embrace Russian language and education in order to modernize through European influence.[77] *Tarjumān* itself was similarly oriented, with bilingual issues in Turkic and Russian, and Gasprinskii in its pages emphasized Muslims' allegiance to Russia and the tsarist empire.[78]

As a newspaper, however, *Tarjumān* fell under considerable official scrutiny. Like all publications in the empire, it was subject to censorship and approval by the state to publish (which could be revoked at any time). Cooperating with tsarist requests for occasional articles that promoted the government's agenda and downplaying problematic political views allowed it to function consistently for decades, at a time when the state authorized only a small handful of Muslim journals.[79] As a rule, periodical publications were treated with wariness by the state, which saw them as greater potential sources of instability than books. Journals were thus subject to much harsher oversight, and publishers, seeking to avoid having whole print runs rejected or their permission canceled, engaged in self-censorship to a large degree, willfully avoiding controversial articles.[80]

The restrictions on Muslim printing were more pronounced than for Russians. Proposals for Muslim journals had been submitted to St. Petersburg as early as 1808, and while Russian journals enjoyed a vibrant existence throughout the 19th century, it wasn't until the 1870s that any periodicals

---

76. Edward Lazzerini. "Ismail Bey Gasprinskii (Gaspirali): The Discourse of Modernism and the Russians." *The Tatars of Crimea: Return to the Homeland.* 2nd ed. Ed. Edward Allworth. Durham, NC: Duke UP, 1998. 48–70.

77. Gasprinskii, *Russkoe musul'manstvo*. This work was originally serialized in 1881 in a Russian journal published in Simferopol, Crimea; Lazzerini, "Gasprinskii" (1973), p. 14.

78. Meyer, *Turks*, pp. 27–28, 40–41. The Russian section of *Tarjumān* ceased in 1905; Bennigsen and Lemercier-Quelquejay, *Presse*, p. 40.

79. Meyer, *Turks*, p. 40; also Lazzerini, "Gasprinskii" (1973), p. 211; Lazzerini, "Gasprinskii" (1998), pp. 64–65; cf. Bennigsen and Lemercier-Quelquejay, *Presse*, p. 46; Usmanova, "Die tatarische Presse," esp. pp. 257–259; also I. P. Foote. "The St. Petersburg Censorship Committee, 1828–1905." *Oxford Slavonic Papers*, vol. 24; 1991. 60–120.

80. Foote, "St. Petersburg," pp. 75, 80. This was certainly the case with Gasprinskii, as Lazzerini notes that more nationalist elements of his thought did not appear in *Tarjumān* until the loosening of censorship restrictions in 1905; cf. Lazzerini, "Gasprinskii" (1973), pp. 224–228.

in Muslim languages were permitted by the government. Even requests by Orientalists in this period were denied.[81]

Though book publishing was less restricted, it was nevertheless subject to government oversight from its very beginnings.[82] Through its censors, the state monitored and regulated the types of books published and their content. Religious texts seem to have been generally unaffected, but political subjects were tightly controlled, and as a result, overt discussions of political topics were largely nonexistent.[83] While working relationships between censors and publishers allowed for a degree of negotiation and flexibility in the approval process for a text, as I. P. Foote points out, a change in policy in the 1870s required that books be submitted to censors already in printed form, meaning that publishers had a financial incentive to produce texts that would be approved without alteration, thereby promoting self-censorship (as was the case with periodicals).[84]

The Muslim public sphere was shaped in this way by state control. Imperial censors inspected the books and pamphlets published across the empire, while St. Petersburg restricted periodicals, all in an effort to regulate the Islamic discourse in Russia. A handful of Muslim journals were permitted around 1900, most of which were narrowly religious in content. Nevertheless, Muslim printing remained strictly limited and entirely depoliticized.[85]

The situation changed drastically in 1905, as widespread protests and civil unrest pushed Tsar Nicholas II (r. 1894–1917) to extend new rights to the empire's population. Faced with open revolt, the government issued guarantees for rights of political representation and freedoms of assembly, conscience, and speech for a wide swath of imperial subjects, ushering in a new political environment with unprecedented opportunities for mass politics by, and including, Muslims.[86]

---

81. Karimullin, *U istokov*, pp. 172–176.

82. Censors were affiliated with the handful of universities around the empire, with censorship of Arabic-script books initially carried out by faculty in Kazan. In 1865 imperial censorship was centralized in St. Petersburg under the Ministry of the Interior, but Kazan Orientalists remained involved; ibid., esp. pp. 108, 112–113; Foote, "St. Petersburg," p. 61; I. P. Foote. "Counter-Censorship: Authors *v*. Censors in Nineteenth-Century Russia." *Oxford Slavonic Papers*, vol. 27; 1994. 62–105; also Geraci, *Window*.

83. The main censor of Turkic-language publications from 1880 to 1905, the St. Petersburg Orientalist Vasilii Smirnov (1846–1922), in fact worked toward limiting publications to *only* religious subjects; Geraci, *Window*, p. 148.

84. Foote, "Counter-Censorship," pp. 63–71.

85. Bennigsen and Lemercier-Quelquejay, *Presse*, pp. 24–25, also 43–46; cf. Khalid, *Politics*, pp. 115–116.

86. For a discussion of the relevant impact of the Revolution of 1905, see Meyer, *Turks*, pp. 81–106; Charles Steinwedel. "The 1905 Revolution in Ufa: Mass Politics, Elections,

The public sphere played a central role in this altered environment. Censorship restrictions were loosened, resulting in an explosion in Muslim publishing, periodicals in particular.[87] In 1904 there were fewer than ten Muslim journals in the whole of the empire, by 1917 there were a total of 172 (sixty of which were published in Kazan alone).[88] Accompanying the political mobilization of Muslims, these periodicals served as the primary venue in which newly important social, political, and cultural issues were debated and discussed. And these journals were written overwhelmingly in the vernacular, reflecting the broad character of the expanded public sphere and their function as organs of a Muslim mass media.

Jadids were at the forefront of the press. Following Gasprinskii's lead, they founded dozens of journals throughout the empire, using them to disseminate their reformist views to a wide audience. In this, there was a clear sense of shared purpose among these publications and a degree of mutual support, evinced in the frequent advertisements in each other's pages.[89]

Nevertheless, these publications were not ideologically uniform.[90] *Al-Iṣlāḥ, Nūr, al-Dīn wa-l-adab, Waqt, Yūldiz,* and *Shūrā* were focused on religious and educational reform, while *Āñ* was a particularly cultural nationalist journal. *Tarjumān, Bayān al-ḥaqq, Bizniñ īl,* and *Idīl* also had a strong nationalist bent, as did the women's journals *Sūyum Bīka* and *ʿĀlam-i niswān,* the latter edited in Bakhchisarai by Gasprinskii's daughter Shafīqa Khānim. *Āzād khaliq* was among the most overtly political, serving as the official organ of Ittifāq, the

---

and Nationality." *Russian Review*, vol. 59, no. 4; 2000. 555–576; S. M. Iskhakov. *Pervaia russkaia revoliutsiia i musul'mane rossiiskoi imperii.* Moscow: izd-vo Sotsial'no-politicheskaia mysl', 2007.

87. The Kazan Orientalist Nikolai Katanov (1862–1922), a Christian Siberian Tatar, was appointed as censor for most publications in Muslim languages, and, Geraci argues, his efforts made this era one of the more liberal in terms of press restrictions; Geraci, *Window*, esp. pp. 331–334.

88. Bennigsen and Lemercier-Quelquejay, *Presse*, pp. 46, 48. Usmanova argues, noting the conservative reaction of 1907, that the boom in publishing in that two-year span should constitute a distinct period, with an ensuing lull before a subsequent boom in 1917; Usmanova, "Die tatarische Presse," esp. pp. 244–253.

89. For example, issues of the journal *al-Iṣlāḥ* from 1907 contain ads for *Idīl, Yūldiz, Bayān al-ḥaqq*, and *Waqt*, as well as for reformist publishing houses in Kazan; e.g., *al-Iṣlāḥ*, no. 2; 17 Ramaḍān 1325/10 October 1907, pp. 15–16.

90. Bennigsen and Lemercier-Quelquejay note that there was at times considerable dissent and contradiction among Jadids, even within the pages of the same journal; Bennigsen and Lemercier-Quelquejay, *Presse*, p. 53.

party dominated by Jadidist intellectuals.[91] In a vein apart from explicitly reformist publications, the bilingual *Ḥuqūq wa-ḥayāt* was published for Muslim students at Kazan University's faculty of law.[92]

Although Jadids founded the majority of journals in this period, many of the publications had tiny circulations and were short-lived, and Jadids hardly had a monopoly on the Muslim press. Indeed, one of the most important and enduring publications was *Dīn wa-maʿīshat*, an Orenburg journal explicitly opposed to Jadidism. It and other more conservative, religious periodicals constituted a significant part of the post-1905 public sphere, within which they were competing with Jadidist organs to shape popular attitudes. The Spiritual Assembly in fact founded its own journal, the *Maʿlūmāt-i maḥkama-i sharʿiyya-i ūrinbūrghiyya*, to publish its official documents, translations of relevant imperial laws, *fetvas*, and messages from the Mufti.[93]

Journals often engaged with each other in their pages, referencing and criticizing other publications' articles and views.[94] The apparent diversity and contestation within this discourse evinces the vibrancy of the Muslim public sphere, which was broadened through the press to constitute a significant component of Muslim society, further linking far-flung communities across the Russian Empire.[95]

But even in this period the Muslim public sphere was larger than the press alone. Book publishing had continued to expand, particularly in the vernacular. In addition, manuscripts remained an important and highly prestigious form of textual production well into the Soviet era. Not only was producing a copy of a religious text by hand considered a pious act with spiritual implications,

---

91. These categorizations are of course simplistic, and there was considerable overlap between them in terms of content. For an overview of publications in the Volga-Urals, see Bennigsen and Lemercier-Quelquejay, *Presse*, esp. pp. 51–103; also Khalid, *Politics*, p. 223.

92. Although short-lived, *Ḥuqūq wa-ḥayāt* was oriented around a certain integrationist vision of late-imperial Russia; D. M. Usmanova and N. V. Gil'mutdinov. "Iz opyta izdaniia spetsializirovannogo iuridicheskogo zhurnala v Kazani: <Khokuk va khaiat>." *Nauchnyi Tatarstan*, no. 1; 2009. 100–105.

93. Cf. Bennigsen and Lemercier-Quelquejay, *Presse*, p. 58.

94. Tuna, *Imperial*, p. 156. In one pointed example, the Baku-based satirical newspaper *Mullā Naṣr al-Dīn* in 1909 published a cartoon depicting a bear, labeled "*Dīn wa-maʿīshat*," about to strike a sleeping *ʿālim*, labeled "Islam," in the head with a rock; reproduced in Bennigsen and Lemercier-Quelquejay, *Presse*, p. 57; see also the retrospective of *Mullā Naṣr al-Dīn*'s cartoons in *Molla Nasreddin: The Magazine That Would've, Could've, Should've*. Zurich: JRP Ringier, 2011.

95. Cf. Stéphane Dudoignon. "Un islam périphérique? Quelques réflexions sur la presse musulmane de Sibérie à la veille de la Première Guerre mondiale." *Cahiers du monde russe*, vol. 41, no. 2–3; 2000. 297–339; see also the debates in Dudoignon, "Status, Strategies."

but manuscripts were a way to avoid censorship restrictions (which had been restored and strengthened in 1907).[96] It is a common perception that beginning in the latter 19th century manuscripts became the domain of conservative *ʿulamāʾ* while reformers and Jadids utilized print, but this is misleading. Authors of all ideological stripes produced manuscripts and printed works; for instance, the staunch anti-Jadidist Īshmuḥammad Dīnmuḥammad (1842–1919), widely known as Īshmī-Īshān or Muḥammad Abū Naqīb Tūntārī, published a number of books and pamphlets against Jadidism, as well as articles in the press.[97] Likewise, reformists continued to disseminate their works in manuscript, even for new genres: some of Zagir Bigiev's novels existed exclusively in manuscript copies (which nevertheless circulated) during his lifetime and were only published years after his death.[98] There was not a firm division between the realms of manuscripts and print; rather debates were carried out simultaneously in both,[99] and the same text could move between them.[100]

Similarly, the intellectual landscape was less bifurcated than often assumed. Though disagreements among individuals could be stark, there was a wide spectrum of positions on the various points of debate, with a range of views as well as rationales to these issues. Contestation over questions of reform, identity, communal and political organization, and approaches to religious authority was a central part of the discourse among Volga-Ural Muslims, and it played out in large part within the public sphere. Printing expanded this discursive space for the tsar's Muslim subjects, and it was conducive to the articulation and spread of social, political, and religious ideas of all types.

---

96. Allen Frank. *Bukhara and the Muslims of Russia: Sufism, Education, and the Paradox of Islamic Prestige*. Leiden: Brill, 2012, pp. 125–127. The avoidance of censors certainly played a role in the continued prominence of manuscripts, which was far from unique to Muslims; cf. Foote, "Counter-Censorship," pp. 63–64.

97. Tuna, *Imperial*, p. 192; R[adik] Salikhov. "Tatarskii traditsionalizm i problema sokhraneniia mnogovekovykh religioznykh ustoev." *Islam v srednem povolzh'e: istoriia i sovremennost'*. Ed. R. M. Mukhametshin. Kazan: Master Lain, 2001. 136–148; e.g., Abū al-Naqīb al-Tūntārī. "Tūntārīdan maktūb." *Dīn wa-maʿīshat*, no. 22; 2 Jumādā al-ākhir 1328/28 May 1910. 343–344. See Rizaéddin Fäxreddin. *Asar*. Vols. 3–4. Kazan: Ruxiyät, 2010, iii, pp. 348–351.

98. Gainullin, *Tatarskaia literatura*, pp. 209–211.

99. Frank notes, for example, the defenses of the hijab and other traditional women's garments, in response to strong criticism from reformers, that appeared in both new manuscript works and Muslim journals; Frank, *Bukhara*, pp. 71–72.

100. A 1902 manuscript from Kazan contains a newspaper article about Muslim settlements in Russia that has been copied into the codex; *Rūsyā, aḥwāl al-muslimīn fī al-mamālik al-rūsiyya*. Ms. SPb IVR, no. A1219. Fols. 90b–92b; cf. A. B. Khalidov. *Arabskie rukopisi Instituta vostokovedeniia Akademii nauk SSSR*. 2 vols. Moscow: izd-vo Nauka, 1986, i, p. 433 (#9429).

The Fragmentation of Authority

The combination of broader education and widely available printed materials expanded engagement with the prevailing Islamic discourse beyond the learned elite, as a greater segment of the Muslim population could interact with the public sphere as readers and as authors. Particularly post-1905, the Muslim press offered myriad venues for Muslims to publicize their views and to both participate in and shape popular discussions and debates.[101]

These phenomena contributed to a fragmentation of Islamic authority, which Dale Eickelman and James Piscatori have described as a situation in which the *ʿulamāʾ*'s foremost ability and authority to determine and articulate Islamic norms is questioned and undermined by other types of actors "compet[ing] to speak for Islam" on a level playing field with scholars.[102] Contestation over religious interpretations and discourse is spurred, they write, by the spread of popular education and literacy and readily available religious texts in the vernacular, which allow broad swaths of Muslims to formulate religious views separate from the *ʿulamāʾ* and in terms external to the scholarly tradition.[103]

The beginning of the 20th century witnessed extended contestation over Islamic authority in the Volga-Ural region between a range of figures whose claims to authority were based not in traditional scholarly knowledge or mystical piety or charisma, but in political or economic stature or in facility in European science or culture. The first moves toward educational reform in the early 19th century began the long process through which Muslims were increasingly schooled outside the scholarly tradition. As noted, the *maktab* and *madrasa* had been the primary unifying force for Muslims, tying the community together through shared knowledge and discourse, but Russian and new-method schools instilled different knowledge (to say nothing of values), lessening the communal cohesion that education had previously supported. At the same time, the growth of book publishing, especially in the later 19th century, helped spread new works and new ideas, and the expanded availability of printed texts and literacy allowed lay Muslims to learn about the religion independent of scholars'

101. Cf. Khalid, *Politics*, pp. 135–136.

102. Dale F. Eickelman and James Piscatori. *Muslim Politics*. 1996. 2nd ed. Princeton, NJ: Princeton UP, 2004, p. 131.

103. Ibid., esp. pp. 42–44, 58–59.

expertise, forming their own, self-taught interpretations, particularly in reformed schools.[104]

The roots of fragmentation, however, stretch back to the takeover of Islamic institutions at the end of the 18th century. The establishment of the Spiritual Assembly not only bounded scholars' religious purview but introduced categorical divisions between scholars as well, granting them official powers based not on their scholarly acumen but on their bureaucratic standing.

This was particularly true for the Mufti, the nature of whose authority differed from that of the rest of the *ʿulamāʾ*. Unlike other scholars, who had at least received the approval of their particular *maḥalla*, the Mufti owed his position over the religious hierarchy entirely to the imperial government. The Mufti was thus set apart from the *ʿulamāʾ* in his standing as tsarist bureaucrat rather than scholar, a fact that was reinforced in 1865 with the appointment of Salimgarei Tevkelev (Salīmgiray b. Tawakkul) (r. 1865–1885), a wealthy officer in the Russian army who lacked all but the most basic religious training and often referred Islamic legal matters to Russian Orientalists. His successor, Mukhamed'iar Sultanov (Muḥammadyār b. Sulṭān) (r. 1885–1915), a military officer and tsarist administrator, had no Islamic education and lacked any knowledge of Arabic or even Tatar-Turkic.[105] But, as with previous Muftis, the position's authority and its exercise came from the state, regardless of a particular Mufti's educational background or scholarly qualifications.[106]

The makeup of the Spiritual Assembly also fostered contestation with lay Muslims over the interpretation of religious matters. Its appellate structure, Crews argues, "substantially broadened lay opportunities to engage in controversies about Islamic interpretations" by providing a venue in which virtually any decision by a scholar could be formally questioned by a member of the community.[107] Moreover, it was common for lay Muslims to make claims to

---

104. Majerczak, "Notes," p. 193; also Khalid, *Politics*, p. 135.

105. See Fakhr al-Dīn's critical, almost sarcastic biographical entries on these figures; Fäxreddin, *Asar*, iii, pp. 128–135, 336–337; also Marjānī, *Mustafād*, ii, pp. 310–312; Danil' D. Azamatov. "The Muftis of the Orenburg Spiritual Assembly in the 18th and 19th Centuries: The Struggle for Power in Russia's Muslim Institution." *Muslim Culture in Russia and Central Asia from the 18th to the Early 20th Centuries. Vol. 2: Inter-Regional and Inter-Ethnic Relations*. Eds. Anke von Kügelgen et al. Berlin: Klaus Schwarz Verlag, 1998. 355–384, pp. 375–377, 380–381.

106. Cf. Robert Crews. *For Prophet and Tsar: Islam and Empire in Russia and Central Asia*. Cambridge, MA: Harvard UP, 2005, p. 177; also Nathan Spannaus. "The Decline of the *Akhund* and the Transformation of Islamic Law Under the Russian Empire." *Islamic Law and Society*, vol. 20, no. 3; 2013. 202–241, pp. 234–241.

107. Crews, *Prophet*, p. 166.

the government of religious impropriety and incorrectness on the *ʿulamāʾ*'s part, appealing scholars' legal decisions to Russian administrators on the grounds that the decisions were unfounded under the *sharīʿa*, or accusing their imams of failing in their religious duties. While, say, an absentee imam was a straightforward problem, claims of misconduct often stemmed from legitimate religious disputes. As much as the Spiritual Assembly was ostensibly the exclusive forum for determining such issues, lay Muslims turned to Russian officials to press their claims over and against the *ʿulamāʾ*, using explicitly religious terms. (*ʿUlamāʾ* of course also appealed to the state for its involvement in Islamic disputes.) To be sure, the state was reluctant to involve itself in intra-Muslim conflicts, but it was also wary of religious dissent, as well as morally unfit members of the *ʿulamāʾ*, undermining the Spiritual Assembly.[108]

In this way, the government itself became an arbiter of Islamic norms, inserting itself into the exercise of religious authority in a manner that was hardly neutral. As Crews argues, St. Petersburg attempted to co-opt Muslim piety as a means of promoting loyalty to the tsar, and the government used the Mufti and Spiritual Assembly hierarchy to issue official pronouncements promoting imperial policy couched in Islamic terminology.[109]

Yet although the state patronized the *ʿulamāʾ*, it was also mistrustful of scholars and their influence over the Muslim community. Tsarist officials were hesitant to support the Spiritual Assembly too strongly out of fear it strengthened Muslims' resistance to Orthodox proselytization and Russification.[110] The government therefore backed the Spiritual Assembly as the sole legitimate Islamic institution while simultaneously working to restrict and undermine its power (as, for instance, when it attempted to take over Muslim schools).

For their part, the *ʿulamāʾ* had to balance their duties to the state with the demands of their communities. In the Russian Empire, speaking for Muslims

108. Ibid., esp. pp. 94–98, 128–129, 134–142. For a discussion of this issue in light of Crews' analysis, see Paul Werth. *The Tsar's Foreign Faiths: Toleration and the Fate of Religious Freedom in Imperial Russia*. Oxford: Oxford UP, 2014, esp. pp. 98–100.

109. Crews, *Prophet*, pp. 66, 76–77, 82; James Meyer. "Speaking Sharia to the State: Muslim Protesters, Tsarist Officials, and the Islamic Discourses of Late Imperial Russia." *Kritika*, vol. 14, no. 3; 2013. 485–505, pp. 490–491.

110. Cf. Werth, *Foreign Faiths*, esp. pp. 71, 163–166; Meyer, "Speaking Sharia," p. 501; Danil' D. Azamatov. "Russian Administration and Islam in Bashkiria (18th–19th Centuries)." *Muslim Culture in Russia and Central Asia from the 18th to the Early 20th Centuries*. Eds. Michael Kemper et al. Berlin: Klaus Schwarz Verlag, 1996. 91–112, p. 110.

was equally as important as speaking for Islam, and the *ʿulamāʾ* generally had served as representatives for their communities, particularly with local and provincial administrators. Likewise, the Muftis retained importance as Muslims' primary representative in the imperial government. Negotiation between the different groups comprising the empire and the autocracy was characteristic of tsarist rule, and the confessional model of governance allotted Muslims a space (*qua* Muslims) to press their communal claims to the state.[111]

But the Great Reform era saw the government expand its administrative reach, particularly on the local level, with new policies and forms of institutional control, marking a shift in the tsarist government's approach away from the older, imperial confessional model toward a more unitary nation-state.[112] Muslims, however, continued to view their place within the empire in religious terms and widely resented the new laws and administrative measures for contradicting what they saw as an agreement with the government dating back to Catherine the Great. These two conceptions of Muslims' relationship with the state came into conflict with the attempted oversight of Muslim schools. Although the imperial Ministry of Education duly considered these schools part of its expanded purview, Muslims rejected this as an excessive intrusion into their communal affairs, and they resisted, at times violently, officials' efforts to carry it out.[113]

Schooling had long been part of the Spiritual Assembly's jurisdiction, which Volga-Ural Muslims sought to defend as *their* institution within the tsarist bureaucracy. Preserving the religious hierarchy was a major priority for Muslims in the post-reform period, and it remained central to their understanding of their imperial subjecthood.[114] In addition, members of the *ʿulamāʾ* were themselves subject to greater scrutiny from lay Muslims. Meyer argues that growing suspicion of the state in the post-reform period meant that participation by *ʿulamāʾ* in even innocuous government ventures could provoke

---

111. Cf. Alfred Rieber. "The Problem of Social Cohesion." *Kritika*, vol. 7, no. 3; 2006. 599–608, esp. pp. 601, 602.

112. Paul Werth. *At the Margins of Orthodoxy: Mission, Governance, and Confessional Politics in Russia's Volga-Kama Region, 1827–1905*. Ithaca, NY: Cornell UP, 2002; Tuna, *Imperial*, esp. pp. 57–63.

113. Meyer, *Turks*, pp. 66–72; Tuna, *Imperial*, esp. pp. 85–97. Resistance to the expansion of state control was widespread and did not follow sectarian lines, with Orthodox Christians and other religious-ethnic groups offering similar protest.

114. Crews, *Prophet*, pp. 346, 359–360; also Spannaus, "Decline," pp. 239–240; cf. Tuna, *Imperial*, esp. pp. 81–82, 84. In fact, a stronger and more independent Spiritual Assembly was a priority shared by reformist and conservative Muslims alike; Rorlich, *Volga Tatars*, pp. 109, 116.

a backlash from the community.[115] The Muftis were particularly susceptible. Tevkelev, for instance, lost considerable support among Muslims in the 1870s for his apparent approval of imperial involvement in Islamic education, which he had not publicly opposed.[116]

Lay Voices

Especially as Muslims' relationship with the state changed in the later 19th century, the *ʿulamāʾ* were undermined in ways that frequently empowered lay Muslims. While the shift away from confessional governance certainly diminished official support for the Spiritual Assembly (Il'minskii and many imperial administrators favored disbanding the hierarchy),[117] new forms of local administration provided avenues for Muslims' civil and political participation beyond the religious sphere, altering the makeup of communal authority.

Merchants were at the forefront of these shifts. They represented an important segment within society, as wealthier merchants, as well as some landowners, constituted the Muslim elite alongside the *ʿulamāʾ*. While the two groups had long cooperated and were closely connected (as noted in Chapter 2), merchants' social standing was quite distinct. The mercantile elite derived their status from their wealth, of course, but also from the explicit support they received from the government, which was institutionalized in the 18th century with the founding of the *ratushas* in Kazan and Qarghālī (themselves Muslim institutions separate from the *ʿulamāʾ*) and their admission into the Russian merchant estate. (The *ʿulamāʾ*, by contrast, were never granted membership in the clerical estate.) With the disbanding of the *ratushas* in 1855, Muslim mercantilism was fully incorporated into mainstream administrative bodies—with Muslims' continued participation—and merchants played a further role in local government as the state introduced new municipal organs beginning in the 1860s.[118] These positions served as source of communal standing for the mercantile elite, as wealthy Muslims took on an increasingly vocal and visible role in protests against the state, pressing for the community's interests through various channels, particularly after 1905.[119]

115. Meyer, *Turks*, pp. 72–73; Meyer, "Speaking Sharia," pp. 502–503.

116. Tuna, *Imperial*, p. 82.

117. Cf. Crews, *Prophet*, pp. 226–227; see also, broadly, Werth, *Foreign Faiths*, pp. 140–146.

118. Cf. Meyer, *Turks*, pp. 52–53; also Geraci, *Window*, esp. pp. 42–44.

119. Meyer, *Turks*, pp. 73–77.

Merchants had been involved with religious institutions primarily through financial support, which was essential for their continued viability and function. This allowed merchants to exert a degree of influence in the religious sphere by supporting scholars in their education and, more importantly, supporting their positions as imams and *mudarris*es. Merchants in this way were integral in the spread of reformed education, patronizing reform-minded *ʿulamāʾ*, with many of the first new-method *madrasas* established and funded by wealthy individuals.[120]

Merchants' support for educational reform had significant communal implications. As Dudoignon points out, Volga-Ural Muslim communities tended to have only a tiny financial base from which they could fund their mosques and schools, and the introduction of new-method schools, often overlapping with existing *madrasas*, served to divide the available resources.[121] Moreover, new-method schooling was disproportionately expensive, requiring not only a new building but also classroom equipment and textbooks, while new-method *muʿallims*, in direct contrast to imams, could command considerable salaries.[122]

Disputes over how to use the community's limited resources converged with questions of handling *zakāt* funds—whether they should be dealt with by the Spiritual Assembly on behalf of the entire community, pooled and collectively distributed by local charitable associations (often connected with Russian civic organizations), or given directly by individuals to any organization or cause they pleased.[123] These disputes deepened existing divisions within the community; Muslims who supported funding schools through charitable associations or individual donations were more likely to support new-method education, while those who held that *zakāt* should go to the Spiritual Assembly were generally inclined to view education in more conservative terms. Though this dispute was not wholly ideological, as individuals who opposed new-method schools on financial grounds were not necessarily hostile to reform (a fact evinced by the greater spread of new-method *maktabs*, which required much less of a financial commitment than *madrasas*),[124] the

120. Tuna, *Imperial*, esp. pp. 138–139.

121. Dudoignon, "Status, Strategies," pp. 63–65.

122. Meyer, *Turks*, pp. 116–117; Ross, "Caught in the Middle," pp. 68–70.

123. Dudoignon, "Status, Strategies," esp. pp. 50, 51, 54.

124. Cf. Tuna, *Imperial*, p. 164.

different sources of funding further distinguished the two types of schooling, reinforcing their mutual separation.[125]

These debates serve to highlight the ongoing fragmentation of authority and contestation within the community. Merchants, who were primarily behind individual donations of *zakāt* as well as charitable associations and participation with Russian administrative bodies, represented a form of communal leadership that was less tied to, and in many ways competing with, religious institutions and strictures, and they used their wealth and influence to promote education that often was not grounded in Islamic tradition at the expense of education that was, thereby shaping the community's religious life. The mercantile elite tended to be more urban and connected with Russian society than most Muslims, and they took a more pragmatic approach to education. They saw traditional education as less useful for current economic circumstances and unsuited to produce graduates prepared for contemporary careers.[126] European and new-method education was far preferable for many of them, and they directed their considerable social and financial resources toward the spread of the latter.

The environment following the 1905 Revolution was more conducive to these efforts, and merchant elites were able to use their existing social standing and political experience to take advantage of new opportunities for authority. They furthered their connection with Muslim intellectuals, who helped articulate ideological—often religious—rationales for non-*ʿulamāʾ* authority (discussed later in this chapter). A category that included figures such as Gasprinskii, these intellectuals predominantly possessed a European-style education, and their numbers and influence had grown with the spread of new-method *madrasa*s and their graduates. They had been the most fervent proponents of reform, and their links with wealthy and politically connected Muslims allowed them to attain a significant level of influence. This new segment of the Muslim elite is exemplified by, for instance, Iusuf Akchurin (Yūsuf Āqchūra) (1876–1935), scion of a prominent Kazan merchant family. Educated in Ottoman military schools and at the Sorbonne, Akchurin was one of the more central voices for Muslim educational and cultural reform, but he was also deeply involved in Muslim politics in Russia as the leader of the Ittifāq party.[127]

---

125. Dudoignon, "Status, Strategies," esp. pp. 54–65, 68–71.

126. Cf. Tuna, *Imperial*, pp. 135–138, also 166.

127. See the brief biography in Meyer, *Turks*, esp. pp. 42–45.

The extensive links between merchants and intellectuals (who had begun to replace *ʿulamāʾ* in terms of family connections—Gasprinskii, as noted, married into the Iunusov family, to which Akchurin was also related) were likewise evident in the latter's publishing activities. While merchants had supported Muslim printing since its very beginnings, toward the turn of the 20th century they became major patrons of reformist periodicals, and they played a significant role in the emergence of the vernacular press.[128] As with funding for new-method schools, merchants used their resources in service of their vision for the Muslim community—often shared with reformers—and promoted and supported it in the avenues available to them.

Their political and publishing activities formed a foundation for asserting claims to communal leadership. For instance, Norihiro Naganawa cites a massive 1910 protest in Kazan against a tsarist policy on religious holidays led not by *ʿulamāʾ* but by Muslim merchants, politicians, and journalists. Elites by this time had the ability and the standing, both with the government and within their communities, to exercise authority equal with *ʿulamāʾ*, even regarding specifically religious matters.[129]

With these opportunities to exercise authority came constant contestation between Muslim political figures, activists, intellectuals, merchants, and *ʿulamāʾ*. And it was not simply elites who participated in this contestation; common people (who, as noted, had long questioned the *ʿulamāʾ* in legal disputes and appeals) began to look beyond scholars for leadership and guidance in their affairs. As early as 1884, Tuna notes, a resident of Kazan wrote to *Tarjumān* asking Gasprinskii about the permissibility of pooling monetary donations to fund a *waqf* endowment. The operation of *waqf*s was a central and often complex issue in the *fiqh* tradition, but Gasprinskii, who was by no means a legal scholar, answered simply that it was a good idea and encouraged the founding of charitable societies modeled after Russian organizations.[130]

Contestation for authority was particularly important in the debates over education, much of which focused on whether it should remain solely the purview of the *ʿulamāʾ*, an issue with obvious religious significance. For some Muslims, new-method education was a moral threat: a 1913 article in *Dīn*

---

128. Most of the journals founded had at least one patron; cf. Bennigsen and Lemercier-Quelquejay, *Presse*.

129. Norihiro Naganawa. "Holidays in Kazan: The Public Sphere and the Politics of Religious Authority Among Tatars in 1914." *Slavic Review*, vol. 71, no. 1; 2012. 25–48. See also Naganawa's discussion of the debates in Kazan over the timing of the *hijrī* calendar involving local *ʿulamāʾ*, the Spiritual Assembly leadership, and the press; ibid., esp. pp. 40–46.

130. Tuna, *Imperial*, p. 141.

wa-maʿīshat, responding to a piece in the reformist journal *Qūyāsh* arguing that teachers' competence should supersede their piety or even religious affiliation, states that only *ʿulamāʾ* could preserve the religion through education, and if piety were irrelevant to schooling, Satan himself could be an instructor.[131] Many petitioned the government against reformed schools. Īshmuḥammad Dīnmuḥammad, for instance, organized a large-scale public campaign against new-method education, with *ʿulamāʾ* and lay Muslims repeatedly denouncing reformist figures to various levels of government and the tsarist police. These denunciations emphasized reformers' irreligious and un-Islamic character while playing on imperial fears of both Muslim separatism and revolutionary politics.[132] They found some success. In 1911, the tsarist security service (*okhrana*) raided the new-method Bubī *madrasa* as a result of such petitions, with Īshmuḥammad Dīnmuḥammad testifying in the ensuing trial that its teachings were both anti-*sharīʿa* and anti-government.[133]

The state was already set against reformed education as a matter of policy, seeing it as infringing upon the government's monopoly on nonreligious schooling. Islamic schools remained the de facto purview of the Spiritual Assembly, but all educational institutions that were not explicitly sectarian fell strictly under the imperial government, thereby precluding any Muslim schools that were not substantively "Islamic" in subject matter.[134]

Proponents of reform frequently viewed their efforts in religious terms, stressing the moral importance of increased knowledge among the community. Gasprinskii presented educational reform as part of Muslims' obligation to learn and a matter of piety and devotion.[135] He grounded his advocacy of the new method within a critique of traditional pedagogy's effectiveness at conveying

131. Cited in Majerczak, "Notes," pp. 197–199.

132. Cf. Meyer, *Turks*, pp. 145–147. Christian Noack notes the efforts by tsarist officials post-1905 to surveil and provoke reformist and leftist Muslims, even falsifying claims against them; Christian Noack. "Retrospectively Revolting: Kazan Tatar 'Conspiracies' During the 1905 Revolution." *The Russian Revolution of 1905: Centenary Perspectives*. Eds. Jon Smele and Anthony Heywood. New York: Taylor & Francis, 2005. 119–136.

133. Rorlich, *Volga Tatars*, pp. 97–99.

134. The government and Orthodox missionaries both saw Russian education as the most effective vehicle for Russification, and they offered it to Muslims as an alternative to the traditional *madrasa*, which they considered patently inferior. Officials concluded, however, that if Islamic schools adopted European methods, Muslims would have little reason to choose Russian schools over them. Jadid *madrasas* were therefore subject to intense government scrutiny, regardless of any political activity on their part; Dowler, *Classroom*, pp. 120–121, 159–160, 183–184; also Khalid, *Politics*, pp. 53; Rorlich, *Volga Tatars*, pp. 92–93.

135. Lazzerini, "Ǧadidism," p. 254.

religious subjects—Arabic literacy specifically—which was a common refrain in reformist writings.[136] Merchants also emphasized their support of Muslim institutions as religious justification for their pursuit of wealth.[137]

But reformers sought greater autonomy for Muslim education as well, including the ability to found schools for Muslims that were not of a specifically religious character. The first platform of the Ittifāq party, drawn up at the second All-Russian Muslim Congress (Vserossiiskii musul'manskii s"ezd), formally adopted the position that state-funded primary education in each group's native language (and alphabet) should be instituted under local administration, and Muslims should be free to establish institutions of higher education of any type with instruction in their own languages.[138] (This congress, held in St. Petersburg in January 1906, was intended to articulate the political priorities and strategy of Ittifāq and petition the tsar accordingly.)[139] By contrast, the All-Russian *ʿUlamāʾ* Congress of April 1905 recommended that the Mufti have exclusive control over all schooling for Muslims.[140]

Education represented a major flashpoint, and these disputes deepened the growing fissures within Muslim communities. At the heart of these disputes was a question of authority: whether the *ʿulamāʾ* should be Muslims' primary leaders and representatives, with judgment over matters of communal importance—education, the relationship with the government, charity, religious interpretation—or whether other segments of society should have a say on these issues equal or superior to that of scholars. But this question, despite its obvious significance, was in many ways moot. It was precipitated by the very fact that lay Muslims had begun to vie for authority in these areas, and there was little that could be done to prevent this. The Spiritual Assembly lacked the power itself to exclude non-*ʿulamāʾ* voices (and it's not clear it had the will to),[141] and individual members of the *ʿulamāʾ* like Īshmuḥammad Dīnmuḥammad were instead left to denounce reformers in petitions to the government, which for its part supported the religious hierarchy only with half measures.

---

136. Ibid., pp. 254–256; also Aktchoura, *État*, pp. 9–11; cf. Majerczak, "Notes," pp. 182–185.

137. Dudoignon, "Status, Strategies," p. 61. Dudoignon notes that Muslim merchants also likened themselves to contemporary Western philanthropists like John D. Rockefeller.

138. Qtd. in Iskhakov, *Pervaia russkaia revoliutsiia*, pp. 337–339.

139. Rorlich, *Volga Tatars*, pp. 112–114.

140. Ibid., p. 109.

141. Meyer notes, for instance, a 1908 petition from some anti-Jadidist scholars that requests the government *force* the Spiritual Assembly to bar graduates of a prominent new-method *madrasa* from religious positions; Meyer, *Turks*, p. 145.

Undermining the Scholarly Tradition

The more or less equal participation in religious discourse with *ʿulamāʾ* by lay Muslims is the essence of the fragmentation of authority as a historical phenomenon, but it also directly relates to the continued validity of the scholarly tradition and the degree to which it remained authoritative. *Madrasa* reform was driven in large part by the belief that this tradition was no longer relevant or useful, and the spread of new-method education led to more and more Muslims holding it in low regard.[142] But as the *ʿulamāʾ*'s authority was premised on their knowledge of it and its discourses, this questioning (if not outright rejection) of the tradition also undermined their authority, not just in terms of education but also as religious interpreters.

The result was further contestation with scholars over matters of religious import, with direct implications for legal and theological discourse. Zaman, following Eickelman and Piscatori's analysis, has argued that the fragmentation of authority is accompanied by a weakening of scholarly consensus, marked by both the opening of established points of doctrine to reinterpretation and the end of the restriction of interpretation to the canonical *madhhabs*. In effect, not only were previously settled questions made subject to revision, but the scope of possible interpretations was also greatly expanded, leading to novel and divergent positions.[143]

The move toward interpretation outside of the scholarly tradition was presented under the heading of "*ijtihād*," which now signified skepticism toward, or abandonment of, the tradition as a discursive framework. "*Taqlīd*" was accordingly recast as strict adherence to the tradition, against *ijtihād*. The relationship between them therefore ceased to be about *fiqh* interpretation, much less primary or secondary legal reasoning, but rather the legitimacy of the tradition itself. *Taqlīd* became associated with blindly following the *ʿulamāʾ*, and proponents of *ijtihād* criticized it as backward and unthinking.[144]

---

142. Cf. Ross, "Caught in the Middle," esp. pp. 85–88; also Mustafa Tuna. "Madrasa Reform as a Secularizing Process: A View from the Late Russian Empire." *Comparative Studies in Society and History*, vol. 53, no. 3; 2011. 540–570.

143. Muhammad Qasim Zaman. *Modern Islamic Thought in a Radical Age: Religious Authority and Internal Criticism*. Cambridge: Cambridge UP, 2012.

144. E.g., Abdullah Bubi. "Is the Period of *Ijtihad* Over or Not?" *Modernist Islam, 1840–1940: A Sourcebook*. Ed. Charles Kurzman. New York: Oxford UP, 2002. 232–237; cf. Kanlidere, *Reform*, pp. 60–65; Thierry Zarcone. "Philosophie et théologie chez les djadids [La question du raisonnement indépendant (iğtihad)]." *Cahiers du monde russe*, vol. 37, no. 1–2; 1996. 53–63.

In response, supporters of the *ʿulamāʾ* attempted to paint *ijtihād* as irreligious. *Dīn wa-maʿīshat,* for instance, published an article defending *taqlīd* as a morally necessary link connecting the present day to the Prophet and his Companions, through deference to Abū Ḥanīfa and the ensuing generations of Hanafis. The article states that religious interpretation without their guidance—that is, outside of the *madhhab*—leads to error and dissension (*iftirāq*).[145] Critically, the article does not focus on any particular position or stance as illegitimate or incorrect, only that *taqlīd* cannot be abandoned. In this way, debates within the tradition had gradually given way to debates *about* the tradition.

It wasn't just *ʿulamāʾ*, merchant elites, and reformers who took part in this process; it seems a wide segment of the Muslim population participated in contestation over religious authority. Even those who ostensibly accepted the *ʿulamāʾ*'s authority sought to assert their own autonomy as interpreters. In fact, *Dīn wa-maʿīshat,* in an issue from 1910, responded to questions from readers about the nature of *taqlīd*: whether, for instance, they had to follow a *madhhab,* or if they could make their own legal interpretations following scriptural proof (*dalīl*).[146] Although the journal supported *taqlīd* of *ʿulamāʾ*, that its readership raised these issues (in the pages of a newspaper, no less) speaks to the broad, ongoing shifts in conceptions of religious authority.

Although the scholarly tradition doubtless continued to be important for many, its necessary connection to its institutions and society had been inexorably weakened. Since the late 18th century, the areas that had formed the *ʿulamāʾ*'s purview—the administration of law, education, textual production, and religious interpretation—each saw the scope of scholars' influence diminished and their authority questioned and contested, whether by the state or by lay Muslims (often both). Thus severed from its institutions—scholarly expertise was no longer essential for serving in the religious hierarchy or teaching in a *madrasa*—the scholarly tradition as a practice ceased to be viable.[147]

This situation did not emerge with the Revolution of 1905; the loosening of publishing restrictions and growth in opportunities for political

---

145. Aḥmad Fāʾiz Manṣūrūf. "Taqlīd wa mutābaʿa." *Dīn wa-maʿīshat,* no. 22; 2 Jumādā al-ākhir 1328/28 May 1910. 339–340; no. 23; 9 Jumādā al-ākhir 1328/4 June 1910. 359–360; no. 24; 16 Jumādā al-ākhir 1328/11 June 1910. 370.

146. *Dīn wa-maʿīshat,* no. 12; 21 Rabīʿ al-awwal 1328/19 March 1910, pp. 178–180.

147. Indeed, the very conflict over the validity of the tradition itself, rather than the discourses within it, shows that it was failing as an operative discursive framework; cf. Alasdair MacIntyre. *After Virtue: A Study in Moral Theory.* 1981. 3rd ed. Notre Dame, IN: U of Notre Dame P, 2007, p. 222.

participation simply made the fissures within the community more visible. Islamic institutions themselves had no power to preclude contestation over their authority, and while Muslims generally continued to accept the *ʿulamāʾ*'s authority, some Muslims' attachment to it (and to them) had waned significantly. The function of speaking for Islam and for Muslims had become fraught with conflict and dissent, which was made manifest throughout the growing public sphere.

Jadidism and the Post-1905 Religious Environment

The prevailing division fell between those who believed that religious authority and communal leadership remained, or should remain, with *ʿulamāʾ* and those who pushed for leadership by other actors—intellectuals, journalists, activists, economic and political elites—and accordingly questioned established methods and forms of religious interpretation. The latter can roughly be equated with Jadidism, which coalesced as a movement with the 1905 Revolution as proponents of educational and religious reform argued for non-*ʿulamāʾ* authority and a corresponding move away from the scholarly tradition.

Internally diverse, Jadidism encompassed a range of positions that shared a basic reformist orientation. Underpinning Jadidism in all its facets was an emphasis on contemporary suitability—that is, that old ways of doing things did not fit current circumstances, and Muslims must reform or abandon those ways in order to evolve and prosper as a community.[148] This attitude was accompanied by a great skepticism toward the past and an embrace of progress (*taraqqī*) as an overarching principle.

The Jadids' notion of progress was couched in terms of cultural and material competition with Europe.[149] Like many at the beginning of the 20th century, they saw peoples or civilizations as developing along a single trajectory, with some societies trailing behind others. Progress, then, meant moving forward along this trajectory and closing the gap with Europe, the leading civilization. Accordingly, many Jadids held an admiration for European culture

148. The Jadid intellectual and activist Hādī Āṭlāsī (1876–1938) sums up this attitude regarding education in a quote from 1913: "Our schools are not adapted to the exigencies of life. They give our children nothing, except a little religious instruction, [but] no understanding of life nor the world"; qtd. in Majerczak, "Notes," p. 182.

149. Meyer, *Turks*, pp. 132–133.

and achievements and a belief in the importance of Muslims adopting these advancements in order to further their own development as a people.[150]

But this emphasis on progress also entailed discarding aspects of their own culture that were seen as hindering their development or contributing to their current state of backwardness. The main culprit the Jadids identified for this situation was the closed-mindedness and rigidity imposed by *taqlīd*, in contrast to their image of the vibrant and sophisticated Islamic civilization that existed prior to the "closure of the gate of *ijtihād*," which marked both the end of freethinking among Muslims and their decline vis-à-vis Europe. The restoration of *ijtihād* and abandonment of *taqlīd* was thus a requisite step in returning Muslims to the path of progress.[151] As argued above, such an understanding of *ijtihād* was tantamount to a rejection of the Islamic scholarly tradition, which Jadids almost unanimously saw as an obstacle to progress. Accordingly, they articulated reforms that broke with the tradition as a discursive and epistemic paradigm. In its place they embraced ways of thinking shaped by the empiricism and materialism of post-Enlightenment Western thought, which formed the foundations for Jadidism as an intellectual movement.

As Jadid author and historian Dzhamaliutdin Validov (1887–1932) writes, there were two primary strains to Jadidism: cultural transformation and religious revivalism.[152] The former was concerned with bringing Muslims' culture and society in line with contemporary European standards. For many Jadids, this involved the development of nationalism. Comparing Muslims with the situation in Western Europe and North America, figures such as Gasprinskii and Akchurin saw national identity and the unity it engendered as essential for their social and cultural advancement.[153] Despite disagreement as to the basis for Muslim nationalism in Russia, there was an understanding among Jadids that mere religious affiliation was no longer sufficient to ensure communal

---

150. Tuna, *Imperial*, pp. 146–170; Mūsā Afandī Bīgīyif. "Madaniyyat dunyāsī taraqqī ītmish īkan, islāmiyyat ʿālamī nīchūn īndī?" *Khalq naẓarīna birnīcha masʾila*. Kazan: èlektro-tipografiia Umid, 1912. 33–39. This ethos is foregrounded even in Gasprinskii's first works; Gasprinskii, *Russkoe musul'manstvo*, esp. pp. 7–9; also Ismāʿīl Ghaṣprinskī. *Awrūpā madaniyyatina bir naẓar mawāzina*. Istanbul: Maṭbaʿa-i Abū Ḍiyā, 1302 [1885].

151. Kanlidere, *Reform*, pp. 60–64; also Zarcone, "Philosophie," pp. 55, 58–59.

152. Dzhamaliutdin Validov. *Ocherk istorii obrazovannosti i literatury Tatar*. 1923. Oxford: Society for Central Asian Studies, 1986, p. 118; cf. Ahmet Kanlidere. "The Trends of Thought Among the Tatars and Bashkirs: Religious Reformism and Secular Jadidism vs. Qadimism (1883–1910)." *Journal of Central Asian and Caucasian Studies*, vol. 5, no. 9; 2010. 48–63.

153. Lazzerini, "Ǧadidism," p. 253; Aktchoura, *État*; cf. Meyer, *Turks*, pp. 134–144.

solidarity, and contemporary society called for a more actively politicized identity (even if religiously grounded).[154]

The focus on nationalism was largely secularist, however, and, though most older Jadids were personally religious, their reformist projects were aimed at lessening the broad influence of religion in Tatar (or Bashkir or Kazakh) society and culture. Yet as new-method and Russian schooling spread at the turn of the 20th century, there emerged a whole cohort of younger Jadids with little attachment to Islam. Educated in modern subjects and European languages, they were able to forge connections with Russian society and the burgeoning political movements therein. They also, Tuna writes, found themselves cut off from the broader Muslim community, less religious and more radical in their political and social views.[155] Accordingly, there was a considerable generation gap separating older reformers from those who came of age in the era of widespread new-method education.[156] (In fact, at the first All-Russian Muslim Congress in August 1905, the organizers—all prominent Jadids—lied to the student factions about the start time of the meeting to prevent them from attending.)[157]

Muslim students in Kazan were particularly inclined toward political and collective action, and new-method *madrasas* were themselves centers for political activity. Students at the Muḥammadiyya *madrasa* often staged walkouts and protests, and they formed multiple associations and organizations that attracted their peers from other *madrasas* while also interacting with similar groups of students at Kazan University.[158] Although founded and led by ʿĀlimjān Bārūdī (1857–1921), one of the foremost *ʿulamāʾ* of the early 20th century—he would be selected by Muslim reformers as the first post-revolutionary Mufti in spring 1917—the Muḥammadiyya had one of the most radical and secularist student bodies. Many of its students became connected with Russian revolutionary politics, including the leaders of the *Tāñchīlar*, a

154. For an example of the complexities of these issues and the efforts of forging a nationalist identity, see the series of questions posed to readers in the journal *Āñ*, under the heading "How do you understand nationalism?"; "Milliyyatnī nīchik āñlīsiz?" *Āñ*, no. 12; 1 Dhū al-ḥijja 1331/27 October 1913. 368.

155. Tuna, *Imperial*, pp. 181–193; also Tuna,"Madrasa," pp. 561–567.

156. Ross, "Caught in the Middle," esp. pp. 74, 80–83.

157. The meeting was held on a riverboat, and when students realized the boat had left without them, some of them rented a second boat to catch up with the meeting. They were eventually allowed onboard to participate, but on the condition that they keep their statements to a minimum; Meyer, *Turks*, p. 87; Rorlich, *Volga Tatars*, p. 110.

158. Ross, "Caught in the Middle," pp. 75, 80–81.

Tatar socialist group that arose in 1905 around the leftist-nationalist newspaper *Tāñ yūldizī*.[159]

Muslim socialists (at least prior to 1917) remained a small but vocal segment within Jadidism.[160] The growth of nationalism was much more far-reaching, however, and for many Jadids nationalism had supplanted religious affiliation as their primary identity. Journals such as *Āñ*, for instance, promoted a vision of Tatar culture based on contemporary European models imbued with romantic nationalism.

This type of political and cultural transformation is widely considered to be the quintessential contribution of Jadidism—a shift away from Islam and Muslim identity toward a "rational," "enlightened," westernized frame of reference, led by dedicated reformers. This historiographical image is of course deeply intertwined with Soviet Marxism, and it obscures the significant religious component within Jadidism.[161] Indeed, religious revivalism by Jadids represents an important movement of specifically Islamic reform (quite similar to connected fin-de-siècle movements in Egypt, the Hijaz, India, and the Ottoman Empire).

There was considerable overlap between the cultural and religious strains of Jadidism. For instance, Fakhr al-Dīn, who would succeed Bārūdī as Mufti in 1921, shared Gasprinskii's project for the creation of a common Turkic language, and he saw national and religious identity as intertwined. While he emphasized *ijtihād* as facilitating advances in natural science and technology, he also criticized other *ʿulamāʾ* from a specifically religious standpoint.[162]

More significant, however, was the revivalists' attachment to new-method education, which for them served as a platform for changing religious praxis and beliefs and adapting them to the modern context. For these figures, improved pedagogy was important for religious and moral purposes: depicting the conventional *madrasa* as ineffective at its basic role of conveying Islamic

159. Validov, *Ocherk*, pp. 87–88; Tuna, *Imperial*, p. 185; Kanlidere, *Reform*, pp. 90–91; Rorlich, *Volga Tatars*, pp. 105–107.

160. Cf. Meyer, *Turks*, p. 126.

161. This image was solidified in the 1930s with the classification in official Soviet scholarship of Islam as a "feudal ideology" and Jadidism as "bourgeois-nationalist" (and therefore part of capitalism and at a more advanced historical stage); e.g., L. I. Klimovich. *Islam v tsarskoi Rossii*. Moscow: Gosudarstvennoe antireligioznoe izd-vo, 1936, pp. 180–182; cf. Nathan Spannaus. "The Ur-Text of Jadidism: Abu Nasr Qursawi's *Irshad* and the Historiography of Muslim Modernism in Russia." *Journal of the Economic and Social History of the Orient*, vol. 59; 2016. 93–125, esp. pp. 97–99.

162. Kanlidere, *Reform*, pp. 130–134.

subject matter, they (as noted) saw new-method education as increasing religious knowledge, in addition to teaching nonreligious subjects. Yet revivalists also sought to alter the content of religious education to reflect their priorities and ideas about normative Islamic knowledge.

For religiously oriented Jadids, skepticism toward the scholarly tradition was not merely an issue of closed-mindedness or cultural backwardness, but rather that it tied Muslims to outmoded (or downright incorrect) beliefs determined by *ʿulamāʾ* centuries earlier. They considered the edifice of the tradition, its "scaffolding," unnecessary for the articulation and fulfillment of Islamic morality, at best irrelevant and at worst obscuring true religious knowledge (in arcane commentaries, for instance). They argued instead for a model of Islam stripped of these extraneous elements and focused on what they saw as both essential to it and of current relevance.[163] This attitude formed the religious basis for new-method schools, which revivalists saw as furthering the spread of correct Islamic knowledge within the community. Toward this end, they strove to make this knowledge widely accessible, creating new texts that emphasized their understanding of the essence of Islam and translating selected older texts into the vernacular.[164]

In this way, Jadidist revivalism sought a significant break in religious discourse. The expunging from that discourse of what was ostensibly irrelevant shows the degree to which Jadids strove to remake Islam to fit their image of the religion. Their treatment of *kalām* stands as a prominent example. To them, theological debates showed the scholarly tradition at its most inane, full of pedantic squabbling and sophistry over issues lacking any practical import or significance beyond the *ʿulamāʾ*.[165] And *kalām* was accordingly ignored in the religious curricula of most new-method schools. Moreover, in line with Zaman's observation about the end of scholarly consensus, Jadids began articulating views on theological questions that had previously been addressed by *mutakallimīn*, but in ways quite separate from *kalām* discourse.[166]

An eclectic attitude toward the past was common among revivalists, reflecting their stance toward extant strains of the tradition. Fakhr al-Dīn, for example, published a series of books on the wide range of Muslim historical

163. Bubi, "Period."

164. See Kanlidere, *Reform*, pp. 94–96.

165. Validov, *Ocherk*, esp. pp. 35–38, 49–50; Bīgīyif, "Madaniyyat dunyāsī," p. 34.

166. Cf. Aidar Khairutdinov. "Musa Bigiev ob universal'nosti Bozhei milosti." *Mir islama*, vol. 1–2; 1999. 175–190.

figures he believed should be better known in the Volga-Ural region.[167] The prominent revivalist Jadid Musa Dzharullakh Bigiev (Mūsā Jār Allāh Bīgī) (1875–1949)—brother of Zagir Bigiev—was especially varied in his use of past authorities, engaging with authors from myriad eras and intellectual trends. For instance, he composed a translation of the *Luzūmiyyāt*, a major work by the Syrian skeptic and esoteric poet Abū al-ʿAlāʾ al-Maʿarrī (973–1058). While the *Luzūmiyyāt* itself deals with issues of religious authority and belief, Bigiev's translation features extended sections in which he explores his own views on these subjects. (In this way, his translation strongly resembles, ironically, a traditional commentary.)[168] But Bigiev also penned translations of an array of works—many of which were external to Volga-Ural scholarship—including Mālik's *Muwaṭṭaʾ* and Abū Isḥāq Ibrāhīm al-Shāṭibī's (?–1388) *Muwāfaqāt*.[169] In addition, he engaged with the ideas of both ibn ʿArabī and his intractable opponent Taqī al-Dīn Ibn Taymiyya (1263–1328). (As did Fakhr al-Dīn, who wrote books on each.)[170] Bigiev, who studied in Kazan, Bukhara, Istanbul, Cairo, and Mecca, did not limit his curiosity to different forms of Islamic thought, but also studied law at St. Petersburg University and Sanskrit and Hinduism in northern India.[171]

Like other revivalist Jadids (to say nothing of Muslim reformers elsewhere), Bigiev seems to have been seeking religious authenticity, the "essence" of Islam. Having abandoned the scholarly tradition as a religious framework, he strove to create a new model for Muslim morality and religiosity in its place.[172]

---

167. Kanlidere, *Reform*, pp. 52, 96.

168. Abū al-ʿAlā Aḥmad b. ʿAbd Allāh al-Maʿarrī. *al-Luzūmiyyāt*. Trans. Mūsā b. Jār Allāh Bīgīyif. Kazan: Tipografiia Sharaf, 1907.

169. Kanlidere, *Reform*, p. 95. (Kanlidere here misidentifies this author as Abū al-Qāsim al-Shāṭibī [1144–1194], a famed scholar of Qurʾanic recitation.) Bigiev's interest in Abū Isḥāq al-Shāṭibī is noteworthy, as his *Muwāfaqāt* has become one of the major sources for Islamic legal reformism in the 20th century; cf. Ebrahim Moosa and SherAli Tareen. "Revival and Reform." *Islamic Political Thought: An Introduction*. Ed. Gerhard Bowering. Princeton, NJ: Princeton UP, 2015. 202–218.

170. Kanlidere, *Reform*, pp. 38–39, 65; cf. Riḍāʾ al-Dīn b. Fakhr al-Dīn. *Ibn Taymiyya*. Orenburg: Waqt maṭbaʿasī, 1911.

171. Kanlidere, *Reform*, pp. 53–54; Elmira Akhmetova. "Musa Jarullah Bigiev (1875–1949): Political Thought of a Tatar Muslim Scholar." *Intellectual Discourse*, vol. 16, no. 1; 2008. 49–71.

172. Olivier Roy has described the eclectic, often idiosyncratic use of varying models in forming modern forms of Islamic religiosity as a type of bricolage, the cobbling together of ideas and beliefs from a diverse array of sources; Olivier Roy. "Les nouveaux intellectuels en monde musulman." *Esprit*, vol. 142; 1988. 58–68; also Olivier Roy. *Globalised Islam: The Search for a New Ummah*. London: Hurst, 2004.

He focused on scripture as the primary basis, sufficient in itself for proper adherence to Islam without the influence of any erroneous or misleading intermediaries, such as overzealous *ʿulamāʾ* or divisive *madhhabs*.[173] This attitude was shared by other movements of the time, most notably Salafism and Wahhabism, both of which viewed scripture as the foremost, if not exclusive, determinant of Islamic correctness, and there was considerable affinity between them and Bigiev's own reformist project.[174] Yet he also had a generally positive view toward Sufism, more esoteric or heterodox Sufi practices notwithstanding, in ways that were at odds with Wahhabism in particular.[175]

Indeed, Bigiev appears to have favored a kind of religious freethinking above any doctrinal or methodological orthodoxy, as well as skepticism toward the received wisdom of religious authorities. This skepticism is the common element between ibn Taymiyya and the Wahhabis on one hand and ibn ʿArabī and al-Maʿarrī on the other, as well as the other varied Muslim figures to whom he referred in his works.[176] Bigiev attempted to connect his thought with theirs—which he did selectively, Kanlidere notes—in order to justify his novel religious constructions and convince Muslims to adopt his more modernist form of Islam.[177] (That very few of these figures were part of the Central Asian tradition further marked his original, reformist position to Volga-Ural audiences.)

---

173. See his *Qawāʿid-i fiqhiyya*, which emphasizes legal reasoning divorced from the methodology of any *madhhab*; Mūsā Jār Allāh Bīgīyif. *Qawāʿid-i fiqhiyya*. Kazan: èlektro-tipografiia Urnek, 1328 [1910].

174. Bigiev was personally connected with early 20th-century Salafis in Cairo and the Hijaz, and he wrote an Arabic-language refutation of Shiʿism that reflects many Salafi and Wahhabi critiques; Mūsā Jār Allāh. *al-Washīʿa fī naqd ʿaqāʾid al-shīʿa*. Lahore: Suhayl Akīdīmī, 1979. (This work, which exists in several editions, has become very popular and influential among contemporary Salafis.) Links with Salafism and Wahhabism were not unique to Bigiev among Jadids; see Dudoignon, "Echoes to *al-Manar*"; for a contemporaneous critique, see ʿ.K. "Firaq-i ḍālla jadīdalardan shikāyat." *Dīn wa-maʿīshat*, no. 23; 9 Jumādā al-ākhir 1328/4 June 1910. 360–362.

175. Kanlidere, *Reform*, pp. 62–63, 65–66. By contrast, Fakhr al-Dīn, Kanlidere writes, grouped Sufism together with *kalām* as one of the main sources of *bidʿa*, though he held a positive view of some historical Sufi scholars; cf. Fakhr al-Dīn, *Ibn Taymiyya*, pp. 132–134.

176. El-Rouayheb's study shows how ibn Taymiyya and ibn ʿArabī's ideas were combined by some 17th-century scholars, including figures associated with the Hijaz network and early Salafism; Khaled El-Rouayheb. *Islamic Intellectual History in the Seventeenth Century: Scholarly Currents in the Ottoman Empire and the Maghreb*. Cambridge: Cambridge UP, 2015, pp. 272–311. Whatever influence these developments had on Bigiev (if at all) remains to be explored.

177. Kanlidere, *Reform*, pp. 95–96.

But Bigiev's eclecticism was not without some apparent contradictions. He emphasized the importance of Islamic authenticity and avoiding overreliance on the West and overt secularism, rejecting the label of "Jadid" for himself on the grounds that "Jadidism" called for dedicated nonreligious schools instead of reformed *madrasas*.[178] Yet he also argued that *ribā* (usury or the charging of interest) was permissible in light of the Qurʾan, in order to facilitate commercial banking by Muslims.[179] In addition, he took positions on women's issues that diverged from Islamic convention, claiming in a text from 1915, for instance, that legal norms allowing polygamy and minimizing women's testimony were no longer necessarily applicable.[180]

The variance within Bigiev's own thought speaks to the diversity within revivalist Jadidism. Figures such as Fakhr al-Dīn and Bārūdī were less critical of established religious institutions than Bigiev, while also disagreeing on the importance of *kalām* and the acceptability of Sufism (both of which Bārūdī endorsed). But revivalist Jadids also engaged with the same kinds of social issues as their culturalist peers, approaching them from a religious perspective. Bigiev and Fakhr al-Dīn, who were both affiliated with Orenburg's Ḥusayniyya *madrasa*, believed that Muslims' civilizational decline was caused by religious error, which must be corrected in order to progress in politics, economics and culture.[181]

The philosophical differences between the two strains of Jadidism were mitigated by the fact that revivalist Jadidism was just as grounded in Western frameworks as the cultural variety. Indeed, the former was based on an understanding of religion and religiosity that emphasized the role of the individual as an educated and rational believer (in other words, that each Muslim should fulfill their personal religious and moral responsibilities with an understanding of both how and why, without necessarily relying on religious authorities in doing so). Thus, carrying out an action simply because it had been done in the past, or it was common, or a *shaykh* ordered it was for Jadids an insufficient form of religiosity, as well as a source of religious error. Doing so amounted to *taqlīd*, which needed to be replaced with a spirit of free and

---

178. Kanlidere, "Trends," pp. 59–60. On the flip side, Tuna notes a radical young author who criticized older, particularly religious forms of Jadidism as little different from religious conservatism, arguing instead that in order to reform their society Tatars must truly embrace the new, which "Jadidism" does not; Tuna, *Imperial*, pp. 182–183.

179. He justified this position as following from his *ijtihād*; Kanlidere, *Reform*, pp. 64–65.

180. Ibid., p. 75.

181. Bīgīyif, "Madaniyyat dunyāsī," pp. 34–37; Fakhr al-Dīn, *Ibn Taymiyya*, esp. pp. 128–134.

FIGURE 6 Husayniyya C: Ḥusayniyya *madrasa*, Orenburg (Anonymous, undated photo)

rational inquiry through *ijtihād*, so that Muslims could understand the religion for themselves, thereby increasing their piety.[182] And Jadids expressed this understanding in frequently "protestant" terms of purifying the religion from false accretions and removing structures of religious authority that hindered believers, discussing explicitly the impact and role of an Islamic "Luther" (often Marjānī in their writings, but also Qūrṣāwī).[183]

There was a common language of historical development connecting the two strains of Jadidism. Islam, they believed, should foster progress and inventiveness and adaptability, all things that are in concert with its essential spirit but were thwarted centuries earlier by intolerant and ignorant *ʿulamāʾ*. Regaining that spirit would strengthen Muslims' piety and attachment to Islam while allowing them to attain a modern civilization on par with Europeans, but it would also require throwing off the shackles of the scholarly tradition and its

182. Cf. Kanlidere, *Reform*, esp. p. 95.

183. Gubaidullin, for instance, compares Qūrṣāwī to Martin Luther in his stand against entrenched religious authorities; Gubaidullin, "K Voprosu," p. 101; cf. also Kanlidere, *Reform*, pp. 58–60; Zarcone, "Philosophie," pp. 57–60. Holidays became a major issue in terms of Islamic correctness, with some Jadid intellectuals and merchants arguing against "folk" festivals such as Ṣabāntūy, and even the Prophet's birthday (traditionally not celebrated in the region), as lacking scriptural grounding and encouraging immorality; Dudoignon, "Status, Strategies," pp. 66–68; Naganawa, "Holidays," pp. 43–44.

backward character. This view was foundational to Jadidism as a movement, which was therefore primarily concerned with discontinuity—intellectual, cultural, religious, political—and breaking with Muslims' immediate past in favor of contemporary suitability.

In this way, the label "Jadidism" was perfectly appropriate. The Jadids' focus on the historical trajectory of their culture encouraged novelty at the expense of older ways, whose insufficiency as far as the Jadids were concerned had been proved by Muslims' current condition behind—to say nothing of subordinate to—Europeans. To continue the old ways was to continue Muslims' backwardness, consigning them to historical regression.

Qadimism

Jadids denounced those who did not share this progressive ethos, characterizing them as static and medieval.[184] Resistance to Jadidism was accordingly labeled "Qadimism," cast as a movement to preserve the status quo the Jadids were so set against and rejecting all change, including educational reform, the press and non-*ʿulamāʾ* religious authority. "Qadimism" is thus a derivative term, created to signify ideological opposition to Jadidism. The label itself comes out of Jadidist discourse; Jadid authors contrasted *uṣūl-i jadīd* as an educational approach with traditional *madrasa* pedagogy, which they termed *uṣūl-i qadīm* (the old method). Just as Jadids embraced "new" reforms, their opponents, they reasoned, clung to "old" ways, and were described accordingly.[185] Qadimism was thus not a self-conscious movement, and indeed Dudoignon has argued that it was primarily financial concerns, rather than religious or ideological resistance, that drove the opposition to new-method schools.[186]

Linking the continued use of traditional teaching methods with a coherent anti-reform movement has the effect of attributing an ideological stance to

---

184. E.g., Saʿdī, *Tātār adabiyātī*, p. 70; Validov, *Ocherk*, p. 21.

185. See the Jadid Fātiḥ Karīmī's (1870–1937) description of the conflicts over education, which he presents as a struggle between the "progressivists" (*taraqqī-parwar*), with their new method, and "conservatives" (*muḥāfiẓa-kār*), who remain attached to old ways (lit. *uṣūl-i qadīm*); F. K. "Rūsīyada īnārūdīs maktablarī." *Shūrā*, no. 10; 27 Rabīʿ al-ākhir 1326/15 May 1908. 306–309.

186. Dudoignon, "Status, Strategies," esp. pp. 57, 63; see also Stéphane A. Dudoignon. "*Qadimiya* as a Historiographical Category: The Question of Social and Ideological Cleavages Between 'Reformists' and 'Traditionalists' Among the Muslims of Russia and Central Asia, in the Early 20th Century." *Reform Movements and Revolutions in Turkistan*. Ed. Timur Kocaoglu. Haarlem: SOTA, 2001. 159–177; Meyer, *Turks*, pp. 114–118.

the mere adherence to tradition, rendering it tradition*alism*. Frank notes that in demonizing their opponents as Qadimists, Jadids presented them as obtusely rejecting all types of change, clinging to a static and inert—not to mention ahistorical and anachronistic—tradition.[187] This is not to say that there weren't Muslims set against Jadidism; Īshmuḥammad Dīnmuḥammad, of course, worked to convince the government to stop new-method *madrasas*, and *Dīn wa-maʿīshat* published frequent attacks on individual Jadids, Musa Bigiev particularly. But there were certainly also those, especially outside of urban settings, who had no opinion on Jadidism and/or were only barely aware of it.[188] Despite their differences, these positions are all grouped under the heading of Qadimism, as examples of strict attachment to Islamic tradition and failure to embrace reform.

The dubious nature of Qadimism as a category notwithstanding, there's also little evidence that would-be Qadimists (a term very few seem to have used for themselves) were necessarily set against all reform. While considerably more research is needed into all manner of religious trends beyond Jadidism, particularly manuscript sources, examples exist that show opponents of Jadidism embracing some kinds of change and adapting to contemporary circumstances in ways that belie their historiographical image as uniformly rigid.[189] The Muftiate, frequently presented as a bastion of Qadimism, advocated for educational and social reform under Mufti Sultanov.[190] Conservatives' role in the formation of the vernacular press is often overlooked as well, with anti-Jadidist newspapers actively engaged in the current Islamic discourse. Dudoignon notes the considerable overlap within the public sphere between pro- and anti-Jadidist factions, signaling the complex ideological relations at work, including, he writes, conservatives' invocations of "progress" and "civilization" to attack Jadidism in the press.[191] And Īshmuḥammad Dīnmuḥammad made extensive use of pamphlets to advocate against new-method schooling, as part of his public campaign to

187. Frank, *Institutions*, p. 219.

188. Cf. ibid., pp. 248–250.

189. Cf. Tuna, *Imperial*, pp. 192–193.

190. Ildus Kotdusovich Zagidullin. "Mahkama-i Shargyya Yrynburgyya (the Orenburg Muslim Spiritual Assembly): The Reformation Centre of the Muslim Society in the Late 19th Century." *Tatarica*, vol. 3; 2014. 122–139. (In English and Tatar.) It's worth repeating that Muftis Tevkelev and Sultanov were not *ʿulamāʾ*, and so the argument that the Muftiate represented unchanging *ʿulamāʾ* authority doesn't quite follow.

191. Dudoignon, "Echoes to *al-Manar*," pp. 105–106; Meyer, *Turks*, p. 133.

close reformed schools.[192] (That campaign, it should be noted, involved constant petitioning of the tsarist administration, thus requiring him to shape his religious message for the state, shifting its moral thrust from a narrowly Islamic frame of reference to one that would appeal to and persuade Russian officials.)[193]

Conservative publications also played a part in bringing about change within Islamic tradition, often in subtle ways. One example is the *fatwās* published in each issue of *Dīn wa-maʿīshat* in response to religious questions submitted by readers. Although conventional in content, these *fatwās* operate in a novel fashion. Rather than coming out of a particular interaction between a *muftī* and a *mustaftī* over the latter's question—impossible in the pages of a newspaper—they are put forward as abstracted norms functioning as religious guidance for a broad audience, ostensibly to follow in similar cases in their own lives. Thus, despite relying on a long-established element of legal discourse, these *fatwās* are necessarily rendered distinct.[194]

Spurred by the emergence of the press and the ability reach an expanding swath of the public, *Dīn wa-maʿīshat* reshapes the *fatwā* here into a mass-media vehicle for spreading moral and legal guidance. *Dīn wa-maʿīshat* therefore used the press in a similar way as its Jadidist opponents—that is, to articulate and spread their religious interpretations and notions of communal authority. Even though the journal argued for the *ʿulamāʾ* as the primary religious authorities and the continuation of the scholarly tradition—in other words, against fragmentation—its altered use of the *fatwā* in mass media ironically reinforced broader, ongoing changes to Islamic authority.

Volga-Ural Islamic Modernism

The alteration of Islamic discourse wasn't unique to *Dīn wa-maʿīshat*, or to newspapers as a medium. Rather, it was common to the opposition to Jadidism in ways that call into question the putative "medieval" character of Qadimism, showing instead how Qadimists in fact adapted to the current context.

---

192. D. F. Galliamov. "Istoricheskie diskursy tiurko-musul'manskoi ideologii vtoroi poloviny XIX-nachala XX stoletii." *Problemy vostokovedeniia*, no. 2; 2011. 90–96, esp. pp. 93–94, 95.

193. Cf. ibid., pp. 93–94; Meyer, *Turks*, pp. 145–148.

194. As Brinkley Messick points out in his study of radio *fatwās* in Yemen, such use of *fatwās* "represent[s] both a significant continuity in the venerable Islamic institution of ifta'" and, through their public dissemination, "an equally significant discontinuity"; Brinkley Messick. "Media Muftis: Radio Fatwas in Yemen." *Islamic Legal Interpretation: Muftis and Their Fatwas.* Eds. Muhammad Khalid Masud et al. Cambridge, MA: Harvard UP, 1996. 310–322, p. 310.

Such adaptations represent discursive discontinuity, driven by the contemporary environment. They are therefore examples of modernism, and indeed, any anti-Jadidist stance is necessarily modernist; if Jadidism is a quintessentially modern movement, then explicit opposition to it must be modern as well. Moreover, as Tuna argues, continued attachment to the *ʿulamāʾ* as social and religious authorities was in part driven by a desire to defend Muslim communal space under the Spiritual Assembly, which (as noted) had been weakened by changes in tsarist governance since the Great Reform period. Jadids' embrace of European cultural norms and Russian institutions, as well as lack of deference for *ʿulamāʾ*, threatened to undermine that space, thus warranting "conservative" resistance.[195] As such, the contemporary political climate formed part of the very impetus for Qadimism.

Qadimism, though conservative, should therefore be seen as part of the intellectual and religious shifts taking place. The *ʿulamāʾ*'s former primacy in religious interpretation had been replaced by a diversity of practices, approaches, and voices: *fatwā*s published in newspapers existed alongside conventional *iftāʾ* from a learned scholar, *fetva*s from the Mufti, lay Muslims forming their own interpretations, and secularist Muslims with little regard for Islamic legal norms, as well as official imams fulfilling their judicial role, Sufi *shaykh*s offering religious guidance, Russian Orientalists weighing in on issues of *fiqh*, and calls for the codification of Islamic family law (proposed by both Fakhr al-Dīn and Gasprinskii).[196] This variation in terms of law reflects the broader intellectual diversity that had developed across the 19th century, spurred by differing/competing educational frameworks, increased literacy, greater circulation of books, the growth of the press, the rise in non-*ʿulamāʾ* interpreters, and growing skepticism toward the scholarly tradition. As historical phenomena, these led to contestation and divergence within the community, rather than a single trajectory of modernization opposed by an equally monolithic traditionalism. Instead, Muslims approached their environment in myriad ways, adopting a wide range of positions.

This diversity is an example of the cultural logic of modernity. Muslims, faced with a constantly shifting historical context, maintained or discarded elements of their tradition based on the transformed environment. Yet they did so as individuals, with minimal social structures to ensure coherence to these changes. The result was a plethora of varying and contradictory

195. Tuna, *Imperial*, esp. p. 193.

196. Fakhr al-Dīn's proposal for codification of family law was adopted as part of the platform of the first congress of Russian *ʿulamāʾ* in 1905; Rorlich, *Volga Tatars*, pp. 57–58.

positions, such that some Muslims abandoned things that others believed to be essential.

More important than the extremes of discourse, however, was the intermixing between continuity and discontinuity. While it's easy to strictly associate Jadidism with discontinuity and Qadimism with continuity, doing so not only privileges Jadidist reasoning on the matter but also ignores instances of discontinuity by conservatives and continuity by Jadids. We can see the latter in Bigiev's focus on various Muslim historical figures, which can be considered a search for antecedents to connect his ideas of normative Islam to an authentic past.[197] Given Jadidism's basis in Western forms of thought, this served as an important legitimating factor. Although Jadidism represents a rejection of the Islamic scholarly tradition in its historical construction, the focus on earlier Muslim authorities (which isn't unique to Bigiev) allows Jadids to justify that rejection, on the grounds that the tradition was itself illegitimate. This approach is most frequently apparent in discussions of the "gate of *ijtihād*," in which its putative closure is presented as a failure on the part of the medieval *ʿulamāʾ* and its reopening by the Jadids as both a stride toward modernization and a return to the freethinking and innovative spirit of early Islam.[198]

In this way, an Islamic heritage for Jadidism was formed. The Jadids' references and allusions to earlier authorities (as with ibn Taymiyya, ibn ʿArabī, al-Maʿarrī, Mālik, Abū Ḥanīfa, and others) were employed as support for their arguments and critiques of traditional education or *taqlīd*, bolstering their bona fides as Islamic reformers. (Their treatment of Qūrṣāwī was not altogether different. Though a local figure and an authority of much more direct importance than, say, al-Maʿarrī, the appeals to Qūrṣāwī and his reformism in Jadidist writings were no less of an appropriation.)

But such references to earlier authorities and Islamic ideals were ultimately claims to religious authenticity and correctness, which others could accept, borrow, question, argue with, reject, or ignore. These claims existed within a much broader discourse that was neither created nor dominated by Jadids but rather was characterized by a profound diversity that they and all others were equally part of and forced to contend with.

---

197. Asad, as noted in Chapter 8, describes the overlapping temporalities of modern discourses, which, despite their novelty, are nevertheless articulated in reference to the past, either by invoking or shunning it; Asad, *Formation*, p. 222.

198. Bigiev explicitly blames the formation of the *madhhab*s as preventing the use of reason (*ʿaql*) in Islamic civilization, condemning Muslims to fall behind Europeans; Bīgīyif, "Madaniyyat dunyāsī," pp. 36–38.

The diversity of views and outlooks among Muslims can be traced to their disembedding, their separation as individuals from the community, and the removal of the *sharīʿa* (as noted in Chapter 8) as an "inescapable framework for social life." Islamic institutions could no longer maintain Muslims' communal coherence, particularly as ever-larger numbers of Muslims were educated in European or new-method schools. With less of a basis of shared knowledge and values, religious and intellectual divergence became inevitable, with more and more Muslims questioning the role of *ʿulamāʾ* and asserting themselves as religious authorities independent of scholars. The result was an environment in which the Islamic scholarly tradition not only held less importance but ceased to serve as the communally accepted domain of orthodoxy and the prevailing framework for articulating correct belief and praxis. It retained that role for some Muslims, of course (and would into the Soviet period), but its normative force had diminished for a growing segment of the community, some of whom—including *ʿulamāʾ*—rejected it outright.

10

Conclusion

SEPARATING QŪRṢĀWĪ AND JADIDISM

THE TRANSITIONS OF the 19th century altered the religious and intellectual environment of the Volga-Ural region. Changes in schooling undermined its communal importance, as Muslims increasingly possessed other kinds of education, and the advent of printing and the public sphere allowed for the articulation and spread of new ideas and discourses. By the 20th century, Muslims were widely adopting ways of thinking and reasoning external to the Islamic scholarly tradition, and/or picking and choosing within it, questioning its construction and validity—all parts of the fragmentation of Islamic authority, with significant contestation between lay Muslims and *ʿulamāʾ*. The discourse of this period became marked by debates over the tradition and its continued relevance, utility, and normative force.

The intellectual landscape following the 1905 Revolution, by which time the full impact of all these changes had been felt, was therefore quite different from Qūrṣāwī's era a century earlier, in which the scholarly tradition still retained its religious and social predominance. A prominent example of the shift away from the tradition was of course Jadidism, which encompassed many of the elements characteristic of the revolutionary period. As a movement of social, cultural, religious, and political reform, it was premised on a severe skepticism toward, if not outright rejection of, the Islamic past—particularly established modes of scholarship and education—in favor of a

European or European-derived future, to be brought about by the embrace of Western intellectual, cultural, and scientific frameworks.[1]

Qūrṣāwī's reformism is based on different premises. The distinctly post-classical character of his thought and the reliance of his legal and theological views on existing *fiqh* and *kalām* discourses set it apart from Jadidism's abandonment of much of *ʿulamāʾ* scholarship and repudiation of it as religiously normative. He considers the scholarly tradition and those who are trained and knowledgeable in it essential for the moral well-being of the community, indeed part of what makes it Muslim. This view is reflected in his belief in the continuous need for primary legal reasoning, which he sees as maintaining a necessary link between the community and the texts of revelation. But for him, *ijtihād*, like all religious interpretation, must be carried out through established interpretive frameworks to avoid falling into error and whim, as well as an overreliance on *ʿaql*.

Qūrṣāwī's stance is thus distinct from the direct, rationalistic approach to scripture outside of any *madhhab* called for by many Jadids.[2] This later view comes out of the fragmentation of authority, which, as Zaman argues, allows for interpretation that is not limited to *ʿulamāʾ* nor adheres to established parameters. He, as noted, equates fragmentation with the abandonment of consensus, in that it can be contradicted by the new exercise of *ijtihād* and that legal interpretation is not limited to the doctrines or methodologies of the four *madhhabs*.[3] Qūrṣāwī's stance allows for neither; he argues for interpretation by lay Muslims, but he holds that legal reasoning by anyone—*ʿulamāʾ* or otherwise—must utilize an established hermeneutic of *uṣūl al-fiqh* and cannot violate consensus. It does not entail the freedom for an individual to interpret scripture any way they see fit. This Qūrṣāwī categorically denies, arguing that every act of *ijtihād* must conform to the basic principles of the religion, as already established by scholars.[4] He also explicitly rejects the possibility of

1. In fact, Gasprinskii, who is easily the most influential figure for the development of Jadidism, expressed the need for educational and social reform in fundamentally "civilizational" terms in his very first works; Ismail Bei Gasprinskii. *Russkoe musul'manstvo: Mysli, zametki, i nabliudeniia musul'manina*. 1881. Oxford: Society for Central Asian Studies, 1985; Ismāʿīl Ghaṣprinskī. *Awrūpā madaniyyatina bir naẓar mawāzina*. Istanbul: Maṭbaʿa-i Abū Ḍiyā, 1302 [1885].

2. E.g., Mūsā Afandī Bīgīyif. "Madaniyyat dunyāsī taraqqī ītmish īkan, islāmiyyat ʿālamī nīchūn īndī?" *Khalq naẓarīna birnīcha masʾila*. Kazan: èlektro-tipografiia Umid, 1912. 33–39, pp. 36–38.

3. Muhammad Qasim Zaman. *Modern Islamic Thought in a Radical Age: Religious Authority and Internal Criticism*. Cambridge: Cambridge UP, 2012, esp. pp. 72–73.

4. Qūrṣāwī, *Irshād*, p. 24.

ijtihād regarding foundational religious tenets, which are beyond doubt and therefore not subject to interpretation or disagreement.[5]

The fragmentation of authority, however, meant that *any* position was subject to reinterpretation or abandonment, as were whole systems of thought, which was done under the banner of *ijtihād*. No longer mere legal reasoning, *ijtihād* had been transformed into a vehicle for the broad rethinking of Islam and Islamic religiosity, and it was rendered a "theological" issue, with its scope extending to all manner of the "Islamic."[6] It was identified with reformism itself, now operating along contemporary Western philosophical and scientific lines, external to and frequently in competition with *ʿulamāʾ* discourses.

By contrast, *ijtihād* in Qūrṣāwī's understanding remained inherently linked to *fiqh*, and, whatever his criticisms of *ʿulamāʾ*, it was nevertheless internal to their frameworks. The same is true of his stance toward *kalām*, his attacks on which revolve around the specifics of its discourse, focusing on the content of particular points of belief and the shortcomings of certain interpretive methodologies. He considers *ʿilm al- tawḥīd wa-l-ṣifāt* a superior form of theological knowledge not because it is wholly separate from *kalām*—it is not—but because it excises unfounded and misguided elements of *kalām* discourse. Jadids, however, widely viewed *kalām* as a worthless exercise, at best a distraction from relevant and worthwhile subjects. Due to its focus on the abstract and transcendent (the latter of course shaped by Sufism, which suffered similar treatment), *kalām* held little meaning for Jadidism's decidedly materialist outlook,[7] and Jadids accordingly rejected it as a necessary or significant field of religious knowledge (a position often justified as an exercise of *ijtihād*).

These two distinct conceptions of *ijtihād* illustrate well the marked divergence between Qūrṣāwī and Jadidism. For Jadids, engaging in *ijtihād* was tantamount to an abandonment of the scholarly tradition, which for them had been rendered obsolete and backward, in favor of religious interpretation guided by new notions of rationalism and civilizational progress. For Qūrṣāwī, not only was the widespread exercise of *ijtihād* intended to preserve the scholarly tradition, but, more significantly, it was part of his broader project to maintain the connection between *ʿulamāʾ* discourse and certain religious knowledge. In this regard, "*ijtihād*" in his reformism is subsumed within the

5. Ibid., p. 27.

6. Thierry Zarcone. "Philosophie et théologie chez les djadids: la question du raisonnement independent (igtihad)." *Cahiers du monde russe*, vol. 37; 1996. 53–64, pp. 57–60; Zaman, *Modern Islamic Thought*, p. 72.

7. That is, philosophically materialist, distinct from legal materialism.

scholarly tradition, while in Jadidism the scholarly tradition is subordinated to "*ijtihād*." Their different understandings of the term therefore separate, rather than connect them.

The main point of similarity between Qūrṣāwī and Jadidism lies with his view that *ijtihād* is an obligation upon all Muslims, which has obvious similarity with the individual, "protestant" religious interpretation entailed in Jadids' conception of *ijtihād* (likewise with his emphasis on increasing lay Muslims' religious understanding, shared with revivalist Jadids). The resemblance between these positions, however, is superficial rather than substantive. Each focuses on the role of the individual, but they approach the issue from opposite perspectives. While Qūrṣāwī was attempting to prevent sweeping legal and moral changes by shifting the responsibility for determining proper action from (now undermined) institutions to the community broadly, Jadids were explicitly encouraging such changes, abandoning the scaffolding of *ʿulamāʾ* discourse that Qūrṣāwī's stance relies upon.

With the publication of the *Irshād* in 1903 (edited by ʿĀlimjān Bārūdī), some Jadids could well have seen a parallel between their own ideas and Qūrṣāwī's discussion of *ijtihād* in that text. But any linkage should be viewed as—at most—indirect. Debates over *ijtihād* had been circulating among Bulghar Muslims since the early 19th century, reflecting the shifting nature of Islamic authority and scholarship and the historical changes faced by the Muslim community. Jadidism is of course part of this discourse, and in this regard it shares a broad context with Qūrṣāwī's stance on *ijtihād*, as both engage with issues ultimately arising out of modernity—namely, the altered role of the individual. Indeed, Qūrṣāwī's prominence into the 20th century can be attributed in part to the fact that his reformism speaks to concerns with continued relevance for this context. But the same can be said of Ūtiz-Īmānī and his radical emphasis on *taqlīd*, which was likewise formulated in response to these changes.[8] (By contrast, Ūriwī, who did not seek to alter or adapt the post-classical legal tradition, seems to have become largely ignored by 1900, despite having more contemporary prominence than either Qūrṣāwī or Ūtiz-Īmānī.) Therefore, both Jadidist uses of *ijtihād* and Qūrṣāwī's position on it are simply part of a larger history of the growing focus on the individual apart from communal structures, which encompasses otherwise divergent views and equally connects Jadidism with Ūtiz-Īmānī despite his absolute rejection of *ijtihād*.

---

8. Some of Ūtiz-Īmānī's works were published in this period as well: ʿAbd al-Raḥīm Ūtiz-Īmānī. *Risāla-i muhimma*. Kazan: Tipografiia Kazanskogo universiteta, 1877; ʿAbd al-Raḥīm Ūtiz-Īmānī. *Tuḥfat al-aḥbāb fī tajwīd kalām al-rabb*. Kazan: Tipo-litografiia Imperatorskogo universiteta, 1900; and his *al-Risāla al-irshādiyya* was translated from Arabic into Tatar.

The Historiography of Reform

The discrepancy between the different conceptions of *ijtihād* in Qūrṣāwī's reformism and Jadidism is obscured—if not hidden entirely—by Soviet-era historiography, which viewed Qūrṣāwī through a lens of modernization and presented him as pioneer of Jadidism. Focusing on *ijtihād* as a kind of rationalist freethinking, the overarching narrative placed Qūrṣāwī in the position of breaking categorically with the *ʿulamāʾ* and rejecting virtually all forms of religious authority in favor of a radical, secularist stance, introducing Europeanized forms of religion and thought, and leading the Tatar nation toward a progressive, enlightened future. His reformism has meaning in this historiography only in terms of its connection to Tatars' social, cultural, and political development, which was understood as a shift away from their feudal or medieval Islamic past. His theological views, which are so important to his thought, were thus entirely elided; the issues they speak to bear no relation to the (Marxist) process of modernization, and so they were not only irrelevant but meaningless to this literature. His controversy with the Bukharan *ʿulamāʾ* was accordingly stripped of its theological content, and it retained significance only as a repudiation of backward dogmatism in favor of modern rationality, which accounted for its historiographical prominence. The same is true of his critiques of *ʿulamāʾ*'s shortcomings, which were transformed into an outright rejection of religious authority.[9]

This presentation of Qūrṣāwī as a *sui generis* voice for a wholly new cultural orientation stemmed from the emphasis in Soviet scholarship on the role of singular enlighteners in the process of modernization.[10] Indeed, as Lowell Tillett has shown in his study of the Soviet historiography of minorities, "enlightenment" in this regard signified Russification, while also overstating Muslim enlighteners' conflicts with other Muslims—particularly religious authorities—and omitting any of their "anti-Russian" (i.e., not

9. See Alfrid Bustanov and Michael Kemper. "From Mirasism to Euro-Islam: The Translation of Islamic Legal Debates into Tatar Secular Cultural Heritage." *Islamic Authority and the Russian Language: Studies on Texts from European Russia, the North Caucasus and West Siberia.* Eds. Alfrid Bustanov and Michael Kemper. Amsterdam: Pegasus, 2012. 29–54, pp. 41–47.

10. Cf. ibid., pp. 36–38; Franz Wennberg. *On the Edge: the Concept of Progress in Bukhara during the Rule of the Later Manghits.* Uppsala: Acta Universitatis Upsaliensis, 2013, pp. 15–17; David Griffiths. "In Search of Enlightenment: Recent Soviet Interpretation of Eighteenth-Century Russian Intellectual History." *Canadian-American Slavic Studies*, vol. 16, no. 3–4; 1982. 317–356.

European-oriented) works.[11] Qūrṣāwī's reformism was therefore reduced to his push for *ijtihād*—continued by Marjānī after his death—but recast with an entirely separate, anachronistic conception suitable for a modernizing narrative.

The origins of the official historiography in the Soviet academy are found in ʿAbdraḥmān Saʿdī's (1889–1956) account, which emphasizes Qūrṣāwī's influence on Marjānī, describing their arguments for *ijtihād* in terms of skeptical rationalism, a rejection of *taqlīd* and *kalām*, and an embrace of modern science.[12] In this way, Marjānī, who is connected to Jadidism through his support for educational reform and personal ties to reformers and early Jadids, was put forward as the key link in the genealogy tying Qūrṣāwī to Jadidism proper, which represents part of Tatars' "Europeanization movement" (*yāwrūpālāshū ḥarakatī*) and "reformation" (*rīfūrmāchinliq*).[13]

Marjānī's own writings, however, do not support such a position within the narrative. His stance on *ijtihād*, despite some similarities, is distinct from Qūrṣāwī's, and it is much less of a departure from the conventional understanding. Marjānī shares with Qūrṣāwī an emphasis on the importance of *ijtihād* and the continued existence of absolute *mujtahids*, on the grounds that their disappearance would be detrimental to the community's religious adherence.[14] He also criticizes the ranks for *fuqahāʾ* within the Hanafi school and attendant restrictions on scholars' interpretive autonomy, and he argues instead that jurists that are capable of *ijtihād* must carry it out, thereby precluding scholars with a high level of expertise from choosing to engage in *taqlīd*.[15] Yet Marjānī's position is more grounded within *madhhab* structures than Qūrṣāwī's and accordingly features a larger role for *taqlīd*. While Marjānī holds absolute *ijtihād* to be possible, he states that most scholars do not reach such a stage of expertise and are thus at most *mujtahids fī al-madhhab*, i.e., *mujtahids* who adopt the legal methodology of their school and uphold the

---

11. Lowell Tillett. *The Great Friendship: Soviet Historians on the Non-Russian Nationalities*. Chapel Hill, NC: U of North Carolina P, 1969, pp. 387–402, and esp. pp. 395–397.

12. Saʿdī, *Tātār adabiyātī tārīkhī*, p. 67; cf. Hélène Carrère-d'Encausse. *Islam and the Russian Empire: Reform and Revolution in Central Asia*. London: I. B. Tauris, 1988, pp. 61–62. On the influence of Saʿdī's account in subsequent scholarship, see Nathan Spannaus. "The Ur-Text of Jadidism: Abu Nasr Qursawi's *Irshad* and the Historiography of Muslim Modernism in Russia." *Journal of the Economic and Social History of the Orient*, vol. 59; 2016. 93–125, esp. pp. 100–102.

13. Saʿdī, *Tātār adabiyātī tārīkhī*, p. 76.

14. Marjānī, *Nāẓūrat al-ḥaqq*, pp. 31–32.

15. Ibid., pp. 58, 27.

positions of the founder. *Fuqahāʾ* who have not attained the level of *mujtahid* are, he argues, not *muqallids*, but can exercise legal reasoning only through *tarjīḥ*. For scholars with less knowledge, however, *taqlīd* becomes obligatory, and they must rely on established texts of *furūʿ*. Laypeople, though they can learn legal norms, are *muqallids* absolutely, obliged to follow scholars' guidance.[16]

Marjānī's view, which shares Qūrṣāwī's limitations on reinterpreting established religious norms and proper subjects for *ijtihād*, is therefore less radical and does not seek to alter the relationship between the *ʿulamāʾ* and the community, instead relying more on the *ʿulamāʾ*'s exercise of religious authority over lay Muslims.[17] Although this view is reformist, its more conventional character puts it at odds with its portrayal as creative religious interpretation.[18]

Neither Qūrṣāwī's nor Marjānī's conception of *ijtihād* thus fits with the "protestant" thrust of Jadidism—Marjānī's even less so than Qūrṣāwī's, his supposed inspiration—which only serves to call into question their roles in the development of the movement. The putative genealogy linking Jadidism to Qūrṣāwī's groundbreaking stand against the *ʿulamāʾ* through Marjānī's further embrace of rational, scientific, progressive ways of thinking relies on a common understanding of *ijtihād* that begins with Qūrṣāwī. Given both Marjānī's support for both early Jadids and Qūrṣāwī, this would seem reasonable. But their differences over *ijtihād* weaken such a link. In fact, Marjānī is primarily indebted to specific views from Qūrṣāwī regarding *kalām*, which obviously was not continued by Jadids.

Pedagogy and Reform

Marjānī's clear connection with pedagogical reform has led to a greater focus in the post-Soviet period on education as the basis for Jadidism's genealogical link to Qūrṣāwī.[19] Yet this narrative is similarly misleading. Qūrṣāwī did indeed

---

16. Ibid., pp. 16–18, 27, 51, 56–58.

17. Cf. ibid., pp. 16, 26.

18. Indeed, Marjānī's stance is praised by the Syrian Hanafi Muḥammad Zāhid Kawtharī (1878–1951), who explicitly rejected *ijtihād* as radical reinterpretation and the removal of the *madhhab* from legal reasoning; Muḥammad Zāhid b. al-Ḥasan Kawtharī. *Ḥusn al-taqāḍī fī sīrat al-Imām Abī Yūsuf al-Qāḍī wa-ṣafḥa min ṭabaqāt al-fuqahāʾ*. Homs: R. Ḥākimī, 1968, pp. 102–116.

19. E.g., Stéphane A. Dudoignon. "Echoes to *al-Manar* Among Muslim of the Russian Empire: A Preliminary Research Note on Riza al-Din b. Fakhr al-Din and the *Shura* (1908–1918)." *Intellectuals in the Modern Islamic World: Transmission, Transformation, Communication.*

call for more widespread and correct religious knowledge, criticizing contemporary *ʿulamāʾ* for failing in their duties as teachers, as did Jadids. However, not only is this vague—such calls are ubiquitous in Islamic reformism—but, like with *ijtihād*, it ignores substantive differences between them. The proper knowledge and learning that Qūrṣāwī advocated for lay Muslims may appear to converge with Jadids' emphasis on broad religious knowledge, but, as with his reformist project as a whole, it was unquestionably grounded within the scaffolding of the scholarly tradition. It's telling that the *Irshād*, his primary work intended for a wide audience, both includes an extensive explication of Hanafi *fiqh* and is written in Arabic; it assumes a basic degree of literacy in scholarly discourse from the reader, even as it seeks to further educate them in that discourse. (His *tafsīr* is of course aimed at an even broader readership, but understanding the Qurʾan is a basic, even minimal element of religious learning. There is no doubt that Qūrṣāwī would consider that in itself an insufficient Islamic education.)

Jadidism, however, was premised upon reshaping Islamic education along Western lines, as part of civilizational reform. For Jadids, established methods of the *ʿulamāʾ* and the makeup of the *madrasa* were ill-suited to the needs of contemporary society, if not inherently flawed, and among the main causes of Muslims' backwardness and failure to progress. In this way, Jadids' efforts toward pedagogical and curricular transformation stand in stark contrast to Qūrṣāwī's reformism. Insofar as he criticized people's learning and scholars' teaching, it was as a matter of degree or quality—*ʿulamāʾ* had not taught people all they should know and, worse, had offered them misguidance and falsehood in the guise of proper knowledge. There's little indication, however, even with his notable disagreements with other *ʿulamāʾ*, that Qūrṣāwī attacked the foundations of Islamic education, nor implemented an altered pedagogy in his own *madrasa*.

Education per se was not a focus for Qūrṣāwī, while its reform represents the very basis of Jadidism, and the remaking of Muslim schooling was part and parcel of Jadids' rejection of old ways in favor of the new. Traditional education for them was identified with the Bukharan *madrasa*, which was presented as the source of the Volga-Ural *ʿulamāʾ*'s backward and closed-minded character, and Jadidism was understood as the shift away from its influence.[20] In fact, the

Eds. Stéphane A. Dudoignon et al. New York: Routledge, 2006. 85–116; Allen Frank. *Bukhara and the Muslims of Russia: Sufism, Education, and the Paradox of Islamic Prestige*. Leiden: Brill, 2012, pp. 155–160.

20. Frank, *Bukhara*, pp. 160–170; cf. M. Mobin Shorish. "Traditional Islamic Education in Central Asia prior to 1917." *Passé Turco-Tatar, Présent Soviétique: études offertes à Alexandre*

embrace of Western approaches and civilizational reform rendered Bukhara's place in Jadidist messaging primarily symbolic, standing not for any unique scholarly or pedagogical modus operandi but rather for the entire edifice of traditional Islamic scholarship. Bukhara of course held immense significance for Volga-Ural Muslims as the wellspring for their Islamic cultural heritage, which was tied to established forms of learning, piety, and scholarly and mystical authority. It thus became an obvious focal point for critique by Jadids in their denigration and rejection of all that was "*qadīm*" (with accompanying connotations).[21]

Accordingly, the image of Qūrṣāwī in Jadidist historiography is primarily utilized in service of this negative portrayal of Bukhara. It focuses overwhelmingly on his condemnation, which is treated both as an example of his resistance against the *ʿulamāʾ* and as an example of their extremism in clinging to old doctrines. Validov, for instance, foregrounds the intransigence of the "kalamists" (*keliamisty*) of the Bukharan *ʿulamāʾ* and their role in Qūrṣāwī's ordeal.[22] Its original significance as a disagreement over the nature of the divine attributes, however, is replaced with a new understanding of it as an instance of violent reaction by conservative *ʿulamāʾ* to an attempt to move away from traditional scholarship. As with other aspects of his reformism, his condemnation was thus stripped of its substance and meaning and repurposed for Jadidist aims. It was used as a precedent to which Jadids could appeal to bolster their message against more conservative (strictly speaking) sectors of Muslim society, connecting Jadidism to a prominent reformist figure and thereby strengthening Jadids' reformist credentials.[23]

Bennigsen. Eds. Ch. Lemercier-Quelquejay et al. Paris: Editions Peeters, 1986. 317–344; see Dzhamaliutdin Validov. *Ocherk istorii obrazovannosti i literatury Tatar*. 1923. Oxford: Society for Central Asian Studies, 1986, esp. pp. 17–25.

21. Cf. Frank, who writes that Bukhara served as a trope for Muslim reformers in Russia to critique their own institutions, which had of course been influenced by Bukharan scholarship; Frank, *Bukhara*, p. 155. He goes on to note, however, the ways in which reformers attacked the sources of Bukhara's religious prestige, which I would argue is an example of shifting notions of Islamic normativity, not away from Bukhara specifically but rather away from older sources of religious authority. Indeed, a 1912 article in the reformist journal *Shūrā* devoted to Muḥammad b. ʿAlī Sanūsī and his Sanūsiyya order compares their struggle for *ijtihād* and reform against Ottoman conservatism with Qūrṣāwī's conflict with the Bukharan *ʿulamāʾ*; "Muḥammad Sanūsī wa-Mahdī Sanūsī." *Shūrā*, no. 11; 29 Jumādā al-ākhir 1330/1 July 1912. 321–324.

22. Validov, *Ocherk*, esp. p. 33.

23. This of course happened with other reformist figures; see, for instance, Ahmad Dallal. "Appropriating the Past: Twentieth-Century Reconstruction of Pre-Modern Islamic Thought." *Islamic Law and Society*, vol. 7, no. 3; 2000. 325–358.

The disconnect between the Jadids' presentation of Qūrṣāwī's condemnation and the reality of it underlines the profound and irreducible differences between his reformist project and Jadidism. While the similarities and points of overlap between them are vague, superficial, and prosaic, their outlook, premises, aims, philosophical foundations, and cultural orientations are substantively distinct. His reform project sought to emend the flawed aspects of scholarship, to ensure that religious beliefs and praxis conformed to certain sources of knowledge and that the prevailing methodologies fostered correct and excluded incorrect views as part of the continuation of the Islamic scholarly tradition. By contrast, Jadidism was underpinned by the abandonment of the scholarly tradition and its replacement by new, self-consciously modern discursive and intellectual frameworks, combining Islamic revivalism, nationalism, and Western thought. Qūrṣāwī's *epistemological* reform focused on the particulars of scholarly discourse and its construction, whereas Jadidism's move away from the scholarly tradition represented a kind of *epistemic* reform, concerned less with specific views or methodologies than with the framework itself.

The vast differences between Qūrṣāwī's reformism and Jadidism make any genealogical connection between the two difficult to maintain. Indeed, given the movement's central focus on remaking Islamic education in emulation of the modern West, a more accurate genealogy for Jadidism would lie with 19th-century figures who worked to incorporate European pedagogical and intellectual paradigms into the *madrasa*, such as Faizkhanov and Nasyri. As for Qūrṣāwī, it could be said that no genealogy follows from him at all. Although his thought was influential and he had followers and champions of his views, historical changes rendered his reform project increasingly untenable. His works speak to his particular context, contemporaries, and concerns. But, as we have seen, the religious and intellectual environment for Volga- Ural Muslims was transformed in subsequent decades, with significant structural shifts, notably the fragmentation of authority, remaking the Islamic discursive space in the region. Debates internal to the tradition in Qūrṣāwī's era gradually gave way to debates about the tradition, its relevance and validity, and the concepts and premises underpinning his thought lost significance and currency, or were reappropriated for different uses in a different setting.

Qūrṣāwī remained influential regarding *ʿishāʾ*, and the historical memory of his general reformist orientation and condemnation was obviously important into the 20th century. But, as we've seen, there seems to have been little correspondence between this memory and the specifics of his reform project, and his two major contributions, on *ijtihād* and the divine attributes, as well as his epistemological critique of scholarship, were obscured by historical circumstance. Ultimately, his efforts to preserve and emend the scholarly tradition were undone by a changing context that saw the tradition itself called into question by significant sections of the Volga-Ural Muslim community.

The failure of Qūrṣāwī's reformism, however, does not negate its importance for the earlier period, but rather is critical for understanding both the nature of his project and Volga-Ural intellectual history, without teleology. His reformism was suited to its period, not a later one shaped by posthumous developments he could not have envisioned, and it has immense significance for understanding very early modern reformism, particularly the adaptation of the scholarly tradition to a new historical context. It shows how discourses and elements from within the tradition could be used and altered to suit a transformed social setting, and relied upon for the continuity of the tradition itself. In addition, it stands as an example of how the tradition could be reformed without direct European influence, but nevertheless in ways that reflect the circumstances under European imperial rule. The disconnect between his reformism and Jadidism is likewise illustrative of the changes in religious discourse that took place over the course of the 19th century, which produced a very different context than his own, with very different concerns. His contributions lie in an earlier era, and so should his legacy.

The vast transformations in the history of Volga-Ural Muslims between the end of the 18th century and the beginning of the 20th complicate such questions of context, continuity, and change, and this chapter, along with Chapters 8 and 9, has attempted both to locate Qūrṣāwī in reference to this posthumous history and to address the real discrepancy between the content of his reformism and his historiographical portrayal. While the study of Volga-Ural intellectual history will surely progress, expanding our understanding of the developments under discussion here, conclusions about the broader environment must remain tentative, circumscribed, and adorned with caveats, particularly in a study devoted to a single figure. But there are nevertheless contributions to be made, to this small field and beyond, as I have tried to do here.

And God knows best.

Bibliography

Manuscript collections: St. Petersburg Institute of Oriental Manuscripts (SPb IVR), Kazan University (KFU), Tiumen Museum (TGM).

CITED WORKS BY QŪRṢĀWĪ

Haftiyak tafsīrī. Ms. KFU T–36.

al-Irshād li-l-ʿibād. Kazan: lito-tipografiia I. N. Kharitonova, 1903. Reprinted with introduction and Russian translation as Abu-n-Nasr Abd an-Nasir al-Kursavi. *Nastavlenie liudei na put' istiny*. Intro. and trans. Gul'nara Idiiatullina. Kazan: Tatarskoe knizhnoe izd-vo, 2005.

Kitāb al-Naṣāʾiḥ. Ms. KFU A–1347. Fols. 18a–22b.

al-Lawāʾiḥ li-l-ʿaqāʾid. Ms. SPb IVR A1241. Fols. 76b–86a.

Mabāḥith al-ism wa-l-ṣifa. Ms. SPb IVR A1241. Fols. 153b–170b.

[On Prayer.] Ms. KFU A–841. Fols. 3b–4a.

Risāla fī Ithbāt al-ṣifāt. Ms. SPb IVR A1241. Fols. 148b–152a.

Sharḥ al-ʿAqāʾid al-nasafiyya al-qadīm. Ms. KFU A–1347. Fols. 17a–18b.

Sharḥ jadīd li-l-ʿAqāʾid al-nasafiyya. Ms. SPb IVR A1241. Fols. 92b–147a.

Sharḥ mukhtaṣar al-Manār. Ms. TGM VF 6765, no. 19064. (Citations from this work utilize the pagination added to the manuscript codex.)

OTHER MANUSCRIPT SOURCES

al-Bukhārī, ʿInāyat Allāh. [Untitled work.] Ms. SPb IVR A914. Fols. 113a–117a.

al-Bukhārī, ʿInāyat Allāh. *Risāla ʿan qism ḥāshiyat al-Khayālī ʿalā Sharḥ al-ʿAqāyid al-nasafiyya li-l-Taftāzānī*. Ms. SPb IVR A914. Fols. 117a–122a.

"al-Dāghistānī, Afandī." *Radd ʿalā Abī al-Naṣr al-Qūrṣāwī*. Ms. SPb IVR B2750. Fols. 1b–7a.

Manāqib Abī Naṣr ʿAbd al-Naṣīr b. Ibrāhīm al-Bulghārī al-Qāzānī. Ms. SPb IVR A1241. Fols. 68a–70a.

al-Mangārī, Baymurād b. Muḥarram. *Risāla fī al-ṣifāt*. Ms. KFU A–1004. Fols. 122b–128a.

al-Marjānī, Shihāb al-Dīn. *Wafiyat al-aslāf wa-taḥiyat al-akhlāf.* Vol. 6. Ms. KFU A–615.

Ṭabaqāt al-ḥanafiyya. Ms. KFU A–1010. Fols. 21b–45a.

al-Ūriwī, Fatḥ Allāh b. al-Ḥusayn. [Untitled work.] Ms. KFU T–3571. Fols. 1a–3a.

al-Ūriwī, Fatḥ Allāh b. al-Ḥusayn. *Risāla fī al-mabāḥith al-mutaʿalliqa bi-ṣifāt al-bārī.* Ms. SPb IVR C234. Fols. 35b–43a.

PUBLISHED WORKS

Abdullin, Ia. G. *Tatarskaia prosvetitel'skaia mysl'.* Kazan: Tatarskoe knizhnoe izd-vo, 1976.

Abou El Fadl, Khaled. "Islamic Law and Muslim Minorities: The Juristic Discourse on Muslim Minorities from the Second/Eighth to the Eleventh/Seventeenth Centuries." *Islamic Law and Society*, vol. 1, no. 2; 1994. 141–187.

Abrahamov, Binyamin. "The 'Bi-la Kayfa' Doctrine and Its Foundations in Islamic Theology." *Arabica*, vol. 42, no. 3; 1995. 365–379.

Abrahamov, Binyamin. "Faḫr al-Din al-Razi on the Knowability of God's Essence and Attributes." *Arabica*, vol. 49, no. 2; 2002. 204–230.

Abrahamov, Binyamin. *Islamic Theology: Traditionalism and Rationalism.* Edinburgh: Edinburgh UP, 1998.

Ahmed, Asad Q. "Post-Classical Philosophical Commentaries/Glosses: Innovation in the Margins." *Oriens*, vol. 41, no. 3–4; 2013. 317–348.

[Akchurin, Iusuf.] Youssouff Aktchoura oglu. *L'état actuel et les aspirations des Turco-Tatares Musulmans en Russie.* Lausanne: imprimeries Réunies, 1916.

[Akchurin, Iusuf.] Yūsuf Āqchūra. *Ūch ṭarz-i siyāsat.* New ed. Istanbul: Maṭbaʿa-yi Qadar, 1327 [1911].

Akhmetova, Elmira. "Musa Jarullah Bigiev (1875–1949): Political Thought of a Tatar Muslim Scholar." *Intellectual Discourse*, vol. 16, no. 1; 2008. 49–71.

Al-Azmeh, Aziz. "Orthodoxy and Hanbalite Fideism." *Arabica*, vol. 35, no. 3; 1988. 253–266.

ʿAlī al-Qārī. *Risāla fī waḥdat al-wujūd.* In *Majmūʿa rasāʾil fī waḥdat al-wujūd.* [Istanbul]: n.p., 1294 [1877]. 52–114.

ʿAlī al-Qārī. *Sharḥ kitāb al-Fiqh al-akbar.* Beirut: Dār al-kutub al-ʿilmiyya, 1984/1404.

Algar, Hamid. "A Brief History of the Naqshbandi Order." *Cheminements et situation actuelle d'un ordre mystique musulman: Actes de la Table Ronde de Sèvres, 2–4 mai 1985.* Eds. Marc Gaborieau, Alexandre Popovic, and Thierry Zarcone. Istanbul: Editions ISIS, 1990. 3–44.

Algar, Hamid. "Shaykh Zaynullah Rasulev: The Last Great Naqshbandi Shaykh of the Volga-Urals Region." *Muslims in Central Asia: Expressions of Identity and Change.* Ed. Jo-Ann Gross. Durham, NC: Duke UP, 1992. 112–133.

Allard, Michel. *Le problème des attributs divins dans la doctrine d'al-Aš ʿari et de ses premiers grands disciples.* Beirut: Imprimerie Catholique, 1965.

Amīrkhān, Ḥusayn. *Tawārīkh-i bulghāriyya*. Kazan: Maṭbaʿat Wiyācheslāf, 1883. Reprinted with Russian translation as Khusain Amirkhanov. *Tavarikh-e Bulgariia (Bulgarskie khroniki)*. Intro. and trans. A. M. Akhunov. Moscow: izd-vo Mardzhani, 2010.

Anisimov, E. V. *The Reforms of Peter the Great: Progress Through Coercion in Russia*. Intro. and trans. John T. Alexander. Armonk, NY: M. E. Sharpe, 1993.

Ansari, Muhammad Abdul Haq. *Sufism and Shariʿah: A Study of Shaykh Ahmad Sirhindi's Effort to Reform Sufism*. Leicester, UK: Islamic Foundation, 1986.

Arberry, A. J. "Introduction." *The Doctrine of the Sufis*. Cambridge: Cambridge UP, 1977. ix–xviii.

Arsharuni, A. M., and Kh. Gabidullin. *Ocherki panislamizma i pantiurkizma*. Moscow: izd-vo Bezobozhnik, 1931.

Asad, Talal. *Formations of the Secular: Christianity, Islam, Modernity*. Stanford, CA: Stanford UP, 2003.

Asad, Talal. "The Idea of an Anthropology of Islam." *Qui Parle*, vol. 17, no. 2; 2009. 1–30. Re-edition of *The Idea of an Anthropology of Islam*. Washington, DC: Center for Contemporary Arab Studies, Georgetown University, 1986.

al-Ashʿarī, Abū al-Ḥasan. *Maqālāt al-islāmiyyīn wa-ikhtilāf al-muṣallīn*. 2nd ed. Ed. Hellmut Ritter. Weisbaden: Franz Steiner Verlag, 1963.

ʿAynī, Ṣadr al-Dīn. *Tārīkh-i amīrān-i Manghitiyya-i Bukhārā*. Tashkent: Turkestanskoe gosudarstvennoe izd-vo, 1923.

Azamatov, Danil' D. "The Muftis of the Orenburg Spiritual Assembly in the 18th and 19th Centuries: The Struggle for Power in Russia's Muslim Institution." *Muslim Culture in Russia and Central Asia from the 18th to the Early 20th Centuries. Vol. 2: Inter-Regional and Inter-Ethnic Relations*. Eds. Anke von Kügelgen, Michael Kemper, and Allen J. Frank. Berlin: Klaus Schwarz Verlag, 1998. 355–384.

Azamatov, Danil' D. *Orenburgskoe magometanskoe dukhovnoe sobranie v kontse XVIII–XIX vv*. Ufa: Gilem, 1999.

Azamatov, Danil' D. "Russian Administration and Islam in Bashkiria (18th–19th Centuries)." *Muslim Culture in Russia and Central Asia from the 18th to the Early 20th Centuries*. Eds. Michael Kemper, Anke von Kügelgen, and Dmitriy Yermakov. Berlin: Klaus Schwarz Verlag, 1996. 91–112.

Babadžanov, Baxtiyor M. "On the History of the Naqšbandiya Muğaddidiya in Central Mawara'annahr in the Late 18th and Early 19th Centuries." *Muslim Culture in Russia and Central Asia from the 18th to the Early 19th Centuries*. Eds. Michael Kemper, Anke von Kügelgen, and Dmitriy Yermakov. Berlin: Klaus Schwarz Verlag, 1996. 385–414.

Baiazitov, Ataulla. *Otnosheniia Islama k nauke i k inovertsam*. St. Petersburg: Tipografiia A. S. Suvorina, 1887.

Baldauf, Ingeborg. "Jadidism in Central Asia Within Reformism and Modernism in the Muslim World." *Die Welt des Islams*, vol. 41, no. 1; 2000. 72–88.

Baljon, J. M. S. *Religion and Thought of Shah Wali Allah Dihlawi 1703–1762*. Leiden: Brill, 1986.

Başkan, Birol. *From Religious Empires to Secular States: State Secularization in Turkey, Iran, and Russia*. New York: Routledge, 2014.

Battal-Taymas, A. "La littérature des Tatars de Kazan." *Philologiae Turcica Fundamenta*. Vol. 2. Eds. Jean Deny, Louis Bazin, Hans Robert Roemer, and Erik-Jan Zürcher. Aquis Mattiacis: Steiner, 1964. 762–778.

Batyev, S. G. "Tatarskii dzhadidizm i ego èvoliutsiia." *Istoriia SSSR*, no. 4; 1964. 53–63.

al-Bazdawī, ʿAlī b. Muḥammad. *Uṣūl al-Bazdawī: Kanz al-wuṣūl ilā maʿrifat al-uṣūl*. [Karachi]: Mīr Muḥammad kutubkhāna-i markaz-i ʿilm wa-adab, n.d.

Beck, Ulrich. *A God of One's Own: Religion's Capacity for Peace and Potential for Violence*. Cambridge: Polity, 2010.

Bennigsen, Alexandre, and Chantal Lemercier-Quelquejay. *La presse et le mouvement national chez les musulmans de Russie avant 1920*. Paris: Mouton, 1964.

Berkes, Niyazi. *The Development of Secularism in Turkey*. Montreal: McGill UP, 1964.

[Bigiev, Musa.] Mūsā Afandī Bīgīyif. "Madaniyyat dunyāsī taraqqī ītmish īkan, islāmiyyat ʿālamī nīchūn īndī?" *Khalq naẓarīna birnīcha masʾila*. Kazan: èlektro-tipografiia Umid, 1912. 33–39.

[Bigiev, Musa.] Mūsā b. Jār Allāh Bīgīyif, trans. Abū al-ʿAlā Aḥmad b. ʿAbd Allāh al-Maʿarrī. *al-Luzūmiyyāt*. Kazan: Tipografiia Sharaf, 1907.

[Bigiev, Musa.] Mūsā Jār Allāh Bīgīyif. *Qawāʿid-i fiqhiyya*. Kazan: èlektro-tipografiia Urnek, 1328 [1910].

[Bigiev, Musa.] Mūsā Jār Allāh. *al-Washīʿa fī naqd ʿaqāʾid al-shīʿa*. Lahore: Suhayl Akīdīmī, 1979.

Brown, Daniel W. *Rethinking Tradition in Modern Islamic Thought*. New York: Cambridge UP, 1996.

Brown, Jonathan A. C. "Is Islam Easy to Understand of Not?: Salafis, the Democratization of Interpretation and the Need for the Ulema." *Journal of Islamic Studies*, vol. 26, no. 2; 2015. 117–144.

Brown, Nathan. "Sharia and State in the Modern Muslim Middle East." *International Journal of Middle East Studies*, vol. 29, no. 3; 1997. 359–376.

Bubi, Abdullah. "Is the Period of *Ijtihad* Over or Not?" *Modernist Islam, 1840–1940: A Sourcebook*. Ed. Charles Kurzman. New York: Oxford UP, 2002. 232–237.

Buehler, Arthur. "The Naqshbandiyya in Timurid India: The Central Asian Legacy." *Journal of Islamic Studies*, vol. 7, no. 2; 1996. 208–228.

Buehler, Arthur. *Sufi Heirs of the Prophet: The Indian Naqshbandiyya and the Rise of the Mediating Sufi Shaykh*. Columbia, SC: U of South Carolina P, 1998.

[al-Bukhārī], Sayyid Muḥammad Naṣīr al-Dīn b. Sayyid Amīr Muẓaffar. *Tuḥfat al-zāʾirīn*. Ed. Mullā Muḥammadī Makhdūm. Bukhara: n.p., 1328 [1910].

al-Bulghārī, ʿAbd Allāh b. ʿAbd Allāh. *ʿUjāla marḍiya fī bayān al-ashʿariyya*. Kazan: Tipo-litografiia imperatorskago universiteta, 1905.

Burton, Audrey. *The Bukharans: A Dynastic, Diplomatic, and Commercial History, 1550–1702*. Richmond, UK: Curzon, 1997.

Bustanov, Alfrid. "ʿAbd al-Rashid Ibrahim's Biographical Dictionary on Siberian Islamic Scholars." *Kazan Islamic Review*, no. 1; 2014. 10–78.

Bustanov, Alfrid. "The Bulghar Region as a 'Land of Ignorance': Anti-Colonial Discourse in Khvarazmian Connectivity." *Journal of Persianate Studies*, vol. 9; 2016. 183–204.

Bustanov, Alfrid, and Michael Kemper. "From Mirasism to Euro-Islam: The Translation of Islamic Legal Debates into Tatar Secular Cultural Heritage." *Islamic Authority and the Russian Language: Studies on Texts from European Russia, the North Caucasus and West Siberia*. Eds. Alfrid Bustanov and Michael Kemper. Amsterdam: Pegasus, 2012. 29–54.

Calder, Norman. "al-Nawawi's Typology of Muftis and Its Significance for a General Theory of Islamic Law." *Islamic Law and Society*, vol. 3, no. 2; 1996. 137–164.

Campbell, Elena. "The Autocracy and the Muslim Clergy in the Russian Empire (1850s–1917)." *Russian Studies in History*, vol. 44, no. 2; 2005. 8–29.

Carrère d'Encausse, Hélène. *Islam and the Russian Empire: Reform and Revolution in Central Asia*. London: I. B. Tauris, 1988.

Casanova, Jose. "The Secular, Secularizations, Secularisms." *Rethinking Secularism*. Eds. Craig Calhoun, Mark Juergensmeyer, and Jonathan VanAntwerpen. New York: Oxford UP, 2011. 54–74.

Chittick, William. "Sadr al-Din Qunawi on the Oneness of Being." *International Philosophical Quarterly*, no. 21; 1981. 171–184.

Chittick, William. *The Self-Disclosure of God: Principles of Ibn al-ʿArabi's Cosmology*. Albany: State U of New York P, 1998.

Chittick, William. *The Sufi Path of Knowledge: ibn al-ʿArabi's Metaphysics of Imagination*. Albany: State U of New York P, 1989.

Chittick, William, and Patrick Lamborn Wilson. "Introduction." In Fakhr al-Din Ibrahim ʿIraqi. *Divine Flashes*. New York: Paulist Press, 1982. 3–32.

Cohn, Bernard. *Colonialism and Its Forms of Knowledge: The British in India*. Princeton, NJ: Princeton UP, 1996.

Copty, Atallah S. "The Naqshbandiyya and Its Offshoot, the Naqshbandiyya-Mujaddidiyya in the Haramayn in the 11th/17th Century." *Die Welt des Islams*, vol. 43, no. 3; 2003. 321–348.

Cracraft, James. *The Church Reform of Peter the Great*. Stanford, CA: Stanford UP, 1971.

Crews, Robert. "Empire and the Confessional State: Islam and Religious Politics in Nineteenth-Century Russia." *American Historical Review*, vol. 108, no. 1; 2003. 50–83.

Crews, Robert. *For Prophet and Tsar: Islam and Empire in Russia and Central Asia*. Cambridge, MA: Harvard UP, 2005.

Dallal, Ahmad. "The Origins and Early Development of Islamic Reform." *The New Cambridge History of Islam. Vol. 6: Muslims and Modernity: Culture and Society Since 1800*. Ed. Robert Hefner. Cambridge: Cambridge UP, 2010. 107–147.

Dallal, Ahmad. "The Origins and Objectives of Islamic Revivalist Thought, 1750–1850." *Journal of the American Oriental Society*, vol. 113, no. 3; 1993. 341–359.

Davidson, Herbert. *Proofs for Eternity, Creation and the Existence of God in Medieval Islamic and Jewish Philosophy*. New York: Oxford UP, 1987.

al-Dawānī, Jalāl al-Dīn Muḥammad. *Risālat al-Zawrāʾ*. In *Sabʿ rasāʾil*. Ed. Aḥmad Tūysirkānī. Tehran: Mīrāth-i maktūb, 1381/2002. 171–184.

DeWeese, Devin. "Islam and the Legacy of Sovietology: A Review Essay on Yaacov Roʾi's *Islam in the Soviet Union*." *Journal of Islamic Studies*, vol. 13, no. 3; 2002. 298–330.

Donnelly, Alton S. *The Russian Conquest of Bashkiria 1552–1740: A Case Study in Imperialism*. New Haven, CT: Yale UP, 1968.

Dorn, B. "Chronologisches Verzeichniss der seit dem Jahre 1801 bis 1866 in Kasan gedruckten arabischen, türkischen, tatarischen und persischen Werke, als Katalog der in dem asiatischen Museum befindlichen Schriften der Art." *Mélanges asiatiques tirés du Bulletin de l'Académie impériale des sciences de St.-Pétersbourg*, vol. 5; 1866. 533–649.

Dowler, Wayne. *Classroom and Empire: The Politics of Schooling Russia's Eastern Nationalities, 1860–1917*. Montreal: McGill-Queen's UP, 2001.

Dudoignon, Stéphane A. "Echoes to *al-Manar* Among Muslim of the Russian Empire: A Preliminary Research Note on Riza al-Din b. Fakhr al-Din and the *Shura* (1908–1918)." *Intellectuals in the Modern Islamic World: Transmission, Transformation, Communication*. Eds. Stéphane A. Dudoignon, Komatsu Hisao, and Kosugi Yasushi. New York: Routledge, 2006. 85–116.

Dudoignon, Stéphane A. "Un islam périphérique? Quelques réflexions sur la presse musulmane de Sibérie à la veille de la Première Guerre mondiale." *Cahiers du monde russe*, vol. 41, no. 2–3; 2000. 297–339.

Dudoignon, Stéphane A. "*Qadimiya* as a Historiographical Category: The Question of Social and Ideological Cleavages Between 'Reformists' and 'Traditionalists' Among the Muslims of Russia and Central Asia, in the Early 20th Century." *Reform Movements and Revolutions in Turkistan*. Ed. Timur Kocaoglu. Haarlem: SOTA, 2001. 159–177.

Dudoignon, Stéphane A. "Status, Strategies and Discourses of a Muslim 'Clergy' Under a Christian Law: Polemics About the Collection of the *Zakat* in Late Imperial Russia." *Islam in Politics in Russia and Central Asia (Early Eighteenth to Late Twentieth Centuries)*. Eds. Stéphane A. Dudoignon and Hisao Komatsu. London: Kegan Paul, 2001. 43–73.

Eickelman, Dale F., and James Piscatori. *Muslim Politics*. 1996. 2nd ed. Princeton, NJ: Princeton UP, 2004.

Eisenstein, Elizabeth. *The Printing Revolution in Early Modern Europe.* Cambridge: Cambridge UP, 1983.

Eklof, Ben. *Russian Peasant Schools: Officialdom, Village Culture and Popular Pedagogy, 1861–1914*. Berkeley: U of California P, 1986.

El-Rouayheb, Khaled. *Islamic Intellectual History in the Seventeenth Century: Scholarly Currents in the Ottoman Empire and the Maghreb.* Cambridge: Cambridge UP, 2015.

Encyclopedia Iranica. London: Routledge and Kegan Paul. [Cited as *EIr.*]

Encyclopedia of Islam. 2nd–3rd eds. Leiden: Brill. [Cited as *EI.*]

Esposito, John, and John Voll. *Makers of Contemporary Islam.* Oxford: Oxford UP, 2001.

Fadel, Mohammad. "The Social Logic of Taqlid and the Rise of the Mukhtasar." *Islamic Law and Society*, vol. 3, no. 2; 1996. 193–233.

Faizkhanov, Khusain. "Reforma medrese (Islakh madaris)." Trans. I. F. Gimadeev. *Khusain Faizkhanov: Zhizn' i nasledie.* Ed. D. V. Mukhetdinov. Nizhnii Novgorod: izd-vo Medina, 2008. 12–28.

Fakhr al-Dīn, Riḍāʾ al-Dīn. *Āthār.* 15 parts in 2 vols. Part 1: Kazan: Tipo-litografiia imperatorskogo universiteta, 1900. Parts 2–15: Orenburg: Tipografiia G. I. Karimova, 1901–1908.

Fakhr al-Dīn, Riḍāʾ al-Dīn. *Ibn Taymiyya.* Orenburg: Waqt maṭbaʿasī, 1911.

[Fakhr al-Dīn, Riḍāʾ al-Dīn.] Rizaéddin Fäxreddin. *Asar.* Vols. 3–4. Kazan: Ruxiyät, 2010.

Faruqi, Burhan Ahmad. *The Mujaddid's Conception of Tawhid: Study of Shaikh Ahmad Sirhindis* [sic] *Doctrine of Unity*. Lahore: Institute of Islamic Culture, 1989.

Fisher, Alan W. "Enlightened Despotism and Islam Under Catherine II." *Slavic Review*, vol. 27, no. 4; Dec. 1968. 542–553.

Foote, I. P. "Counter-Censorship: Authors v. Censors in Nineteenth-Century Russia." *Oxford Slavonic Papers*, vol. 27; 1994. 62–105.

Foote, I. P. "The St. Petersburg Censorship Committee, 1828–1905." *Oxford Slavonic Papers*, vol. 24; 1991. 60–120.

Frank, Allen. *Bukhara and the Muslims of Russia: Sufism, Education, and the Paradox of Islamic Prestige*. Leiden: Brill, 2012.

Frank, Allen. *Islamic Historiography and "Bulghar" Identity Among the Tatars and Bashkirs of Russia*. Leiden: Brill, 1998.

Frank, Allen. *Muslim Religious Institutions in Imperial Russia: The Islamic World of Novouzensk District and the Kazakh Inner Horde, 1780–1910*. Leiden: Brill, 2001.

Frank, Allen. "Tatarskie mully sredi kazakhov i kirgizov v XVIII i XIX vv." *Kul'tura, isskustvo tatarskogo naroda: istoki, traditsii, vzaimosviazi.* Eds. M. Z. Zakiev, D. M. Iskhakov, and G. F. Valeeva-Suleimanova. Kazan: IIaLI AN RT, 1993. 124–128.

Frank, Richard. "The Science of *Kalam*." *Arabic Sciences and Philosophy*, vol. 2; 1992. 7–37.

Friedmann, Yohanan. *Shaykh Ahmad Sirhindi: An Outline of His Thought and a Study of His Image in the Eyes of Posterity*. Montreal: McGill-Queen's UP, 1971.

Gainullin, M. Kh. *Tatarskaia literatura XIX veka*. Kazan: Tatarskoe knizhnoe izd-vo, 1975.

Galliamov, D. F. "Istoricheskie diskursy tiurko-musul'manskoi ideologii vtoroi poloviny XIX-nachala XX stoletii." *Problemy vostokovedeniia*, no. 2; 2011. 90–96.

Gasprinskii, Ismail Bei. *Russkoe musul'manstvo: Mysli, zametki, i nabliudeniia musul'manina*. 1881. Oxford: Society for Central Asian Studies, 1985.

[Gasprinskii, Ismail.] Ismāʿīl Ghaṣprinskī. *Awrūpā madaniyyatina bir naẓar mawāzina*. Istanbul: Maṭbaʿa-i Abū Ḍiyā, 1302 [1885].

Geraci, Robert. *Window on the East: National and Imperial Identities in Late Tsarist Russia*. Ithaca, NY: Cornell UP, 2001.

al-Ghazālī, Abū Ḥāmid Muḥammad. *Iḥyāʾ ʿulūm al-dīn*. 5 vols. Beirut: Dar Sader, 2000.

al-Ghazālī, Abū Ḥāmid Muḥammad. *al-Mustaṣfā fī ʿilm al-uṣūl*. 2 vols. Baghdad: Maktabat al-muthannā, 1970. Reprint, 1324 Būlāq edition.

Gould, Rebecca. "*Ijtihad* Against *Madhhab*: Legal Hybridity and the Meanings of Modernity in Early Modern Daghestan." *Comparative Studies in Society and History*, vol. 57, no. 1; 2015. 35–66.

Griffiths, David. "In Search of Enlightenment: Recent Soviet Interpretation of Eighteenth-Century Russian Intellectual History." *Canadian-American Slavic Studies*, vol. 16, no. 3–4; 1982. 317–356.

[Gubaidullin, Gaziz.] ʿAzīz ʿUbaydullīn. "Marjānīniñ tārīkhī khidmatlārī." *Marjānī*. Ed. Ṣāliḥ b. Thābit ʿUbaydullīn. Kazan: Maʿārif, 1333 [1915]. 333–359.

Gubaidullin, Gaziz. "Ismail Gasprinskii i iazyk." 1927. *Gasırlar awazı/Ekho vekov*, no. 3–4; 1997. 205–214.

Gubaidullin, Gaziz. *Istoriia Tatar*. 1925. 3rd ed. Moscow: Moskovskii litsei, 1994.

Gubaidullin, Gaziz. "K Voprosu ob ideologii Gasprinskogo." 1929. *Gasırlar awazı/Ekho vekov*, vol. 4, no. 3–4; 1998. 98–118.

Gutas, Dimitri. *Avicenna and the Aristotelian Tradition*. Leiden: Brill, 1988.

Gyekye, Kwame. *Tradition and Modernity: Philosophical Reflections on the African Experience*. New York: Oxford UP, 1997.

Hallaq, Wael. *Authority, Continuity and Change in Islamic Law*. New York: Cambridge UP, 2001.

Hallaq, Wael. *A History of Islamic Legal Theories: An Introduction to Sunni Usul al-Fiqh*. New York: Cambridge UP, 1997.

Hallaq, Wael. "Ifta' and Ijtihad in Sunni Legal Theory: A Developmental Account." *Islamic Legal Interpretation: Muftis and Their Fatwas*. Eds. Muhammad Khalid Masud, Brinkley Messick, and David Powers. Cambridge, MA: Harvard UP, 1996. 33–44.

Hallaq, Wael. *The Impossible State: Islam, Politics, and Modernity's Moral Predicament*. New York: Columbia UP, 2013.

Hallaq, Wael. *Shariʿa: Theory, Practice, Transformations*. New York: Cambridge UP, 2009.

Hallaq, Wael. "Was the Gate of Ijtihad Closed?." *International Journal of Middle East Studies*, no. 16; 1984. 3–41. Reprinted in Wael B. Hallaq. *Law and Legal Theory in Classical and Medieval Islam*. Brookfield, VT: Variorum, 1995.

Hallaq, Wael. "What Is Shariʿa?" *Yearbook of Islamic and Middle Eastern Law, 2005–2006*, XII. Leiden: Brill, 2007. 151–180.

Hamamoto, Mami. "Tatarskaia Kargala in Russia's Eastern Policies." *Asiatic Russia: Imperial Power in Regional and International Contexts*. Ed. Tomohiko Uyama. London: Routledge, 2012. 32–51.

Haykel, Bernard. "Reforming Islam by Dissolving the Madhahib: Shawkani and His Zaydi Detractors in Yemen." *Studies in Islamic Legal Theory*. Ed. Bernard Weiss. Leiden: Brill, 2002. 337–364.

Haykel, Bernard. *Revival and Reform in Islam: The Legacy of Muhammad al-Shawkani*. Cambridge: Cambridge UP, 2003.

Heyd, Uriel. *Studies in Old Ottoman Criminal Law*. Oxford: Clarendon, 1973.

Humphreys, R. Stephen. *Islamic History: A Framework for Inquiry*. Rev. ed. Princeton, NJ: Princeton UP, 1991.

Ibn ʿArabī, Muḥy al-Dīn. *Inshāʾ al-dawāʾir*. In *Kleinere Schriften des Ibn al-ʿArabi*. Ed. H. S. Nyberg. Leiden, Brill, 1919. 1–39.

Ibn Idrīs, Aḥmad. *Risālat al-Radd ʿalā ahl al-raʾy*. In *The Exoteric Ahmed ibn Idris: A Sufi's Critique of the Madhahib and the Wahhabis*. Eds. Bernd Radtke, John O'Kane, Knut Vikor, and R. S. O'Fahey. Leiden: Brill, 2000. 47–131.

Idiiatullina, Gul'nara. "Dukhovno-religioznaia atmosfera v Povolzh'e v XVII–XVIII vv." *Islam v srednem povolzh'e: istoriia i sovremennost'*. Kazan: IIaLI AN RT, 2001. 176–201.

Idiiatullina, Gul'nara. "Vvedenie." In Abu-n-Nasr Abd an-Nasir al-Kursavi. *Nastavlenie liudei na put' istiny*. Kazan: Tatarskoe knizhnoe izd-vo, 2005. 10–88.

Iskhakov, S. M. *Pervaia russkaia revoliutsiia i musul'mane rossiiskoi imperii*. Moscow: izd-vo Sotsial'no-politicheskaia mysl', 2007.

Istoriia Kazakhskoi SSR s drevneishikh vremen do nashikh dnei. 5 vols. Alma-Ata: izd-vo Nauka Kazakhskoi SSR, 1979.

Iusupov, M. Kh. *Shigabutdin Mardzhani kak istorik*. Kazan: Tatarskoe knizhnoe izd-vo, 1981.

Iuzeev, Aidar. *Filosofskaia mysl' tatarskogo naroda*. Kazan: Tatarskoe knizhnoe izd-vo, 2007.

Iuzeev, Aidar. *Mirovozzrenie Sh. Mardzhani i arabo-musul'manskaia filosofiia*. Kazan: IIaLI AN RT, 1992.

Jackson, Sherman. "Fiction and Formalism: Toward a Functional Analysis of *Usul al-fiqh*." *Studies in Islamic Legal Theory*. Ed. Bernard Weiss. Leiden: Brill, 2002. 177–204.

Jackson, Sherman. *Islamic Law and the State: The Constitutional Jurisprudence of Shihab al-Din al-Qarafi*. Leiden: Brill, 1996.

Jackson, Sherman. "Taqlid, Legal Scaffolding and the Scope of Legal Injunctions in Post-Formative Theory: Mutlaq and ʿAmm in the Jurisprudence of Shihab al-Din al-Qarafi." *Islamic Law and Society*, vol. 3, no. 2; 1996. 165–192.

Jameson, Fredric. *A Singular Modernity*. 2nd ed. London: Verso, 2012.

Jāmī, ʿAbd al-Raḥmān. *al-Durra al-fākhira fī taḥqīq madhhab al-ṣūfiya wa-l-mutakallimīn wa-l-ḥukamāʾ al-mutaqaddimīn*. Eds. Nicholas Heer and ʿAlī Mūsāwī Bihbihānī. Tehran: Dānishgāh-i MakGīll, 1980/1358.

Jāmī, ʿAbd al-Raḥmān. *Naqd al-nuṣūṣ fī sharḥ Naqsh al-fuṣūṣ*. Ed. William Chittick. Tehran: Anjuman-i Shāhanshāhī-i Falsafa-i Īrān, 1398/1977.

Johansen, Baber. *Contingency in a Sacred Law: Legal and Ethical Norms in the Muslim* Fiqh. Leiden: Brill, 1999.

Johansen, Baber. "Legal Literature and the Problem of Change: The Case of Land Rent." *Islam and Public Law: Classical and Contemporary Studies*. Ed. Chibli Mallat. London: Graham and Trotman, 1993. 29–47.

Kalābādhī, Abū Bakr Muḥammad b. Ishāq. *Kitāb al-Taʿarruf li-madhhab ahl al-taṣawwuf*. Ed. A. J. Arberry. Cairo: Maktabat al-khānjī, 1934.

Kamali, Mohammad Hashim. *Principles of Islamic Jurisprudence*. 3rd ed. Cambridge: Islamic Texts Society, 2003.

Kanlidere, Ahmet. *Reform Within Islam: The Tajdid and Jadid Movement Among the Kazan Tatars (1809–1917): Conciliation or Conflict?* Istanbul: Eren, 1997.

Kanlidere, Ahmet. "The Trends of Thought Among the Tatars and Bashkirs: Religious Reformism and Secular Jadidism vs. Qadimism (1883–1910)." *Journal of Central Asian and Caucasian Studies*, vol. 5, no. 9; 2010. 48–63.

Karimullin, A. G. *U istokov tatarskoi knigi: ot nachala vozniknoveniia do 60-kh godov XIX veka*. Kazan: Tatarskoe knizhnoe izd-vo, 1992.

Katalog knig otpechatannykh v tipografii imperatorskago kazanskago universiteta c 1800 do 1896. Eds. N. F. Katanov and A. Solovev. Kazan: Tipografiia kazanskago universiteta, 1896.

Kawtharī, Muḥammad Zāhid b. al-Ḥasan. *Ḥusn al-taqāḍī fī sīrat al-Imām Abī Yūsuf al-Qāḍī wa-ṣafḥa min ṭabaqāt al-fuqahāʾ*. Homs: R. Ḥākimī, 1388/1968.

Kazem Beg, Mirza. "Notice sur la marche et les progrès de la jurisprudence musulmane parmi les sectes orthodoxes." *Journal asiatique*, ser. 4, no. 15; Jan. 1850. 154–210.

Keddie, Nikki R. "The Revolt of Islam, 1700 to 1903: Comparative Considerations and Relations to Imperialism." *Comparative Studies in Society and History*, vol. 36, no. 3; 1994. 463–487.

Kemper, Michael. "Imperial Russia as Dar al-Islam? Nineteenth-Century Debates on Ijtihad and Taqlid Among the Volga Tatars." *Encounters: An International Journal for the Study of Culture and Society*, vol. 6; 2015. 95–124.

Kemper, Michael. "Şihabaddin al-Marğani als Religionsgelehrter." *Muslim Culture in Russia and Central Asia from the 18th to the Early 20th Centuries*. Eds. Michael Kemper, Anke von Kügelgen, and Dmitriy Yermakov. Berlin: Klaus Schwarz Verlag, 1996. 129–166.

Kemper, Michael. "Şihabaddin al-Marğani über Abu n-Nasr al-Qursawis Konflikt mit den Gelehrten bucharas." *Muslim Culture in Russia and Central Asia. Vol. 3: Arabic, Persian and Turkic Manuscripts (15th–19th Centuries)*. Eds. Anke von Kügelgen, Aširbek Muminov, and Michael Kemper. Berlin: Klaus Schwarz Verlag, 2000. 353–383.

Kemper, Michael. *Sufis und Gelehrte in Tatarien und Baschkirien, 1789–1889: Der islamische Diskurs unter russischer Herrschaft*. Berlin: Klaus Schwarz Verlag, 1998.

Khairullin, A. N. "Mesto G. Kursavi v istorii obschestvennoi mysli." *Iz istorii tatarskoi obschestvennoi mysli*. Ed. Iakh''ia Abdullin. Kazan: IIaLI AN SSSR, 1979. 72–78.

Khairutdinov, Aidar. "Musa Bigiev ob universal'nosti Bozhei milosti." *Mir islama*, vol. 1–2; 1999. 175–190.

Khalid, Adeeb. *The Politics of Muslim Cultural Reform: Jadidism in Central Asia*. Berkeley: U of California P, 1998.

Khalid, Adeeb. "What Jadidism Was, and What It Wasn't: The Historiographical Adventures of a Term." *Central Eurasian Studies Review*, vol. 5, no. 2; 2006. 3–6.

Khayrutdinov, Ramil. "The Tatar *Ratusha* of Kazan: National Self-Administration in Autocratic Russia, 1781–1855." *Islam in Politics in Russia and Central Asia (Early Eighteenth to Late Twentieth Centuries)*. Eds. Stéphane A. Dudoignon and Hisao Komatsu. London: Kegan Paul, 2001. 27–42.

Khodarkovsky, Michael. "'Not by Word Alone': Missionary Policies and Religious Conversion in Early Modern Russia." *Comparative Studies in Society and History*, vol. 38, no. 2; 1996. 267–293.

Khodarkovsky, Michael. *Russia's Steppe Frontier: The Making of a Colonial Empire, 1500–1800*. Bloomington: Indiana UP, 2002.

Kirmse, Stefan. "Law and Empire in Late Tsarist Russia: Muslim Tatars Go to Court." *Slavic Review*, vol. 72, no. 4; 2013. 778–801.

Kivelson, Valerie. "Kinship Politics/Autocratic Politics: A Reconsideration of Early-Eighteenth-Century Political Culture." *Imperial Russia: New Histories for the Empire*. Eds. Jane Burbank and David Ransel. Bloomington, IN: Indiana UP, 1998. 5–31.

Klimovich, L. I. *Islam v tsarskoi Rossii*. Moscow: Gosudarstvennoe antireligioznoe izd-vo, 1936.

Knysh, Alexander. *Ibn ʿArabi and the Later Islamic Tradition: The Making of a Polemical Image in Medieval Islam*. Albany: State U of New York P, 1999.

Knysh, Alexander. "Razmyshleniia po povodu russkogo perevoda knigi Mikhaèla Kempera." *Ab Imperio*, no. 2; 2011. 333–344.

Knysh, Alexander. "Sufism as an Explanatory Paradigm: The Issue of the Motivations of Sufi Resistance Movements in Western and Russian Scholarship." *Die Welt des Islams*, vol. 42, no. 2; 2002. 139–173.

Kreindler, Isabelle. "Ibrahim Altynsarin, Nikolai Il'minskii and the Kazakh National Awakening." *Central Asian Survey*, vol. 2, no. 3; 1983. 99–116.

Landau-Tasseron, Ella. "The 'Cyclical Reform': A Study of the Mujaddid Tradition." *Studia Islamica*, no. 70; 1989. 79–117.

Lapidus, Ira M. "Islamic Revival and Modernity: The Contemporary Movements and the Historical Paradigms." *Journal of the Economic and Social History of the Orient*, vol. 40, no. 4; 1997. 444–460.

Lazzerini, Edward. "Ǧadidism at the Turn of the Twentieth Century: A View from Within." *Cahiers du monde russe et soviétique*, vol. 16, no. 2; 1975. 245–277.

Lazzerini, Edward. "Ismail Bey Gasprinskii and Muslim Modernism in Russia, 1878–1914." Diss. University of Washington, 1973.

Lazzerini, Edward. "Ismail Bey Gasprinskii (Gaspirali): The Discourse of Modernism and the Russians." *The Tatars of Crimea: Return to the Homeland*. 2nd ed. Ed. Edward Allworth. Durham, NC: Duke UP, 1998. 48–70.

Leaman, Oliver, and Sajjad Rizvi. "The Developed *Kalam* Tradition." *The Cambridge Companion to Classical Islamic Theology*. Ed. Timothy Winter. Cambridge: Cambridge UP, 2008. 77–96.

Lemercier-Quelquejay, Chantal. "Les missions orthodoxes en pays musulmans de moyenne- et basse-Volga." *Cahiers du monde russe et soviétique*, vol. 8; 1967. 369–403.

Lemercier-Quelquejay, Chantal. "Un réformateur tatar au XIXe siècle ʿAbdul Qajjum al-Nasyri." *Cahiers du monde russe et soviétique*; vol. 4; 1963. 117–142.

Levtzion, Nehemia, and John O. Voll. "Introduction." *Eighteenth-Century Renewal and Reform in Islam*. Eds. Nehemia Levtzion and John O. Voll. Syracuse, NY: Syracuse UP, 1987. 3–20.

Libson, Gideon. "On the Development of Custom as a Source of Law in Islamic Law." *Islamic Law and Society*, vol. 4, no. 2; 1997. 131–155.

MacIntyre, Alasdair. *After Virtue: A Study in Moral Theory*. 1981. 3rd ed. Notre Dame, IN: U of Notre Dame P, 2007.

Madelung, Wilferd. "The Spread of Maturidism and the Turks." *Actas IV congresso de estudos arabes e islamicos, Coimbra-Lisboa, 1968*. Leiden: Brill, 1971. 109–168.

Makdisi, George. "The Guilds of Law in Medieval Legal History: An Inquiry into the Origins of the Inns of Court." *Cleveland State Law Review*, vol. 34, no. 3; 1985. 3–18.

Majerczak, R. "Notes sur l'enseignement dans la Russie musulmane avant la révolution." *Revue du monde musulman*, vol. 34; 1917–1918. 179–248.

al-Marjānī, Shihāb al-Dīn. *Ḥāshiya ʿalā sharḥ al-ʿAqāʾid al-ʿaḍudiyya*. Printed alongside Ismāʿīl b. Muṣṭafā Kalanbawī. *Ḥāshiya ʿalā sharḥ Jalāl al-Dīn Dawānī ʿalā al-ʿAqāʾid al-ʿaḍudiyya*. Dersaadat [Istanbul]: Maṭbaʿa ʿUthmāniyya, 1316/1898.

al-Marjānī, Shihāb al-Dīn. *al-Ḥikma al-bāligha al-jāniyya fī sharḥ al-ʿaqāʾid al-ḥanafiyya*. Kazan: Maṭbaʿat Wiyācheslāf, 1888.

al-Marjānī, Shihāb al-Dīn. *Mustafād al-akhbār fī aḥwāl Qazān wa-Bulghār*. 2 vols. Vol. 1: Kazan: tipografiia B. L. Dombrovskago, 1897. Vol. 2: Kazan: tipografiia Universitetskago, 1900. Reprinted as Şehabeddin Mercani. *Müstefad'ül-ahbar fi ahval-i Kazan ve Bulgar*. 2 vols. Ankara: Ankara Üniversitesi basımevı, 1997.

al-Marjānī, Shihāb al-Dīn. *Nāẓūrat al-ḥaqq fī farḍiyyat al-ʿishāʾ wa-in lam yaghib al-shafaq*. Kazan: n.p., 1870.

al-Marjānī, Shihāb al-Dīn. *Risālat Tanbīh abnāʾ al-ʿaṣr ʿalā tanzīh anbāʾ Abī Naṣr*. Published in Michael Kemper. "Sihabaddin al-Margani über Abu n-Nasr al-Qursawis Konflikt mit den Gelehrten bucharas." *Muslim Culture in Russia and Central Asia. Vol. 3: Arabic, Persian and Turkic Manuscripts (15th–19th Centuries)*. Eds. Anke von Kügelgen, Aširbek Muminov, and Michael Kemper. Berlin: Klaus Schwarz Verlag, 2000. 353–383. [Cited as Marjānī, *Tanbīh*.]

Martin, Virginia. *Law and Custom in the Steppe: The Kazakhs of the Middle Horde and Russian Colonialism in the Nineteenth Century*. Richmond: Curzon, 2001.

Materialy po istorii Bashkirskoi ASSR. 5 vols. Moscow/Leningrad: izd-vo Akademii Nauk SSSR, 1936–1960.

Mayer, Toby. "Theology and Sufism." *The Cambridge Companion to Classical Islamic Theology*. Ed. Timothy Winter. Cambridge: Cambridge UP, 2008. 258–287.

McChesney, Robert. "Islamic Culture and the Chinggisid Restoration: Central Asia in the Sixteenth and Seventeenth Centuries." *New Cambridge History of Islam. Vol. 3: The Eastern Islamic World Eleventh to Eighteenth Centuries*. Eds. David Morgan and Anthony Reid. Cambridge: Cambridge UP, 2010. 239–265.

Messick, Brinkley. *The Calligraphic State: Textual Domination and History in a Muslim Society*. Berkeley: U of California P, 1993.

Messick, Brinkley. "Media Muftis: Radio Fatwas in Yemen." *Islamic Legal Interpretation: Muftis and Their Fatwas*. Eds. Muhammad Khalid Masud, Brinkley Messick, and David Powers. Cambridge, MA: Harvard UP, 1996. 310–322.

Meyendorff, John. "Russian Bishops and Church Reform in 1905." *Catholicity and the Church*. Crestwood, NY: St. Vladimir's Seminary P, 1983. 143–156.

Meyer, James. "Speaking Sharia to the State: Muslim Protesters, Tsarist Officials, and the Islamic Discourses of Late Imperial Russia." *Kritika*, vol. 14, no. 3; 2013. 485–505.

Meyer, James. *Turks Across Empires: Marketing Muslim Identity in the Russian-Ottoman Borderlands, 1856–1914*. New York: Oxford UP, 2014.

Mitchell, Timothy. *Colonising Egypt*. 2nd ed. Berkeley: U of California P, 1991.

Moaddel, Mansoor. *Islamic Modernism, Nationalism, and Fundamentalism: Episode and Discourse*. Chicago: U of Chicago P, 2005.

Morris, James. "Ibn ʿArabi and His Interpreters Part II: Influences and Interpretations." *Journal of the American Oriental Society*, vol. 106, no. 4; 1986. 733–756.

Morris, James. "Ibn ʿArabi and His Interpreters Part II (Conclusion): Influences and Interpretations." *Journal of the American Oriental Society*, vol. 107, no. 1; 1987. 101–119.

Khwāja Muḥammad Maʿṣūm. *Maktūbāt*. 3 vols. Karachi: Asrār Muḥammad Khān, 1977.

Mustafa, Abdul-Rahman. *On Taqlid: Ibn al Qayyim's Critique of Authority in Islamic Law*. Oxford: Oxford UP, 2013.

Nafi, Basheer M. "Tasawwuf and Reform in Pre-Modern Islamic Culture: In Search of Ibrahim al-Kurani." *Die Welt des Islams*, vol. 42, no. 3; 2002. 307–355.

Nafi, Basheer M. "A Teacher of ibn ʿAbd al-Wahhab: Muhammad Hayat al-Sindi and the Revival of *Ashab al-Hadith*'s Methodology." *Islamic Law and Society*, vol. 13, no. 2; 2006. 208–241.

Naganawa, Norihiro. "Holidays in Kazan: The Public Sphere and the Politics of Religious Authority Among Tatars in 1914." *Slavic Review*, vol. 71, no. 1; 2012. 25–48.

Naganawa, Norihiro. "Maktab or School? Introduction of Universal Primary Education Among the Volga-Ural Muslims." *Empire, Islam, and Politics in Central Eurasia*. Ed. Tomohiko Uyama. Sapporo: Slavic Research Center, 2007. 65–98.

Noack, Christian. "Les musulmans de la region Volga-Oural au XIXe siècle. L'arrière-plan économique, social et culturel du mouvement d'émancipation." *L'Islam de Russie: conscience communautaire et autonomie politique chez les Tatars de la Volga et de l'Oural depuis le XVIIIe siècle*. Eds. Stéphane Dudoignon, Damir Is'haqov, and Rafyq Mohammatshin. Paris: Maisonneuve et Larose, 1997. 89–114.

Noack, Christian. "Retrospectively Revolting: Kazan Tatar 'Conspiracies' During the 1905 Revolution." *The Russian Revolution of 1905: Centenary Perspectives*. Eds. Jon Smele and Anthony Heywood. New York: Taylor & Francis, 2005. 119–136.

Noack, Christian. "State Policy and Its Impact on the Formation of a Muslim Identity in the Volga-Urals." *Islam in Politics in Russia and Central Asia (Early Eighteenth to Late Twentieth Centuries)*. Eds. Stéphane Dudoignon and Hisao Komatsu. London: Kegan Paul, 2001. 3–26.

O'Fahey, R. S. *Enigmatic Saint: Ahmad ibn Idris and the Idrisi Tradition*. Evanston, IL: Northwestern UP, 1990.

O'Fahey, R. S. "Pietism, Fundamentalism and Mysticism: An Alternative View of the 18th and 19th Century Islamic World." *Festskrift til Historisk Institutts 40-ars jubileum 1997*. Ed. Geir Atle Ersland. Bergen: Historik institutt, Universitetet i Bergen, 1997. 151–166.

O'Fahey, R. S., and Bernd Radtke. "Neo-Sufism Reconsidered." *Der Islam*, vol. 70; 1993. 52–87.

Ostrowski, Donald. "The Military Land Grant along the Muslim-Christian Frontier." *Russian History*, vol. 19, no. 1–4; 1992. 327–359.

Peters, Rudolph. "Ijtihad and Taqlid in 18th and 19th Century Islam." *Die Welt des Islams*, vol. 20, no. 3–4; 1980. 131–145.

Peters, Rudolph. "Reinhard Schulze's Quest for an Islamic Enlightenment." *Die Welt des Islams*, vol. 30, no. 1; 1990. 160–162.

Polnoe sobranie zakonov Rossiiskoi Imperii. Series 1. 40 vols. St. Petersburg: Gosudarstvennaia tipografiia, 1830. [Cited as *PSZ.*]

Pourjavady, Reza. *Philosophy in Early Safavid Iran: Najm al-Din Mahmud al-Nayrizi and his Writings.* Leiden: Brill, 2011.

al-Quhistānī, Shams al-Dīn Muḥammad. *Jāmiʿ al-rumūz.* Intro. Qāḍīzāda Sharīf Makhdūm. Kazan: Maṭbaʿat Kūkūbīn 1299 [1882].

Radtke, Bernd. "Ijtihad and Neo-Sufism." *Asiatische Studien: Zeitschrift der Schweizerischen Gesellschaft für Asienkunde*, vol. 48, no. 3–4; 1994. 909–921.

Rahman, Fazlur. *Islam.* 2nd ed. Chicago: U of Chicago P, 2002.

Ramzī, Muḥammad Murād. *Talfīq al-akhbār wa-talqīḥ al-āthār fī waqāʾiʿ Qazān wa-Bulghār wa-mulūk al-Tatār.* 2 vols. 1908. Ed. Ibrāhīm Shams al-Dīn. Beirut: Dār al-kutub al-ʿilmiyya, 2002.

Reichmuth, Stefan. "Arabic Literature and Islamic Scholarship in the 17th/18th Century: Topics and Biographies: Introduction." *Die Welt des Islams*, vol. 42, no. 3; 2002. 281–288.

Reinhart, Kevin A. "'Like the Difference Between Heaven and Earth': Hanafi and Shafiʿi Discussions of *Wajib* and *Fard*." *Studies in Islamic Law and Society*. Ed. Bernard Weiss. Leiden: Brill, 2002. 205–234.

Renard, John. "Introduction." *Knowledge of God in Classical Sufism: Foundations of Islamic Mystical Theology.* New York: Paulist Press, 2004. 11–64.

Rieber, Alfred. "The Problem of Social Cohesion." *Kritika*, vol. 7, no. 3; 2006. 599–608.

Romaniello, Matthew. *The Elusive Empire: Kazan and the Creation of Russia, 1552–1671.* Madison, WI: U of Wisconsin P, 2012.

Rorlich, Azade-Ayşe. *The Volga Tatars: A Profile in National Resilience.* Stanford: Hoover Institution Press, 1986.

Ross, Danielle. "Caught in the Middle: Reform and Youth Rebellion in Russia's Madrasas, 1900–10." *Kritika*, vol. 16, no. 1; 2015. 57–89.

Roy, Olivier. "Les Nouveaux intellectuels en monde musulman." *Esprit*, vol. 142; 1988. 58–68.

Rudolph, Ulrich. *Al-Maturidi and the Development of Sunni Theology in Samarqand.* Leiden: Brill, 2012.

Saʿdī, ʿAbdraḥmān [*sic*]. *Tātār adabiyātī tārīkhī.* Kazan: Tātārstān dawlat nashriyātī bāsmāsī, 1926.

Safiullina, R. R. *Arabskaia kniga v dukhovnoi zhizni tatarskogo naroda.* Kazan: izd-vo Alma-Lit, 2003.

Salikhov, R. "Tatarskii traditsionalizm i problema sokhraneniia mnogovekovykh religioznykh ustoev." *Islam v srednem povolzh'e: istoriia i sovremennost'.* Ed. R. M. Mukhametshin. Kazan: Master Lain, 2001. 136–148.

al-Sālimī, Abū Shukūr. *Tamhīd*. Delhi: al-Maṭbaʿ al-Fārūqī, 1309 [1892].

al-Sanūsī, Muḥammad b. ʿAlī. *ʿIqāẓ al-wasnān fī al-ʿamal bi-l-ḥadīth wa-l-Qurʾān*. In *al-Majmūʿa al-mukhtāra*. Ed. M. A. ibn Ghalbūn. Manchester: n.p., 1990.

al-Sanūsī, Muḥammad b. ʿAlī. *al-Masāʾil al-ʿashr al-musammā bughyat al-maqāṣid fī khulāṣat al-marāṣid*. In *al-Majmūʿa al-mukhtāra*. Ed. M. A. ibn Ghalbūn. Manchester: n.p., 1990.

al-Sanūsī, Muḥammad b. Yūsuf. *ʿUmdat ahl al-tawfīq wa-l-tasdīd fī sharḥ ʿaqīdat ahl al-tawḥīd*. Cairo: Maṭbaʿat jarīdat al-Islam, 1316 [1898]. [Cited as *Sharḥ al-kubrā*.]

Schimmelpenninck van der Oye, David. "Know Thine Enemy: The Travails of the Kazan School of Russian Missionary Orientology." *Religion and Identity in Russia and the Soviet Union: A Festschrift for Paul Bushkovitch*. Eds. Nikolaos Chrissidis, Cathy Potter, David Schimmelpenninck van der Oye, and Jennifer Spock. Bloomington, IN: Slavica, 2010. 145–164.

Schimmelpenninck van der Oye, David. "Mirza Kazem-Bek and the Kazan School of Russian Orientology." *Comparative Studies of South Asia, Africa and the Middle East*, vol. 28, no. 3; 2008. 443–458.

Schulze, Reinhard. "Das Islamische 18. Jahrhundert. Versuch einer historiographischen Kritik." *Die Welt des Islams*, vol. 30, no. 1; 1990. 140–159.

Schulze, Reinhard. "Was ist die islamische Aufklärung?." *Die Welt des Islams*, vol. 36, no. 3; 1996. 276–325.

Shāh Walī Allāh Aḥmad b. ʿAbd al-Raḥīm al-Fārūqī al-Dihlawī. *al-Inṣāf fī bayān asbāb al-ikhtilāf*. Beirut: Dār al-nafāʾis, 1397/1977.

Shāh Walī Allāh Aḥmad b. ʿAbd al-Raḥīm al-Fārūqī al-Dihlawī. *ʿIqd al-jīd fī aḥkām al-ijtihād wa-l-taqlīd*. Ed. Muḥammad ʿAlī al-Ḥalabī al-Atharī. Sharjah: Dār al-fatḥ, 1415/1995.

Al-Shahrastani, Muhammad. *Book of Religious and Philosophical Sects*. Ed. William Cureton. London: Society for the Publication of Oriental Texts, 1846.

Sharaf, Shahr. "Marjānīniñ tarjima-i ḥālī." *Marjānī*. Ed. Ṣāliḥ b. Thābit ʿUbaydullīn. Kazan: Maʿārif, 1333 [1915]. 2–193.

al-Shawkānī, Muḥammad b. ʿAlī. *al-Badr al-ṭāliʿ bi-maḥāsin man baʿd al-qarn al-sābiʿ*. 2 vols. Cairo: Dār al-kitāb al-islāmī, n.d.

al-Shawkānī, Muḥammad b. ʿAlī. *al-Qawl al-mufīd fī adallat al-ijtihād wa-l-taqlīd*. Cairo/Beirut: Dār al-kutub al-miṣrī/Dār al-kutub al-lubnānī, 1411/1991.

Sherif, Mohamed. *Ghazali's Theory of Virtue*. Albany: State U of New York P, 1975.

Shorish, M. Mobin. "Traditional Islamic Education in Central Asia prior to 1917." *Passé Turco-Tatar, Présent Soviétique: etudes offertes à Alexandre Bennigsen*. Eds. Ch. Lemercier-Quelquejay, G. Veinstein, and S. E. Wimbush. Paris: Editions Peeters, 1986. 317–344.

Sirhindī, Aḥmad. *Maktūbāt-i imām-i rabbānī ḥaḍrat mujaddid-i alf-i thānī*. 3 vols. Ed. Nūr Aḥmad Amritsarī. Istanbul: Ishīq, 1397/1977. Reprint (with altered pagination) of 1392/1972 Karachi edition by H. M. Saʿīd Kampanī.

Spannaus, Nathan. "The Decline of the *Akhund* and the Transformation of Islamic Law Under the Russian Empire." *Islamic Law and Society*, vol. 20, no. 3; 2013. 202–241.

Spannaus, Nathan. "Formalism, Puritanicalism, Traditionalism: Approaches to Islamic Legal Reasoning in the 19th-Century Russian Empire." *Muslim World*, vol. 104, no. 3; 2014. 354–378.

Spannaus, Nathan. "Islamic Thought and Revivalism in the Russian Empire: An Intellectual Biography of Abu Nasr Qursawi (1776–1812)." Diss. McGill University, 2012.

Spannaus, Nathan. "Šihab al-Din al-Marǧani on the Divine Attributes: A Study in *Kalam* in the 19th Century." *Arabica*, vol. 62, no. 1; 2015. 74–98.

Spannaus, Nathan. "Theology in Central Asia." *Oxford Handbook of Islamic Theology*. Ed. Sabine Schmidtke. Oxford: Oxford UP, 2016. 587–605.

Spannaus, Nathan. "The Ur-Text of Jadidism: Abu Nasr Qursawi's *Irshad* and the Historiography of Muslim Modernism in Russia." *Journal of the Economic and Social History of the Orient*, vol. 59; 2016. 93–125.

Steinwedel, Charles. "The 1905 Revolution in Ufa: Mass Politics, Elections, and Nationality." *Russian Review*, vol. 59, no. 4; 2000. 555–576.

al-Taftāzānī, Saʿd al-Dīn. *Sharḥ al-ʿaqāʾid al-nasafiyya*. Ed. Aḥmad Ḥijāzī al-Saqqā. Cairo: Maktabat al-Kulliyyāt al-azhariyya, 1407/1988.

[Pseudo-]Taftāzānī. *Risāla fī waḥdat al-wujūd*. In *Majmūʿa rasāʾil fī waḥdat al-wujūd*. [Istanbul]: n.p., 1294 [1877]. 2–50.

Tahir, Mahmud. "Rizaeddin Fahreddin." *Central Asian Survey*, vol. 8, no. 1; 1989. 111–115.

Taylor, Charles. *Modern Social Imaginaries*. Durham, NC: Duke UP, 2004.

Taylor, Charles. *A Secular Age*. Cambridge, MA: Harvard UP, 2007.

ter Haar, J. G. J. *Follower and Heir of the Prophet: Shaykh Ahmad Sirhindi (1564–1624) as Mystic*. Leiden: Het Oosters Instituut, 1992.

ter Haar, J. G. J. "The Importance of the Spiritual Guide in the Naqshbandi Order." *The Heritage of Sufism*, Vol. II: *The Legacy of Medieval Persian Sufism (1150–1500)*. Ed. Leonard Lewisohn. Oxford: Oneworld, 1999. 311–322.

Tillett, Lowell. *The Great Friendship: Soviet Historians on the Non-Russian Nationalities*. Chapel Hill, NC: U of North Carolina P, 1969.

Tonaga, Yasushi. "The School of Ibn Arabi in Mashriq and Turkey with Special Reference to Abd al-Karim al-Jili." *III. Uluslar Arasi Mevlana Kongresi, 5–6 Mayis 2003: Bildirler*. Ed. Nuri Şimşekler. Konya: Selcuk Universitesi Matbaasi, 2004. 315–330.

Tuna, Mustafa. "Gaspirali v. Il'minskii: Two Identity Projects for the Muslims of the Russian Empire." *Nationalities Papers*, vol. 30, no. 2; 2002. 265–289.

Tuna, Mustafa. "Imperial Russia's Muslims: Inroads of Modernity." Diss. Princeton University, 2009.

Tuna, Mustafa. *Imperial Russia's Muslims: Islam, Empire, and European Modernity, 1788–1914*. Cambridge: Cambridge UP, 2015.

Tuna, Mustafa. "Madrasa Reform as a Secularizing Process: A View from the Late Russian Empire." *Comparative Studies in Society and History*, vol. 53, no. 3; 2011. 540–570.

Türkyılmaz, Selçuk. "Usul-i Cedid Türkçe Öğretim Kitapları ve İsmail Gaspıralı." *Modern Türklük Araştırmaları Dergisi*, vol. 11, no. 4; 2014. 47–78.

Usmanov, Mirkasym. "Avtografy Mardzhani na poliakh podlinnika proekta Khusaina Faizkhanova o shkol'noi reforme." *Mardzhani: uchenyi, myslitel', prosvetitel'*. Ed. Ia. G. Abdullin. Kazan: Tatarskoe knizhnoe izd-vo, 1990. 119–128.

Usmanov, Mirkasym. "Istochniki knigi Sh. Mardzhani 'Mustafad al-akhbar fi akhval Kazan va Bulgar.'" *Ocherki istorii povolzh'ia i priural'ia*, no. 2–3; 1969. 144–154.

Usmanov, Mirkasym. "The Struggle for the Reestablishment of Oriental Studies in Twentieth-Century Kazan." *The Heritage of Soviet Oriental Studies*. Eds. Michael Kemper and Stephan Conermann. New York: Routledge, 2011. 169–202.

Usmanova, Dilara. "Die tatarische Presse 1905–1918: Quellen, Entwicklungsetappen und quantitative Analyse." *Muslim Culture in Russia and Central Asia*. Eds. Michael Kemper, Anke von Kügelgen, and Dmitriy Yermakov. Berlin: Klaus Schwarz Verlag, 1996. 239–278.

Usmanova, D. M., and N. V. Gil'mutdinov. "Iz opyta izdaniia spetsializirovannogo iuridicheskogo zhurnala v Kazani: <Khokuk va khaiat>." *Nauchnyi Tatarstan*, no. 1; 2009. 100–105.

[Ūtiz-Īmānī], ʿAbd al-Raḥīm b. ʿUthmān al-Bulghārī. *Jawāhir al-bayān*. Ms. Institut iazyka literatury i istorii Akademii nauka Respublika Tatarstan (IIaLI RT), fond 39, no. 2982. Fols. 23–87. Facsimile printed in G. Utyz-Imiani al-Bulgari. *Izbrannoe*. Ed. R. Adygamov. Kazan: Tatarstan knizhnoe izd-vo, 2007.

[Ūtiz-Īmānī], ʿAbd al-Raḥīm b. ʿUthmān al-Bulghārī. *Risāla-i Dibāghāt*. Ms. IIaLI RT, fond 39, no. 46. Facsimile printed in G. Utyz-Imiani al-Bulgari. *Izbrannoe*. Ed. R. Adygamov. Kazan: Tatarstan knizhnoe izd-vo, 2007.

[Ūtiz-Īmānī], ʿAbd al-Raḥīm b. ʿUthmān al-Bulghārī. *Risāla-i Irshādiyya*. Kazan: èlektro-tipografiia Ürnäk, 1910. Reprinted in G. Utyz-Imiani al-Bulgari. *Izbrannoe*. Ed. R. Adygamov. Kazan: Tatarstan knizhnoe izd-vo, 2007.

[Ūtiz-Īmānī, ʿAbd al-Raḥīm b. ʿUthmān al-Bulghārī.] G. Utyz-Imiani al-Bulgari. "Spasenie pogibaiushchikh." *Izbrannoe*. Ed. and trans. R. Adygamov. Kazan: Tatarstan knizhnoe izd-vo, 2007. 132–165.

Validov, Dzhamaliutdin. *Ocherk istorii obrazovannosti i literatury Tatar*. 1923. Oxford: Society for Central Asian Studies, 1986.

Vikor, Knut. *Sufi and Scholar on the Desert Edge: Muhammad b. ʿAli al-Sanusi and His Brotherhood*. London: Hurst, 1995.

Voll, John O. "ʿAbdallah ibn Salim al-Basri and 18th Century Hadith Scholarship." *Die Welt des Islams*, vol. 42, no. 3; 2002. 356–372.

Voll, John O. "Hadith Scholars and Tariqahs: An Ulama Group in the 18th Century Haramayn and Their Impact in the Islamic World." *Journal of Asian and African Studies*, vol. 15, no. 3–4; 1980. 264–273.

Voll, John O. *Islam: Continuity and Change in the Modern World*. Boulder, CO: Westview Press, 1982.

Voll, John O. "Muhammad Hayya al-Sindi and Muhammad ibn ʿAbd al-Wahhab: An Analysis of an Intellectual Group in Eighteenth-Century Madina." *Bulletin of the School of Oriental and African Studies, University of London*, vol. 38, no. 1; 1975. 32–39.

Voll, John O. "Neo-Sufism: Reconsidered Again." *Canadian Journal of African Studies*, vol. 42, no. 2–3; 2008. 314–330.

Voll, John O. "Renewal and Reform in Islamic History: Tajdid and Islah." *Voices of Resurgent Islam*. Ed. John L. Esposito. New York: Oxford UP, 1983. 32–47.

von Kügelgen, Anke. "Die Entfaltung der Naqsbandiya Mugaddidiya im mittleren Transoxanien vom 18. bis zum Beginn des 19. Jahrhunderts: Ein Stück Detektivarbeit." *Muslim Culture in Russia and Central Asia from the 18th to the Early 20th Centuries. Vol. 2: Inter-Regional and Inter-Ethnic Relations*. Eds. Anke von Kügelgen, Michael Kemper, and Allen J. Frank. Berlin: Klaus Schwarz Verlag, 1998. 101–151.

von Kügelgen, Anke. *Die Legitimierung der mittelasiatischen Mangitendynastie in den Werken ihrer Historiker (18.–19. Jahrhundert)*. Istanbul: Ergon Verlag Würzburg, 2002.

Weickhardt, George. "Modernization of Law in Seventeenth-Century Muscovy." *Modernizing Muscovy: Reform and Social Change in Seventeenth-Century Russia*. Eds. Jarmo Kotillaine and Marshall Poe. London: Routledge, 2004. 76–92.

Weismann, Itzchak. *The Naqshbandiyya: Orthodoxy and activism in a worldwide Sufi tradition*. New York: Routledge, 2007.

Weiss, Bernard. "Interpretation in Islamic Law: The Theory of Ijtihad." *American Journal of Comparative Law*, vol. 26, no. 2; 1978. 199–212.

Weiss, Bernard. "The Madhhab in Islamic Legal Theory." *The Islamic School of Law: Evolution, Devolution, and Progress*. Eds. Peri Bearman, Rudolph Peters, and Frank Vogel. Cambridge: Harvard UP, 2005. 1–9.

Weiss, Bernard. "The Primacy of Revelation in Classical Islamic Legal Theory as Expounded by Sayf al-Din al-Amidi." *Studia Islamica*, no. 59; 1984. 79–109.

Wennberg, Franz. *On the Edge: The Concept of Progress in Bukhara During the Rule of the Later Manghits*. Uppsala: Acta Universitatis Upsaliensis, 2013.

Wensinck, A. J. *The Muslim Creed: Its Genesis and Historical Development*. London: Frank Cass & Co., 1965.

Werth, Paul. *At the Margins of Orthodoxy: Mission, Governance, and Confessional Politics in Russia's Volga-Kama Region, 1827–1905*. Ithaca, NY: Cornell UP, 2002.

Werth, Paul. "Coercion and Conversion: Violence and the Mass Baptism of the Volga Peoples, 1740–1755." *Kritika*, vol. 4, no. 3; 2003. 543–569.

Werth, Paul. "Empire, Religious Freedom, and the Legal Regulation of 'Mixed' Marriages in Russia." *Journal of Modern History*, vol. 80; 2008. 296–331.

Werth, Paul. "In the State's Embrace: Civil Acts in an Imperial Order." *Kritika*, vol. 7, no. 3; 2006. 433–458.

Werth, Paul. "*Soslovie* and the 'Foreign' Clergies of Imperial Russia: Estate Rights or Service Rights?" *Cahiers du monde russe*, vol. 51, no. 2–3; 2010. 419–440.

Werth, Paul. *The Tsar's Foreign Faiths: Toleration and the Fate of Religious Freedom in Imperial Russia*. Oxford: Oxford UP, 2014.

Wiederhold, Lutz. "Legal Doctrines in Conflict: The Relevance of Madhhab Boundaries to Legal Reasoning in the Light of an Unpublished Treatise on Taqlid and Ijtihad." *Islamic Law and Society*, vol. 3, no. 2; 1996. 234–304.

Wisnovsky, Robert. "Avicenna and the Avicennian Tradition." *The Cambridge Companion to Arabic Philosophy*. Eds. Peter Adamson and Richard C. Taylor. New York: Cambridge UP, 2005. 92–136.

Wisnovsky, Robert. *Avicenna's Metaphysics in Context*. Ithaca, NY: Cornell UP, 2003.

Wisnovsky, Robert. "Avicennism and Exegetical Practice in the Early Commentaries on the *Isharat*." *Oriens*, vol. 41, no. 3–4; 2013. 349–378.

Wisnovsky, Robert. "Essence and Existence in the Eleventh- and Twelfth-Century Islamic East (*Mašriq*): A Sketch." *The Arabic, Hebrew and Latin Reception of Avicenna's Metaphysics*. Eds. A. Bertolacci and D. Hasse. Berlin: de Gruyter, 2011. 27–50.

Wisnovsky, Robert. "One Aspect of the Avicennian Turn in Sunni Theology." *Arabic Sciences and Philosophy*, vol. 14; 2004. 65–100.

Wisnovsky, Robert. "Towards a Genealogy of Avicennism." *Oriens*, vol. 42, no. 4; 2014. 323–363.

Wolfson, Harry Austryn. *The Philosophy of the Kalam*. Cambridge, MA: Harvard UP, 1976.

Zagidullin, Ildus Kotdusovich. "Mahkama-i Shargyya Yrynburgyya (the Orenburg Muslim Spiritual Assembly): The Reformation Centre of the Muslim Society in the Late 19th Century." *Tatarica*, vol. 3; 2014. 122–139.

Zaitsev, Il'ia. "Murad Ramzi i Arminii Vamberi." *Gasırlar awazı/Ekho vekov*, no. 3–4; 2001. n.p.

Zakiev, M. Z. "Vliianie kazanskogo universiteta na razvitie tiurkologii v pervoi polovine XIX veka (do 1855 g.)." *Voprosy tatarskogo iazykoznaniia*. Ed. M. Z. Zakiev. Kazan: izd-vo kazanskogo universiteta, 1965. 357–393.

Zaman, Muhammad Qasim. *Modern Islamic Thought in a Radical Age: Religious Authority and Internal Criticism*. Cambridge: Cambridge UP, 2012.

Zaman, Muhammad Qasim. "Transmitters of Authority and Ideas Across Cultural Boundaries, Eleventh to Eighteenth Centuries." *New Cambridge History of Islam. Vol. 4: Islamic Cultures and Societies to the End of the Eighteenth Century*. Ed. Robert Irwin. Cambridge: Cambridge UP, 2010. 582–610.

Zaman, Muhammad Qasim. *The Ulama in Contemporary Islam: Custodians of Change.* Princeton, NJ: Princeton UP, 2002.

Zarcone, Thierry. "Philosophie et théologie chez les djadids: la question du raisonnement independent (igtihad)." *Cahiers du monde russe*, vol. 37; 1996. 53–64.

Zenkovsky, Serge A. *Pan-Turkism and Islam in Russia.* Cambridge: Harvard UP, 1960.

Ziai, Hossein. "Recent Trends in Arabic and Persian Philosophy." *The Cambridge Companion to Arabic Philosophy.* Eds. Peter Adamson and Richard C. Taylor. Cambridge: Cambridge UP, 2005. 405–425.

al-Ziriklī, Khayr al-Dīn. *al-Aʿlām: qāmūs tarājim li-ashhar al-rijāl wa-l-nisāʾ min al-ʿarab wa-l-mustaʿribīn bayn al-mustashriqīn.* 8 vols. Beirut: Dār al-ʿilm li-l-milāyīn, 1980.

Zysow, Aron. "The Economy of Certainty: An Introduction to the Typology of Islamic Legal Theory." Diss. Harvard University, 1984.

Zysow, Aron. "Mu'tazilism and Maturidism in Hanafi Legal Theory." *Studies in Islamic Legal Theory.* Ed. Bernard Weiss. Leiden: Brill, 2002. 235–266.

Index

Abū Ḥanīfa, 106–7, 109, 117–18, 121, 129, 132, 155–56, 192–93, 198, 213, 272, 286

Akchurin, Iusuf, 255n.72, 267–68, 274–75. *See also* merchants

ākhūnds. See *ʿulamāʾ*

ʿAlī Qārī Harawī, 165n.115, 166n.123, 182, 192–93, 209–10

Amīrkhān, Ḥusayn, 32–33, 46, 51–52

ʿaql (reason), 57, 95–96, 100–2, 165, 167–70, 173–74, 193n.71, 194–96, 200, 211–12, 286n.198, 289

Āqyigit, Mūsā, 252–53

Asad, Talal, 16–20, 34n.21, 81, 225, 229, 233–35, 254n.71, 286n.197

Ashʿaris/Ashʿarism, 154–55, 158, 160n.84, 166, 176–77, 184n.39, 195–96

Āshiṭī, Muḥammad Raḥīm, 48–49, 51–52, 57–58, 59n.154, 166n.123, 208–9

Astrakhan, 43, 65–66

ʿAṭāʾ Allāh Bukhārī, 56–58, 64, 72, 87, 101n.51, 183n.38, 193n.71

attributes of God, 61–62, 64, 68, 85, 87–89, 145–47, 158, 170–71, 173, 179–87, 193–202, 214–15, 234, 296–98

ʿayniyya, 146, 158–59, 170–73, 182, 184–85, 196–97

contingency, 61n.170, 147–49, 153–54, 159, 171–73, 181–82, 184, 186–88, 190–91, 193–95, 197–200, 204

differentiation, 61n.170, 148, 153–54, 157, 161–62, 169–71, 186–87, 191–92, 194–95, 198

ghayriyya, 146, 148, 153–55, 158–62, 170–71, 182–83, 196–97

multiplicity, 61n.170, 148, 153–58, 160–62, 169–71, 186–89, 192–95, 197–200, 204

Muʿtazilite position, 63n.178, 152–53, 155, 170–73, 181, 184–85, 189n.61, 196–97

necessity, 147–51, 153, 169–71, 173, 181–82, 184, 189–91, 193–95, 198–99, 204

superaddition, 61n.170, 148, 153–54, 157–58, 161, 170–71, 183, 187–88, 193–95, 199

authority, religious, 3, 18–19, 23–24, 34, 35–37, 68–69, 77–85, 89, 91–93, 97–99, 104–5, 108, 135–39, 141–43, 201, 204–6, 214–27, 229–31, 234–36, 277–79, 279, 287, 292. *See also* *ʿulamāʾ*

fragmentation, 238, 261–71, 273, 284–85, 289–90, 297

Avicenna (ibn Sīnā), 147–48, 164n.106, 166, 177, 178n.12

Avicennian modalities. *See* metaphysics

Bārūdī, ʿĀlimjān, 275–76, 280, 291
Beck, Ulrich, 224n.13, 227–28
Bigiev, Musa, 252–53, 277–80, 282–83, 286
Bigiev, Zagir, 252–53, 259–60, 277–78
Bukhara, 1–2, 31, 52–53, 72, 87–89, 120. *See also* Qūrṣāwī, Abū Nasr: condemnation
  ʿulamāʾ, 31–32, 54–58, 62, 65–69, 85–86, 145, 193n.71, 198, 216–17, 225, 295–96

Cairo, 8, 51n.104, 86, 207n.22, 243, 255n.72, 277–78
Catherine II (the Great), 44–50, 78–79, 89, 219, 239, 264
commentary (*sharḥ*), 96–99, 101, 199, 202–3, 277–78
consensus (*ijmāʿ*), 91, 95–96, 108–9, 115, 119, 121–24, 132, 141, 154–55, 167n.126, 168, 173–74, 195, 201–2, 213, 271, 277, 289–90
contingency. *See* metaphysics
Crews, Robert, 83–84, 229, 262–63
Crimea, 45n.70, 48, 77n.258, 78, 241, 250, 253–55, 256n.77

Dagestan, 48, 63, 208–9
"Dāghistānī, Afandī," 66–67, 145n.4, 161–62, 171–73, 192–94, 196–97, 199n.93
Dallal, Ahmad, 10–12, 214
Dawānī, Jalāl al-Dīn, 87–88, 101, 178–79, 183n.38, 184n.39, 194
Dīn wa-maʿīshat (journal), 259, 268–69, 272, 282–84
disembedding, 221, 227, 230, 233–35, 287
divine essence, 177–80, 183. *See also* attributes of God
  knowability of, 151, 164, 169–70, 172
  simplicity, 145–46, 151–52, 156–63, 170, 187
  transcendence (*tanzīh*), 61n.170, 145–46, 149, 151–53, 155–57, 162, 165, 169–74, 179–86, 191, 196–200
  uniqueness, 61n.170, 145–50, 152–58, 160–63, 170–73, 184–86, 195–200

education, 35, 37, 48–49, 59, 61–62, 77–78, 86–88, 166n.123, 215, 226, 238–39, 241–46, 248–49, 266, 272, 286. *See also* Bukhara: *ʿulamāʾ*
  European, 239–40, 242, 246, 252–53, 267, 275, 287, 295–97
  funding, 49–51, 266–68
  reform, 234–35, 238, 249–52, 261–62, 266–71, 273n.148, 275–77, 280, 282–85, 287, 293–94 (*see also* Jadidism)
  tsarist supervision, 242, 251n.62, 263–65, 269
Eisenstein, Elizabeth, 248–49
enlightenment, 3–4, 13, 22, 228, 232–33, 237–38, 274, 276, 292–93
epistemology, 23, 59–62, 67–68, 91–93, 95–96, 102, 107–12, 124–28, 132, 133–34, 141, 144–45, 167–69, 194–95, 201–2, 204, 297. *See also* legal theory

Faizkhanov, Khusain, 239–41, 251–53, 297
Fakhr al-Dīn, Riḍāʾ al-Dīn, 29–33, 209, 253, 262n.105, 276–78, 280, 285
Fakhr al-Dīn b. Ibrāhīm b. Khūjāsh, 57–58, 63, 183n.38, 193–94
Fatwā and *iftāʾ*, 36–37, 105, 123, 127–28, 136–37, 284, 285. *See also* Muftiate
Fayḍ Khān Kābulī, 54–55, 72
formalism. *See* legal theory

Gasprinskii, Ismail, 3–4, 241, 244n.28, 250, 253, 256, 258–59, 267–70, 273n.150, 274–76, 285, 288n.1

Ghazālī, Abū Ḥāmid, 59–61, 67–68, 99n.44, 135–36, 137n.110, 163
God. *See* attributes of God; divine essence

hadith, 10, 95, 115–16, 123–27, 130n.83, 131, 168, 205–10, 212–13. *See also* scripture
Hallaq, Wael, 34, 103–4, 228n.23, 230n.30
Hanafism, 21, 23–25, 37, 47–48, 67, 83–85, 105–7, 109, 118, 124, 127–29, 130–33, 135–36, 139–42, 163, 202–4, 209–11, 213, 248–49, 272
Hanbalism, 107n.73, 203–4, 207
Ḥaydar, amir of Bukhara, 56–58, 64–67, 87, 171, 193–94
Ḥusayniyya *madrasa*, 280

ibn ʿArabī, Muḥy al-Dīn, 97n.37, 175–85, 277–79, 286
ibn Idrīs, Aḥmad, 8–9, 205–6, 207n.21
ibn Kullāb, ʿAbd Allāh, 146–47, 154–55, 158, 173–74, 189n.61
ibn Taymiyya, Taqī al-Dīn, 277–79, 286
Ibrāhīm b. Khūjāsh, 48, 57–58, 74
ijtihād
  absolute, 114–18, 122, 128–29, 141, 293–94
  debates over, 85, 88–89, 130, 133, 234, 291
  as *fiqh* interpretation, 83–84, 94–95, 103–4, 107, 110–15, 127–28, 130–37, 144, 167–68, 197–98, 202, 204, 214–18, 229–30, 289–91, 293–94, 297–98
  gate of, 85, 128, 274, 286
  infallibilism, 119
  and Jadidism, 1, 271–72, 274, 276, 280–81, 290–91, 294–95
  and reformism, 10, 14, 24, 204–7, 208–10, 211–12, 231–32, 234–35, 295–96n.21
impossibility. *See* metaphysics
ʿInāyat Allāh Bukhārī, 56, 64, 101n.51, 167, 193n.74
India, 8–9, 53, 55–56, 61–62, 86n.292, 175–76, 216, 233n.38, 254–55, 276–78
individualism/individualization, 3, 134–35, 139, 217, 222–34, 236, 280–81, 285–86, 291
ʿishāʾ, 83–85, 88–89, 94, 96, 130, 132–33, 144–45, 201–2, 204, 297–98
Īshmuḥammad Dīnmuḥammad (Īshmī-Īshān), 259–60, 268–70, 282–84
Īshniyāz b. Shīrniyāz Khwārizmī, 47–48, 52, 86
Istanbul, 8, 29, 86, 243, 253–54, 277–78. *See also* Ottoman Empire
Ittifāq party, 258–59, 267, 270

Jadidism, 24, 26, 237–38, 256, 258–60, 273–84, 288–91, 294
  historiography of, 3, 15, 22, 237–38, 283–84, 292, 294–95
  uṣūl-i jadīd (new method), 241, 243–47, 254, 266, 268–71, 282 (*see also* education)
Jameson, Fredric, 232–35
Jāmī, ʿAbd al-Raḥmān, 176, 178n.13, 180–82, 184n.41, 185–86

Kalābādhī, Abū Bakr, 120, 157n.73, 163, 165n.115, 173–74, 191–93, 213
kalām, 1, 22, 24, 48–49, 61–62, 87–88, 93n.16, 99–101, 134, 175–79, 187–88, 193–94, 211–12, 214–15, 240–41, 249, 271, 277, 278n.175, 280, 289–90, 292–94, 296. *See also* attributes of God; divine essence; metaphysics
  Qūrṣāwī's critique, 56–59, 85, 102, 107, 109–10, 144–45, 160n.84, 165–68, 174, 193, 202, 217, 290

Kazakhs/Kazakh steppe, 4, 36, 47–48, 71–72, 78, 246n.34, 275
Kazan, 29, 30–31, 38–40, 41n.45, 43–44, 47–51, 62n.171, 65–66, 68, 74, 77n.257, 129, 225–26, 239–44, 246n.34, 250–54, 257n.82, 258n.87, 259n.100, 265, 267–68, 275–78
  conquest, 32–34, 37–40, 42–43, 207n.22
  mosques, 33, 43–45, 48, 50–52, 59n.153, 86–87
  publishing, 67n.206, 87, 247, 248n.40, 250n.53, 252–53, 255, 258–59
  university, 103n.59, 239–40, 242, 251–52, 255, 258–59, 275–76
Kemper, Michael, 5–7, 14, 22, 203, 208–9, 231–32, 236
Khal'fin, Ibragim, 239–40, 242, 249–50, 255
Khān-Kirmānī, ʿAbd al-Raḥmān, 54, 65–66, 68, 188, 192

language, 5–6, 8, 68, 87, 103n.59, 179–80, 239–42, 249–54, 255–56, 258–62, 269–70, 275–77, 291n.8, 294–95
law
  Islamic, 1, 21, 23–25, 34–37, 46–47, 102, 112–13, 140, 215–17, 272, 285 (*see also ijtihād*; legal theory; *madhhab; sharīʿa; taqlīd*)
  restriction of Islamic law, 46–47, 70, 79–83, 137–38, 220–24, 226, 227, 229
  Russian, 38–42, 75–78, 220–21, 228, 258–59, 277–78
legal theory (*uṣūl al-fiqh*), 48–49, 59, 93n.16, 95, 103–5, 112–13, 129, 131–32, 135–36, 167–68, 271–72
  formalism, 105–7, 118, 139–40, 142, 202–4, 207–8
  materialism, 107, 203–4, 206–7, 290n.7
  Qūrṣāwī on, 67, 109, 113–14, 116–19, 121–23, 135, 139, 217, 289–90, 294–95

Maʿarrī, Abū al-ʿAlāʾ, 277–79, 286
MacIntyre, Alasdair, 18–20, 35, 98n.40, 236n.46, 272n.147
madhhab, 10, 97–100, 102, 108–10, 116, 121, 133, 139, 202–3, 205–8, 212, 217, 271–72, 278–79, 286n.198, 289–90. See also *taqlīd*
  ranks of scholars, 106–7, 116–18, 128–29, 142, 202, 293–94
madrasa/maktab. *See* education
Mālik b. Anas, 10, 129n.77, 207n.19, 277–78, 286
Malikism, 206, 207n.21
Mangārī, Baymurād, 51–52, 87, 132–33, 173, 183n.38, 193–94, 209, 239–40
Marjānī, Shihāb al-Dīn, 2–4, 26–27, 29–33, 48n.90, 64n.189, 66–67, 87–89, 141, 161, 184n.39, 240–41, 292–95
Marxism, 4, 15, 233n.39, 275–76. *See also* Soviet academia
materialism. *See* legal theory
Maturidism, 21, 23–25, 145, 154, 195–96, 210–11, 213. *See also* Hanafism
merchants, Muslim, 45, 49–53, 76, 219, 233–34, 242, 247–48, 265–70, 272, 280n.183
metaphysics. *See also* attributes of God
  Avicennian modalities, 147–48, 176–79, 189–94, 202–4
  contingency (*imkān*), 147–48, 150–52, 173, 177–79, 189–90
  impossibility (*imtināʿ*), 147–48, 177–79, 181–82
  necessity (*wujūb*), 147–51, 154, 177–81, 189–91, 193–94
  taʿayyun (individuation), 177, 179–82, 187

wujūdī metaphysics, 175–80, 187–88, 191, 193–94, 199, 202–3
Moaddel, Mansoor, 19, 214n.42
modernity, 16, 22, 24, 26, 213, 232, 237–38, 284, 291–93
Moscow/Muscovy, 8, 38–41, 50–51, 241
Muftiate, 69, 70–71, 74–77, 79–81, 85–86, 136, 215–16, 225, 262–65, 270, 275–76, 283–85
Muḥammad Maʿṣūm, 54, 159n.83, 161, 183, 189, 209–10
Muḥammadiyya *madrasa*, 244, 275–76
Muḥammadjān b. Ḥusayn, Mufti, 54, 69n.214, 70–77, 79–81, 84–86, 93, 130, 193–94, 225, 234, 243. *See also* Muftiate
Mujaddidiyya. *See* Naqshbandiyya
Muscovy. *See* Moscow
Muʿtazila/Muʿtazilism, 120, 166, 173–74, 184–85, 195–96. *See also* attributes of God

naql, 57, 95–96, 100–2, 110, 119, 132, 144–45, 165–70, 173–74, 193n.71, 195–204
Naqshbandiyya, 25, 55–56, 83n.277, 210–11
  Mujaddidiyya, 23, 29, 47–48, 53–59, 65n.190, 72, 76–77, 86, 134, 187–88, 192, 195–96, 208–10 (*see also* Sirhindī, Aḥmad)
Nasafī, Najm al-Dīn, 61–62, 68, 101, 120, 125n.63, 146–47, 151n.27, 154–55, 191–93, 195, 213
Nasyri, Kaium, 240–41, 250–53, 297
nationalism, 4, 22, 237n.2, 256n.80, 258–59, 274–76, 297. *See also* Jadidism
necessity. *See* metaphysics
New method. *See* Jadidism

ontology. *See* metaphysics
Orenburg, 45n.70, 47, 71–73, 242, 246n.34, 255, 259, 280. *See also* Qarghālī
Orientalists/Orientalism, 36n.24, 103n.59, 230n.30, 239–41, 249–52, 255n.75, 256–57, 258n.87, 262, 285
Ottoman Empire, 6, 36n.25, 61–62, 134n.100, 175, 183n.38, 243, 248–49, 252n.64, 255, 267, 276, 295n.21

Peter I (the Great), 41–42, 219–20, 226n.17, 247n.37
postclassical period, 1, 2, 10, 21, 23, 24, 38–39, 88–89, 93–102, 116, 167–68, 175–80, 194, 199, 202–3, 212–13, 217–18, 235–36, 289, 291
prayer. See *ʿishāʾ*
printing, 238, 247–53, 261–62, 268, 272–73, 283–85, 291. *See also* Kazan: publishing
  censorship, 256–58

Qadimism, 237–38, 282, 284–86
Qarabāghī, Yūsuf, 57n.146, 178n.14, 183n.38
Qarghālī, 47–52, 54, 65–66, 68, 72, 265. *See also* Orenburg
Qudūqī, Muḥammad b. Mūsā, 208–10
Qūrṣā, 29, 32, 38n.32, 48, 51–52, 57n.142, 59–63, 65–67, 85–86, 178n.15
Qūrṣāwī, ʿAbd al-Khāliq, 30n.5, 51, 58–59, 86, 207n.22
Qūrṣāwī, Abū Naṣr
  condemnation, 1–2, 26, 31–32, 57–58, 62, 65–67, 85–86, 145, 157–58, 171–72, 192–93, 216–17, 225, 292, 296–98
  early life and family, 29, 51–52, 58n.152, 66–67, 86 (*see also* Qūrṣāwī, ʿAbd al-Khāliq)
  death, 29, 86
  education, 32, 48–49, 56–57, 58

Qūrṣāwī, Abū Naṣr (*cont.*)
followers and companions, 58–59, 86–89, 166n.123
historiographical portrayal, 3–8, 280–81, 292–93, 295–96, 298
Irshād, 6, 67–68, 108–9, 114, 122, 125, 127, 135, 138, 229–30, 291, 294–95
Lawāʾiḥ, 61–62
Mabāḥith, 67, 189–91
Naṣāʾiḥ, 67, 68n.212, 189
Sharḥ jadīd, 67, 138n.115, 166n.123, 184, 195
Sharḥ Manār, 67, 114n.12, 125, 127n.73, 135, 229–30
Sharḥ qadīm, 61–62, 187n.53
tafsīr, 68, 87, 294–95

Ramzī, Muḥammad Murād, 29–31, 33
ratusha, 49–50, 265
reason. See *ʿaql*
reformism, 2, 12, 25, 224, 276, 294–95, 298
eighteenth-century, 7–12, 25, 141, 204–11, 214–15
Hijaz network, 9–10, 12, 30, 207, 208–11
Revolution of 1905, 256n.80, 257–58, 261, 265, 267, 268n.132, 272–73, 288–89
Russian government, 2, 8–9, 45, 49–50, 219–20, 242, 264–65, 285
control of Islamic institutions, 21, 44–45, 68, 74, 82–83, 89, 110, 134–36, 141, 214, 219–23, 242, 262–65
relationship to Muslim subjects, 1–2, 15, 20–22, 24–26, 30, 32–34, 38–46, 71–77, 89, 134–35, 211, 214, 219–21, 223–24, 232, 237, 246–47, 256–57, 262–65, 268–69, 283–85
Russian Orthodox Church, 38, 41–42, 44–45, 78–79, 81, 219–20, 228–29
proselytization, 39–44, 251–52, 263, 269n.134

salaf, 59–60, 63, 91, 95, 213
Salafis/Salafism, 6, 25, 203–4, 213, 278–79. *See also* reformism
Sālimī, Abū Shukūr, 149n.19, 163, 173–74, 192–93, 213
Samarqand, 8, 66–67, 167n.126
Sanūsī, Muḥammad b. ʿAlī, 8–9, 14, 204, 211, 295n.21
Sanūsī, Muḥammad b. Yūsuf, 211–12
scripture, 3, 10, 57, 59, 60, 68, 91, 93, 102, 108–13, 115–17, 119–25, 127, 132, 141, 144–45, 154–55, 161–65, 191, 204–6, 213, 221–22, 229–30, 278–79, 280n.183, 289–90, 294–95. See also *naql*
secularity, 25, 227, 232–34, 236
Shāh Walī Allāh, 8–9, 11–12, 204–5, 207–9, 211, 212n.37
sharḥ. *See* commentary
sharīʿa, 34–39, 46n.75, 81, 89, 136–37, 214–17, 220–22, 224, 226–32, 262–63, 287. *See also* law
Shawkānī, Muḥammad b. ʿAlī, 9–11, 14, 204–9, 211, 213
Shirdānī family, 52, 58, 74, 86
Siberia, 43, 46–48, 84n.282, 258n.87
ṣifāt. *See* attributes of God
Sirhindī, Aḥmad, 54–56, 67–68, 134, 150n.25, 159, 161–63, 164n.106, 173–74, 178n.14, 179–87, 208
Soviet academia, 3–4, 6–7, 15, 276, 292–93
Spiritual Assembly, 29–30, 33, 45, 49, 68, 72–74, 78–81, 129–30, 134, 219–20, 241, 259, 263–67, 269, 270n.141, 285. *See also* Muftiate; *ʿulamāʾ*
impact, 79–83, 89, 136–38, 214–17, 225, 234–35, 262–63
St. Petersburg, 41, 50–51, 103n.59, 239–40, 247n.37, 250–51, 255, 257n.83, 270, 277–78
Sufism, 9–10, 13, 53, 89, 120, 134, 163, 175–76, 189, 208, 213, 249,

278–80, 285, 290, 295–96. *See also* Naqshbandiyya
Sultanov, Mufti Mukhamed'iar, 262, 283–84

taʿayyun. *See* metaphysics
Taftāzānī, Saʿd al-Dīn, 61–62, 97n.34, 101, 145–61, 169–74, 177n.11, 178–79, 181–82, 184–87, 189, 192–97, 204, 207n.22
taḥqīq (verification), 92, 94, 102, 107, 110–12, 114, 127–28, 132, 141, 168, 174, 195, 199–202, 204, 211–12, 214–15, 217–18, 229–30
tajdīd, 8–9, 13, 141, 204–6, 212–13. *See also* reformism
taqlīd, 3, 93, 97–102, 175, 293–94. *See also madhhab*; postclassical period
  defense of, 85, 128, 132, 216–17, 230–32, 234–36, 271–72, 291
  Qūrṣāwī on, 1, 93–95, 102, 108, 112, 114–18, 122, 124, 138, 141, 199, 201–4
  and reformism, 10, 204–9, 211–12, 274, 280–81, 286, 293
tarjīḥ, 104–5, 114, 121–22, 129, 138, 229–30, 293–94
Tarjumān (journal), 253, 256, 258–59, 268
tawḥīd. *See* divine essence
Taylor, Charles, 221–22, 227, 254n.71
Tevkelev, Mufti Salimgarei, 262, 264–65, 283n.190
theology. See *kalām*
tradition. See also *naql*
  concept, 16, 22–25, 233–34, 244
  rejection, 203, 236–38, 271–73, 276–82, 288–93, 295–97
  scholarly, 2–3, 18–19, 20–25, 34–36, 83, 89, 92, 94–102, 142, 145, 192, 202–4, 214–18, 235–36, 238–39, 244, 249–50, 261–62, 267, 269–71, 273, 282–83, 285–91, 294–98
Tuna, Mustafa, 15, 237n.2, 254n.71, 285
Tūntārī, Muḥammad Abū Naqīb. *See* Īshmuḥammad Dīnmuḥammad
Turkmānī, Niyāzqulī, 54–59, 62–67 , 209–10
Tursūn Bāqī, 63n.184, 64–66, 85–86, 171–72

Ufa, 69–71, 75, 246n.34
ʿulamāʾ, 32–37, 39, 44–56, 72–74, 82, 134–35, 137–39, 225–26, 244–49, 265–85, 287, 295–96. *See also* authority, religious; Bukhara: *ʿulamāʾ*; education; Spiritual Assembly
  ākhūnd (office), 69–81, 136–37, 215–16
  bureaucratization, 70–71, 74, 79–81, 85, 89, 92, 137–38, 142, 216, 229, 262–63
  imam (office), 30–31, 42, 44–45, 51–52, 69–71, 74–76, 79–81, 215–16, 223, 285
  interactions with Russian state, 33, 44–46, 68–70, 75
  Qūrṣāwī's critique, 60, 62–63, 91, 94, 110, 142, 216–18, 294–95
Ūriwī, Fatḥ Allāh, 54, 76–77, 83–87, 93, 129–33, 183n.38, 185–88, 192–96, 199n.93, 208, 216–17, 225, 234–36, 291
Ūriwī, Ḥabīb Allāh, 54, 76–77, 82n.276
uṣūl-i jadīd. *See* Jadidism
Ūtiz-Īmānī, ʿAbd al-Raḥīm, 54, 59n.153, 82–85, 132–35, 138n.115, 142, 196, 216–17, 230–32, 234–36, 291

verification. See *taḥqīq*
Voll, John, 9–15, 24–25, 207–11, 213. *See also* reformism

wujūdī metaphysics. *See* metaphysics

Yūnus b. Īwānāy, 36–37, 129n.77